Trade and Environment in the EC and the WTO

Europa Law Publishing, Groningen 2003

Trade and Environment in the EC and the WTO
A Legal Analysis

Jochem Wiers

Paperback edition

Europa Law Publishing is a publishing company
specializing in European Union Law.
For further information please contact Europa Law
Publishing via email: info@europalawpublishing.com
or visit our website at: www.europalawpublishing.com.

© Europa Law Publishing, Jochem Wiers, 2003

Typeset in Scala and Scala Sans, Graphic design by
G2K Designers, Groningen/Amsterdam

NUR 828; ISBN 90-76871-20-5

British Library Cataloguing-in-Publication Data
A catalogue record for this book is available from the
British Library

Preface

There are a lot of people who have contributed to the successful completion of this work. I will mention the most important ones explicitly, but the list is not exhaustive. First, my supervisors: Professors Jan H. Jans and Friedl Weiss in Amsterdam and, during the initial phase Claus-Dieter Ehlermann in Florence. The last-mentioned also kindly agreed to serve on my PhD committee, together with Professors Gráinne De Búrca, Pieter-Jan Kuijper, André Nollkaemper, and Hanna Sevenster. I would like to thank all of them for their intellectually stimulating comments. I am grateful to my colleagues of the Department of International Law of the University of Amsterdam and elsewhere for the discussions in our weekly EC Courtwatch and in several other meetings. Jim Mathis and Annette Schrauwen deserve special mention. With them, I had frequent and fruitful discussions and we co-operated on the journal *Legal Issues of Economic Integration*. I would further like to thank Otto Genee, Denise Prevost, and Mark Jacobs, for their comments on earlier drafts of parts of my work, Gabrielle Marceau, for enabling a successful internship in Geneva, and Andrew Martin, for many stimulating discussions in Bruges and Florence.

My family provided an intellectually stimulating environment and supported my undergraduate studies. Nuffic (*Netherlands Organisation for International Education Exchange*) made my subsequent stays in Bruges and Florence financially possible, and NWO (*Netherlands Organisation for Scientific Research*) contributed to my stay in Geneva and covered the editing costs. The editing itself was swiftly and carefully done by Peter Morris, and the fast and efficient production of the book you have before you is the merit of Jacqueline Lensink of Europa Law Publishing. Finally, my deepest thanks go to Eveline. For enduring my frequent absent-mindedness over the past years, while I was pondering on such things as national treatment or proportionality. But most importantly, for the most joyous event: the birth of our son Gillis.

Much of the work in preparing this thesis has gone into studying and describing the evolution of the case-law of the European Court of Justice and of GATT panels and WTO panels and the Appellate Body. This work is reflected in Chapters 2 and 4. Chapters 3 and 5 identify a number of recurring themes in the case-law of both organisations. Chapters 6, 7 and 9 build upon these earlier Chapters, while Chapter 8 addresses a somewhat singular issue, the legal status in the EC of goods from non-EC Member States that are WTO Members. Chapter 10 contains concluding remarks. The law is reflected as it was in December, 2001, although, an occasional reference to subsequent case-law may have slipped into the footnotes during the final revision. The changes made to the EC Treaty by the Treaty of Nice are not reflected, as these had not come into force by the time the manuscript was closed. The author welcomes comments at jochem.wiers@minbuza.nl or jochem.wiers@zonnet.nl.

Jochem Wiers
Amsterdam, April 2002

Contents

CHAPTER 7   **Harmonisation, Extraterritoriality and Production and Processing Methods**

CHAPTER 8   **National Environmental Measures and Third-Country Products in the EC**

PART ONE

Introduction

Brunel Library
Check out receipt

Customer ID: ******8360

Title: Legal aspects of implementing the Kyoto
Protocol mechanisms : making Kyoto work
Item ID: 6025347918
Due: 6/5/2008,23:59

Title: Trade and environment in the EC and the
WTO : a legal analysis
Item ID: 6040327299
Due: 6/5/2008,23:59

Total items: 2
27/04/2008 17:49

Renewals:
http://brunel.ac.uk/library_catalogue
01895 266 141

CHAPTER I

Introduction

1.1 Trade and Environment Dilemmas

According to the rules of the World Trade Organisation and the European Community, is Denmark allowed to prohibit the use of metal beverage cans while allowing the use of other drink containers? Can the Netherlands require all wood products sold on its market to carry a label indicating whether they have been sustainably produced or not? Can the European Community enact a ban on beef containing growth hormones? Can it limit the importation of products containing genetically modified organisms? Can the United States impose gasoline quality standards allowing foreign refiners less possibilities to adapt to these standards than domestic refiners? The above are just some of the questions that have arisen in recent years over the interpretation of trade liberalisation commitments and environmental concerns in the context of the European Community (EC) and the World Trade Organisation (WTO). This study describes and compares the rules of the EC and the WTO on the liberalisation of trade in goods, and how they relate to measures taken by the members of these organisations for the protection of the environment and health.

All of the above examples concern measures that are currently being contemplated by domestic authorities, or have already led to proceedings within the European Community or the World Trade Organisation. The proposed Dutch labelling requirement for wood products aptly illustrates some of the problems involved. In the Netherlands, deforestation caused by unsustainable wood management is widely regarded as a pressing international environmental problem. The Netherlands supports international efforts to address this problem, but these have so far only resulted in non-binding agreements and recommendations on forest management. Some political parties and groups would like to make a more forceful contribution towards addressing the environmental problem. They attempt to do so by enacting policy measures that have an impact on trade. Examples are a ban on unsustainably produced wood products, or a mandatory labelling requirement. Both have been proposed in the Netherlands. The impact of such policies on trade triggers the application of trade agreements to which the state in question is a party, such as the WTO Agreements and the EC Treaty.[1] The national policy measure may be challenged as an unjustifiable violation of the disciplines in these agreements. If this occurs, and the measure is not withdrawn or modified, the issue may be taken to dispute settlement proceedings. It will then be up to those deciding disputes in the WTO and EC (the WTO Dispute Settlement Body, and the European Court of Justice, respectively), to resolve the matter.

---

[1]   The term "WTO Agreements" as used here refers to the WTO Agreement and the Annexed Agreements, i.e. the Multilateral Agreements on Trade in Goods, the General Agreement on Trade in Services (GATS), the Agreement on Trade-Related Aspects of Intellectual Property Rights (TRIPS), the Understanding on Rules and Procedures Governing the Settlement of Disputes (Dispute Settlement Understanding, DSU), and the Trade Policy Review Mechanism (TPR).

Why are these trade liberalisation disciplines there in the first place, if they seem to obstruct national policies pursuing such laudable goals as environmental protection? The simple answer is that most countries believe that it is to their benefit to conclude international agreements containing such disciplines. The economic theory of "comparative advantages" argues that nations can mutually benefit from opening their markets to trade, even when their levels of productivity differ, and even when they open their markets unilaterally. In spite of various challenges made against it over the past two centuries, this theory still stands strong.[2] The World Trade Organisation has practically been built upon it.[3] Even if in theory, unilateral liberalisation is beneficial, states generally feel more comfortable when other states agree to liberalise too. Thus, in order to reap the benefits from trade on a more permanent basis, states and other independent customs territories have concluded trade agreements throughout modern history[4]. In these agreements, they committed themselves to reducing government-induced trade barriers. Such trade barriers include, first and foremost, tariffs and quantitative restrictions, which may be dubbed "classical" trade policy instruments. Under the 1947 General Agreement on Tariffs and Trade (GATT), the predecessor to the WTO, the most important trading nations in the world agreed to control such barriers. Tariffs were bound to negotiated maximum rates, while quantitative restrictions were in principle prohibited.[5] Moreover, rules were agreed upon to discipline such trade policy instruments as anti-dumping and anti-subsidy measures, rules of origin and customs valuation methods. At the regional level, the 1957 European Community Treaty not only prohibited quantitative restrictions, but phased out tariffs entirely over a transitional period.[6]

---

[2] For an instructive overview of the origins of this theory, as well as the major subsequent challenges against it, see Irwin (1996). For a recent critique on the model built on comparative advantage, see Dunoff (1998a) and (1999a), arguing that this model is being challenged by the linkages between trade and such non-trade issues as environmental protection.

[3] See e.g. the 'About the WTO' introductory section at the WTO webpages, http://www.wto.org.

[4] Although trade arrangements have been reported as far back as 2500 BC, "modern history" refers to the state system as it developed in Europe from the mid-17th Century onwards. Although historic developments obviously do not usually start in a particular year, the 1648 Peace of Westphalia is often taken as the reference point for the beginning of this development. See Irwin (1996).

[5] See Articles II and XI of the 1947 General Agreement on Tariffs and Trade, GATT.

[6] In the EC Treaty as it was before it was amended by the 1997 Amsterdam Treaty, the relevant provisions were Articles 30 and 34 for quantitative restrictions and Articles 12 to 17 for tariffs. The EC Treaty is based on the 1957 Rome Treaty Establishing the European Economic Community. Since the amendments to the EEC Treaty made by the 1992 Maastricht Treaty on European Union, the adjective "Economic" was dropped to reflect the Community's reach beyond the merely economic sphere, and the official name is now the European Community. Hence the use of the abbreviation EC in this work.

Yet barriers to international trade do not only result from such "classical" trade policy instruments as tariffs or quotas. They are also caused by a wide variety of government policies which do not necessarily or specifically target trade, but are nevertheless capable of hindering it. Such policies range from the taxation of products to the allocation of subsidies to domestic industries, and to all sorts of regulations addressing, for example, standards for the safety of products. From the point of view of trade liberalisation efforts, such internal government policies may be typified as "internal barriers".[7] The effects of such internal barriers on international trade often equal or even surpass those of "classical" trade instruments. For instance, if producers have to meet technical regulations that differ from country to country, they will need to adapt their production processes for each country they wish to export their products to. The trade-impeding effects of "internal barriers" became a point of attention in both the GATT and EC in the late 1960s and early 1970s.[8] States and other customs territories committing themselves to reducing trade barriers were in agreement that many "internal barriers" at the same time pursue legitimate domestic policy objectives, such as national security, public morality, and human, animal or plant life and health. Considering the obvious need for domestic policy action in such areas, it was not a viable option to subject internal regulations and taxes to outright prohibitions or negotiated maximum levels, as had been deemed suitable for disciplining border measures such as quantitative restrictions and tariffs. Therefore, trade agreements rather subjected "internal barriers" to agreed principles such as non-discrimination and non-protectionism. This had the effect of leaving members the liberty to pursue their societal goals through regulatory and taxation policies, as long as they did not unduly discriminate against imports or protect domestic industries.

Thus, trade agreements usually contain strict disciplines as regards the use of "classical" trade instruments, as well as less strict disciplines addressing trade barriers resulting from other, "internal" government policies, such as taxation or regulation. Still, countries felt that they sometimes needed to enact measures pursuing legitimate objectives that could not avoid contravening these disciplines. For example, it is sometimes necessary to ban imports of a dangerous product, or to tax or regulate in ways that may turn out to be discriminatory. Therefore, legitimate objectives such as the protection of life and health were expressly acknowledged in the trade liberalisation agreements. This was done by

---

[7] The more common term "non-tariff barriers" is avoided here, because some of the "classical" trade policy instruments such as quantitative restrictions are, technically speaking, also non-tariffs, yet are included in the "classical" trade instruments in this work.

[8] See the questions in the European Parliament during 1966-67 discussed in Chapter 2, and accounts of trade barriers in "GATT Activities" publications from the early 1970s onwards (see also Chapter 4 on the Tokyo Round Standards Code, the precursor of the TBT Agreement).

inserting clauses providing exceptions to both the commitments on "classical" trade instruments and the agreed principles regarding "internal barriers". In order for the trade liberalisation objectives not to be too easily undermined by extensive invocations of these exceptions, they were accompanied by conditions to be met in order for such legitimate objectives to trump trade liberalisation interests. An example of such a condition is the requirement that a measure for which an exception is invoked should not result in "arbitrary discrimination" or a "disguised restriction on trade".

From the start, both the EC Treaty and the GATT contained an exception clause referring to the protection of human, animal and plant life and health. In addition, the GATT provided an exception to its disciplines for the conservation of exhaustible natural resources. Initially, "environmental protection" as such was not among the agreed legitimate objectives in the founding treaties. However, in the EC, through the case-law of the European Court of Justice, "environmental protection" as such became accepted as a legitimate objective capable of hindering the free movement of goods. Similarly, while "environmental protection" as such is not mentioned in the text of the GATT, it now figures in a number of other WTO agreements, notably the Agreement on Technical Barriers to Trade (TBT).[9]

The trade liberalisation commitments and exceptions clauses that are the focus of this study were to a large extent agreed upon in the late 1940s and 1950s. Since then, important developments have occurred. The successful reduction of "classical" trade barriers diminished their relative importance. Accordingly, trade liberalisation efforts increasingly focused on "internal" barriers. In the EC, the relevant rule even developed into a general prohibition on trade obstacles, unless justified. At the same time, large-scale human-induced environmental problems, some of which had transboundary implications, received widespread attention. Moreover, internal government regulation multiplied in many states as it addressed increasingly complex and technical subject matters, correspondingly adding to the risk of interfering with trade commitments. Thus, since the mid-twentieth century, there has been increased attention to environmental problems, an increased scope and intensity of governmental action, and an increasing reach of trade disciplines into governments' regulatory authority. As a corollary to these developments, tensions between trade liberalisation and national environmental policies have come to the fore. Since the 1980s, various national policy measures pursuing environmental goals have been challenged as being violations of the trade liberalisation commitments in both the EC Treaty and the GATT/WTO Agreements. Likewise, the environmental exceptions and justification grounds in these treaties were invoked to justify them.

---

[9] The TBT Agreement in its current form was negotiated during the Uruguay Round from 1986 to 1993, while its predecessor dates from the Tokyo Round, which lasted from 1973 to 1979.

I.2 Similar Conflicts, Different Structures

The EC Treaty and the WTO contain trade liberalisation commitments and environmental justifications that operate according to a roughly similar pattern. Tariffs and quantitative restrictions are restrained or abolished, principles are laid down regarding internal regulations and taxes causing trade barriers, as well as exceptions for measures pursuing legitimate objectives.[10] In the context of the EC, this pattern is often referred to as "negative integration", as it focuses on limiting trade barriers caused by national regulatory activity, rather than replacing such activity by international or supranational regulatory activity ("positive integration"). Although the term "integration" derives from the study of regional agreements such as the EC, it is also increasingly applied to trade liberalisation on a global scale taking place under the auspices of the WTO.[11] Not only the relevant rules in the EC and the WTO, but also the conflicts between members' environmental policies and trade liberalisation commitments are to a considerable extent similar. However, there are also obvious and important differences between the EC and the WTO. These differences relate not only to their membership, but also to the goals, institutional set-up, functions and powers of these organisations.

I.2.1 EC Background

The trade liberalisation commitments in the 1957 Rome Treaty Establishing the European Economic Community and their objectives were far-reaching. The Treaty of Rome sought to establish a common market and a customs union.[12] These concepts both refer to the "free movement of goods", which has been interpreted by the ECJ as a "general principle of Community law" and as a "fundamental Community provision."[13] The common market is

---

[10] As will be extensively discussed below, the EC goes even further by inserting into the EC Treaty a prohibition on 'measures having equivalent effect to quantitative restrictions', as well as accepting justifications not explicitly acknowledged in the Treaty.

[11] See Tinbergen (1954); Balassa (1961); Pelkmans (1997)

[12] Article 8 of the original Rome Treaty Establishing the European Economic Community. The 1986 Single European Act replaced the reference to the "common market" with the notion of "internal market", currently found in Article 14 EC. See on both concepts, Schrauwen (1997). The reference to "common market" can still be found in Article 2 EC as it stands. On the customs union, see Article 9 of the original Rome Treaty, presently Article 23 EC.

[13] See e.g. the ECJ in Case 240/83 *ADBHU*, para. 9: '[...] the principles of free movement of goods and freedom of competition, together with freedom of trade as a fundamental right, are general principles of Community law of which the court ensures observance.' And in Case C-49/89 *Corsica Ferries*, para. 8: 'the articles of the EEC Treaty concerning the free movement of goods, persons, services and capital are fundamental Community provisions and any restriction, even minor, of that freedom is prohibited.'

supposed to resemble as closely as possible a domestic internal market.[14] The European Union, of which the EC forms an integral part, is built upon a foundation of common values. These are expressed in the Preambles to the EC and EU Treaties as well as in Article 6 EU, which speaks of 'the principles of liberty, democracy, respect for human rights and fundamental freedoms, and the rule of law'.[15] The EU has recently adopted a Charter of Fundamental Rights, although its exact legal status is as yet unclear.[16] In addition to pursuing "negative integration" through trade liberalisation commitments, the European enterprise from the very start encompassed an even more ambitious project. In the aftermath of the devastating consequences of the Second World War, economic prosperity was expected to go hand in hand with peace and stability for the continent. The interests of individual Member States were to be tied together through the pooling of their resources and the setting up of common institutions. The origin of the idea of a forging of interests can be found in the 1950 Schuman Plan, which led to the European Community for Coal and Steel (ECSC): 'World peace cannot be safeguarded without the making of creative efforts proportionate to the dangers which threaten it' [...] 'the contribution to civilisation made by an organised and living Europe is indispensable to the maintenance of peaceful relations'.[17] Moreover, the Community institutions were given the power to enact legislation binding the Member States.

The same ideas underlied the 1957 EEC Treaty.[18] For example, the pooling of resources in the literal sense was to be realised by a common agricultural policy. More generally, common action through common institutions was apparent from the tasks and activities given to the Community in Articles 2 and 3 of the Treaty. Among the tasks in Article 2 EC the following are mentioned:

---

[14] See e.g. the ECJ in Case 15/81 *Gaston Schul*, para. 33: 'The concept of a common market as defined by the Court in a consistent line of decisions involves the elimination of all obstacles to intra-community trade in order to merge the national markets into a single market bringing about conditions as close as possible to those of a genuine internal market.'

[15] 1992 Maastricht Treaty on European Union. That Treaty established a so-called "pillar structure", with the the first pillar consisting of the three European Communities (EC, ECSC, and Euratom), a second pillar consisting of a 'common foreign and security policy', and a third pillar regarding 'cooperation in the fields of justice and home affairs', which was subsequently redubbed 'police and judicial cooperation in criminal matters' by the 1997 Amsterdam Treaty. This work addresses certain aspects of the EC Treaty, i.e., a part of the first pillar. Only very occasionally is the term European Union (EU) used to denote the larger entity.

[16] See http://www.europarl.eu.int/charter.

[17] Excerpts from the Schuman Declaration of 9 May 1950, http://europa.eu.int/abc/symbols/9-may/decl_en.htm.

[18] See the Preamble to the EC Treaty: 'common action to eliminate the barriers which divide Europe', 'the removal of existing obstacles calls for concerted action', 'by thus pooling their resources'.

a 'harmonious, balanced and sustainable development of economic activities', a 'high level of protection and improvement of the quality of the environment', and the 'raising of the standard of living and quality of life'. The activities in Article 3 include *inter alia* a 'common commercial policy', a 'common policy in the sphere of agriculture and fisheries', a 'policy in the sphere of the environment', and a 'contribution to the attainment of a high level of health protection'. These tasks and activities implied the attribution of powers to the Community and its institutions. This attribution of powers was made more explicit by the 1992 Maastricht Treaty's addition to the EC Treaty of the current Article 5 EC (then Article 3b). Article 5 EC requires that the Community acts within the limits of the powers conferred upon it by the Treaty and of the objectives assigned to it therein. Article 7 EC (Article 4 of the original Rome Treaty) lists the individual institutions and reiterates the attribution principle as far as they are concerned.

Perhaps the most salient feature of the powers attributed to the European institutions is their ability to bind the Community's Member States and their inhabitants by enacting legislation, often by a qualified majority of the Member States' representatives in the Council and in a co-decision procedure with the directly elected European Parliament. Such legislation, in the form of regulations, directives and decisions, has its legal basis in a number of provisions throughout the Treaty. It is usually referred to as "secondary" EC law, as opposed to the "primary" rules in the EC Treaty itself. Importantly, secondary legislation is not confined to those areas where the Community pursues "common policies" or has an "exclusive competence", meaning that powers have been entirely transferred from the Member States to the Community, such as in external trade.[19] The Community also enacts legislation in all those policy areas where it shares competencies with its Member States. There is a general mandate in the EC Treaty to legislate in order to contribute to the establishment of an internal market.[20] Moreover, the Treaty includes mandates to enact environmental legislation,[21] and to pursue action in the field of public health to complement the Member States' own public health policies.[22] Further references to environmental protection and health are found in Article 2 EC, which lists the Community's tasks and objectives,[23] in Article 3, listing the Community's poli-

---

[19] See Articles 26 and 133 (formerly 28 and 113) EC.

[20] See Article 95 EC.

[21] See Articles 174-176 EC (ex Articles 130r-t, as inserted in the EC Treaty by the 1986 Single European Act and amended by the 1992 Maastricht and 1997 Amsterdam Treaties).

[22] See Article 152 EC (ex Article 129, as inserted in the EC Treaty by the 1992 Maastricht Treaty and amended by the 1997 Amsterdam Treaty).

[23] 'The Community shall have as its task, [...] to promote throughout the Community [...] a high level of protection and improvement of the quality of the environment [...]'

cies,[24] and in Article 6, prescribing the integration of environmental protection requirements into the definition and implementation of all Community policies, with a view to promoting sustainable development.[25] The Treaty on European Union, of which the EC forms an integral part, refers in its Preamble to 'the principle of sustainable development' and to environmental protection.

Another important characteristic of European integration is the participation of Europe's citizens in the process. Citizens participate formally through direct representation in the European Parliament. National parliaments control national governments' input in the Council of Ministers. In addition, their participation in the European integration process was greatly enhanced by the possibility to invoke European law before national courts in the Member States, and to have national law set aside by it. The case-law on the "direct effect" and "supremacy" of Community law that brought about these opportunities for citizens has been described and commented on extensively elsewhere.[26] Through its case-law, the ECJ has effectively lifted the question of the effects of an international agreement between states in the internal legal orders of those states to the level of the institutions set up by that agreement, especially the ECJ itself, irrespective of what national constitutions had to say about the effects of international law in their national legal orders. Such effects had not been explicitly agreed upon by the Member States when they negotiated the EC Treaty. Arguably, however, the drafters of the EC Treaty had already laid the foundation for the participation of citizens in the enforcement (and formation through case-law) of European law, by designing the preliminary ruling procedure in the Treaty.[27] This procedure not only connects citizens to European law, it also ensures direct participation of national courts in its development. In addition, it ensures the uniform interpretation and application of European law by those courts. Arguably, the entire construction of "direct effect" and "supremacy" of EC law erected by the ECJ would not have worked without the preliminary ruling procedure.

Finally, citizens also have direct access to the European Court of Justice, albeit under certain conditions. The EC Treaty allows individuals direct access to the ECJ in certain circumstances, such as when they seek to challenge the legality of an act of one of the EC's institutions that directly and individually concerns them.[28] In addition to providing preliminary rulings and hearing

---

[24] 'For the purposes set out in Article 2, the activities of the Community shall include [...] a policy in the sphere of the environment; [...] a contribution to the attainment of a high level of health protection [...]'

[25] Article 6 EC, inserted as part of the title on environment by the Single European Act, and transferred to the general first part on Principles of the EC Treaty by the 1997 Treaty of Amsterdam.

[26] See, in addition to the numerous textbooks on European Law covering these subjects, e.g. Weiler (1981) and (1991); Spiermann (1999).

[27] Article 234 (formerly 177) EC.

[28] See Article 230 EC.

challenges to Community acts, the Court also deals with procedures against Member States for failure to correctly implement and apply Community law. These infringement procedures may be initiated by other Member States or by the European Commission.[29] Infringement procedures between Member States are very rare.[30] Action against Member States for failure to correctly apply Community law is normally left to the Commission in its function as the 'guardian of the Treaty'.[31] Rulings by the Court of Justice are considered to be authoritative, and both the compliance rate with its judgments and the level of acceptance of its preliminary rulings by the national courts are high. Regarding infringement procedures against Member States, the Treaty even provides for a fine to be imposed by the Court in the case of a continued failure to comply with the judgment in which the infringement was found. Although this stage has seldom been reached, it illustrates the vigour of the Court's judgments.[32]

Thus, as supranational institutions supervising the implementation and application of European law, the Court and the Commission play a vital role in the European structure. Another highly idiosyncratic feature of this structure is the institutional interplay in the creation of secondary Community legislation. Even if the Council of Ministers, which consists of representatives of the Member States, adopts Community legislation, this is done in most cases by qualified majority, and according to a procedure of co-decision with the European Parliament.[33] The Commission is the sole initiator of Community legislation. Its proposals can only be amended by the Council with unanimity, and the Commission may alter its proposal as long as the Council has not acted.[34] This allows the Commission to play an active part in the legislative process. Thus, Member States are not the only ones to affect the outcome of the legislative process in the Community through their representatives in the Council; the Commission and Parliament as reflecting Community or "supranational" interests have an important influence in the process too. Moreover, in many cases Member States can be bound by legislation they do not favour, when it has been adopted by qualified majority. In the making of *primary* Community law, i.e. the devising of new treaties and the amendment of existing ones, the Member States play a more autonomous role. An intergovernmental confer-

---

[29] See Articles 227 and 226 EC, respectively.

[30] For a recent example, see e.g. Case C-388/95 *Belgium* v. *Spain* (*Rioja wine*).

[31] See Article 211 EC.

[32] The Court recently imposed a fine for the first time in Case C-387/97 *Commission* v. *Greece*. The fine amounted to EUR 20,000 for each day of delay in implementing the measures necessary to comply with the judgment in Case C-45/91, in which the Court had found that Greece had failed to put into effect an obligation to implement waste disposal plans.

[33] Article 251 EC, which is increasingly becoming the standard procedure for Community legislation.

[34] Article 250 EC.

ence is convened where representatives of the Member States must agree by common accord to any Treaty changes, which must moreover be ratified by all Member States in accordance with their domestic constitutional requirements.[35] Nevertheless, the European Parliament and the Commission play an important part in the run-up to the actual intergovernmental conference, so even that process is not purely intergovernmental.

In almost every aspect of the European structure, the institutional interplay is evident in continuing power struggles between the various Community institutions. Examples are disputes concerning the legal basis of Community legislation and the ensuing roles of various institutions in the process.[36] Such struggles may be dubbed manifestations of "horizontal federalism".[37] Interestingly, these horizontal institutional struggles often also have a "vertical" pendant, in that Member States are involved in them not just through their representation in the Council of Ministers, but also directly. Examples are "comitology", i.e. the way Member States control the exercise of powers delegated by the Council to the Commission through expert committees,[38] and disputes concerning the Community's competence to legislate internally and externally.[39]

1.2.2 GATT/WTO Background

The 1947 GATT Agreement in its Preamble mentions as its objectives the raising of standards of living, employment, real income and effective demand growth, full use of resources and expanding production and exchange. Such objectives were to be contributed to by 'reciprocal and mutually advantageous arrangements directed to the substantial reduction of tariffs and other barriers to trade and to the elimination of discriminatory treatment in international commerce'. The GATT was provisionally applied for almost 50 years. Although it had an administrative secretariat, there was no further institutional structure. The GATT was legally speaking not an international organisation, although regarded as one *de facto*.[40] The 1994 WTO, which incorporates the GATT, is a fully-fledged international organisation, and has a somewhat

---

[35] Article 48 Treaty on European Union.

[36] See e.g. Case C-300/89 *Commission* v. *Council*, on the legal basis of a directive on waste from the titanium dioxide industry.

[37] See Trachtman (1996a).

[38] Mentioned by way of example are Lenaerts and Verhoeven (2000).

[39] See e.g. Case C-376/98 *Germany* v. *Parliament and Council*, on the legal basis of a directive on tobacco advertising, and the Court's Opinion 1/94 on the competence to conclude the Uruguay Round Agreements.

[40] See Krueger in Krueger (1998). However, Seidl-Hohenveldern (1999 and 1992) always treated the GATT as an international organisation.

more elaborated institutional structure. The Preamble to the WTO Agreement essentially builds upon the GATT Preamble. It reiterates the objectives described above. In addition, it refers to the objectives of sustainable development, environmental protection and the needs of developing countries. However, all of these additional objectives should be contributed to by 'reciprocal and mutually advantageous arrangements'.

Thus, while new objectives like environmental protection and sustainable development have been identified by the WTO in comparison with its precursor, no new strategies to achieve them are envisaged. Apparently, these new objectives, just like the "traditional" GATT objectives, are supposed to be attained by the reduction of trade barriers and the elimination of discrimination in trade. Thus, the Preamble to the WTO Agreement suggests that there is no tension between objectives like the full use of resources and expanding production on the one hand, and sustainable development on the other. The Preamble also refers to the aim of developing 'an integrated, more viable and durable multilateral trading system, preserving its basic principles and furthering the objectives underlying this multilateral trading system'.[41] However, despite the references to an "integrated system" based on "principles", the WTO has no legislative powers of its own, and does not pursue common actions or policies as regards subject areas such as the environment, culture or social issues. Moreover, common values that explicitly underlie the EU, such as liberty, democracy, respect for human rights and fundamental freedoms, and the rule of law, are not expressly mentioned in the WTO Agreements.

The WTO Agreements do explicitly recognise the values of environmental and health protection, however. Exceptions in the GATT refer to human, animal or plant life or health and to the conservation of exhaustible natural resources, and environmental protection is mentioned in a number of the WTO's annexed Agreements.[42] Moreover, as said, the Preamble to the Agreement Establishing the WTO refers to 'the objective of sustainable development' and uses the words 'seeking both to protect and preserve the environment and to enhance the means for doing so [...]'. Trade and environment issues are discussed in the Committee on Trade and Environment.[43] The Committee has a fairly extensive work programme, and by the year 2000 had issued over a hundred reports.[44] However, no environmental or health policies as such are pursued by the WTO itself. Therefore, there is no question of competencies shared by the organisation and its members, as there is in the EC.

---

[41] Preamble to the WTO Agreement.

[42] See e.g. Articles 2.2, 2.10, 5.4, 5.7 TBT Agreement; Article 5.2 SPS Agreement; Article 20 Agreement on Agriculture; Article 8 Subsidies Agreement; Article XIV GATS; Article 27.2 TRIPS.

[43] WTO Trade and Environment Decision, MTN/TNC/45(MIN).

[44] See WTO documents WT/CTE/W1-100 and WT/CTE/1-3.

It is clear that the WTO does not aim to establish a common or internal market, and no such thing as a "principle" of the free movement of goods can be read into its provisions. The WTO Preamble merely speaks of 'expanding [...] trade', 'the substantial reduction of tariffs and other barriers to trade', and 'the elimination of discriminatory treatment in international trade relations'. Is there a general 'principle of trade liberalisation' in the WTO? This question could be of great importance. If such a principle were to exist, and were to be placed 'at the top of the list' and thus be overriding, as is sometimes asserted, it could be instrumental in tilting interpretations of WTO law towards liberalisation in cases of doubt.[45] This would imply that members of the WTO have adhered to an inherent commitment to trade liberalisation.[46] It should be stressed, however, that a "substantial reduction" of trade barriers and the elimination of trade discrimination do not presuppose a final objective of free trade.[47]

At most, the WTO could be said to contain a dynamic principle of progressive trade liberalisation. Moreover, trade liberalisation as a goal has always, from the early days of the ITO and GATT onwards, been intrinsically linked with safeguards guaranteeing members sufficient leeway to pursue their policies, be they of a monetary, labour, employment, or social character. Thus, trade liberalisation has never been the sole goal of the GATT or the WTO; it has been and is "embedded" in other goals, pursued primarily by its Members. This important qualification of the trade liberalisation objective of the GATT and WTO has been stressed by a number of authors.[48] Overlooking it easily leads to a presentation of 'trade and...' conflicts as contradictory, presenting the goal of "free" or "unfettered" trade as absolute and as opposed to the societal goals pursued by national legislation. Accordingly, some authors conclude that the WTO regime gives primacy to trade interests over other interests.[49] It is submitted that rather than doing that, the WTO, as a result of its functions and rules, is bound to regard non-trade interests from a trade angle. It is therefore of the utmost importance to decide *what* national policies are affected by its trade

---

[45] Hilf (1999) at 10 and (2001) at 117 appears to read a general trade liberalisation principle into the WTO. He refers to the textual references in the WTO Preamble and in the Preamble to GATT 1994, and to Articles II and XXVIII bis GATT, and the TBT Agreement. In addition, he mentions the Appellate Body reports in *Australia-Salmon* and *Korea-Alcohol*. However, it is unclear to the current author how the paragraphs in these reports cited can be read as manifestations of an (overarching) principle of trade liberalisation.

[46] *Contra*, see Bronckers (2001).

[47] Cf. the following statement by a former US State Department trade policy analyst with regard to the GATT, as quoted by Dunoff (1999a) at 371: 'No one was committed to "free trade"; no one expected anything like it; the term does not appear in the GATT, which simply calls for a process of liberalisation with no stated objective.'

[48] Roessler (1998); Dunoff (1999a) at 370, referring to Ruggie (1982).

[49] See e.g. Nichols (1996a) at 700; Atik (1998) at 248.

liberalisation disciplines in the first place, and then whether trade liberalisation is indeed an overriding requirement in the interpretation of these disciplines.

In the WTO, there is no direct citizens' representation in the form of a directly elected supranational parliamentary body. National parliaments, to the extent that these exist in WTO Members, are supposed to control what their governments' delegates say and do in the WTO. As to the role of WTO law before national courts, whether citizens can invoke GATT/WTO law before their national courts and whether national laws can be set aside in such procedures is entirely up to individual Members to decide. It is clear from Article XVI.4 of the WTO Agreement that Members are obliged, as a matter of international law, to ensure the conformity of their internal laws with their WTO obligations. However, it remains up to national legal systems and their constitutions *how* these international obligations are incorporated into the national legal orders. Thus, WTO law does not prescribe that domestic courts should set aside domestic laws found to be incompatible with WTO rules. Although national legislatures or courts could in principle decide to allow individuals to invoke WTO law to challenge domestic laws, this appears unlikely to happen. Important WTO Members such as the US and the EC have explicitly stated that they do not intend WTO law to have such effects in their domestic courts.[50] The case-law of the ECJ confirms the indirect nature of the effects of WTO law in the European legal order.[51]

Significantly, there is no such thing as a preliminary ruling procedure in the WTO. No direct actions are possible before the DSB either; only states can bring disputes before the Dispute Settlement Body. Therefore, individuals depend upon their own national legal and political system to enforce the benefits of trade liberalisation commitments. In some WTO Members, they can ask their government to take action against another WTO Member when their trading rights are impaired.[52] But that possibility does not allow individuals to challenge

---

[50] See Council Decision 94/800/EC concerning the conclusion on behalf of the Community of the WTO Agreements, OJ (1994) L 336/1, and Introductory Note to the Schedules of Commitments under GATS of both the EC and the MS (Legal Instruments Embodying the Uruguay Round Results, Vol. 28 at p. 23557). For the US positions, see Sections 102(a)1 and 2 of the Uruguay Round Agreements Act and the Statement of Administrative Action, at p. 14.

[51] On the status of GATT/WTO law in the EC legal order, see Eeckhout (1997), with further references. On the status of GATT 1947 in the EC, see e.g. Cases 21-24/72 *International Fruit Company*, 70/87 *Fediol*, C-69/89 *Nakajima*, C-280/93 *Germany-Council*. On the status of the WTO Agreements in the EC, see e.g. Cases C-53/96 *Hermès* and C-300/98 *Dior*, both preliminary rulings on national courts' questions, and C-149/96 *Portugal-Council* regarding a direct challenge to Community legislation before the ECJ.

[52] Such possibilities for individuals to trigger action under WTO dispute settlement procedures have been laid down in legislation in some WTO Members, such as the EC (Trade Barriers Regulation, Reg. 3286/94) and the US (Sections 301-310 of the 1974 Trade Act).

the laws of their own country because of inconsistencies with WTO commitments.[53] The WTO Secretariat cannot commence procedures before the Dispute Settlement Body against Members for infringements of the Agreements.[54] There is also no equivalent to secondary Community law in the WTO. Logically, then, there is no possibility of judicial action against acts of the WTO institutions. Institutionally, there is no equivalent to supranational bodies like the European Commission or the European Parliament in the WTO. The WTO Secretariat does not function as the guardian of the Agreements in the way the Commission does in the EC. Thus, the kind of intensive institutional interplay witnessed in the EC does not occur in the WTO.

1.3 Context of Trade and Environment Conflicts

Worries concerning the WTO and other international institutions in that they may be obstacles to pursuing environmental policies have been among the major causes of criticism aimed at and protests against these organisations. Within Europe, although somewhat milder, similar antagonisms between trade liberalisation and environmental goals are present. It therefore seems appropriate, before examining the relevant rules and their interpretations, to have a look at the contexts in which these rules operate, and at the underlying interests and values of trade and environment conflicts in the EC and the WTO.

1.3.1 Environmental Protection, Sustainable Development, and Globalisation

The dilemmas faced when interpreting the relevant provisions in conflicts concerning trade and environment go beyond those which are purely legal. They are embedded in a political, economic and cultural context. Discussions on trade-environment issues on a global scale take place against the background of the discourse on "sustainable development" and "globalisation". Behind both terms lies a wealth of academic and policy discourse, which to a considerable degree concerns their meaning and scope. The 1987 report of the World Commission on Environment and Development (Brundtlandt Report) described the term "sustainable development" as 'development that meets the needs of the present without compromising the chances of future generations to meet their needs'.[55] "Sustainable development" seeks to address concerns

---

[53] Which, according to authors such as Petersmann, is a most important function of trade liberalisation rules.

[54] Cf. Lasok (2000).

[55] Brundtlandt Report (1987). For more information, see the United Nations Sustainable Development webpage at http://www.un.org/esa/sustdev.

about development inequalities, both intragenerational and intergenerational. It seeks to do so not just in an economic sense, but also with regard to the social and environmental components of development. Hence trade and environment problems are clearly within its ambit.[56] Although there is no one agreed definition, "globalisation" is widely understood to encompass the increasing international flows of goods, services and finance.[57] Increasing transboundary and global environmental problems may equally be regarded as aspects of "globalisation".

Starting with bilateral fisheries treaties, environmental concerns have been addressed in international law from the 19th century onwards.[58] However, it was not until the late 1960s that the need for more comprehensive policies to manage the environment was internationally recognised.[59] At the 1972 Stockholm United Nations Conference on the Human Environment, an action plan, recommendations and a set of principles were adopted. In the same year, the United Nations Environment Programme (UNEP) was established. After the Brundtlandt Report on sustainable development had been issued in 1987, preparations began for the 1992 United Nations Conference on Environment and Development (UNCED). At that conference, three non-binding instruments were adopted: the Rio Declaration on Environment and Development, the UNCED forest principles, and Agenda 21.[60] These instruments explicitly addressed the relationship between trade and environmental protection. Although non-binding, some principles in the Rio Declaration may reflect rules of customary international law. Moreover, it provides guidance as to future legal developments.[61] Principle 12 of the Rio Declaration stipulates that:

States should cooperate to promote a supportive and open international economic system that would lead to economic growth and sustainable development in all countries, to better address the problems of environmental degradation. Trade policy measures for environmental purposes should not constitute a means of arbitrary or unjustifiable discrimination or a disguised restriction on international trade.[...][62]

---

[56] On trade and sustainable development, see e.g. Weiss, Denters, and De Waart (eds.) (1996); Repetto (1994); IISD (1994).

[57] A web search for a definition of "globalisation" in November 2001 produced around 50,000 hits. Recent works on trade and globalisation include Richardson (2000); WTO (1998). Critical approaches are found in e.g. Wallach (1999); Klein (1999); Hertz (2000).

[58] For an overview of the history of international environmental law, see Sands (1996).

[59] See the final report of the 1968 Biosphere Conference, cited in Sands (1996) at 34.

[60] In addition, two international environmental agreements were opened for signature: the Convention on Biological Diversity and the UN Framework Convention on Climate Change.

[61] Sands (1996) at 50.

[62] See also Section 5.4.3 on Principle 12 of the Rio Declaration and paragraphs 2.22 and 3.39(d) of Agenda 21, regarding the need for multilateral solutions over and above unilateral solutions to environmental problems.

Agenda 21 does not provide principles, but rather a more elaborate action plan to tackle the challenges of sustainable development in the 21st century. It also addresses trade and environment:

> *Environment and trade policies should be mutually supportive. An open, multilateral trading system [...] contributes to an increase in production and incomes and to lessening demands on the environment. [...] A sound environment, on the other hand, provides the ecological and other resources needed to sustain growth and underpin a continuing expansion of trade. An open, multilateral trading system, supported by the adoption of sound environmental policies, would have a positive impact on the environment and contribute to sustainable development.*[63]

In the GATT, attention was paid to trade and environment for the first time in a 1971 report by the Secretariat, compiled in the context of the preparations for the 1972 Stockholm Conference.[64] In the same year, a GATT expert group on environmental measures and international trade (EMIT) was set up, which however convened for the first time only in 1991, just before UNCED. The final phase of the Uruguay Round negotiations that led to the establishment of the WTO coincided with UNCED. It is no surprise that the WTO Decision on Trade and Environment refers to the Rio Declaration and Agenda 21, and contains similar language. The Preamble to the WTO Agreement refers to sustainable development.[65]

According to the international instruments referred to above, trade, environmental protection and sustainable development are not regarded as being incompatible. On the contrary, they are seen as complementary and mutually reinforcing. This depiction of their relationship may appear somewhat simplistic and idealistic. The relationship between trade, environment and development is highly complex and differs from case to case. In some cases, trade can have

---

[63] Paragraphs 2.19 of Agenda 21. Cf. Paragraphs 2.3 and 2.5 of Agenda 21:

'The international economy should provide a supportive international climate for achieving environment and development goals by: (a) Promoting sustainable development through trade liberalization; (b) Making trade and environment mutually supportive; [...] An open, equitable, secure, non-discriminatory and predictable multilateral trading system that is consistent with the goals of sustainable development and leads to the optimal distribution of global production in accordance with comparative advantage is of benefit to all trading partners. Moreover, improved market access for developing countries' exports in conjunction with sound macroeconomic and environmental policies would have a positive environmental impact and therefore make an important contribution towards sustainable development.'

[64] GATT (1971).

[65] As the Appellate Body noted in *US-Shrimp-Turtle*, para. 153: 'As this preambular language reflects the intentions of negotiators of the WTO Agreement, we believe it must add colour, texture and shading to our interpretation of the agreements annexed to the WTO Agreement, in this Case, the GATT 1994.'

concrete detrimental effects on the environment; one can here think of pollution caused by transport.[66] In other cases, trade disciplines can have direct positive environmental effects, e.g. when resulting in subsidies for unsustainable fisheries being abolished. The above principles and understandings therefore certainly should not be understood to mean that there can or will be no concrete conflicts between trade and environmental policies. How such conflicts are dealt with in interpreting trade liberalisation rules is precisely the subject of this study.

In the EC, the year 1972 also marked an important step in the development of an environmental policy. Before then, occasional Community measures were taken that pursued environmental objectives, but without an underlying environmental policy. In 1972, the European Council stated that economic expansion should lead to raising quality and standards of living, and stressed the importance of a Community environmental policy.[67] After 1972, the Community started to draw up environmental action plans. In 1987, with the Single European Act, environmental protection received treaty status.[68] The Title on Environment in the EC Treaty provided *inter alia* that 'environmental protection requirements must be integrated into the definition and implementation of other Community policies'. With the 1992 Maastricht Treaty on European Union, "respect for the environment" and a "policy in the sphere of the environment" were added to the Community's tasks and activities in Articles 2 and 3 of the EC Treaty.[69] Finally, the modifications to the EC Treaty made by the 1997 Amsterdam Treaty have resulted in a reference to a 'harmonious, balanced and sustainable development of economic activities' and to a 'high level of protection and improvement of the quality of the environment' among the Community's tasks. Moreover, the integration principle has moved forward and is now placed among the Community's general principles. The Preamble and Article 2 of the Treaty on European Union now also refer to sustainable development.

1.3.2   "Trade and...": Trade Liberalisation and Non-Trade Interests

Trade liberalisation commitments may come into conflict not only with the protection of life and health and of the environment, but with other societal goals as well. Often, the expression "trade and..." is used when referring to conflicts between trade liberalisation and other societal interests. Generally speaking, the basic mechanisms examined in this study, i.e. trade liberalisation commitments, and justifications for 'non-trade interests' with accompanying

---

[66] As recognised in WTO (1999), commented upon by Charnovitz (2000).

[67] Bulletin EC 1972, No. 10, cited in Jans (2000a) at 3.

[68] In what then were Articles 130r-t and 100a EC, now 174-176 and 95 EC.

[69] The preamble to the Treaty on European Union also refers to "environmental protection".

conditions, are to a large extent relevant to policies pursuing other non-trade interests. The societal goals that make up the other end of 'trade and...' conflicts are referred to as "non-trade interests". Examples are labour rights, collective social benefit systems, cultural diversity, or the protection of intellectual property rights. Conflicts are also possible between trade liberalisation and such interests as national security, public morality, and public policy, or *ordre public*. The latter interests are generally perceived as part of the *domaine réservé*, expressions of state sovereignty *par excellence*. Accordingly, it has been argued that they are less likely to become the subject of multilateral agreement than the other interests mentioned.[70] Admittedly, multilateral agreement will be more difficult to reach with regard to some interests than to others. However, even with respect to the interests part of the *domaine réservé*, it is possible that international legislative or adjudicatory institutions determine the margins of interpretation, as the European Community demonstrates.[71]

There are similarities as well as differences in the range of "non-trade interests" recognised in the EC and the WTO. In their provisions providing general exceptions to liberalisation commitments for trade in goods, both the EC and the WTO refer to the protection of life and health.[72] Environmental protection as a legitimate cause potentially overriding trade liberalisation commitments has been recognised in the ECJ's case-law, as well as in a number of the WTO Uruguay Round Agreements, such as the TBT Agreement. On the other hand, the exception in the GATT separately provides for the protection of exhaustible natural resources, which are not mentioned in the EC Treaty. Outside the environmental realm, similarities between the EC and the WTO include exceptions for public morality, national treasures of artistic, historic or archaeological value, and national or public security. In addition, the EC Treaty refers to public policy and the protection of industrial and commercial property, while the WTO includes a number of general exceptions not found in the EC, among which are the import and export of gold and silver, the products of prison labour, and products in short supply.

In the WTO context, "trade and..." conflicts are normally presented as pitching international trade liberalisation commitments versus national non-trade interests. While this is true in many cases, this picture needs to be refined. First of all, the non-trade interest may also be transnational. This is illustrated both by the unilateral efforts by WTO members to address international environmental problems, and by multilateral environmental agreements (MEAs)

---

[70] See e.g. Weiss (1999), and further discussion in Section 3.2.5.

[71] See with regard to public policy and the free movement of persons e.g. Case 41/74 *Van Duyn*; Joined Cases 115-116/81 *Adoui and Cornuaille*. With regard to public morality and the free movement of goods, see Cases 121/85 *Conegate* and 34/79 *Henn and Darby*.

[72] Article 30 EC and Article XX GATT, respectively.

that may conflict with trade liberalisation commitments. Secondly, while trade liberalisation commitments are made internationally, the interests behind them are national, i.e. the interests of producers, consumers, importers and exporters. At the same time, the interests of an open, rules-based and non-discriminatory trading system are ideally shared by actors in all members of the trade liberalisation agreement, and in that sense are transnational. Thus, a "trade and..." conflict in reality often pitches transnational interests against each other. However, these interests are supposed to be represented in the *national* political process preceding the implementation of a national policy that may lead to a "trade and..." conflict. The transnational trade interests are supposedly represented in trade agreements. The transnational non-trade interests will be represented in relevant international environmental agreements or standards, and if there are none, they will only be represented to the extent that they are taken into account in the national political process.

The EC does not pursue its own policies with regard to, for example, public morality or *"ordre public"*. Thus, with regard to such interests, the picture is largely similar to the WTO situation; national non-trade interests are pitched against international trade liberalisation commitments. The Court of Justice determines the margins within which the Member States may invoke these interests to interfere with free movement rights derived from Community law. The same refinement made above applies here too; trade liberalisation is at the same time a national and a transnational interest. As regards those non-trade interests that are the subject of this work, the EC has legislative competencies of its own, so the transnational nature of these interests has treaty status. The EC Treaty differentiates between "public health" and "environment". The Community pursues an environmental policy of its own, and shares competencies with its Member States in this field. Therefore, a trade and environment conflict in the EC involves an international trade liberalisation commitment and a non-trade interest that may be both national and Community-wide. The degree to which the non-trade interest is perceived as a national or also as a Community interest depends on the environmental problem at issue. Accordingly, "trade and..." conflicts in the EC may be considered to lie somewhere in the middle of a scale with completely or mostly national non-trade interests like public order at the one end, and completely Community (or "communitarised") non-trade interests at the other end. The Community's public health policy is only supplementary to the Member States' policies. Nonetheless, life and health protection is also an internal market issue, and through that avenue increasingly comes to the forefront in Community legislation. Thus, trade and health conflicts lie somewhere between trade and public policy conflicts and trade and environment conflicts on the scale proposed above.

Some authors present 'trade and...' problems as value conflicts.[73] Of course, whether one agrees with such a view depends on how one defines "values". Non-trade interests such as environmental protection may well be values or express values. It seems less clear that trade liberalisation itself is a value. It has also been suggested that trade linkage problems involve conflicting claims of justice in the context of international economic law. Accordingly, a concept of justice is central to international economic law.[74] In this view, each 'trade and...' debate has, at its root, a series of questions concerning justice. Identifying trade linkage questions as justice questions suggests an 'integrated view', which recognises that conflicts between traditional trade policy and other areas of social policy involve branches of the same tree, the tree being the construction of a "just society". The resolution of 'trade and...' disputes cannot be sought exclusively at the doctrinal level. It has to be articulated normatively, as an attempt to resolve dilemmas and tensions within the liberal vision and between liberalism and other candidates for 'right order'.[75]

1.3.3 "Trade And...", International Law and Other Disciplines

Much of the literature concerning the WTO forms part of what is called 'international trade law' or 'international economic law'.[76] The latter term is usually also taken to include regional economic agreements, among which is the European Community. The debate on "trade and..." conflicts in international law is often linked to much more than trade and certain societal interests. Discussions involve notions such as democracy, human rights, liberalism, sovereignty, legitimacy and equality.

Proponents usually point out that trade liberalisation increases economic opportunities, thus giving countries and their populations the chance to reap the economic gains from trade.[77] World Bank studies suggest that developing countries that have liberalised their trade regimes have shown much better growth rates than developing countries that have remained relatively closed to trade.[78] In addition, liberalised trade is said by its proponents to stimulate peace

---

[73] See e.g. Nichols (1996a) and Atik (1998).

[74] Garcia (1998a).

[75] Ibid.

[76] For discussions on the meaning of these terms, see (1996) 17 *U. Pa. J. Int'l. Econ. L*, special issue dedicated to international economic law.

[77] See e.g. 'The Case for Globalisation', *The Economist*, 22 September 2000 and 29 September 2001.

[78] World Bank (2001) shows that 24 developing countries that increased their integration into the world economy over two decades ending in the late 1990s achieved higher growth in incomes, longer life expectancy and better schooling. These countries, home to some 3 billion people, enjoyed an average 5 percent growth rate in income per capita in the 1990s compared to 2 percent in rich countries. On

between trading nations and peoples. Trade interests increase knowledge and understanding of each other, and even in the event of conflicts, established trade contacts make war too costly an option to consider. The main source of inspiration for this view are the writings of Kant.[79] The idea that trade stimulates or even guarantees peaceful coexistence underlies the European integration project.[80] Although less explicitly, it may be said to underlie global trade liberalisation too.[81] As early as 1947, when the Havana Conference that sought to establish an International Trade Organisation was held, it was stated that '[t]rade had been man's main peacetime activity almost since the time he had begun to live in society, which led people to believe that the success to be attained by the work of the Conference would become an invaluable pillar of that lasting peace that all the peoples were so anxiously seeking.'[82] On the basis of Kantian ideas, it has been argued that "liberal democracies" do not wage war on each other.[83] They will form a 'league of democratic nations' in international organisations, and to some extent already do so in organisations such as the OECD, the EC and the GATT.[84] This view has been criticised as ignoring the tensions between democracy and liberalism, and implicitly favouring the latter over the former.

---

the other hand, some 2 billion people - particularly in sub-Saharan Africa, the Middle East, and the former Soviet Union - live in countries that are being left behind. These countries have been unable to increase their integration with the world economy. On average, these economies have contracted and poverty has risen.

[79] '[N]ature also unites nations which the concept of cosmopolitan right would not have protected from violence and war, and does so by means of their mutual self-interest. For *the spirit of commerce* sooner or later takes hold of every people, and it cannot exist side by side with war.' Kant (1991) at 114.

[80] See the Preamble to the EC Treaty: 'Resolved by thus pooling their resources to preserve and strengthen peace and liberty [...]', and the excerpt from the Schuman Declaration, *supra* note 17.

[81] See the 'About the WTO' introductory section at the WTO webpages, http://www.wto.org.

[82] Speech at the first plenary meeting by the President of Cuba, host of the 1947-48 Havana Conference on Trade and Employment that was to prepare the International Trade Organisation. E/CONF.2/SR.1 at 1.

[83] When Francis Fukuyama (1992) proclaimed the "end of history", he argued that the victory of "liberal democracy" marked the end of ideological clashes. Simplifying his thesis, he argued that this victory is driven by two main factors: the 'logic of modern natural science' that leads to the triumph of capitalism, and man's desire for recognition, manifested in such feelings as self-respect and dignity. A "liberal democracy" in Fukuyama's view is a societal order built on the logic of modern science and capitalism, and able to satisfy the desire for recognition of all citizens. The international dimension of Fukuyama's thesis is much less elaborated.

[84] Fukuyama (1992) at 276-284. Interestingly, in this view, even if the GATT does not require its members to be democratic, it does require them to have "liberal economies". Fukuyama, at 283, note 9. This point is debatable, however, as the GATT accommodated a number of non-market economies as contracting parties.

Moreover, it has been added, liberal democracy has never been under so much strain as it is today.[85]

The word "liberal" takes on different meanings in discussions on "trade and..." problems. First, the liberal view in international relations theory challenges the realist and positivist assumptions that states are the sole or predominant actors on the international scene, focusing instead on individuals, interest groups and companies. Secondly, when international trade lawyers speak of a "liberal trade order", they refer to open markets enabling international trade flows without undue discrimination on the grounds of the national origin of goods and unnecessary trade obstacles. Thirdly, "liberal" may also denote the kind of *domestic* system that states should be based on in order to successfully take part in the international trade system. The latter meaning of "liberal" has an economic as well as a political pendant. It is not only associated with a capitalist, property-based economy, but frequently also with respect for human rights and fundamental freedoms, democracy and the rule of law. Proponents of a "liberal" international trade system do not necessarily argue that all participating states should be democratic, or even capitalist. The history of the GATT shows in fact that its rules were quite apt to take in state-driven economies. And although the WTO's expanded scope *vis-à-vis* the GATT makes it more difficult for non-capitalist states to participate, this does not seem to be an impossibility.[86] Moreover, the WTO does not lay down any demands for membership in terms of human rights, democracy or the rule of law. It is debatable to what extent such values are enshrined in the WTO agreements.[87]

It may be argued that through trade contacts, open economies gradually absorb and adopt certain values relating to democracy and human rights. However, in some countries that have shown impressive economic performance, little or no improvement in terms of democracy and human rights has taken place.[88] The view that trade spreads such essential assets of (Western) neoliberal societies as democracy, the rule of law, individualism and human rights may

---

[85] Marks (1997).

[86] For instance the TRIPS Agreement requires a domestic system of intellectual property rights, which may be difficult to introduce in a non-market economy. Nevertheless, Myanmar and Cuba are just two obvious examples of WTO Members that are largely based on non-market economies.

[87] It has accordingly been argued that the WTO should not attempt to 'micromanage world social policy' for three reasons. First, it would not work between polities ranging from democracies to totalitarian dictatorships. Second, many conflicts between trade and societal values are local in nature. Third, social policy co-ordination and imposition does not create universal values. Nichols (1996a). For an opinion that the WTO does enshrine basic liberties and human rights, see various writings by Petersmann.

[88] See UN doc A/55/342, "Globalization and its impact on the full enjoyment of all human rights", preliminary report of the UN Secretary-General.

be criticised from a cultural relativist perspective.[89] Trade itself is sometimes presented as a human right, often linked to the right to property.[90] The main source of inspiration appears to be the German constitution. However, most of the world's constitutions do not recognise a constitutional right to trade.[91]

Considering the fact that trade and environment conflicts go beyond those which are merely legal, it comes as no surprise that they are also studied by other than legal disciplines. Particularly influential in the study of international trade law are international relations theory,[92] and economics.[93] In international relations, institutionalism has proved a viable alternative to the dichotomy between realism (focusing on states as the primary and unitary actors in world affairs) and liberalism (viewing other actors, such as individuals, business, and interest groups as essential). Regime theory is increasingly applied to issues of public international law, including WTO law. Such applications are usually categorised as institutionalist.[94]

The application of economic insights to legal issues is captured by the law and economics movement.[95] Public choice theory applies insights from the study of private economic behaviour to collective action problems, including government action.[96] Institutional economics focuses on the transaction costs involved in obtaining information needed to take rational decisions. The relationship between transaction costs and institutions is regarded as being critical to understanding economic exchange and the existence of institutions. Transactions are sometimes left to the market, where they take place on the spot and spontaneously, and sometimes institutionalised in a firm or in government regulation.[97]

---

[89] See e.g. Hungtington (1996) at 183-195: 'The central problem in the relations between the West and the rest is [...] the discordance between the West's - particularly America's - efforts to promote a universal Western culture and its declining ability to do so. [...] Double standards in practice are the unavoidable price of universal standards of principle. [...] If democracy comes to additional Asian countries it will come because the increasingly strong Asian bourgeoisies and middle classes want it to come'.

[90] See various writings of Petersmann.

[91] As noted by Kuijper (1997).

[92] See e.g. Slaughter (1995) and Abbott (1989).

[93] See e.g. Bhagwati and Hudec (eds.) (1996) and Bhandari and Sykes (eds.) (1997).

[94] See Nichols (1996b) and (1998), arguing that the notion of institutionalism encompasses more than just than regime theory, providing an overview of institutionalist approaches, and proposing historical and sociological institutionalism as alternative ways of looking at the WTO.

[95] For an overview of this discipline, see Bouckaert and De Geest (ed.) (2000).

[96] See e.g. Stephan (1995).

[97] The leading work on the theory of the firm is Coase (1988), incorporating Coase's papers 'The Theory of the Firm' and 'The Problem of Social Cost'. For a criticism of the way the 'law and economics' movement has subsequently modified the Coase theorem, see Fletcher (1999).

"New" institutional economics enables comparative institutional analysis by providing for the analysis of different institutions and organisations at the same time.[98] Examples of these approaches which are relevant to the topic of this study include a comparative institutional analysis of the various 'trade-off devices' applied in 'trade and...' conflicts before international and federal dispute resolution bodies.[99] The same author has taken a first step in building on new institutional economics to develop a theory on international economic organisations.[100] The theory builds on previous works in institutional economics that focused on transaction costs to compare the market with the firm, and the market with government regulation. It seeks to apply a transaction costs analysis to assess international regulation as compared to business firms and national regulation.[101] Finally, the issue of non-tariff barriers in international trade and the concepts of "regulatory competition" and "regulatory harmonisation" between states have attracted economists and lawyers alike.[102]

1.4 Aim, Structure and Scope of the Research

1.4.1 Aims and Structure of this Work

The aim of this work is to review the way "negative integration" clauses as well as "environmental justifications" operate in the EC and the WTO, and how they limit the environmental policy choices of the members of these organisations. As accounted earlier in this introductory Chapter, trade and environment conflicts are increasingly coming to the fore in both the EC and WTO. With a thorough study of the commitments in this respect in both organisations it is hoped to provide some clarity in a heated yet often poorly informed debate. In addition to raising academic interest, this work also hopes to provide information for national and European policy-makers on the possibilities and problems of conducting environmental policies in the light of trade liberalisation commitments. In addition, the author hopes to provide some insight into the important question as to whether the rules on trade and environ-

---

[98] An important work of institutional economics, written in the context of the US federal system, is Komesar (1994). It has inspired Poiares Maduro (1998a), an interesting study of the role of the European Court of Justice in EC law on the free movement of goods.

[99] Trachtman (1998).

[100] Trachtman (1996a), building on Coase (1988) and Komesar (1994).

[101] A first attempt has also been made to apply this theoretical framework to actual international economic organisations, particularly the Association of South East Asian Nations (ASEAN), by Kiriyama (1998).

[102] See e.g. Sykes (1999a and 1999b) and (1995), Pelkmans (1997); Trebilcock and Howse (1998); and the special issue (2000-2) of JIEL devoted to "Regulatory Competition".

ment in the EC and the WTO enable adjudicators to strike a reasonable balance between conflicting interests.

Why compare trade and environment in the EC and the WTO? The differences between these organisations as described above are clear. However, there are several reasons for a comparison. First and foremost, the nature of the provisions studied, as well as the kind of disputes in which they have been invoked, are similar to an important extent. The basic question that can be asked in both the EC and the WTO is what room their rules leave to their members to pursue environmental policies by measures affecting trade. Moreover, the provisions of the EC Treaty studied in this work have largely been modelled on the relevant GATT provisions. Secondly, the EC and WTO do not live in separate worlds. On the one hand, the EC is a regional agreement which is supposed to be in conformity with the basic principles of the multilateral trading system. The EC's own policies, *inter alia* in the environmental field, must comply with WTO commitments. On the other hand, the WTO is a young organisation whose reach into the domestic legal and policy arenas of its Members goes well beyond that of its predecessor, the GATT. It is only natural, then, for the WTO to look at experiences in other trade liberalisation contexts when it is increasingly confronted with trade-environment conflicts. Among the sources of inspiration, the EC with its well-developed case-law is a prime candidate. This is not to suggest, however, that the WTO can only learn from the EC. Conversely, as already stated, the EC is bound to comply with WTO law, and the WTO may be expected to increasingly affect developments in the EC.[103]

Approaches based on legal theory in general, conventional treaty interpretation or the specifics of European integration will not suffice in bringing to the fore the similarities and differences of the two organisations under examination. There are no ready-made theories on comparing regional economic integration with the youthful World Trade Organisation.[104] Accordingly, the approach of this study is modest; it does not attempt to design an overall theoretical framework. Its point of departure is the interpretation of a number of rules in the EC Treaty and the WTO Agreements. The approach is largely based on case-law and academic literature. Occasional references are made to the different structures and institutional contexts in which the studied rules function. Perceived similarities between EC and WTO law have prompted some to speak of "convergence", while others have even advocated taking the EC as a "model" for further developments in the WTO.[105] As a scholarly observer, the tendency to look for similarities and generalities between two sets of rules comes almost naturally.

---

[103] Cf. De Búrca and Scott (2001); Eeckhout (1997).

[104] To the present author's knowledge, the only tentative start towards a comprehensive theoretical framework encompassing both the EC and the WTO is found in Trachtman (1996a).

[105] See Weiler (1999), Trachtman (1996b), and Prodi (2000), further discussed in Chapter 9.

At the same time, the intention in this work is to consider both similarities and differences as neutral, in the sense that there is no presumption that similarities or convergence are desirable, or that differences or divergence are unwanted.

Merely concentrating on environmental justifications in the EC and the WTO is of little use without a thorough preliminary study of their basic prohibitions. Before contemplating justifications, the question as to whether a measure possibly infringes a prohibition should be addressed. The structure of this work is as follows. After this introductory part, the evolution of EC law in the field of study will be analysed in part two (Chapters 2 and 3). The analysis will revolve around the interpretation of the basic prohibition in Article 28 EC, including the central notion of 'measures of equivalent effect to quantitative restrictions', and the exclusion of "selling arrangements" from that basic prohibition as developed in the case-law. Next, the focus turns to the exceptions laid down in the EC Treaty (Article 30), and the justifications for "mandatory requirements" as accepted in the case-law of the ECJ. Finally, the conditions attached to the application of these justifications are discussed. In Chapter 3, an analysis of a number of recurring themes is made, i.e., basic disciplines and typologies, justifications and conditions, the role of discrimination, and the issue of production and processing methods (PPMs). Part three (Chapters 4 and 5) analyses the evolution of GATT/WTO rules and their interpretation. Here, there are not just two pivotal provisions as in the EC, but various rules applicable to the regulatory measures of Members and their justifications in the GATT, TBT and SPS Agreements. For these Agreements, the relevant obligations, exceptions and conditions for those exceptions to apply are discussed, as well as the relationships between them. Again, a second part addresses essentially the same recurring themes as in the EC Part. In the fourth part (Chapters 6 to 10), Chapter 6 takes a comparative approach as regards the operation of the "negative integration" clauses and environmental justifications in the EC and the WTO. Chapter 7 addresses two issues in whose respect it is more difficult to compare the EC and WTO, i.e., international harmonisation and trade-restrictive measures based on production and processing methods and with extraterritorial protection goals. Chapter 8 addresses a somewhat separate question, which the author nonetheless thinks is worth consideration: the legal status of the application by EC Member States of trade-restrictive environmental measures to products from third countries that are WTO members. The study ends with a discussion of whether the EC could be regarded as a "model" for the WTO in Chapter 9, and concluding remarks in Chapter 10.

1.4.2   Research Limitations and Working Definitions

One of the most difficult aspects of a research topic is its proper delimitation. The focus in this study on 'unilateral regulatory environmental and health measures that restrict trade in goods' needs some further explanation.

(a)   "Measures"

This work focuses on the prohibitions aimed at ensuring trade liberalisation commitments, and what are provisionally called "environmental justifications" in the EC Treaty and WTO Agreements, and how they legally affect domestic policy.[106] Manifestations of domestic policy-making in the environmental sphere are manifold, and no attempt is made to categorise them. Often, the word "measure" is used to refer to such manifestations of domestic policy. Especially in the WTO, the use of the word "measure" sometimes causes confusion. For the sake of clarity, a "measure" is here defined as the application to imported (or exported) products of domestic laws, regulations, requirements, administrative practices, etc., that trigger the application of EC or WTO disciplines.

The extension of the prohibitions and justifications in the EC and the WTO to that which falls within the competence of domestic policy will obviously depend on their wording and scope. Generally speaking, a domestic measure's alleged discriminatory, protectionist, or otherwise hindering effect on international trade, will trigger the application of the prohibitions in the EC Treaty or WTO Agreements. The trigger thus lies in a measure's (potential) application to foreign products. In some cases, the measure will not be covered by these disciplines. In other cases, it will be covered by these disciplines and will need to be justified. Then, the claimed environmental purpose of the measure will come into play.

(b)   Trade Obstacles and Discrimination; "Life and Health" and "Environment"

The relevant provision of the EC Treaty prohibits quantitative restrictions and measures having equivalent effect thereto. The GATT in one provision prohibits quantitative restrictions, and in another it prohibits discrimination, or to be more precise, it prohibits internal regulations from giving less favourable treatment to imported products in comparison with their domes-

---

[106] Henceforth, the term "domestic" should be understood to refer to policies of the Member States of the EC as well as policies of WTO Members, including the EC itself.

tic counterparts. This is called the National Treatment principle. The TBT Agreement provides specific rules for technical regulations and the SPS Agreement for sanitary and phytosanitary measures. There is another important non-discrimination provision in the GATT, which does not consider discrimination of imported products *vis-à-vis* domestic products, but rather discrimination of products imported from country A *vis-à-vis* products imported from country B. Despite its great importance to the WTO system, this principle of Most-Favoured Nation treatment is not addressed in this work. There are two reasons for this. First of all, there is no explicit mention of the Most-Favoured Nation principle in the EC Treaty, although it is implicit.[107] Secondly, up to now, all trade and environment conflicts in the GATT and the WTO have focused on the prohibition of quantitative restrictions and the National Treatment obligation, rather than on Most-Favoured Nation treatment.

Both the GATT and EC Treaty provide an exception to their trade liberalisation disciplines for the protection of human, animal or plant life and health. The GATT in addition contains an exception for the conservation of exhaustible natural resources. "Environmental protection" as such is not found in either the EC Treaty exceptions to the free movement of goods, or in the GATT. However, the European Court of Justice has accepted "environmental protection" as a "mandatory requirement" that may in principle justify trade-restricting measures. And in the WTO, "environmental protection" is explicitly mentioned in a number of Agreements, notably the TBT. These differences lead to the question whether "life and health", "conservation" and "environmental protection" are different objectives, or whether they overlap, and if so, to what extent. Moreover, these concepts do not necessarily have to receive the same interpretation in the WTO and the EC.

The notion of environmental protection at first sight appears to be less clear than the protection of the life and health of humans, animals and plants, or the conservation of exhaustible natural resources. A wide interpretation of environmental protection could include both life and health protection and resource conservation. A stricter interpretation of environmental protection, however, would exclude at least life and health protection, and thus only cover those environmental objectives not directly concerned with life or health. Although much narrower than the wide interpretation, such a strict concept of environmental protection would not be devoid of meaning. Examples would include noise pollution, "horizon pollution", and non-dangerous waste. As to resource conservation,

---

[107] EC Member States are supposed to treat all products in the internal market equally, in whichever Member State they originate. They are supposed to do the same for all products originating from third countries, once the products are put into free circulation. Article XXIV GATT provides room for preferential treatment of products from within a customs union *vis-à-vis* products from third countries. See Chapter 8.

in the WTO, this concept has received a wide interpretation as including the protection of living species, even if that might have been expected to have been covered by life and health protection. In the EC, resource conservation is not separately mentioned. It could be covered by environmental protection and by life and health protection. In this work, "environmental protection" as a general term is loosely used in the broadest sense, including life and health protection, environmental objectives not directly related to life and health, resource conservation, and the protection of "global commons" such as the ozone layer, the atmosphere, and biological diversity. However, when specific treaty provisions and judgments are discussed below, "environmental protection" usually has a narrower scope, not covering "life and health" protection.[108]

(c) Trade in Goods; Non-fiscal Measures; Focus on Imports

There are three important limitations to the kind of rules under scrutiny in this work. First of all, this study addresses trade in goods, not services.[109] The author is aware of the increasing role of services in both global and European trade. Trade in services has been covered by the EC Treaty from its entry into force, along with goods and the other free movement subjects (capital and persons, in the form of freedom of movement for workers and freedom of establishment). Not covered by the 1947 GATT, trade in services is now covered by WTO disciplines in the GATS, although in a less far-reaching manner than goods.[110] Despite the growing importance of trade in services and its increasing coverage by WTO disciplines, however, there are good reasons to concentrate the analysis on goods. First, the interface between environmental regulation and trade in goods has a longer and richer history than the interface with trade in services (or other EC freedoms). Experiences in the environment-goods interface will most probably have an influence on developments regarding services as well. Secondly, domestic environmental policies interfere more easily with disciplines on trade in goods than with disciplines on trade services. Thirdly, constraints of space and time urge a limitation of the scope of the analysis.

The second limitation lies in this work's focus on non-fiscal environmental policies. Domestic measures interfering with trade can roughly be divided into fiscal and non-fiscal measures. Fiscal measures include duties or charges levied on imported products only (border measures) such as tariff duties and other charges, and duties levied on imported products to offset dumping or subsidies. They also include internal taxation levied on products, which may be imported.

---

[108] See further Section 6.2.

[109] Although occasional reference is made to trade in services: see Section 5.3.3.

[110] In the GATS, some of the most important disciplines, such as National Treatment, are not generally applicable as in the GATT, and are only binding upon the regulations of WTO Members with respect to those services regarding which they have made specific commitments.

Examples are excise duties and value-added taxes (VAT). Fiscal measures are disciplined by separate provisions in both the EC and WTO contexts. This work does not purport to address those disciplines exhaustively, although occasional reference is made to them.[111] Non-fiscal measures, on the other hand, comprise quantitative restrictions and other limitations to or prohibitions on imports or exports (border measures) as well as the application of any internal regulatory manifestation of policy (laws, regulations, administrative practices, etc.) to imported or exported products. This wide range of non-fiscal "internal measures" includes product requirements, labelling requirements, restrictions on the transportation, distribution, selling and advertising of products, and so on. When applied to imports, all such measures may in principle trigger the application of EC and WTO rules.

Finally, although occasional reference is made to exports, the focus of the study is on rules that address measures applied to imported goods. Although domestic environmental measures may well interfere with export flows, the bulk of the attention in both case-law and literature has been on effects on imports. This is no great surprise, as much of the discussion on the compatibility of domestic measures with international disciplines is influenced by the dilemma between allowing the pursuance of legitimate objectives and precluding such objectives from being abused for undesirable protectionist purposes. Obviously, protectionist voices will generally advocate restricting imports rather than exports.

(d)   States and the EC as Actors

In the EC, there are currently 15 Member States, while accession is being negotiated with 12 states in Central and Eastern Europe, as well as with Turkey.[112] In the WTO, there are over 140 Members.[113] The large majority of WTO Members are states, among which are the EC Member States, but there are also non-state WTO Members. According to the WTO Agreement, the Contracting parties to the GATT and the European Communities became original Members of the WTO.[114] Thus, the EC itself has become a Member of

---

[111] See Section 3.4.5.

[112] Accession negotiations are currently taking place between the EC and Latvia, Lithuania, Estonia, Poland, the Czech Republic, Hungary, Slovenia, Cyprus, Malta, and the Slovak Republic, whose accession is expected by some as early as 2004, and with Bulgaria, Romania, and Turkey, which will need more time.

[113] In late 2001, China became the 143th WTO Member, and negotiations with *inter alia* Russia are being held.

[114] Article XI:1 WTO Agreement. Moreover, any 'separate customs territory possessing full autonomy in the conduct of its external commercial relations and in the other matters provided for in this Agreement and the Multilateral Trade Agreements' may accede to the WTO. Article XII:1 WTO Agreement.

the WTO and is therefore bound by the WTO rules just as its Member States are. The emphasis in this work on states and the European Community as actors is by no means self-evident. Non-state actors, such as private individuals, business enterprises, and non-governmental organisations, play an important role in the EC legal order and an increasingly important one in the international legal order(s). However, for a comparison between the EC and WTO, the basis chosen are these organisations' rules concerning the limitations posed by trade liberalisation commitments to their members' regulatory behaviour for environmental reasons, and the interpretations of these rules in dispute settlement procedures. A focus on states (and the EC as a WTO Member) as main actors then seems appropriate. This is of course not to say that other actors are irrelevant, or that state action is not viewed as a series of outcomes of internal interest clashes. Yet laying the emphasis on, for example, the role of individuals and national courts as actors in the development of the free movement of goods in the EC legal order provides a difficult basis for a comparison with an organisation like the WTO, which does not impose the direct applicability of its rules in national courts, in whose dispute settlement body citizens have no standing, and to which national courts cannot refer questions on the interpretation of WTO rules.

(e)   PPMs; Harmonisation and Unilateral Action

Measures affecting trade flows are often enacted because of worries concerning global or transboundary environmental problems.[115] They pose particular problems to the EC and WTO rules when they are framed in terms of production or processing methods (PPMs). In contrast to product characteristics, such PPM-based policies do not just impose requirements as to products as they are traded, but seek to prescribe how their production should take place in the exporting country. In the remainder of this work, PPMs and related problems are discussed in separate Sections both in the EC and WTO contexts.

Another issue that is addressed with regard to both EC and WTO rules is international harmonisation or standard-setting as a way of tackling regulatory differences that may disturb trade. The main focus of this work is on how the relevant rules relate to unilateral measures of members of the WTO and the EC. However, in the EC, the room for unilateral action is disciplined not only by the provisions of "primary EC law" on the free movement of goods, but also by relevant "secondary EC law", i.e. Community legislation in the field of environmental or health standards. Such legislation represents a multilateral solution to striking a balance between the demands of market integration and

---

[115] The Dutch legislative proposal on mandatory wood labelling referred to above provides an example of such a measure.

safeguarding legitimate non-economic interests. Often, though, the balance struck is not uniform and all-encompassing. The standards agreed upon at the Community level in many cases only establish a minimum level of protection, leaving individual Member States with room to go beyond that level. Although this study discusses secondary Community legislation, it does not elaborate on its intricacies. Secondary Community legislation in some cases renders recourse to the primary EC Treaty rules impossible. In assessing national policies going beyond Community standards, the primary Community rules on the free movement of goods often come into play. Thus, the primary EC Treaty provisions that are the main focus of this study cannot be considered in isolation from secondary EC law.

In the WTO, as argued above, there is no legislative capacity to set standards in fields such as health or environmental protection. Here too, the focus of the WTO provisions studied is on disciplining the unilateral domestic policies of members. However, that is not to say that at the global level, no multilateral action is taken to address environmental and health problems. First, environmental and health standards may be agreed upon multilaterally in international bodies and organisations, such as the International Standardisation Organisation and the Codex Alimentarius. The SPS and TBT Agreements refer to such multilateral standards, and provide more lenient disciplines to national measures that are in conformity with relevant standards than to measures that deviate from them. Secondly, numerous so-called multilateral environmental agreements (MEAs) address environmental and health issues. These MEAs sometimes directly affect trade relations by containing provisions regulating trade in the products or species concerned.[116] Even without explicitly regulating trade, they may present issues of compatibility with WTO provisions.[117] The WTO Agreements do not explicitly refer to any specific MEA.[118] This study does not focus on the relationship between WTO rules and international standards and MEAs. The provisions of the SPS and TBT Agreements as they relate to international standards are discussed, and at various occasions, reference is

---

[116] The most important examples are the Basel Convention on Dangerous Waste, the Convention on International Trade in Endangered Species, and the Montreal Protocol on Substances containing CFCs.

[117] For example, the Kyoto Protocol provides for emissions trading as one of the mechanisms to achieve reductions of greenhouse gas emissions in order to curb global warming. Emissions trading rules still need to be elaborated, but their compatibility with WTO rules has already been discussed. See Werksman (1999).

[118] With the exception of the SPS Agreement, which in Article 3.4 refers to standards developed in organisations operating under the framework of the International Plant Protection Convention. The absence of further references to MEAs in the WTO may be contrasted with the NAFTA, which in Article 104 explicitly provides that in case of conflict, the provisions of a number of MEAs shall have priority over those of the NAFTA.

made to the relevance of MEAs to the interpretation of WTO rules.[119] This is a logical consequence of the fact that the WTO rules are not self-contained, but are part of general public international law.[120] Nevertheless, the main focus of the analysis is on situations where a WTO member takes a measure in the absence of relevant international standards.

---

[119] See especially Sections 4.6, 5.4.3, 5.4.5, and 7.1.

[120] As recognised and emphasised by the Appellate Body in various dispute settlement reports, e.g.
  US-Gasoline and US-Shrimp-Turtle.

PART TWO

Trade and Environment in the European Community

.

CHAPTER 2

The Main Provisions and Their Interpretation

2.1 Prohibition of Import Restrictions and Measures Having Equivalent Effect

2.1.1 Article 28 EC

The wording of Article 28 of the EC Treaty is short and simple:[1]

Quantitative restrictions on imports and all measures having equivalent effect shall be prohibited between Member States.

The importance of Article 28 in the pursuit of a Community-wide integrated market can hardly be overstated. Its use in the removal of intra-Community trade barriers is attributable to the wide interpretation that has been given to the words 'measures having equivalent effect', rather than to the prohibition of quantitative restrictions as such. Quantitative restrictions are so clearly incompatible with the very notion of a common market that it has not often been necessary to have recourse to Article 28 to remove them. Most quantitative restrictions between Member States had in fact already been removed under the auspices of the Organisation for European Economic Co-operation (OEEC, the precursor of the OECD) during the 1950s.[2] On the contrary, the interpretation of 'measures having equivalent effect' has enabled the European Court of Justice to tackle many national regulations having an effect on Community trade, even if they were not specifically aimed at limiting imports. The Court's case-law reflects a continuing search for the appropriate ambit of the prohibition in Article 28. Some questions regarding this search are the following: Should Article 28 merely prohibit discriminatory and protectionist measures? Or should it rather preclude any unjustified obstacle to intra-Community trade? Should some types of national measures receive different treatment than others? The search for the scope of Article 28 is discussed in general terms, but it has repercussions for national measures aimed at protecting health or the environment.

2.1.2 Place in the EC Treaty

In the original 1957 Rome Treaty Establishing the European Economic Community, Article 3 mentioned among the "activities" of the Com-

---

[1]   Hereinafter, references to EC Treaty provisions appear with the suffix "EC" only when they are first introduced.

[2]   Weatherill and Beaumont (1995) at 429. For an account of the liberalisation of quantitative restrictions under the OEEC Liberalisation Code, see Hieronymi (1973), Chapter V; Veil (1965), Drittes Kapitel. On the origins of the OEEC, see http://www.oecd.org/about/origins/conf-oeec.htm.

munity the 'elimination, as between Member States, of customs duties and quantitative restrictions on the import and export of goods, and of all other measures having equivalent effect'.[3] Also mentioned as an "activity" of the Community was the abolition as between Member States of obstacles to the free movement of persons, services and capital.[4] The latter was changed by the 1992 Maastricht Treaty on European Union into a comprehensive reference to an internal market characterised by the 'abolition, as between Member States, of obstacles to the free movement of goods, persons, services and capital'.[5] Article 3 is located in Part One of the Treaty, entitled Principles. The Treaty provisions which this work is primarily concerned with, Articles 28-30, are placed in Chapter Two, entitled 'Elimination of Quantitative Restrictions Between Member States', belonging to Title One, entitled 'Free Movement of Goods', which in turn forms part of what in the original EEC Treaty was called Part Two, the Foundations of the Community. The 1992 Maastricht Treaty changed this into Part Three, Community Policies.

2.1.3 Context: Other Treaties

The concept of 'measures having equivalent effect' to quantitative restrictions introduced in Article 28 was a novelty in international law. Whereas the notion of quantitative restrictions was found in earlier trade agreements[6], the concept of 'measures having equivalent effect' neither appeared in the 1947 GATT, nor in the legal texts of the 1948 OEEC.[7] The specific wording 'measures having equivalent effect' to quantitative restrictions also does not figure in the instruments establishing the other two European Communities, the 1952 European Coal and Steel Community (ECSC) Treaty and the 1957 Euratom Treaty.[8] After the entry into force of the EC Treaty, the term did appear in the Convention establishing the European Free Trade Association (EFTA)[9] as well as in various trade agreements between the EC and third

---

[3] Article 3(a) of the original EEC Treaty. The English version of this phrase only became official after the United Kingdom and Ireland had joined the Community in 1973.

[4] Article 3(c) of the original EEC Treaty.

[5] After the 1986 Single European Act had introduced the term "internal market" into the EEC Treaty. On this concept, see Schrauwen (1997).

[6] Such as the 1927 Geneva Convention on Import and Export Prohibition and Restriction, Geneva, League of Nations Publications, Economic and Financial, 1927. See Winham (1992) at 28.

[7] As noted by Béraud (1968) at 266-7; Graf (1972) at 59-60.

[8] Both Treaties lay down the prohibition of quantitative restrictions, but not of measures having equivalent effect. See Article 4 Treaty establishing the European Community for Coal and Steel; Article 93 Euratom Treaty.

[9] EFTA Treaty, http://secretariat.efta.int/efta/library/legal/stockhconv, Article 10.11: '"Quantitative restrictions" means prohibitions or restrictions on imports from the territory of other Member States

countries[10], albeit sometimes with qualifications.[11] The 1958 Benelux Economic Union Treaty[12], which was concluded shortly after the EC Treaty, instead used the terms 'quantitative or qualitative restrictions'.[13]

Although the concept of 'measure having equivalent effect' did not as such occur in earlier and contemporary trade agreements, such agreements did employ language on the elimination of measures that hinder trade, rather than merely discriminatory or protectionist measures.[14] As early as 1950, plans were put forward in the OEEC Council for a single European market.[15] In the same year, the OEEC laid down a liberalisation code, which provided for the abolition of quantitative restrictions, but not of measures of equivalent effect.[16] In 1961, the OECD replaced the OEEC, and Canada and the United States became members of the new organisation. In the OECD Convention, members agreed to 'pursue their efforts to reduce or abolish *obstacles* to the exchange of goods and services [...]'.[17]

---

whether made effective through quotas, import licences or other measures with equivalent effect, including administrative measures and requirements restricting import'. Note the similarity with GATT Article XI, and the addition to its wording, probably inspired by the EC Treaty, of the term 'with equivalent effect'.

[10] See e.g. Article 11 of the Treaty Establishing the European Economic Area, OJ L 1 (1994) at p. 3; Article 13 Europe Agreement between the European Communities and Hungary, OJ L 347 (1993) at p. 2.

[11] Treaty establishing an Association between the European Economic Community and Turkey, OJ 217 (1964) 3687, Article 10.2: 'L'union douanière comporte : - l'interdiction entre les Etats membres de la Communauté et la Turquie, à l'importation comme à l'exportation, des droits de douane et taxes d'effet équivalent et des restrictions quantitatives, ainsi que de toute autre mesure d'effet équivalent visant à assurer à la production nationale une protection contraire aux objectifs de l'accord [...]'. (no authentic English version available).

[12] This Treaty established an economic union comprising the free movement of goods, persons, capital and services. See Benelux Economic Union Treaty, Brussels, Benelux Secretariat, 1958, Article 1.

[13] Benelux Economic Union Treaty, Article 3: 'La circulation des marchandises [...] est [...] exempte de toutes prohibitions ou entraves d'ordre économique ou financier, notamment de restrictions quantitatives, qualitatives ou de change' (no authentic English version available).

[14] Article 4 of the Convention for European Economic Co-operation, reproduced in OECD (1996), provided that 'Contracting Parties will develop, in mutual co-operation, the maximum possible interchange of goods and services. To this end they [...] will co-operate in relaxing *restrictions* on trade and payment between one and another, with the object of abolishing as soon as possible those restrictions which at present *hamper* such trade and payments.' Emphasis added.

[15] Plans by Stikker and amendments by Petsche and Pella, see http://www.oecd.org//about/origins/oeec.htm.

[16] See Veil (1965) at 99; Graf (1972) at 59.

[17] 1960 Convention on the Organisation for Economic Co-operation and Development, text available at http://www.oecd.org/about/origins/convention/conventn.htm. Emphasis added.

The EC Treaty was inspired by the GATT rules. When the GATT was designed in 1946-47, it was foreseen that regional integration agreements, such as free trade areas and customs unions, would want to liberalise their internal trade more drastically than the trade between its constituent members and other GATT contracting parties. GATT Article XXIV therefore provides an exemption from GATT obligations (notably the Most-Favoured Nation requirement) for customs unions and free trade areas. In order to qualify for this exemption, such areas of further integration needed to meet certain conditions. These require *inter alia* that 'duties and other restrictive regulations of commerce' should be eliminated with respect to 'substantially all the trade' between the members.[18] The customs union in the EC Treaty was designed to meet these GATT requirements.

As discussed in Chapter 4, Article XI of the GATT prohibits 'prohibitions or restrictions other than duties, taxes, or other charges, whether made effective through quotas, import or export licences or *other measures*'. In the GATT, the words "other measures" have not received a similarly wide scope as 'measures having equivalent effect' in the EC Treaty. Although a further analysis follows in Chapter 4, it may be noted at this point that Article XI GATT is not needed to challenge national regulatory measures having the effect of restricting imports, since the GATT makes a distinction between "border" and "internal" trade restricting measures, and contains a separate provision addressing the latter. Simply put, the GATT forbids import and export prohibitions or restrictions, and disciplines internal regulatory measures through a non-discrimination requirement. The GATT provides essentially the same framework for fiscal barriers such as duties, charges and taxes, distinguishing between border and internal charges. Interestingly, whereas the designers of the EC Treaty followed the GATT framework by laying down two separate provisions for fiscal trade barriers and internal taxes, the same was not done as regards regulatory barriers. No distinction was made in the EC Treaty between border and internal regulatory measures; they were covered by one and the same provision, Article 28. The extent to which internal regulatory measures were within the scope of this provision thus depended upon the interpretation of the notion of 'measures having equivalent effect'.

2.1.4 History of Article 28 EC

Considering its absence in previous and contemporary trade treaties, one wonders where the term 'measures having equivalent effect' comes from, and how and when it was introduced. In December of 1952, the Dutch government sent a Memorandum on the task and competencies of a European

---

[18] Article XXIV:8(a)(i) GATT. Emphasis added. Article XXIV GATT is further discussed in Chapter 8.

customs union to the members of the ECSC. This memorandum spoke, in addition to a tariff community of 'autres obstacles dans le commerce'.[19] The memorandum with the attached proposals for treaty provisions became known as the Beyen plan. These documents discuss the abolition of quantitative restrictions between member states, but do not mention 'measures of equivalent effect'.[20] The same is true for the economic part of the 1953 Report to the Foreign Ministers from the intergovernmental conference for a European Political Community.[21] The Commission for a European Political Community, however, in the economic part of its report to the Foreign Ministers, proposed the following formula as part of the definition of the common market:

> *Dans le marché commun réalisé:*
> *1. les marchandises pourront circuler librement sur le territoire de la Communauté, les restrictions quantitatives, les droits de douane* ainsi que les autres mesures et pratiques ayant le même effect, *[...] ayant été abolis; [...]*[22]

In May of 1955, the Benelux countries proposed general economic integration in a Memorandum which spoke of 'la suppression progressive des obstacles aux échanges'.[23] In June of the same year, the Messina Resolution established an Intergovernmental Committee ("Comité Directeur") presided over by Spaak to study aspects of the proposed economic integration plans, one of which was on the establishment of a common market. The Spaak Report, issued in April of 1956, elaborated the requirements for the establishment of a common market. Its chapter on quotas, however, did not mention measures of equivalent effect or anything similar.[24] The Spaak Report was endorsed in May of 1956, and a second Spaak Committee was established to prepare the Treaties establishing the European Economic Community and the European Atomic Energy Community. A document from June-July of 1956 of the sub-group on the common market mentioned among the Community's activities in Article 3 sub (a) of the draft

---

[19] Memorandum of 11 December 1952, point 2.b. Translated into English as 'other obstacles hampering trade', in Harryvan and Van der Harst (1997) at 74.

[20] See also the letter by Beyen of 14 February 1953 and the Memorandum from the Dutch government of 5 May 1953, reproduced in *Jaarboek Buitenlandse Zaken* 1952-53.

[21] Report to the Foreign Ministers from the intergovernmental conference for a European Political Community, Rome, 22 September to 9 October 1953.

[22] Commission for a European Political Community, Report to the Foreign Ministers, Title VII, 'formules de synthese et textes alternatives', Formule no. 3, 'définition du marché commun'. Text proposed by the German, Belgian, Italian, Luxembourg and Dutch delegations in March 1954. Emphasis added.

[23] Memorandum by the Benelux countries, Doc.MAE 10/55, as quoted in Neri and Sperl (1960).

[24] 'Rapport des chefs de délégation aux ministres des affaires étrangères', also known as the Spaak Report, 21 April 1956, Title I, Chapter 2.

Treaty the elimination of, *inter alia*, price and sales regulations having equivalent effect to quantitative restrictions.[25] Later in the same year, Italian proposals introduced the term 'measures having equivalent effect' into the provision that is now Article 28 EC.[26] These proposals were approved by the group on the common market in March of 1957, the same month in which the Treaties were signed in Rome.[27]

(a) Early Doctrinal Debate

Before the ECJ had first delivered a decision on this aspect in 1974, considerable uncertainty existed as to the scope of the concept of 'measures having equivalent effect'. This uncertainty appears from a number of discussions of the concept in early doctrine.[28] Roughly, three approaches have been identified in this debate. Some advocated a narrow interpretation of the concept of 'measures having equivalent effect' as only covering discriminatory measures.[29] Of course, the scope of this interpretation still varies according to one's view of what actually constitutes "discrimination". Others insisted on a broader view, bringing within the concept even measures that were equally applicable to imported and domestic products, and insisting that in principle all measures having as their effect a restriction of intra-Community trade are covered.[30] All sorts of intermediary positions emerged, *inter alia* among Commission officials, to the effect that Article 28 covers some measures that are equally applicable, e.g. when they preclude imports or make them more difficult than the disposal of domestic products, and their restrictive effect is unnecessary or disproportionate.[31]

---

[25] 'L'élimination progressive des droits de douane et des restrictions quantitatives à l'entrée ou à la sortie des produits, et des taxes, fixations de tarifs ou réglementations d'achat et de vente comportant un effet équivalent a ces droits ou restrictions'. Groupe du Marché Commun, file I, archives of the Dutch Ministry of Foreign Affairs, the Hague.

[26] Documents MAE 504f/56js and 545f/56js, files IV and V, archives of the Dutch Ministry of Foreign Affairs, the Hague.

[27] Document MAE 823f/57mp, file VII, archives of the Dutch Ministry of Foreign Affairs, the Hague.

[28] In addition to the works cited supra in note 7, see e.g. VerLoren van Themaat (1967) and (1970); Dona-Viscardini (1973); Gormley (1985).

[29] See Seidl (1967) and Graf (1972).

[30] The main proponents of this expansive view were VerLoren van Themaat (1967) and Waelbroeck (1970).

[31] See Béraud (1968).

(b) Questions from the European Parliament

The Commission outlined its views on the scope of the concept of 'measures having equivalent effect' for the first time in 1967, in response to two questions in the European Parliament. In its answer to the first question, the Commission emphasised that it was the effect of a measure and not its nature or contents that was decisive for being considered a measure having equivalent effect or not.[32] Although the emphasis on the effects of national measures makes perfect sense, one may wonder how the contents of a measure can be non-decisive, as mostly it is the contents of the measure which are looked at when determining its (potential) trade-hindering effect.[33] The Commission listed a number of national measures it had addressed during the previous years. It had dealt with both existing measures through its mandate in what was then Article 33(7) (now deleted)[34], and new measures through its general mandate in Articles 211 (ex 155) and 226 (ex 169) of the Treaty. In the first category, the Commission mentioned among other measures the application to imports of minimum prices. In the second category, the Commission reported having eliminated a national measure increasing the minimum amount of nitrogen required in certain manure products to a higher level than the level required in all other Member States. Whereas the domestic industry adapted to this requirement in order to be able to continue to sell the larger part of its production domestically, such adaptation was not profitable for industries from other Member States which only sold a small part of their production in the Member State in question. Thus, the Commission said, measures *indistinctly applicable* to imported and domestic products may also *in certain cases* constitute measures having an equivalent effect to quantitative restrictions.[35] It appears that this is the origin of the categorisation between indistinctly and distinctly applicable measures that would subsequently lead to so much discussion.

In a second question, the Commission was explicitly asked what concept and definition of 'measures having equivalent effect' had been the basis for address-

---

[32] JO 59 (1967) 901. Response to written question no. 118 posed in December 1966 by Mr. Deringer, JO 9 (1967) 122. Translation from the French original by the author.

[33] It has further been observed that the purpose of the measure might well have been added to the non-decisive characteristics. Gormley (1985) at 10.

[34] Article 33(7) of the original EEC Treaty: 'Des directives de la Commission déterminent la procédure et le rythme de suppression entre les Etats membres des mesures d'effet équivalant à des contingents, existant à la date de l'entrée en vigueur du présent traité.' The original Article 31 laid down the prohibition of introducing new quantitative restrictions and measures having equivalent effect, while the original Article 32 precluded Member States from making existing quantitative restrictions and measures having equivalent effect more restrictive. Both provisions have been deleted.

[35] JO 59 (1967) 901 at 903. Translation and emphasis by the author.

ing the variety of measures it had mentioned in its answer to the previous question.[36] In response, the Commission spoke of 'certain common traits' in the examples given in its previous answer, which at that point in time allowed the following measures to be ranged among measures having equivalent effect:

'des dispositions législatives, réglementaires et administratives ainsi que des pratiques administratives, qui font obstacle à des importations ou à des exportations qui pourraient avoir lieu en leur absence, y compris celles qui rendent les importations ou les exportations plus onéreuses ou plus difficiles au regard de l'écoulement de la production nationale sur le marché national. Il est rappelé, toutefois, que les dispositions indistinctement applicables aux importations et à la production nationale ne constituent pas, dans la plupart des cas, des mesures d'effet équivalant aux restrictions quantitatives'.[37]

The Commission added that new assessment factors could be added by experience, and that it was ultimately up to the Court of Justice to decide on the matter.

2.1.5 Commission Directive 70/50

Commission Directive 70/50 elaborated the views of the Commission and thus provides a further insight into the scope which the Commission intended Article 28 to have at that time.[38] Although formally this Directive has lost much of its relevance, it still has importance as the basis of the Commission's view and as a source of inspiration for the Court.[39] The Directive in its preamble defined the word "measure" for the purposes of Article 28 et seq. as 'laws, regulations, administrative provisions, administrative practices, and all instruments issuing from a public authority, including recommendations'. Furthermore, the Directive distinguished between
  (a) measures 'other than those applicable equally to domestic or imported products', and
  (b) measures 'governing the marketing of products which deal, in particular, with shape, size, weight, composition, presentation, identification or putting up and which are equally applicable to domestic and imported products'.

---

[36] JO 169 (1967) 11. Written question no. 64 by Mr. Deringer.

[37] JO 169 (1967) 11 at 12.

[38] Commission Directive 70/50 of 22 December 1969, OJ L 13 (1970) 29.

[39] The Directive was based on the original Article 33(7) (now removed), which only had formal relevance during the transitional period. According to the original Article 7, that period ended in 1970. See Oliver (1996) at 73.

Measures in category (a) were covered by the Directive (and thus by Article 28), and hence were to be abolished where they 'hinder imports which could otherwise take place, *including* measures which make importation more difficult or costly than the disposal of domestic production'.[40] In particular, the Directive covered 'measures which make imports or the disposal, at any marketing stage, of imported products subject to a condition - other than a formality - which is required in respect of imported products only, or a condition differing from that required for domestic products and more difficult to satisfy'. Equally covered 'in particular' were 'measures which favour domestic products or grant them a preference, other than an aid, to which conditions may or may not be attached'.[41] The Directive then listed nineteen examples of measures 'other than those applicable equally'.

The effects of Category (b) measures were considered as a general rule not to be equivalent to those of quantitative restrictions, since such effects are 'normally inherent in the disparities between rules applied by Member States in this respect'.[42] Such measures, however, may have a restrictive effect on the free movement of goods 'over and above that which is intrinsic to such rules'.[43] The Commission deemed this to be the case where imports

are either precluded or made more difficult or costly than the disposal of domestic production and where such effect is not necessary for the attainment of an objective within the scope of the powers for the regulation of trade left to Member States by the Treaty; [...] such is in particular the case where the said objective can be attained just as effectively by other means which are less of a hindrance to trade; [...] such is also the case where the restrictive effect of these provisions on the free movement of goods is out of proportion to their purpose.[44]

These preambular considerations were reflected in Article 3 of the Directive. This Article stipulated that the Directive also covered

measures governing the marketing of products which deal, in particular, with shape, size, weight, composition, presentation, identification or putting up and which are equally applicable to domestic and imported products, where the restrictive effect

---

[40] See Article 1 of the Directive: 'The purpose of this Directive is to abolish the measures referred to in Articles 2 and 3, which were operative at the date of entry into force of the EEC Treaty', and Article 2:1 of the Directive. Emphasis added.

[41] Article 2(2) of the Directive.

[42] Preamble to the Directive.

[43] Ibid.

[44] Ibid.

of such measures on the free movement of goods exceeds the effects intrinsic to trade
rules. This is the case, in particular, where:
- the restrictive effects on the free movement of goods are out of proportion to their
  purpose;
- the same objective can be attained by other means which are less of a hindrance
  to trade. [45]

The main themes that would subsequently recur in the interpretation of Article
28 and justifications for infringements thereof can be seen in the Directive. It
contained a typology of the "measures" covered by Article 28, as well as the
seeds of the "means-end tests" of least-trade restrictiveness and proportionality
that condition the justification of national measures. Moreover, the Directive
repeated the distinction between "distinctly applicable" and "indistinctly applicable" measures, which had been introduced in the Commission's response to
the first parliamentary question discussed above. This distinction relates to the
role played by the concept of discrimination in the scope of Article 28 and the
justifications. The following observations may be made with regard to the above
citations.

   First of all, the reference to 'measures governing the marketing of products
which deal, *in particular,* with shape, size, etc.' suggests that more measures
governing the marketing of products may be covered. Secondly, the question
arises which restrictive effects of equally applicable measures are "inherent" or
"intrinsic" and which are not. Thirdly, the words 'This is the case, *in particular,*
etc.' in Article 3 suggest that even equally applicable measures which are not
out of proportion and whose objective cannot be attained by less trade-restrictive
means may still have a restrictive effect exceeding those effects intrinsic to trade
rules. Fourthly, are the two conditions in the last phrase of Article 3 cumulative
or alternative? The Preamble ('this is also the case etc.') suggests that they are
alternatives, implying that least-trade restrictiveness and proportionality were
considered to be different concepts by the Commission. Finally, it may be noted
that Article 3, in contrast with the Preamble, does not refer to situations in
which imports are precluded or made more costly or difficult than domestic
sales. Thus, between the Preamble and Article 3, the reference to the barring
of market access or the imposition of heavier burdens for imports than for
domestic products was dropped, paving the way for a more extensive coverage
of "equally applicable" measures by focusing on restrictive effects *per se,* not
in relation to domestic products or limited to measures barring market access
altogether.

---

[45] Article 3 of the Directive. René Joliet, former Judge of the ECJ, has described the first phrase as 'd'une
   obscurité telle que, malgré des efforts répétés, je ne suis jamais parvenu à en discerner le sens'. Joliet
   (1994).

Directive 70/50 was subsequently invoked before and by the Court in a number of cases.[46] In only a few of these was reference made to "equally applicable" measures as covered by Article 3 of the Directive.[47] In *Commission-Italy (car purchasing subsidies)*, the Court emphasised that the Directive would not impede it from interpreting Article 28: 'Directive 70/50 must be read in the light of Article 30 [now 28] of the Treaty and it may not be relied upon as a means of defeating the objective set out in that article [...]'.[48] Indeed, most of the interpretation activity would subsequently be carried out by the European Court of Justice on the basis of actual disputes concerning Article 28, both in Treaty infringement procedures and in preliminary rulings answering questions asked by national courts. In an impressive series of cases based primarily on the *effects* of national measures on the free movement of goods in the Community, the Court has shown remarkable flexibility, creativity, and sometimes even inconsistency in its interpretation of Article 28.[49] As the major cases have been discussed in all textbooks on EC law as well as a host of academic articles, they are only briefly addressed in the next Section. As these landmark cases determine the scope of the basic prohibition in Article 28 EC, their relevance to national measures pursuing health and environmental protection will be clear.

2.1.6 Interpretation by the Court of Justice

When interpreting the phrase 'quantitative restrictions and measures having equivalent effect', the Court initially emphasised their charac-

---

[46] See Cases 155/73 *Sacchi*, 12/74 *Commission-Germany*, 4/75 *Rewe* v. *Landwirtschaftskammer*, 13/77 *GB-Inno-BM* v. *ATAB*, 13/78 *Eggers*, 159/78 *Commission-Italy*, 113/80 *Commission-Ireland*, 75/81 *Blesgen*, 95/81 *Commission-Italy*, 247/81 *Commission-Germany*, 249/81 *Commission-Ireland*, 155/82 *Commission-Belgium*, 18/84 *Commission-France*, 103/84 *Commission-Italy*, 56/87 *Commission-Italy*, 253/87 *Sportex*, 145/88 *Torfaen Borough Council* v. *B&Q*; C-249/88 *Commission-Belgium*, C-304/90 *Reading Borough Council* v. *Payless*; and AG Opinions in Cases 103/84 *Commission-Italy*, 20/87 *Ministère public* v. *Gauchard*, 56/87 *Commission-Italy*, 253/87 *Sportex*, 382/87 *Buet*, 21/88 *Du Pont de Nemours*, and C-249/88 *Commission-Belgium*.

[47] See Cases 155/73 *Sacchi* (on an exclusive right to advertise on cable television, otherwise addressed under the services and competition rules of the EC Treaty), 75/81 *Blesgen* (on a law prohibiting the stocking and the consumption of spirits of an alcoholic strength exceeding 22% in all places open to the public), 145/88 *Torfaen Borough Council* v. *B&Q* (one of the famous cases on Sunday shop-closing laws that came to the Court before its judgment in *Keck*, discussed later in this Chapter); and the Advocate Generals' opinions in those cases as well as in Cases 20/87 *Ministère public* v. *Gauchard* and 382/87 *Buet*.

[48] Case 103/84, *Commission-Italy*, para. 20.

[49] On the Court and its interpretation of Article 28, an equally impressive range of textbook chapters and review articles have appeared. See e.g. Gormley (1985), Oliver (1996), Weatherill and Beaumont (1995) and Craig and De Búrca (1998).

ter as 'restrictions or discriminations' and 'prohibitions'.[50] After the transitional period foreseen in the Treaty for the abolition of quantitative restrictions and measures having equivalent effect had ended, the Court began to give a wider interpretation to 'measures of equivalent effect'. This occurred first in the specific context of regulations forming part of the agricultural policy.[51] In *Dassonville*, the Court for the first time applied the wider interpretation to Article 28 in general terms. In *Cassis de Dijon*, the Court confirmed that Article 28 applies to "indistinctly applicable" measures, but at the same time acknowledged that Member States may have legitimate reasons to apply such measures. In *Keck*, the Court decided that certain types of measure, i.e. "certain selling arrangements", are not covered by the prohibition in Article 28. In a number of other cases, the application of Article 28 was refused as a result of the type of measure at issue (when the effects on trade were too 'remote and uncertain'), or of the situation that gave rise to a question for a preliminary ruling ('purely internal situations').

(a) *Dassonville*

This case concerned the compatibility with the EC Treaty of a Belgian law requiring spirits bearing a designation of origin that were imported, sold, displayed for sale, in possession or transported for the purpose of sale or delivery in Belgium, to bear a certificate certifying the right to such designation of origin. In other words, any spirit sold on the Belgian market not only had to have a designation of origin duly adopted by the Belgian government, but also a certificate to the effect that the spirit was entitled to that designation.[52] The Court chose to adopt a broad interpretation and laid down the following well-

---

[50] See, respectively, Case 20/64 *SARL Albatros*: '[the Treaty involves] the prohibition of any new restriction or discrimination, the obligation progressively to abolish existing restrictions and discriminations and the necessity that they should disappear totally at the latest by the end of the transitional period', and Case 7/68 *Commission v. Italy*: '[The subject of] the chapter relating to the elimination of quantitative restrictions between Member States [...] is state intervention in intra-Community trade by measures *in the nature of prohibitions, total or partial*, on import, export or transit'. Emphasis added.

[51] See Case 2/73 *Geddo*. The Court in this case, in its decision delivered a year before *Dassonville*, said as regards Article 23 of Regulation 359/67 on the common organisation of the rice market, prohibiting quantitative restrictions and measures having equivalent effect: 'The prohibition on quantitative restrictions covers measures which amount to a total or partial restraint of, according to the circumstances, imports, exports or goods in transit. Measures having equivalent effect not only take the form of restraint described; whatever the description or technique employed, they can also consist of *encumbrances having the same effect*.' Emphasis added. The French version applies the words 'd'entraves, quelle que soit leur appellation ou leur technique, ayant le meme effet'.

[52] Case 8/74 *Dassonville* at 839.

known definition of measures having equivalent effect to quantitative restrictions:

> *All trading rules enacted by Member States which are capable of hindering, directly or indirectly, actually or potentially, intra-Community trade are to be considered as measures having an effect equivalent to quantitative restrictions.*[53]

Although this formula was repeated by the Court on a number of occasions in subsequent cases,[54] it was only in 1979 that the Court expressly referred to the judgment for the first time.[55] The doctrinal debate had centred on whether or not Article 28 covered non-discriminatory trade barriers, and the Commission's contributions made a distinction between distinctly applicable and equally applicable measures. In that context, it strikes one as being remarkable that the Court in *Dassonville* did not use the terms "discriminatory" or 'distinctly or equally applicable' at all. Instead, it clearly focused on obstacles to trade. The Court in subsequent cases did not decide on the question to what extent "equally applicable" measures were caught by its "obstacles" test[56], until it was confronted with the *Cassis de Dijon* case.

(b)   *Cassis de Dijon*

In 1979, the Court delivered a judgment which, if not as regards its theoretical definition, greatly widened the scope of Article 28 as regards its practical application. The *Cassis* judgment was the first in a series of cases where national measures that were clearly indistinctly applicable to domestic and imported goods, but nevertheless restricted intra-Community trade, were tested against Articles 28-30. At the same time, by this judgment Member States were given the opportunity to argue that such measures were justified as 'necessary in order to satisfy *mandatory requirements*.' In other words, the strictly interpreted list of justifications expressly mentioned in Article 30 was added to by the Court.[57] At issue in *Cassis* was German legislation fixing minimum

---

[53] Para. 5 of the judgment.

[54] See e.g. Cases 190/73 *Van Haaster*, 41/76 *Donckerwolcke*, 104/75 *De Peijper*, 31/78 *Bussone*.

[55] This was in a case concerning the same Belgian law that was at issue in *Dassonville* itself, in a Treaty infringement against Belgium, Case 2/78 *Commission* v. *Belgium*. The first stage of this infringement procedure had begun even before the *Dassonville* judgment had been delivered. The original letter from the Commission to Belgium was sent in March 1974, whereas the *Dassonville* judgment was delivered in July of that same year.

[56] The Court explicitly refused to decide the point in Case 13/78 *Eggers*, para. 28. In the same case, it observed erroneously that Directive 70/50 relates solely to 'measures, other than those applicable equally' (para. 27).

[57] See *infra*, Section 2.2.

alcohol contents for specified categories of liqueurs and other spirits, including a minimum content of 25% for "Cassis de Dijon", while the alcohol content of that product as freely marketed in France was between 15 and 20%.[58] The following key quotes are taken from the Court's judgment:

Obstacles to movement within the Community resulting from disparities between the national laws relating to the marketing of the products in question must be accepted in so far as those provisions must be recognised as being necessary in order to satisfy mandatory requirements [...][59]

[...] the requirements [...] do not serve a purpose which is in the general interest and such as to take precedence over the requirements of the free movement of goods, which constitutes one of the fundamental rules of the Community.

There is therefore no valid reason why, provided they have been lawfully produced and marketed in one of the Member States, [the products in question] should not be introduced into any other Member State [...][60]

Consider also the following quotes from a case decided 16 months after *Cassis*, laying down some of the principles contained in *Cassis* in more general terms:

In the absence of common rules relating to the production and marketing of the product in question it is for the Member States to regulate all matters relating to its production, distribution and consumption on their territory subject, however, to the condition that those rules do not present an obstacle, directly or indirectly, actually or potentially, to intra-Community trade.[61]

It is only where national rules, which apply without discrimination to both domestic and imported products, may be justified as being necessary in order to satisfy imperative requirements [...] that they may constitute an exception to the requirements arising under Article 30 [now 28].[62]

It is clear from the paragraphs cited that the *Cassis* line of cases on the one hand establishes that even indistinctly applicable national rules may fall under the *Dassonville* definition. On the other hand, it recognises a certain degree of

---

[58] Case 120/78 *Cassis*, para. 3.

[59] Ibid., para. 8

[60] Ibid., para. 14.

[61] Case 788/79 *Gilli and Andres*, para. 5.

[62] Ibid., para. 6.

domestic legislative autonomy in the absence of Community harmonisation and opens the door to justifications for the infringement of Article 28 in the form of "mandatory" or "imperative" requirements.[63] These may however only justify "indistinctly applicable" measures. The reference to "fundamental rules" shows the importance attached by the Court to the free movement of goods.[64] The third quote from *Cassis* establishes what has become known as the concept of *mutual recognition*.[65] This obliges the Member States in principle to recognise as equivalent each other's production and marketing standards, so that they cannot, save in exceptional circumstances, insist on compliance with their own rules on production and marketing as a condition for market access.[66] The principle of mutual recognition raises a strong presumption that a product lawfully produced and marketed in another Member State will comply with the importing Member State's national rules.[67] That presumption will only be rebutted if the importing Member State applies non-equivalent, stricter standards, which it can justify as being necessary to satisfy mandatory requirements or grounds mentioned in Article 30.[68]

Subsequent to the *Cassis* judgment, the Commission issued an interpretative Communication on its consequences and noted that, in its view, a whole body of national rules had to be tackled. The Commission referred in particular to 'rules covering the composition, designation, presentation and packaging of products as well as requiring compliance with certain technical standards.'[69] The Court in *Cassis* had mentioned that national rules concerning a product's 'production and marketing' had to comply with the *Dassonville* formula, and had subsequently added in *Gilli and Andres* national rules on 'distribution' and 'consumption'. The Commission concluded in its Communication that:

---

[63] *Cassis* mentions particularly the effectiveness of fiscal supervision, protection of public health, the fairness of commercial transactions and the defence of the consumer. But as shall be seen *infra*, that list is not exhaustive.

[64] See however Opinion 1/91 *Re the European Economic Area*, paras. 17-18, where the Court stated that the free movement of goods is not an end in itself, but merely a means for establishing an internal market and economic and monetary union.

[65] This concept has also been dubbed "functional parallelism". See Weiler (1999), referring to Dashwood without further reference.

[66] For more references on the concept of mutual recognition, see Weatherill and Beaumont (1995) at 495.

[67] Emiliou (1996a) at 233.

[68] Oliver (1996) at 116, mentions mandatory requirements only. The Commission's Communication, discussed *infra*, enables wider justification grounds as it mentions 'a purpose in the general interest which is compelling enough to justify an exception to a fundamental rule of the Treaty such as the free movement of goods'.

[69] OJ 1980 C 256/2.

[a]ny product imported from another Member State must in principle be admitted to the territory of the importing Member State if it has been lawfully produced, that is, conforms to rules and processes of manufacture that are customarily and traditionally accepted in the exporting country, and is marketed in the territory of the latter.

Thus, 'where a product "suitably and satisfactorily" fulfils the legitimate objective of a Member State's own rules, the importing Member State cannot justify prohibiting its sale in its territory by claiming that the way it fulfils the objective is different from that imposed on domestic products.'[70]

(c) *Keck*

The Court in 1993 set an outer limit to the applicability of Article 28. At issue in the *Keck* case was a French general prohibition of resale at a loss. The Court first observed that the measure at issue was *not designed to regulate trade* in goods.[71] Although such legislation may restrict the volume of sales, and hence the volume of sales of products from other Member States in so far as it deprives traders of a method of sales promotion, the Court deemed this effect insufficient to characterise it as a measure having equivalent effect. The Court noted an 'increasing tendency of traders to invoke Article 30 [now 28] of the Treaty as a means of challenging any rules whose effect is to limit their commercial freedom even where such rules are not aimed at products from other Member States'[72], and considered it necessary to 're-examine and clarify its case-law'. It stated as follows:

It is established by the case-law beginning with "Cassis de Dijon" [...] that, in the absence of harmonisation of legislation, obstacles to free movement of goods which are the consequences of applying, to goods coming from other Member States where they are lawfully manufactured and marketed, rules that lay down requirements to be met by those goods (such as those relating to designation, form, size, weight, composition, presentation, labelling, packaging) constitute measures of equivalent effect prohibited by Article 30 [now 28]. This is so even if those rules apply without distinction to all products unless their application can be justified by a public-interest objective taking precedence over the free movement of goods.

By contrast, contrary to what has previously been decided, the application to products from other Member States of national provisions restricting or prohibiting certain selling arrangements is not such as to hinder directly or indirectly, actually

---

[70] Ibid.

[71] Joined Cases C-267/91 and C-268/91 *Keck* [1993] ECR I-6097, at para. 12. Emphasis added.

[72] Ibid. at para. 14.

or potentially, trade between Member States [...] so long as those provisions apply to all relevant traders operating within the national territory and so long as they affect in the same manner, in law and in fact, the marketing of domestic products and of those from other Member States.

Provided that those conditions are fulfilled, the application of such rules to the sale of products from another Member State meeting the requirements laid down by that State is not by nature such as to prevent their access to the market or to impede access any more than it impedes the access of domestic products. Such rules therefore fall outside the scope of Article 30 [now 28] of the Treaty.[73]

(d)   After *Keck*

The exact scope of the limitation to Article 28 laid down in *Keck* is not entirely clear. The Court did not clarify what it meant by "certain selling arrangements", as seemingly opposed to 'rules that lay down requirements to be met by goods'.[74] By adding 'certain' to "selling arrangements", the Court suggested that not all selling arrangements are outside the scope of Article 28, but only those that fulfil the conditions laid down in the judgment. However, those conditions are not entirely clear. Did the Court add something to the discrimination criterion in paragraph 16 when it spoke of market access in paragraph 17, the last paragraph quoted above? Or does paragraph 17 merely confirm paragraph 16? The Court has confirmed that selling arrangements that do not 'affect in the same manner, in law and in fact, the marketing of domestic products and of those from other Member States' (para. 16 of the *Keck* judgment) may indeed impede market access of imports more than that of domestic products.[75] But it seems that national provisions *prohibiting* certain selling arrangements could well prevent market access of an imported product altogether, even if they affected imports and domestic products identically in law and in fact. If the first part of paragraph 17 really means that measures that prevent market access altogether are covered by Article 28, this does not follow from the discrimination test in paragraph 16. It has therefore been argued that the market access prevention should operate, and in fact already operates, as an isolated requirement narrowing the application of *Keck*, to the effect that selling arrangements may fall within the scope of Article 28 when they prevent market

---

[73] Joined Cases C-267/91 and C-268/91 *Keck*, paras. 15, 16 and 17.

[74] Weatherill (1996) proposes to drop the reference to selling arrangements altogether.

[75] Case C-254/98 *TK Heimdienst*, para. 26. The same approach was taken in the advertising cases *De Agostini* and *Gourmet*, discussed hereafter.

access of imports.[76] Several Advocates-General have taken the same view.[77] The Court has up to now not delineated the full consequence of its statement in the first part of paragraph 17. The Court's Sixth Chamber has arguably suggested that it perceives paragraph 17 as functioning separately from paragraph 16.[78]

Another uncertainty ever since the *Keck* ruling is the extent to which advertising restrictions are "selling arrangements". The Court decided in *Leclerc-Siplec* that French legislation prohibiting the broadcasting of televised advertisements for the distribution sector fell within the *Keck* formula of "selling arrangements" and fulfilled the conditions laid down in *Keck*.[79] In *De Agostini*, it repeated this application of *Keck*, adding however that 'it cannot be excluded that an outright ban, applying in one Member State, of a type of promotion for a product which is lawfully sold there might have a greater impact on products from other Member States'.[80] The Court further noted that television advertising is sometimes the only effective form of sales promotion enabling foreign companies to penetrate the Swedish market.[81] While the Court left the actual assessment of whether the *Keck* requirements had been fulfilled to the national court in *De Agostini*, in *Gourmet* the Court decided on the matter itself.[82]

Some types of advertising bear directly on the product as it is traded, and do not fall within the term "certain selling arrangements".[83]

---

[76] See e.g. Weatherill (1996), and Eeckhout (2000), referring to two cases in which Keck was not mentioned, but a market access test was applied to conclude that a measure that was arguably a selling arrangement was covered by Article 28: Cases C-189/95 *Franzén* and C-337/95 *Dior*; Barnard (2001) at 48.

[77] See AG Tesauro in his opinion in Case C-368/95 *Familiapress*, para. 9, referring to Case C-384/93 *Alpine Investments*, which regarded the free movement of services and C-415/93 *Bosman* regarding the free movement of workers; AG Elmer in his opinion in Case C-189/95 *Franzén*, paras. 57-61, referring to Cases C-391/92 *Commission-Greece (Baby Milk)* and C-387/93 *Banchero*.

[78] Case C-405/98 *Gourmet*, para. 18: '[A]ccording to paragraph 17 of its judgment in *Keck and Mithouard*, if national provisions restricting or prohibiting certain selling arrangements are to avoid being caught by Article 30 [now 28] of the Treaty, they must not be of such a kind as to prevent access to the market by products from another Member State or to impede access any more than they impede the access of domestic products.' However, the case did not involve a situation in which the market access of imports was prevented altogether.

[79] Case C-412/93 *Leclerc-Siplec*.

[80] Joined Cases C-34-36/95 *De Agostini*, para. 42.

[81] Ibid., para. 43. This case has been interpreted as involving a measue that prevented market access: Barnard (2001) at 44. However, the advertising ban at issue did not ban market access of the products at issue, but only prohibited certain television advertisements for such products.

[82] Case C-405/98 *Gourmet*, para. 21. AG Jacobs had proposed the same approach in his opinion.

[83] Case C-470/93 *Mars*; Case C-368/95 *Familiapress*.

A final uncertainty arising from the judgment in *Keck* is what role, if any, is played by the Court's observations that the measure at issue was not *designed* to regulate trade and not *aimed* at imports. Does this imply that the aim and objective of a measure clarify whether it is covered by Article 28? The Court in a subsequent case said that the *Keck* judgment was concerned only with domestic provisions which limit or prohibit certain selling arrangements, and not with national legislation *designed to regulate trade* in goods between Member States *or* which relate to the requirements to be met by the goods in question.[84] It could be inferred from this that the design and aim of the national measure indeed play a role when assessing whether a measure is covered by the *Keck* limitation to Article 28, albeit perhaps a subsidiary one.

(e)   Other Limitations to (the Invocation of) Article 28

In addition to those covered by the notion of "selling arrangements" and complying with the requirements laid down in *Keck*, there are a number of other national measures that the Court has deemed to fall outside the ambit of Article 28.

First, the Court has been confronted with claims regarding Article 28 that concerned national measures whose link with the free movement of goods was tenuous. The Court held in *Peralta* and other cases that Article 28 does not preclude national legislation if it makes no distinction according to the origin of the goods covered, its purpose is not to regulate trade in goods with other Member States and the restrictive effects which it might have on the free movement of goods are too uncertain and indirect to be regarded as being of a nature to hinder trade between Member States.[85] The 'uncertain and indirect effects' on intra-Community trade concern the connection between the measure and its effects on trade. These cases may be considered a further interpretation of the *Dassonville* formula.

The connection between the measure and possible trade effects should not be confused with the argument that measures with a *minimal* effect on intra-Community trade are outside the scope of Article 28. If a national measure is capable of hindering imports it must be regarded as a measure having an effect equivalent to a quantitative restriction, even though the hindrance is slight and even though it is possible for imported products to be marketed in other ways.[86] Attempts to introduce a *de minimis* rule in Article 28 are sometimes put forward,

---

[84] Case C-158/94 *Commission* v. *Italy*, para. 31. Emphasis added.

[85] See Case C-379/92 *Peralta*, referring to Case C-69/88 *Krantz*, and Case C-93/92 *CMC Motorradcenter*. See also Joined Cases C-140/94 to C-142/94 *DIP*.

[86] See Joined Cases 177/82 and 178/82 *Van de Haar*, and Cases 269/83 *Commission* v. *France*; 103/84 *Commission* v. *Italy*.

but have never been accepted by the Court.[87] An environmental case in point is *Bluhme*, where Denmark argued that Article 28 was not applicable to a national measure only covering 0.3% of Danish territory. Although the effects of such a measure on trade will indeed be minimal, that does not mean that the connection between the measure and those effects is uncertain or indirect. The measure is covered by the prohibition in Article 28 and needs justification. The difference between the *Peralta* and *Bluhme* situations is illustrated by Advocate-General Fennelly, who in his opinion in the latter case spoke of the "remoteness" v. the "scale" of effects on trade.[88]

Secondly, Article 28 does not apply to "internal situations" without any connection to intra-Community trade. Thus, a trader or producer operating within a Member State cannot invoke Article 28 to challenge an obstacle to the marketing in the same Member State of goods produced in that same Member State. However, there are signs that this limitation to the applicability of Article 28 is becoming less and less important. The Court has held in *Pistre* that 'whilst the application of a national measure having no actual link to the importation of goods does not fall within the ambit of Article 30 [now 28] of the Treaty, Article 30 [now 28] cannot be considered inapplicable simply because all the facts of the specific case before the national court are confined to a single Member State.'[89] The Court has confirmed this in *Guimont*, another case concerning French food laws.[90]

In situations of "reverse discrimination", producers or traders attempt to challenge domestic laws and regulations that disfavour them in comparison with their competitors from other Member States. When such laws are challenged with reference to the EC Treaty, the Court has held that the purpose of Article 28 is to eliminate obstacles to the importation of goods and not to ensure that goods of national origin always enjoy the same treatment as imported goods. Reverse discrimination is not covered by Article 28.[91] Despite this limitation to the applicability of Article 28, traders and producers may challenge domestic laws and regulations on the basis of *domestic* requirements of equal treatment and prohibitions of reverse discrimination. They will have a case under such requirements if they can show that the domestic laws and regulations do not apply to imports and therefore disfavour domestic products. In this respect, judgments such as *Pistre* and *Guimont* are helpful to them. They may base their domestic claim of reverse discrimination on the infringement of Article 28 caused by the potential application to imports of the domestic laws and

---

[87] See e.g. AG Jacobs in Case C-412/93 *Leclerc-Siplec*.

[88] AG Fennelly in Case C-67/97 *Bluhme*.

[89] Joined Cases C-321/94 to C-324/94 *Pistre and Others*, para. 44.

[90] Case C-448/98 *Guimont* (Emmenthal).

[91] See Cases 98/86 *Mathot* and 355/85 *Cognet*.

regulations in question. Thus, the Court accepts questions on Article 28 in cases with a potential link with trade, where its answer may assist a national judge in determining whether national non-discrimination requirements have been violated.

The measures in the above examples were not applied to imports in the particular case leading to ECJ proceedings, but could at least potentially be so applied. By contrast, national laws that really only apply internally and cannot be applied to imports (or exports) appear to be excluded from the scope of Article 28. An example in the environmental sphere is a prohibition on the transport of local waste between regions within a Member State. However, it is not inconceivable that even such measures may in the future fall within the ambit of Article 28, if the Court were to extend its case-law on the application of Article 25 (customs duties and charges having equivalent effect) to measures having equivalent effect to quantitative restrictions under Article 28.[92]

(f)   Summary

The scope of the prohibition in Article 28 is very wide. In principle, it captures any domestic environmental or health measure that has possible effects on trade. This means that any such measure may be challenged as violating Article 28 and accordingly will need justification under EC law. Many examples of environmental measures falling within the prohibition in Article 28 are discussed *infra*, when their justification is addressed. Environmental measures will only fall outside the scope of Article 28 if they are "selling arrangements" that do not discriminate against imports in law or in fact and do not impede market access altogether. An example is a requirement that certain toxicants can only be sold in designated shops or to authorised persons. Further, environmental measures whose effects on trade are very remote or indirect fall outside Article 28, but the Court has not often found this to be the case. Finally, Article 28 does not allow traders to challenge national environmental measures under Article 28 if their situation has no connection to trade with other Member States whatsoever, or if domestic products are discriminated against *vis-à-vis* imported products. However, these limitations on the invocability of Article 28 seem to be increasingly confined.

---

[92]   See Joined Cases C-363/93, C-407/93-C-411/93, *Lancry*, and Joined Cases C-485/93 and C-486/93 *Simitzi*. Oliver (1999) at 786 argues for such an extension.

2.1.7 Article 29 EC: Export Restrictions and Measures having Equivalent Effect

Although not the central focus of this research, Article 29 of the EC Treaty is mentioned here. It is the counterpart of Article 28 which prohibits quantitative restrictions on exports and measures having equivalent effect. Although it employs the same terms as Article 28,[93] it has been interpreted more narrowly. Article 29 in the Court's interpretation comprises a discrimination test. The Court has declared in various cases that Article 29:

> concerns national measures which have as their specific object or effect the restriction of patterns of exports and thereby the establishment of a difference in treatment between the domestic trade of a member state and its export trade in such a way as to provide a particular advantage for national production or for the domestic market of the state in question at the expense of the production or of the trade of other member states.[94]

This is not so, the Court continued, in the case of a prohibition applied objectively to the production of goods of a certain kind, without drawing a distinction depending on whether such goods are intended for the national market or for export. In other words, Article 29 does not prohibit indistinctly applicable measures. As a consequence, export restrictions for environmental reasons will only be covered by the prohibition in Article 29 if distinctly applicable; if they do fall under that provision, however, they can only be justified by Article 30 with its strict interpretation and conditions discussed *infra*. Article 29 has understandably caused a much less abundant case-law than Article 28. Nonetheless, the formula cited above also has been repeated in environmental cases, particularly in the waste sector. A number of national measures requiring that certain domestic waste goods such as oil filters and poultry offal be delivered to domestic companies, have thus been found to contravene Article 29 because they imply a prohibition to export such goods.[95]

The narrower reading of Article 29 *vis-à-vis* Article 28 is interesting because of their identical wording. The rationale behind the different interpretations is understandable, as Member States will be much less inclined to restrict their exports than their imports for reasons other than legitimate objectives.

---

[93] The only difference other than referring to "exports" instead of "imports" is the use of commas in Article 29: 'Quantitative restrictions on exports, and all other measures having equivalent effect, shall be prohibited between Member States.'

[94] Case 15/79 *Groenveld*, para. 7.

[95] See Cases 172/82 *Inter-Huiles*, 118/86 *Nertsvoederfabriek*, C-37/92 *Vanacker* and C-203/96 *Dusseldorp*.

Nevertheless, a broader interpretation of Article 29 has been advocated.[96] It should be noted that the range of measures covered by Article 29 but not by Article 28 is limited. Many measures that may restrict exports may at the same time potentially hinder imports and be covered by the wide interpretation of Article 28 discussed above. This is the case for e.g. product requirements. Measures not covered by Article 28 that may be covered by Article 29 will mostly be production requirements applied to domestic producers, including waste management.

2.2 Justifications

2.2.1 Article 30 EC: Treaty Exceptions

Measures infringing Article 28 may be justified under Article 30. The wording of Article 30 is as follows:

The provisions of Articles 28 and 29 shall not preclude prohibitions or restrictions on imports, exports or goods in transit justified on grounds of public morality, public policy or public security; the protection of health and life of humans, animals or plants; the protection of national treasures possessing artistic, historic or archaeological value; or the protection of industrial and commercial property. Such prohibitions or restrictions shall not, however, constitute a means of arbitrary discrimination or a disguised restriction on trade between Member States.

Immediately striking in this provision is that it speaks of 'prohibitions or restrictions', and not of 'quantitative restrictions and measures having equivalent effect', as do Articles 28 and 29. This difference has not received much attention, however. It may be assumed that the reference to "restrictions" is to be interpreted in the same way as 'measures having equivalent effect'.[97]

According to the Court, Article 30 as an exception is to be interpreted strictly: 'Article 36 [now 30] is an exception to the fundamental principle of the free movement of goods and must, therefore, be interpreted in such a way that its scope is not extended any further than is necessary.'[98] The Court has also repeatedly stressed that 'the purpose of Article 30 [...] is not to reserve certain matters to the exclusive jurisdiction of the Member States; it merely allows

---

[96] See Opinions of AG Jacobs in Case C-384/93 *Alpine Investments* and AG Lenz in Case C-415/93 *Bosman*; see also Oliver (1999), as well as Weatherill (1996) at 903, arguing that export restraints ought to be justified by Member States where they prevent export market access.

[97] Oliver (1988) at 166.

[98] Case 13/78 *Eggers*, para. 30.

national legislation to derogate from the principle of free movement of goods to the extent to which this is and remains justified in order to achieve the objectives set out in the Article.'[99] As a Community concept, the scope for national derogations from free movement is defined by the ECJ and not by the Member States themselves. No other justifications than those specifically mentioned are allowed under Article 30.[100] Thus, general economic difficulties or policies are excluded as justifications, and Article 30 cannot be invoked for a measure aimed at safeguarding the survival of an undertaking.[101] However, if one of the exception grounds in Article 30 justifies a measure, the justification is not nullified by additional or accessory economic advantages. Thus, a measure justified by the need to protect life and health, or by security interests, may have as an additional effect that an undertaking is supported by it.[102]

The 'protection of the environment' as such is not mentioned among the justification grounds. Moreover, Article 30, unlike its GATT counterpart, does not mention the 'conservation of exhaustible natural resources' among its justification grounds.[103] The difference is possibly attributable to the fact that the EC aims to achieve an internal market in which production factors freely flow, including natural resources. Coal and steel have been regulated by the ECSC Treaty rather than the EC Treaty, but will be part of the general EC Treaty regime from 2002 onwards. As to other natural resources, the Community does not pursue a common natural resource policy within the internal market, even if according to Article 174 EC, 'prudent and rational utilisation of natural resources' is one of the objectives of the Community's environmental policy. Therefore, differences in national natural resource policies between the Member States are quite conceivable. If they restrict trade, resource protection measures will largely be covered by the exception on plant life and health and the mandatory requirement of environmental protection which is discussed below. However, in order to qualify, such measures should genuinely pursue a protection goal. The difference with economic motives will not always be easy to establish, as in the case of an export restriction on waste in order to ensure the viability of a national recycling plant.[104]

The strict interpretation of Article 30 as providing exceptions to the general prohibition in Articles 28 and 29 also implies that the scope of the justification grounds themselves is interpreted narrowly.[105] Accordingly, an environmental

---

[99] See e.g. Cases 35/76 *Simmenthal*; 72/83 *Campus Oil*.

[100] See e.g. Cases 113/80 *Commission* v. *Ireland*, and 95/81 *Commission* v. *Italy*, where the ECJ refused to accept consumer protection and the defence of a Member State's currency, respectively, as justifications under Article 30 EC.

[101] See Cases 7/61 *Commission* v. *Italy*; 238/82 *Duphar*.

[102] See Cases 118/86 *Nertsvoederfabriek*; C-324/93 *Evans Medical*; 72/83 *Campus Oil*.

[103] GATT Article XX(g).

[104] See Case C-203/96 *Dusseldorp*.

[105] See e.g. Cases 7/68 *Commission* v. *Italy*; 29/72 *Marimex*.

problem that poses no direct health risks will not be covered by Article 30, but it may be justified by "mandatory requirements" as discussed below.[106] However, the Court is not always crystal clear in its considerations of what is acceptable under Article 30. It sometimes mentions environmental protection when discussing the justification of a measure under Article 30.[107] Moreover, it has made reference to Article 30 in a case concerning

The Court has explicitly stated that 'the health and life of humans rank foremost among the property or interests protected by Article 36 [now 30] of the Treaty'.[108] Thus, once within the scope of Article 30, the interest of life and health protection is granted high importance. Considering this statement, it may be assumed that the Member States will generally be left with less room to manoeuvre when enacting measures to protect animals or plants than with respect to measures aimed at human health protection. Recently, however, the Court has also interpreted the protection of the life and health of animals some-what broadly. It accepted trade-restricting measures to preserve an indigenous bee subspecies with distinctive characteristics. Cross-breeding threatened this subspecies with extinction, so the measure contributed to the conservation of biodiversity. The Court referred to the Convention on Biodiversity and added that:

[f]rom the point of view of such conservation of biodiversity, it is immaterial whether the object of protection is a separate subspecies, a distinct strain within any given species or merely a local colony, so long as the populations in question have characteristics distinguishing them from others and are therefore judged worthy of protection either to shelter them from a risk of extinction that is more or less imminent, or, even in the absence of such risk, on account of a scientific or other interest in preserving the pure population at the location concerned.[109]

In the case-law on Article 30, the large majority of the cases in which the "health and life" justification was invoked have concerned human health and life.[110]

---

[106] See Section 3.2.1.

[107] See e.g. Case C-473/98 *Toolex Alpha*, para. 39.

[108] See Cases 104/75 *De Peijper*; C-320/93 *Ortscheit*; C-473/98 *Toolex Alpha*.

[109] Case C-67/97 *Bluhme*.

[110] The main ones are Cases 104/75 *De Peijper*; 53/80 *Officier van Jusitie v. Koninklijke Kaasfabriek Eyssen BV*; 272/80 *Frans-Nederlandse Maatschappij voor Biologische Producten*; 124/81 *Commission v. UK* ('*UHT Milk*'); 174/82 *Sandoz*; 227/82 *Van Bennekom*; 94/83 *Heijn*; 216/84 *Commission v. France* ('*Substitute Milk Powder*'); 178/84 *Commission v. Germany* ('*Beer Purity Laws*'); 188/84 *Commission v. France* ('*Wood-working Machines*'); C-304/88 *Commission v. Belgium* ('*Live Animals*'); 25/88 *Bouchara née Wurmser*; 125/88 *Criminal Proceedings against Nijman*; C-228/91 *Commission v. Italy* ('*Fish*'); C-293/94 *Criminal Proceedings against Brandsma*; C-189/95 *Franzén*; C-358/95 *Morellato*; C-389/96 *Aher-Waggon*; C-400/96 *Harpegnies*.

Considerably fewer cases relate to plant and animal life and health. They have concerned mostly the prevention of animal or plant diseases, and in some cases the protection of rare or endangered species and animal welfare.[111]

The existence of a hazard to life or health must be demonstrated by the Member State invoking the exception in Article 30 to justify its trade-hindering measure.[112] This is not to say that the Member State invoking the justification must provide conclusive and incontestable evidence. In various cases, the Court has held that in the absence of complete harmonisation, it is for the Member States to decide what degree of protection of the health and life of humans they intend to assure. The Court has said this in cases regarding food and additives,[113] pharmaceuticals,[114] and pesticides and biocides.[115] The Member States thus enjoy a considerable margin of appreciation, especially in cases of scientific uncertainty, where it is impossible to establish the threshold above which the product in question poses health hazards.[116] The lenient attitude of the Court may be understood in the light of the precautionary principle as laid down in the EC Treaty.[117] However, in a number of cases concerning product composition, especially additives, Member States have been unable to adduce any evidence whatsoever as to the perceived health risk. The Court in such cases rejected the argument based on Article 30. Moreover, even if accepting the life or health protection ground as such, the Court has usually added that Member States must at the same time have regard to the requirements of the free movement of goods within the Community, in particular the last sentence of Article 30.[118] The way these requirements are taken into account in the application of the proportionality principle is discussed *infra*.[119]

---

[111] Cases 64/75 *Rewe*; 35/76 *Simmenthal*; 46/76 *Bauhuis*; 251/78 *Denkavit*; 124/81 *Commission v. UK ('UHT Milk')*; Joined Cases 141-143/81 *Holdijk*; 40/82 *Commission v. UK ('Newcastle Disease')*; 74/82 *Commission v. Ireland ('Newcastle Disease')*; 73/84 *Denkavit*; C-304/88 *Commission v. Belgium ('Live Animals')*; C-128/89 *Commission v. Italy ('Grapefruits')*; C-169/89 *Criminal Proceedings against Gourmetterie van den Burg ('Van den Burg' or 'Red Grouse')*; C-131/93 *Commission v. Germany ('Crayfish')*; C-5/94 *Hedley Lomas*; C-149/94 *Vergy*; C-202/94 *Van der Feesten*; C-1/96 *Compassion*; C-67/97 *Bluhme*; C-162/97 *Nilsson*; C-350/97 *Monsees*.

[112] See e.g. Cases 174/82 *Sandoz*, 227/82 *Van Bennekom*, 304/84 *Muller*, 178/84 *Commission v. Germany (Beer Purity)*, C-42/90 *Bellone*, and Joined Cases C-13/91 and C-113/91 *Debus*.

[113] See e.g. the cases mentioned in footnote 112, and 97/83 *Melkunie*.

[114] See e.g. Case 104/75 *De Peijper*.

[115] See e.g. Cases 272/80 *Frans-Nederlandse Maatschappij voor Biologische Producten*, C-293/94 *Brandsma*.

[116] See e.g. Cases 53/80 *Eyssen*, 227/82 *Van Bennekom*, C-473/98 *Toolex Alpha*.

[117] Article 174(2) EC. See EC Commission (2000b).

[118] E.g. in Case 125/88 *Criminal Proceedings against Nijman*.

[119] See Section 2.3.4.

2.2.2 "Mandatory Requirements": Justifications Accepted in Case-Law

Measures that may infringe Article 28 cannot only be justified under Article 30, but also by the so-called "mandatory requirements" as accepted by the Court of Justice in its interpretation of Article 28. It is recalled that the Court in *Cassis* and subsequent cases determined that obstacles to the free movement of goods in the Community must be accepted in so far as necessary to satisfy mandatory requirements. This formula has been widely referred to as the "rule of reason", although the Court does not itself use this term in this context.[120] Even if usually associated with the *Cassis* case, the origins of the "rule of reason" were already present in *Dassonville*. There, having expressed the broad formula for 'measures having equivalent effect', the Court stated that in the absence of a Community system guaranteeing the objective pursued by a Member State's measures, those measures should be *reasonable*.[121] It was only in *Cassis*, however, that this idea received a clearer definition. This is not surprising, considering the fact that the Court in that case complemented the widening of the ambit of Article 28 by broadening the reasons as to why trade-hindering national measures could be found to be compatible with the EC Treaty.

As seen above, in *Cassis* the Court mentioned 'mandatory requirements relating in particular to the effectiveness of fiscal supervision, the protection of public health, the fairness of commercial transactions and the defence of the consumer.'[122] To mention the protection of public health among these interests seems superfluous, as it is already explicitly covered by Article 30.[123] As appears from the words 'in particular', the enumeration of "mandatory requirements" was not meant to be exhaustive. In later case-law, a number of mandatory requirements have been added, including the protection of the environment.[124]

---

[120] The Court has explicitly used the term "rule of reason" in competition law cases, albeit without accepting it; see e.g. Case T-112/99 *Métropole*.

[121] *Dassonville*, para. 6. Emphasis added. It remained unclear in the judgment whether the objective - the prevention of unfair practices with regard to designations of origin - was covered by the grounds mentioned in Article 30.

[122] Case 120/78 *Cassis*, para. 8. Consumer protection was confirmed as mandatory requirement in Case 178/84 *Commission* v. *Germany*. There is overlap between this requirement and that of the fairness of commercial transactions, cf. Case 286/81 *Oosthoek*.

[123] As Article 30 may cover both distinctly and indistinctly applicable measures, there seems to be no reason why "public health" should be a mandatory requirement under the rule of reason. See Emiliou (1996a) at 241.

[124] Environmental protection was accepted in Case 302/86 *Commission* v. *Denmark*. Other mandatory requirements accepted by the Court are e.g. press diversity in Case C-368/95 *Familiapress*, the financial equilibrium of social security systems in Case C-120/95 *Decker*, the improvement of working conditions

Consideration to environmental concerns in relation to Article 28 was provided as early as 1976, in the *Kramer* case that concerned measures aimed at the conservation of fish stocks.[125] Advocate-General Trabucchi disapproved of treating the measures as falling outside Article 28, fearing that this would lead to a too flexible view as regards the concept of measures having equivalent effect.[126] Thus, he rejected the idea of accepting an environmental justification within the application of Article 28, and rather opted for considering the measure to be prohibited but nevertheless justified under Article 30. He was rather hesitant about the latter point, though, because of the extraterritorial nature of the fish whose protection was sought by the measure.[127] The Court did not follow the Advocate-General, and applied a sort of "rule of reason" by finding that the catch quotas were not prohibited by Article 28 because of their conservation objectives:

> *Measures for the conservation of the resources of the sea through fixing catch quotas and limiting the fishing effort, whilst restricting "production" in the short term, are aimed precisely at preventing such "production" from being marked by a fall which would seriously jeopardize supplies to consumers. Therefore, the fact that such measures have the effect, for a short time, of reducing the quantities that the states concerned are able to exchange between themselves, cannot lead to these measures being classified among those prohibited by the treaty, the decisive factor being that in the long term these measures are necessary to ensure a steady, optimum yield from fishing.*[128]

In its 1980 Communication on the interpretation of the *Cassis* judgment, the Commission had already mentioned the protection of the environment among the mandatory requirements.[129] The Court followed a few years later. In the 1985 *ADBHU* case, the Court considered the validity of a Community Directive in the light of primary Community law. The Court observed that the directive at issue must be seen in the perspective of environmental protection, which is *one of the Community's essential objectives*.[130] This judgment was delivered before environmental protection had received Treaty status in the 1986 Single

---

by regulating working hours in Case 155/80 *Oebel* [1981] ECR 1993. Even more "mandatory requirements" have been added within the realm of the free movement of services. See the overview in Kapteijn and VerLoren van Themaat (1998) at 759-60.

[125] Joined Cases 3,4,6/76 *Kramer* [1976] ECR 1279.

[126] Opinion of Advocate-General Trabucchi in Joined Cases 3,4,6/76 *Kramer*, at 1324.

[127] See *infra*, Section 3.4.

[128] Ibid., paras. 56/59.

[129] OJ 1980 C 256/2.

[130] Case 240/83 *ADBHU*, at 549.

European Act. The express recognition of environmental protection as a mandatory requirement occurred in the *Danish Bottles* case, where the Court stated that 'the protection of the environment is a mandatory requirement which may limit the application of Article 30 [now 28] of the Treaty'.[131] The Court in that judgment referred to the *ADBHU* case and to the 1986 Single European Act. It did not define the scope of the mandatory requirement of environmental protection, however. That scope will have to be assessed by additional case-law, which is still scarce on the subject.

2.3   Conditions for the Application of the Justifications

2.3.1   Introduction

Merely invoking the protection of health or life or environmental protection as a mandatory requirement for hindering intra-Community trade will not suffice for a Member State. Additional conditions concerning the relationship between means and ends have to be satisfied.[132] The Court has developed a set of conditions with which national measures have to comply in order to be justified under both Article 30 and the "mandatory requirements". The Court varies the terminology used. However, recurring themes in this language are the "suitability" of the measure to pursue the goal sought, its "necessity", its "proportionality", and the question whether there are alternative measures available that would attain the same goal by means that are less restrictive of intra-Community trade.

What is the basis of these conditions as developed by the Court? Article 30 uses the words '*justified* on grounds of...the protection of health and life...'.[133] The Court has interpreted this word as implying a necessity test.[134] The terms most commonly employed by the Court when applying the "rule of reason" are '*necessary* to satisfy mandatory requirements', although it sometimes varies, referring instead to e.g. '*justified* by an imperative requirement',[135] or 'overriding requirements of general public importance which may *justify* obstacles to the free movement of goods'.[136]

---

[131] Case 302/86 *Commission* v. *Denmark*, para. 9.

[132] Moreover, a measure satisfying a mandatory requirement should be "indistinctly applicable" to imported and domestic goods. This point is further discussed *infra*, in Section 3.3.

[133] Emphasis added.

[134] Case 153/78 *Commission* v. *Germany*: 'Since the restrictive measures authorised by article 36 [now 30] derogate from the fundamental principle of the free movement of goods, they are in accordance with the treaty only in so far as they are "justified", that is to say, necessary in order, in this case, to ensure the protection of human health and life.'

[135] See e.g. Case C-209/98 *Sydhavnens*, para. 49. Emphasis added.

[136] See e.g. Case C-34/95 *De Agostini*, para. 46. Emphasis added.

2.3.2 The Requirement of "Proportionality"

The conditions to be fulfilled by national measures in order to be justified by Article 30 or a mandatory requirement are often taken together and referred to as the proportionality requirement.

The proportionality of means and ends has been considered a general principle of Community law from the early years of the Coal and Steel Community.[137] First pronounced by the Court of Justice in a case in 1955,[138] the principle was invoked and applied in hundreds of subsequent cases before it. The principle of proportionality works in two ways. On the one hand, it provides a check on Community legislative action, and in that sense it may be seen as an expression of the principle of attributed powers.[139] The principle thus operates to balance Community action in the general interest with individual interests. This manifestation of proportionality has Treaty status. The Court of Justice may be confronted with questions regarding the proportionality of Community legislation in two ways: through direct actions based on Article 230, and in preliminary questions from national courts based on Article 234 regarding the validity of Community acts.[140]

On the other hand, the principle also provides a check on Member State legislative and regulatory action through its application in cases involving the compatibility of such action with the Treaty, e.g. with the free movement of goods. Proportionality in this sense is assessed both by national courts applying Community law and by the European Court of Justice when answering preliminary questions on the interpretation of Community law. It is this manifestation of proportionality which is most relevant to this study. Although not explicit in the Treaty, it forms part of the general principles of Community law, and may arguably be read into the term "justified" in Article 30 as well as the Court's judgments on measures that are "justified" by mandatory requirements.

The Court has never made explicit the origin of the proportionality principle as applied in Community law.[141] The principle has its roots in the legal traditions of a number of Member States. In international law, proportionality is regarded as one aspect of a broader concept of "reason". That notion has formal as well as substantive elements. Focusing on the substantive elements, proportionality

---

[137] Neville Brown (1985).

[138] Case 8/55 *Fédéchar*.

[139] Emiliou (1996a) at 138.

[140] See Section 2.3.4.

[141] Even though both Advocates-General and national courts have discussed this issue. See e.g. the opinion of AG Dutheillet de Lamothe in Case 11/70 *Internationale Handellsgesellschaft*, and a statement by the Verwaltungsgericht Frankfurt that the principle of proportionality is derived from the prohibition against the abuse of rights in public international law, both in Emiliou (1996a) at 135-37.

may be described as the sufficiency of the causal link between a measure and its legitimate objective, the causal link and the objective being the other substantive elements.[142] It has been suggested that proportionality is essentially the same as "reasonableness", a term commonly used in English law.[143] Proportionality as such is found in French administrative law,[144] but the concept as applied in the EC appears to have been inspired principally by German administrative law.[145] According to German law, a measure is deemed proportional if it fulfils a three-pronged test. First, the measure must be appropriate for attaining the objective sought by it. Second, it must be necessary, in the sense that no other measure less restrictive of freedom is available. Third, it must not be disproportionate to its objective: proportionality in the narrow sense.[146]

Thus, there is, on the one hand, a large proportionality concept, encompassing basically all the requirements which a measure has to fulfil in order to justify a restriction on the free movement of goods.[147] On the other hand, a stricter concept of proportionality, proportionality *stricto sensu*, posits proportionality as only one of the conditions a measure has to fulfil in order to justify trade restrictions. The other conditions which a measure pursuing a legitimate aim has to meet in addition would in that view be "appropriateness", "necessity" and "least trade-restrictiveness".

2.3.3   Proportionality of National Measures

Where the proportionality of national measures is concerned, the elements identified above occur in all sorts of variations in the Court's judgments, the opinions by Advocates-General, and academic literature. The first criterion of proportionality in the wider sense, the measure's appropriateness, is also referred to as "suitability", "usefulness" or "effectiveness".[148] This element is often clear enough and not made explicit by the Court. As regards the second

---

[142] Corten (1999).

[143] Advocate-General Warner in his opinion in Case 34/79 *Henn and Darby*, at 3830, referring to Neville Brown (1985), as noted by De Búrca (1993) at 108.

[144] See Emiliou (1996a) at Chapter 2.

[145] See Emiliou (1996a) at Chapter 3.

[146] See, with slight variations but all listing essentially these three elements, Schwarze (1992) at Chapter 5; De Búrca (1993) at 113; Emiliou (1996a) at 26; Jacobs (1999); at 1; Jans (2000b) at 240-41.

[147] E.g. Krämer (1993b) at 120: 'A measure is proportional when it aims to pursue a legitimate political objective, when the measure is appropriate to approach this objective, when the measure is necessary to reach or approach the objective and when there is no measure which is less restrictive for the free circulation of goods.' Note, however, that this author lists necessity and least trade-restrictiveness as separate requirements, and does not identify the third prong of the test, proportionality *stricto sensu*.

[148] See e.g. De Búrca (1993) at 113.

criterion, often "necessity" and "least trade-restrictiveness" are equated by the Court and in academic literature.[149] The third and most controversial element of the test as described above, proportionality in the strict sense, is rarely applied in the Court's case-law. However, the words "proportional" or "proportionate" are frequently used by the Court, often to refer to what has been described above as the "necessity" and "least trade-restrictive" tests.[150] Sometimes, the Court has separately mentioned proportionality, necessity and least trade-restrictiveness.[151] The Court also sometimes suggests that proportionality and least trade-restrictiveness are cumulative conditions.[152] On other occasions, the Court has found a measure to be "manifestly disproportionate".[153] In a number of cases, the Court has applied a negative formulation of the principle of proportionality, accepting a national measure as "not disproportionate".[154] The Court has in a number of cases pointed out that 'where a Member State relies on overriding requirements to justify rules which are likely to obstruct the exercise of free movement of goods, such justification must also be interpreted in the light of the general principles of law and in particular of fundamental rights.'[155]

(a)   Proportionality and Article 30

In the absence of Community harmonisation addressing the objective pursued, Member States are entitled to decide what *degree of protection* of life and health they wish to assure. However, they must take account of the requirements of the free movement of goods.[156] As argued above, the Court does not require exclusive proof of a "health and life" hazard. Genuine doubt about

---

[149] See the Court in Case C-131/93 *Commission* v. *Germany (Crayfish)*: '[R]ules restricting intra-Community trade are compatible with the Treaty only in so far as they are *indispensable* for the purposes of providing effective protection for the health and life of animals. They cannot therefore be covered by the derogation provided for in Article 36 [now 30] if that aim may be achieved just as effectively by measures having less restrictive effects on intra-Community trade.' Emphasis added. Cf. Jans (2000b) at 240, and Jacobs (1999) at 1.

[150] Case C-217/99 *Commission* v. *Belgium*; Case 302/86 *Commission* v. *Denmark (Danish Bottles)*, at para. 6.

[151] Case C-67/97 *Bluhme*.

[152] Case C-189/95 *Franzèn*, para. 76, referring to Cases 120/78 *Cassis de Dijon*, C-470/93 *Mars* paragraph 15; Case C-368/95 *Familiapress*, paragraph 19; and Joined Cases C-34/95, C-35/95 and C-36/95 *De Agostini*, paragraph 45.

[153] Cases C-241/89 *SARPP* at para. 21; C-369/88 *Delattre* at para. 56.

[154] Cases C-39/90 *Denkavit* at para. 24; C-312/89 *Conforama* at para. 12; C-389/96 *Aher-Waggon*, para. 25.

[155] See in the context of goods, Case C-368/95 *Familiapress*, para. 24; and in the context of services, Case C-260/89 *ERT*, para. 43, both referring to the freedom of expression laid down in Article 10 of the European Convention on Human Rights.

[156] See eg. Case 125/88 *Nijman*.

a product's safety may justify action under Article 30 even if scientific evidence is not unequivocal, and even if other Member States consider the product to be acceptable.[157] Nonetheless, the proportionality test requires that the Member State take into consideration whether a component in imported products it wishes to prohibit is harmless according to international scientific data, and whether it meets a genuine technical or other need. The concept of technological need must be assessed in the light of the raw materials utilised, bearing in mind the assessment made by the authorities of the Member State where the product is lawfully manufactured and marketed. Account must also be taken of the findings of international scientific research, in particular of the work of the Community's Scientific Committees for Food, the Codex Alimentarius Committee of the FAO and the WHO.[158] Furthermore, the Member State must make available to importers and foreign companies an administrative procedure for seeking general authorisation for products containing such components.[159]

As argued above, in the absence of any health risk, the Court will reject an Article 30 justification. But whenever there is at least the possibility of a health risk, the Court will demonstrate more deference to national authorities' policy decisions. Thus, in cases concerning products causing health risks, Member States may require prior authorisation for the marketing of such products, and even complete prohibitions are not *per se* unacceptable. This is not only so in cases concerning obviously dangerous products such as biocides and pesticides,[160] but also in cases concerning medicines,[161] and food additives posing only a potential health risk.[162] In such cases, the Court has shown that it is ready to accept national governments' arguments.[163]

Sometimes, Member States invoke both health risks and the mandatory requirement of consumer protection. The latter argument will be based on the perceived confusion caused to domestic consumers when confronted with products from other Member States that differ from the domestic products they have traditionally known. This has been put forward in relation to marketing requirements for e.g. beer,[164] other alcoholic beverages[165], vinegar[166] and pasta[167].

---

[157] See e.g. Case 53/80 *Eyssen* .

[158] Cases C-13/91 and C-113/91 *Debus* at para. 29, citing Case 178/84 *Commission v. Germany.*

[159] See e.g. Case 174/82 *Sandoz.*

[160] See e.g. Cases 272/80 *Frans-Nederlandse Maatschappij voor Biologische Producten*; C-293/94 *Brandsma*; C-400/96 *Harpegnies.*

[161] Case C-55/99 *Commission v. France.*

[162] Case 53/80 *Officier van Jusitie v. Koninklijke Kaasfabriek Eyssen BV* ; Case 174/82 *Sandoz*; Case 227/82 *Van Bennekom.*

[163] Case C-473/98 *Toolex Alpha*, at paras. 40-48. See further on this case Heyvaert (2001).

[164] See Case 178/84 *Commission v. Germany* ('*Beer Purity Laws*').

[165] See Case 120/78 *Cassis de Dijon.*

[166] See Case 788/79 *Gilli and Andres.*

[167] See Case 407/85 *Drei Glocken.*

The Court usually not only rejects the health justification, but also the invocation of the mandatory requirement of consumer protection in such cases. It will consider that Member States may ensure that consumers make an informed choice by means which do not prevent the importation of products which have been lawfully manufactured and marketed in other Member States and, in particular, 'by the compulsory affixing of suitable labels giving the nature of the product sold'.[168]

It is contrary to the principle of proportionality for national rules to require imported products to comply strictly and exactly with the provisions or technical requirements laid down for products manufactured in the importing Member State, when those imported products afford users the same level of protection. However, in a case concerning French requirements for woodworking machines, the Court acknowledged that approaches to protection may differ between Member States, and that such differences should be taken into account when applying the proportionality test. In Germany, the approach to life and health protection included compulsory training for the users of such machines, whereas the French applied stricter requirements to the machines themselves. The Court accepted that it had not been established that the two approaches guaranteed users the same level of protection. Statistics on accidents with woodworking machines in both countries did not take into account these different approaches and were not conclusive.[169]

The proportionality principle has up until now been applied in relation to measures aimed at animal and plant protection in only a relatively small number of cases.[170] Roughly, the same principles apply as in relation to measures for human life or health protection, although it is recalled that human life and health are considered more important than animal or plant life and health.[171] In most of these cases, the emphasis has been on the least trade-restrictiveness test.[172] The *Crayfish* case provides a clear example; the Court found a German import ban to be disproportionate, since Germany had not convincingly shown that measures which were less restrictive for intra-Community trade were incapable of effectively protecting the interests pleaded.[173] In *Monsees*, the subject-

---

[168] See e.g. Case 407/85 *Drei Glocken* at para. 16. A more elaborate discussion of these types of cases can be found in Weatherill (1999).

[169] Case 188/84 *Commission v. France (woodworking machines)*, paras. 16-22.

[170] See Case 64/75 *Rewe*; Case 251/78 *Denkavit*; Case 124/81 *Commission v. UK*; Case 40/82 *Commission v. UK*; Case 74/82 *Commission v. Ireland*; Case 73/84 *Denkavit*; Case C-304/88 *Commission v. Belgium*; Case C-128/89 *Commission v. Italy*; Case C-131/93 *Commission v. Germany*.

[171] Cases 104/75 *De Peijper*; C-320/93 *Ortscheit* [1994] ECR I-5243.

[172] Notably the first *Denkavit* case, *Commission v. UK* ('*UHT Milk*'), the *Newcastle Disease* cases, *Commission v. Belgium* ('*Live Animals*'), *Commission v. Italy* ('*Grapefruits*') and *Commission v. Germany* ('*Crayfish*'), all in note 111.

[173] Case C-131/93 *Crayfish*, at para. 26.

matter of the national measure was Austrian limitations to live animal transportation. The Court observed that the effect of the measure was to make all international transit of animals for slaughter by road almost impossible in Austria. Furthermore, measures appropriate to the objective of protecting the health of animals and less restrictive of the free movement of goods were conceivable.[174]

The proportionality requirement not only applies to national laws laying down, for example, food standards, but also to the assessment of conformity with such standards. To the extent that conformity checks are not covered by Community legislation, the Court has accepted the possibility for a Member State to apply checks even if the product has been checked and approved in another Member State.[175] However, the Court has at the same time prohibited tests where similar tests have been applied in the other Member State, whose results are available.[176] Moreover, the Court has consistently held that, where co-operation between the authorities of the Member States makes it possible to facilitate and simplify frontier checks, the authorities responsible for health inspections must ascertain whether the documents issued within the framework of that co-operation give rise to a presumption that the imported goods comply with the requirements of domestic health legislation, thus enabling the checks carried out upon importation to be simplified.[177] From this case-law, it has been concluded that 'a product accompanied by a certificate that declares that it has been tested in its state of origin is in principle free to circulate throughout the Community without being subjected to further tests.'[178] Thus, the importing state will have to justify why a second test is necessary. This can be considered a manifestation of the principle of mutual recognition as laid down in the *Cassis* and subsequent cases.

In sum, the proportionality principle as applied to justifications for the life and health of humans balances deference to national authorities' chosen levels of health protection with the need to secure market access throughout the Community for products lawfully manufactured and marketed in any Member State. Article 30, it is recalled, is applicable in those instances where the health risk at issue has not been (fully) addressed by Community harmonisation. The balance between health protection and market access depends on the

---

[174] Case C-350/97 *Monsees*. The Court relied on pending Community harmonisation to prove its point that less trade-restrictive measures were conceivable; see Langer and Wiers (2000). On harmonisation, see Section 2.4.

[175] See e.g. Case 251/78 *Denkavit* [1979] ECR 3369.

[176] See e.g. Case 272/80 *Frans-Nederlandse Maatschappij voor Biologische Producten*; Case C-293/94 *Brandsma*.

[177] Case 104/75 *de Peijper*; Case 251/78 *Denkavit*; Case 124/81 *Commission v. UK*.

[178] Weatherill and Beaumont (1995) at 470.

perceived health risk. In cases of established health risks, the Member States have more leeway to restrict or even completely prevent market access. Where risks are minimal or absent, labelling or certification is usually found to be the least-trade restrictive alternative, making more restrictive measures disproportionate. Factors taken into account when striking the necessary balance are international scientific evidence; whether the substance posing a health risk meets a genuine need; and how other Member States deal with the perceived health risk. All this, however, must be seen in the light of the principles of prevention and precaution, as laid down in Article 174 EC and elaborated in a communication by the Commission.[179] Although the Communication was only meant as 'input in an ongoing debate', it did outline requirements to be met by precautionary measures.[180] Arguably, this principle not only applies to Community legislation, but also to Member State measures. Thus, it seems that the existence of a risk as perceived in one Member State, even if disputed elsewhere, may suffice to justify trade-restrictive measures.

The second sentence of Article 30 reflects the preamble of GATT Article XX.[181] It stipulates that prohibitions or restrictions that may be justified under the first sentence of Article 30 shall not constitute a means of arbitrary discrimination or a disguised restriction on trade between Member States. As the Court has held in various cases, the function of the second sentence of Article 36 is to prevent restrictions on trade based on the grounds mentioned in the first sentence from being diverted from their proper purpose and used in such a way as to create discrimination in respect of goods originating in other Member States or indirectly to protect certain national products.[182] Thus, the prohibition in the second sentence is designed to prevent abuse of the permitted justifications in the first sentence of Article 30. The Court has applied the term "misuse" explicitly in cases concerning another ground mentioned in Article 30, the protection of commercial and industrial property.[183]

---

[179] EC Commission (2000b).

[180] Ibid.: 'Where action is deemed necessary, measures based on the precautionary principle should be, *inter alia*:
- proportional to the chosen level of protection,
- non-discriminatory in their application,
- consistent with similar measures already taken,
- based on an examination of the potential benefits and costs of action or lack of
action (including, where appropriate and feasible, an economic cost/benefit analysis),
- subject to review, in the light of new scientific data, and
- capable of assigning responsibility for producing the scientific evidence necessary for a more comprehensive risk assessment.'

[181] See Chapter 4.

[182] See Case 34/79 *Henn and Darby* para. 21; Joined Cases C-1/90 and C-176/90 *Aragonesa*, para. 20.

[183] See e.g. Case 15/74 *Sterling Drug*.

The Court has said that the principle of proportionality *underlies* the second sentence of Article 30.[184] Some authors contend that the proportionality test and the second sentence of Article 30 are equivalent,[185] while others argue that the second sentence of Article 30 includes the principles of proportionality and alternative means.[186] Still others contend that proportionality and the second sentence of Article 30 are different things. Proportionality is part of the question whether a measure is justified or not, while the second sentence of Article 30 acts as an overriding requirement. In this view, a measure that is justified as proportionate may still infringe the second sentence.[187]

(b) Proportionality and the Mandatory Requirement of Environmental Protection

The *Danish Bottles* case was the first case in which the Court discussed the mandatory requirement of environmental protection and the proportionality of a national measure taken to pursue that requirement.[188] The case concerned a Danish measure under which beer and soft drinks could only be marketed in returnable containers, for which a system of collection and refilling was required. Containers had to be approved by the Danish Environmental Protection Agency. Non-approved containers, except any form of metal containers, could be used to market a maximum of 2,800 hectolitres per year per producer, provided that for those containers a deposit-and-return system was established. The case is especially interesting in the light of the proportionality principle, as the Court ruled the infringements to the free movement of goods brought about by the Danish system to be partially proportionate and partially disproportionate to the objective pursued.

The Court found the obligation to establish a deposit-and-return system, which went hand in hand with the requirement that beer and soft drinks be marketed only in returnable containers to be 'an indispensable element of a system intended to ensure the re-use of containers and therefore necessary to achieve the aims pursued by the contested rules', and it determined that this obligation was proportionate.[189] The Court did not expressly consider whether there were less trade-restrictive means available; perhaps the word "indispensable" implies that the Court thought that there were no such alternatives available. Probably the Court did not itself go into the question of the requirement that

---

[184] E.g. in Cases 174/82 *Sandoz*, para. 18; 227/82 *Van Bennekom*, para. 39; C-400/96 *Harpegnies*, para. 34.

[185] See e.g. Krämer (1993b) at 127.

[186] Weatherill and Beaumont (1995) at 455. The principles mentioned are discussed in more detail below.

[187] Gormley (1985) at 210-11.

[188] Case 302/86 *Commission* v. *Denmark*. On this case, see e.g. Krämer (1993a) at 89-105; Kromarek (1990).

[189] Para. 13 of the judgment.

only returnable containers be marketed, because the Commission had accepted this requirement and had expressed its view that it did not wish to see the system in force replaced by another system.[190]

As to the quantitative limit for non-approved containers, the Court acknowledged that a system for returning *approved* containers 'ensures a maximum rate of re-use and therefore a *very considerable degree of protection of the environment* since empty containers can be returned to *any* retailer of beverages.'[191] Non-approved containers, on the contrary, could only be returned where they had been bought. The Court however argued:

> *Nevertheless, the system for returning non-approved containers is capable of protecting the environment and, as far as imports are concerned, affects only limited quantities of beverages compared with the quantity of beverages consumed in Denmark owing to the restrictive effect which the requirement that containers should be returnable has on imports. In those circumstances, a restriction of the quantity of products which may be marketed by importers is disproportionate to the objective pursued.[192]*

Subsequent case-law on the mandatory requirement of environmental protection and proportionality is scarce. The Court did not discuss proportionality in the *Walloon Waste* case. In *Aher-Waggon*, the Court assessed under Articles 28-30 a German measure concerning noise standards for aircraft, which was stricter than the relevant Community harmonisation. The Court observed that the measure fell within the *Dassonville* formula, but could be justified by considerations of public health and environmental protection, as long as it was proportionate and met the least trade-restrictiveness test. The Court found that 'limiting noise emissions from aircraft is the most effective and convenient means of combating the noise pollution which they generate', and concluded that the measure was not disproportionate.[193] Without making explicit whether it regarded the justification as falling within Article 30 or within the mandatory requirement of environmental protection, the Court appears to have opted for the latter by suggesting that the measure was indistinctly applicable,[194] and concluding that Article 28 did not preclude the German measure.

---

[190] Krämer (1993a) at 101.

[191] Para. 20 of the judgment. Emphasis added.

[192] Para. 21 of the judgment.

[193] Case C-389/96 *Aher Waggon*, paras. 21-24.

[194] Case C-389/96 *Aher Waggon*, para. 22. This point is debatable, see Section 3.3.3.

2.3.4   Proportionality of Community Measures

The third sentence of Article 5 of the EC Treaty provides that '[a]ny action by the Community shall not go beyond what is necessary to achieve the objectives of this Treaty'. Without explicitly mentioning the term, this is a clear formulation of the proportionality principle. It has been somewhat further elaborated in the Protocol on the Application of the Principles of Subsidiarity and Proportionality attached to the 1997 Amsterdam Treaty, although that Protocol deals mostly with subsidiarity. The relevant text provides that '[t]he shape of Community action is as simple as possible without impeding satisfactory realisation of the goal of the action and of its effective execution'.[195] This means that the Community should only legislate where necessary, and should choose directives rather than regulations.

In the *ADBHU* case, the Court said that Community environmental measures restricting trade must 'neither be discriminatory nor *go beyond the inevitable restrictions* which are *justified by the pursuit of the objective* of environmental protection'.[196] The Court, in assessing the proportionality of Community measures, clearly distinguishes between the several elements of the test:

> *the lawfulness of the prohibition of an economic activity [by a Community measure] is subject to the condition that the prohibitory measures are appropriate and necessary in order to achieve the objectives legitimately pursued by the legislation in question; when there is a choice between several appropriate measures recourse must be had to the least onerous, and the disadvantages caused must not be disproportionate to the aims pursued.*[197]

The Court usually explicitly identifies and assesses these elements individually. At the same time, it is reluctant to impose its own judgement over and above that of the Community's legislative authorities when applying the test, especially when common policies are concerned, such as the common agricultural policy. For example, in the same judgment cited above, the Court stated that 'with regard to judicial review of compliance with those conditions it must be stated that in matters concerning the common agricultural policy the Community legislature has a discretionary power which corresponds to the political responsibilities given to it [...] Consequently, the legality of a measure adopted in that sphere can be affected only if the measure is *manifestly inappropriate* having regard to the objective which the competent institution is seeking to pursue'.[198]

---

[195] Amsterdam Protocol, para. 6.

[196] Case 240/83 *ADBHU*, para. 15. Emphasis added.

[197] See e.g. Case C-331/88 *Fedesa*, para. 13.

[198] Ibid., para. 14, referring to Case 265/87 *Schraeder*, paras. 21 and 22. Emphasis added.

It should be noted that "manifestly inappropriate" concerns the first part of the proportionality test as described by the Court and cited above, i.e., the appropriateness of the measure, rather than the last part, i.e. the relationship between 'disadvantages caused and aims pursued'.[199]

The Court is equally reserved when assessing the necessity of the measure and the availability of less trade-restrictive measures. In the *Boehringer* case, the Court of First Instance was asked to judge on the proportionality of Community measures largely prohibiting the use of clenbuterol for bovines, which practically put a company producing that substance out of business. The Court, having found that the measures were not manifestly inappropriate to their aims, assessed their necessity by looking at alternatives. The Court found that the Council had not made a 'manifest error of assessment' when deciding that a prohibition was the preferable solution.[200] This illustrates the Court's unwillingness to challenge the Community's legislator. Interestingly, the Court at the same time applied a balancing test as part of the necessity requirement. The Court not only argued that the alternatives proposed would be less effective, but it also observed that control measures that would be warranted by the application of less restrictive measures would entail a significant cost for the public purse, and that that cost must be balanced against the loss caused to the company by the prohibition.[201] Recently, Advocate-General Alber proposed a more intrusive "necessary" test of Community legislation.[202]

The last part of the test applied to Community legislation assesses proportionality *stricto sensu*, 'that is to say the weighing of damage to individual rights against the benefits accruing to the general interest'.[203] Again, the Court appears unwilling to challenge the balance struck by the competent institutions. In a context where the Community legislature makes social policy choices, or undertakes 'complex assessments based on technical and scientific information which is liable to change rapidly', the Court limits its judicial review to examining whether the exercise of the legislature's power 'has been vitiated by a manifest error of assessment or a misuse of powers or whether the legislature has manifestly exceeded the limits of its discretion.'[204] In practice, the Court indeed applies the strict proportionality test with much restraint. For example, in *Fedesa*, the Court confined itself to observing that the importance of the objectives pursued was such as to justify even substantial negative financial consequences for certain traders.[205] In the *Boehringer* case, the Court concluded

---

[199] This is confirmed by the Court of First Instance in Case T-125/96 *Boehringer*, at para. 76.

[200] Case T-125/96 *Boehringer*, paras. 97 and 100.

[201] Ibid., paras. 92-96.

[202] Opinion in Joined Cases C-27/00 and C-122/00 *Omega Air*.

[203] Ibid., para. 102.

[204] Cases C-84/94 *UK v. Council*, para. 58, and C-127/95 *Norbrook Laboratories*, para. 90.

[205] Case C-331/88 *Fedesa*, para. 17.

on this point that 'the importance of the aims pursued [...] is such as to justify adverse economic consequences, even of a substantial nature, for individual traders [...]', and that 'the maintenance of public health must take precedence over all other considerations'.[206]

To sum up, in assessing the proportionality of Community measures, the Court distinguishes much more clearly between the different elements of proportionality *senso latu* than in assessing national measures. Moreover, its proportionality test for Community legislation includes a strict proportionality test, i.e. a full balancing of the interests at issue. At the same time, however, the Court, apparently very conscious of the division of competencies between the Community's institutions, is reluctant to step into the role of the Community legislator. It usually only applies a marginal test in assessing all of the elements.

2.4 Community Harmonisation and the Right to Go Beyond Community Standards

The goal of this work is not to discuss the intricacies of Community harmonisation instruments,[207] or the problems associated with their appropriate legal basis.[208] However, an assessment of Member States' environmental and health measures as they relate to Community law is incomplete when looking only at the primary Treaty Articles on the free movement of goods. If an environmental subject-matter is outside the scope of secondary Community legislation, it remains within the competence of the Member States to regulate, albeit within the limits of primary Community law. On the other hand, if the subject-matter is covered by secondary Community legislation, what action Member States may still take unilaterally with respect to that subject-matter primarily depends on the relevant secondary legislation. In principle, Articles 28-30 are no longer relevant to national measures in such situations, and a Member State cannot invoke Article 30 or the mandatory requirement of environmental protection to justify a trade-restrictive environmental or health measure.[209] Only if the relevant secondary legislation enables the Member States to deviate from or go beyond the set environmental or health standards will primary Community law on the free movement of goods come into play.[210]

---

[206] Case T-125/96 *Boehringer*, para. 102.

[207] On Community environmental harmonisation, see Geradin (1993); Faure (1998); Jans (2000a).

[208] These problems were more pressing until the 1997 Amsterdam Treaty made the legislative procedure for environmental Community legislation under Article 175 the same as for internal market legislation under Article 95. See e.g. London and Llamas (1995), at 34-44; Jans (1995), at 50-61.

[209] See e.g. Cases C-169/89 *Van den Burg*, C-5/94 *Hedley Lomas*, C-1/96 *Compassion*.

[210] See e.g. Cases C-389/96 *Aher Waggon*, C-383/97 *Van der Laan*.

For the above reasons, the assessment of national environmental and health measures must begin by investigating whether there is any relevant Community legislation addressing the subject-matter which the national measure seeks to regulate. However, it is not always easy to determine the respective coverage of Community and national legislation. In assessing whether a subject-matter is covered by harmonisation, the personal, territorial and substantive scope of the Community legislation at issue must be examined. Often, the legislation lists explicitly the areas, persons or products to which it applies. Generally speaking, anything outside the personal, territorial or substantive scope of Community legislation is for the Member States to regulate.[211]

The substantive scope of secondary Community law is not only determined by the subject-matter which is regulated, but is also closely related to its objectives, which can usually be discerned from the preamble. If the objectives of Community legislation and a national measure regulating the same persons or products coincide, the ability of individual Member States to regulate in pursuance of these objectives is circumscribed by the Community legislation. Thus, if a Community directive lays down maximum transit hours for live animal transports to protect animal welfare, a Member State can only pursue the same objective (animal welfare) regarding the same subject-matter (live animal transports) within the limits set by the directive.[212] On the other hand, a Member State was allowed to apply national measures on the dimensions of boxes for fattening calves as long as there were no Community measures regulating such dimensions, even if there was a common market organisation scheme in place for the animals concerned.[213] The common market organisation scheme did not contain any provision for animal protection, so it regulated calves but not their protection.

However, such a situation will not often arise. In the majority of cases, Community measures refer to both internal market and environmental or health concerns. The Court in such cases readily accepts that both objectives are covered by the Community measure. For example, subsequent to the case referred to above, a directive regulating the dimensions of boxes for fattening calves has come into force. The Court subsequently stated that this directive 'provides for harmonisation of the measures necessary to achieve the specific objective [of animal protection], thus making recourse to Article 36 [now 30] impossible.'[214] Apparently, the Court sees no problem in Community secondary

---

[211] C.f. Cases 94/83 *Heijn*, 125/88 *Nijman*, 380/87 *Balsamo*, C-473/98 *Toolex Alpha*.

[212] See Directive 91/628, OJ (1991) L 340/1, as amended by Directive 95/29 OJ (1995) L 148/52. This directive was at issue in Case C-350/97 *Monsees*, but did not yet apply to Austria when the facts of the case arose, thus making Articles 28-30 applicable.

[213] Joined Cases 141-143/81 *Holdijk*.

[214] See Case C-5/94 *Hedley Lomas*, para. 18; Case C-1/96 *Compassion in World Farming*, para. 47.

legislation having several "specific objectives". National action pursuing any of these objectives is precluded, even if internal market concerns appear to have weighed at least as heavily as environmental concerns in enacting the Community legislation, as in the case of the directive on the dimensions of calf boxes.[215]

Having established the extent to which the subject-matter of a national measure is covered by secondary Community legislation, a close look at that legislation must be taken in order to determine whether, and if so to what extent and under what conditions, individual Member States are still allowed to regulate the subject-matter at issue. Community environmental legislation often lays down minimum or maximum values. This is true for standards concerning production aspects, and general standards concerning e.g. air or water quality, but also sometimes for product standards.[216] Member States are in principle free to impose stricter production and quality standards on their own producers than those laid down in Community legislation. Of course, they do not have the jurisdiction to do the same for producers in other Member States.[217] The situation is different for product standards. If Member States were allowed to impose stricter product requirements than the standards set at Community level on products imported from other Member States, they could replace Community standards by their own standards for all goods marketed in their territory. This would seriously endanger the harmonising effect and the accompanying scale advantages of Community product standards. Therefore, Community legislation laying down product standards often contains a so-called "free movement clause", stipulating that a Member State cannot impede the marketing of any product imported from another Member State that meets the Community standards. Accordingly, a product meeting the Community standards can be marketed throughout the Community.[218]

Community legislation is sometimes categorised in terms of "minimum", "total", or "exhaustive" harmonisation. A Community directive can be called

---

[215] Cf. the following considerations in the preamble of Directive 91/629/EEC, at issue in Cases C-5/94 *Hedley Lomas* and C-1/96 *Compassion in World Farming*: '[...] Whereas differences which may distort conditions of competition interfere with the smooth running of the organisation of the common market in calves and calf products; Whereas there is therefore a need to establish common minimum standards for the protection of rearing calves or calves for fattening in order to ensure rational development of production [...]'

[216] See by way of examples, Directive 92/112 OJ (1992) L 409/11 (waste from the titanium dioxide industry), and Directive 99/30 OJ (1999) L 163/41 (air quality standards), and Directive 94/62 OJ (1994) L 365/10 (maximum values for heavy metals in packaging materials), respectively.

[217] What happens when a Member State attempts to impose production standards on imported products is discussed in Sections 2.3.4 and 7.2.

[218] See e.g. Article 18 of Directive 94/62 OJ (1994) L 365/10.

"minimum harmonisation" because it lays down minimum standards, "total" harmonisation because it provides a free movement clause, and "exhaustive" harmonisation because it entirely covers the subject-matter a national policy aims to regulate and the room left to act unilaterally. However, such categories do not assist much in determining the scope for national policy measures after harmonisation has taken place. They seem to be partially overlapping. With regard to product standards, minimum requirements are often combined with a free movement clause, in which case Member States may apply stricter standards only to domestic production.[219] In the absence of a free movement clause, stricter standards may be applied to imports too, but such application will be tested against the Treaty, notably Articles 28-30.[220] However, there appear to be exceptions to this scheme. In a case concerning the Wild Birds directive, the Court pointed at the fact that a directive allowed Member States to apply stricter measures, and 'therefore regulated exhaustively the Member States' powers'. The Court found that with regard to species that did not receive special protection under the Directive and did not occur within their territory, Member States were not allowed to adopt stricter protective measures than those provided under the Directive.[221] In another case, concerning a directive laying down minimum standards for the protection of calves, the Court stated that the Community legislature 'laid down exhaustively common minimum standards'. The fact that the directive itself authorised Member States to adopt stricter measures within their territory did not mean that the directive had not exhaustively regulated the powers of the Member States in the area of the protection of veal calves.[222] In both instances, the Court thus refused to assess under Articles 28-30 EC national measures aiming at higher protection levels than provided for in the directive at issue. These cases may be peculiar in that they both concerned national measures pursuing extraterritorial protection goals.[223] Be that as it may, they show how difficult it is to categorise harmonising legislation. Thus, rather than to attempt to establish what type of harmonisation is at issue, the appropriate way to proceed seems to determine the coverage of the national measure and the Community legislation, and then to look at the possibilities for national policies offered by the legislation. Depending on how such possibilities, if any, are phrased, Articles 28-30 may come into play.

When assessing the Member States' scope of action after harmonisation, not only the text of secondary Community legislation itself is relevant, but also its legal basis. The EC Treaty's Title on Environment consists of Articles

---

[219] See e.g. Case C-11/92 *Gallaher*.

[220] See e.g. Case C-389/96 *Aher-Waggon*, paras. 15-16.

[221] Case C-169/89 *Van den Burg*, paras. 9 and 12.

[222] Case C-1/96 *Compassion in World Farming*, paras. 56 and 63, referring to *Van den Burg*.

[223] Cf. Scott (2000) at 128. See further on these cases, Section 3.4.

174, 175 and 176. Article 174 lays down as the objectives of the Community's environmental policy 'preserving, protecting and improving the quality of the environment', as well as 'protecting human health'. It further stipulates that the Community environmental policy shall aim at a high level of protection, and mentions a number of principles on which the policy shall be based and aspects that shall be taken into account in preparing it. Where appropriate, environmental harmonisation measures shall include a safeguard clause allowing Member States to take provisional measures for non-economic environmental reasons. Article 175 provides the legal basis for Community environmental legislation. This has led to an important body of Community environmental law, both "sectoral", e.g. various directives setting air and water quality standards, and "horizontal", e.g. the directive on integrated pollution prevention and control.[224] The Court has observed that the Community rules do not seek to effect complete harmonisation in the area of the environment.[225]

Article 176 stipulates that Member States may apply more stringent measures than those laid down in Community legislation based on Article 175. Article 176 further restates the obvious requirement that such national measures must be compatible with the Treaty, which includes Articles 28-30. It also stipulates that Member States must notify such measures to the Commission. However, Member States do not need the Commission's approval to apply their stricter measures. If the Commission is unhappy about the effects of such measures on the internal market, it may prepare new legislative proposals on the subject-matter or start infringement proceedings against the Member State concerned. It will thus be the Court of Justice and not the Commission which will ultimately assess the measure's compatibility with Community law in such cases.

The Treaty Title on Public Health consists of Article 152. According to Article 152(1), Community action shall complement national policies and be directed towards improving public health. Article 152(4) gives the Council the power to adopt by co-decision (a) quality standards for human organs, substances, blood and blood derivatives, without preventing individual Member States from applying more stringent measures; (b) veterinary and phytosanitary measures having as their direct objective the protection of public health; and (c) incentive measures to protect and improve human health, however excluding any harmonisation. As regards measures of type (b), the possibility for Member States to apply stricter standards would seem to depend on the text of the specific Community measure at issue. Considering the above enumeration, the legislative powers of the Community in the field of public health protection are limited. Nevertheless, human health is an important objective that pervades all policy areas. Article 152(1) provides that a high level of human health protection shall

---

[224] See Jans (2000a).

[225] Case C-318/98 *Fornasar*, para. 46.

be ensured in the definition and implementation of all Community policies and actions, so human health concerns are to be integrated in other Community policies. It is also recalled that human health is expressly mentioned in Article 174 as one of the objectives of the Community's environmental policy.

Apart from the specific Treaty provisions on health and environmental protection, there is a general mandate in Article 95 to adopt measures 'which have as their object the establishment and functioning of the internal market'. A great deal of health and environmental protection measures have been based on Article 95. That this is possible is underscored by paragraph 3 of the same Article, which stipulates that the Commission will take a high level of protection as a basis for legislative proposals concerning health, safety, environmental and consumer protection, and the European Parliament and Council will also seek to achieve this objective. Harmonisation based on Article 95 mostly concerns product standards. Often, such harmonisation contains a free movement clause to ensure that products meeting the requirements laid down in the harmonising legislation can be marketed throughout the Community. Derogations must meet the strict conditions laid down in Article 95, discussed *infra*.

The Court has made it clear that the extent to which Article 95 may be used to harmonise health standards is not unlimited. For example, it has overturned Community legislation based on Article 95 which harmonised rules on advertising and sponsorship of tobacco products, and was to a large extent inspired by public health policy objectives.[226] In the Court's interpretation, the limits to Article 95 seem to be determined by the requirement that the Community legislation must as a whole promote the free movement of goods or other market freedoms. The Court stated that 'a measure adopted on the basis of Article 100a [now 95] of the Treaty must genuinely have as its object the improvement of the conditions for the establishment and functioning of the internal market.'[227] The Court subsequently subdivided this requirement into two aspects; (a) the elimination of obstacles to the free movement (of goods or services in this case); (b) the elimination of distortions of competition.

The above considerations should be seen against the background of the limited competence to harmonise health standards under Article 152. As regards environmental standards, there is no doubt as to the Community's competence to harmonise, although the choice of the appropriate legal basis between Articles 95 and 175 is not always clear. Both aspects mentioned by the Court with regard to health protection measures, i.e. the elimination of obstacles to free movement and the elimination of distortions of competition, have also featured in disputes on the proper legal basis for environmental legislation[228] These disputes often

---

[226] Case C-376/98 *Germany v. Parliament and Council.*

[227] Ibid., at paras. 83-84.

[228] See Cases 70/88 *Parliament v. Council (Chernobyl II)*, C-300/89 *Commission v. Council (Titaniumdioxide)*, C-155/91 *Commission v. Council (Waste Directive)*, C-187/93 *Parliament v. Council (Basle Regulation)*, Joined Cases C-164-165/97 *Parliament v. Council.*

centre around the question whether the legal basis should be Article 95 or 175, or both. The Court's case-law suggests that Community legislation harmonising environmental *product standards* should as a general rule be based on Article 95, although in exceptional cases, the incidence on the internal market is to be regarded as merely accessory and not warranting the choice of Article 95.[229] It is as yet unclear to what extent legislation harmonising *production methods* to eliminate distortions of competition should have Article 95 as its basis. Perhaps such legislation should be based on Article 95 when it affects particular industries, but not when it has more incidental effects.[230] Alternatively, Article 95 should be chosen when the production method significantly affects production costs, and Article 175 when that is not the case. Probably, these criteria run parallel to a considerable extent. Finally, a double legal basis is conceivable, but only in exceptional cases.[231]

The conditions for derogating from legislation based on Article 95 are laid down in that Article itself. Article 95(4) allows Member States to maintain national provisions on grounds of "major needs" referred to in Article 30 (among which is human, animal or plant life or health), or relating to the protection of the environment or the working environment. Article 95(5) addresses the introduction of national provisions based on new scientific evidence, but only relating to the protection of the environment or working environment, not to the grounds mentioned in Article 30. The problem must be specific to the Member State introducing the measure and must have arisen after the adoption of the Community harmonising legislation. According to Article 95(6), the Commission verifies whether national measures notified on the basis of paragraphs 4 and 5 are 'a means of arbitrary discrimination, a disguised restriction on trade, or an obstacle to the functioning of the internal market'. The first two elements are equivalent to the second sentence of Article 30. The Commission has interpreted the third element of Article 95(6) as follows: '[T]he concept of an obstacle to the functioning of the internal market has to be understood as a disproportionate effect in relation to the pursued objective'.[232] Article 95(7) obliges the Commission, in cases where a derogation has been granted under paragraph 6, to immediately examine whether Community harmonisation should be adapted. Article 95(10), finally, provides that harmonisation measures based on Article 95 shall in appropriate cases include a safeguard

---

[229] As in Case 70/88 *Parliament* v. *Council (Chernobyl II)*. There, Article 31 Euratom was considered to be the proper legal basis for measures laying down permitted levels of radioactivity in foodstuffs. That Article provides for basic standards to be laid down 'for the protection of the health of workers and the general public against the dangers arising from ionising radiations'.

[230] See Jans (2000a) at 53.

[231] See Case C-42/97 *Parliament* v. *Council* and Opinion 2/00 *Re the Cartagena Protocol*.

[232] See Commission Decisions 99/830-836, OJ (1999) L 329/1 et seq.

clause allowing Member States to take provisional measures for one or more of the 'non-economic reasons referred to in Article 30', but not for reasons of protection of the environment or working environment.

Judging from the first applications of Article 95(6), the Commission's proportionality test appears to go beyond the test applied by the Court when applying Articles 28-30 to national measures. This is not entirely surprising. When the Commission assesses a national measure under Article 95(6), a balance between internal market and environmental interests has already been struck at the Community level, while this is not the case when the Court assesses a national measure under Articles 28-30. The freedom for Member States to adopt unilateral policies is narrower in the first case than in the second. This view is also supported by the very wording of Article 95(6). This adds the "obstacles" test to the requirements that occur in the second sentence of Article 30, thus suggesting a stricter test than the Court normally adopts under Articles 28-30. On the other hand, it could be argued that a Member State should still be free to strike its own balance between trade and environment interests when adopting stricter measures than those provided by Community legislation based on Article 95; this is precisely the idea behind the possibility created by paragraphs 4-6 of Article 95.

Despite the above considerations, the Commission may be expected to encounter difficulties when overturning measures under Article 95(6) because of a disproportionate impact on the internal market. The Commission has so far overturned invocations of Article 95(4) because of the absence of scientific evidence to support the stricter national measure. Considering the hostility which these decisions have met in the Member States concerned, resistance may be expected to be even greater if the Commission overturns stricter environmental measures for being disproportionate.[233] It will also be interesting to see to what extent the Court will review the Commission's assessment of proportionality when confronted with a challenge (under Article 230) by a Member State against a Commission decision taken on the basis of Article 95(6).

Finally, it should be noted that Article 6 of the EC Treaty states in general terms that environmental protection requirements must be integrated into the definition and implementation of the Community policies and activities referred to in Article 3 of the Treaty, 'in particular with a view to promoting sustainable development'. Article 3 lists among the Community's activities common policies in the sphere of agriculture, fisheries, and transport, but also 'a contribution to the attainment of a high level of health protection'. Thus, environmental protection requirements must be integrated into the Community's contribution to a high level of health protection. At the same time, as noted above, protecting

---

[233] See Van Calster (2000).

human health is one of the objectives of the Community's environmental policy. This example and the above account of the various legal bases of Community measures demonstrate that the demarcation line between "environmental protection", "public health" and "human health" is far from clear.

CHAPTER 3

Analysis of Recurring Themes

3.1 Basic Disciplines and Typologies

3.1.1 'Measures Having Equivalent Effect': From "Trading Rules" to Inaction

The wording 'capable of hindering, directly or indirectly, actually or potentially, intra-Community trade' in *Dassonville* strikes one as being almost a catch-all provision. Interestingly, the definition employs the words "trading rules", which could be interpreted as a limitation on the type of national regulations covered by the concept of 'measures having equivalent effect'. However, in subsequent case-law repeating the *Dassonville* formula, the reference to "trading rules" was dropped in favour of broader concepts, such as "national measures"[1], "national rules"[2], "all commercial rules"[3] and even "any national rule"[4]. According to the Court, measures adopted by the government of a Member State which do not have binding effect may also be capable of influencing the conduct of traders and consumers in that state, and are thus covered by the concept of 'measures having equivalent effect'.[5]

The Court has suggested that since an internal tax on a product of which there is no comparable domestic production is not covered by Article 90, the adverse effect on the free movement of goods resulting from such a tax may be assessed under Article 28 et seq.[6] Article 28 even includes, under certain conditions, inaction by a Member State to safeguard the free movement of goods. France was found to have infringed Article 28 when it failed to act against farmers blocking roads to prevent imports of Spanish strawberries.[7] The Court used quite sweeping language, stating that 'the fact that a Member State abstains from taking action [...] is just as likely to obstruct intra-Community trade as is a positive act.[8]

---

[1] See e.g. Case 104/75 *De Peijper*.

[2] See e.g. Case 31/78 *Bussone*.

[3] See e.g. Case 247/81 *Commission-Germany*.

[4] See e.g. Case 94/79 *Vriend*.

[5] See e.g. Case 249/81, *Commission v. Ireland*, paras. 28-29.

[6] Cf. Case C-47/88 *Commission v. Denmark*, referring to Case 31/67 *Stier*. Demaret (2000) at 187 criticises the Court's suggestion, arguing that taxes should not be assessed under Article 28.

[7] Case C-265/95 *Commission v. France*.

[8] Case C-265/95 *Commission v. France*, para. 31.

3.1.2 Selling Arrangements, Product Requirements and Other Measures

The Court in *Keck* only spoke of product requirements and selling arrangements. However, the dividing line between "selling arrangements" and "product requirements" is sometimes difficult to establish, for example as regards labelling and advertising.[9] Moreover, there are other measures capable of hindering trade that fit into neither of these categories. Examples of measures that are neither product requirements nor selling arrangements, but have nevertheless been assessed under Article 28 include a national law on the reimbursement of spectacles by social security institutions, an administrative requirement concerning the registration of cars, and, in the environmental sphere, national rules making aircraft registration dependent on noise emission standards.[10] Such measures do not restrict or prohibit selling arrangements, but they also do not lay down requirements to be met by goods in order to be marketed. They do however constitute potential trade barriers. Judging from the Court's case-law in the examples above, such "third category" measures do in principle fall within the *Dassonville* formula and accordingly require justification, unless their trade effects are too remote or uncertain.

Keck does not clarify whether Article 28 covers national rules regulating aspects of consumption other than "selling arrangements". Examples range from restrictions on the use of cars to compulsory waste collection schemes. Such measures may affect the marketing, use or disposal of imported products in the Member State of consumption. Therefore, they also seem to fall within the "third category", and accordingly within the broad *Dassonville* formula as qualified by the *Peralta* case-law.

In *Keck* the Court clarified that the *Cassis* case-law applies to 'obstacles to the free movement of goods which are the consequences of applying, to goods coming from other Member States where they are lawfully manufactured and marketed, rules that lay down requirements to be met by those goods'. This statement could be interpreted as suggesting that Article 28 essentially addresses rules laying down product requirements.[11] On the basis of such a reading of *Keck*, one might argue that the *Keck* limitation applies to all measures not laying down product requirements. Accordingly, Article 28 would deal with all other national rules only to the extent that they do not 'apply to all relevant traders operating within the national territory and affect in the same manner, in law and in fact, the marketing of domestic products and of those from

---

[9] See Oliver (1996) at 100-102.

[10] Cases C-120/95 *Decker*, C-314/98 *Snellers*, and C-389/96 *Aher-Waggon*, respectively.

[11] This seems to be the view of Petersmann, who concludes from *Keck* that 'the scope of application of Article 28 of the EC Treaty seems to be essentially limited to product regulations.' Petersmann (1995) at 55-56.

other Member States', thus 'preventing their access to the market or impeding their access any more than the access of domestic products'. In this view, only product requirements fall automatically within the ambit of Article 28 and require justification. All other measures will only require justification if they discriminate *de jure* or *de facto*. If the market access requirement in *Keck* plays a role in addition to the discrimination test, measures completely barring market access for imports would also require justification.[12] Thus, any discriminatory measure has to be justified, as well as any other measure barring market access for imports, which would include product requirements.[13]

Logically appealing as the above interpretation may be, it is difficult to reconcile with the Court's continued use of the term "selling arrangements", which could not easily be given such a broad ambit. According to the Court's case-law in its present state, only national measures falling within the concept of "selling arrangements" will be outside the scope of Article 28 unless they fail to meet the test laid down in *Keck*. All other measures are in principle covered by the *Dassonville* formula unless their trade effects are too remote and uncertain. That general rule is further further specified in *Cassis de Dijon* as regards product requirements, in the sense that differences between Member States' product requirements will always require justification since by their very nature they hinder intra-Community trade. The situation created by the use of the term "selling arrangements" is unsatisfactory. The milder treatment of selling arrangements *vis-à-vis* "third category measures" is not warranted by their respective trade effects. It is for the Court to tackle this problem. It would seem to make sense to apply a similar test to "third category measures" as applied in *Keck* to "selling arrangements". It is submitted that the Court should at the same time clarify the status of the reference in *Keck* to measures completely impeding market access for imported goods. If that reference means that such measures do not benefit from the *Keck* limitation and are to be assessed under Articles 28-30 EC, the same should be true for "third category measures" that completely bar market access for imported goods.

When they do fall within the scope of Article 28, can "third category" measures be justified under both Article 30 and "mandatory requirements"? It would seem perfectly acceptable that they enjoy both justification possibilities. It seems clear from the Court's statement in *Gilli* that the mandatory requirements were not intended by the Court to be limited to the justification of product requirements:

---

[12] Cf. Weiler (1999) at 372-3, arguing that the term "selling arrangements" should be dropped and further advocating a Community 'national treatment overarching principle', combined with a 'special rule of free movement', according to which national provisions preventing market access for imported goods must be justified.

[13] See for a similar proposal Barnard (2001).

In the absence of common rules relating to the production and marketing of the product in question it is for the Member States to regulate all matters relating to its production, distribution and consumption on their territory subject, however, to the condition that those rules do not present an obstacle, directly or indirectly, actually or potentially, to intra-Community trade.[13a]

3.2 Justifications and Conditions: "Means-Ends Tests", Interests, and "Reason"

3.2.1 Mandatory Requirements as an Additional Justification Possibility

During the Intergovernmental Conference preparing the 1997 Amsterdam Treaty, a proposal to insert a reference to "environmental protection" in Article 30 was not accepted. The question arises what the mandatory requirement of environmental protection adds to the justification grounds in Article 30 EC. The scope of the concepts of 'protection of health and life of humans, animals or plants' in Article 30 and the 'protection of the environment' as a "mandatory requirement" justifying obstacles to the free movement of goods, and the relationship *inter se* are not entirely clear. The Court in the *Walloon Waste* case stated that 'the accumulation of waste, even *before* it becomes a *health hazard*, constitutes a danger to the *environment*.' It then accepted the measure as being justified, not by Article 30, but by 'imperative requirements of environmental protection'.[14] Similar reasoning was applied in later cases concerning waste.[15] This suggests that in order for the life and health justification to be applicable, there has to be a *direct threat* to health or life.[16]

In *Preussen Elektra*, the Court deemed a national measure obliging electricity suppliers to buy local green electricity to be compatible with Article 28. The Court did not specify whether the measure was justified by Article 30 or the mandatory requirement of environmental protection. It observed that the measure was capable of hindering intra-Community trade and that it had to be determined whether the measure was 'nevertheless compatible with Article 30 [now 28]'. It remarked that the measure was 'useful for protecting the environment in so far as it contributes to the reductions in emissions of greenhouse gases which are amongst the main causes of climate change', before referring to the Community's obligations in this respect, and observed that 'that policy

---

[13a] Case 788/79 *Gilli and Andres*, para. 5.

[14] Case C-2/90 *Commission* v. *Belgium*, at paras. 28 and 32 respectively. Emphasis added.

[15] Cases C-203/96 *Dusseldorp* and C-209/98 *Sydhavnens*.

[16] Krämer (1993b) at 118 speaks of the "direct effect" of a measure on the protection of humans or flora or fauna, which in the present author's view is a somewhat unfortunate term in the EC context.

is also designed to protect the health and life of humans, animals and plants'.[17] What 'that policy' refers to is not clear from the judgment, but it appears to refer to the Community's energy and climate change policy, rather than to national policies. In its dictum the Court concluded that the measure was not incompatible with Article 28. This suggests that it was looking at the mandatory requirement of environmental protection rather than at Article 30. The Court's reference to Article 30 was made as part of its observations that the national measure was in accordance with the objectives of Community policies, which also seek to protect human, animal and plant life and health. It thus seems that the reference to Article 30 should not be taken as applying to the national measure. The measure aimed at stimulating the use of renewable energy and combating climate change. It seems that the life and health hazard posed by that problem was too indirect to be covered by Article 30. Thus, the requirement of a direct life or health risk for invoking Article 30 would still seem to stand.

If a direct threat to health or life is needed in order to successfully invoke Article 30, some national measures that are not eligible for justification under Article 30 may be justified as being necessary to satisfy the mandatory requirement of environmental protection. Does this mean that the scope of environmental protection encompass that of life and health protection? If this is the case, any measure justified under the life and health exception must also be within the scope of "environmental protection". Or should the two grounds rather be seen as existing side by side, with some overlap? The question is mostly academic, as a measure justified under either one of the grounds no longer needs justification under the other ground. However, as will be seen, the conditions for invoking the different grounds are not entirely the same. Member States will therefore want to know which justification ground to invoke.

Theoretical discussion is also possible concerning the precise meaning of the "rule of reason" in its relationship with Article 28 and Article 30. This debate centres on the question whether the "rule of reason" adds exceptions to Article 30 for measures that in principle infringe Article 28, or rather delimits the scope of Article 28, causing those measures to fall outside the scope of Article 28 in the first place. Confining oneself to the text of the Treaty, the "rule of reason" cannot be read into Article 30, and must therefore be seen as part of the interpretation of the basic obligation in Article 28. Thus, a national measure posing an obstacle to intra-Community trade, but justified by a 'mandatory requirement', should be deemed not to infringe Article 28. However, there is an important difference between on the one hand, measures deemed to fall outside Article 28 because they do not pose a sufficiently serious hindrance to intra-Community trade (the *Keck* and *Peralta* situations), and, on the other, measures that do pose such a hindrance but must be allowed when they propor-

---

[17]   C-379/98 *Preussen Elektra*, paras. 73-75.

tionately pursue non-economic public objectives that have not (exhaustively) been addressed by Community legislation. Substantially, the latter category of measures resemble the measures found to infringe Article 28 but are justified under Article 30 more than they resemble the types of measures found to fall outside Article 28 in *Keck* and *Peralta*.

In practice, the Court does not treat justifications under the "rule of reason" any differently from justifications under Article 30, except for the additional requirement that the measure must be 'indistinctly applicable' to qualify for the "rule of reason".[18] Thus, "mandatory requirements" are increasingly treated as additional exceptions to the prohibition in Article 28. The Court often uses the term "justified" for both Article 30 and the mandatory requirements.[19] On the other hand, even in the case of Article 30, the Court sometimes uses the words 'falls outside the prohibition in 28 and 29'.[20]

What seems most important in this respect is the order of assessing things and the burden of proof. The Court's order of proceeding is usually to establish whether there is an obstacle to the free movement of goods in the sense of *Dassonville* (as qualified by *Keck*), after which it looks at possible justifications for the national measure. Although it has stated that it will look at the justifications in Article 30 first,[21] the Court is not consistent in whether first to assess Article 30 or the rule of reason. The Court rarely deals with a measure it has found to be indistinctly applicable under Article 30.[22] Rather, the Court often looks at Article 30 without having to decide whether the measure is equally applicable or not. That appears to be an approach which is informed not by systemic but by practical considerations. Article 30 applies to both distinctly and indistinctly applicable measures, so there is no need to determine whether a measure is distinctly or indistinctly applicable. From a systemic point of view, it would seem to make more sense to look at mandatory requirements which are part of Article 28, and only after this to move on to Article 30.

In principle, Member States bear the burden of proving that their measure, once found to be an obstacle to trade, is justified by Article 30 or a mandatory requirement, and that it meets the conditions for justifications that are discussed below. In many cases, the existence of a ground for justification will not be contested. Moreover, as discussed above, the Court has in the context of the life and health justification in Article 30 allowed the Member States a considerable degree of leeway in cases of scientific uncertainty. However, this leeway has its limits. Thus, Member States cannot require traders to prove that a product is

---

[18] On that requirement, see Section 3.3.3.

[19] See e.g. Case C-389/96 *Aher-Waggon*, at para. 19.

[20] See Case 53/80 *Eyssen*, para. 16

[21] See Joined Cases C-1/90 and C-176/90 *Aragonesa* [1991] ECR I-4151, para. 13.

[22] E.g. Case 124/81 *Commission v. UK*.

not dangerous.[23] They may, however, within reasonable limits, require a trader to verify that a product he wishes to market conforms to their health and safety standards.[24] Although case-law on the mandatory requirement of environmental protection is still scarce, that mandatory requirement will generally be argued in cases where a direct life or health hazard is lacking. Accordingly, in such a case the Court may be less tolerant in cases of scientific uncertainty. Scientific uncertainty may also play a role in the fulfilment of the means-end requirements discussed below.

When a national measure is challenged in national court proceedings and the Court is asked for a preliminary ruling, it will be up to the Member State to show that its measure is justified. In principle, the same is true when the Commission challenges a Member State in proceedings for a failure to fulfil its Treaty obligations under Article 226 EC. However, in such cases, it is for the Commission to place before the Court the information needed to enable it to determine whether the obligation has not been fulfilled.[25] In the Court's practice, the picture is less clear and more varied, especially with regard to the condition of proportionality, which is further discussed below. In many cases before the ECJ, all parties, including intervening parties, present arguments that relate to the proportionality of the contested measure. Thus, for example, if the Commission presents detailed arguments as to why a measure is not proportionate, the Member State will be forced to respond to those arguments in detail too. The question of the burden of proof will only arise if factual aspects have not been resolved by the end of the hearing.[26]

It has been argued that the requirements in the second sentence of Article 30 also apply to justifications under the "rule of reason".[27] This is theoretically problematic in view of the Court's insistence that the "rule of reason" is contained in Article 28 and not in Article 30, as a result of which, logically speaking, the second sentence of the latter Article could not apply to any other justifications than those contained in its first sentence.[28] From a practical point of view, however, it seems acceptable to assume that since the proportionality principle, which also applies to "rule of reason" justifications, underlies the requirement in the second sentence of Article 30, that requirement may be taken together with the proportionality test as applied to both Article 30 and "rule of reason" justifications. In fact, it has been noted that the two overlap to a significant

---

[23] See e.g. Case 174/82 *Sandoz.*

[24] Case 25/88 *Bouchara née Wurmser.*

[25] Case C-159/94 *Commission* v. *France*, para. 102; Case C-55/99 *Commission* v. *France*, para. 30.

[26] See for examples, Jans (2000b); Krämer (2000).

[27] Ziegler (1996), at 90, mentioning the *Dassonville* case as a reference for this assertion.

[28] Cf. Oliver (1996) at 181.

extent and should not be considered in isolation.[29] Perhaps the second sentence of Article 30 is best regarded as a *concretisation* of the general principle of proportionality. The "added value" of the prohibition of arbitrary discrimination or a disguised restriction on intra-Community trade as compared to the general proportionality requirement may be that it stresses the *intention* with which national measures are taken, rather than their *effect*. Its aim is to prevent trade restrictions from being diverted from their proper purpose.[30] However, it is generally difficult to assess the intention behind national measures. Moreover, the case-law on the protection of intellectual and commercial property suggests that the application of the second sentence of Article 30 depends on the *effect* of artificially dividing the market, and that proof of subjective intentions is not required.[31]

3.2.2 Observations on Proportionality

The relationship between means and ends required for the justification of national trade-restrictive measures under Article 30 or a mandatory requirement has been referred to earlier in this Chapter as proportionality in the wide sense. That concept consists of three elements; suitability (or appropriateness), necessity (or least trade-restrictiveness), and proportionality in the strict sense. The Court does not consistently describe the means-ends requirements for the justification of national measures in terms of the three elements outlined above, but it does usually refer to some of them. There is support for this view of proportionality in the academic literature and in several opinions by Advocates-General.[32]

It has been argued elsewhere that the three elements of proportionality *lato sensu* constitute 'an ascending series in terms of the intensity with which the Court of Justice can review national measures.'[33] However, none of the three criteria are without problems as regards their application. The first element looks

---

[29] Emiliou (1996a) at 259. Examples of cases where both sentences of Article 30 were applied without a clear distinction are Case 64/75 *Rewe* and Case 40/82 *Newcastle Disease*. The same author however contends at 260 that the second sentence of Article 30 acts as an overriding requirement to ensure that apparently justified measures are not applied so as to divide the internal market artificially.

[30] Case 34/79 *Henn and Darby* and Case 40/82 *Newcastle Disease*. AG Van Gerven, in his Opinion in Case C-131/93 *Crayfish*, uses the words '*improper use* of the grounds of justification' and '*only* serve protectionist purposes'. Emphasis added.

[31] Kapteijn and VerLoren van Themaat (1998) at 674, referring to AG Capotorti in Case 1/81 *Pfizer*.

[32] For example, AG Fennelly in Case C-217/99 *Commission v. Belgium* endorsed the view of proportionality as consisting of the three elements. See also the other Advocates-General discussed in the current Section. For the literature, see the references in note 146 of Chapter 2.

[33] Jans (2000b) at 241.

at the legitimate aim invoked and assesses whether the measure is appropriate
to pursue that aim, i.e. whether it can actually attain the objective sought. In
other words, the first element of the proportionality test requires some causal
link between the measure and its objective. Although this part of the test seems
relatively straightforward, it will not always be easy to assess the suitability of the
measure to achieve its aims. In the sphere of health and environmental legislation, such assessments often involve complex technical and economic analysis,
which the Court is ill-equipped to undertake. The discussion of the Court's
deference in situations of scientific uncertainty illustrates that risk assessment
is to a great extent left to the Member States. Thus, the Court will often have to
accept a Member State's arguments as to the objective sought by a measure and
its suitability to achieve that objective.

Only rarely will the Court find that a measure does not fulfil the first
element. When addressing a Belgian measure requiring foodstuff labels to
contain the reference number under which they had been notified to the national
health inspection service, the Court found that such a requirement is *not capable*
of enabling consumers to decide whether or not they should consume the
product and, if they do consume it, in what quantities. Arguably, the Court
could have stopped its analysis there and then, as a measure that is not capable
of attributing to the aim pursued can never be proportionate. Nevertheless, in
cautious words the Court concluded that the requirement was *not sufficiently*
useful for consumers for its inclusion *to be fully justified* on the ground of protection of public health. It stated that, *moreover*, a national measure imposing an
obligation such as the disputed obligation must, in any event, be "proportionate"
to the aim pursued, and it thereby applied a necessity test.[34]

The second element, the "necessity" or "least trade-restrictiveness" of the
measure, also gives rise to a lot of questions. To what extent should the Court
take alternative measures into account in its analysis of a measure's necessity?
If a regulatory measure is chosen, should the Court accept arguments to the
effect that a different type of measure, e.g. a tax, is equally effective and less
trade-restrictive?[35] How can the trade-restrictiveness of hypothetical alternatives
by assessed? To what extent should the Court look at practices in other Member
States? And, perhaps most importantly, how can the Court know whether an
alternative measure which is less trade-restrictive is *equally effective* in achieving
the objective sought? This question closely relates to the chosen level of protection and whether the Court should interfere with it. If an alternative measure
is available which will (possibly) achieve the desired objective slightly less effectively, but is much less trade-restrictive, what should the Court do?

---

[34] Case C-217/99 *Commission* v. *Belgium*, at paras. 26-28. Emphasis added.

[35] This question is referred to as "diagonal proportionality" by Jans (2000a) at 263.

In *Toolex Alpha*, the Court indicated that the necessity test looks at less trade-restrictive alternatives that are equally effective in attaining the aim pursued:

[N]ational rules or practices having, or likely to have, a restrictive effect on the importation of products are compatible with the Treaty only to the extent that they are necessary for the effective protection of the health and life of humans. A national rule or practice cannot therefore benefit from the derogation provided for in Article 36 [now 30] of the Treaty if the health and life of humans may be protected just as effectively by measures which are less restrictive of intra-Community trade.[36]

In the case concerning the Belgian foodstuff labelling requirement discussed above, the Court also looked at the necessity of the requirement to indicate the notification number. It observed that the notification number did not provide any additional information enabling the consumer's health to be more effectively protected. By contrast, the labelling included other data such as the name of the product, the identity of the manufacturer or distributor, the nutritional content, the date of minimum durability or the recommended intake, which were *equally useful* information in that respect. Thus, the disputed obligation was *not necessary* for the protection of public health.[37]

The third element of the test, proportionality *stricto sensu*, implies an assessment of any excessive or disproportionate impacts on intra-Community trade, even if there were no alternative measures available to the Member State to attain its legitimate objective. If it should fail, such a test would allow free movement to prevail over legitimate non-economic objectives pursued by Member States in cases where no Community legislation has been agreed on to harmonise the ways in which the objective at issue is pursued. The controversial nature of this part of the test becomes clear if one realises that in such cases the Court of Justice takes the place of democratically legitimised national legislative procedures.

Advocate-General Van Gerven analysed the principle of proportionality in Articles 28-30 in his opinion in the *Van den Burg* case, which dealt with a Dutch prohibition on keeping, buying or selling red grouse.[38] He considered that national measures have to meet two tests. First, a necessity requirement, in which Van Gerven included the first criterion of appropriateness or causal connection. He left open the question of what degree of causal connection is required.[39] Secondly, a proportionality requirement, concerned with the exist-

---

[36] Case C-473/98 *Toolex Alpha*, at para. 40. Emphasis added.

[37] Case C-217/99 *Commission* v. *Belgium*, para. 29. Emphasis added.

[38] Case C-169/89 *Gourmetterie Van den Burg*, at 2157-2159. The Court itself did not decide the case on the basis of the proportionality test. It only discussed a relevant Community Directive, and then concluded that Article 30, read in conjunction with the Directive, could not justify the import prohibition at hand. It had not discussed Article 30 as such when it reached that conclusion.

[39] Cf. Jans (1995) at 215.

ence of 'a proportional relationship between the obstacle introduced, and the objective pursued thereby and its actual attainment'. In the remainder of his opinion, however, Van Gerven changed the word "and" into "and/or", and then into "or".[40] It appears to the current author that the objective of a measure is not necessarily the same as the result actually achieved by it, so that comparing either one with the obstacle introduced are different exercises. The relationship between the obstacle to trade and the objective of a measure can be assessed *in abstracto*, while the relationship between the trade obstacle and the actual attainment of the objective can only be assessed by looking at the concrete facts of the case. The former test appears to coincide with proportionality stricto sensu as described above. However, Van Gerven in his opinion in *Van den Burg* rather seemed to propose that the latter test should be applied. He stated that the import prohibition at hand was capable of making only a small contribution *in concreto* to the achievement of the objective pursued. Such a test shades into the first element of proportionality in the wide sense as described above, because it really assesses the quality of the causal relationship between the measure and its objective.

In his opinion in *Danish Bottles*, Advocate-General Slynn said that the Danish authorities had to prove the necessity and proportionality of the measures alleged by the Commission to infringe Article 28.[41] This is somewhat strange, as he had just previously argued that the Danish measures could not be justified by either Article 30 or the "rule of reason". It seems that in such a case, there is no longer any reason to look into the proportionality of the measure.[42] Slynn accepted that the Danish measures achieved the highest standard of environmental protection, and that it might be difficult to achieve the same high standard by other measures. Nevertheless, he contended that the Commission did not have to show that the same standard can be achieved by other specified means. Rather, '[t]here has to be a balancing of interests between the free movement of goods and environmental protection, even if in achieving the balance the high standard of the protection sought has to be reduced. *The level of protection sought must be a reasonable level [...]*'. The interesting question following from this is who is to assess what is "reasonable". Slynn seemed to think that assessment was a Community affair. Thus, he opted for the Court's fully-fledged assessment of the proportionality of a national measure, even if that could result in lowering the level of the protection sought. It should be noted that there were no direct health hazards at issue in the *Danish Bottles* case.

---

[40] See para. 10 of his Opinion.

[41] Case 302/86 *Danish Bottles* at 4625.

[42] Apparently, AG Slynn addressed the proportionality and necessity question in case the Court would not agree with his opinion that neither Article 30 nor the "rule of reason" could apply to them.

3.2.3 Proportionality and "Reason"

The acceptance by the Court in *Cassis* of national measures capable of hindering trade because they are necessary to fulfil a "mandatory requirement" is often dubbed the "rule of reason" in academic literature. The Court, however, does not apply the term "rule of reason". Moreover, a survey of its case-law concerning Articles 28-30 of the Treaty shows that the Court's use of the word "reason" is not limited to situations where mandatory requirements are invoked.

It is recalled that the Court in *Dassonville* stated that as long as there was no relevant Community legislation guaranteeing for consumers the authenticity of a product's designation of origin, Member States could take measures to prevent unfair practices in this connection, *on condition that the measures were reasonable*.[43] After the judgment in *Dassonville*, the Commission challenged Belgium for persisting in its trade-restrictive measures. The Court stated that '[t]he essential question to be resolved is therefore whether the measures taken by the kingdom of Belgium [...] are *unreasonable in that they are disproportionate* in relation to that objective.'[44] In a number of cases, the Court has qualified its refusal to accept administrative or financial reasons as justifications for trade-restrictive measures by a "reason test": '[A]rticle 36 [now 30] cannot be relied on to justify rules or practices which, even though they are beneficial, contain restrictions which are explained primarily by a concern to lighten the administration's burden or reduce public expenditure, unless, in the absence of the said rules or practices, this burden or expenditure clearly would exceed the limits of what can *reasonably* be required.'[45] The Court has also looked at the reasonableness of national regulatory distinctions. In *Aragonesa*, where the proportionality of a measure prohibiting advertising in public places for drinks having an alcoholic strength of 23 degrees or more was at issue, the Court observed that '[i]n principle, the latter criterion does not appear to be *manifestly unreasonable* as part of a campaign against alcoholism'.[46]

From the above account of the Court's references to "reason" in its case-law concerning Articles 28-30, it may be argued that in the Court's view, the concept of "reason" is strongly related to the conditions applying to justifications for trade-hindering measures, which may be captured by the term proportionality in the wide sense. Therefore, it is submitted that the term "rule of reason" is more appropriately used to refer to these conditions as they apply to both the

---

[43] Case 8/74 *Dassonville*, para. 6.

[44] Case 2/78 *Commission* v. *Belgium*, para. 38. Emphasis added.

[45] Case 104/75 *De Peijper*, para. 18. See in a similar vein Cases 251/78 *Denkavit*, 32/80 *Kortmann*, and C-128/89 *Commission* v. *Italy*.

[46] Joined Cases C-1/90 and C-176/90 *Aragonesa* at para. 17.

grounds in Article 30 and to "mandatory requirements", than to refer only to the acceptance of mandatory requirements as justification grounds in addition to those found in the Treaty.

3.2.4 The Court and Proportionality in the Strict Sense

If the proportionality of a national measure to pursue a certain objective is assessed, does that mean that the assessment of the objective itself is also a Community matter? The objective of a measure must be accepted under Community law.[47] In the environmental and health sphere, the acceptability of the objective of a national measure under Community law is often undisputed. However, a more thorny question is whether the objective should be pursued by the measure chosen and at the level of protection chosen, and who is to decide whether this is the case. Should the Court confine its proportionality test to assessing whether there were less trade-restrictive measures available in order to attain the objective, irrespective of the objective itself? Or should the objective itself be weighed against the infringement of the free movement of goods? In other words, what has to be proportionate to what?[48] This question may appear somewhat trivial, but nevertheless it has great importance. If the objective is weighed against the trade restriction, a strict proportionality test is applied. As appears from the earlier discussion of the Court's case-law, the Court usually confines itself to testing the suitability of a national measure and its necessity in the absence of less trade-restrictive alternatives. However, in some instances, the Court appears to have gone somewhat further. One case concerns the mandatory requirement of environmental protection, and the other animal life and health protection.

In *Danish Bottles*, the Court found the obligation to set up a deposit-and-return system, and thereby the requirement that containers be returnable, to be necessary and proportionate. However, it found the quantitative limit to non-approved containers disproportionate, although it admitted that it ensured a very considerable degree of environmental protection. The Court arguably came to this conclusion because the objective of "environmental protection" as such, as opposed to 'a very considerable degree of environmental protection', could be reached by less trade-restrictive means, i.e. by merely requiring a deposit-and-return system without a limit on non-approved containers. This assessment by the Court goes beyond a mere comparison of various alternatives to pursue the same environmental aim. It actually looks at the level of protection attained by

---

[47] Cf. AG Fennelly in his Opinions in Cases C-149/94 *Vergy* and C-202/94 *Van der Feesten*, looking for a justification for the national measures at issue in accordance with Community environmental objectives.

[48] Cf. Jans (1995) at 218-222.

the various alternatives. Thus, the Court in this case applied the third element of the proportionality test, a fully-fledged weighing of the impact on intra-Community trade and the aim of the measure. It has rightly been criticised for not explicitly clarifying how it undertook this assessment.[49]

In the meantime, a directive on packaging and packaging waste has been agreed upon at the Community level, and a new case concerning Danish beverage containers is pending before the Court.[50] The Danish legislation no longer contains a limit on non-approved containers that was deemed incompatible with the EC Treaty more than a decade ago. Nevertheless, the requirement that drinks may only be marketed in returnable packaging, which the Court found to be compatible with the EC Treaty back in 1988 when there was no directive, has now been challenged anew. The Commission argued that this requirement infringes the packaging Directive, which prohibits Member States to impede the placing on their market of packaging satisfying the provisions of the Directive. Moreover, Danish legislation prohibits *imported* drinks in metal packages. In case the packaging directive does not fully apply to the Danish legislation, the Commission invoked Articles 28-30 to support these challenges. In that context, the Commission stated that '[e]xtensive measures for environmental protection, such as a total ban on the use of metal cans and non-returnable packaging for beer and carbonated drinks, even though the packaging is lawfully used in all other Member States, calls [sic] for *a reasonably unambiguous and certain scientific basis.*'[51] The Commission deemed that the life-cycle analysis provided by Denmark does not constitute such a basis. Moreover, according to the Commission, a complete ban on the use of certain types of packaging runs counter to the proportionality principle. Return and deposit systems along with, if appropriate, labelling and environmental taxes, can secure *the same or identical environmental advantages as a ban.*[52]

Thus, in this new Danish case, the Commission advocated strong scrutiny of the national measures in the form of a far-reaching application of the necessity and proportionality requirements. This implies even some interference with the level of protection as chosen by the Danish authorities. It should be noted, however, that this case concerns a situation in which the Member States have agreed on the balance to be struck between the free movement of goods and environmental protection in the relevant field, such as in this case packaging

---

[49] Krämer (1993a) at 102.

[50] See Directive 94/62 EC of 20 December 1994, OJ 1994 L 365, at p. 10. There are actually two cases pending, C-233/99 (reference for a preliminary ruling) and C-246/99 (action brought by the Commission). Their registration at the Court was reported in OJ 1999 C 246 at p. 14 and p. 19, respectively. See Langer and Wiers (2000).

[51] C-246/99, OJ 1999 C 246 p. 19 at 20. Emphasis added.

[52] Ibid. Emphasis added.

waste. Whether Member States may go beyond that agreed level will depend on the terms of the harmonisation instrument and the Treaty provision on which it is based.[53] The Directive at issue is based on Article 95 EC, but Denmark has not invoked paragraphs 4 or 5 of that provision. The Court will assess the measure under Articles 28-30 EC only if it finds that the Directive does not entirely cover the matters regulated by the Danish measures. Advocate-General Ruiz-Jarabo Colomer argued that the Directive completely harmonised national measures on packaging recovery and disposal. In case the Court would find otherwise, he deemed the measure to be a violation of Article 28 EC which is not justified by the mandatory requirement of environmental protection.[54]

In *Monsees*, the Court condemned as disproportionate certain Austrian measures restricting the transport of live animals on its territory. The Court applied an extremely concise proportionality test in this case. It observed that the effect of the Austrian rules was to make all international transit of animals for slaughter almost impossible in Austria. Furthermore, measures appropriate to the objective and less restrictive of the free movement of goods were conceivable, as was demonstrated by a relevant Community Directive, even if at the time it did not yet formally apply to Austria.[55] The Court ignored the fact that the Austrian rules at issue contained two separate requirements. First, animals were to be transported only as far as the nearest suitable abattoir in Austria. Apparently, in the Court's view, this aspect of the national measure implied such a serious infringement of the free movement of goods that it was disproportionate, even if it ensured a very high level of protection. The Directive showed that less drastic measures could protect live animals during transport. The second aspect of the Austrian law laid down a maximum total journey time and distance. In contrast with the first aspect, these requirements reflected an approach similar to that taken in the animal transport Directive, however with stricter limits than in the Directive. It is submitted that even if the first aspect of the Austrian measure could be regarded as too trade-restrictive an approach, the second requirement could well have been judged to be compatible with the Treaty, as long as the transposition date of the Directive had not expired.[56]

With regard to the first requirement of the Austrian legislation, the Court appears to have applied a real balancing test between the seriousness of the

---

[53] See Section 2.4.

[54] Opinions issued on 13 September 2001. The Advocate-General advised the Court to rule in Case C-246/99 that the Danish requirements that beer and sodas can only be marketed in reusable containers and that imported drinks cannot be marketed in metal containers amount to infringements of the Directive and of Article 28 EC, and to state the same in Case C-233/99 with regard to the prohibition to market imported drinks in metal cans.

[55] Case C-350/97 *Monsees*, paras. 29-30.

[56] For a more detailed analysis, see Langer and Wiers (2000).

trade restriction and the attainment of the aim of animal protection, i.e. a proportionality test stricto sensu, just as in *Danish Bottles*. Because of the rarity of such applications, it would have been preferable if the Court had done so more openly and clearly. Regardless of whether one deems such a test appropriate for the Court to undertake, a more balanced and clear judgment could have been made in this case if the two aspects of the measure had been separated when considering their justification and proportionality.

3.2.5 Proportionality, Objectives, Competencies, and Interests

According to the Court, what counts in assessing proportionality is the national interest in attaining an aim found to be legitimate under Community law:

Appraising the proportionality of national rules which pursue a legitimate aim under Community law involves weighing the national interest in attaining that aim against the Community interest in ensuring the free movement of goods.[57]

Thus, when applied to national measures, the principle of proportionality operates to balance a national interest such as health or environmental protection with the general interest of the Community to ensure the free movement of goods. The latter normally coincides with the individual interests of economic operators, such as producers, importers or exporters, but also with the general interest of European consumers in having a wide choice of goods from all over the Community. The interest pursued by the national measures is sometimes purely or primarily of a national nature, e.g. in some instances of public morality and public policy. In other cases it is only partly national and may partly coincide with Community interests. Thus, in many cases of environmental or health protection, the interest sought to be protected by national authorities is at the same time a Community interest, which competes with the Community interest in ensuring unimpeded intra-Community trade.

It is recalled that the Court, when assessing the proportionality of Community measures, only marginally tests strict proportionality. The Court weighs 'the damage to individual rights against the benefits accruing to the general interest'.[58] The proportionality of a Community measure applies to a situation where the Community legislative process has led to a supposedly acceptable balance between the different interests at stake, including the interests of the free movement of goods and of non-economic goals such as environmental or heath protection. Obviously, the compromise laid down in each piece of Commu-

---

[57] Case C-169/91 *Stoke-on-Trent* at para 15. Emphasis added.

[58] Case T-125/96 *Boehringer.*

nity legislation leads to different levels of satisfaction in different Member States, and among different interested persons within the Member States. It reflects the relative power positions of the Member States, in most cases according to the official weighting of their rights in qualified majority voting, but probably also in a more concealed way, as a result of, e.g., the strength of national and sectoral lobbies and of the importance attached by Member States to the matter at hand. It has been argued that Community harmonisation suffers from "majoritarian bias" in that it tends to neglect the interests of consumers and producers in a minority of Member States.[59] Arguably, however, there is no reason to assume that Community legislation *systematically* favours interests in *certain Member States*, whether it be trading interests or, for example, environmental interests.

Taking the foregoing considerations into account, should the Court assess the proportionality of national measures differently from the proportionality of Community measures? On the one hand, it may be argued that with regard to subject-matters which have not been harmonised, it is for the national legislative process to balance the damage to trade and traders with the benefits to the environmental or health interest pursued. This would be a reason for the Court to be even more reluctant to weigh these interests than when it assesses Community measures. On the other hand, the Community interest in the free movement of goods may not always be fully represented in the weighing of interests which is part of the national legislative process. This will especially be the case where those standing to gain from the free movement of goods are under-represented in the national policy process. Likewise, it will occur when non-economic interests such as environmental protection coincide with protectionist or discriminatory motives of national producers. In the words of Poiares Maduro, 'even when national legislation is not enacted with protectionist intents or does not discriminate against foreign nationals, the institutional structure of the State's regulatory process tends, in any case, to favour home interests'.[60]

In the view of Poiares Maduro, the problem of interest representation transcends the application of the principle of proportionality. According to him, it is not desirable to submit all kinds of national measures to a cost-benefit analysis by the Court of Justice under Article 28, without first assessing *when* the Court is the appropriate institution to undertake such a cost-benefit analysis. He rather proposes to curtail the instances in which the Court undertakes a cost-benefit analysis in the first place, thus allowing Member States to make different cost-benefit analyses on the basis of different values and measurement mechanisms. At the same time, the representation of the interests of foreign nationals in

---

[59] Poiares Maduro (1998a) at 116-126 and 172.

[60] Ibid. at 148.

the national policy-making processes should be ensured by the Court.[61] To this end, Poiares Maduro suggests tests to identify measures that are suspect of representative malfunction in the national political process. He proposes a distinction between "cross-national" and "national" interests. If a national measure regulates cross-national interests, it will not *prima facie* fall under Article 28, and will only be subjected to a balance test when shown to be discriminatory.

The test proposed moves the identification of the interests at stake to centre stage. This task will presumably be performed by national courts and the Court of Justice. However, such an identification exercise appears to be problematic, as is apparent from the examples provided by the author himself.[62] Even apart from the practical difficulties involved in identifying the interests in question, it seems questionable as a matter of principle that the Court of Justice should attempt to correct biases in the domestic political systems of the Member States caused by the under-representation of foreign interests, with regard to those matters not (yet) regulated at the Community level.[63]

With regard to the objectives invoked to justify trade-restrictive measures and the interests they represent, a distinction has been proposed between two categories of non-economic factors. On the one hand, factors that 'partake essentially of the nature and function of public order', such as public security, public health and public morality, i.e. the *"domaine reservé"* in the strict sense. On the other hand, 'those factors in respect of which governmental action is directly substituted for sections of civil society, reflecting their particular interests', including *inter alia* environmental policies, social policies and labour

---

[61] Ibid. at 169.

[62] The examples provided by Poiares Maduro are not entirely convincing to the present author, as they partially rely on the same typologies which Poiares Madure earlier on rejects. See ibid. (1998a), at 173-174, arguing that many national measures 'regulating market circumstances' concern interests that are equal in the different Member States, and mentioning by way of example a prohibition on selling sex-articles in non-licensed establishments. Arguably, this is precisely the kind of measure that may well reflect national idiosyncrasies. The author also contends that "product characteristics" will often affect divergent national and foreign interests, but not when they are 'of a technical nature' and 'not part of national production habits', or when 'aiming to regulate a recently discovered environmental or health risk'. Arguably, health risks may rightfully be perceived differently in different Member States.

[63] In this respect, it should be noted that Poiares Maduro largely bases his argument on the institutional analysis by Komesar (1994), which was made in the different context of the United States. See Poiares Maduro (1998a) at 172, note 40. The political characteristics of the US federal system in terms of vertical and horizontal relationships are only partially reflected in the context of the European Union. Arguably, differences between the US and the EU in these respects may have important consequences for the analysis of institutional malfunctions.

standards.[64] However, the current author submits that such a distinction is not based on essential or principal differences in the nature of the interests involved. Even if interests such as public security and public morality are within the core of national *"domaine reservé"*, and accordingly are less likely to be transferred to the European polity than other interests, there is essentially no reason why they could not be transferred. It may be recalled that the Court has stated that Article 30 does not reserve matters to Member States' exclusive jurisdiction.[65] The Court, although accepting Member States' ability to define such "hard core" areas of *"domaine réservé"* as public order, public security and public morality, has not shied away from assessing Member States' measures, thus defining the limits to those objectives in Community terms.[66]

The difference between the two groups of interests would rather seem to be gradual. This makes it difficult to categorise interests in either one of the groups. For example, if public health is part of the *"domaine reservé"*, how is it explained that it is increasingly regulated at the European level? Why is it that social policies are so difficult to harmonise if they are not part of the *"domaine reservé"*? How should animal and plant life and health protection as mentioned in Article 30 be categorised? It also appears that environmental protection does not always reflect the particular interests of a section of civil society. Arguably, there are numerous environmental problems that are of concern to entire societies, within a Member State, within the Community and world-wide.

The complicated interest patterns involved are reflected in the institutional roles played by the principle of proportionality. In its function of a check on Community legislation, this role concerns the "horizontal" relationship between the Community legislator and the Community judiciary, and also the "vertical" relationships between the Community legislator and individual Member States as well as their inhabitants. In its function as a check on Member States' measures, the institutional role of proportionality concerns the "vertical" relationship between the Community and its Member States in terms of their scope to regulate, by way of trade-restrictive measures, in pursuance of non-trade interests. At the same time, proportionality affects the "horizontal" relationship between the national legislative and administrative authorities and the national judiciary, as it is informed by the Court of Justice through preliminary rulings.[67]

If the Court informs a national court to the effect that a national environmental measure violates the EC Treaty because of a disproportionate effect on the free movement of goods, in a way it curtails national legislative and

---

[64] Weiss (1999).

[65] See Cases 35/76 *Simmenthal*; 72/83 *Campus Oil*.

[66] See e.g. Cases 231/83 *Cullet-Leclerc* and C-265/95 *Commission v. France* on public order, Case 72/83 *Campus Oil* on public security, and 121/85 *Conegate* on public morality.

[67] Cf. Trachtman (1996a) on 'horizontal and vertical federalism'.

administrative authorities. Yet this is not done in a straightforward "vertical" manner, by legislative action at the Community level precluding or setting the limits for legislative action by Member States. Instead, it is done through Community judicial action. Thus, to some extent, the principle of proportionality operates to remove competencies from national authorities to the Community level in fields of mixed competence such as the environment. Such removal of competencies through judiciary action may cause a "regulatory gap" when national authorities are precluded from legislating to pursue an objective, while Community legislative action on the subject-matter at issue has not (yet) taken place.[68]

It has been suggested that the degree of scrutiny with which the Court will assess the proportionality of a national measure will relate to the division of competencies between the Community and the Member State with regard to the subject-matter which the measure aims to regulate.[69] Thus, it has been argued that the margin of discretion left to the Member States is likely to diminish in the public health context as health standards are increasingly harmonised both at the Community level and internationally, a tendency which has been contrasted with the public policy and public morality grounds in Article 30 EC.[70] In the environmental field, the proportionality question is a particularly thorny issue considering the hybrid nature of the competencies shared by the Community and its Member States, and the applicability of the principle of subsidiarity in Article 5 EC to such competencies. In the field of public health, too, competencies are shared, although the Treaty confers less competencies upon the Community than in the environmental field, as observed earlier in this Chapter. Nonetheless, the Community makes frequent use of Article 95 EC to harmonise health standards. The link between proportionality testing and competencies suggests that the extent to which the Community has occupied a policy field will also determine the room which is left for a Member State to act concerning those subject-matters not (yet) harmonised at the Community level. However, strictly speaking, this does not seem to be correct, because in policy fields where the Community and the Member States share competencies the Member States remain competent to determine how strict their protection measures will be.

---

[68] Cf. Micklitz and Weatherill (1994) at 33-34.

[69] See De Búrca (1993) at 112 and 127.

[70] Ibid. at 139.

3.2.6 Proportionality and the Appropriate Level of Environmental Protection

It may be recalled that the Court has stated in relation to Article 30 that in the absence of harmonised Community rules, it is for the Member States to establish their desired levels of protection.[71] The freedom to do so would be curtailed by the application of a strict proportionality test. If, as argued above, there is no essential difference between the interests of life and health protection and of environmental protection, and the competence to regulate in their pursuance is shared between the Community and the Member States, can it be assumed that Member States are free to set their own levels of *environmental* protection just as they are to set their own levels of *health* protection? If this is the case, a strict proportionality test would seem to be equally inappropriate for environmental protection measures as for life and health protection measures with regard to those matters not (yet) covered by Community legislation.

It has been suggested that Member States enjoy a wider margin of discretion to establish high protection levels under the Treaty exception for life and health protection than under the mandatory requirement of environmental protection.[72] A possible willingness by the Court to subject national environmental measures to stricter scrutiny than national health measures may be explained by the fact that the life and health exception has Treaty status, whereas the mandatory requirement of environmental protection is an invention of the Court. It may also be connected with the difference regarding the division of competencies to regulate health and environmental aims. The specific Community mandate to enact environmental legislation is larger than the mandate to enact health legislation, leaving the Member States more competence and thus discretion in health than in environmental matters.[73] On the other hand, as argued above, the Community also sets a lot of health standards on the basis of Article 95 EC.

The current author submits that to the extent that Member States' competencies in environmental matters are untouched by Community harmonisation, they should have the same discretion in establishing their desired protection levels as with regard to the grounds mentioned in Article 30. It has been argued that it follows from Articles 174-176 and 95 that the environment cannot be left unprotected.[74] This argument was reinforced by the relocation of the require-

---

[71] See e.g. Cases 104/75 *De Peijper,* 272/80 *Frans-Nederlandse Maatschappij voor Biologische Producten,* C-131/93 *Commission* v. *Germany (crayfish),* C-473/98 *Toolex Alpha.* See also on public morality Case 34/79 *Henn and Darby.*

[72] Temmink (2000), at 89.

[73] See Section 2.4.

[74] Krämer (1993b) at 95 and 122-127 arguing that the degree of protection should not be part of the assessment of the national measure under Articles 28-30, basing this argument on *inter alia* his interpretation of Article 95(4).

ment of environmental integration from the environmental title to the Community's general principles.[75] Even if the Court's concept of "environment" does not include situations constituting direct life or health hazards, environmental problems may have health implications in the longer term, which are often uncertain. Taking into consideration the principles of precaution and prevention as laid down in Article 174 and of subsidiarity in Article 5, it seems reasonable to assume that where the Community has not (yet) acted to address an environmental problem, the Member States are free to do so at the level of protection they deem appropriate.

Confirmation of the assumption that Member States enjoy similar discretion with regard to protection goals under mandatory requirements as under Treaty exceptions may possibly be found in the Court's judgment in *Läärä*. The caveat should be made that that case mostly concerned trade in services rather than goods, and did not deal with environmental protection measures, but rather restrictions on gambling for the protection of gamblers and the maintenance of order in society. The Court made it clear that it was up to the Member State to determine the extent of the protection to be afforded, and added that how other Member States had regulated the matter would not affect the proportionality of the Finnish measures[76] When discussing the proportionality of the measure, the Court accepted that the restrictions were more effective than less restrictive alternatives in achieving part of the measure's goal, namely the setting of limits to the lucrative nature of gambling.[77] It is as yet an open question to what extent the deference shown by the Court in this case is confined to the particular field of gambling. It is true that there are no specific legislative competencies to be found in the Treaty for the Community to regulate gambling, and that gambling constitutes an important source of government income in many Member States. However, it seems clear from this case that the level of protection is to be set by Member States also in relation to mandatory requirements. The present author sees no reason why similar deference should not be applied by the Court to environmental measures relating to subject-matters not (yet) regulated by the Community.

3.3 The Role of Discrimination

It is as yet unclear from the Court's case-law how its distinction between "distinctly applicable" and "indistinctly applicable" measures relates to the concept of discrimination. Although the Court in most cases appears to

---

[75] The integration principle is now found in Article 6 EC.

[76] Case C-124/97 *Läärä*, paras. 35-36.

[77] Case C-124/97 *Läärä*, para. 41.

equate "distinctly applicable" with "formally" or *"de jure"* discriminatory, it has sometimes also found a measure that is *de facto* discriminatory to be distinctly applicable. With respect to these concepts, there are important differences in leading textbooks.[78] As has been remarked by Scott, it is remarkable that 'in an area as apparently well trodden as free movement of goods there remains such scope for legitimate debate as regards the "basics"'.[79] Moreover, the condition of 'affecting in the same manner in law and in fact the marketing of domestic and imported products' in *Keck* has raised new questions as to the role of discrimination. The existing confusion is illustrated by the Commission's 1999 Communication on the Single Market and the Environment. There, the Commission states that where no harmonised rules exist, national environmental rules are compatible with Article 28 of the Treaty if they are indistinctly applicable, 'i.e., they should apply, *de jure* and *de facto*, without distinction to domestic products and those of other Member States'.[80]

The continuing lack of clarity as to the role played by discrimination in Article 28 has consequences throughout the field of the free movement of goods.[81] It not only has a bearing upon the scope of the prohibition in Article 28 as qualified by *Keck*, but also upon the applicability of justification possibilities, since the Court has decided that only "indistinctly applicable" measures can be justified by mandatory requirements. Moreover, discrimination plays a role in the conditions applied to justifications. The second sentence of Article 30 provides that measures which are justified under that provision may not constitute arbitrary discrimination. Sometimes, discrimination even seems to inform the proportionality test.[82]

The inspiration for the Court's distinction between "distinctly applicable" and "indistinctly applicable" measures is found in Commission Directive 70/50, which made a distinction between "equally applicable" and "other measures". However, it is already unclear from that Directive whether "equally applicable" measures included all measures not formally distinguishing between domestic and imported goods, or only measures that applied equally in law and in fact. The indicative list of 'measures other than those equally applicable' in the Directive included as an example the fixing of product prices 'solely on the basis of the cost price or the quality of domestic products at such a level as to create a hindrance to importation'.[83] This is arguably a formally equally

---

[78] See e.g. the differences between Craig and De Búrca (1998) and Weatherill and Beaumont (1995), as accounted in Scott (1998) and Hilson (1999). See also Kapteijn/VerLoren (1998) at 675, note 592, suggesting that the Court 'looks behind the measure to see if it really is indistinctly applicable'.

[79] Scott (1998) at 74.

[80] COM(99)263f, at 7.

[81] And also concerning other market freedoms such as the free movement of services and workers; see Hilson (1999).

[82] Case C-169/91 *Stoke-on-Trent* at para 15.

[83] Article 2(3)(e) of the Directive.

applicable measure. Thus, the Directive suggests that 'measures other than those applicable equally' includes formally equally but materially not equally applicable measures. If that is the case, "equally applicable" measures in the sense of Article 3 of the Directive must logically refer to measures that are equally applicable *both in law and in fact*. However, as said, the Court in most cases has equated "distinctly applicable" with formally distinguishing measures. Indeed, it may be questioned whether "distinctly applicable" or "indistinctly applicable" measures can meaningfully be distinguished on any basis other than a formal criterion.

The word "discrimination" does not occur in Articles 28 and 29, but does occur in the exceptions in Article 30. This term also features in other parts of the Treaty.[84] It even occurs in some of the other provisions on free movement.[85] The word "discrimination" as such is also not explicitly used in Directive 70/50, or in any of the landmark cases that have shaped the interpretation of Article 28. Nevertheless, it has been argued that a discrimination test has always underlied the Court's approach to Article 28.[86] Moreover, national courts sometimes refer to Article 28 as containing a prohibition of discrimination, or as not covering equally applicable measures.[87] That opinion seems difficult to maintain in view of judgments in which the Court has determined that measures may create barriers to intra-Community trade covered by Article 28, even if they do not have the purpose of regulating trade patterns and their effect is not to favour national production as against the production of other member states.[88] The view of Article 28 as essentially a non-discrimination requirement is a recurring theme in the doctrine, however, and has been aired on numerous occasions in disputes involving Article 28.[89]

The argument that discrimination is the conceptual basis of the concept of measures of equivalent effect has received renewed impetus especially after the

---

[84] I.e., Articles 11 (closer co-operation), 12 (discrimination on grounds of nationality), 13 (discrimination based on sex, racial or ethnic origin, religion or belief, disability, age or sexual orientation), the common agricultural policy (Article 34(2)), transport policy (Article 75), state aids (Article 87), national measures going beyond Community internal market harmonisation (Article 95(6)), discrimination based on sex (Article 141), and trade with overseas countries and territories (Article 184(5)).

[85] I.e., those regarding commercial monopolies (Article 31), the free movement of workers (discrimination based on nationality between workers of the Member States as regards employment, remuneration and other conditions of work and employment, Article 39(2)), and the exceptions to the free movement of capital (Article 58(3))

[86] See in particular Marenco (1984).

[87] E.g. a German court in Case C-383/97 *Van der Laan*, and a French court in Case C-448/98 *Guimont*. For references to national courts applying Article 28 as if equally applicable measures are not covered by it, see Jarvis (1998) at 54-55.

[88] E.g. Joined Cases 60-61/84 *Cinethèque*.

[89] See for example, Cases 13/78 *Eggers* and 153/78 *Commission-Germany (meat preparations)*.

Keck judgment. The argument is that the imposition by the importing Member State of *product requirements* on goods imported from other Member States by its very nature constitutes indirect discrimination. This is not the case for the imposition on imports of measures regulating selling arrangements. One may add that the same is true for any other measure applied to imports that does not impose product requirements and does not regulate a "selling arrangement", i.e. measures outside the two main categories created by the Court's case-law that have been dubbed "third category" measures in this work. In this view, product requirements are by nature discriminatory and prohibited, while a discrimination test is applied to all other measures.

3.3.1 What is "discrimination"?

The very definition of the word "discrimination" is not devoid of problems.[90] Its meaning may vary according to whether it applies to the treatment of goods, persons, or services. Generally speaking, there is little doubt that the concept of discrimination covers different treatment of identical situations, often dubbed "formal" discrimination. Yet a first root of discord is the question whether such differential treatment should only be dubbed "discrimination" when it is not objectively justified, and merely "differentiation" or "different treatment" when it is justified. In addition, the question arises whether "discrimination" also covers identical treatment of different situations. This is usually dubbed "material" discrimination. The question is then, what are "different situations"? Sometimes, a distinction is made between "direct" and "indirect" discrimination. While the former refers to a difference in treatment based on the use of a distinguishing criterion such as nationality or sex, the latter refers to the use of a neutral criterion which has the same effect. Indirect discrimination can also occur when no such criterion is applied, but requirements are imposed which are easier to fulfil for one category of goods (or persons) than for another category.[91] Other terms applied in combination with discrimination are "de facto" or "factual", "in substance", "relative", and "arbitrary".[92]

The Court's case-law on the concept of discrimination does not apply any clear or consistent definitions. Sometimes the Court refers to different treatment of similar situations only, but in other instances it also includes identical treatment of different situations. In an early judgment, the Court found that 'the different treatment of non-comparable situations does not lead automatically to the conclusion that there is discrimination. An appearance of discrimination

---

[90] See e.g. Scott (1998), Bernard (1996), Hilson (1999), Drijber and Prechal (1997).

[91] Drijber and Prechal (1997).

[92] Timmermans (1982).

in form may therefore correspond in fact to an absence of discrimination in substance. Discrimination *in substance* would consist in treating either similar situations differently or different situations identically.'[93] The Court's definition of discrimination often includes objective justifications for differentiation. As early as 1961, the Court found that 'for the High Authority to be accused of discrimination it must be shown to have treated like cases differently, thereby subjecting some to disadvantages as opposed to others, without such differentiation being justified by the existence of substantial objective differences'.[94] The Court regards non-discrimination as part of the principle of equal treatment: '[t]he prohibition of discrimination [...] is merely a specific enunciation of the general principle of equality which is one of the fundamental principles of Community law. This principle requires that similar situations shall not be treated differently unless differentiation is objectively justified.'[95]

As will be seen below, discrimination tests play a role in the prohibition in Article 28 EC, although it is not entirely clear what role. If such tests include the consideration of objective justifications, confusion may arise in a context where the justification of national measures also refers to objective justifications, as is the case both for Article 30 and for the "mandatory requirements". For instance, objective justifications for indirect discrimination in the context of Article 28 have been equated with the mandatory requirements doctrine,[96] while others regard these as two separate phenomena.[97] However, in order to avoid discrimination, it is the *differentiation* that needs to be justified, not the measure as a whole. If the differentiation made by a measure is not objectively justified, it is discriminatory. But the measure as a whole, even if discriminatory, may still be justified under Article 30 or the mandatory requirements, as will be discussed below.[98] Thus, although there will be an overlap, the justification of measures as such cannot be equated with the justification of differential treatment. The difficulties involved in assessing regulatory distinctions and categorisations under Article 28 and the relationship with justifications under Article 30 and mandatory requirements are illustrated by the *Bluhme* case discussed *infra*.

3.3.2 Discrimination and Article 28 EC

When assessing national measures under Article 28, the Court usually applies the obstacles test developed in *Dassonville* and subsequent cases,

---

[93] Case 13/63 *Commission v. Italy*, para. 4. Emphasis added. See also e.g. Case 817/79 *Buys*, para. 29.

[94] See Case 17/61 *Klöckner*. Cf. Case 245/81 *Edeka*, paragraph 11.

[95] Joined Cases 117/76 and 16/77 *Ruckdeschel*, para. 7; see also Case C-217/91 *Brandy*, para. 37.

[96] Bernard (1996) at 92.

[97] Weatherill and Beaumont (1995) at 445, as noted by Hilson (1999) at 449.

[98] Cf. Timmermans (1982) at 441.

without referring to discrimination. However, there are exceptions to this practice.[99] Price regulations have almost always been subjected to a discrimination
test by the Court.[100] The test seems to include formal as well as material
discrimination. It possibly also includes a prohibition for pricing measures to
prevent imported products from competing on the market altogether: 'price
control systems applicable to domestic products and imported products alike,
although not in themselves constituting measures having an equivalent effect to
a quantitative restriction contrary to Article 30 of the Treaty, may nevertheless
have such an effect when the prices are fixed at a level such that the sale of
imported products becomes either impossible or more difficult than that of
domestic products.'[101]

The famous limitation on the scope of Article 28 in the *Keck* case did not
employ the term "discrimination" as such. Rather, it stipulated that the application to imports of national provisions restricting or prohibiting "certain selling
arrangements" would not fall within the *Dassonville* formula,

'so long as those provisions apply to all relevant traders operating within the
national territory and so long as they *affect in the same manner, in law and in fact,
the marketing* of domestic products and of those from other Member States'.[102]
This test calls for a comparison of the marketing possibilities of domestic and
imported products, and therefore closely resembles if not equals a discrimination test. However, the *Keck* conditions do not seem to invite consideration of
objective justifications for any differences in treatment.

3.3.3   Discrimination and Justifications

The logical starting point of a discussion on the role of discrimination in the justifications is the second sentence of Article 30, which
explicitly provides that measures that may be justified under the first sentence of
Article 30 shall not constitute 'a means of arbitrary discrimination or a disguised
restriction on trade between Member States'. However, although often mentioning it, the Court very rarely addresses the second sentence individually.[103] It often
merges into the proportionality test, which, in the Court's words, underlies it.[104]

What role does discrimination play in justifications based on mandatory
requirements? According to the Court' s case-law, 'the question of imperative

---

[99] See Cases 152/78 *Commission v. France (Advertising of Alcoholic Beverages)*; C-21/88 *Du Pont de Nemours*;
    C-260/89 *ERT*; Joined Cases C-321-324/94 *Pistre and others*, referring to Case 13/78 *Eggers*.

[100] See Cases 65/75 *Tasca*; 82/77 *Van Tiggele*; Joined Cases 16 to 20/79 *Danis*; 90/82 *Commission v. France*;
    181/82 *Roussel*; 229/83 *Leclerc/Au Blé Vert*; 231/83 *Cullet/Leclerc*; Joined Cases 80 and 159/85 *Edah*.

[101] Case C-249/88 Commission v. Belgium, para. 15, referring to Case 181/82 *Roussel*, para. 17.

[102] Joined Cases C-267/91 and C-268/91 *Keck et Mithouard* at para. 16.

[103] An exception is found in Joined Cases C-1/90 and C-176/90 *Aragonesa*.

[104] See e.g. Cases 174/82 *Sandoz*, 227/82 *Van Bennekom*, and C-400/96 *Harpegnies*.

requirement for the purposes of the interpretation of Article 30 [now 28] cannot arise unless the measure in question applies *without distinction* to both national and imported products.'[105] Sometimes, the Court has used the words "without discrimination" instead of "without distinction".[106] Generally, the Court treats measures as "indistinctly applicable" if they formally apply to domestic and imported goods without distinction. In other words, "distinctly applicable" measures would seem to be equated with formal discrimination. Obviously, measures that apply only to imports do not apply without distinction and cannot be justified by a mandatory requirement.[107] However, in some cases, the Court has also denied national measures justification under the mandatory requirements rule because of their *de facto* discriminatory nature or character, even if they were applicable without distinction between domestic and imported goods.[108]

How "applicable without distinction" is defined is of obvious importance for a measure's justification possibilities. If a formal criterion is taken for distinguishing between distinctly applicable and indistinctly applicable measures, indistinctly applicable measures could be justified by mandatory requirements in addition to Article 30, even if they *de facto* disfavour imports. Distinctly applicable measures could only be justified by Article 30. On the other hand, if a material criterion is taken, all measures that discriminate in law or in fact are "distinctly applicable", and only measures that do not discriminate formally or materially are genuinely "indistinctly applicable" and may enjoy the justification possibilities offered by the mandatory requirements. Accordingly, if a formal criterion is taken for distinguishing between distinctly applicable and indistinctly applicable measures, a measure failing the "in law" part of the *Keck* test could only be justified by Article 30, while a measure failing only the "in fact" part of the *Keck* test could be justified by both Article 30 and mandatory requirements. If, on the other hand, the view is taken that a *de facto* discriminatory measure really cannot be called "indistinctly applicable", it would seem inconsistent to allow such a measure to enjoy justification by mandatory requirements if it has failed the "in fact" part of the *Keck* test. The Court appears to take the former view.[109]

The question whether discriminatory measures may be justified under "mandatory requirements" is of particular importance in the environmental field. As discussed earlier, "environmental protection" is a "mandatory requirement", but is not as such mentioned in Article 30 EC. As noted above, an attempt

---

[105] See e.g. Joined Cases C-1/90 and C-176/90 *Aragonesa*, at para. 13. Emphasis added.

[106] See e.g. Case 788/79 *Gilli and Andres*.

[107] See e.g. Cases 113/80 *Irish Souvenirs*, 59/82 *Weinvertriebs-GmbH*.

[108] See e.g. Cases 177/83 *Kohl* v. *Ringelhan*; C-21/88 *Du Pont de Nemours*; Joined Cases C-321-324/94 *Pistre and others*.

[109] See e.g. Joined Cases C-34-36/95 *De Agostini* [1997], paras. 44-45.

to add "environmental protection" to the list of exceptions in Article 30 at the 1997 intergovernmental conference failed. To read another justification ground into Article 30 appears difficult to reconcile with the Court's approach to Article 30 as a closed list. However, from a policy point of view, the need is sometimes felt for environmental protection measures to differentiate between domestic and imported goods, or to make differentiations that may turn out to be unfavourable to imported goods. In a number of cases, the Court has referred to "the environment" in the context of Article 30.[110] Although these cases cannot be said to prove that environmental protection as such now forms part of Article 30, they do indicate that the Court is not insensitive to the problem that some environmental measures need to differentiate in order to be effective.

The problem came to light most poignantly in the *Walloon Waste* case.[111] This case concerned a measure by the region of Wallonia prohibiting imports of waste from other Belgian regions and from foreign countries. Although the Court in that case repeated that the mandatory requirements may only be invoked with respect to indistinctly applicable measures, it in fact allowed a distinctly applicable measure to be justified by the mandatory requirement of environmental protection.[112] The discriminatory character of the national measure was convincingly argued by Advocate General Jacobs and the Commission.[113] Nonetheless, the Court took a different view, stating that in assessing whether or not the measure was discriminatory, account must be taken of the particular nature of waste. The Court found that 'having regard to the differences between waste produced in different places and to the connection of the waste with its place of production, the contested measures cannot be regarded as discriminatory'.[114] The Court based this finding on the Community principle that environmental damage should be remedied at its source, as laid down in Article 174(2) EC, according to which 'waste should be disposed of as close as possible to the place where it is produced, in order to limit as far as possible the transport of waste.'[115] The Court argued that this principle is consistent with the internationally agreed principles of self-sufficiency and proximity, as laid down in the 1989 Basle Convention on the control of transboundary movements of hazardous wastes and their disposal, to which the Community is a signatory.[116]

---

[110] See Cases 94/83 *Heijn*, 125/88 *Nijman*, C-389/96 *Aher-Waggon*, C-473/98 *Toolex Alpha*. See also AG Trabucchi in his Opinion in Case 3,4,6/76 *Kramer* at 1324, equating the protection of animal and plant life with environmental protection.

[111] Case C-2/90 *Commission v. Belgium*.

[112] See para. 29 of the judgment.

[113] See para. 20 of his first opinion and para. 33 of the judgment respectively.

[114] See para. 37 of the judgment.

[115] See para. 29 of the judgment.

[116] See para. 35 of the judgment.

This judgment has been widely criticised for its reasoning.[117] For one thing, the Court completely omitted to apply any form of proportionality test to the measure. Moreover, it is questionable that the principle of remedy at source, invoked by the Court to limit the transport of waste, should be applied within the Community in a manner resulting in the upholding of intra-Community trade barriers. The consistency of this principle with the international principles of proximity and self-sufficiency should not necessarily have to result in its being interpreted according to Member States' national borders. Would it not be more in line with the internal market to say that the Community should apply these principles *as a whole*? This could in practice mean that waste generated in Northern France, within 20 km. of the Belgian border, should preferably be treated and disposed of in Wallonia rather than at the nearest French waste treatment site, if that were located at a greater distance from the place where the waste was generated. It is as yet unclear to what extent the Court's reasoning is confined to the specific area of waste, which in the same case was recognised as being a good, but which poses particular problems.[118] Moreover, the Court did not formally acknowledge the application of the mandatory requirement of environmental protection to a measure which was distinctly applicable. Rather, the Court applied creative reasoning to come to the conclusion that the measure was not discriminatory. This suggests that a measure that differentiates between domestic and imported products for legitimate reasons does not discriminate, and can be justified by the mandatory requirement of environmental protection.

More cracks in the wall between mandatory requirements and Article 30 seem to be appearing, also outside the area of waste. In the *Aher-Waggon* case, at issue were German rules making aircraft registration dependent on noise emission standards. The German standards were stricter than those laid down by a relevant Community directive, but aircraft which had obtained registration in national territory before the Directive was implemented were exempt from the stricter standards. Thus, second-hand aircraft from other Member States seeking to be registered were disadvantaged *vis-à-vis* second-hand aircraft that had already been registered in Germany.[119] The Court found that the German measure could be justified by considerations of public health and environmental protection, in other words, both on the grounds of Article 30 and of "mandatory requirements". This is interesting in that the rules differentiated on the basis of whether the aircraft had been previously registered in Germany or in other Member States. Thus, although not differentiating on the basis of where the aircraft had been produced, the measure did apply a differentiating criterion

---

[117] Another point of criticism is the complete absence of any application of the proportionality principle. See on the case e.g. Krämer (1993a), at 77-87; Jans (1995) at 227-228.

[118] On the specific features of waste and the Community waste regime, see London and Llamas (1995).

[119] Case C-389/96 *Aher-Waggon*, at para. 18.

linked to where the aircraft had been registered. The measure was arguably "distinctly applicable", and could nevertheless be justified by mandatory require-ments.

A somewhat similar issue is found in *Bluhme*, which concerned Danish legis-lation prohibiting bees being kept on the island of Laesø other than a certain subspecies that only existed on that island, in order to avoid cross-breeding which would lead to the extinction of the subspecies. Although the Court did not tackle the question whether the measure was "indistinctly applicable", as it found the measure justified under Article 30, Advocate-General Fennelly did pay attention to "mandatory requirements", in case the justification based on Article 30 would not be accepted. He argued that even if there were indications to the contrary, the measure was indistinctly applicable, for two reasons. First, the measure did not discriminate against other subspecies if the distinction made by it was objectively justified:

> [G]olden bees, as members of a separate subspecies, can more readily be recognised as materially different in character, so that rules favouring one subspecies over the other need not, if they serve a legitimate public-interest objective related to that distinction, be regarded as discriminatory.

This reasoning essentially boils down to the view that there is no discrimination if a measure differently treats situations that are different, and the distinction made relates to a legitimate objective. Secondly, Fennelly referred to the *Walloon Waste* judgment and contended that the Danish measures took preventive action against inter-breeding, which may be seen as an attempt to rectify at source the environmental damage arising from such inter-breeding. In the light of these legislative objectives, there were relevant differences between the bee population protected by the measure and other populations of bees. Albeit somewhat hesitantly, Fennelly concluded that the exclusion of the other popula-tions was not discriminatory in character, and may therefore be justified by the mandatory requirement of environmental protection.[120]

In *Preussen Elektra*, the compatibility with EC rules of a national measure obliging electricity suppliers to buy local green electricity was at issue. Advocate-General Jacobs in his opinion advised the Court not to follow its reasoning in *Walloon Waste* (i.e. the measure is really not discriminatory because of the specific nature of the good and certain environmental principles, so it may be justified by environmental protection), which he deemed flawed. He pointed out that 'it is desirable that even directly discriminatory measures can sometimes be justified on grounds of environmental protection'.[121] He therefore urged the

---

[120] Conclusion by AG Fennelly in Case 67/97 *Bluhme*, at paras. 24-25.

[121] Conclusion by AG Jacobs in Case C-379/98 *Preussen Elektra*, para. 225-26.

Court to clarify its position on this point so as to provide the necessary legal certainty, arguing that a more flexible approach to the mandatory requirement of environmental protection was called for, for two reasons. First, the heightened concern for the environment in the Community, and secondly, because to deny the justification of environmental protection to distinctly applicable measures would risk defeating their purpose:

> National measures for the protection of the environment are inherently liable to differentiate on the basis of the nature and origin of the cause of harm, and are therefore liable to be found discriminatory, precisely because they are based on such accepted principles as that 'environmental damage should as a priority be rectified at source' [...] Where such measures necessarily have a discriminatory impact of that kind, the possibility that they may be justified should not be excluded.[122]

The argument appears somewhat overstretched, because it seems obvious that not all national environmental measures necessarily need to discriminate. However, the opinion convincingly drives home the point that in some cases, environmental measures need to discriminate. However, the Court did not provide the desired clarity. It observed that the measure was capable of hindering intra-Community trade and that it had to be determined whether the measure was 'nevertheless compatible with Article 30 [now 28]'. It remarked that the measure was 'useful for protecting the environment', referred to Community measures aiming at a reduction in the emission of greenhouse gases, and observed that 'that policy is also designed to protect the health and life of humans, animals and plants'.[123] The Court in its *dictum* concluded that the measure was not incompatible with Article 28. It is submitted that all this suggests that it was looking at the mandatory requirement of environmental protection rather than at Article 30. The measure was clearly discriminatory.[124] But by mentioning Article 30 as well, the Court did not provide explicit clarity as to the possibility of justifying discriminatory measures by mandatory requirements. It seems to have taken a similar approach as in *Walloon Waste*, referring to the 'particular features of the electricity market' and to international and Community instruments with the same objective which the national measure pursues. Also, just as in *Walloon Waste* the Court did not apply any kind of proportionality requirement, which seems strange, to say the least.

In cases involving waste exports, the Court appears to suggest that justifying distinctly applicable measures infringing Article 29 by mandatory requirements

---

[122] Ibid., para. 233.

[123] Case C-379/98 *Preussen Elektra*, paras. 73-75.

[124] Cf. a similar requirement to purchase a percentage of domestic goods in Case C-21/88 *Du Pont de Nemours*.

is possible.[125] This would be difficult to reconcile with the limited scope of Article 29, prohibiting only discriminatory export restrictions.

Outside the realm of environmental protection, similar developments may be observed to the effect that the difference between indistinctly and distinctly applicable measures becomes blurred. As early as 1984, the Court was willing to consider a "mandatory requirement" invoked to justify a measure that reserved the use of a certain type of wine bottle to a limited list of domestic wines, and thus seemed clearly distinctly applicable.[126] In the *Decker* case, the Court arguably accepted a mandatory requirement to justify a measure only applied to spectacles purchased abroad.[127] In *Snellers*, the Court did a similar thing for an administrative requirement concerning the registration of cars, which applied separate rules to cars having been registered in the Netherlands and cars having been registered abroad.[128] It is furthermore recalled that the Court has suggested that a measure that does not meet the *Keck* test because it does not equally affect in fact the marketing of imports and domestic products, i.e. a *(de facto) discriminatory* measure, can be justified by mandatory requirements.[129]

As early as 1982, it was suggested to discard the dichotomy between the two justification venues in Article 30 and accepted in the Court's case-law on "mandatory requirements".[130] However, the Court only hesitantly appears to be willing to drop its distinction between indistinctly applicable and distinctly applicable measures, and to consider mandatory requirements as justifications for measures that do not treat imported and domestic goods the same in law and in fact. Even if all measures could benefit from both venues, the concept of discrimination would not have disappeared from the ambit of Articles 28-30. It still plays a central role in Article 29. It keeps on surfacing in the doctrinal debate and occasionally in the case-law on Article 28. Discrimination is expressly mentioned in the second sentence of Article 30. Those wishing to get rid of discrimination tests and to concentrate on obstacles to the free movement of goods and justifications have been shown by the *Keck* line of cases that discrimination is difficult to eliminate from the discussion. There are even suggestions that it is returning to centre stage in the application of Article 28.[131]

---

[125] See Case C-203/96 *Dusseldorp*, paras. 44 and 49. The Court's unclear position on this point is evident from Case C-209/98 *Sydhavnens*, paras. 49-50.

[126] Case 16/83 *Prantl* ('*Bocksbeutel*').

[127] Case C-120/95 *Decker*, especially. paras. 36 and 39 of the judgment. Cf. Oliver (1999) at 805. It is not entirely clear, however, whether the measure was discriminatory, at least formally, in terms of goods' origin. See also the opinion of Advocate-General Tesauro, at para. 47.

[128] Case C-314/98 *Snellers*.

[129] Joined Case C-34-36/95 *De Agostini*.

[130] Oliver (1982) at 230-31.

[131] Weiler (1999).

3.4 Production Methods, Extraterritoriality, and Unilateral Action

This Section addresses three issues that are often, but not necessarily related. First, what is the status under Articles 28-30 EC of measures based on production and processing methods? Second, are extraterritorial environmental protection goals and measures targeting the behaviour of producers and/or governments in other Member States acceptable under Articles 28-30 EC? Third, what is the scope for Member States to take unilateral measures with extraterritorial effects and/or objectives when there is relevant Community legislation, and when there is no such legislation? After a general discussion of these issues, the scarce relevant case-law of the ECJ will be discussed.

3.4.1 Articles 28-29 EC and Production and Processing Methods (PPMs)

Can a Member State infringe the Community rules on the free movement of goods by restricting *production* under its own jurisdiction? In the absence of Community legislation on production and processing methods (PPMs), Member States are in principle free to regulate production within their respective jurisdictions. Normally, national production restrictions will not constitute specific export restrictions and will not be caught by the *Groenveld* interpretation of Article 29.[132] Likewise, unless the regulating Member State attempts to apply a production regulation to imports, a possibility which is discussed hereafter, a measure regulating national production will not affect imports and will not be covered by Article 28.[133] Nevertheless, the Court has not altogether discarded the possibility that a production limitation can as such be covered by Article 28 EC. In *Kramer,* the Court observed that the fish catch quotas at issue and the prohibition laid down in Article 28 'relate to different stages of the economic process, that is to say, to production and marketing respectively'.[134] However, it did not conclude from this that limitations to produc-

---

[132] Case 15/79 *Groenveld*, at para. 6: Article 29 concerns measures which have as their 'specific object or effect the restriction of patterns of exports and thereby the establishment of a difference in treatment between the domestic trade of a Member State and its export trade in such a way as to provide a particular advantage for national production or for the domestic market of the State in question at the expense of the production or of the trade of other Member States.' Cf. Case 155/80 *Oebel*, paras. 12-16.

[133] Cf. Petersmann (1995) at 57.

[134] Joined Cases 3,4,6/76 *Kramer,* at para. 55. AG Trabucchi, at 1323, argued that production limitations are 'liable to affect trade in the product by limiting from the beginning the quantities which can be offered on the market'. Thus, such restrictions in principle fall within the *Dassonville* formula and require justification. Cf. Case 190/73 *Van Haaster* on national rules limiting the cultivation of hyacinth bulbs.

tion are *per se* outside the scope of Article 28. The Court rather said that whether
a measure limiting production impedes trade between Member States depends
on relevant Community rules and their objectives, and the nature and circumstances of the production of the product in question. The Court concluded that
fish conservation measures were not covered by Article 28 because their long-
term objective is to ensure a steady, optimum yield from fishing.[135] This suggests
that production limitations for other products and in other circumstances could
be covered by Article 28.

Can a Member State infringe the Community rules on the free movement
of goods by restricting *imports* for reasons of their production process abroad?
It follows from the *Cassis de Dijon* line of cases that a Member State should
in principle accept the marketing in its territory of goods lawfully produced
and marketed in another Member State. Thus, Article 28 will be violated if an
imported product is refused because of the way it has been produced abroad,
unless the measure is justified and proportionate. If the production method
cannot be traced back in the product as it is traded, how can the importing
Member State assess the production process which takes place outside its jurisdiction? It will have to either rely on foreign authorities to provide information
on the production processes, or send officials to the importing country to carry
out checks. Alternatively, the importing Member State may require the imported
product to carry a certificate or label specifying that the PPM in the exporting
Member State meets the requirements imposed by the importing country.

Insisting on carrying out checks on the territory of other Member States
appears to be contrary to the spirit of mutual trust underlying the Community.
There is no reason why the emphasis on mutual trust and acceptance of test
results from other Member States as laid down by the Court in its case-law
on product requirements should not apply to the acceptance of information on
PPMs provided by the exporting Member State.[136] Assuming that there is no
relevant Community legislation, a certification or labelling requirement specifying a product's PPM would be covered by Article 28. It would effectively impede
market access of products lawfully produced and marketed in another Member
State. If a Member State regulates its own producers directly through production
requirements and accordingly requires a label only for imported products, the
requirement would be a distinctly applicable measure. Justification on grounds
of mandatory requirements would be problematic. A labelling requirement
applying to imported and domestic products alike could in principle be justified
by Article 30 or mandatory requirements. If extraterritorial protection goals were
to be accepted in principle under the justification grounds, a matter discussed

---

[135] Ibid., paras. 56-59. This judgment can be regarded as an application of the "rule of reason" *avant la lettre*.

[136] See e.g. Cases 272/80 *Frans-Nederlandse Maatschappij voor Biologische Producten*; C-293/94 *Brandsma*.

in the next subsection, the importing Member State would still have to demonstrate that the production process in the exporting Member State was not equivalent to its requirements, and that its measure was necessary and proportionate.

Can a Member State infringe the Community rules on the free movement of goods by restricting *exports* for reasons of their domestic production process? A specific export restriction is covered by the *Groenveld* formula and thus requires justification. Although not very likely, it is conceivable that a Member State, in view of idiosyncrasies in other Member States as regards taste or morals, wishes to restrict the export but not the domestic consumption of products produced in a certain manner. The *Groenveld* situation is itself a case in point, where the Member State wanted to safeguard the image of its meat processing industry abroad.[137] However, in that case, the measure did not specifically restrict exports, but rather applied at the production level. Export restrictions because of environmental or health effects which a product may have *abroad* are also conceivable. Such restrictions do not normally concern PPMs, but effects caused by the product's use or disposal. However, export restrictions applied because of what is going to happen to the product after it has been exported may also relate to further production or processing abroad. In that case they do concern PPMs, but not the PPMs of the exporting Member State. A case in point would be an export restriction or prohibition of live animals because of raising or slaughtering methods abroad which are perceived as cruel in the exporting Member State.[138]

3.4.2 Extraterritorial Protection Goals

There are arguments for and against accepting extraterritorial protection goals under Article 30 and the mandatory requirement of environmental protection. On the one hand, the solidarity requirement laid down in Article 10 EC Treaty generally applies to unilateral measures aimed at protecting the environment outside the territory of the Member State taking them. Considering the fact that the Member States have the possibility to pursue environmental goals that exceed their own borders through the sophisticated system of international co-operation provided by the Community, it appears to be against the spirit of European integration to pursue environmental protection in another Member State through trade-restrictive measures. Moreover, it has been argued that the grounds in Article 30 and the mandatory requirements may justify trade-restrictive measures to the extent that these account for social and moral differences between Member States, as long as the interests at hand are not or are insufficiently protected by Community harmonisation.[139] If that

---

[137] Cf. in the field of services, Case C-384/93 *Alpine Investments*.

[138] Such situations are discussed below, however in cases where there was relevant Community harmonisation on raising and slaughtering methods.

[139] Weatherill and Beaumont (1995), at 478-9.

is the function of the justifications, it is questionable whether trade-restrictive measures pursuing protection goals in another Member State can be acceptable. Indeed, pursuing such interests has been equated with imposing one Member State's standards or morality on other Member States.[140]

On the other hand, neither the text of Article 30, nor the expression of environmental protection as a mandatory requirement in the Court's case-law hint at a limitation to a Member State's national territory for the protection of environmental or life or health interests. Article 30 mentions "national" in relation to the protection of 'treasures possessing artistic, historic or archaeological value', and places "public" in front of "morality", "policy" and "security". Although "public" does not necessarily refer to the national public and could be understood as 'the European public', the interests which this adjective precedes strongly suggest that the national public is meant. Thus, on the basis of the absence of any adjective in front of 'health and life of humans, animals or plants', one could conclude *a contrario* that no territorial limitation was intended. An argument against such a conclusion would be the general rule that the grounds in Article 30 must, according to the case-law, be strictly interpreted as an exception to the fundamental principle of the free movement of goods.

3.4.3   Unilateral Action and Community Solidarity

All national environmental measures assessed under Articles 28-30 are unilateral in the sense that they either address a subject not covered by secondary Community legislation, or, if there is relevant Community legislation, go beyond that legislation. However, particular problems in the internal market are raised by unilateral trade-restrictive measures that have extraterritorial environmental aims, and/or aim to influence foreign producers' or authorities' behaviour affecting the environment.

It is established Community law that a Member State is not entitled to 'take the law into its own hands'. This follows from the general obligation of "solidarity" in Article 10 EC. If a Member State deems that another Member State infringes Community law, the appropriate way to deal with the problem is not to enact unilateral measures. The Member State should raise the issue within the institutional setting of the Community, including eventually the possibility of an infringement procedure before the Court of Justice on the basis of Article 227 EC. Thus, if production methods are covered by secondary Community legislation, and a Member State thinks that another Member State is not complying with that legislation, it may not take unilateral trade restrictive measures to address the perceived failure of the other Member State to live up to its

---

[140] Cf. Oliver (1996) at 186.

Community obligations.[141] Also, a Member State may not compromise pending Community legislation by its unilateral measures.[142]

In the absence of relevant Community legislation on the production method concerned, may Member States take unilateral trade-restrictive measures to protect the environment outside their borders, or to affect the behaviour of producers or the policies of governments in other Member States to ensure environmental protection? It is submitted that the existence of a sophisticated political and legal system and the solidarity obligation in Article 10 EC have consequences in such situations too. Perceived deficiencies in a foreign production process should lead the importing Member State to push for the adoption of Community standards in the field, rather than to restrict trade in the product at issue. Production processes do not have to be uniform throughout the Community.[143] Arguably, although unilateral action would not seem to be prohibited *per se*, trade obstacles caused by measures based on PPMs in other Member States would only be acceptable as necessary and proportionate under Article 30 or the mandatory requirements in limited circumstances.

3.4.4 The Court's Case-Law

The Court of Justice has not taken a clear position with regard to the issues addressed above. In *Dassonville*, Advocate General Trabucchi discussed Article 30 as an exception enabling Member States to protect various *national* interests. He posited that Member States can under Article 30 derogate from the prohibition of Article 28 only for the protection of their own interests, not of the interests of other Member States. Thus, in his view, export restrictions cannot be justified for the protection of the public health of the populations in other Member States.[144] Trabucchi further elaborated this view in his opinion in *Kramer*. He there spoke of the 'essential spirit and purpose of this exempting clause' in Article 30, which implied that the restrictive measures justified by it should have 'the genuinely unilateral character, confined to a particular State, which results from the fact that the interest for which Article 36 [now 30] provides protection is essentially national and internal to the State.' He then queried whether the essential purpose of Article 30, 'to protect an individual Member State from more general Community principles concerning free movement', was sufficient to rule out reliance on the Article in the case at hand. He

---

[141] Case 5/94 *Hedley Lomas*, referring to Joined Cases 90/63 and 91/63 *Commission v. Luxembourg and Belgium*, and Case 232/78 *Commission v. France*.

[142] Case C-129/96 *Inter-Environnement Wallonie* [1997] ECR I-7411

[143] It is economically disputable that a country should be able to compensate at the border for differences in production methods. See e.g. Esty and Geradin (1998).

[144] AG Trabucchi in Case 8/74 *Dassonville* at 860.

decided it was not, albeit with some struggle. Trabucchi seemed to say that the action was really in the Member State's own interest of safeguarding future fish stocks for its own "production", even if the fish is not in its own waters; and its interest really coincided with the Community interest, and was therefore allowed as long as the Community had not acted to safeguard that interest. The Court concluded that fish quotas were not prohibited by the Treaty, thereby implying that migratory fish stocks could be protected extraterritorially through a production limitation. However, although they possibly affected trade flows in the sense of limiting the volume produced by Dutch fishermen and thus the volume of fish traded in the Community, there was no restriction or prohibition of the *importation* of the fish sought to be protected.

Few if any examples of the assessment under Articles 28-30 EC of efforts by a Member State to protect the environment outside its borders by measures restricting imports are known. The *Van den Burg* case therefore deserves specific mention. The Wild Birds directive covers all species of naturally occurring birds in the wild state in the EC (Article 1).[145] It lays down a general prohibition on killing or capturing those species (Article 5) and selling, keeping or offering them (Article 6), but provides exceptions that oblige, respectively allow Member States to permit the sale and keeping of certain species listed in Annexes to the directive.[146] The directive moreover provides for special protection measures for endangered and migratory species (Article 4), and allows Member States to introduce stricter protective measures than those provided for under the directive (Article 14). The Scottish Red Grouse that was at issue in *Van den Burg* did not occur in the Netherlands, which prohibited its marketing and importation. The bird was mentioned in Annex III/1 and was lawfully killed or captured in the UK. Thus, the only way the Netherlands could avoid infringing Article 6 of the directive was to invoke Article 14 that allowed stricter measures.

The Commission put forward a number of arguments to the effect that Article 30 could be invoked for protecting animals in another Member State. These arguments were based on the wording of Article 30; on a case which dealt with veterinary inspections;[147] and on the 'transfrontier nature of the protection of birds' as recognised in Community and international legal instruments. In response to these arguments, Advocate General Van Gerven argued that the wording of Article 30 did not yield any clue on the issue of extraterritorial protection goals, and that the veterinary inspections at issue in the case mentioned by the Commission were imposed by a Community directive and were thus not unilateral. He also had doubts about the relevance of the instruments mentioned by the Commission to support its third argument. However, he did agree that

---

[145] Directive 79/409, OJ 1979 L 103/1.

[146] Annex III/ and III/21 respectively.

[147] Case 46/76 *Bauhuis*.

it is possible to justify measures to protect extraterritorial interests, adding that the necessity and proportionality requirements should in such a case be assessed 'with the customary vigour'.[148]

The Court found that Article 30, 'read in conjunction with' the Wild Birds directive, cannot justify extraterritorial protection measures of species that are neither migratory nor endangered, when those species only occur in another Member State and are there lawfully hunted in accordance with the directive. In its dictum, the Court mentioned Article 30 'in conjunction with' the Wild Birds directive, so the Court's position might have been different if unilateral measures had been taken in the complete absence of relevant harmonisation. Indeed, when interpreting the provision in the directive allowing Member States stricter protection measures, the Court implicitly interpreted the room left for Member States after harmonisation in accordance with Articles 28-30 EC. Thus, the Court's mentioning of Article 30 in *Van den Burg* suggests that it did not favourably regard import restrictions for extraterritorial protection reasons under that provision, except when animals deserving special protection are at stake. Indeed, the *Van den Burg* case has been said to hint at 'scepticism on the part of the Court as regards the legitimacy of trade restrictions adopted with a view to protecting "foreign" environmental goods, at least in so far as these are not conceived as "shared"-representing part of the common heritage of mankind.'[149] However, despite the Court's scepticism, *Van den Burg* does not appear to exclude the theoretical possibility that Article 30 (and arguably the mandatory requirements) allow for extraterritorial measures pursuing transnational and global environmental protection objectives.

In *Vergy* and *Van der Feesten*, the Court again interpreted the Wild Birds directive. It found that the directive obliged Member States to ensure the protection of all bird species protected by the directive, i.e. not just those receiving special protection under Article 4. This is so even if the particular subspecies at issue does not occur in the wild in the European territory but the species to which it belongs or other subspecies of that species do so occur (*Van der Feesten*),[150] and even if the species in question does not have its natural habitat in the Member State concerned but does in other Member States (*Vergy*).[151] Thus, it appears that extraterritorial protection is allowed and even mandated by the general prohibition on hunting and trading all species protected by the Wild Birds directive. Any other position would endanger the protection goals of the directive, which are of a transnational nature.[152] The directive, it is recalled, also

---

[148] Para. 7 of his Opinion in Case C-169/89 *Van den Burg*. Sevenster (1998) at 31 agrees with this view.

[149] Scott (2000) at 128.

[150] Case C-202/94 *Van der Feesten*.

[151] Case C-149/94 *Vergy*.

[152] See Case C-149/94 *Vergy*, para. 17; Case C-202/94 *Van der Feesten*, paras. 16-17.

allows Member States to take stricter protection measures. However, considering *Van den Burg*, Member States may only take stricter extraterritorial protection measures with respect to endangered or migratory species that receive special protection under the directive.[153]

While the Commission in *Van den Burg* argued that Article 30 could accommodate extraterritorial protection goals, it appears to take a different approach with regard to the mandatory requirement of environmental protection. In its comments on a Dutch legislative proposal for a mandatory PPM-based label for wood products, the Commission remarked that the Court has only accepted environmental protection as a mandatory requirement to the extent that it concerns trade-restrictive measures aimed at protecting the environment of the Member State taking the measures.[154] In *Preussen Elektra*, the Court appears to have accepted extraterritorial protection goals when it deemed a national measure obliging electricity suppliers to buy local green electricity to be compatible with Article 28. The Court, however, did not make explicit whether the measure was justified by Article 30 or the mandatory requirement of environmental protection. It remarked that the measure was 'useful for protecting the environment in so far as it contributes to the reductions in emissions of greenhouse gases which are amongst the main causes of climate change', referred to the Community's obligations in this respect, and observed that 'that policy is also designed to protect the health and life of humans, animals and plants'.[155]

In contrast with the scarcity of cases concerning import restrictions, there is a considerable number of cases dealing with *export* restrictions in order to pursue extraterritorial environment or health objectives. They are not consistent, however. The *Inter-Huiles* case could be taken to imply that protective measures aimed at another Member State's environment might be justified, if that state does not adequately protect the interest invoked.[156] On the other hand, the *Nertsvoederfabriek* case may be invoked to argue against the acceptance of

---

[153] Notaro (2000) at 470 sees a sharp contrast between *Van den Burg* on the one hand, and *Vergy* and *Van der Feesten* on the other, although he concludes that they are reconcilable. However, it should be emphasised that the former case concerned stricter measures under Article 14 of the Wild Birds directive, while the latter two cases concerned the scope of the basic obligations in the directive, not stricter national measures.

[154] Comments by the Commission within the framework of Article 9(2) of Directive 98/34 on the provision of information in the field of technical standards and regulations. See on the Dutch law, Dutch Parliament, proposal to amend the Wet milieubeheer (Environmental Management Act), Kamerstukken nos. 23 982 and 26 998, available in Dutch at http://www.overheid.nl/op. An account of the Dutch Act in English can be found in WTO document G/TBT/Notif.98.448, available at http://docsonline.wto.org.

[155] C-379/98 *Preussen Elektra*, paras. 73-75.

[156] Case 172/82 *Inter-Huiles*. See Jans (1995) at 229.

extraterritorial environmental protection goals. In that case, the Court found Article 29 to be applicable to a national system for poultry offal to the extent that exports were restricted by it. When examining its justification under Article 30, the Court said 'it does not appear necessary to prohibit the exportation of poultry offal, provided that the conditions relating to health laid down by those provisions [the exporting state's health safeguards] are satisfied with respect to removal and transport *on national territory.*'[157] In the *Dusseldorp* case, the Court did appear to accept the possibility of extraterritorial protection through export restrictions. When the Netherlands argued that an export ban on oil filters was justified by the protection of human life and health, the Court replied that such a justification would be relevant if the processing of oil filters *in other Member States* and their shipment over a greater distance as a result of their being exported posed a threat to the health and life of humans.[158] However, in a subsequent case dealing with very similar circumstances, the Court dropped the reference to the processing in other Member States and merely pointed at transport over a larger distance.[159] Thus, again, there is no conclusive evidence in the Court's case-law for or against extraterritorial application.

In *Hedley Lomas* and *Compassion in World Farming*, the Court did not address the question whether extraterritorial protection is in principle possible. In both cases, relevant Community harmonisation existed. The Court held that 'recourse to Article 36 [now 30] is no longer possible where Community directives provide for harmonisation of the measures necessary to achieve the specific objective which would be furthered by reliance upon this provision.'[160] In *Hedley Lomas*, the relevant Community legislation concerned requirements for slaughtering animals.[161] The UK prohibited exports to Spanish slaughterhouses because it believed that Spain did not apply these requirements. Thus, the case really centred on the unilateral character of the British measure. The Court stressed that no Member State is allowed to unilaterally adopt corrective or protective measures designed to obviate any perceived breach of rules of Community law by another Member State.[162] In *Compassion*, the Community directive at issue set minimum standards for boxes and stalls used to house calves.[163] The directive allowed Member States to apply stricter provisions for the protection of calves, but only *within their territories*. The Court held that measures permitted on that basis were limited to strictly territorial boundaries, and could relate only

---

[157] Case 118/86 *Nertsvoederfabriek*, para. 16. Emphasis added. This is also noted by Jans (1995) at 229.

[158] Case C-203/96 *Dusseldorp*, para. 46. See Jans (1999).

[159] Case C-209/98 *Sydhavnens*, and Vedder (2001).

[160] Cases C-5/94 *Hedley Lomas*, para. 18, and C-1/96 *Compassion*, para. 47.

[161] Directive 74/577/EEC, OJ 1974 L 316/10.

[162] Case C-5/94 *Hedley Lomas*, para. 20.

[163] Directive 91/629, OJ 1991 L 340/28.

to cattlefarms falling within the jurisdiction of the Member State in question. Member States were not entitled to adopt stricter measures for the protection of calves other than provisions applying within their territory. An export ban imposed on account of conditions prevailing in other Member States which had implemented the directive would fall outside the derogation provided in the directive. Such a ban would strike at the harmonisation achieved.[164]

In his opinions in *Hedley Lomas* and *Compassion*, Advocate General Léger largely disapproved of the possibility of extraterritorial protection goals. However, in his Opinion in *Compassion*, he did suggest a possibility to justify export restrictions, not on the basis of animal life and health, but where an unjustified impairment of the life or health of animals as a result of the manner in which cattle are raised in another Member State damages public morality or public policy in the *exporting* state. For such a justification to succeed, the damage caused to animals by the manner in which cattle are raised in the other Member State should be objectively demonstrated, and the measure should of course be necessary and proportionate.[165] The Court did not follow Léger's argument and found that the public morality justification was really not self-standing, but accessory to the animal life and health justification.[166]

3.4.5   Tax Parallel

Regarding trade restrictions based on production and processing methods outside the jurisdiction of the Member State taking the measure, a slight side-step is made at this point to the ECJ's jurisprudence on internal taxation. The ECJ has accepted tax differentiation on the basis of PPMs in a number of cases. In *Bobie*, the Court accepted a German beer tax based on the quantity of beer produced by each brewery (to protect small breweries), as long as foreign beer was taxed on the same basis.[167] In *Hansen*, the Court confirmed that Article 90 EC does not prevent Member States from granting tax exemptions to certain classes of producers, when legitimate economic or social purposes are served, such as the use of certain raw materials or the continuance of certain classes of undertakings. However, any such tax advantages must be extended to imported Community spirits fulfilling the same conditions.[168] In *Commission-Italy (Regenerated Oil)*, Italy fiscally favoured regenerated oil over oil of primary distillation in order to protect the Italian regenerating industry. The end-products were physically identical and served the same economic ends,

---

[164] Case C-1/96 *Compassion*, paras. 59, 60 and 62.

[165] AG Léger in Case C-1/96 *Compassion*.

[166] Case C-1/96 *Compassion*, para. 66.

[167] Case 127/75 *Bobie*.

[168] Case 148/77 *Hansen*.

but the production costs of regenerated oil were much higher than of primary destination oil. The Court accepted that the tax favour was justified to help regenerators meet the high costs of regeneration and compete with primary oils, but insisted that this favour should be extended to imported regenerated oils. Difficulties in comparing imported with domestic products were no reason to deny advantages to imports. It was for the importers wishing to qualify for the reduced rate to produce evidence that the oils they imported were regenerated, and Italy could require evidence of this, e.g. demanding certificates from the authorities or other appropriate bodies of the exporting Member States.[169]

Thus, internal taxes may differentiate on the basis of objective criteria without regard to product origin, including the raw materials used or production processes employed, as long as there is no discrimination or protection, i.e. as long as any tax advantages are extended to imports. This implies that a differentiated rate according to production methods for domestic products, accompanied by a flat rate for imports will only be acceptable if no domestic product is charged less than the flat rate for imports. Moreover, tax differentiation is compatible with Community law only if it pursues objectives which are themselves compatible with the Treaty and its secondary legislation. These principles were confirmed in *Chemial Farmaceutici* and more recently in *Outukumpu Oy*, where the Court explicitly said that a tax differentiation according to PPMs based on environmental considerations is acceptable, as long as importers are given an opportunity to demonstrate the PPM applied in producing the imported electricity so as to qualify for a favourable rate.[170]

This consistent case-law regarding tax differentiations may be taken to suggest that a national *regulatory* measure differentiating products according to their production methods and allowing imported products to be marketed if accompanied by a certificate or label stating their production method might be acceptable under Articles 28-30 EC. However, there are several problems with a parallel reading of the tax and regulatory EC Treaty regime. First, no exceptions provision like Article 30 (ex 36) EC exists for taxes as it does for regulatory measures. Secondly, Article 90 finds its counterpart in Articles 23 and 25 (ex 9 and 12). Thus, the EC Treaty separates border taxes and internal taxes. No such separation exists for regulatory measures, Article 28 covering both quantitative restrictions (border regulation) and measures having equivalent effect (which may be either border or internal regulatory measures). Thirdly, it is generally easier to ascertain whether an imported product is "discriminated" against in tax cases than in regulatory cases. For taxes, it is a matter of establishing whether two products are similar, and whether one is taxed in excess of the other.

---

[169] Case 21/79 *Commission* v. *Italy* (*Regenerated Oils*).

[170] Cases 140/79 *Chemial Farmaceutici* and C-213/96 *Outukumpy Oy*.

Arguably, parallel interpretations of provisions differently structured and located in the Treaty should not readily be assumed.

3.4.6   Evaluation

Thus, neither the Court's case-law, nor the opinions of Advocates-General provide any conclusive answer to the question whether unilateral extraterritorial protection is acceptable under Articles 28-30, and if so, under what circumstances or conditions. Despite the scarce case-law on the subject and the contradictory opinions of Advocates-General, a number of authors argue that, in principle, Article 30 does not preclude protection of the environment, life and health in another Member State.[171]

Although the Court's findings in *Compassion* could be read as an outright denial of the possibility of extraterritorial environmental protection measures, it should be borne in mind that the case concerned a situation of existing relevant Community legislation. If a Community directive lays down minimum environmental standards on production circumstances, allowing a Member State to be stricter within its territory, it is not allowed to limit its exports to another Member State that has chosen to implement the minimum Community standards, but not to be stricter. The balance between environmental objectives and the free movement of goods has been struck at Community level, whereby the minimum standards are to be deemed acceptable to all Member States. A Member State is allowed to go beyond the acceptable level, but it cannot impose stricter standards on other Member States. Arguably, the situation is different in the absence of any relevant Community harmonisation. No acceptable minimum level has been agreed upon in that situation, so Member States should have more leeway to decide what is acceptable to them. The current author would therefore disagree with those interpreting the *Compassion* judgment as an outright prohibition of any extraterritorial protection.

Nevertheless, unilateral actions aimed at protecting the environment outside the borders of the Member State taking the measure will not be easily accepted, as the institutional structure of the Community risks being undermined when Member States take action according to their own judgements rather than following the appropriate path of setting items on the Brussels agenda. When the Court is confronted with such unilateral actions, it will have to decide whether they are in principle contrary to Articles 28 or 29, and if so, whether they are justified. When assessing their justifications, the Court will have to make clear whether it views extraterritorial protection as illegitimate *per se*, i.e.

---

[171] Sevenster (1998); Jans (1995) at 232. Krämer (1993b) at 118-119, noticeably only mentions life and health of animals and plants, not of humans. He does not explain why he thinks that only the stricter application area of "life and health", and not the "rule of reason" could possibly justify such measures.

as a justification ground not covered by Article 30 or the mandatory requirements, or whether it is acceptable in principle. If the Court takes the latter view,
it will apply the proportionality test to the measure. Both the suitability and the
necessity of the measure may be expected to be severely scrutinised, and perhaps
the Court will apply a strict proportionality test too.

Considerations that may play a role in the assessment of extraterritorial
measures are the following: whether imports or exports are affected; whether
protection of the environment as a mandatory requirement, or the life and health
protection grounds in Article 30 are invoked; and the extent to which harmonisation is in place. Also important will be the location of the interest protected. The
object of the environmental or life and health protection aim may be located fully
within another Member State, or partially in another Member State, or outside
any jurisdiction. It may be transboundary or migratory.

3.5 Concluding Remarks

This Chapter has described and analysed the rich case-law of
the European Court of Justice in the field of the free movement of goods and
justifications for national measures pursuing environmental and health protection. Much attention has been paid to the scope of the prohibition of 'measures
having equivalent effect to quantitative restrictions' in Article 28. The findings
by the Court as to the scope of this concept are of paramount importance, even if
they do not directly concern environmental or health measures. This is because
environmental or health justifications and the conditions laid down for their
acceptance only come into play once a measure has been found to fall within the
scope of the prohibition of 'measures having equivalent effect'.

As regards the scope of the prohibition in Article 28, several recurring
themes may be identified. First of all, the Court has proclaimed that as a matter
of principle, any national action - or even inaction - may infringe Article 28
if posing an *obstacle* to intra-Community trade. Secondly, in order to further
specify and also to delimit this very wide prohibition, the Court has applied
various *typologies* of national measures. The most important types of measures
identified by the Court are "selling arrangements" and "product requirements".
The Court has also found that a number of measures are outside the scope of
Article 28 because their link with trade is remote and tenuous. Thirdly, the
Court has applied *discrimination tests* in various instances. One is the requirement that national "selling arrangements" are outside the scope of Article 28 if
they affect in the same manner in law and in fact the marketing of domestic
and imported goods. Another is the formula applied to price measures, and yet
another the interpretation of Article 29, which prohibits export restrictions and
measures having equivalent effect. Finally, other themes recur in the Court's

case-law, whose role is difficult to define. These are, market access, e.g., the obligation in *Cassis* to grant market access to goods lawfully produced and marketed in another Member State; the as yet unclear role of market access with regard to selling arrangements in *Keck*; and the aim or intent of national measures, e.g. when finding that measures fall outside the scope of Article 28, the Court sometimes observes that they are not designed to regulate trade, or are not aimed at imports.

Tests delimiting the ambit of Article 28 identify the cases in which the Court is not the appropriate institution to assess the interests involved by assessing justifications and applying conditions to justifications. As seen, such tests may be based on typologies of measures, or on obstacles to trade, or on discriminatory or protectionist effects or intent, or on combinations of these criteria. History has shown that discrimination and protectionism tests sometimes do not go far enough, while obstacle tests go too far. Typologies alone cannot delimit the ambit of Article 28, as they leave open the question what kind of criterion (Obstacle? Discrimination? Market access?) should apply to what type of measures. Moreover, as clearly shown by *Keck*, typologies result in grey areas. On the basis of criticisms of all tests applied so far to delimit the ambit of Article 28, it has been argued that the interests involved should already play a role in the delimitation of Article 28, and thereby of the identification of situations in which the Court should be balancing interests.[172] However, how these interests should be identified and how they should affect the ambit of Article 28 is difficult to imagine.

Although none of the tests identified above are satisfactory, some test or combination of tests will have to be applied by the Court in order to delimit the ambit of Article 28. But that is not the end of the exercise. Once the Court has been established as the institution best suited to balancing the interests involved, it will balance the interest of the free movement of goods and the justifications put forward. The question then arises how the Court should perform this balancing exercise. The Community interest in the free movement of goods will coincide with the economic interests of traders and consumers in the importing country, but also with those of producers in Member States which have possibly been under-represented in the national decision-making process. Whether the Court should also take into account non-economic interests in other Member States will mostly be relevant in the context of so-called extraterritorial protection measures.

Once found to fall within the scope of Article 28, a national measure may be justified under the exceptions in Article 30 or under the "mandatory requirements" as recognised by the Court, if it complies with certain conditions. In this respect, the following observations may be made on the basis of the analysis

---

[172] Poiares Maduro (1998a).

in this Chapter. The conditions applied by the Court to justifications based on both Article 30 and mandatory requirements are often dubbed "proportionality". Proportionality in the wide sense comprises the suitability of the measure to contribute to the aim pursued; the necessity of the measure in the sense that no equally effective but less trade-restrictive measures are available; and finally and most controversially, "strict proportionality", which requires a proportionate relationship between the aim of the measure and its trade-hindering effect. The Court applies these conditions in essentially the same way with regard to justifications under Article 30 and under the mandatory requirements, usually refraining from testing "strict proportionality".

Should the Court confine itself to assessing the suitability and necessity of the measure, or also apply a strict proportionality test, i.e. actually weighing the interests involved, balancing the degree to which trade is restricted with the perceived importance of the non-trade aim pursued, and in some cases also the contribution of the measure to that aim? The current author submits that in the absence of an agreed Community-wide level of protection, the Court should be very reluctant to interfere with levels of protection chosen by Member States by applying the proportionality test *stricto sensu*. This is so even if the high level of protection chosen by a Member State necessitates measures that severely restrict trade. Possibly, the Court in applying a strict proportionality test to national measures can correct national biases and thereby protect the Community interest in safeguarding the free movement of goods.[173] However, to the extent that biases in the national decision-making process are the result of interests reflected in national democratic procedures, it seems questionable whether the Court and not the Community legislator is the appropriate institution to correct such biases. Apart from this possibility to correct national biases, there is no reason for the Community Court to replace the national legislature any more than to replace the Community legislature.

Thus, if the "appropriateness" and "necessity" tests are fulfilled, i.e. there is a causal connection between the measure and the goal, and there are no alternative less trade-restrictive measures that are likely to result in similar levels of attainment of the environmental or health objective, the Court should condemn a national measure only when its trade effects are manifestly disproportionate to its goal.[174] Measures will mostly be deemed manifestly disproportionate when the Court suspects national authorities of pursuing objectives other than merely the environmental or health goal claimed. It may have recourse to the second sentence of Article 30 in cases where life and health justifications are invoked, and may read a similar requirement into the proportionality test for mandatory

---

[173] Cf. Poiares Maduro (1998a).

[174] Cf. the Court's reference to the effectiveness of alternative measures in attaining the protection aim in cases C-473/98 *Toolex Alpha* and C-124/97 *Läärä*.

requirements. This approach seems to be in line with the division of competencies between the Community and Member States and between legislative and judicial bodies.

The one difference the Court applies with regard to the mandatory requirements *vis-à-vis* the grounds in Article 30 is that it only accepts the former as justification for measures that are "indistinctly applicable" to imported and domestic goods. It is submitted, however, that this limitation to the invocation of mandatory requirements is no longer tenable. Of course, national legislators should still preferably choose "indistinctly applicable" means to pursue legitimate aims, but sometimes a "distinctly applicable" measure will be necessary to pursue a mandatory requirement. An additional benefit of dropping the requirement *per se* that mandatory requirements can only be pursued through indistinctly applicable measures is that the confusion may be ended over how to define and distinguish distinctly and indistinctly applicable measures, and over what role the various concepts of discrimination play in this respect. The preference for indistinctly applicable measures does not need to be dropped by the Court. It can still be reflected in the necessity requirement. A distinctly applicable measure will be deemed unnecessary if an indistinctly applicable measure is available as a less trade-restrictive alternative.

According to the principle of "mutual recognition", Member States must accept goods lawfully produced and marketed in other Member States; if they do not, they have to justify why. Thus, production methods in other Member States should in principle be accepted. Moreover, any Member State wishing to apply its own production requirements to products imported from other Member States encounters the practical problem of how to check whether those products conform to its production standards. It would either have to perform checks on production sites in other Member States, or require imported products to be labelled or certified. Both possibilities appear problematic in the light of the principle of "mutual recognition" and the mutual trust on which the relations between Member States of the Community is built. Mutual trust and the solidarity requirement in Article 10 EC may also be an obstacle in accepting unilateral measures by Member States aimed at protecting the environment outside their borders, and especially in other Member States. Such measures do not necessarily concern production methods. The case-law on extraterritorial protection has in fact addressed more export restrictions than import restrictions. Although the case-law is inconclusive as to the acceptability of extraterritorial protection, the current author contends that it should not be prohibited *per se*, but should be assessed with strong scrutiny in terms of its suitability and necessity.

Finally, it should be noted that more and more Community harmonising legislation is being enacted in the fields of environmental and health protection. Within the material scope of such legislation, the room for national measures is primarily determined by the provisions in the relevant Community legislation. However, Articles 28-30 of the Treaty remain applicable when Member States apply stricter measures, sometimes directly, as provided in Article 176, sometimes indirectly, as a source of inspiration in the Commission's assessment under paragraphs 4-6 of Article 95. And of course, Articles 28-30 remain fully applicable to all those situations where Member States take measures regarding subject-matters of environmental or health protection not covered by Community harmonisation.

There is a certain interaction between Community harmonising legislation on the one hand, and the control over Member States' measures under the primary Treaty Articles on the other. First, the Commission acts as a "watchdog" through its competencies under the infringement procedure in Article 226. It can thus ask the Court to find that a national environmental or health measure infringes Article 28 without being justified as reasonable. At the same time, the Commission can initiate legislation to remove trade barriers caused by national measures, including if the Court upholds a national measure. Secondly, as the Commission is instrumental in devising Community legislation, it is involved in determining the room left for Member States under such legislation. Under Article 95, it actively controls and assesses the reasonability of Member States' measures that are more stringent.

PART THREE

Trade and Environment in the World Trade Organisation

CHAPTER 4

The Main Provisions and Their Interpretation

4.1 Introduction: The Havana Charter, GATT 1947, and GATT 1994

Conscious of the role that increasing trade protectionism had played in the run-up to World War II, countries started multilateral trade negotiations shortly after the war. The prelude to these negotiations was essentially an Anglo-American affair. The United States and the United Kingdom had already discussed plans on reconstructing the world trading system in the postwar period. In December 1945, the US Department of State issued a document entitled 'Proposals for Consideration by an International Conference on Trade and Employment', which was part of its 'Proposals for Expansion of World Trade and Employment'. On the same day, the Government of the UK published the same proposals expressing its full agreement on all important points therein and accepting them as a basis for international discussion. The UN Economic and Social Council thereupon called a UN Conference on Trade and Employment (UNCTE) in February 1946. It also established a Preparatory Committee of the UNCTE to prepare for consideration at the Conference an agenda and a draft convention or charter for an International Trade Organisation (ITO). On the basis of the proposals by the US and the UK, deliberations were held under the United Nations' auspices in London, New York, Geneva and Havana.[1] In Geneva, a draft ITO charter was agreed upon in August 1947.

Parallel to its second session, the Preparatory Committee held a round of trade and tariff negotiations. This round was to result in 'Procedures for Giving Effect to Certain Provisions of the Charter of the International Trade Organization by Means of a General Agreement on Tariffs and Trade Among the Members of the Preparatory Committee'. The text of the General Agreement on Tariffs and Trade (GATT), signed in October 1947, was based on the commercial policy provisions of the Geneva draft Charter. The Havana Conference, which was held from late 1947 to March 1948, resulted in the 'Final Act and Related Documents of the United Nations Conference on Trade and Employment, including the text of the Havana Charter for an International Trade Organization'. The fifth chapter of the Final Act included roughly the same provisions on commercial policy as the Geneva draft and the GATT. The Havana Conference also established an Interim Commission for the International Trade Organization (ICITO). However, the Havana Charter never entered into force and the ITO was not realised.[2] The General Agreement on Tariffs and Trade

---

[1]   See UN Documents E/CONF.2/.. and GATT (1995).

[2]   The main reason for this appears to be that the Charter had never been accepted by the United States Congress, which restrained other countries from depositing their acceptances of the Charter. In late 1950, the US Department of State issued a statement of policy to the effect that the Havana Charter would not again be submitted to Congress.

was definitively accepted by only two governments, and as such never entered into force either. However, in contrast to the Havana Charter, the GATT did become operational in practice. It was applied provisionally by its contracting parties under the Protocol of Provisional Application and subsequent Protocols of Accession.

At the first three sessions of the GATT contracting parties held in 1948 and 1949, amendments were agreed to bring the GATT text closer to that of the Havana Charter. It was decided to replace Articles III, VI and XVIII GATT by their Havana counterparts. These changes entered into force in 1948.[3] In 1955, a Protocol Amending the Preamble and Parts II and III of the GATT entered into force. This Protocol resulted in the insertion into the GATT text of the interpretative notes to *inter alia* Article III which had been agreed upon in Havana. Since then, the text of GATT 1947 has only been changed by the 1965 Protocol to Introduce a Part IV on Trade and Development. GATT 1947, as provisionally applied, has provided the working basis for the regulation of international trade relations for almost 50 years.

During the provisional application of the GATT, a number of negotiating rounds on tariff bindings and other commitments were held. The last of these, the Uruguay Round, lasted from 1986 to 1994 and resulted in the Agreement Establishing the World Trade Organisation. Annexed to the WTO Agreement are several multilateral agreements on trade in goods, among which are the GATT 1994, agreements on trade in services and on trade-related aspects of intellectual property rights, an understanding on dispute settlement, a trade policy review mechanism, and a small number of "plurilateral agreements". With the exception of the latter, the WTO Agreements constitute a "single package" for all WTO Members. On 1 January 1996, a year after the WTO Agreements entered into force, the provisional application of the GATT was terminated. "GATT 1994" now forms an integral part of the WTO "single package" cluster of agreements, as part of Annex 1A to the WTO Agreement. GATT 1994 is no more than GATT 1947 as subsequently amended, to which a number of Understandings on specific GATT provisions and the Marrakesh Protocol containing the tariff commitments agreed upon in the Uruguay Round have been added.

4.1.1 Interpretation in Accordance with the Vienna Convention

Article 23 of the WTO Dispute Settlement Understanding (DSU) essentially provides that WTO Members when making a claim concerning WTO rules, must have recourse to and abide by the DSU rules. This

---

[3] Likewise, Article XXIX was reworded and some other minor amendments were made. Protocol Modifying Part II and Article XXVI of the General Agreement on Tariffs and Trade, signed at Geneva 14 September 1948, entered into force 14 December 1948, 62 UNTS 80.

requirement may be read as a claim to exclusive jurisdiction for panels and the Appellate Body in any dispute involving WTO rules. This claim may result in conflicts where other rules of public international law are also involved in a dispute, and concurring claims are made at other tribunals.[4] However, this strong jurisdictional claim should not be taken to imply that WTO rules are to be interpreted in "clinical isolation" from other public international law. On the contrary, according to Article 3.2 DSU, the WTO dispute settlement system serves *inter alia* to clarify the existing provisions of the covered agreements 'in accordance with customary rules of public international law'.

The Appellate Body has on various occasions stressed the need to achieve such clarification of the WTO rules by reference to the fundamental rule of treaty interpretation set out in Article 31(1) of the *Vienna Convention*.[5] According to that rule, 'a treaty shall be interpreted in good faith in accordance with the ordinary meaning to be given to the terms of the treaty in their context and in the light of its object and purpose.'[6] Accordingly, the interpretation of WTO provisions must 'begin with, and focus upon, the text of the particular provision to be interpreted. It is in the words constituting that provision, read in their context, that the object and purpose of the states parties to the treaty must first be sought. Where the meaning imparted by the text itself is equivocal or inconclusive, or where confirmation of the correctness of the reading of the text itself is desired, light from the object and purpose of the treaty as a whole may usefully be sought.'[7] As the Appellate Body has emphasised, the general rule of interpretation in Article 31 of the Vienna Convention has attained the status of a rule of customary or general international law.[8] So has Article 32 of the Vienna Convention on supplementary means of interpretation.[9] That provision however only becomes relevant when the interpretation according to Article 31

---

[4] That such a situation is far from inconceivable in the environmental sphere is illustrated by the Swordfish dispute between the EC and Chile. In this dispute, provisions of both WTO Agreements and the UN Convention on the Law of the Sea (UNCLOS) were invoked. The dispute was settled amicably, and proceedings were suspended both in the WTO and before the UNCLOS tribunal. See OJ (2000) L 96/67, and http://www.europa.eu.int/comm/trade/miti/dispute/swordfish.html.

[5] See the Appellate Body Reports in *US-Gasoline*, at p. 17; *Japan-Alcohol*, at pp. 10-12; *India-Patent Protection*, paras. 45-46; *Argentina-Footwear*, para. 47; and *EC-LAN*, adopted 22 June 1998, para. 85. Hereinafter, WTO Appellate Body reports are referred to as 'AB in [...]', followed by their abbreviated title, WTO panel reports as 'panel in [...]' followed by their abbreviated title, and GATT panel reports simply by their abbreviated title.

[6] The text of Article 31 of the Vienna Convention on the Law of Treaties is found in the Annex to this work. On the Vienna Convention, see Reuter (1995).

[7] AB in *US-Shrimp-Turtle*, para. 114.

[8] AB in *US-Gasoline*, at p. 17.

[9] See the text of Article 32 in the Annex to this work.

leaves the meaning ambiguous or obscure, or leads to a manifestly absurd or unreasonable result.[10] As the Appellate Body has put it, the words of the treaty form the foundation for the interpretative process. The provisions of the treaty are to be given their ordinary meaning in their context. The object and purpose of the treaty are also to be taken into account in determining the meaning of its provisions. That is, the treaty's "object and purpose" are to be referred to in determining the meaning of the "terms of the treaty" and not as an independent basis for interpretation. A fundamental tenet of treaty interpretation flowing from the general rule of interpretation set out in Article 31 is the principle of effectiveness.[11]

Article 31.2 of the Vienna Convention defines the context as comprising the text, including its preambles and annexes, and in addition any agreement relating to the treaty entered into between all the parties in connection with the conclusion of the treaty, and any instrument made by one of the parties in connection with the conclusion of the treaty and accepted by the other parties as an instrument related to the treaty. It would appear that the Marrakesh Decision on Trade and Environment qualifies as an agreement relating to the treaty. The WTO Committee on Trade and Environment was set up under that Decision. It contains *inter alia* the following language:

> *Considering that there should not be, nor need be, any policy contradiction between upholding and safeguarding an open, non-discriminatory and equitable multilateral trading system on the one hand, and acting for the protection of the environment, and the promotion of sustainable development on the other,*

> *Desiring to coordinate the policies in the field of trade and environment, and this without exceeding the competence of the multilateral trading system, which is limited to trade policies and those trade-related aspects of environmental policies which may result in significant trade effects for its members [...]*[12]

Article 31.3 further stipulates that the following are to be taken into account together with the context: (a) subsequent agreement between parties; (b) subsequent practice in the application of the treaty; and (c) 'any relevant rules of international law applicable in the relation between parties'.

The Appellate Body has made it clear that adopted GATT and WTO panel reports do not constitute "subsequent practice" within the meaning of Article 31.3(b) of the *Vienna Convention*.[13] Nevertheless,

---

[10] AB in *Japan-Alcohol*, at p. 10.

[11] Ibid., at pp. 11-12.

[12] Marrakesh Decision on Trade and Environment, available at http://www.wto.org.

[13] AB in *Japan-Alcohol*, at p. 14. Adopted panel reports also do not constitute 'other decisions of the CONTRACTING PARTIES to GATT 1947' for the purposes of paragraph 1(b)(iv) of Annex 1A incorporating the GATT 1994 into the WTO Agreement.

[a]dopted panel reports are an important part of the GATT acquis. They are often considered by subsequent panels. They create legitimate expectations among WTO Members, and, therefore, should be taken into account where they are relevant to any dispute.[14]

The Appellate Body provides 'interpretative guidance for future panels'.[15] Thus, although adopted panel and Appellate Body reports are only binding as between the parties to the dispute, and even if it is not entirely clear how they fit into the terms of Article 31 of the Vienna Convention, they play an important role in the interpretation of WTO provisions. When the relevant provisions in this work are examined *infra*, occasional reference will also be made to relevant rules of international law, as these are pursuant to Article 31.2(c) of the Vienna Convention to be taken into account when interpreting WTO provisions.

4.2 Article III:4 GATT: National Treatment Requirement for Internal Regulation

It is self-evident that in an exercise of their sovereignty, and in pursuit of their own respective national interests, the Members of the WTO have made a bargain. In exchange for the benefits they expect to derive as Members of the WTO, they have agreed to exercise their sovereignty according to the commitments they have made in the WTO Agreement. One of those commitments is Article III of the GATT 1994 [...][16]

Because the national treatment obligation affects internal government action so directly, it becomes more quickly embroiled in domestic politics than any other GATT obligation and it may be one that is often breached.[17]

4.2.1 Text and History of Article III GATT

The parts of Article III of the General Agreement on Tariffs and Trade which are relevant for the purpose of this study are reproduced in its Annex. The principle of national treatment dates back to at least the twelfth century, albeit in the context of the treatment of persons rather than

---

[14] Ibid., at p. 14.

[15] AB in *US-Shrimp-Turtle Implementation*, para. 107.

[16] AB in *Japan-Alcolhol*, at p. 16.

[17] Jackson (1969) at 274.

goods.[18] Many commercial treaties concluded around the time of the ITO and GATT negotiations featured national treatment provisions for goods. These often concerned internal taxation.[19] Some provided for national treatment with regard to internal regulation.[20] The 1945 US-UK Proposals contained a National Treatment requirement, which provided that 'Members should undertake: 1. To accord to products from other members treatment no less favorable than that accorded to domestic products with regard to matters affecting the internal taxation and regulation of the trade in goods [...].'[21]

Article 18 of the Geneva draft charter and of the 1947 version of Article III GATT both did not contain a general introductory clause as is now found in Article III:1 GATT. They started off with a national treatment provision on internal taxation, which was substantially different from what was eventually to become Article III:2 GATT.[22] In contrast, the provision on national treatment for internal regulation had almost reached its final shape by the time of the Geneva session. Only during the Havana Conference was a new first paragraph of the

---

[18] VerLoren van Themaat (1981) at 19 et seq.

[19] See e.g. Article II of the 1946 Agreement and Supplemental Exchanges of Notes Between the United States of America and Paraguay; Article IV of the 1946 Agreement between the United States of America and the Republic of the Philippines Concerning Trade and Related Matters During a Transitional Period Following the Institution of Phillippine Independence, reproduced in Kress (1949).

[20] Article XVI:1 of the 1948 Treaty of Friendship, Commerce and Navigation Between the United States of America and the Italian Republic provided that 'Articles the growth, produce or manufacture of either High Contracting Party, imported into the territories of the other High Contracting Party, shall be accorded treatment with respect to all matters affecting internal taxation, or the sale, distribution or use within such territories, no less favorable than the treatment which is or may hereafter be accorded to like articles of national origin.' Reproduced in Kress (1949).

[21] GATT (1995) at 205.

[22] Article 18 of the Geneva Draft provided as follows:
1.The products of any Member country, imported into the territory of any other Member country shall be exempt from internal taxes and other internal charges of any kind in excess of those applied directly or indirectly to like products of domestic origin. Moreover, in cases in which there is no substantial domestic production of like products of national origin, no Member shall apply new or increased internal taxes on the products of the territories of other Member countries for the purpose of affording protection to the production of directly competitive or substitutable products which are not similarly taxed [...].
2.The products of the territory of any Member country imported into the territory of any other Member country shall be accorded treatment no less favourable than that accorded to like products of national origin in respect of all laws, regulations and requirements affecting their internal sale, offering for sale, purchase, transportation, distribution, or use. The provisions of this paragraph shall not prevent the application of differential transportation charges which are based exclusively on the economic operation of the means of transport and not on the nationality of the product. [...]

National Treatment provision introduced, which states in a general manner that both internal taxation and internal regulation should not be applied so as to afford protection to domestic production.[23] The provision on National Treatment for internal regulation was not discussed to a great extent and not substantially amended during the Havana Conference. It was simply renumbered Paragraph 4 instead of Paragraph 2.[24] Subsequently, GATT Article III was replaced by the National Treatment provision of the Havana Charter. The working party on modifications to the General Agreement recognised that '[T]he wording adopted at Havana was clearer and more precise than the text as it now stood.'[25]

At Havana, various delegations proposed amendments and additions to Article 18 of the Geneva draft.[26] Most of the discussions on National Treatment centred on what would become Article III:2 on internal taxation, and more specifically on the reference to protectionism in the second sentence of that paragraph. Already at this early stage, there were differences of opinion between the various delegations as to what exactly the principle of National Treatment embodied and how it related to protectionism.[27] The Committee's draft report to the Conference remarked that 'Article 18 [...] was extensively revised and clarified, but the *general principle* that internal taxes *and regulations* should not be applied in such a manner *as to afford protection* to domestic production was *preserved*'.[28] Apparently, the Committee understood the National Treatment provision as containing a general principle of non-protectionism, both in its Geneva and Havana drafts and concerning both internal taxation and internal regulation. This is striking, as the general formulation of the principle in the new first paragraph referring to both taxation and regulation was only introduced at Havana.

---

[23] According to the documents, the new paragraph 1 was inserted somewhere between 9 January 1948 (see E/CONF.2/C.3/6/Add.5) and 16 February 1948 (see E/CONF.2/C.3/59).

[24] This was the result of the insertion of the general clause that became the first paragraph, and of a clause on existing national taxes, which became the third paragraph of the National Treatment provision.

[25] GATT/CP. 2/22/Rev.1, II/39, paras. 4 and 11.

[26] For an overview, see E/CONF.2/C.3/6.

[27] E/CONF.2/11/Add.9: proposal by China to delete the second sentence, arguing that a rule on protection did not form part of National Treatment as it was generally understood. E/CONF.2/C.3/SR.11, at p. 1: US opinion that this particular provision strengthened the principle of national treatment and prevented its abuse. E/CONF.2/C.3/SR.9, at p. 7: The Chairman of Committee 3, dealing with *inter alia* the National Treatment provision, thought that this provision embodied 'the principle that domestic industries should not be protected through taxation'.

[28] The Committee further observed that a special Working Party had been established on the subject of protection, whose report, however, contained no definite recommendations, and did not result in changes in the text. Report of the Working Party: E/CONF.2/C.3/71. See also E/CONF.2/C.3/89/Add.3, at p. 9.

The proposals at Havana regarding regulatory National Treatment were mostly limited to the second sentence thereof, which addresses differential transportation charges.[29] The only proposal in more general terms was made by Norway, which suggested adding a new paragraph to Article 18, to the effect that the national treatment requirement would not apply to 'laws, regulations and requirements which (a) have the purpose of standardizing products in order to improve the quality or to reduce the costs of production, or (b) have the purpose of facilitating an improved organization of internal industry; provided they have no harmful effect on the expansion of international trade.'[30] The Norwegian delegation withdrew the proposal when it was reassured by the Sub-Committee that such internal regulatory measures as envisaged by its proposal would not contravene Article 18 anyway.[31] Thus, apparently, little or no discussion was needed to agree on the fact that internal rules regarding product standards would not be prohibited by Article 18.[32]

4.2.2 Eliminating Discrimination and Avoiding Protectionism

The general context of Article III GATT is constituted by the last paragraph of the preamble to GATT 1994 and the third paragraph of the preamble to the WTO Agreement, which both read:

Being desirous of contributing to these objectives by entering into reciprocal and mutually advantageous arrangements directed to the substantial reduction of tariffs and other barriers to trade and to the elimination of discriminatory treatment in international commerce

In *Japan-Alcohol*, the Appellate Body stated that the broad and fundamental purpose of Article III is to avoid protectionism in the application of internal tax and regulatory measures.[33] The Appellate Body observed that Article III protects expectations not of any particular trade volume, but rather of the equal competitive relationship between imported and domestic products.[34] It has since repeated these statements in a number of reports.[35] The purpose of avoiding protectionism is most clearly present in the first paragraph of Article III, which

---

[29] E/CONF.2/C.3/1/Add. 43 and 52.

[30] E/CONF.2/C.3/1/Add. 39.

[31] E/CONF.2/C.3/59, at p. 10.

[32] The final text of Article 18 of the Havana Charter appeared in the Report of the Conference - Final Act and Related Documents, E/CONF.2/78, also published as ICITO/4.

[33] AB in *Japan-Alcohol*, page 16.

[34] Ibid., referring (in the original footnote 36) to *US-Superfund*, para. 5.1.9.

[35] AB in *Korea-Alcohol*, para. 119; AB in *Chile-Alcohol*, para. 135. Cf. the panel in *Chile-Alcohol*, para. 7.8.

constitutes the immediate context of Article III:4. However, the adhortative wording ("should") in the first paragraph of Article III contrasts with the more forceful language of the second paragraph addressing internal taxation and the fourth paragraph addressing internal regulation.

The GATT panel in *US-Beer* observed that because Article III:1 is a more general provision than either Article III:2 or III:4, it would 'not be appropriate' for the panel to consider Canada's Article III:1 allegations to the extent that the panel were to find US measures to be inconsistent with the 'more specific provisions' of Article III:2 and III:4.[36] This panel considered that Article III:1 would only come into play separately if and when Article III:4 (and for that matter, Article III:2) had been found not to have been infringed. The WTO panel in *US-Gasoline* agreed with the above reasoning, and therefore did not examine the consistency of the US Gasoline Rule with Article III:1 after having found that it infringed Article III:4.[37] The Appellate Body in *Japan- Alcohol* observed that:

> *Article III:1 articulates a general principle that internal measures should not be applied so as to afford protection to domestic production. This general principle informs the rest of Article III. The purpose of Article III:1 is to establish this general principle as a guide to understanding and interpreting the specific obligations contained in Article III:2 and in the other paragraphs of Article III, while respecting, and not diminishing in any way, the meaning of the words actually used in the texts of those other paragraphs.*[38]

As the italicised passage from *Japan-Alcohol* shows, in the Appellate Body's view the principle in Article III:1 also informs Article III:4. This was confirmed by the Appellate Body in *EC-Asbestos*, which noted that Article III:1 has particular contextual significance in interpreting Article III:4, as it sets forth the "general principle" pursued by that provision.[39] The panels in *Canada-Periodicals* and in *EC-Bananas III* considered it necessary to make a separate finding on Article III:1 after having found an infringement of Article III:4.[40] In *Canada-Periodicals*, neither of the parties raised this point on appeal and the Appellate Body did not correct the panel. However, in *EC-Bananas III*, the Appellate Body decided that this was not a correct reading of the way in which Article III:1 informs Article III:4. As Article III:4 does not specifically refer to Article III:1, a determination of whether Article III:4 has been violated does not require any separate consid-

---

[36] *US-Beer*, para. 5.2.

[37] Panel in *US-Gasoline*, para. 6.17.

[38] AB in *Japan-Alcohol*, at p. 17-18.

[39] AB in *EC-Asbestos*, paras. 93 and 98.

[40] Panel in *Canada-Periodicals*, paras. 5.37-38; panel in *EC-Bananas III*, paras. 7.181 and 7.249.

eration of whether a measure affords protection to domestic production.[41] The Appellate Body in *EC-Asbestos* said that the term "less favourable treatment" expresses the general principle, in Article III:1, that internal regulations 'should not be applied ... so as to afford protection to domestic production'.[42]

4.2.3 Article III:2 GATT: National Treatment for Internal Taxation

Also part of the immediate context of Article III:4 is Article III:2, its counterpart regarding internal taxation. Contrary to Article III:4, Article III:2 does not contain a single sentence covering "like products". It consists of two separate sentences, one dealing with "like products" and the other expressly referring to the principles set forth in paragraph 1 of Article III. The Note Ad Article III:2 clarifies that the second sentence applies to 'directly competitive or substitutable products'. In *Japan-Alcohol*, the Appellate Body made it clear that in order to show that a tax measure is inconsistent with the general principle set out in the first sentence, the presence of a protective application need not be established separately from the specific requirements laid down in the first sentence. However, this does not mean that the general principle of Article III:1 does not apply to the first sentence. Rather, the first sentence of Article III:2 is an application of this general principle. Thus, the first sentence of Article III:2 merely requires a finding of "like" imported and domestic products and taxes applied to the imported products 'in excess of' those applied to the like domestic products.[43] The second sentence does require a separate finding of protectionist application, in addition to a finding of directly competitive or substitutable products and dissimilar taxation which is not *de minimis*.[44] As regards the interpretation of "protective application", the Appellate Body noted in *Japan-Alcohol* that '[t]his is not an issue of *intent*. [...] This is an issue of how the measure in question is *applied*.'[45] Examining this requires a comprehensive and objective analysis of the structure and application of the measure in question on domestic as compared to imported products:

[I]t is possible to examine objectively the underlying criteria used in a particular tax measure, its structure, and its overall application to ascertain whether it is applied in a way that affords protection to domestic products. Although it is true that the aim of a measure may not be easily ascertained, nevertheless its protective application can most often be discerned from the design, the architecture, and the revealing structure of a measure.[46]

---

[41] AB in *EC-Bananas III*, para. 216.

[42] AB in *EC-Asbestos*, para. 100.

[43] AB in *Japan-Alcohol*, at p. 18-19

[44] Ibid., at p. 24.

[45] Ibid., at p. 28.

[46] Ibid., at p. 29.

The Appellate Body further noted that the very magnitude of the dissimilar taxation in a particular case may be evidence of protective application. Most often, there will be other factors that need consideration as well. In conducting this inquiry, panels should give full consideration to all the relevant facts and all the relevant circumstances in any given case. For example, in *Canada-Periodicals*, the Appellate Body looked *inter alia* at statements by government officials regarding the policy objectives pursued by the measure at issue, and found ample evidence that the very design and structure of the measure at issue was such as to afford protection to domestic periodicals.[47] In *Korea-Alcohol*, the panel found that the tax scheme in question had a discriminatory structure, with domestic producers being almost exclusively the beneficiaries, a finding that was upheld by the Appellate Body.[48]

In *Chile-Alcohol*, the Appellate Body made it clear that the objective of Article III is to 'provide equality of competitive conditions for *all* directly competitive or substitutable imported products in relation to domestic products, and not simply for *some* of these imported products.'[49] Therefore, the assessment under the second sentence of Article III:2 must take into account the whole group of directly competitive or substitutable products, also when it is broader than simply the products within each fiscal category.[50] Likewise, the relative proportion of domestic versus imported products *within* a particular fiscal category is not in and of itself decisive as regards the appropriate characterisation of the total impact of the measure under Article III:2, second sentence; it is the *cumulative consequences* of the measure as a whole that will be assessed.[51] In the same case, the panel had considered the absence of a clear relationship between a tax measure and its stated objectives as 'evidence confirming the discriminatory design, structure and architecture of the measure.'[52] On appeal, Chile argued that the panel had been wrong to consider the objectives underlying the measure. In response, the Appellate Body said that the purposes of a measure, objectively manifested in its design, architecture and structure, are 'intensely pertinent' to whether or not the measure is applied so as to afford protection. The Appellate Body noted that explanations regarding the structure of the tax scheme might have been helpful in understanding what *'prima facie* appeared to be anomalies in the progression of tax rates'. Thus, concluding that there is a case of protective application [on the basis of the design and structure of the measure] becomes very difficult to resist in the absence of 'countervailing

---

[47] AB in *Canada-Periodicals*, at p. 31.

[48] Panel in *Korea-Alcohol*, paras. 10.101-102; AB in *Korea-Alcohol*, para. 150.

[49] AB in *Chile-Alcohol*, para. III.9. Emphasis in the original.

[50] Ibid.

[51] Ibid., para. V.12. Emphasis added.

[52] Panel in *Chile-Alcohol*, para. 7.154.

explanations' and 'effective rebuttal'. The Appellate Body added that it would be inappropriate under Article III:2, second sentence to examine whether the tax measure is *necessary* for achieving its stated objectives or purposes. However, it considered that the task of relating the observable structural features of the measure with its declared purposes is unavoidable in appraising whether or not the application of the measure is protective of domestic production.[53]

4.2.4 Article III:4 GATT: National Treatment for Internal Regulation

(a) 'Laws, Regulations, and Requirements Affecting their Internal Sale...'

Considering the words 'all laws, regulations and requirements affecting their internal sale, offering for sale, purchase, transportation, distribution or use', the material scope of the National Treatment requirement in Article III:4 is wide.[54] These terms cover basically all laws applicable to a product from the moment it has entered a country's market, i.e. when all customs formalities have been fulfilled. This includes national regulations dealing with circumstances that are not product characteristics, such as laws regulating opening hours for retail outlets, general advertising bans, prohibitions on heavy goods vehicles using roads at night, etc. Although such laws in general will not readily be found to treat imports any less favourably than their domestic counterparts, or otherwise to protect domestic production, they are not *a priori* excluded from the material scope of Article III. Moreover, several GATT and WTO panel reports have found that actions by private parties can constitute "requirements" within the meaning of Article III:4.[55]

As early as 1958, a GATT panel dealt with an Italian argument as to the scope of the GATT in general, and Article III:4 in particular. The panel was confronted with an alleged violation of Article III:4 by Italian measures regarding credits for agricultural machinery. Italy argued the GATT was a trade agreement and its scope was limited to measures governing trade. Therefore, Article III:4 applied only to rules concerned with the actual conditions for the sale, transportation etc., of the good in question and should not be interpreted extensively. In Italy's view, broadly construing the provisions of Article III would limit the rights of GATT contracting parties in the formulation of their domestic economic policies in a way not contemplated when they accepted the terms of the GATT.[56] The

---

[53] AB in *Chile-Alcohol*, paras. V.16-17.

[54] For a comprehensive account of interpretations of the terms in Article III, see GATT (1995).

[55] See e.g. *Canada-FIRA*, para. 5.4; *EEC-Parts and Components*, para. 5.21; panel in *Canada-Auto*, paras. 10.107 and 10.118.

[56] *Italy-Agricultural Machinery*, paras. 6 and 10.

panel rejected these arguments. It had the impression that Italy's contention might have been influenced by the different wording of Article III:4 in the French version.[57] However, the panel did not go into the question whether this textual difference could have any implications for the scope of the provision.[58] Rather, the panel stated that the fact that the Italian law did not specifically prescribe conditions of sale or purchase appeared irrelevant. The intention of the drafters of the GATT was clearly to treat the imported products in the same way as the like domestic products once they had been cleared through customs. Otherwise, indirect protection could be given.[59] The panel noted that the drafters of Article III, when they selected the word "affecting", intended to cover in Paragraph 4 not only the laws and regulations which *directly governed* the conditions of sale or purchase but also any laws or regulations which *might adversely modify the conditions of competition* between the domestic and imported products on the internal market.[60]

More recently, the WTO panel in the *EC-Bananas III* dispute observed that the word "affecting" suggests a coverage of Article III:4 beyond legislation *directly* regulating or governing the sale of domestic and like imported products. According to the panel, when assessing the scope of Article III:4, account should also be taken of the Interpretative Note Ad Article III, which clarifies that the mere fact that an internal charge is collected or a regulation is enforced in the case of an imported product at the time or point of importation does not prevent it from being subject to the provisions of Article III.[61] The panel in *Canada-Auto* stated that the ordinary meaning of the word "affecting" implies a measure that has 'an effect on', which indicates a broad scope of application.[62] The implementation panel in *US-FSC* rejected the argument by the US that when a generally applicable measure is at issue in Article III:4, a "meaningful nexus" must be established between the measure and adverse effects on competitive conditions for a like class of imported products.[63]

---

[57] The French text provided that the imported products *'ne seront pas soumis à un traitement moins favorable'*, i.e. in a negative, prohibitive manner.

[58] It is submitted that the English wording, far from being genuinely imperative as opposed to prohibitive, merely relates to the location of the negation in the sentence. Instead of 'shall be accorded treatment no less favourable', Article III:4 could have read 'shall not be accorded treatment less favourable'. Given the fact that the panel did not even look at this point, and that Article III:2, although having a close relationship with Article III:4, is prohibitively worded, this textual issue probably has little genuine importance.

[59] *Italy-Agricultural Machinery*, para. 11.

[60] Ibid., para. 12. Emphasis by the author.

[61] Panel in *EC-Bananas-III* (Guatemala), para. 7.175. Emphasis added.

[62] Panel in *Canada-Auto*, para. 10.80, referring to the AB report in *EC-Bananas III*, para. 220, interpreting "affecting" in GATS Article XVII, and to *Italian Agricultural Machinery*.

[63] Panel in *US-FSC Implementation*, para. 8.134.

(b) Focus on Products?

To what extent can the sale, offering for sale, etc. of products be affected by laws, regulations and requirements applying to persons and companies rather than to products? There is a great deal of uncertainty surrounding this question. Article III:4 uses the words "the products" and "like products". The GATT panel in *Canada-FIRA* observed that generally, 'the national treatment obligations of Article III of the General Agreement do not apply to foreign persons or firms but to imported *products* and serve to protect the interests of producers and exporters established on the territory of any contracting party'.[64] However, as demonstrated by *Italy-Agricultural Machinery*, this does not mean that laws and regulations not directly bearing on products as such are outside the scope of Article III:4. Other panel reports confirm that products may also be treated less favourably in terms of this provision by measures addressing producers or importers. In *US-Section 337*, the panel observed that the applicability of Article III:4 could not be denied because most of the procedures in the case before it were applied to persons rather than products, since the factor determining whether persons might be susceptible to Section 337 proceedings or federal district court procedures was the source of the challenged products.[65]

In spite of the broad scope of "affecting...", a number of GATT panels and the WTO panel in *US-Gasoline* have taken the view that Article III:4 prohibits the application on imported products of regulations not relating to the product as such. This view has been referred to as the "product-process distinction".[66] Both panels in *US-Tuna-Dolphin I and II* were unclear as to whether Article III only *covers* measures applied to products, or rather only *permits* such measures, which implies it also covers other measures but does not permit them.[67] The panel in *US-Auto Taxes* observed that for a measure to be subject to Article III, it does not have to regulate a product directly. It only has to affect the conditions of competition between domestic and imported products.[68] The panel considered that since conditions of competition could easily be modified by regulations applied directly to producers or importers and not to a product, the direct application of a regulation to a producer did not mean that the regulation could not "affect" the product's conditions of competition.[69] However, when confronted with other measures, the same panel took a different approach. In a textual analysis of Article III, the panel observed that the activities listed in

---

[64] *Canada-FIRA*, para. 6.5.

[65] *US-Section 337*, para. 5.10.

[66] Hudec (2000); Howse and Regan (2000).

[67] These panels are more extensively discussed in Section 5.4.

[68] *US-Auto Taxes*, unadopted, para. 5.45.

[69] Ibid., referring to *US-Section 337*, para. 5.10.

Article III:4 (sale, offering for sale, etc.) 'relate to the *product as a product*, from its introduction into the market to its final consumption. They do not relate directly to the producer'.[70]

The panel noted that a similar principle underlies the treatment of taxes under Article III:2. Referring to the 1970 GATT Working Party Report on Border Tax Adjustments, the panel noted that the domestic taxes permitted to be applied to imports in that Report were based on factors directly related to the product, while those that could not be so applied were not directly related to the product, but to other factors, such as the income of the producer.[71] The panel considered that this 'limitation on the range of domestic policy measures that may be applied also to imported products' reflected one of the central purposes of Article III, i.e. to ensure the security of tariff bindings. Contracting parties could not be expected to negotiate tariff commitments if these could be frustrated through the application of measures affecting imported products subject to tariff commitments and triggered by factors unrelated to the products as such. If it were permissible to *justify under Article III* less favourable treatment to an imported product on the basis of factors not related to the product as such, Article III would not serve its intended purpose.[72] These considerations confirmed, in the view of the panel, the fact that Article III:4 'does not permit' treatment of an imported product less favourable than that accorded to a like domestic product based on factors not directly relating to the product as such. Thus, to the extent that treatment under the US measure was based on factors relating to the control or ownership of producers or importers, it could not 'in accordance with Article III:4 be applied in a manner that also accorded less favourable treatment to products of foreign origin'.[73]

In *US-Gasoline*, The panel observed that the Gasoline Rule distinguished between refiners on the one hand, and importers and blenders on the other, which affected the treatment of imported gasoline with respect to domestic gasoline. This distinction was related to certain differences in the characteristics of refiners, blenders and importers, and the nature of the data held by them. However, the panel observed, 'Article III:4 of the General Agreement deals with the treatment to be accorded to like *products*; its wording *does not allow*

---

[70] Ibid., para. 5.52. Emphasis added.

[71] Ibid., para. 5.52, referring to the Report of the Working Party on Border Tax Adjustments, BISD 18S/97. The panel asserted that the Working Party had interpreted Article III:2 as permitting the application of domestic taxes to imports only when the taxes were directly levied on products. However, the Working Party had only noted that 'there was convergence of views to the effect that *certain* taxes that were not directly levied on products were not eligible for border tax adjustment.' Working Party Report, para. 14. Emphasis added. See further Section 5.4.

[72] Ibid., para. 5.53. Emphasis added.

[73] Ibid., para. 5.54. Emphasis added.

less favourable treatment dependent on the characteristics of the producer and the nature of the data held by it.'[74] The panel noted that in *US-Beer*, a tax regulation according less favourable treatment to beer on the basis of the size of the producer had been rejected.[75] Although this finding had been made under Article III:2 concerning fiscal measures, the panel considered that the same principle applied to regulations under Article III:4. Accordingly, it rejected the US argument that the requirements of Article III:4 had been met because imported gasoline was treated similarly to gasoline from similarly situated domestic parties.[76]

(c) "Like Products"

Whether products are in fact "like" is of obvious importance in the context of Article III:4. Imported products that are not "like" domestic products do not have to be treated "not less favourably" than those domestic products. Therefore, the narrower the term "like" is interpreted, the less the treatment of imports under national regulations will be scrutinised under Article III, and the more room there will be for national regulatory autonomy. The term "like products" occurs in various GATT and WTO provisions, and does not necessarily have the exact same meaning in those different provisions.[77] A 1970 Working Party on Border Tax Adjustments concluded that problems arising from the interpretation of the terms should be examined on a case-by-case basis. The Working Party suggested 'some criteria' for determining whether products qualified as "like" products, which included the product's end-uses in a given market; consumers' tastes and habits, which change from country to country; and the product's properties, nature and quality.[78] Often, in addition to the criteria mentioned by the 1970 Working Party, the tariff classification of products has played a part in "likeness" assessments.[79] However, in the context of tax measures, the WTO Appellate Body has observed that tariff bindings that include a wide range of products are not a reliable criterion for determining or confirming product "likeness" under Article III:2.[80] This could be relevant to

---

[74] Panel in *US-Gasoline*, para. 6.11.

[75] Referring to *US-Beer*, para. 5.19.

[76] Panel in *US-Gasoline*, para. 6.11.

[77] See GATT (1995) at 35: The Preparatory Committee stated that 'the expression had different meanings in different contexts of the Draft Charter'. As noted by Jackson (1969) at 259, the terms "like products" appear in Articles I:1, II:2(a), III:2 and 4, VI:1(a) and (b), IX:1, XI:2(c), XIII:1, and XVI:4. "Like commodity", "like merchandise", and "like or competitive products" occur in Articles VI:7, VII:2, and XIX:1, respectively. The term "like" also features in a number of other WTO Agreements.

[78] Report of the Working Party on Border Tax Adjustments, BISD 18S/97, at 102.

[79] See e.g. *EEC-Food Proteins*, paras. 4.1-4.2, *Japan-Alcohol 1987*, para. 5.6; panel in *US-Gasoline*, para. 6.9.

[80] AB in *Japan-Alcohol Taxes*, at p. 25.

likeness determinations under Article III:4 too. GATT panels, as well as WTO panels and the Appellate Body, have stated that "likeness" cannot be generally defined, and have taken a case-by-case approach, based on the above criteria.[81] A different approach to "likeness" taken by two GATT panels that took into account the objectives of regulatory distinctions in order to determine whether products are "like", known as the "aim and effect" test, appears not to have been accepted under GATT 1994.[82]

When interpreting "like" in the first sentence of Article III:2, the Appellate Body in *Japan-Alcohol* used the following metaphor to illustrate its view of the "likeness" concept:

> *...there can be no one precise and absolute definition of what is "like". The concept of "likeness" is a relative one that evokes the image of an accordion. The accordion of "likeness" stretches and squeezes in different places as different provisions of the WTO Agreement are applied. The width of the accordion in any one of those places must be determined by the particular provision in which the term "like" is encountered as well as by the context and the circumstances that prevail in any given case to which that provision may apply.[83]*

The interpretation of "like products" in Article III:4 was extensively discussed in the *EC-Asbestos* dispute. The panel in that dispute analysed the 'properties, nature and quality' of the products at issue, noting that these have to be evaluated with a view to market access. Even if the structure or chemical composition of the products compared was different, the panel found "likeness", seemingly focusing on the similarity of the products' "end-uses". It found other criteria, such as consumers' tastes and habits or tariff classification, irrelevant or not decisive, and declined to introduce the element of the risk of the products in the likeness determination.[84] *EC-Asbestos* provided the Appellate Body with its first opportunity to interpret the "likeness" issue in the specific context of Article III:4. The Appellate Body reiterated the image of an accordion it had evoked in *Japan-Alcohol*, and noted that three interpretative issues must be resolved: the relevant *characteristics or qualities*; the *degree or extent to which products must share qualities or characteristics* in order to be "like"; and from whose perspective "likeness" should be judged.[85]

---

[81] See e.g., *Germany-Sardines*, at 57; *Australia-Ammonium Sulphate*, at 191; and more recently, e.g. *US-Superfund*, para. 5.1.1, and *Japan-Alcohol 1987*, para. 5.5.

[82] See Section 5.3.3.

[83] AB in *Japan-Alcohol*, at p. 23.

[84] Panel in *EC-Asbestos*, paras. 8.112-8.150. See Wiers (2001).

[85] AB in *EC-Asbestos*, paras. 88 and 92.

The Appellate Body recalled its narrow interpretation of "like" in the first sentence of Article III:2 in *Japan-Alcohol*. However, it pointed to the textual difference between paragraphs 2 and 4 of Article III. This led the Appellate Body to the conclusion that the 'accordion of likeness stretches in a different way in Article III:4.'[86] In its view, if "like" were to be interpreted just as narrowly in paragraph 4 as it had been interpreted in paragraph 2, Members could protect their production by regulatory means while they were prevented from doing so by taxation, which would be incongruous. Thus, in the absence of a second sentence in paragraph 4, "like" in that paragraph has a wider meaning than in paragraph 2, although not broader than the combined product scope of the two sentences of paragraph 2.[87] The Appellate Body further remarked that the general principle in Article III:1 has particular contextual significance in interpreting Article III:4. In its view, "like" in Article III:4 is to be interpreted as applying to products in a competitive relationship in the marketplace. 'Thus, a determination of "likeness" under Article III:4 is *fundamentally* a determination about the nature and extent of a competitive relationship between and among products.'[88] Admitting that by thus interpreting "likeness", it gave Article III:4 a 'relatively broad product scope', the Appellate Body added that if two products are "like", that does not in itself mean that a measure is inconsistent with Article III:4. The other element, "less favourable treatment", must still be established.[89]

Before assessing the panel's "likeness" findings in the actual dispute, the Appellate Body referred to the four general criteria developed in the GATT and the WTO, while slightly rephrasing them.[90] The Appellate Body noted that these criteria do not form a closed list and are often interrelated. At the same time, it criticised the panel for not having examined the evidence 'relating to *each* of those criteria and, then, weighed *all* of that evidence, along with any other relevant evidence, in making an overall determination' of likeness.[91] It also criticised the panel for having used arguments relating to end-uses for its conclusion on properties.[92] The Appellate Body further overturned the panel's

---

[86] Ibid., paras. 94-96.

[87] Ibid., para. 99.

[88] Ibid., paras. 93 and 99. Emphasis added.

[89] See the AB's *obiter dictum* on less favourable treatment quoted in Section 4.2.4, and the discussion in Section 5.3.3.

[90] AB in *EC-Asbestos*, para. 101: (1) physical properties (including nature and quality), (2) the extent to which the products are capable of serving the same or similar end-uses; (3) the extent to which consumers perceive and treat the products as alternative means of performing similar functions in order to satisfy a particular want or demand (in short, consumers' tastes and habits); and (4) tariff classification.

[91] Ibid., para. 109. Emphasis in the original.

[92] Ibid., paras. 110-111.

refusal to introduce "risk" as a factor into the analysis of physical properties
of products as part of the "likeness" assessment. It observed that no evidence
should be *a priori* excluded from a panel's examination of "likeness". On the
contrary, evidence relating to health risks may be pertinent to both physical
properties and consumers' tastes and habits.[93] Noting that chrysotile asbestos
fibres are carcinogenic and the fibres whose "likeness" is examined are not,
or at least not to the same extent, the Appellate Body did not see how 'this
highly significant physical difference' could not be a consideration in examining
physical properties.[94] The Appellate Body noted that in cases where the products
at issue are physically quite different, in order to overcome this indication that
products are *not* "like",

*a higher burden is placed on complaining Members to establish that, despite
the pronounced physical differences, there is a competitive relationship between the
products such that* all *of the evidence, taken together, demonstrates that the products
are "like" under Article III:4 of the GATT 1994.*[95]

In establishing this competitive relationship, the second and third criteria for
"likeness", i.e. end-uses and consumers' tastes and habits, are highly relevant
evidence. A panel cannot conclude that products are "like" if their properties
are very different without examining consumers' tastes and habits.[96] Having
overturned the panel's assessment and findings of "likeness", the Appellate Body
completed the analysis itself, concluding that the appellant, Canada, had not met
its burden of proving that the products at issue were "like".[97] Interestingly, in a
"concurring statement", one of the members of the Appellate Body noted that
in his view the Appellate Body should have gone a step further by finding that
the products at issue were not "like" on the basis of their physical differences
in terms of carcinogenity. This definitive characterisation of the products as not
"like" in his view 'may and should be made even in the absence of evidence
concerning [...] end-uses and consumers' tastes and habits.' It was difficult for
him to imagine how evidence relating to the economic competitive relationship
reflected in those criteria could 'outweigh and set at naught' the physical differences between the products if one of them has been scientifically proven
to be potentially lethal.[98] This further step of turning the physical properties
criterion into a decisive one irrespective of the other criteria was not taken

---

[93] Ibid., para. 113.

[94] Ibid., para. 114.

[95] Ibid., para. 118. Emphasis in the original.

[96] Ibid., para. 121.

[97] Ibid., paras. 141 and 147.

[98] Ibid., para. 152.

by the Appellate Body, he added, because of the other members' conception of the "fundamental", perhaps decisive, role of economic competitive relationships in determining "likeness" under Article III:4. He disagreed with such a "fundamentally" market-based interpretation of "likeness".[99]

The implementation panel in *US-FSC* viewed the principal purpose of the "like product" inquiry under Article III:4 of the *GATT 1994* as 'ascertaining whether any formal differentiation in treatment between an imported and a domestic product could be based upon the fact that the products are different -i.e. not like- rather than on the origin of the products involved.' It observed that the mere fact that a good is of US origin does not render it "unlike" an imported good.[100]

(d) "Treatment No Less Favourable"

Regarding the interpretation of the words "treatment no less favourable", the panel in *Italy-Agricultural Machinery* noted that the intent of the drafters was to provide equal conditions of competition once goods had been cleared through customs.[101] The panel in *US-Section 337* noted that the words "treatment no less favourable" are an expression of the underlying principle of equality of treatment of imported products, and that '[t]he words "treatment no less favourable" in paragraph 4 call for effective equality of opportunities for imported products'.[102] The panel noted that a previous panel had found that the purpose of the first sentence of III:2 on internal taxation is to protect 'expectations on the *competitive relationship* between imported and domestic products'.[103] In the panel's view, Article III:4, which is the parallel provision of Article III dealing with the non-charge elements of internal legislation, had to be construed as serving the same purpose. The *potential* impact of laws, regulations or requirements is decisive, rather than their actual consequences for specific imported products.[104] The requirement of Article III:4 is addressed to 'relative competitive opportunities created by the government in the market, not to the actual choices made by enterprises in that market.'[105] Thus, a measure *capable* of resulting in less favourable treatment of like imported products may infringe Article III:4.[106]

---

[99] Ibid., para. 154: 'The necessity or appropriateness of adopting a "fundamentally" economic interpretation of the "likeness" of products under Article III:4 of GATT 1994 does not appear to me to be free from substantial doubt.'

[100] Panel in *US-FSC Implementation*, paras. 8.132-133.

[101] *Italy-Agricultural Machinery*, para. 13.

[102] *US-Section 337*, para. 5.11. See also *Canada-Beer II*, para. 5.5; *US-Beer*, para 5.30.

[103] Ibid., referring to *US-Superfund*. Emphasis by the author.

[104] *US-Section 337*, para. 5.13. Emphasis by the author.

[105] *US-Malt Beverages*, para. 5.31.

[106] *EC-Oilseeds*, paras. 140-141; panel in *Canada-Auto*, para. 10.78.

Also in *US-Section 337*, the panel made it clear that in its view, *de jure* difference of treatment between imports and like domestic products does not necessarily lead to less favourable treatment:

On the one hand, contracting parties may apply to imported products different formal legal requirements if doing so would accord imported products more favourable treatment. On the other hand, it also has to be recognised that there may be cases where application of formally identical legal provisions would in practice accord less favourable treatment to imported products and a contracting party might thus have to apply different legal provisions to imported products to ensure that the treatment accorded them is in fact no less favourable.[107]

Thus, according to the panel, in cases of formally different treatment, it has to be assessed whether or not such differences in the applicable legal provisions do or do not accord less favourable treatment to imported products. Given that the underlying objective is to guarantee equality of treatment, it is incumbent on the contracting party applying differential treatment to demonstrate that, in spite of such differences, the no less favourable treatment standard of Article III is being met.[108] Apparently ignoring the findings in *US-Section 337*, the WTO panel in *Korea-Beef* found that any regulatory distinction based exclusively on criteria relating to the nationality or origin of products is incompatible with Article III:4.[109] The Appellate Body reversed this finding, emphasising that a measure whose treatment of imported products is *different* from that accorded to like domestic products is not necessarily *inconsistent* with Article III:4. It is the competitive conditions that are decisive:

A formal difference in treatment between imported and like domestic products is thus neither necessary, nor sufficient, to show a violation of Article III:4. Whether or not imported products are treated "less favourably" than like domestic products should be assessed instead by examining whether a measure modifies the conditions of competition in the relevant market to the detriment of imported products.[110]

The Appellate Body in this case focused on 'the fundamental thrust and effect of the measure itself', and concluded that the conditions of competition had indeed been modified to the disadvantage of imported products.[111] The implementation

---

[107] *US-Section 337*, para. 5.11. Emphasis added.

[108] Ibid.

[109] Panel in *Korea-Beef*, para. 627.

[110] AB in *Korea-Beef*, para. 137.

[111] Ibid., paras. 142-148.

panel in *US-FSC* also emphasised that a formal difference in treatment does not necessarily amount to less favourable treatment, and that the analysis does not stop there. It found that the measure at issue created an incentive to use domestic rather than imported goods, which inherently advantaged domestic goods, and thereby concluded that there was a case of less favourable treatment.[112]

Both in relation to Article III:2 and Article III:4, it has been established that the actual trade effects of a disputed measure are not a decisive criterion in determining whether the requirements of these provisions have been met in a given case.[113] In *US-Section 337*, the panel remarked that the no less favourable treatment requirement of Article III:4 has to be understood as being applicable to each individual case of imported products. The panel rejected any notion of balancing the more favourable treatment of some imported products against the less favourable treatment of other imported products.[114] This observation was repeated and concurred with by the WTO panel report in the *US-Gasoline* dispute.[115] It is recalled that although Article III:1 informs Article III:4, a determination of whether there has been a violation of Article III:4 does not require a separate consideration of whether a measure affords protection to domestic production.[116]

In *EC-Asbestos*, the Appellate Body made interesting remarks on the issue of "less favourable treatment", although it did not rule on the issue in the particular case before it. Having said that "like" in Article III:4 covers a potentially broad range of products, the Appellate Body emphasised the significance of the other condition in Article III:4, i.e. less favourable treatment. The Appellate Body stated that the term "less favourable treatment" expresses the general principle in Article III:1 and added that:

> *If there is "less favourable treatment" of the group of "like" imported products, there is, conversely, "protection" of the group of "like" domestic products. However, a Member may draw distinctions between products which have been found to be "like", without, for this reason alone, according to the group of "like" imported products "less favourable treatment" than that accorded to the group of "like" domestic products.[117]*

In the implementation dispute in *US-FSC*, the US argued that there must be evidence that any particular 'class of imported goods' will be accorded less

---

[112] Panel in *US-FSC Implementation*, paras. 154-158.

[113] AB in *Japan-Alcohol*, at p. 16; panel in *EC-Bananas III (ECU)*, para. 7.179.

[114] *US-Section 337*, para. 5.14.

[115] Panel in *US-Gasoline*, para. 6.14.

[116] AB in *EC-Bananas III*, para. 216.

[117] AB in *EC-Asbestos*, para. 100. Emphasis in the original.

favourable treatment than a 'class of like domestic products'. The US further contended that in cases of a generally applicable measure, evidence must be introduced to establish a "meaningful nexus" between the measure and adverse effects on competitive conditions for a like class of imported goods. The panel rejected these arguments in the context of the "likeness" issue, but they appear to refer to all the aspects of Article III:4 discussed above, i.e. the kind of measures covered by Article III:4, "likeness", and "less favourable treatment". The measure at issue was explicitly based on product origin.

4.3   Article XI GATT: Prohibition of Quantitative Restrictions

Article XI is the principal provision of the four GATT Articles containing obligations regarding quantitative restrictions.[118] The text of Article XI GATT is found in the Annex to this work. The second paragraph of Article XI contains a number of exceptions to the general prohibition in the first paragraph, for (a) temporary export prohibitions or restrictions to prevent or relieve critical shortages, (b) import and export prohibitions or restrictions necessary to the application of standards or regulations for the classification, grading or marketing of commodities in international trade,[119] and (c) import restrictions on agricultural or fisheries products necessary to enforce government action to restrict domestic production or marketing, to remove temporary domestic surpluses, or to restrict the production of animal products. During the preparations leading to the GATT and the Havana Charter, the principal prohibition of quantitative restrictions was relatively undisputed.[120] A general ban was laid down in Article XI, albeit accompanied by a number of exceptions in the same Article, and by a number of specific provisions dealing with balance-of-payments problems (see Articles XII and XIV GATT). No amendments were proposed to the first paragraph containing the general prohibition.[121] The discussions focused on the width of the exceptions to the principal prohibition in the second paragraph, with countries taking positions closely related to the relative importance of their agricultural sectors.

---

[118] The others are Article XII, providing an exception to Article XI for balance-of-payments reasons; Article XIII, requiring non-discrimination in the application of quantitative restrictions enacted in accordance with the exceptions in Article XI; and Article XIV, providing an exception to Article XIII in certain balance-of-payments circumstances.

[119] According to Jackson (1969) at 317, this exception refers to measures such as orderly marketing arrangements.

[120] However, a number of developing countries (India, the Phillipines, and a number of South-American countries) and Western European countries (mainly France, whose economy had been ravaged by the Second World War) felt the need to apply quotas for reasons of economic development.

[121] See document E/CONF.2/C.3/54.

The decisive criterion in assessing whether Article XI:1 is being infringed appears to be whether the measure prevents the importation (or exportation) of goods as such.[122] Article XI applies 'to all measures instituted or maintained [...] prohibiting or restricting the importation, exportation, or sale for export of products [...]'.[123] Whereas 'made effective through quotas, import or export licences' seems to be sufficiently clear, the words 'other measures' call for a further definition. Such measures may consist of, for example, outright import or export prohibitions, or import or export restrictions other than quotas.[124] They may also take the form of minimum price systems, allowing imports only above a certain price.[125] 'Other measures' have also been interpreted to include restrictions made effective through an import monopoly.[126] However, where state monopolies extend to both importation and distribution, the distinction between measures on importation and internal measures may blur, as illustrated by the *Canada-Beer I* panel report, discussed *infra*.[127] The scope of Article XI explicitly excludes 'duties, taxes and other charges' instituted or maintained 'on the importation'(or exportation) of products. Thus, whereas Article II:1(b) prohibits all *fiscal* barriers to importation in excess of those agreed upon in the tariff schedules, Article XI prohibits all *non-fiscal* barriers to importation.[128] The delimitation between Articles XI and III is discussed *infra*.[129]

Despite the general prohibition, quantitative restrictions have in reality persisted throughout GATT history, albeit that they have increasingly adopted

---

[122] *Canada-FIRA*, para. 5.14: The panel observed that purchase undertakings do not prevent the importation of goods as such, and reached the conclusion that they are not inconsistent with Article XI:1.

[123] Panel in *India-Quantitative Restrictions*, para. 5.128, referring to *Japan-Trade in Semi-conductors*, para. 104.

[124] An example of an import prohibition is the American measure at issue in the *US-Tuna-Dolphin* cases. An example of a restriction other than a quota is an import restriction by way of a sanction or retaliation, which will be contrary to Article XI if not sanctioned by other WTO provisions (such as the Dispute Settlement Understanding). Cf. the 1950 Report of the Working Party on 'The Use of Quantitative Restrictions for Protective and Commercial Purposes', cited in GATT (1995) at 324.

[125] See e.g. *EEC-Fruits and Vegetables*, para. 4.9.

[126] *Japan-Restrictions on Imports of Certain Agricultural Products*, para. 5.2.2.2.

[127] See Section 4.3.1.

[128] There is a difference in wording between 'duties, taxes or other charges' in Article XI on the one hand, and 'ordinary customs duties' and 'all other duties and charges' in Article II:1(b) on the other. According to Jackson, there are no *travaux préparatoires* nor any GATT practice to suggest that the scope of the Article XI phrase was meant to differ from the complement of the scope of the reference in Article II:1(b). Jackson, (1969), at 315.

[129] See Section 4.3.1, and with regard to the special case of measures based on production and processing methods, Section 5.4.

in the guise of voluntary export restraints and orderly market arrangements.[130] However, contrary to those which are specifically allowed under the exceptions laid down in the GATT, such persisting quotas have not been given legal status. The absolute character of the prohibition in Article XI was explicitly confirmed by a GATT panel in 1983, rejecting an argument by the European Community that 'quantitative restrictions had become a general problem and had gradually come to be accepted as negotiable, and that Article XI could not and had never been considered to be a provision prohibiting residual restrictions irrespective of the circumstances specific to each case'.[131] Voluntary export restraints and orderly market arrangements are now explicitly prohibited by the WTO Safeguards Agreement.[132]

Generally, whether or not there is an import restriction or prohibition is not a contentious issue, apart from cases where it is unclear whether Article XI or Article III is applicable. Accordingly, the discussion in Article XI cases usually focuses not on whether that Article has been infringed, but on the possible justifications of the infringement under the specific exceptions in Article XI itself and/or the general exceptions, mainly to be found in Article XX. Trade-environment disputes involving Article XI have often addressed trade in fish. GATT panels have dealt with tuna import restrictions,[133] salmon and herring export restrictions,[134] and tuna import prohibitions,[135] and WTO disputes have arisen over salmon quarantine measures,[136] and shrimp import restrictions.[137] Other measures concerned import restrictions on cigarettes,[138] and a prohibition of asbestos and asbestos products.[139]

4.3.1   Relationship Between Article XI and Article III

Article XI complements Article III:4, which addresses "internal regulations", i.e. non-fiscal restrictions affecting products *once they have been imported*. Article III and XI 'essentially have the same rationale, namely to protect expectations of the contracting parties as to the competitive relationship between their products and those of the other contracting parties."[140] Sometimes,

---

[130] See on such measures Petersmann (1988).

[131] *EEC- Imports from Hong Kong*, paras. 15 and 28-31.

[132] Article 11.1(b) Safeguards Agreement.

[133] *US-Tuna 1982.*

[134] *Canada-Herring and Salmon.*

[135] *US-Tuna-Dolphin I and II*, unadopted.

[136] Panel in *Australia-Salmon*, paras. 4.227-31and 8.185, and AB in *Australia-Salmon*, paras. 97-105.

[137] Panel in *US-Shrimp-Turtle*, paras. 5.162-9.

[138] *Thailand-Cigarettes.*

[139] Panel and AB in *EC-Asbestos.*

[140] *US-Superfund*, para. 5.2.2; *EC-Oilseeds*, para. 150.

it is difficult to decide whether a national measure is to be properly assessed under Article III or XI GATT. Simply put, "border measures" are dealt with under Article XI, while "internal measures" are assessed under Article III. However, many national laws and regulations comprise both "border" and "internal" aspects. Should these be separated into parts to be assessed under Article III and parts to be assessed under Article XI, or should they be treated in their entirety? Could Articles III and XI be cumulatively applicable, or are they mutually exclusive? The relationship between Articles XI and III is important because of the different nature of the requirements which these provisions contain. If a measure falls within the scope of Article XI, it is in principle prohibited and recourse to exceptions to justify it is needed. If a measure falls within the scope of Article III, the complaining party will still have to make a case that the requirement not to provide imports with less favourable treatment than their like domestic counterparts is being violated. Only then will possible justifications come into play. In determining whether Article III or Article XI covers a measure, the Note Ad Article III must be taken into account, which stipulates that internal measures enforced upon imports at the border may still fall under Article III.[141]

Within the realm of fiscal measures, the delimitation between duties or charges covered by Article II and internal taxes covered by Article III:2 has been interpreted according to a rather formal criterion: 'The relevant fact, according to the text of these provisions, is not the policy purpose attributed to the charge but rather whether the charge is due on importation or at the time or point of importation or whether it is collected internally.'[142] Panels and the Appellate Body have been less clear about the delimitation of regulatory border and internal measures. In *Canada-FIRA*, the panel noted that the GATT distinguishes between measures affecting the "importation" of products, which are regulated in Article XI:1, and those affecting "imported products", which are dealt with in Article III. According to the panel, if Article XI:1 were interpreted broadly to cover also internal requirements, Article III would be partly superfluous. Moreover, the exceptions to Article XI:1, in particular those contained in Article XI:2, would also apply to internal requirements restricting imports, which would be contrary to the basic aim of Article III. The panel did not find any evidence justifying such an interpretation of Article XI, either in the *travaux préparatoires* of the General Agreement or in previous cases.[143]

However, in other cases, panels have been less clear about the relationship between Article III and XI. A number of GATT dispute settlement reports

---

[141] For the text of the Note Ad Article III, see the Annex to this work.

[142] *EEC-Parts and Components*, para. 5.6.

[143] *Canada-FIRA*, para. 5.14.

have addressed both Article III and XI in the context of the same measure.[144] In *US-Spring Assemblies*, the panel considered both Articles III and XI to be relevant, but did not choose between the two.[145] A second panel that addressed the same US legislation applied Article III:4 to the measure and did not consider Article XI. The panel, referring to the Note Ad Article III, noted that the fact that the Section 337 legislation was being used as a means of enforcing US patent law at the border did not 'provide an escape from the applicability of Article III:4'.[146]

In *Canada-Beer I*, the panel considered that in the case of enterprises enjoying a monopoly of both importation and distribution in the domestic market, the distinction normally made by the GATT between restrictions affecting the importation and restrictions affecting imported products had lost much of its significance, since both types of restriction could be made effective by means of a decision by the monopoly.[147] The panel suggested that both Articles XI and III:4 could be applicable to one and the same measure.[148] The 1992 follow-up panel Report on persisting Canadian measures (*Canada-Beer II*) did not bring the required clarity. The panel *ex officio* applied Article III to Canadian listing requirements, while the complainant had alleged an infringement of Article XI only.[149] Moreover, Canada now considered Article III:4 to be applicable to provincial restrictions on access to points of sale that had been found to be inconsistent with Article XI in *Canada-Beer I*. The panel 'saw great force in the argument that the restrictions on access to points of sale were covered by Article III:4'. However, the panel considered it unnecessary to choose between Article XI:1 or III:4 and simply concluded that the restrictions were contrary to the GATT in general.[150]

In *US-Tuna-Dolphin I*, Mexico argued that the US tuna embargo was a quantitative restriction prohibited by Article XI. While the US did not disagree,

---

[144] In other disputes, both provisions have been invoked, but not with regard to the same measures. These were *Australia-Ammonium sulphate*, which decided that neither Article III nor XI were applicable to a subsidy; *Thailand-Cigarettes*, which applied Article III:2 to a tax and Article XI to an import restriction; and *Bananas II*, unadopted, which applied Article III to the allocation of import licences and Article XI to a tariff quota.

[145] Instead, the panel went straight to Article XX(d). *US-Spring Assemblies*, paras. 49-50. On this case, see Klabbers (1992).

[146] *US-Section 337*, para. 5.10.

[147] *Canada-Beer I*, para. 4.24, referring to the Note Ad Articles XI, XII, XIII, XIV and XVIII, which provides that throughout these Articles, the terms "import restrictions" and "export restrictions" include 'restrictions made effective through state-trading operations'.

[148] Ibid., paras. 4.25-.26.

[149] *Canada-Beer II*, para. 5.4.

[150] Ibid., paras. 5.6 and 5.7.

it also contended that its measures were internal regulations enforced at the time or point of importation under Article III:4 and the Note Ad Article III. The panel observed that the text of the Note Ad Article III suggests that 'this Note *covers only* measures applied to imported products that are *of the same nature* as those applied to the domestic products, such as a prohibition on importation of a product which enforces at the border an internal sales prohibition applied to both imported and domestic products.'[151] Although suggesting that the US measures violated Article III if covered by that provision, the panel went on to conclude that the US tuna embargo did not constitute internal regulations covered by the Note Ad Article III, and assessed the measure under Article XI.[152]

Under the WTO dispute settlement procedures, the EC as a defendant in *EC-Bananas III* clearly stated that in its view, Articles III and XI were mutually exclusive. However, neither the panel nor the Appellate Body specifically went into the matter of the delimitation between Articles XI and III; both thought the measures at issue were internal measures falling within the scope of Article III rather than XI.[153] In *EC-Hormones*, the question of the relationship between Articles III and XI arose again in one of the complainants' arguments.[154] However, it was not addressed by the panel and the Appellate Body, since the panel decided to assess the EC measures at stake exclusively under the SPS Agreement.[155]

In *EC-Asbestos*, the measure at issue consisted of a prohibition to produce, import, market, sell, offer or transfer asbestos and asbestos-containing products. The complainant, Canada, argued that the part of the measure imposing an import ban should be assessed under Article XI. The panel made it clear that a measure prohibiting both the domestic production of a material and its importation is covered by the Note Ad Article III. The fact that domestic production no longer existed did not cause the measure to fall under Article XI.[156] The regulations applicable to domestic products and foreign products led to the same result: the halting of the spread of asbestos and asbestos-containing products on French territory.[157] The panel further considered that the wording of the Note Ad Article III and the practice under GATT 1947 did not support the view that an *identical* measure must be applied to the domestic product and the like imported product if the measure applicable to the imported product is to fall under Article III.[158] Without referring to the panel's reference to 'measures of the same nature'

---

[151] *US-Tuna-Dolphin I*, unadopted, para. 5.11. Emphasis added.

[152] Ibid., para. 5.14. See also Section 5.4.

[153] Panel in *EC-Bananas III* (GTM), para. 7.177; AB in *EC-Bananas III*, para. 211.

[154] Panel in *EC-Hormones* (CND), paras. 4.304 and 4.337.

[155] Ibid., paras. 8.272-73 (US); paras. 8.275-76 (CND).

[156] Panel in *EC-Asbestos*, para. 8.91.

[157] Ibid., para. 8.92.

[158] Ibid., para. 8.93.

in *US-Tuna-Dolphin I*, the panel observed that the word "and" in the Note Ad Article III does not have the same meaning as 'in the same way as'.[159] The panel considered that *US-Section 337* supported its view, and that *Canada-Beer I* did not confirm the non-applicability of Article III:4 to the part of an internal measure dealing with the treatment of imported products. At most, it could confirm the application of both provisions.[160] The panel decided, however, that it was outside its terms of reference to decide on a claim for the cumulative application of Articles III:4 and XI.[161] These issues were not appealed.

In sum, the basic rule as regards the delimitation between import restrictions covered by Article XI and internal measures covered by Article III would seem to be that measures affecting the "importation" of products are regulated in Article XI:1, while those affecting "imported products" are dealt with in Article III. Thus, measures that do not prevent the importation of goods as such will be assessed under Article III, not Article XI. Moreover, in accordance with the Note Ad Article III, measures applying to both domestic and imported product which are enforced at the border for imported products will be assessed under Article III. Thus, when a measure includes an import prohibition as part of a more general prohibitory regime, as in *EC-Asbestos*, it is assessed as a whole under Article III and the Note thereto. However, it is as yet unclear to what extent the measures applied to imports may differ in their nature from the measures applied to domestic products. An extreme case is a measure that does not apply to domestic products but to domestic producers, coupled with a prohibition on imported products. Such a measure was not covered by the Note Ad Article III in the eyes of the panel in *US-Tuna-Dolphin I*. This point is further discussed in Section 5.4. The borderline between import measures and internal measures is somewhat blurred in the case of state trading companies that combine monopolies on import and on distribution, or for that matter, any of the other activities described in Article III:1 and III:4, i.e. sale, offering for sale, purchase, transport or use. In such situations, and where measures combine internal regulations of sale, marketing etc. and import restrictions or prohibitions, as in *EC-Asbestos*, panels have left open the possibility of the cumulative application of Articles III and XI.

---

[159] Ibid., para. 8.94. The panel, the first in GATT/WTO history to issue its original report in French, observed that "and" in the Note Ad Article III does not have the same meaning as 'in the same way as', which is another meaning of the word "comme" that features in the French version of the Note Ad Article III.

[160] Ibid., paras. 8.95 and 8.98.

[161] Ibid., para. 8.100.

4.4 Exceptions in Article XX GATT and the Conditions Attached Thereto

The text of the parts of Article XX GATT most relevant to this study is found in the Annex to this work. Article XX provides general exceptions to GATT obligations. It may be invoked to justify a measure that would otherwise be incompatible with GATT obligations, such as Most-Favoured Nation Treatment or National Treatment, or the prohibition on quantitative restrictions. In addition to these general exceptions, the GATT also provides exceptions for security reasons in Article XXI. Both "general" and "security" exceptions have been termed "universal" exceptions.[162] In addition to these "universal" exceptions, the GATT contains a number of exceptions that are particular to certain GATT obligations. An example of the latter is Article XI:2, discussed earlier, which only applies as an exception to the obligation in Article XI:1.

Originally, the provision that was to become Article XX GATT consisted of the chapeau, an introductory clause, followed by two parts. The exceptions now found under paragraphs (a) to (j) constituted the first part, while a second part concerned various situations of domestic short supply. Throughout the Havana negotiations, the counterpart of Article XX GATT essentially retained this two-part structure, and it appeared as such in the Havana Charter.[163] At Havana, a sub-committee of the Committee on Commercial Policy discussed the general exceptions article.[164] The version of the exceptions article drawn up by this sub-committee contained two new provisions as compared to the Geneva draft, which were maintained throughout the negotiations, and also appeared in the Havana Charter.[165] One related to public safety, and was intended to include the concept of "public order" (*"ordre public"*).[166] The other related to measures

---

[162] Jackson distinguishes three types of universal exceptions: those requiring approval, such as waivers (Article XXV:5 GATT); those requiring notification, such as customs unions (Article XXIV GATT); and those requiring neither approval nor notification, such as the exceptions in Articles XX and XXI GATT. Jackson (1969) at 536-37.

[163] See Article 43 of the draft ITO Charter and Article 45 of the Havana Charter; GATT (1995) at 592-4, and Jackson (1969) at 742, footnote 10.

[164] Sub-Committee D on Articles 40, 41 and 43 (which became Articles XIX, XXII and XX GATT, respectively) The sub-committee proposed a text to Committee III in late January of 1948, E/CONF.2/C.3/37.

[165] See the proposed redraft of Article 43 by the Central Drafting Committee, E/CONF.2/C.8/5, the report to the conference by Committee III on Commercial Policy, E/CONF.2/70, and Article 45 of the Havana Charter.

[166] The precursor of Article XX was meant to provide exceptions only to the commercial policy chapter of the intended ITO charter. It originally contained four national security exceptions. At the Geneva session, these were separated from the other exceptions in order to create a general security exceptions provision that applied to all obligations in the Charter, which became Article XXI GATT. See GATT (1995) at 596.

'undertaken in pursuance of any inter-governmental agreement relating solely to the conservation of fisheries resources, migratory birds and wild animals (...)'.[167] This exception for international animal conservation agreements appeared both in the commodities chapter and in the commercial policy chapter of the Havana Charter.[168] However, the GATT Working Party on Modifications to the General Agreement that met in September 1948 decided not to include either of these exceptions in the GATT text.[169]

As compared to the GATT text which is currently applicable, neither the text containing the exceptions of particular relevance to environmental measures nor the chapeau to Article XX were changed at Havana.[170] The main difference between the provision in the Geneva and Havana drafts on the one hand, and in the GATT on the other, is that the former applied only to the commercial policy chapter of the proposed ITO Charter, whereas GATT Article XX applies to the whole of the GATT, which contains more than just the commercial policy chapter of the ITO Charter. Before Havana, a second sentence for paragraph (b) was proposed and subsequently rejected. Various wordings were proposed, such as 'provided that corresponding safeguards are applied in the importing country if similar conditions exist in that country'[171], and 'if corresponding domestic safeguards under similar conditions exist in the importing country'.[172] What follows are some aspects of Article XX which are relevant to trade and environment.[173]

GATT panels have stated that Article XX provides a limited and conditional exception to obligations under other GATT provisions.[174] One unadopted GATT panel report also stated that Article XX does not establish obligations in itself, asserting that 'previous panels had established' this. However, in a footnote the panel referred to only one other panel, which moreover never made such a statement.[175] In other words, if the structure and function of Article XX suggest

---

[167] The remainder of this exception referred to the requirements of paragraph 1(d) of Article 67 [Article 70 in the Havana Charter], the exceptions provision in the chapter of the ITO Charter dealing with intergovernmental commodity agreements. See E/CONF.2/C.8/3 (proposed Article 67), and the Havana Charter (Article 70:1(d)).

[168] Charnovitz (1991) at 46.

[169] GATT (1995) at 596.

[170] Cf. Charnovitz (1991) at 43.

[171] Fauchald (1998) at 331.

[172] GATT (1995) at 565.

[173] For a comprehensive overview, see document WT/CTE/W/53, 'GATT/WTO Dispute Settlement Practice Relating to Article XX, Paragraphs (b), (d) and (g) of GATT, Note by the Secretariat', and the revision thereof, WT/CTE/W/53/Rev.1.

[174] See *US-Section 337*, para. 5.9; *US-Tuna-Dolphin I*, para. 5.22.

[175] *US-Tuna-Dolphin I*, unadopted, para. 5.22, referring to *US-Section 337*, para. 5.9 and incorrectly attributing to that paragraph the statement that Article XX does not establish obligations. Cf. Appleton (1999) at 482.

that this Article indeed was not intended to establish obligations in itself, this conclusion cannot be drawn from GATT panel history. As a matter of fact, one could argue that Article XX does establish an obligation, namely to respect GATT principles when pursuing non-trade goals. The panel in *Canada-Herring and Salmon* stated that:

> *the purpose of including Article XX(g) in the General Agreement was not to widen the scope for measures serving trade policy purposes but merely to ensure that the commitments under the General Agreement do not hinder the pursuit of policies aimed at the conservation of exhaustive [sic] natural resources.*[176]

The function of Article XX, then, is to ensure that the GATT commitments are respected in the pursuit of non-trade policy goals. The following quotes from the panels in *Thailand-Cigarettes* and *US-Gasoline* support this view:

> *[the objective of paragraphs (b) and (d) of Article XX is] to allow contracting parties to impose trade restrictive measures inconsistent with the General Agreement to pursue overriding public policy goals to the extent that such inconsistencies were unavoidable.*[177]

> *Under the General Agreement, WTO Members were free to set their own environmental objectives, but they were bound to implement these objectives through measures consistent with its provisions [...].*[178]

The "measures" to be analysed under Article XX are the same as those that have been found to infringe substantive GATT obligations, such as Article XI or Article III:4.[179] Panels will first examine whether a measure falls within the scope of one or more of the exceptions in paragraphs (a) to (j), before scrutinising whether the measure in its application conforms to the chapeau to Article XX.[180] In *US-Shrimp-Turtle*, the Appellate Body stressed that '[t]he sequence of steps [...] in the analysis of a claim of justification under Article XX reflects, not inadvertence or random choice, but rather the *fundamental structure and logic of Article XX.*'[181] It could be argued that the chapeau and paragraphs of Article XX

---

[176] *Canada-Herring and Salmon*, para. 4.6.

[177] *Thailand-Cigarettes*, para. 74.

[178] Panel in *US-Gasoline*, para. 7.1. This observation is a "concluding remark", and not a "finding" by the panel.

[179] On Articles XX and III:4, see AB in *US-Gasoline*, at p. 13, referring to *Canada-FIRA*, *US-Section 337*, *US-Auto Taxes*. On the difficulties involved in identifying what the "measure" is, see Section 4.4.3.

[180] AB in *US-Gasoline*, at p. 22.

[181] AB in *US-Shrimp-Turtle*, para. 119. Emphasis added.

are independent from each other, as the former addresses a measure's *application* and the latter a measure's relation to its policy goal and trade impacts. If this were so, the assessment sequence should not make any difference to the outcome. However, despite occasional deviations,[182] the sequence of starting with the provisional justification under the relevant paragraphs and then assessing whether the conditions in the chapeau have been met now appears to be accepted practice.

4.4.1   Exception Grounds and Their Specific Conditions

The paragraphs discussed hereunder address specific exception grounds, and contain two different conditions regarding the required means-end relationship; "necessary" in paragraphs (a), (b) and (d), and "relating to" and 'made effective in conjunction with..' in paragraph (g). As the Appellate Body made clear in *US-Gasoline*, 'it does not seem reasonable to suppose that the WTO Members intended to require, in respect of each and every category, the same kind or degree of connection or relationship between the measure under appraisal and the state interest or policy sought to be promoted or realized."[183] Defying an alphabetical order, the analysis starts with paragraph (d), as the interpretation of paragraph (b) draws upon it.

(a)   Article XX(d): Necessary to Secure Compliance with other Laws and Regulations

Paragraph (d) of Article XX refers to measures 'necessary to secure compliance with laws or regulations which are not inconsistent with the provisions of this Agreement', providing by way of example measures relating to customs enforcement, import monopolies and intellectual property protection. The material scope of paragraph (d) is somewhat difficult to establish. Should 'measures necessary to secure compliance with laws or regulations' be understood as procedural measures only? "Substantive" laws and regulations often include measures securing compliance. Examples in the environmental sphere are administrative and criminal control mechanisms, and sanctions enforcing environmental standards.

With regard to "necessary" in paragraph (d), the panel in *Section 337* stated that

a contracting party cannot justify a measure inconsistent with another GATT provision as "necessary" in terms of Article XX(d) if an alternative measure which

---

[182] See e.g. the panel in *US-Shrimp-Turtle*.

[183] AB in *US-Gasoline*, at p. 17.

it could reasonably be expected to employ and which is not inconsistent with other GATT provisions is available to it. By the same token, in cases where a measure consistent with other GATT provisions is not reasonably available, a contracting party is bound to use, among the measures reasonably available to it, that which entails the least degree of inconsistency with other GATT provisions.[184]

Thus, "necessary" requires that there is no 'GATT consistent or less GATT-inconsistent' measure reasonably available to secure compliance.[185] In both the *US-Tuna-Dolphin* disputes and in *US-Auto Taxes*, the measures at issue could not be justified by Article XX(d) because the underlying measures with which they were to secure compliance were themselves GATT-inconsistent.[186] The WTO panel in *US-Gasoline* found that maintaining discrimination contrary to Article III:4 under the baseline establishment methods did not 'secure compliance' with the baseline system, as these methods were not an enforcement mechanism. As such, they were not the types of measures with which Article XX(d) was concerned.[187] This would seem to indicate that the scope of Article XX(d) is limited to actual enforcement measures, and a close relationship with the laws and regulations they are supposed to enforce will be needed in order for a measure to fall within the material ambit of paragraph (d).

In *Korea-Beef*, the Appellate Body set out the main factors involved in determining whether a measure is "necessary" in the context of Article XX(d). It noted that the word "necessary" may have different meanings, depending on the context in which it is used. In the continuum of meanings of "necessary", its meaning in Article XX(d) is 'located significantly closer to the pole of "indispensable" than to the opposite pole of simply "making a contribution to"'.[188] Considering the context in which "necessary" is found in Article XX(d), the Appellate Body observed that:

a treaty interpreter assessing a measure claimed to be necessary to secure compliance of a WTO-consistent law or regulation may, in appropriate cases, take into

---

[184] *US-Section 337*, para. 5.26.

[185] The only instance in which the words "least trade-restrictive" were used instead of "least GATT-inconsistent" was the GATT panel report in *US-Beer*, when addressing a justification claim under Article XX(d).

[186] *US-Tuna-Dolphin I*, unadopted, para. 5.40; *US-Tuna-Dolphin II*, unadopted, para. 5.41; *US-Auto Taxes*, unadopted, para. 5.67. Other GATT disputes in which Article XX(d) was involved are *US-Spring Assemblies* and *US-Beer*.

[187] *US-Gasoline*, para. 6.33, referring to panel in *EEC-Parts and Components*, paras. 5.12-18. The AB was not asked to reverse any of the panel's findings other than those on Article XX(g), and accordingly did not address paragraph (d) of Article XX.

[188] AB in *Korea-Beef*, para. 161, referring in a footnote to its reports on Article XX(g) and noting that the condition set out therein is more flexible than "necessary" in Article XX(d).

account the relative importance of the common interests or values that the law or regulation to be enforced is intended to protect. The more vital or important those common interests or values are, the easier it would be to accept as "necessary" a measure designed as an enforcement instrument.[189]

According to the Appellate Body, determining whether a measure is "necessary" within the contemplation of Article XX(d), involves in every case:

a process of weighing and balancing a series of factors which prominently include the contribution made by the compliance measure to the enforcement of the law or regulation at issue, the importance of the common interests or values protected by that law or regulation, and the accompanying impact of the law or regulation on imports or exports.[190]

The Appellate Body made it clear that it did not consider this interpretation to be a break with the previous GATT panel reports that had interpreted "necessary" as requiring the absence of a reasonably available GATT-consistent or less GATT-inconsistent alternative measure. In the words of the Appellate Body, the 'least GATT-inconsistent alternative' interpretation 'encapsulates' the general considerations made by the Appellate Body quoted above. The weighing and balancing process is comprehended in the determination of whether a WTO-consistent alternative measure which the Member concerned could reasonably be expected to employ is available, or whether a less WTO-inconsistent measure is reasonably available.[191] The panel in this case had found that alternative measures consistent with the WTO Agreement were reasonably available and that the Korean measure at issue was 'a disproportionate measure not necessary to secure compliance [...]'.[192] Korea argued on appeal that alternative measures must not only be reasonably available, but they must also guarantee the level of enforcement sought, which had been set very high by Korea in this particular case, i.e. the complete elimination of fraud. Whilst recognising that Members have the right to determine for themselves the level of enforcement of their WTO-consistent laws and regulations, the Appellate Body refused to accept the Korean argument about its protection level and instead assumed that Korea intended to considerably reduce fraud.[193] The Appellate Body was not persuaded

---

[189] Ibid., para. 162.

[190] Ibid., para. 164.

[191] Ibid., paras. 165-6.

[192] Panel in *Korea-Beef*, para. 675.

[193] AB in *Korea-Beef*, para. 178: 'We think it unlikely that Korea intended to establish a level of protection that *totally eliminates* fraud with respect to the origin of beef (domestic or foreign) sold by retailers. The total elimination of fraud would probably require a total ban of imports. Consequently, we assume that in effect Korea intended to *reduce considerably* the number of cases of fraud occurring with respect to the origin of beef sold by retailers.' Emphasis in the original.

that Korea could not achieve its desired enforcement level through "conventional" WTO-consistent enforcement measures if it devoted more resources to its enforcement efforts. Such measures would moreover not involve such onerous shifting of enforcement costs on imports as the measures at issue had done.[194]

(b) Article XX(b): Necessary to Protect Human, Animal or Plant Life or Health

The two specific elements that have to be established by the party invoking Article XX(b) are:

(1) that the policy in respect of the measures for which the provision was invoked fell within the range of policies designed to protect human, animal or plant life or health;
(2) that the inconsistent measures for which the exception was being invoked were necessary to fulfil the policy objective; [...][195]

Whether the environmental policy falls within the 'range of policies designed to protect human, animal or plant life or health' will usually not be very strictly scrutinised. Panels do not normally include environmental specialists. Panels and the Appellate Body have emphasised on various occasions that WTO Members are free to set the level of protection of their choice for their populations.[196] Thus, although they will check the necessity of the measure taken to achieve that goal, as discussed below, panels and the Appellate Body will not check the necessity of a measure's environmental *policy goal* as such. For example, in *US-Tuna-Dolphin II*, the panel accepted that a policy to protect the life and health of dolphins in the eastern Tropical Pacific Ocean pursued by the US within its jurisdiction over its nationals and vessels fell within the range of policies covered by Article XX(b).[197] In the *Thailand-Cigarettes* case, the panel accepted that smoking constitutes a serious risk to human health, and that measures designed to reduce the consumption of cigarettes fell within the scope of Article XX(b).[198]

---

[194] Ibid., paras. 180-82.

[195] See the panel in *EC-Asbestos*, para. 8.169; the panel in *US-Gasoline*, para. 6.20, referring to *US-Tuna-Dolphin II*, unadopted, para. 5.29. The panels actually outlined three elements, the third element being conformity with the chapeau of Article XX, which has to be fulfilled when invoking any of the paragraphs in Article (XX).

[196] Panel in *EC-Asbestos*, paras. 8.171 and 8.179; AB in *US-Gasoline*, at p. 33; *US-Section 337*, para. 5.26.

[197] *US-Tuna-Dolphin II*, unadopted, paras. 5.30 and 5.33.

[198] *Thailand-Cigarettes*, para. 73.

Under the WTO dispute settlement procedures, the panel in *US-Gasoline* agreed with the parties to the dispute that a policy to reduce air pollution resulting from the consumption of gasoline was within the range of policies covered by Article XX(b).[199] In *EC-Asbestos*, the panel accepted that the French policy of prohibiting chrysotile asbestos fell within the range of policies designed to protect human life or health, and the Appellate Body upheld this finding.[200]

The second condition in Article XX(b), the necessity requirement, is more controversial. According to a number of GATT and WTO dispute settlement reports, "necessary" requires that there is no 'GATT consistent or less GATT-inconsistent' measure reasonably available to pursue the policy objective. The root of this interpretation of "necessary" is found in the GATT panel report in *Thailand-Cigarettes*, which in turn referred to the interpretation of "necessary" in paragraph (d) by the panel in *US-Section 337*. The panel considered that Thailand's health objective consisted of a qualitative aspect in protecting the population from harmful ingredients, and a quantitative aspect in reducing the quantity of cigarettes sold in Thailand. The panel considered that Thailand could reasonably be expected to address the quality-related objectives it pursued through non-discriminatory labelling and ingredient disclosure regulations coupled with a ban on unhealthy substances.[201] As to the objectives in terms of the quantity of cigarettes consumed, the panel implicitly stated that Thailand could reasonably have been expected to impose a non-discriminatory cigarette advertising ban. A cigarette import ban infringing Article XI did not meet the "necessary" test because the alternative of an advertising ban, even if inconsistent with Article III:4, would be justified under Article XX(b) as 'unavoidable and therefore necessary'.[202]

The Appellate Body in *EC-Asbestos* further elaborated the necessity requirement. It referred to its observations in *Korea-Beef* in the context of Article XX(d), discussed *supra*, to the effect that assessing "necessary" involves a process of weighing and balancing factors, such as the contribution of the measure to the goal, the importance of the interest protected, and trade impacts. This weighing and balancing process is 'comprehended in the determination of whether a WTO-consistent alternative measure is reasonably available'.[203] The Appellate Body observed that in the particular case at issue, the value pursued was both vital and important in the highest degree. The remaining question was whether there was an alternative measure that would achieve the same end and that was less restrictive of trade than a prohibition. The Appellate Body concluded

---

[199] Panel in *US-Gasoline*, para. 6.21.

[200] Panel in *EC-Asbestos*, paras. 8.181-2 and 8.194; AB in *EC-Asbestos*, para. 163.

[201] *Thailand-Cigarettes*, para. 77.

[202] Ibid., para. 78.

[203] AB in *EC-Asbestos*, para. 172.

that France could not reasonably be expected to employ any alternative measure if that measure would involve a continuation of the very risk that the Decree sought to "halt". Such an alternative measure would, in effect, prevent France from achieving its chosen level of health protection.[204]

As regards the reasonable availability of alternative measures, the panel in *US-Gasoline* held that alternative measures did not cease to be "reasonably available" because they involved administrative difficulties for the Member invoking Article XX.[205] The panel in *EC-Asbestos* observed that the existence of a reasonably available measure must be assessed in the light of the economic and administrative realities facing the Member concerned, but also by taking into account the fact that the State must provide itself with the means of implementing its policies.[206] The Appellate Body in the same dispute observed that the chosen level of health protection by France was high, i.e. "halting" the spread of asbestos-related health risks. The measure at issue was 'clearly designed and apt to achieve that level of health protection', and that conclusion was not altered by the fact that competing products that were not prohibited also posed a health risk, but a lesser one.[207]

The GATT panel in *Thailand-Cigarettes* and the Appellate Body in *EC-Asbestos* were both inspired by the interpretation of "necessary" in Article XX(d).[208] However, there is an interesting difference between them. The GATT panel in *Thailand-Cigarettes* took the view that the meaning of the term "necessary" in paragraph (d) should be the same as in paragraph (b).[209] On the other hand, the Appellate Body in *Korea-Beef* suggested that "necessary" need not have the same meaning in different provisions. This leaves open the possibility of having different tests for "necessary" in paragraphs (b) and (d), and also in paragraph (a) for that matter.

(c) Article XX(g): Relating to the Conservation of Exhaustible Natural Resources

In contrast with Article XX(b), the provision in paragraph (g) was not based on any historical precedents when it appeared in the "Suggested Charter" proposed by the US.[210] There are strong indications that this paragraph

---

[204] Ibid., paras. 172-4.

[205] Panel in *US-Gasoline*, para. 6.28.

[206] Panel in *EC-Asbestos*, para. 8.207.

[207] AB in *EC-Asbestos*, para. 168, referring to para. 8.204 of the panel report.

[208] They referred to the interpretation of "necessary" in paragraph (d) in *US-Section 337* and *Korea-Beef*, respectively.

[209] *Thailand-Cigarettes*, para. 74.

[210] Charnovitz (1991) at 45.

was originally intended to address export restrictions.[211] Nevertheless, it has been invoked in several disputes concerning import-restricting measures under the GATT and WTO dispute settlement practice. The requirements which are specific to this paragraph have been outlined as follows:

> (1) that the policy in respect of the measures for which the provision was invoked fell within the range of polices related to the conservation of exhaustible natural resources;
> (2) that the measures for which the exception was being invoked - that is the particular trade measures inconsistent with the General Agreement - were related to the conservation of exhaustible natural resources;
> (3) that the measures for which the exception was being invoked were made effective in conjunction with restrictions on domestic production or consumption.[212]

In the preparatory meetings to prepare a draft trade charter, the natural resources were usually referred to as "raw material" or "mineral". One author asserts that "exhaustible" referred to "stock" resources, in contrast to "renewable" or "flow" resources, such as animals, plants, soil and water.[213] However, the very first GATT panel report dealing with paragraph (g) already interpreted "exhaustible natural resources" to include fish.[214] Subsequently, salmon and herring, dolphins, gasoline, turtles, and even clean air have been found to fall within the meaning of "exhaustible natural resources".[215] Already under GATT dispute settlement practice, animals that were not in danger of extinction were considered "exhaustible natural resources". It can therefore be safely assumed that animals do not have to be threatened by extinction to qualify.

In *US-Gasoline*, the panel observed that clean air 'was a resource (it had value), and it was natural. It could be depleted. The fact that the depleted resource was defined with respect to its qualities was not decisive for the panel. Likewise, the fact that a resource was renewable could not be an objection.'[216] In *US-Shrimp-Turtle*, the Appellate Body observed that '[t]extually, Article XX(g) is *not* limited to the conservation of "mineral" or "non-living" natural resources', and that '[it did] not believe that "exhaustible" natural resources and "renewable" natural resources are mutually exclusive'.[217] The Appellate Body referred to the

---

[211] See Fauchald (1998) at 330, and Charnovitz (1991) at 45.

[212] Panel in *US-Gasoline*, para. 6.35. The fourth condition is compliance with the chapeau to Article XX.

[213] Charnovitz (1991) at 45.

[214] *US-Tuna 1982*, para. 4.9.

[215] See, respectively, *Canada-Salmon and Herring*, para. 4.4; *US-Tuna-Dolphin II*, unadopted, para. 5.13; *US-Auto Taxes*, unadopted, para. 5.57; AB in *US-Shrimp-Turtle*, paras. 127-134; panel in *US-Gasoline*, para. 6.37.

[216] Ibid., para. 6.37.

[217] AB in *US-Shrimp-Turtle*, para. 128. Emphasis in the original.

objective of sustainable development in the preamble to the WTO Agreement. It noted that from the perspective of sustainable development, the generic term "natural resources" in Article XX(g) is not static but is rather 'by definition, evolutionary'. The latter concept was taken from an advisory opinion of the International Court of Justice.[218] Pointing in addition at a number of international treaties protecting living resources, the Appellate Body believed that it was 'too late in the day' to suppose that Article XX(g) covers only non-living resources. Referring also to the earlier mentioned *US-Tuna 1982* and *Canada-Herring and Salmon* panel reports, and 'in line with the principle of effectiveness in treaty interpretation', the Appellate Body found that both living and non-living exhaustible resources could fall within paragraph (g).[219] Thus, the two instances in which the meaning of "exhaustible natural resources" were discussed under WTO dispute settlement render the definition of such resources, and thereby the material scope of the exception in paragraph (g), potentially very wide.

In comparison with paragraphs (a), (b) and (d), paragraph (g) is characterised by a more loosely formulated means-end test, i.e. "relating" or "related" instead of "necessary". On the other hand, paragraph (g) contains an additional condition to be fulfilled, i.e. being made effective in conjunction with domestic restrictions. The GATT panel in *Canada-Salmon and Herring* interpreted "relating to" in paragraph (g) as "primarily aimed at", an interpretation which was subsequently applied in *US-Tuna-Dolphin I* and *II*, and *US-Auto Taxes*.[220] The Appellate Body in *US-Gasoline* observed that all the parties to the dispute accepted the "primarily aimed at" interpretation. It added however that "primarily aimed at" is not itself treaty language and was not designed as a simple litmus test for inclusion or exclusion from Article XX(g).[221] The Appellate Body went on to apply the "relating to" test in that case, finding that it required a "substantial relationship" between measure and purpose. The measure under appraisal must be 'not merely incidentally or inadvertently aimed at' the conservation goal.[222]

In *US-Shrimp-Turtle*, the Appellate Body repeated its findings on "relating to" in *US-Gasoline*, observing that the relationship it had found there was a 'close and genuine relationship of ends and means'.[223] The Appellate Body examined

---

[218] Ibid., para. 130, referring to *Namibia (Legal Consequences) Advisory Opinion* (1971) I.C.J. Reports, at p. 31, where the International Court of Justice stated that where concepts embodied in a treaty are 'by definition, evolutionary', their 'interpretation cannot remain unaffected by the subsequent development of law [...] Moreover, an international instrument has to be interpreted and applied within the framework of the entire legal system prevailing at the time of the interpretation.'

[219] Ibid., para. 131.

[220] *Canada-Salmon and Herring*, paras. 4.5-4.7; *US-Tuna-Dolphin I*, unadopted, para. 5.31; *US-Tuna-Dolphin II*, unadopted, para. 5.22; *US-Auto Taxes*, para. 5.67.

[221] AB in *US-Gasoline*, at pp. 19-20.

[222] Ibid., at p. 20. Emphasis added.

[223] AB in *US-Shrimp-Turtle*, para. 136.

the general structure and design of the measure at stake in *US-Shrimp-Turtle*, and the policy goal the measure purported to serve. The US measure required a country wishing to export shrimp to the US to adopt a regulatory program requiring its shrimp fishers to use turtle excluder devices (TEDs). This requirement was in the view of the Appellate Body *directly connected* with the policy of sea turtle conservation.[224] Focusing on the design of the measure at stake, the Appellate Body thought that the measure was 'not disproportionately wide in its scope and reach in relation to the policy objective of protection and conservation of sea turtle species'. The means were, in principle, 'reasonably related to the ends'. The Appellate Body added that the means-ends relationship was a 'close and real one' and every bit as substantial as that found in *US-Gasoline*.[225] The conclusion was that the US measure was indeed "relating to" the conservation of an exhaustible natural resource.

'Made effective in conjunction with' was interpreted by the GATT panel in the *Canada-Salmon and Herring* case as 'primarily aimed at rendering effective'.[226] This reading has been criticised, as it appears to exclude from its scope domestic restrictions that are subsidiary to the contested measure, which is not warranted by the words 'in conjunction with'.[227] In *US-Tuna-Dolphin I and II* and in *US-Auto Taxes*, the panels referred to the *Canada-Salmon and Herring* panel report. The panel in *US-Auto Taxes*, when it dealt with fleet averaging requirements for imported cars, observed that 'the application of fleet averaging *in a similar manner* to its application to domestic cars [...] served to render effective the conservation measure.'[228] It should be noted that although the panel report in *Canada-Salmon* and *Herring* was adopted, the interpretation of 'in conjunction with' in that report was contested by Canada.[229] The three panel reports that followed remained unadopted. Therefore, the interpretation of 'in conjunction with' as 'primarily aimed at' did not have a very firm basis when dispute settlement entered the WTO era.

In *US-Gasoline*, the Appellate Body observed that the clause 'made effective in conjunction with':

---

[224] Ibid., para. 140. Emphasis added.

[225] Ibid., para. 141.

[226] *Canada-Salmon and Herring*, para. 4.6.

[227] Fauchald (1998) at 334. As he rightly points out at 332, Article XI:2(c)(i) does warrant the exclusion of domestic measures subsidiary to an import measure, by referring to 'Import restrictions...necessary to the enforcement of governmental measures which operate: (i) to restrict the quantities of the like domestic product [...]'.

[228] *US-Auto Taxes*, unadopted, para. 5.65. Emphasis added.

[229] Fauchald (1998) at 336.

is appropriately read as a requirement that the measures concerned impose restric-
tions, not just in respect of imported gasoline but also with respect to domestic
gasoline. The clause is a requirement of even-handedness in the imposition of restric-
tions, in the name of conservation, upon the production or consumption of exhaustible
natural resources.[230]

The Appellate Body added that *identical* treatment of domestic and imported
products is not required. On the other hand, if *no* restrictions at all are imposed
on domestically-produced like products, then the clause is obviously not being
complied with.[231] The dividing line between what does and what does not constitute 'made effective in conjunction with' must be somewhere between these two
extremes. Further indications as to where the line may be drawn can be found
in the actual application by the Appellate Body in this case of its interpretation
of the clause. It observed that '[r]estrictions on the consumption or depletion
of clean air by regulating the domestic production of "dirty" gasoline are established *jointly* with *corresponding* restrictions with respect to imported gasoline.'[232]

In *US-Shrimp-Turtle*, the Appellate Body explicitly recalled "even-handedness", but not 'established jointly' and "corresponding". In examining whether
the US measure which was being applied to shrimp imports was 'an even-
handed measure', the Appellate Body noted that that specific measure addressed
the mode of harvesting of imported shrimp only. It went on to note that the
US had enacted legislation two years earlier regulating the fishing methods of
US vessels. Having noted that these internal measures were now fully effective
and that the US had measures for enforcement at its disposal, the Appellate
Body remarked that the US government has the ability to seize shrimp catches
from trawl vessels fishing in US waters and had done so in cases of egregious
violations. It believed that the import measure was in principle an even-handed
measure.[233]

Finally, the Appellate Body in *US-Gasoline* noted that the clause 'if made
effective in conjunction with restrictions on domestic production or consumption' was in its view not intended to establish an empirical "effects test". If a
specific measure cannot realistically in any possible situation have any positive
effect on conservation goals, it would very probably be because that measure was
not designed as a conservation regulation to begin with. In other words, it would
not have been "primarily aimed at" the conservation of natural resources at
all.[234] Such a measure would therefore not only fail to meet the 'made effective..'
requirement but also to meet the "relating to" requirement. In other words,

---

[230] AB in *US-Gasoline*, at p. 21. Emphasis added.

[231] Ibid., at p. 21. Emphasis added.

[232] Ibid., at p. 22. Emphasis added.

[233] AB in *US-Shrimp-Turtle*, para. 144.

measures that fail the "relating to" test because they cannot have a conservation effect will logically also fail the 'made effective...' test.

(d)   Other Paragraphs of Article XX

Article XX(a) refers to measures 'necessary to protect public morals'. No panel has ever been asked to rule on this particular provision.[235] Public morals obviously differ from country to country. It will be difficult to find common agreement among all WTO members on even the core contents of this concept. A uniform interpretation therefore appears not to be an option. However, this clause is apt to determine the limits to Members' discretion in interpreting public morality. With so-called "consumer concerns" relating to trade on the rise, the public morals exception may be discussed in the near future in relation to some of the most difficult aspects of the trade-environment nexus in the WTO, i.e. unilateral actions affecting trade based on production methods in other Members on which no international consensus can be found, precisely because the arguments condemning foreign production methods are based on moral arguments in the importing country.[236] Another situation in which Article XX(a) may be invoked is where a Member wishes to ban a product on grounds of public opinion, without being able (for the time being) to provide 'sufficient scientific evidence' within the meaning of Article 2.2 SPS Agreement.[237]

Article XX(h) contains a generally phrased exception for 'international commodities agreements', which in principle allows trade restricting measures pursuant to e.g. fisheries or other commodities agreements to be justified.[238] However, the text of paragraph (h) and the Note thereto contain important limitations that have resulted in their being rarely invoked.[239] An intergovernmental commodity agreement can be brought within this exception only if it conforms to criteria that have been submitted to the Members (formerly "Contracting

---

[234] AB in *US-Gasoline*, at p. 23.

[235] On Article XX(a), see Feddersen (1998).

[236] The most obvious examples are measures based on animal welfare considerations, such as EC initiatives on animal testing, minimum requirements for laying hens, and leghold traps used to catch fur-bearing animals. See further on such measures, Section 5.4.

[237] See Section 4.5.2.

[238] At Geneva, it was agreed that a general exception for commodities agreements should be applicable not just to the commodities chapter, but to all the provisions of the commercial policy chapter of the Charter. That exception was also included in the 1947 text of the GATT (Article XX:1(h) of GATT 1947) and as Article 45:1(a)(ix) of the Havana Charter. It now appears as Article XX(h) GATT. GATT (1995) at 588.

[239] A 1991 Secretariat Note on Trade and Environment mentions a small number of countries having invoked Article XX(h) as a justification for quantitative restriction. GATT (1991) at p. 95.

Parties") and they have not disapproved of such criteria, or if the agreement itself is so submitted and it has not been disapproved of, or, finally, if the agreement conforms to the principles in a resolution of the United Nations Economic and Social Council (ECOSOC) from 1947. When the European Communities raised Article XX(h) to justify their banana import regime in the *Bananas II* case, the panel simply noted that none of these three scenarios were applicable to the case. Article XX(h) could therefore not justify the inconsistency of the banana regime with Article I GATT.[240]

4.4.2 General Conditions: The Chapeau to Article XX

The introductory clause to Article XX is often referred to as the chapeau to that Article, a practice that is adhered to here. The chapeau was not part of the original exceptions article as proposed by the US and the UK. It was inserted during the London sessions of the Preparatory Committee.[241] According to the chapeau, a measure taken to protect a legitimate interest as described in the various sub-paragraphs of Article XX should in its application not constitute arbitrary or unjustifiable discrimination between countries where the same conditions prevail or a disguised restriction on international trade. Thus, the chapeau contains three requirements, two of which appear closely inter-related because they both refer to discrimination. The term "unjustifiable" was only inserted into the chapeau at the New York session of the Preparatory Committee.[242] The Appellate Body has made it clear that 'between countries where the same conditions prevail' includes discrimination between exporting Members and the importing Member concerned.[243]

The chapeau to Article XX has only been addressed in two GATT dispute settlement cases. In both instances, the panel dealt with the chapeau first, and then proceeded to examine whether specific exceptions in Article XX had rightfully been invoked.[244] Later GATT panels developed the practice of first inquiring whether one of the exceptions in paragraphs (a) to (j) applied. As none of these panels concluded that this was the case, none of them reached the stage of testing the measure for compatibility with the chapeau.[245] In the WTO, the Appellate Body in *US-Gasoline* for the first time provided a fully-fledged analysis of the chapeau, its function and its wording. The Appellate Body noted that

---

[240] *EC-Bananas II*, unadopted, para. 166.

[241] GATT (1995) at 563-4.

[242] Charnovitz (1991) at note 41. The term "unjustifiable" is absent in the equivalent of the chapeau of Article XX in the EC Treaty, i.e. the second sentence of Article 30 EC.

[243] AB in *US-Gasoline*, at pp. 23-24; AB in *US-Shrimp-Turtle*, para. 150.

[244] See *US-Tuna 1982*, para. 4.8, and *US-Spring Assemblies*, paras. 54-56.

[245] Document WT/CTE/W/53/Rev.1, para. 13.

the provisions of the chapeau cannot logically refer to the same standard(s) by which a violation of a substantive rule has been determined to have occurred.[246] It further observed that the sentence '[n]othing in this Agreement shall be construed...' in the chapeau indicates that Article XX relates to all of the obligations under the GATT, including Article III.[247] Having remarked that the purpose and object of the chapeau is to prevent any abuse of the exceptions, the Appellate Body said that:

> The chapeau is animated by the principle that while the exceptions of Article XX may be invoked as a matter of legal right, they should not be so applied as to frustrate or defeat the legal obligations of the holder of the right under the substantive rules of the General Agreement. If those exceptions are not to be abused or misused, in other words, the measures falling within the particular exceptions must be applied reasonably, with due regard both to the legal duties of the party claiming the exception and the legal rights of the other parties concerned.[248]

The Appellate Body went on to observe that the three standards in the chapeau may be read side-by-side, and that 'they impart meaning to one another.' It was clear to the Appellate Body that "disguised restriction" includes "disguised *discrimination*" and is not exhausted by '*concealed* or *unannounced* restriction or discrimination'. Moreover, "disguised restriction" embraces restrictions amounting to arbitrary or unjustifiable discrimination.[249] The Appellate Body applied these interpretations to the dispute at issue and found two failures in the national measures assessed: To explore means to mitigate problems arising from accepting individual foreign baselines, in particular to seek co-operation with foreign governments, and to count the costs for foreign refiners. The Appellate Body concluded that the resulting discrimination 'must have been foreseen, and was not merely inadvertent or unavoidable'.[250] In their application, the US measures constituted "unjustifiable discrimination" and a "disguised restriction on international trade".

In *US-Shrimp-Turtle*, the Appellate Body stated that the policy goal of a measure cannot amount to its rationale or justification under the standards of the chapeau of Article XX.[251] The chapeau requires the striking of a balance between the right of the party invoking an exception and the duty of that same

---

[246] AB in *US-Gasoline*, at p. 23.

[247] Ibid., at p. 24.

[248] Ibid., at p. 24.

[249] Ibid., at p. 26. Original emphasis. The limitation to 'concealed or unanounnenced' restrictions had been suggested by the GATT reports mentioned in note 244.

[250] Ibid., at p. 31.

[251] AB in *US-Shrimp-Turtle*, paras. 148-49.

party to respect the treaty rights of the other parties concerned.[252] 'The language of the chapeau makes clear that each of the exceptions in paragraphs (a) to (j) of Article XX is a *limited and conditional* exception from the substantive obligations contained in the other provisions of the GATT 1994, that is to say, the ultimate availability of the exception is subject to the compliance by the invoking Member with the requirements of the chapeau'.[253] The chapeau is but one expression of the principle of good faith, which is at once a general principle of law in general and of international law in particular.[254] The Appellate Body added that:

> *The task of interpreting and applying the chapeau is, hence, essentially the delicate one of locating and marking out a line of equilibrium between the right of a Member to invoke an exception under Article XX and the rights of the other Members under varying substantive provisions [...] The location of the line of equilibrium, as expressed in the chapeau, is not fixed and unchanging; the line moves as the kind and the shape of the measures at stake vary and as the facts making up specific cases differ.[255]*

The Appellate Body considered the application of the US measure at issue in the light of these observations.[256] First of all, the Appellate Body stressed the coercive effect of the measure, that required all other exporting Members wishing to exercise their GATT rights to adopt essentially the same policy as that applied in the US. Different conditions prevailing in different countries were not taken into account, which resulted in discrimination.[257] According to the Appellate Body, discrimination results not only when countries in which the same conditions prevail are treated differently, but also when the application of the measure at issue does not allow for any inquiry into the appropriateness of the regulatory programme for the conditions prevailing in those exporting countries.[258] The second major aspect of the application of the US measure criticised by the Appellate Body was the fact that the US had not engaged in 'serious, across-the-board negotiations' to seek international agreement before enforcing the import prohibition. The fact that the US had negotiated an Inter-American Convention on the protection of sea turtles demonstrated that 'an alternative course of action was reasonably open to the United States for securing the legitimate policy goal

---

[252] Ibid., para. 156.

[253] Ibid., para. 157. Emphasis in the original.

[254] Ibid., para. 158.

[255] Ibid., para. 159.

[256] For more elaborate discussions, see Appleton (1999); Wiers (1999).

[257] AB in *US-Shrimp-Turtle*, paras. 161-165.

[258] Ibid., para. 165.

[259] Ibid., paras. 166-171.

of its measure'.[259] The US had negotiated with some shrimp exporters, but not with others. The resulting discrimination was unjustifiable.

The US measure was operated completely unilaterally in its actual application. Detailing the required conservation policies, as well as the process of granting, denying or withdrawing certification to exporting countries took place without any participation by those countries. The unilateral character of the application of the American measure 'heightened the disruptive and discriminatory influence of the import prohibition and underscored its unjustifiability.'[260] Moreover, some countries were granted a phase-in period to comply with the US requirements, while others were not; and the level of efforts made by the US to transfer the required technology also differed from country to country. All these differences in their cumulative effect amounted to "unjustifiable discrimination".[261] The Appellate Body also found that the rigidity of the US requirements and the inflexible way in which they were applied constituted "arbitrary discrimination". The Appellate Body in its further considerations on this element of the chapeau placed emphasis on the lack of transparency and predictability in the application of the measure. It made a connection with Article X:3 GATT in this respect.[262]

In *EC-Asbestos*, the panel's first step in addressing the measure under the chapeau was to determine whether the measure was "discriminatory" in its application. In a footnote the panel added that what is prohibited by the introductory clause to Article XX is a particular form of discrimination (i.e. that which is arbitrary or unjustifiable between countries where the same conditions prevail) and not all forms of discrimination. If the measure is not in general discriminatory in its application, then *a fortiori* it cannot constitute arbitrary or unjustifiable discrimination between countries where the same conditions prevail.[263] The panel went on to note that

if the application of the measure is found to be discriminatory, it still remains to be seen whether it is arbitrary and/or unjustifiable between countries where the same conditions prevail. It is in this context, and not in the stage of the existence of discrimination - which is an objective fact, that we shall determine whether the measures falling within the particular exceptions of Article XX(b) [...] have been applied reasonably, with due regard to both the legal duties of the party claiming the exception and the legal rights of the other parties concerned.[264]

---

[260] Ibid., para. 172.

[261] Ibid., para. 176.

[262] Ibid., paras. 177-184.

[263] Panel in *EC-Asbestos*, original footnote 191, referring to *US-Spring Assemblies*, para. 55.

[264] Ibid., para. 8.226. Emphasis in the original.

The panel concluded that since Canada had not established discrimination in relation to the application of the French Decree, there was no need to consider the question of its arbitrariness or unjustifiability.[265] Turning the analysis to 'disguised restriction on international trade', the panel focused on the word "disguised". A restriction which formally meets the requirements of Article XX(b) will constitute an abuse if such compliance is in fact only a disguise to conceal the pursuit of trade-restrictive objectives. Although the aim of a measure may not be easily ascertained, the protective application of a measure can most often be discerned from its design, architecture and revealing structure.[266] The panel referred to the Appellate Body in *Japan-Alcohol*.[267] It saw no reason why it should not be applicable in other circumstances where it is necessary to determine whether a measure is being applied for protective purposes.[268] The panel found nothing in the design, architecture and revealing structure of the French Decree to suggest that the French measure had protectionist *objectives*. It admitted that there is always the possibility that such measures might have the *effect* of favouring the domestic substitute product's manufacturers. However, 'this is a natural consequence of prohibiting a given product and in itself cannot justify the conclusion that the measure has a protectionist *aim*, as long as it remains within certain limits'. The panel observed that the information made available to it did not suggest that the import ban had benefited French industry, to the detriment of third country producers, *to such an extent* as to lead to the conclusion that the Decree has been applied so as to constitute a disguised restriction on international trade.[269] The panel's interpretation of the chapeau was not appealed.

The panel in *US-Shrimp-Turtle* was reconvened to determine the compatibility with the WTO rules of the measures taken by the US in order to implement the Appellate Body report. The panel concentrated on the chapeau of Article XX as a standard for determining the extent of the obligation to negotiate an international agreement before resorting to unilateral import restrictions. The panel referred to the Marrakesh Decision establishing the Committee on Trade and Environment, and noted that

> recourse to trade-related measures not based on international consensus is generally not the most appropriate means of enforcing environmental measures, since it leads to the imposition of unwanted constraints on the multilateral trading system and may affect sustainable development.[270]

---

[265] Ibid., para. 8.230.

[266] Ibid., para. 8.236.

[267] The panel erroneously stated that this approach by the AB had been developed in relation to Article III:4, whereas in actual fact it had been developed in relation to Article III:2, second sentence.

[268] Ibid., original footnote 199.

[269] Ibid., paras. 8.238-9. Emphasis added.

[270] Panel in *US-Shrimp-Turtle Implementation*, para. 5.55.

The panel added that both the factual context, i.e. sea turtles being highly migratory species, and the legal framework, i.e. the recognition in the WTO and other international agreements that the protection of migratory species is best achieved through international cooperation, 'significantly move the line of equilibrium referred to by the Appellate Body towards a bilaterally or multilaterally negotiated solution, thus rendering recourse to unilateral measures less acceptable'. Hence, applying a unilateral import prohibition without having made "serious efforts" to negotiate a multilateral agreement might amount to an abuse or misuse of Article XX. Moreover, the notion of good faith as expressed by the chapeau to Article XX implies a continuity of efforts.[271] However, the obligation is to *negotiate* an agreement before resorting to unilateral measures, not to *conclude* one.[272] The US in this case was obliged to take the initiative of negotiating with all interested parties and to make serious efforts in good faith to negotiate, taking into account the situations in the other negotiating countries.[273] The panel regarded the Inter-American Convention on Sea Turtle Protection as evidence that an international agreement was feasible in the circumstances, and observed that it was reasonable to expect a great deal of the US in terms of good faith efforts, considering it was a *"demandeur"* in this field and given its capacity of persuasion. However, the US cannot be exclusively responsible for reaching an agreement.[274] The panel found that the US efforts met the standards established. However, it added that:

> in a context such as this one [...], the possibility to impose a unilateral measure[...] is more to be seen, for the purposes of Article XX, as the possibility to adopt a provisional measure allowed for emergency reasons than as a definitive "right" to take a permanent measure. The extent to which serious good faith efforts continue to be made may be reassessed at any time. For instance, steps which constituted good faith efforts at the beginning of a negotiation may fail to meet that test at a later stage.[275]

The panel subsequently assessed the other elements of "unjustifiable discrimination" as identified by the Appellate Body. As regards the lack of flexibility of the original US implementing measures, the panel interpreted the AB report as implying that while demanding other Members to adopt 'essentially the same' regulatory programme would amount to unjustifiable discrimination, demanding them to adopt programmes that are 'comparable in effectiveness' would not. Such a requirement must in practice be applied with sufficient flexibility, taking

---

[271] Ibid., paras. 5.59-60.

[272] Ibid., paras. 5.63-64, referring to paras. 166 and 172 of the AB report in *US-Shrimp-Turtle*.

[273] Ibid., paras. 5.66 and 5.73.

[274] Ibid., paras. 5.75-76 and 5.78.

[275] Ibid., para. 5.88.

into account the conditions prevailing in the exporting country.[276] The panel then addressed an additional argument by the complainant, Malaysia, which merits consideration. Malaysia argued that the United States, by imposing a unilaterally defined standard of protection, violated the sovereign right of Malaysia to determine its own sea turtle protection and conservation policy. The panel responded as follows:

> [I]t is the understanding of the Panel that the Appellate Body Report found that, while a WTO Member may not impose on exporting members to apply the same standards of environmental protection as those it applies itself, this Member may legitimately require, as a condition of access of certain products to its market, that exporting countries commit themselves to a regulatory programme deemed comparable to its own. [...][277]

The panel added that this could have consequences on policy priorities of exporting countries:

> If Malaysia exported shrimp to the United States, it would be subject to requirements that may distort Malaysia's priorities in terms of environmental policy. As Article XX of the GATT 1994 has been interpreted by the Appellate Body, the WTO Agreement does not provide for any recourse in the situation Malaysia would face under those circumstances.[278]

The second additional element of unjustifiable discrimination in the AB report consisted of the prohibition of imports of shrimp from uncertified countries, even if the shrimp in question had in fact been caught using turtle excluder devices (TEDs). The panel found that the US had changed its guidelines sufficiently in this respect, even if the new guidelines were the subject of appeal in US domestic courts at the time the panel issued its report and were under threat of being repealed in the future.[279] The third and fourth additional elements concerned discrimination between exporting countries in terms of the granted phase-in periods, and differences in the level of efforts by the US to transfer technology. The panel considered that the problems identified by the AB in these respects were not very relevant in this instance, as Malaysia had so far not sought certification and therefore it was impossible to assess whether it would incur more costs than the countries granted longer phase-in periods had incurred. Neither had Malaysia sought technology transfer.[280]

---

[276] Ibid., paras. 5.93-102.

[277] Ibid., para. 5.103.

[278] Ibid.

[279] Ibid., paras. 5.106-111.

[280] Ibid., paras. 5.14-116 and 5.117-120.

With regard to the issue of "arbitrary discrimination", the panel essentially reiterated its findings under "unjustifiable discrimination" to the effect that the US measures now provided sufficient flexibility. The second aspect of "arbitrary discrimination" concerned requirements of due process, i.e. the *ex parte* nature of inquiries and certifications, and the absence of a formal opportunity to be heard, of a formal written decision, and of a procedure for review. The panel found that the revised US measures, as well as their application in practice, sufficiently addressed the concerns raised by the AB in this regard.[281]

Finally, the panel assessed whether the US implementing measures consti-tuted a disguised trade restriction. The panel referred to the *EC-Asbestos* panel to the effect that there would be an abuse of Article XX if compliance with Article XX was in fact only a disguise to conceal the pursuit of trade-restrictive objec-tives.[282] Like the panel in *EC-Asbestos*, it further referred to the Appellate Body in *Japan-Alcohol* to the effect that the protective application of a measure can most often be discerned from its design, architecture and revealing structure.[283] The panel, looking at the US law and implementing measures as actually applied by the US, concluded that there were no indications of protective application. By allowing exporting countries to apply programmes not based on the mandatory use of turtle excluder devices (TEDs), and by offering technical assistance to develop the use of TEDs in third countries, the United States had demonstrated that its measures were not being applied so as to constitute a disguised restric-tion on trade.[284]

4.4.3 Relationship Between Article XX and Article III

According to the Appellate Body in *US-Gasoline*, the relation-ship between the "affirmative commitments" set out in Articles I, III and XI GATT, and the policies and interests embodied in the "general exceptions" listed in Article XX GATT can only be given meaning within the framework of the GATT and its object and purpose by a treaty interpreter on a case-to-case basis.[285] In both *US-Gasoline* and *US-Shrimp-Turtle*, the Appellate Body contrasted the right to invoke the exceptions in Article XX with the "substantive" rules, provi-sions, rights, and obligations that are found in provisions such as Articles III or XI.[286] Also in *US-Gasoline*, the Appellate Body stated that '[t]he chapeau by its express terms addresses, not so much the questioned measure or its specific

---

[281] Ibid., paras. 5.126-136.

[282] Referring to the panel in *EC-Asbestos*, para. 8.236. This finding was neither reversed nor modified by the AB.

[283] AB in *Japan-Alcohol*, at p. 29.

[284] Panel in *US-Shrimp-Turtle Implementation*, paras. 5.138-144.

[285] AB in *US-Gasoline*, at p. 18.

[286] AB in *US-Gasoline*, at pp. 22-25; AB in *US-Shrimp-Turtle*, paras. 156-160.

contents as such, but rather *the manner* in which that measure is *applied*.'[287]
The provisions of the chapeau 'cannot logically refer to the same standard(s) by
which a violation of a substantive rule has been determined to have occurred'.[288]
In *US-Shrimp-Turtle*, the Appellate Body specified that the nature and quality of
the discrimination in the chapeau of Article XX is 'different from the discrimination in the treatment of products which was already found to be inconsistent
with one of the substantive obligations of the GATT 1994, such as Articles I,
III or XI'.[289]

In *US-Gasoline*, the Appellate Body said that '[t]he chapeau of Article XX
makes it clear that it is the "measures" which are to be examined under Article
XX(g), and not the legal finding of less favourable treatment [under Article
III:4].'[290] The AB thereby corrected the panel, which had asked itself whether
the "less favourable treatment" of imported gasoline "related to" the conservation
of natural resources, rather than the "measure", i.e. the baseline establishment
rules. In *Argentina-Hides*, the panel argued that although the above statement
was made by the Appellate Body with regard to Article XX(g), it was based on
the chapeau and should therefore apply to Article XX(d) too.[291] Thus, it is not the
actual *violation* of a substantive obligation such as Article III that has to meet
the "means-ends tests" in Article XX, but rather the measure. The same would
seem to apply to the chapeau of Article XX, which refers to "measures" and not
to "violations". However, the assessment of a measure's application under the
chapeau will focus on discriminatory or protective aspects. Even if the Appellate
Body has emphasised that the discrimination standard for the chapeau of Article
XX cannot be the same as the standard in substantive GATT provisions, there
will likely be some overlap with the analysis under e.g. Article III. However, the
analysis in the chapeau requires an extra step, i.e., focusing on the justifiability
or arbitrariness of a difference in treatment that may have already been found
under Article III.[292]

---

[287] AB in *US-Gasoline*, at p. 22, referring to the GATT panel in *US-Spring Assemblies*.

[288] Ibid., at p. 23.

[289] AB in *US-Shrimp-Turtle*, para. 150.

[290] AB in *US-Gasoline*, at p. 16.

[291] Panel in *Argentina-Hides*, para. 11.303 and footnote 560. The panel considered that the Appellate Body's
approach overruled that taken by the GATT panel in *US-Section 337*, para. 5.27, which had stated that
what had to be justified as "necessary" under Article XX(d) was 'each of the inconsistencies with another
GATT Article found to exist'.

[292] Cf. the panel in *Argentina-Hides*, footnote 564, with regard to the justification of tax differences between
domestic and imported products: 'It is true that the European Communities disputes that the higher
rates applied to imported products [...] are "necessary" in order to secure compliance with the IVA Law
and IG Law. [...] We consider that this contention goes to the question of whether Argentina makes
improper use of the exception set out in Article XX(d) and not to the question of whether [the measures],

The two GATT panel reports in *US-Beer* and *US-Auto Taxes* introduced an "aim and effect" test into Article III. According to that test, if a regulatory or tax distinction is not applied with the aim or effect of protecting domestic production, but has a legitimate aim, the products at issue are not "like" and the measure will not thereby violate Article III. This test has been criticised for introducing the consideration of regulatory objectives into the analysis of Article III, while they should be properly considered in Article XX.[293] In *Japan-Alcohol*, the panel expressly rejected the "aim and effect" test for the first sentence of Article III:2, noting *inter alia* that 'the list of exceptions contained in Article XX of GATT 1994 could become redundant or useless because the aim-and-effect test does not contain a definitive list of grounds justifying departure from the obligations that are otherwise incorporated in Article III.' According to the panel, a WTO Member could invoke the protection of health in the context of the aim-and-effect test. If this were the case, the standard of proof established in Article XX would effectively be circumvented; WTO Members would not have to prove that a health measure is "necessary" to achieve its health objective.[294] Likewise, the panel in *EC-Asbestos* refused to take into account health risks of different products in determining "likeness" under Article III:4, for fear of thereby rendering Article XX(b) inutile, especially the "necessary" and chapeau requirements.[295] However, the Appellate Body reversed this approach, emphasising that different inquiries occur under Articles III:4 and XX:

> *Under Article III:4, evidence relating to health risks may be relevant in assessing the* competitive relationship in the marketplace *between allegedly "like" products. The same, or similar, evidence serves a different purpose under Article XX(b), namely, that of assessing whether a Member has a sufficient basis for "adopting or enforcing" a WTO-inconsistent measure on the grounds of human health.*[296]

---

in light of their general design and structure, fall within the terms of Article XX(d). We therefore address the justifiability of applying higher rates to imported products when we appraise [the measures] under the chapeau of Article XX. This approach is in accordance with that followed by the Appellate Body in *United States-Gasoline.*'

[293] See e.g. Mattoo and Subramanian (1998).

[294] Panel in *Japan-Alcohol*, paras. 6.16-17.

[295] Panel in *EC-Asbestos*, para. 8.130.

[296] AB in *EC-Asbestos*, para. 115. Emphasis in the original.

4.5 Technical Barriers to Trade and Sanitary and Phytosanitary Measures

In addition to GATT 1994, two WTO Agreements of particular relevance to the scope of unilateral environmental measures are the Agreement on Technical Barriers to Trade (TBT) and the Agreement on the Application of Sanitary and Phytosanitary Measures (SPS). Both agreements resemble and elaborate upon the GATT disciplines. However, there are important differences between the two agreements, regarding their scope and disciplines, as well as their relationship to GATT 1994. Their relationship *inter se* will also be discussed.

4.5.1 The Agreement on Technical Barriers to Trade (TBT)

Trade barriers can result from divergences between technical requirements between countries. A producer in country A has to comply with requirement A in its home market, and also with requirement B in country B if it wishes to sell its goods on that market. If requirements A and B are so different as to necessitate changes in the production process, the additional costs incurred are clear. Trade barriers can also result from certification and approval procedures. The emphasis in this work, however, is on diverging requirements themselves, and more particularly, those with which compliance is mandatory. Such requirements often do not discriminate on the basis of product origin, and usually reflect valid national regulatory concerns over such interests as safety, health and environmental protection. They therefore represent the tensions between such interests and that of liberalising trade *par excellence.*

In principle, all products, including industrial and agricultural products, are subject to the TBT Agreement.[297] The Agreement lays down obligations concerning technical regulations, standards and conformity assessment procedures. Only those national measures falling within the definitions of either of these three categories will therefore be covered by the Agreement. The definitions and the most relevant provisions of the TBT Agreement are found in the Annex to this work. The definitions differentiate between "technical regulations" and "standards". Whereas compliance with a technical regulation is mandatory, compliance with a standard is voluntary.[298] Although voluntary standards may have certain trade effects, especially when they receive some form of government support, the focus in this analysis is on technical regulations. Their potential trade effects are indisputable, as foreign producers will have to comply with such

---

[297] Article 1.3 TBT Agreement, hereinafter refererred to as TBT.

[298] Cf. the Explanatory Note to Definition 2 of Annex 1 TBT: '[...] For the purpose of this Agreement standards are defined as voluntary and technical regulations as mandatory documents.[...]'

regulations if they wish to sell their products on the market of the Member applying those regulations. The central provisions regarding technical regulations are found in Article 2 of the TBT Agreement. The main obligations of Members with respect to standards are found in the Code of Good Practice for the Preparation, Adoption and Application of Standards, which is found in Annex 3 to the TBT Agreement. Materially, these obligations strongly resemble the obligations with respect to technical regulations that are discussed hereafter.[299] Article 5 of the TBT Agreement deals with conformity assessment, and again, its obligations resemble those applying to technical regulations.

The panel in *EC-Asbestos* stated that a measure constitutes a "technical regulation" if it affects one or more given products, specifies the technical characteristics of the product(s) which allow them to be marketed in the Member that took the measure, and compliance is mandatory.[300] On the basis of this description, the panel found that the part of the pertinent French law constituting a general prohibition on marketing asbestos and asbestos-containing products was not a "technical regulation". The part of the French law providing exceptions to the asbestos ban did constitute a "technical regulation", but the panel declined to come to any findings since the claimant had not made specific claims concerning those exceptions.[301] The Appellate Body disagreed with the panel's separation of the prohibitions and exceptions in the national measure at issue. It was of the opinion that the measure had to be examined as a whole, and that the exceptions in the measure would have no autonomous legal significance in the absence of the prohibitions.[302] According to the Appellate Body, with respect to products, a "technical regulation" has the effect of *prescribing* or *imposing* one or more "characteristics". 'Product characteristics may be prescribed or imposed in a positive or negative form. Although a technical regulation must be applicable to an *identifiable* product or group of products, these do not have to be explicitly named, identified or specified in the national measure.'[303] Applying these interpretations to the French measure at issue, the Appellate Body observed that the products covered by a prohibition of *products containing a substance* (in this case asbestos fibres) were identifiable. The measure laid down "characteristics" for all products that might contain asbestos. Its exceptions laid down the 'applicable administrative provisions' for certain products containing asbestos fibres that were excluded from the prohibition. The measure as a whole was a "technical regulation" under the TBT Agreement.[304] Interestingly, the Appellate Body added that if the French measure had consisted only of

---

[299] The TBT Agreement contains only one provision specifically dealing with standards, Article 4, which refers to the Code of Good Practice.

[300] Panel in *EC-Asbestos*, para. 8.57. Original footnote omitted.

[301] Ibid., paras. 8.58 and 8.70-72.

[302] AB in *EC-Asbestos*, para. 64.

a prohibition on asbestos fibres as such, it might not constitute a "technical regulation".[305]

Article 2.1 TBT encapsulates both the Most-Favoured Nation (MFN) and National Treatment (NT) requirements from the GATT. As the National Treatment requirement is phrased in essentially the same terms as in Article III:4 GATT, the crucial elements being "like product" and "treatment no less favourable", the discussion of that Article and those terms in Section 4.2 is referred to. The remainder of Article 2 TBT contains obligations that go beyond the MFN and NT standards. Arguably, the pivotal provision is Article 2.2, reproduced in the Annex to this work. The 1979 TBT Agreement already contained a provision similar to Article 2.2 TBT. In its Article 2.1 it combined the National and Most-Favoured Nation Treatment requirements with two requirements; (a) to ensure that technical regulations and standards were not prepared, adopted or applied *with a view to* creating trade obstacles, and (b) to ensure that technical regulations, standards or their application did not have the *effect* of creating unnecessary trade obstacles.[306] The difference between technical regulations with the *purpose* and with the *effect* of creating trade obstacles has been removed in the 1994 TBT Agreement.[307] Another difference is that Article 2.1 of the 1979 Agreement did not elaborate upon the notion of "unnecessary" with reference to protection goals, as Article 2.2 TBT does. However, the Preamble to the 1979 Agreement did clarify that countries could take measures to pursue such goals, and moreover mentioned them among the reasons why relevant international standards could be inappropriate.[308] Presumably, therefore, a member could enact a technical regulation if it deemed it "necessary" to do so for the protection of non-trade goals. A complainant had to prove that a technical regulation went beyond what was necessary.[309]

---

[303] Ibid., paras. 68-70.

[304] Ibid., paras. 72-76.

[305] Ibid., para. 71.

[306] Emphasis added. Article 2.1 of the 1979 TBT Agreement reads in full: 'Parties shall ensure that technical regulations and standards are not prepared, adopted or applied with a view to creating obstacles to international trade. Furthermore, products imported from the territory of any Party shall be accorded treatment no less favourable than that accorded to like products of national origin and to like products originating in any other country in relation to such technical regulations and standards. They shall likewise ensure that neither technical regulations nor standards themselves nor their application have the effect of creating unnecessary obstacles to international trade.' 1979 TBT Agreement, as reproduced in EC Official Journal L 71 (1980) 29-43.

[307] Article 2.2 TBT combines the phrases 'with a view to' and 'with the effect of' with 'creating unnecessary trade obstacles'.

[308] Article 2.2 of the 1979 TBT Agreement.

[309] See Stewart (1993) at 1068, Middleton (1980) at 206.

Contemporary GATT publications suggest that the 1979 Agreement was already intended to go beyond the National Treatment and Most Favoured Nation requirements which it incorporated.[310] A GATT publication from 1979 notes that standards were covered in a general way in Article III, XI and XX GATT, but that the TBT Agreement went *"well beyond* these provisions".[311] This was confirmed in its account of the results of the Tokyo Round.[312] The 1979 TBT Agreement was a plurilateral agreement, a "side-code" binding only the signatories to it and having its own dispute settlement procedures.[313] When it was transformed into the 1994 TBT Agreement, it became part of the single WTO undertaking. Thus, the possibility of challenging internal measures beyond those violating the GATT was extended from an option chosen by a limited membership to a general standard applicable to all WTO members, and subjected to the general procedures of the Dispute Settlement Understanding. Little attention appears to have been paid to this important extension of the capacity to challenge the internal regulations of Members.[314]

The non-exhaustive list of "legitimate objectives" in Article 2.2 contains elements from Article XX(b) GATT and Article XXI GATT, as well as objectives not found in those provisions, i.e. the prevention of deceptive practices, and the protection of the environment and of human safety. The second non-exhaustive list in Article 2.2 contains elements to be taken into account in assessing the risk of the non-fulfilment of a legitimate objective, when determining whether a technical regulation is 'not more trade-restrictive than necessary to fulfil a legitimate objective'. So far, no dispute settlement reports have assessed a measure under either Article 2.1 of the 1979 TBT Agreement, or Article 2.2 of the 1994 TBT Agreement.[315]

---

[310] GATT (1979a) at 41: 'These regulations are often adopted for perfectly legitimate reasons, and are not intended in themselves as barriers to trade. However, they can create trade barriers in many different ways, and so can the testing requirements and certification systems which are designed to ensure that the regulations are met. International trade can be complicated and inhibited by disparities between regulations at local, State, national or regional levels'.

[311] GATT (1979b) at 62. Emphasis added.

[312] Ibid., at 139: 'The relevant provisions of the GATT are not sufficient in themselves to enable all the problems that arise in the field of technical barriers to trade to be dealt with. There was a need to go beyond the GATT provisions. [...] The objective of the Agreement cannot be to abolish all restrictions. Its aim is to remove unnecessary barriers to trade.' Original underlining.

[313] Jackson (1988); Bernier (1982); Middleton (1980).

[314] This author has found no account of the significance of the combination of the far-reaching "trade obstacles" provision and its extension to the entire membership of the WTO. Accounts of the ongoing negotiations during the Uruguay Round merely stated that the new TBT Agreement would extend and clarify the 1979 version. See e.g. GATT Activities in 1991, Geneva, GATT, 1992, at 25.

[315] Under the WTO dispute settlement procedures, Article 2 TBT was invoked in a number of disputes but not applied by panels or the Appellate Body. See Section 5.1.2. Its predecessor, Article 2.1 of the 1979 TBT Agreement, was also not the subject of dispute settlement. See Annex B in Petersmann (1997a).

According to the first sentence of Article 2.5, Members must, upon request by other Members, justify in terms of the provisions of Article 2.2 to 2.4 their technical regulations which may have significant trade effects. Thus, they will have to explain that their technical regulations do not create unnecessary trade barriers (Article 2.2), and are not maintained while circumstances or objectives giving rise to their adoption no longer exist (Article 2.3). Moreover, they will need to explain why any relevant international standards that they have not used as a basis for their technical regulations were ineffective or inappropriate means for the legitimate objectives pursued by their technical regulations. This may be the case as regards fundamental climatic or geographical factors or fundamental technological problems (Article 2.4). Apart from the obligation to explain technical regulations, there are general notification and information requirements in Articles 2.9 and 2.10. The provisions of the TBT Agreement regarding the use of international standards are further discussed *infra*.[316]

Article 2.7 obliges Members to 'give positive consideration to accepting as equivalent' technical regulations of other Members, even if these regulations differ from their own, provided they are satisfied that these regulations adequately fulfil the objectives of their own regulations.[317] This is a first step towards the recognition of equivalent standards.[318] It should be noted that Article 2.7 does not provide for positive consideration to be given to *mutual* recognition, but to *unilaterally* recognising another Member's technical regulations.[319] Article 2.8 requires Members to specify technical regulations in terms of performance rather than design or descriptive characteristics. This requirement is of great potential value in overcoming the problems arising from different national regulatory approaches. Focusing on performance rather than design will create more instances in which foreign producers can enter markets without having to redesign their products.[320] However, the requirement in Article 2.8 is accompanied by the qualification 'wherever appropriate', which may significantly diminish its importance.

The provisions in the TBT Agreement addressing the procedures applied by Members to assess the conformity with their technical regulations and

---

[316] See Section 4.6.2.

[317] Article 2.7 TBT.

[318] It has been proposed to extend the obligation in Article 2.7 to voluntary standards too. See e.g. G/TBT/W/88 and 145, and G/TBT/W/143.

[319] Appleton (1997a) at 120 nonetheless speaks of "mutual recognition" in the context of Article 2.7 TBT.

[320] Cf. the reference to Article 2.8 TBT in interpreting EC law by Advocate General Alber in his opinion in Joined Cases C-27/00 and C-122/00 *Omega Air*.

standards largely mirror the provisions on technical regulations themselves.[321] However, Article 6, the provision on the recognition of foreign conformity assessment procedures, is more elaborate than the parallel provision on the recognition of technical regulations. There is a basic obligation to recognise foreign conformity assessment procedures, which is farther-reaching than the mere obligation to 'give positive consideration to accepting as equivalent foreign technical regulations' in Article 2.7. Moreover, Article 6 contains elements of *mutual* recognition not found in the parallel provision on the recognition of technical regulations. However, this wider basic obligation is subject to important qualifications. Members are only to ensure the acceptance of the results of foreign conformity assessment 'whenever possible', and provided 'they are satisfied that those procedures offer an assurance of conformity with applicable technical regulations or standards equivalent to their own procedures'.[322]

4.5.2   The Agreement on the Application of Sanitary and Phytosanitary Measures (SPS)

In the GATT era, to the extent that sanitary and phytosanitary measures violated GATT obligations, they could be justified under Article XX(b) of GATT 1947. However, when negotiations on agricultural trade liberalisation were taking place during the Uruguay Round, the need was felt to elaborate more detailed rules for these types of measures, which resulted in the SPS Agreement. The application of sanitary and phytosanitary measures to imports could otherwise undo the progress which had already been made in terms of market access commitments in agricultural goods. Thus, the SPS Agreement intends to ensure that human, animal and plant life and health can be effectively protected, but at the same time to prevent SPS measures from being abused as 'thinly-disguised barriers to trade'.[323]

As is the case for TBT, the starting point as far as the coverage of the SPS Agreement is concerned lies in its definitions. Article 1.2 SPS refers to Annex A to the SPS Agreement, which defines a sanitary or phytosanitary measure in terms of the objective of its application. A measure is an SPS measure if it is applied to protect human, animal or plant life or health from risks arising from pests or diseases;[324] to protect human or animal life or health from food-borne risks;[325] and to prevent or limit other damage caused by pests.[326] The

---

[321] Cf. Article 5.1.2 with 2.2; 5.2.7 with 2.3; 5.4 with 2.4; 5.5 with 2.6; 5.6 with 2.9; and 5.7 with 2.10.

[322] Article 6.1 TBT.

[323] Stewart (1993) at 41.

[324] Annex A of the SPS Agreement, 1.(a) and 1.(c); hereinafter referred to as SPS.

[325] Annex A SPS, 1.(b).

[326] Annex A SPS, 1.(d).

second leg of the definition states that SPS measures include 'all relevant laws, decrees, regulations, requirements and procedures including *inter alia* product criteria; processes and production methods; [...] and packaging and labelling requirements directly related to food safety'.

Once within the SPS Agreement and in accordance with its definitions that refer to the measure's objective, Article 1.1 SPS suggests a broad coverage *ratione materiae* by stating that the Agreement applies to all SPS measures 'which may directly or indirectly affect international trade'. This includes a wide range of measures, including border measures that would be covered by Article XI GATT and internal regulations that would be covered by Article III GATT.[327] In fact, the words "indirectly affect" make it difficult to imagine any SPS measures not covered by Article 1.1. Perhaps a local SPS measure, such as the temporary closure of a nature reserve after the outbreak of an animal or plant disease, could be seen as not even indirectly affecting trade. Potentially more troublesome seems to be the reference to the measure's objective in the definitions. What if a Member challenged with a violation of the SPS Agreement argues that its measure is not being applied to protect life or health and is therefore not covered by the SPS Agreement? Such a scenario is not entirely inconceivable, because the SPS Agreement imposes more duties upon the Members in terms of risk assessment than does the GATT or the TBT Agreement, as will be shown below. However, it should be noted that the question whether a measure is being applied to protect life or health should not be equated with the legislator's subjective intent. It seems that this question could be objectivised to an important extent.[328]

The central substantive obligations contained in the Agreement are found in Articles 2, 3 and 5.[329] Article 3 relates to international standards and is discussed in Section 4.6.3. Article 2.1 reaffirms the right of WTO Members to take any SPS measures which are necessary for life or health protection, provided that such measures are consistent with the SPS Agreement. Article 2.2 lays down the basic obligations of the SPS Agreement. It contains the "necessary" requirement that is also found in Article XX(b) GATT, and the requirement that SPS measures have a scientific basis, which is further elaborated in Article 5. Article 2.3 appears largely to have been inspired by the requirements found in the chapeau of Article XX GATT. However, there is a subtle difference. While Article XX refers to the *application* of measures in a manner constituting discrimination, Article 2.3 SPS refers to discriminatory measures as such.[330] Moreover, the

---

[327] An overview of trade concerns related to SPS measures raised in the SPS Commitee is found in G/SPS/GEN/204.

[328] See Section 5.1.2.

[329] See the Annex to this work.

[330] The AB in *EC-Hormones*, para. 238, ignored this difference when it misquoted Article 2.3 SPS as if it did contain the exact same wording as the chapeau to Article XX GATT.

SPS provision posits "identical or similar" instead of "the same" conditions, and makes it clear that discrimination is covered not only between exporting Members but also between an exporting Member and the Member applying the measure. Article 2.3 SPS not only closely resembles the chapeau to Article XX GATT, it has also been said to correspond to the GATT's MFN and National Treatment principles.[331] As the Appellate Body put it in *Australia-Salmon*, '[Article 2.3] takes up obligations similar to those arising under Article I:1 and Article III:4 of the GATT 1994 and incorporates part of the "chapeau" to Article XX of the GATT 1994.'[332] Thus, Article 2.3 SPS unites substantive obligations and exceptions from the GATT.

Article 5.1 obliges Members to ensure that their SPS measures are based on 'an assessment, as appropriate to the circumstances, of the risk to human, animal or plant life or health [...]'. This language elaborates the requirements in Article 2.2. A measure not based on a risk assessment in the sense of Article 5 is presumed not to be based on scientific principles or to be maintained without sufficient scientific evidence in the sense of Article 2.2.[333] The panel in *EC-Hormones* considered that Article 5 provides for more specific rights and obligations than the 'basic rights and obligations' set out in Article 2.[334] The Appellate Body agreed, adding that Articles 2.2 and 5.1 should constantly be read together, that Article 2.2 informs Article 5.1, and that 'the elements that define the basic obligation set out in Article 2.2 impart meaning to Article 5.1.'[335] At the same time, Article 2.2 is broader than Article 5.1: '[g]iven the more general character of Article 2.2, not all violations of Article 2.2 are covered by Articles 5.1 and 5.2.'[336] Thus, a measure can be challenged for inconsistency with Article 2.2 SPS alone.

In Annex A to the SPS Agreement, "risk assessment" is defined as the 'evaluation of the *likelihood* of entry, establishment or spread of a pest or disease [...] according to the SPS measures which might be applied, and of the associated [...] consequences'. For food-borne risks, the definition is the 'evaluation of the *potential* for adverse effects on human or animal health'.[337] Thus, a risk assessment requires more for pests and diseases than for food-borne risks, which is understandable as human life or health may be at stake in the latter case. Evaluating the likelihood of entry or establishment 'according to the SPS measures which might be applied' entails a comparison of risks according to various alternative measures.[338] Article 5 SPS mentions a number of elements to

---

[331] Pauwelyn (1999) at 653.

[332] AB in *Australia-Salmon*, para. 251.

[333] Ibid., paras. 137-138.

[334] Panel in *EC-Hormones* (US), para 8.271; (CND), para. 8.274.

[335] AB in *EC-Hormones*, para. 180, as repeated by the AB in *Australia-Salmon*, para. 130.

[336] Panel in *Australia-Salmon*, para. 8.52, confirmed by the AB, para. 137.

[337] Annex A, paragraph 4, SPS Agreement.

[338] As confirmed by the AB in *Australia-Salmon*, para. 121, and in *Japan-Varietals*, para. 112.

be taken into account when assessing risk, such as international risk assessment techniques (Article 5.1), factors such as available scientific evidence and relevant environmental conditions (Article 5.2), and economic factors (Article 5.3). This does not appear to be an exhaustive enumeration, which leads to the question whether consumer concerns and societal value judgements that are not based on scientific evidence may be taken into account in assessing risks. In *EC-Hormones*, the panel stated that a risk assessment required by Article 5.1 is 'a *scientific* process aimed at establishing the *scientific* basis for the sanitary measure a Member intends to take'.[339] The panel opined that such non-scientific factors should not be part of a risk *assessment*, but of risk *management*, i.e. determining the appropriate risk level and selecting the measure to meet that level.[340] The Appellate Body reversed this approach to the extent that the Panel purported to exclude from the scope of a risk assessment 'all matters not susceptible of quantitative analysis by the empirical or experimental laboratory methods commonly associated with the physical sciences', noting that

the risk that is to be evaluated in a risk assessment under Article 5.1 is not only risk ascertainable in a science laboratory operating under strictly controlled conditions, but also risk in human societies as they actually exist, in other words, the actual potential for adverse effects on human health in the real world where people live and work and die.[341]

The Appellate Body referred by way of illustration to factors mentioned in Article 5.2 SPS, i.e. 'relevant processes and production methods' and 'relevant inspection, sampling and testing methods', which are not necessarily or wholly susceptible to investigation according to laboratory methods. Although the point is not entirely clear, the above considerations would seem to indicate that the Appellate Body did not intend to include subjective factors in risk assessment, such as societal perceptions of risk not based on scientific evidence. Indeed, at issue in *EC-Hormones* were factors such as the detection and control of a failure to observe good veterinary practice. Such failure, while not a laboratory risk, is still a real, identifiable risk to health, unlike consumer concerns and societal values.

Also in *EC-Hormones*, the Appellate Body found that the "risk" evaluated in a risk assessment must be an ascertainable risk; theoretical uncertainty is not the kind of risk which, under Article 5.1, is to be assessed. However, a panel cannot require a risk assessment to establish a minimum magnitude of risk; it is authorised only to determine whether a given SPS measure is "based on" a

---

[339] Panel in *EC-Hormones* (US), para. 8.107; (CND), para. 8.110.
[340] Panel in *EC-Hormones* (US), para. 8.146, (CND), para. 8.149.
[341] AB in *EC-Hormones*, para. 187.

risk assessment.[342] "Based on" in this context was interpreted by the panel in
EC-Hormones as a procedural requirement of demonstrating that the results of
a risk assessment had been taken into account when enacting the measure. The
Appellate Body overturned this view and interpreted "based on" as a substantive
requirement requiring that the results of the risk assessment must 'sufficiently
warrant - that is to say, reasonably support - the SPS measure at stake', thus, that
there is 'a rational relationship between the measure and the risk assessment.'[343]
A risk assessment does not have to come to a "monolithic conclusion" that
coincides with the scientific conclusion or view implicit in the SPS measure; it
may well represent minority opinions. An SPS measure may even be based on
'a divergent opinion coming from qualified and respected sources'.[344] However,
considering the way the Appellate Body applied these insights in *EC-Hormones*,
a considerable amount of specificity in the scientific material will be required for
such a measure to be considered to be "based on" a risk assessment.[345]

The economic factors mentioned in Article 5.3 must be taken into account
not only in the risk assessment, but also in determining the appropriate level
of protection from such risk. The appropriate level of sanitary or phytosanitary
protection is defined in Annex A as 'the level of protection deemed appropriate
by the Member establishing a SPS measure [...]'. Although the SPS Agreement
does not contain any explicit obligation to determine the appropriate level of
protection, it is implicit in several of its provisions.[346] In cases where a Member
does not determine its appropriate level of protection, or does so with insufficient precision, the appropriate level of protection may be established by panels
on the basis of the level of protection reflected in the SPS measure actually
applied.[347] Determining the appropriate level of protection is a prerogative of the
Members and the appropriate level could even be set at zero risk.[348]

Article 5.5 adds the requirement to 'avoid arbitrary or unjustifiable distinctions in the levels it considers to be appropriate in different situations, if such
distinctions result in discrimination or a disguised restriction on international
trade'. The express objective of this requirement is to achieve consistency in the
application of the concept of an appropriate level of sanitary or phytosanitary
protection against risks to human life or health, or to animal and plant life
or health; in other words, Members are supposed to be consistent in applying

---

[342] Ibid., para. 186.

[343] Ibid., para. 193.

[344] Ibid., para. 194.

[345] Ibid., paras. 197-200.

[346] See paragraph 3 of Annex B, Article 4.1, Article 5.4 and Article 5.6 SPS, as referred to by the AB in
Australia-Salmon, para. 205.

[347] AB in *Australia-Salmon*, para. 207.

[348] Ibid., paras. 125 and 199.

SPS measures to various products in different situations. The three-step analysis required by Article 5.5 is made up of whether different appropriate protection levels have been adopted in different situations, whether those protection levels exhibit arbitrary or unjustifiable differences, and whether the measure embodying these differences results in discrimination or a disguised restriction on international trade. The analysis has been applied by panels and the Appellate Body,[349] and has also been interpreted by the SPS Committee in guidelines.[350] These guidelines expressly provide that they do not add or diminish rights and obligations. However, they may play an important role in the future application of the SPS Agreement, as they contain detailed and extensive elaborations of what Members are supposed to do under Article 5.5:

> [A] Member should compare any proposed decision on the level of protection in a particular situation with the level it has previously considered or is considering to be appropriate in situations which contain sufficient common elements so as to render them comparable [...]. If differences are observed in comparable situations, either the proposed level may need to be modified, or the level of protection previously determined may need to be revised [...][351]

According to the Appellate Body in *EC-Hormones*, 'Article 5.5, when read together with Article 2.3, may be seen to be marking out and elaborating a particular route leading to the same destination set out in Article 2.3'.[352]

In applying Article 5.5 in *EC-Hormones*, the Appellate Body concluded that neither the *architecture and structure* of the measures, nor the evidence submitted to the panel supported the conclusion that the distinctions resulted in discrimination or a disguised restriction on international trade.[353] In *Australia-Salmon*, the Appellate Body observed that a finding under Article 5.1 that an SPS measure is not based on a risk assessment is a strong indication that it is really a disguised trade restriction within the meaning of Article 5.5.[354] Article 5.5 refers to distinctions in appropriate protection levels in different situations, which suggests that it prohibits any discrimination caused by arbitrary or unjustifiable distinctions in protection levels. Thus, it has been argued that SPS measures could be found to be inconsistent with this provision even if equally applicable to imports and domestic products.[355] However, inconsistency would only be found

---

[349] Panel in *EC-Hormones* and panel and AB in *Australia-Salmon*.

[350] Document G/SPS/W/104, 'Proposed Guidelines to Further the Practical Implementation of Article 5.5'.

[351] Point A.4 of the proposed Guidelines.

[352] AB in *EC-Hormones*, para. 212.

[353] AB in *EC-Hormones*, para. 246. Emphasis added.

[354] AB in *Australia-Salmon*, para. 166.

[355] Pauwelyn (1999) at 653-4.

if the distinctions made were arbitrary or unjustifiable, *and* if they resulted in discrimination or a disguised trade restriction. Thus, it is uncertain whether indistinctly applicable SPS measures can be challenged under Article 5.5.

"Equally applicable" SPS measures can certainly be challenged under Article 5.6. This provision elaborates upon the more general Article 2.2.[356] It requires that SPS measures are not more trade-restrictive than necessary in order to achieve their appropriate level of protection, taking into account technical and economic feasibility. A footnote to this provision clarifies that a measure fulfils this requirement when three cumulative elements are fulfilled: There is no other measure (a) reasonably available taking into account technical and economic feasibility, (b) that achieves the appropriate level of protection, and (c) is significantly less trade-restrictive.[357] The second element seems problematic, as it invites panels to judge whether alternative measures are equally effective in reaching the protection level chosen by a Member.[358] In *Australia-Salmon*, the Appellate Body emphasised that assessing the second element of the test in Article 5.6 involves no interference with the appropriate level of protection chosen by the Member.[359] The Appellate Body said that the *SPS Agreement* contains an implicit obligation to determine the appropriate level of protection. In cases where a Member does not determine its appropriate level of protection, or does so with insufficient precision, the appropriate level of protection may be established by panels on the basis of the level of protection reflected in the SPS measure actually applied.[360] In the dispute at issue, the Appellate Body overturned the panel's application of Article 5.6 because the panel had used an incorrect "measure" as a yardstick for comparison. The Appellate Body could not complete the analysis of Article 5.6, because there were no indications as to whether alternative measures would achieve the appropriate protection level.[361] In *Japan-Varietals*, the Appellate Body overturned the panel's application of Article 5.6, because that panel had deduced the existence of an alternative measure that would meet the protection level on the basis of experts' opinions instead of on parties' arguments.[362] Importantly, in the same dispute the Appellate Body made it clear that a panel's consideration and weighing of the evidence relates to its assessment of the facts and, therefore, falls outside the scope of appellate review under Article 17.6 of the DSU.[363] In other words, a panel's

---

[356] Although the panel in *Australia-Salmon*, para. 8.165, saw no reason to explore the relationship between Articles 2.2 and 5.6, it did say that Article 5.6 should, in particular, be read in the light of Article 2.2.

[357] See also AB in *Australia-Salmon*, para. 123.

[358] Cf. the "necessary" test in Article XX(b) GATT, discussed in Section 5.2.1.

[359] AB in *Australia-Salmon*, para. 204. Emphasis in the original.

[360] Ibid., paras. 206-207.

[361] Ibid., paras. 208-213.

[362] AB in *Japan-Varietals*, paras. 125,130-31.

[363] Ibid., para. 98.

finding that an alternative measure can achieve a Member's appropriate level of protection cannot be appealed.

Article 5.7 allows Members in cases where scientific evidence is insufficient to adopt provisional SPS measures on the basis of available pertinent information. A provisional measure may only be maintained if the Member applying it seeks additional information which is necessary for a more objective risk assessment, and accordingly reviews the measure within a reasonable period of time. According to the Appellate Body in *Japan-Varietals*, the "additional information" sought must be 'germane to conducting such a risk assessment', and what constitutes a 'reasonable period of time' depends on the specific circumstances of each case, including the difficulty in obtaining the additional information which is necessary for the review *and* the characteristics of the provisional SPS measure.[364] In *EC-Hormones*, the Appellate Body said that the precautionary principle, at least outside the field of international environmental law, still awaits authoritative formulation. It noted that the principle had not been written into the SPS Agreement as a ground for justifying SPS measures that are otherwise inconsistent with the obligations of Members as set out in particular provisions of that Agreement, and that it finds reflection in Article 5.7 as well as in the sixth paragraph of the preamble and in Article 3.3 of the SPS Agreement.[365] The relationship between Article 5.7 and the "precautionary principle" in more general terms has been much discussed in academic literature as well as in policy papers.[366] The Appellate Body in *Japan-Varietals* observed that Article 5.7 forms part of the context of Article 2.2, and operates as a qualified exemption from the obligation under Article 2.2 not to maintain SPS measures without sufficient scientific evidence.[367]

In sum, according to the complicated scheme of obligations arising out of the SPS Agreement, Members are required to take the following steps when enacting measures to protect their populations, animals and plants from health risks. They can determine the level of protection they deem to be appropriate, but should avoid arbitrary or unjustifiable distinctions in the appropriate levels of protection that lead to discrimination or disguised restrictions. They must base their SPS measures on a risk assessment. The risk assessment must include available scientific evidence and other relevant factors. Members must decide whether the risk assessed is unacceptable, and if so, they must select an SPS measure to address the risk. The measure selected should not discriminate,

---

[364] Ibid., paras. 92-93. Original emphasis.

[365] Panel in *EC-Hormones*, paras. 124-5.

[366] See e.g. Hey (2000), Pauwelyn (1999), Douma and Jacobs (1999), and the European Council Resolution, document G/SPS/GEN/225, G/TBT/W/154, WT/CTE/W/181, and Communication from the European Commission, document WT/CTE/W/147, G/TBT/W/137, G/SPS/GEN/168.

[367] AB in *Japan-Varietals*, para. 80.

and there should be no alternative measure reasonably available that achieves the protection level deemed to be appropriate and which is significantly less trade-restrictive. The role played by international standards in the SPS Agreement is discussed *infra*.[368]

4.6 International Standards and the Right of Members to Go Beyond Them

4.6.1 GATT 1994 and International Standards

Except for Article XX(h), which has so far played no significant role in the trade-environment debate, the GATT does not contain any explicit references to international environmental or health standards. Such standards can be agreed upon in international organisations or agencies, and/or may be included in international environmental agreements. During the 1980s and 1990s, the EFTA countries and later the EC proposed to insert a general clause into Article XX referring to international environmental agreements.[369] An example of a similar clause is found in the NAFTA, albeit that it explicitly refers to a number of international environmental agreements. Applying the same approach to the GATT would have the disadvantage that it would require an amendment to Article XX every time an international environmental agreement would be added to the list. If the need arises, the relationship between Article XX GATT and other WTO provisions on the one hand, and international environmental agreements or standards on the other, could be clarified by means of an authoritative interpretation of WTO provisions.[370] In the absence of any explicit clause in Article XX apart from paragraph (h), or of other institutional devices regarding the relationship between the GATT and international environmental agreements, the relationship between the GATT and internationally agreed environmental and health standards will depend on how panels and the Appellate Body take such standards into account in interpreting GATT provisions. Of particular relevance in this context are the chapeau and subparagraphs of Article XX.

On the basis of paragraph 3(a) or (c) of Article 31 of the Vienna Convention, internationally agreed health or environmental standards are to be 'taken into account' in interpreting WTO provisions, such as Article XX GATT. Arguably, paragraph 3(c) of Article 31 includes interpretations of the relevant rules of

---

[368] See Section 4.6.3.

[369] See WTO Documents Press/TE 014,14 November 1996, Press/TE 008, 29 April 1996; and the full EC contributions at http://europa.eu.int/comm/trade/miti/envir/contrib.htm.

[370] In accordance with Article IX:2 WTO Agreement.

international law by international courts or tribunals, to which WTO panels and the Appellate Body may thus refer. In addition, Article 32 of the Vienna Convention provides that recourse may be had to 'supplementary means of interpretation', including the preparatory work of the treaty and the circumstances of its conclusion, in order to confirm the meaning resulting from the application of Article 31, or to determine the meaning when the interpretation according to Article 31 leaves the meaning ambiguous or obscure, or leads to a result which is manifestly absurd or unreasonable. There are several examples of references to international environmental agreements by panels and the Appellate Body.[371] In *US-Shrimp-Turtle*, the Appellate Body explicitly mentioned the example of a multilateral environmental agreement in which the parties had 'together marked out the equilibrium line' that is expressed in the chapeau to Article XX GATT. That is, a multilateral environmental agreement was taken to determine the equilibrium line between the right of a Member to invoke an exception under Article XX and the rights of the other Members under varying substantive provisions (e.g., Article XI) of the GATT 1994.[372]

International environmental agreements may also contain specific provisions that regulate trade in certain goods between its members, and sometimes even trade with non-signatories. Well-known examples of MEAs containing provisions trade-restrictive measures are the Basel Convention on transboundary movements of waste,[373] the Montreal Protocol on substances damaging the ozone layer,[374] CITES,[375] and the Biosafety Protocol.[376] Other environmental agreements may have WTO repercussions even if not directly regulating trade in goods, such as the Kyoto Protocol.[377] Trade-restrictive measures taken pursuant to such MEAs may be difficult to reconcile with substantive GATT obligations such as those in Articles I, III or XI. However, the existence of an MEA will generally facilitate their justification under Article XX GATT. The issue is more complicated when the MEA does not specifically provide for or prescribes trade restrictions, but merely suggests them or sets certain objectives which might be

---

[371] See Section 5.4.3 and Howse (2000).

[372] AB in *US-Shrimp-Turtle*, paras. 159 and 170.

[373] See e.g. OECD, COM/ENV/TD(97)41/FINAL, Trade Measures in the Basel Convention on the Control of Transboundary Movements of Hazardous Wastes and their Disposal, at http://www.oecd.org.

[374] See e.g. OCDE/GD(97)230, Experience with the Use of Trade Measures in the Montreal Protocol on Substances that Deplete the Ozone Layer, at http://www.oecd.org.

[375] See e.g. OCDE/GD(97)106, Experience With the Use of Trade Measures in the Convention on International Trade in Endangered Species of Wild Fauna and Flora, at http://www.oecd.org.

[376] Article 4 of the Biosafety Protocol provides that '[t]his Protocol shall apply to the transboundary movement, transit, handling and use of all living modified organisms that may have adverse effects on the conservation and sustainable use of biological diversity, taking also into account risks to human health.'

[377] See Werksman (1999).

attained through trade-restrictive measures, such as the Kyoto Protocol. Another complication presents itself when trade restrictions are applied to a non-party to an MEA that is a WTO member. The WTO Committee on Trade and Environment has been discussing the issue for some time.[378] It has issued a matrix of trade measures pursuant to selected MEAs.[379] Moreover, a rapidly increasing body of academic literature is addressing the subject.[380] At the fourth Ministerial Conference in Doha, Members agreed to put the relationship between WTO rules and MEAs on the agenda for negotiations in the new round, albeit only with respect to the relationship between parties of MEAs.[381] This study does not focus on the relations between MEA provisions and WTO rules, a subject that deserves a study in itself. However, as argued in the Introduction, WTO rules do not exist in isolation from other public international law, so at various points in this work, reference is made to other international law.

4.6.2 The TBT Agreement and International Standards

Article 2.4 to 2.6 TBT establish a preference for the use of international standards as the basis for national technical regulations. Article 2.4 lays down a qualified obligation to use international standards. The obligation is qualified by the conditions that the standards must be relevant and not be ineffective or inappropriate to attain the legitimate goal pursued, which is up to the Member applying the technical regulation to determine.[382] However, that Member will have to comply with the requirements of notification and explanation in Article 2.9 and the first sentence of Article 2.5. Article 2.4 may be applicable both in situations where a country cannot live up to international standards, and where a country wishes to apply stricter technical regulations than provided for in the relevant international standard. Developing countries may have climatological or technical difficulties in applying standards suited to more developed countries. In many cases, this will imply that developing countries cannot live up to the level of the international standard. On the other hand, a WTO Member may think that the relevant international standard is the

---

[378] Items 1 and 5 of its Work Program address the issue. See various documents available at http://docsonline.wto.org.

[379] Document WT/CTE/W/160.

[380] See e.g. various issues of the UNEP Environment and Trade series addressing the Montreal and Basel provisions in relation to the GATT.

[381] See document WT/MIN(01)/DEC/1.

[382] The list of possible reasons for the ineffectiveness or inappropriateness of international standards is non-exhaustive, as Article 2.4 states 'for instance because of fundamental climatic or geographical factors or fundamental technological problems.'

result of an international compromise and constitutes the minimum level of protection, and may have good reasons to wish to go further.

The second sentence of Article 2.5 lays down a rebuttable presumption of TBT-consistency for technical regulations in accordance with international standards and pursuing one of the legitimate objectives explicitly mentioned in Article 2.2.[383] By reserving the rebuttable presumption for the legitimate objectives listed in Article 2.2, Article 2.5 creates two categories of legitimate objectives. Legitimate objectives other than those explicitly listed in Article 2.2 may be invoked to demonstrate that a measure does not create an unnecessary trade obstacle, but cannot raise a rebuttable presumption of TBT-consistency even if they are in accordance with relevant international standards. Article 2.6 provides that 'Members *shall* play a full part in the preparation by appropriate international standardizing bodies of international standards for products for which they either have adopted, or expect to adopt, technical regulations', albeit within the limits of their resources.[384] This is another qualified obligation, but one that is not likely to lead to dispute settlement proceedings.

A difficult question is what exactly is meant by "international standards" in the context of the TBT Agreement. It is recalled that the TBT distinguishes between mandatory technical regulations and voluntary standards. The term "standard" is here given a more restricted interpretation than is usual, and certainly more so than is applied by, for instance, the International Standardisation Organisation (ISO). An explanatory note in the definitions in Annex 1 to the TBT Agreement adds to the lack of clarity. It provides that whereas standards prepared by 'the international standardisation community' - a term that remains undefined - are based on consensus, the TBT Agreement also covers documents that are not based on consensus.[385] It is unclear whether "documents" refers to documents laying down standards that are internationally agreed upon, but not by 'the international standardisation community', or national standards, or both. What is probably meant are international standards not based on consensus.

In view of the above and since the TBT Agreement does not specify the organisations whose standards may be used by Members as a basis for their technical regulations, there appear to be no inherent limitations in the TBT Agreement on the type of international co-operation leading to standards that may be used. This would make it possible for standards agreed upon in multilateral environmental agreements, and even in regional agreements, to be used for its purpose. The definitions in Annex 1 to the TBT Agreement provide that an "international body or system" is a body or system whose membership is open to the relevant bodies of at least all Members. Strangely, however,

---

[383] See also Section 4.7 on the burden of proof.

[384] Article 2.6 TBT, emphasis added.

[385] Explanatory Note to the definition of "standard" in Annex 1 TBT.

the term "international body" is found nowhere in the text of the TBT Agreement. Therefore, it is by no means certain that only standards by bodies whose membership is open to all WTO Members can be used in the sense of Articles 2.4 and 2.5 TBT. The fact that "international standards" are not clearly and precisely defined in the TBT has been identified by several WTO Members as one of the areas in which the Agreement is in need of improvement.[386] Concrete proposals have been tabled.[387]

4.6.3 The SPS Agreement and International Standards

Annex A to the SPS Agreement defines "international standards" as standards established by or under the auspices of the Codex Alimentarius, the International Office of Epizootics, and the International Plant Protection Convention, as well as other relevant international organisations open for membership to all WTO Members for matters not covered by those organisations. Article 3 of the SPS Agreement, entitled "Harmonisation", refers to "international standards" in a number of ways. According to the Appellate Body, the object and purpose of Article 3 is to promote the harmonisation of the SPS measures of Members on as wide a basis as possible, while at the same time recognising and safeguarding the right and duty of Members to protect the life and health of their people.[388]

Article 3.1 establishes an obligation to *base* SPS measures *on* international standards, where they exist, 'except as otherwise provided for in this Agreement, and in particular in paragraph 3'.[389] Article 3.2 lays down a presumption of consistency with SPS and GATT obligations as regards SPS measures that *conform to* international standards. Such standards 'shall be deemed to be necessary to protect human, animal or plant life or health, and presumed to be consistent with the relevant provisions of this Agreement and of GATT 1994.'[390] Article 3.3 allows Members to introduce or maintain SPS measures 'resulting in a higher level of protection than would be achieved by measures *based on* the relevant international standards, if there is a scientific justification, or as a consequence of the level of protection a Member determines to be appropriate in accordance with [...] Article 5'.[391] A footnote to Article 3.3 adds that there is a

---

[386] See e.g. the proposals on the TBT for the Millennium Round by the EC (document WT/GC/W/274) and Japan (document WT/GC/W/241).

[387] See e.g. documents G/TBT/W/121 (Japanese proposal, with correction); G/TBT/W/87 and 133 (EC proposals); G/TBT/W/143 (Canadian proposal), and G/TBT/W/131 (Communications from the IEC and ISO).

[388] AB in *EC-Hormones*, para. 177.

[389] Emphasis added.

[390] Emphasis added.

[391] Emphasis added.

"scientific justification" if a Member determines that the relevant international standard is not sufficient to achieve its appropriate level of protection, on the basis of 'an examination and evaluation of available scientific information' in accordance with the SPS Agreement. As the Appellate Body observed, this 'examination and evaluation would appear to partake of the nature of the risk assessment required in Article 5.1'.[392] Thus, the difference in Article 3.3 between the two possible reasons to deviate from relevant international standards is unclear. 'It may have very limited effects and may, to that extent, be more apparent than real.'[393] The application of SPS measures resulting in lower levels of protection than would be achieved by the relevant international standard is unlikely and probably even impossible to challenge under the SPS Agreement.

As the Appellate Body made clear in *EC-Hormones*, "conform[ing] to" requires much more than "based on".[394] Thus, an SPS measure that conforms to an international standard within the meaning of Article 3.2 completely embodies the international standard and, for practical purposes, converts it into a municipal standard. Such a measure enjoys the benefit of a presumption (albeit a rebuttable one) that it is consistent with the relevant provisions of the SPS Agreement and of the GATT 1994. As the Appellate Body said, 'harmonization of SPS measures of Members on the basis of international standards is projected in the Agreement, as a *goal*, yet to be realized *in the future*. To read Article 3.1 as requiring Members to harmonize their SPS measures *by conforming those measures with international standards*, guidelines and recommendations, *in the here and now*, is, in effect, to vest such international standards, guidelines and recommendations (which are by the terms of the Codex *recommendatory* in form and nature) with *obligatory* force and effect'.[395] It should be noted, however, that international standards arguably do obtain a similar effect *de facto*, through the presumption of SPS consistency in Article 3.2.

SPS measures *based on* the existing relevant international standard, guideline or recommendation within the meaning of Article 3.1 may adopt some, but not necessarily all, of the elements of the international standard. The Member imposing an SPS measure based on an international standard does not benefit from the presumption of consistency laid down in Article 3.2. However, that Member 'is not penalized by exemption of a complaining Member from the normal burden of showing a *prima facie* case of inconsistency with Article 3.1 or any other relevant Article of the SPS Agreement or of the GATT 1994'.[396]

---

[392] AB in *EC-Hormones*, para. 175.

[393] Ibid., para. 176.

[394] Ibid., para. 163: 'A measure that "conforms to" and incorporates a Codex standard is, of course, "based on" that standard. A measure, however, based on the same standard might not conform to that standard, as where only some, not all, of the elements of the standard are incorporated into the measure.'

[395] Ibid., para. 165. Emphasis in the original.

[396] Ibid., para. 171.

The above considerations lead to an important question which has not yet been settled. Is there a difference in terms of challenging SPS measures based on international standards and alternatively SPS measures not based on international standards? Even if the former do not benefit from a general presumption of SPS-consistency, they are based on an international standard and therefore on internationally agreed upon scientific evidence and risk assessment. Arguably, therefore, a complainant cannot challenge an SPS measure based on an international standard for a violation of the sufficient scientific evidence requirement in Article 2.2 and the risk assessment requirement in Article 5. Admittedly, this interpretation leads to a *de facto* presumption of consistency with important parts of the SPS Agreement. However, to interpret Article 3.1 any differently would render that provision meaningless. There would be no difference between the status of SPS measures based on and those not based on international standards. This would also run counter to the goal of harmonising SPS measures on as wide a basis as possible as laid down in Article 3.1, and the desire 'to further the use of harmonised SPS measures between Members on the basis of international standards' as laid down in the Preamble of the SPS Agreement.

Under Article 3.3, a Member may decide to establish its own level of protection which is different from that which is implicit in the relevant international standard, and to implement or embody that level of protection in a measure not "based on" the international standard. The Member's appropriate level of protection may be higher than that implied in the international standard.[397] According to the Appellate Body in *EC-Hormones*, the right of a Member to establish its own level of sanitary protection under Article 3.3 is an autonomous right and *not* an "exception" from a "general obligation" under Article 3.1, as the panel had found.[398] Even if Article 3.3 is not an exception to Article 3.1, they are connected. Thus, it would seem, a complainant will not confine itself to claiming that the defendant violates Article 3.1 because its SPS measure is not based on an existing relevant international standard. The complainant will also assert a violation of Article 3.3: the defendant is deviating from a relevant international standard without meeting the requirements in that provision. The burden of proof is further discussed below.

In sum, the following different situations are conceivable with regard to the SPS Agreement and international standards. First, there is no relevant international standard, and Article 3 SPS is not relevant. Second, there is a relevant international standard, and an SPS measure conforms to it, raising the presumption of consistency in Article 3.2. Third, there is a relevant international

---

[397] Ibid., para. 172.
[398] Ibid., paras. 104 and 173.

standard, and an SPS measure is based on it. Arguably, although this is not clear, the measure cannot be challenged for a lack of scientific basis, although it may be challenged under other SPS requirements. Fourth, there is a relevant international standard, and an SPS measure not based upon it achieves a higher level of protection, in which case the conditions in Article 3.3 must be met.[399] Finally, there is a relevant international standard, and an SPS measure not based upon it does not achieve a higher level of protection with the necessary scientific basis, in which case Article 3.3 has been violated.

4.7 Burden of Proof

The basic principle as regards the burden of proof in dispute settlement under GATT 1947 was that the complainant had to adduce a *prima facie* case of a violation of a substantive GATT provision, such as Article III or XI. The defendant could rebut that *prima facie* case. If it did not succeed in doing so or conceded that there was a violation, the defendant could seek to "revalidate" or justify its measure under an exception, such as Article XX. Article 3.8 of the Dispute Settlement Understanding codifies this practice for all WTO Agreements, unless they specifically provide otherwise:

> *In cases where there is an infringement of the obligations assumed under a covered agreement, the action is considered* prima facie *to constitute a case of nullification or impairment. This means that there is normally a presumption that a breach of the rules has an adverse impact on other Members parties to that covered agreement, and in such cases, it shall be up to the Member against whom the complaint has been brought to rebut the charge.*

The Appellate Body in *US-Shirts and Blouses* referred to the 'generally-accepted canon of evidence in civil law, common law and, in fact, most jurisdictions' that the burden of proof rests upon the party who asserts the affirmative of a particular claim or defence. 'If that party adduces evidence sufficient to raise a presumption that what is claimed is true, the burden then shifts to the other party, who will fail unless it adduces sufficient evidence to rebut the presumption.'[400] The Appellate Body went on to state that in the context of the GATT 1994 and the WTO Agreements, precisely how much and precisely what kind of

---

[399] Arguably, Article 3.3 covers both the situation in which the appropriate level of protection of the Member imposing the measure is higher than the level that would be achieved by the international standard, and the situation that the appropriate level of protection is the same, but the international standard does not achieve that level of protection in that country for specific reasons, e.g. climatological circumstances.

[400] AB in *US-Shirts and Blouses*, at p. 14.

evidence will be required to establish such a presumption will necessarily vary from measure to measure, provision to provision, and case to case.[401] A *prima facie* case of a violation of Article III:4 will involve adducing evidence that a measure may result in imported goods being treated less favourably than like domestic products. When the measure complained of makes an origin-based distinction, there is no need to demonstrate the existence of products actually traded.[402] Article XX GATT provides exceptions to "substantive" GATT obligations, and the Member invoking it as a defence must show that the requirements of Article XX have been met. As the Appellate Body in *US-Shirts and Blouses* stated:

> *Articles XX and XI:(2)(c)(i) are limited exceptions from obligations under certain other provisions of the GATT 1994, not positive rules establishing obligations in themselves. They are in the nature of affirmative defences. It is only reasonable that the burden of establishing such a defence should rest on the party asserting it.*[403]

This means that the Member invoking Article XX will have to demonstrate that its measure falls under at least one of the exceptions listed in paragraphs (a) to (j), that it fulfils the means-ends requirements provided therein, and that the application of the measure satisfies the requirements in the chapeau of Article XX.[404] This seems clear enough as a principle. However, in the actual application of the requirements in the various paragraphs as well as the chapeau to Article XX, the burden of proof may cause difficulties. For instance, what does the party invoking the exception in Article XX(b) have to prove in order to acceptably argue that its measure is "necessary"? Does that party have to show that all other possible alternatives to its measure were unfeasible? And as regards the chapeau, as discussed above, the Appellate Body appears to have applied various tests; does that imply that all of them have to be satisfied by the party invoking Article XX? The combination of both requirements would make it virtually impossible to justify a measure under Article XX. In reality, therefore, the burden of proof in Article XX will be less demanding. For example, in *EC-Asbestos*, the panel observed that it is not for the party invoking Article XX to prove that the arguments put forward in rebuttal by the complaining party are incorrect until the latter has backed them up with sufficient evidence.[405]

---

[401] Ibid., at p. 14.

[402] See e.g. the panel in *US-FSC Implementation*, para. 8.133. This may be different with regard to 'origin-neutral measures'. See Section 5.3.3.

[403] AB in *US-Shirts and Blouses*, at p. 16. Original footnotes omitted.

[404] See document WT/CTE/W/53/Rev.1, at p. 3, citing the GATT panel reports in *Canada-FIRA* and *US-Section 337*, as well as the WTO panel report in *US-Gasoline*.

[405] Panel in *EC-Asbestos*, para. 8.178.

With regard to Article XX(b), the panel found that France, the defendant, had made a *prima facie* case to the effect that its measure did satisfy both the requirements of falling within the range of policies covered by Article XX(b) and of being "necessary".[406] With regard to the chapeau, the panel observed that the defendant had made a *prima facie* case that its measure did not constitute arbitrary or unjustifiable discrimination, establishing a presumption which could not be rebutted by the complainant.[407]

As said above, the same principles apply to the division of the burden of proof in the other Agreements on Trade in Goods in Annex 1A to the WTO Agreement. However, each Agreement has its peculiarities, and the burden of proof will accordingly be assessed on a case-to-case basis.[408] In many of these Agreements, not least in the TBT and SPS Agreements, the dividing line between "substantive obligations" and "exceptions" is far less clear than in the GATT. In SPS cases, where scientific arguments will usually play an important role, the division of the burden of proof is vital, as witnessed by the fact that it has been addressed in all disputes involving the SPS Agreement to date. As the Appellate Body made clear in *EC-Hormones*,

> The initial burden lies on the complaining party, which must establish a prima facie *case of inconsistency with a particular provision of the SPS Agreement on the part of the defending party, or more precisely, of its SPS measure or measures complained about. When that* prima facie *case is made, the burden of proof moves to the defending party, which must in turn counter or refute the claimed inconsistency.*[409]

The Appellate Body reversed the panel's decision, which had found that the *SPS Agreement* as a general rule allocates the burden of proof to the Member imposing an SPS measure if a measure does not conform to international standards.[410] Thus, the party asserting a claim under the SPS Agreement, e.g. that an SPS measure is not based on a risk assessment, or a fact, e.g. the existence of a relevant international standard, must establish a *prima facie* case, which the defending party will then have to rebut.[411] The complainant may, for example,

---

[406] Ibid., paras. 8.194 and 8.222, respectively.

[407] Ibid., para. 8.229.

[408] See e.g. the AB in *US-Shirts and Blouses*, at 16, as to the burden of proof in the Textiles Agreement.

[409] AB in *EC-Hormones*, para. 98, referring to the panel report in the same dispute and to its own report in *US-Shirts and Blouses*.

[410] Ibid., paras. 99-102.

[411] See e.g. AB in *EC-Hormones*, footnote 180, clarifying that the complainant must adduce a *prima facie* case that a measure is not based on a risk assessment and that it considered this to be the case in the dispute at hand.

assert that an SPS measure is being maintained without sufficient scientific evidence, does not conform to international standards, is not based on existing international standards, or applies a stricter standard than the relevant international standard without scientific justification. If the complainant adduces a *prima facie* case, the defendant will need to rebut it. If the complainant fails to adduce a *prima facie* case, the measure will be presumed to be consistent with the SPS Agreement, and therefore also with the GATT.[412] A panel's decision as to whether a *prima facie* case has been established is not within the scope of appellate review.[413]

Although the burden of proof in the TBT Agreement has not yet been the subject of dispute settlement proceedings, some inspiration may be drawn from the case-law on the burden of proof in the SPS Agreement. Based on that case-law and the provisions in the TBT Agreement, it appears that at least three situations may be distinguished. First, there is a rebuttable presumption that a technical regulation does not violate the TBT Agreement if it pursues one of the legitimate objectives identified in Article 2.2 and is in accordance with relevant international standards (Art. 2.5). Second, if the technical regulation deviates from the relevant international standard, there is no presumption of consistency or inconsistency with the TBT (Art. 2.4). The complaining Member will have to demonstrate a *prima facie* case of inconsistency with one or various provisions of the TBT. Third, in the absence of any relevant international standards, there is no presumption of consistency or inconsistency with the TBT Agreement.[414] Again, the complaining Member will have to demonstrate a *prima facie* case of inconsistency with one or various provisions of the TBT. When a Member challenges a technical regulation of another Member under Article 2.2 TBT, it may for example argue that the technical regulation does not pursue any legitimate objective and/or that it is more trade-restrictive than is necessary in order to fulfil a legitimate objective. Panels and the Appellate Body will then have to assess whether the defending Member has established a legitimate objective and whether this is either listed in Article 2.2 or is otherwise acceptable. Next, they will have to apply the least trade-restrictiveness test. The question arises to what extent a defending Member has to show that it has applied

---

[412] See Article 2.4 SPS.

[413] AB in *Australia-Salmon*, para. 261; *Japan-Varietals*, paras. 98 and 136.

[414] *Contra* see Völker (1995) at 291, who asserts that it follows *a contrario* from Article 2.5 that the notion of 'unnecessarily restrictive obstacle' in Article 2.2 includes trade restrictions not using available and suitable international standards. This could be interpreted as an assertion that the Member not using available and suitable international standards is rebuttably presumed to violate the TBT. In that view, the defending Member should establish a reasonable case that the international standard was 'ineffective or inappropriate'.

the least trade-restrictive measure reasonably available to pursue its stated objective. Considering the text of Article 2.2 TBT, the defendant should at least be expected to state a legitimate objective, and to show that it has considered the available alternatives as well as the risk that the non-fulfilment of its stated objective would have created.[415]

---

[415] *Contra* see Howse and Tuerk (2001) asserting that under Article 2.2 the challenging Member must prove 'on the balance of probabilities' that the regulating state has failed to ensure within the regulatory process that its measure is the least trade-restrictive.

CHAPTER 5

Analysis of Recurring Themes

5.1   Basic Disciplines and Typologies

National environmental measures as defined in this work may be covered by the provisions of the GATT and the SPS or the TBT Agreement. The main obligations in the relevant provisions of GATT 1994 discussed above are a prohibition of import-specific restrictions (Article XI) and a prohibition of discrimination for internal regulatory measures (Article III). It has also been seen that both the TBT and the SPS Agreements discipline national environmental measures to an extent beyond those in GATT 1994. Under both Agreements, non-discriminatory internal laws and regulations may be challenged. The existence of various possibly applicable disciplines in these Agreements renders the typology of the measure scrutinised an important issue. The word "measure" itself features in some of these provisions, like Article XI GATT and the definitions and key provisions of the SPS Agreement, but is not as such defined in either of these agreements. However, the TBT Agreement does not refer to "measures", but lays down disciplines for "technical regulations", "standards" and "conformity assessment procedures", as defined in that Agreement. Thus, in order to decide which WTO disciplines apply to a "measure", one needs to determine what the pertinent national environmental "measure" encompasses, and into which of the typologies found in these agreements the measure fits. The main questions to be asked in that respect are the following: Is the measure being applied to protect human, animal, or plant life or health from food-borne risks or diseases (SPS)? If not, is the measure a document laying down product characteristics or their related processes and production methods (TBT)? Is it an import prohibition or restriction (Article XI), or a law, regulation or requirement affecting the sale, transport, distribution or use of products (Article III), even if applied at the border (Note Ad Article III)?

5.1.1   Relationship between Obligations and Exceptions in GATT 1994

The basic rule regarding the relationship between Articles III and XI GATT is that border measures are covered by Article XI and internal regulations by Article III:4. It is only different when border measures are merely the enforcement of internal regulations at the border, in which case the Note to Article III provides that they are covered by Article III.[1] Although Articles III and XI appear to be mutually exclusive, some hints have been made by panels as to the possibility of their cumulative application.[2]

---

[1]   Whether measures applied to both imported *products* and domestic *production* are covered by the Note Ad Article III is discussed *supra* in Section 4.3.1 in general, and *infra* in Section 5.4.5 in the specific context of measures based on production or processing methods.

[2]   See Section 4.3.1.

The relationship between the substantive obligations in Articles III and XI on the one hand, and the exceptions in Article XX on the other, is even more complicated. In cases of violations of Article XI, few problems present themselves, as the violation usually coincides with the measure. However, separating the analysis of a violation in Article III, the provisional justification under one of the paragraphs of Article XX, and the assessment of the conditions in the chapeau is not always easy. The chapeau invites panels and the Appellate Body to determine whether there is arbitrary or unjustifiable discrimination or a disguised trade restriction in the application of a measure. "Disguised trade restriction" has been interpreted with reference to the same indicators as used in the context of "protectionist application" in Article III:2. The whole analysis of Article III revolves around the themes of discrimination and protection. Some overlap between the analysis under Article III and the chapeau of Article XX therefore appears to be inevitable. Problems of overlap may result in questions concerning the burden of proof. The current author doubts whether the emphasis on the difference between the *measure* and its *application* (See Section 4.4.3) is capable of preventing these problems. Arguably, the SPS Agreement reinforces the impression that the difference between the measure and its application is not always clear, by referring in its title to the "application" of SPS measures, while laying down obligations for SPS measures themselves, not just their application.

Problems regarding the relationship between Articles III:4 and XX may become especially poignant as measures that do not discriminate *de jure* against imported products are increasingly assessed under Article III:4.[3] The Appellate Body report in *EC-Asbestos* suggests that there may be flexibility in the interpretation of "less favourable treatment" in Article III:4. It is not inconceivable that policy goals may be taken into account in determining whether there is "less favourable treatment". If this were the case, and a violation was to be found, could the subsequent Article XX assessment still lead to a justification? Would not a finding of protectionist application under Article III almost inevitably lead to the conclusion that the measure either does not meet the means-ends requirements, or does not meet the conditions in the chapeau? This scenario with regard to "less favourable treatment" may be highly speculative. However, the *EC-Asbestos* dispute itself illustrated that a consideration of the same issues may arise in the context of Articles III and XX, in this case the role of the health risks of certain products. The Appellate Body may have said in *EC-Asbestos* that these two Articles require different inquiries, one into the market and the other into the basis of government policy objectives. But government action is able to affect market perceptions, so presenting the analyses under Articles III and XX in isolation from each other seems somewhat illusionary.

---

[3] See Section 5.3.

Finally, the relationship within Article XX itself between the means-ends tests in the different paragraphs and the tests in the chapeau may result in an overlap. The question whether the discrimination is arbitrary or unjustifiable invites considerations that resemble those which play a role in determining whether the measure meets the means-ends tests in paragraphs (g) and (b). The panel in *US-Gasoline* inquired whether it was not the "less favourable treatment" caused by the measure at issue, rather than the measure itself, that was "relating to" the objectives of the measures. According to the Appellate Body, this approach would 'turn Article XX on its head'. Arguably, however, the analysis by the Appellate Body itself in that case shows how difficult it is to separate the measure, the less favourable treatment, the means-end tests and the requirements in the chapeau of Article XX.[4]

5.1.2 Relationships between GATT 1994, TBT and SPS Agreements

(a) General Considerations of the Relationship between WTO Agreements

The Vienna Convention applies to the WTO Agreement, including its annexed Agreements.[5] However, the Vienna Convention does not contain any specific provisions regarding the interrelationships between provisions within a constellation of agreements in a "single package". The WTO Agreement itself contains an interpretative note that sheds some light on the question of the relationship between the GATT 1994 on the one hand, and Agreements such as the SPS and the TBT on the other. The General Interpretative Note to Annex 1A provides that in the event of conflict between a provision of the GATT and a provision of another Agreement in Annex 1A, the provision of the other Agreement shall prevail. Annex 1A to the WTO Agreement contains all the multilateral WTO Agreements on trade in goods, including the GATT 1994, the TBT and the SPS Agreement. The interpretative note has been said to ensure that the GATT 1994 applies only to the extent that it has not been overtaken by the results of the Uruguay Round incorporated in the other Multilateral Trade Agreements.[6] Although "conflict" is not defined in the interpretative note, it may

---

[4] It would seem that the Appellate Body in that case really looked at whether the "less favourable treatment" was "necessary" while applying the chapeau. On this case, see Waincymer (1996), Appleton (1997b).

[5] According to Article 2.1(a) of the Vienna Convention, "treaty" means an international agreement concluded between States in written form and governed by international law, whether embodied in a single instrument or in two or more related instruments and whatever its particular designation.

[6] See Roessler (1996) at 71.

be understood to refer to those situations in which compliance with a provision in one Agreement goes hand in hand with a violation of a provision in the GATT 1994, i.e. when the application of the two Agreements is mutually exclusive.[7] There is a presumption against conflict in public international law, so panels and the Appellate Body will interpret provisions of the WTO Agreements so as to avoid any conflict.[8]

Obviously, the notion of *conflicts* thus defined does not exhaust the possible relationships between the GATT 1994 and other Annex 1A Agreements. In fact, at least three other relationships have been identified.[9] First, *express derogation*, i.e. an Annex 1A Agreement specifically allows Members to act inconsistently with an obligation under GATT 1994.[10] This is a variation of the conflict situation, but here the prevalence of the other Agreement over GATT 1994 is stipulated in the Agreement itself. The other two relationships do not result in conflict, but rather occur when obligations in different Agreements can be cumulatively applied. One is *overlap*, i.e. the provisions in question deal with the same subject, although one such provision often does so more specifically or in more detail.[11] The other is *complementarity*, i.e. one of the other Agreements in Annex 1A provides for different or complementary obligations in addition to those laid down in GATT 1994.[12] In these cases, both Agreements apply cumulatively. As a general principle following from the fact that the WTO Agreement is a single undertaking, Members must comply with all WTO obligations at all times, unless there is a formal conflict between them.[13] This principle also appears to apply between two Annex 1A Agreements other than the GATT 1994,[14] and even outside the realm of Annex 1A, to the relationship between GATT 1994 and GATS (Annex 1B) and TRIPS (Annex 1C),[15] and between the Agreement on Antidumping (Annex 1A) and the Dispute Settlement Understanding (Annex 2).[16]

---

[7] See Montaguti and Lugard (2000) at 476, referring to the panel in *Indonesia-Auto*, para. 14.99, concerning the relationship between Article III:2 GATT and the Subsidies Agreement.

[8] See e.g. the panel in *Indonesia-Auto*, para. 14.28.

[9] The following list is largely based upon Montaguti and Lugard (2000).

[10] See Articles 5 and 13 Agriculture Agreement, as identified by the AB in *EC-Bananas III*, para. 157.

[11] E.g. Article X:3(a) GATT and Article 1.3 of the Licensing Agreement, or Article XIX:1(a) GATT and Article 4.1(a) of the Safeguards Agreement.

[12] E.g. Article VI GATT and Part V of the Subsidies Agreement, as discussed by the AB in *Brazil-Coconut*, at p. 16; Article XIX:1 GATT and Article 2.1 of the Safeguards Agreement, discussed by the AB in *Argentina-Footwear*, paras. 76-98.

[13] Panel in *Turkey-Textiles*, para. 9.92.

[14] See e.g. the panel in *Indonesia-Auto*, paras. 14.47-55.

[15] See e.g. the AB in *Canada-Periodicals*, at p. 19, and in *EC-Bananas III*, paras. 219-222.

[16] See e.g. the AB in *Guatemala-Cement*, para. 65.

(b)   The Relationship Between the TBT and SPS Agreements

Article 1.4 SPS stipulates that the SPS Agreement does not affect the rights of Members under the TBT Agreement with respect to measures not within the scope of the SPS Agreement. Article 1.5 TBT stipulates that TBT does not apply to sanitary and phytosanitary measures as defined in Annex A to the SPS Agreement. Applying Article 1.5 TBT in *EC-Hormones*, the panel found that the measures at issue were SPS measures and that the TBT was therefore not applicable to them. Thus, SPS and TBT appear to be mutually exclusive in their application.[17] This conclusion should nonetheless be drawn with some caution. As said above, Members must comply with all WTO obligations, unless there is a formal conflict between them. Different aspects of a measure may be addressed under the TBT and SPS Agreements. It is even not entirely inconceivable that one aspect of a measure is covered by both Agreements, on different grounds. It may be recalled that the definition of an SPS measure in Annex A to the SPS Agreement attaches a certain degree of importance to the aim of a measure. The definitions in the TBT Agreement, on the other hand, contain more objective descriptions focusing on the typology of the measure at issue. However, the subjective element in the SPS definitions, based on the aim of the measure as presented by the Member applying it, can and needs to be objectified to some extent. It is submitted that whether a measure is an SPS measure or not cannot depend solely on the national legislator's subjective intent. Indeed, whether a measure is being applied so as to protect human, animal or plant life or health can to an important extent be objectified by looking at the measure's structure, design and context.

A panel may need to address these problems in a dispute where both the TBT and SPS Agreements are argued by the parties. A prohibition on certain products containing genetically modified organisms (GMOs) could trigger this question. Should the SPS and not the TBT Agreement apply in cases where the health risk is dubious, but the Member taking the measure presents it as an SPS measure?[18] Such a scenario is not very likely, because it appears more difficult to justify a measure under the SPS Agreement than under the TBT Agreement. A GMO labelling requirement would only fall within the definitions in the SPS Agreement if 'directly related to food safety'. If not 'directly related to food safety'

---

[17]   The official United States view is that the TBT and SPS Agreements 'differ fundamentally in the means used to determine whether a measure is protectionist in nature. The TBT agreement relies primarily on a test of whether a measure discriminates against imported products [...]. By contrast, the SPS agreement focuses on whether a measure is based on scientific principles and on a risk assessment.' US Statement of Administrative Action Uruguay Round Agreements Act, as quoted in Jackson (1997) at 222.

[18]   Cf. Pardo Quintillan (1999) at 191.

but to, for example, consumer protection, then it would be assessed under the terms of the TBT Agreement.

(c) The Relationship Between the GATT and the SPS Agreement

The SPS Agreement explicitly states in its preamble that it stems from the desire to 'elaborate rules for the application of the provisions of GATT 1994 which relate to the use of sanitary or phytosanitary measures, in particular the provisions of Article XX(b), including the chapeau to Article XX."[19]. In Article 2.3, the SPS Agreement repeats the terms found in paragraph (b) and the chapeau to Article XX GATT. Article 2.4 SPS stipulates that SPS measures which are in conformity with the SPS Agreement are presumed to be in accordance with GATT 1994, in particular Article XX(b). Unlike the TBT Agreement, the SPS Agreement does not repeat verbatim the Most Favoured Nation and National Treatment obligations in Articles I and III GATT. Nor for that matter does it refer to the prohibition of quantitative restrictions in Article XI GATT. The references to Article XX(b) could be taken to imply that the SPS Agreement applies to measures infringing a substantive GATT provision, such as Articles I, III or XI, and whose justification is sought under Article XX(b), as elaborated by the SPS Agreement.[20] However, the standard laid down in Article 1.1 SPS ('all sanitary and phytosanitary measures which may directly or indirectly affect trade') and the text of Articles 2.2 and 5.6 SPS suggest that measures not violating any of these GATT provisions can also be challenged under the SPS Agreement. In other words, the SPS agreement also disciplines non-discriminatory measures, thereby extending beyond the scope of the GATT.

In EC-Hormones, the panel noted that the dispute related to trade in goods (imports of meat and meat products) and that, on its face, the GATT applied. However, the panel observed that the SPS Agreement contains no explicit requirement of a prior violation of a GATT provision which would govern the applicability of the SPS Agreement. Moreover, it noted that many provisions of the SPS Agreement impose "substantive" obligations which go significantly beyond and are additional to the requirements for the invocation of Article XX(b).[21] The panel found that the general approach adopted in Article XX(b) of GATT is fundamentally different from the approach adopted in the SPS Agreement. Article XX(b) provides for a general exception which can be invoked to justify any violation of another GATT provision. The SPS Agreement, on the other hand, provides for specific obligations to be met in order for a Member to

---

[19] SPS Agreement, eigth paragraph of the Preamble and first footnote.

[20] Thus, Thorn and Carlson (2000), at 841 assert that the SPS Agreement is an "affirmative defence".

[21] Panel in EC-Hormones, para. 8.38, referring by way of example to the obligation contained in Article 3.1 SPS.

enact or maintain specific types of measures, namely sanitary and phytosanitary measures. Thus, the panel concluded that the SPS Agreement contains obligations which are not already imposed by GATT, and that there is no requirement *in any of the provisions of the SPS Agreement* that a prior violation of a GATT provision need be established before the SPS Agreement applies.[22] The latter approach has been criticised for *a priori* placing the SPS Agreement above the GATT.[23]

In *Australia-Salmon*, the panel found that both GATT 1994 and the SPS Agreement applied to the measure in dispute. It noted that the SPS Agreement specifically addresses the type of measure in dispute, and that it would in any case need to examine the SPS Agreement, whether or not it found a GATT violation. In order to consider this dispute in the most efficient manner, the panel decided to first address the claims made by Canada under the SPS Agreement before addressing those put forward under GATT 1994.[24] Having found that the measure in dispute was inconsistent with the requirements of the SPS Agreement, the panel saw no need to further examine whether it was also inconsistent with Article XI of GATT 1994.[25] The Appellate Body in the same dispute found that Article 2.3 SPS 'takes up obligations similar to those arising under Article I:1 and Article III:4 of the GATT 1994 and incorporates part of the "chapeau" to Article XX of the GATT 1994'.[26]

(d) The Relationship Between the GATT and the TBT Agreement

Unlike the SPS Agreement, the TBT Agreement does not refer to any specific GATT provision in its preamble, provisions or annexes, and it also does not contain an express presumption that measures that conform to the TBT Agreement are GATT-consistent. It has been asserted that TBT 'explains the obligations contained in GATT Article III'.[27] However, the substantive obligation in Article 2.2 is not to create unnecessary *obstacles* to international trade. This

---

[22] Ibid., paras. 8.39-41, referring to Articles 2.4 and 3.2 SPS to support its view. Emphasis added.

[23] *See* Pescatore (1998) at 23, arguing that the EC would have had a stronger position in this litigation had it insisted on having its measures first examined under Article III:4 GATT, then Article XX(b) GATT and only finally under the SPS Agreement.

[24] Panel in *Australia-Salmon*, paras. 8.38-39. The panel followed the approach taken in the panel reports in *EC-EC-Hormones*, para. 8.42 (US), and para. 8.45 (CND), respectively.

[25] Ibid., para. 8.185.

[26] AB in *Australia-Salmon*, paras. 250-51.

[27] Thorn and Carlson (2000) at 841. See also the US arguments in the panel report in *US-Gasoline*, para. 3.77: '[T]he TBT Agreement had been designed to elaborate on the disciplines of Article III of the General Agreement for a very specific subset of measures (technical regulations, standards and conformity assessment procedures).'

obligation arguably interferes with national regulatory powers to a larger extent than the non-discrimination requirements in Article III GATT. Thus, arguably, internal regulations that are consistent with Article III GATT may be found to be inconsistent with Article 2.2 TBT.[28] Moreover, as this obligation applies to all technical regulations as defined in Annex 1 to the TBT Agreement, the prohibition of unnecessary obstacles has a much wider reach than the prohibition of quantitative restrictions in Article XI GATT, which only applies to border measures. On the other hand, the panel in *EC-Asbestos* noted that the criteria in Article 2.2 TBT are very similar to those in Article XX GATT, and that the Preamble to the TBT Agreement repeats some of the wording of the chapeau to Article XX.[29] The same panel noted that the Tokyo Round version of the TBT Agreement 'was already seen as being a development of the existing rules of the GATT, notably Article XX.'[30] However, Article 2.2 TBT provides a non-exhaustive list of legitimate objectives that may prevent a trade obstacle from being unnecessary. This list includes objectives not found in Article XX, such as environmental protection. Thus, the TBT Agreement appears to build upon both the substantive obligations and exceptions in the GATT, but at the same time extends beyond these obligations and exceptions.

Article 2.2 TBT takes a different approach from the usual GATT-scheme. Under the GATT 1994, a violation of a substantive obligation (such as Article III) is alleged; if that violation is found, the defendant may invoke exceptions such as Article XX. Here, the substantive obligation and the exceptions are integrated into one analysis. Unnecessary obstacles to international trade only occur where technical regulations are more trade-restrictive than necessary to fulfil a legitimate objective, taking account of the risks of non-fulfilment. It has been argued that Article 2.2 is so general that it is difficult to apply, and is therefore only useful in the most egregious cases, which can normally also be addressed under GATT provisions.[31] However, the fact that Article 2.2 has not so far been applied in dispute settlement could also be seen as a result of its very potential. Wherever they can, panels and the Appellate Body tend to avoid it and apply the GATT instead.

In *US-Gasoline*, both the complainants and certain third parties argued that the TBT Agreement applied to the measures complained of.[32] The panel,

---

[28] Cf. Petersmann (1993a) at 66; Appleton (1997a) at 111.

[29] Panel in *EC-Asbestos*, para. 8.55.

[30] Ibid., original footnote 41, referring to document MTN/3E/W26, quoted in document TRE/W/21.

[31] Thorn and Carlson (2000) at 842.

[32] See the parties' arguments in the panel report in *US-Gasoline*, paras. 3.73-3.84; third parties' arguments, paras. 4.6-4.7 (EC, referring to 'the increased legal protection resulting from Article 2.2 of that Agreement compared, for instance, with Article XX of the General Agreement'; para. 4.9 (Norway).

however, simply examined the GATT claims and then decided that it was not necessary to decide on issues raised under the TBT Agreement, without making any statements on the relationship between GATT and TBT or the correct order in which claims should be examined.[33] This decision by the panel was not appealed against as such, although the complainants did raise a conditional argument that, if their appeal as regards Article XX would turn out to be unfavourable to them, the Appellate Body would need to examine their claims under TBT. The Appellate Body disagreed and did not examine the TBT Agreement.[34] It has been argued that in *US-Gasoline*, a "golden opportunity" to apply the TBT Agreement was missed, because the TBT Agreement is to be considered *lex specialis vis-à-vis* the GATT, and should prevail in the case of conflict.[35] However, it is recalled that a conflict between the two Agreements only occurs where their application would lead to different results. In most cases, as in *US-Gasoline*, the TBT Agreement and the GATT would seem to be cumulatively applicable, not mutually exclusive. They appear to be partially overlapping (e.g. Article 2.1 TBT and III:4 GATT), and to be partially complementary, in the sense of adding disciplines to those of the GATT, without however being in conflict according to the definition given above.

This view seems to be confirmed by the Appellate Body in *EC-Asbestos*.[36] The panel in that case did not see any reason to conclude that the TBT Agreement imposes stricter disciplines than those in GATT 1994.[37] The Appellate Body, however, observed that the TBT Agreement furthers the objectives of GATT 1994

> 'through a specialized legal regime that applies solely to a limited class of measures. For these measures, the TBT Agreement imposes obligations on Members that seem to be different from, and additional to, the obligations imposed on Members under the GATT 1994'.[38]

As regards the scope of the TBT, judging from the Appellate Body report in *EC-Asbestos*, it seems that a measure prohibiting all products from containing a substance considered to be dangerous to health or environmentally harmful will be covered, while a measure prohibiting a substance *per se* may not be covered by the TBT Agreement. The latter may thus be assessed under GATT rules.

---

[33] Panel in *US-Gasoline*, para. 6.43.

[34] AB in *US-Gasoline*, at pp. 10-12.

[35] Zedalis (1997a) at 205.

[36] See Section 4.5.1.

[37] Panel report in *EC-Asbestos*, para. 8.56.

[38] AB in *EC-Asbestos*, para. 80. Emphasis added.

The TBT Agreement repeats in Article 2.1 the National Treatment obligation of Article III GATT, without however providing an exceptions article equivalent to Article XX. This gives rise to the question of whether the National Treatment obligation in TBT should be interpreted in the same way as in GATT. Another question is what should a Member do when it has been charged with infringing Article 2.1 TBT? The absence of an Article XX-like exception could imply that under the TBT Agreement, discriminatory technical regulations are simply prohibited without any possibility of justification.[39] Alternatively, a defendant charged with a violation of Article 2.1 could either invoke a legitimate objective under Article 2.2, or invoke Article XX GATT. According to the first option, a link should be established between Articles 2.1 and 2.2, although it is debatable whether such a link was intended by the drafters of the TBT Agreement. Discriminatory technical regulations could be presumed to create unnecessary trade obstacles unless they were not more trade-restrictive than necessary to fulfil a legitimate objective in the sense of Article 2.2. The other alternative appears to be even more problematic. The chapeau to Article XX GATT clearly states that 'nothing *in this Agreement* shall be construed to prevent the adoption or enforcement [...] of measures [...]'.[40] Thus, to invoke Article XX GATT in order to justify a TBT violation seems to stretch the application of Article XX GATT beyond what the ordinary meaning given to the terms of its text allows.

Although most technical regulations are origin-neutral, a challenge under Article 2.1 of the TBT Agreement is not inconceivable. The same technical regulation could at the same time be challenged as a violation of Article III:4 GATT, raising the question of whether the two Agreements can apply cumulatively. The cumulative application of the TBT Agreement and the GATT is also possible in the case of technical regulations that do not distinguish on the basis of national origin, i.e., "facially neutral" technical regulations. These could be challenged under both Article III:4 GATT and Article 2.2 TBT. It has been argued that measures that do not make origin-based distinctions will normally be assessed under the TBT Agreement, and measures that do make such distinctions will be assessed under the GATT.[41] However, the current author submits that the definitions in the TBT Agreement should be the benchmark for determining the applicability of that Agreement, rather than a distinction between facially neutral and facially discriminatory technical regulations that cannot be found in the TBT Agreement or the GATT.

---

[39] This view is expressed by Hudec (1998) at 644.

[40] Emphasis added.

[41] Howse and Tuerk (2001) at 24 (manuscript).

5.2   Exceptions, Justifications and Conditions

5.2.1   Article XX GATT

(a)   Justification Grounds, "Means-Ends Tests" and other Conditions in Article XX GATT

The fact that the Appellate Body in *US-Shrimp-Turtle* found that turtles were "exhaustible natural resources" is hardly surprising, as earlier panel reports had done the same for tuna, salmon and herring. Moreover, the turtle species in question were all listed as 'threatened by extinction' by the Convention on International Trade in Endangered Species of Wild Fauna and Flora (CITES). The Appellate Body in the same case said that "exhaustible natural resources" are to be interpreted in an evolutive way, in the context of the objective of sustainable development to which the Preamble to the WTO Agreement refers.[42] This approach, together with the panel report in *US-Gasoline*, warrant the conclusion that the concept of "exhaustible natural resources" in paragraph (g) of Article XX GATT has a wide potential. According to the panel in *US-Gasoline*, anything natural that can be given a market value and that may be depleted, including in terms of its qualities, may in principle qualify as "exhaustible natural resources". Arguably, if air that is not "depleted" by pollutants emitted through the consumption of gasoline qualifies as "exhaustible natural resource", then air that is not "depleted" by excessive concentrations of greenhouse gases might also qualify. That would imply that measures taken to reduce greenhouse gas emissions could be covered by the exception in paragraph (g), subject of course to the other conditions in that paragraph as well as the chapeau to Article XX. Another important resource that might be covered by paragraph (g) is potable water. Water shortages already exist in many regions of the world, and may be expected to become one of the greatest environmental problems of the 21st century.[43]

It has been suggested that the "evolutionary approach" to "exhaustible natural resources" adopted by the Appellate Body in *US-Shrimp-Turtle* may give rise to interpretative problems in the future.[44] The argument is that this approach may cause uncertainty and result in a disrupted balance between the exception for natural resources *vis-à-vis* the exception for life and health protection, especially for the protection of humans. It has even been argued that the evolutionary approach 'implies the possibility of altering previous GATT/WTO interpreta-

---

[42] *AB in Shrimp-Turtle*, paras. 129-131.

[43] A discussion has developed on the relevance of WTO rules to planned Canadian export restrictions of bulk water. See e.g. http://www.waterbank.com/Newsletters/nws15.html.

[44] Appleton (1999) at 482.

tions and thus could affect the balance of rights and obligations negotiated by the parties in contravention of Article 19.2 [DSU]'.[45] However, although panels will normally respect interpretations by previous panels and the Appellate Body, nothing in the DSU obliges them to do so. It is submitted that if a (semi)-adjudicatory body is asked to interpret open terms, it will inevitably bring around some changes in the balance of those rights and obligations pertaining to the WTO Members. This is an inherent feature of an evolving legal framework. If Members think that the balance of their rights and obligations has been excessively altered, they can seek an authoritative interpretation under Article 3.9 DSU, which may overturn a panel or Appellate Body finding. An "evolutionary approach" in the light of the objective of sustainable development as integrated in the WTO preamble could also be applied to the substantive provisions in the GATT.[46]

The Appellate Body in *US-Gasoline* observed that Article XX uses different terms in different paragraphs, and that it would be unreasonable to suppose that the WTO Members intended to require the same kind or degree of connection between the measure and its purpose in each of those paragraphs.[47] "Necessary", which features in paragraphs (a), (b) and (d), may have a different meaning in different contexts, and there are indications in *EC-Asbestos* that it is being more loosely interpreted when serious health risks are at stake in paragraph (b) than when such is not the case, as in paragraph (d). Still, looking at the terms "necessary" in paragraph (b) and "relating to" in paragraph (g), it seems clear that the ordinary meaning of the former demands a stricter means-ends relationship than the latter. As a somewhat counterintuitive result, it is in principle easier to justify a measure protecting natural resources than a measure protecting human, animal or plant life or health. Members may therefore be expected to continue to resort to paragraph (g) when animal protection is at stake.

(b) "Necessary"

It may be recalled that when applying the "necessary" test, panels traditionally referred to the "least GATT-inconsistent" measure reasonably available. However, as the GATT does not contain any order of "GATT-inconsistency", a measure is either GATT-consistent or GATT-inconsistent, and "less GATT-inconsistent" seems a nonsensical phrase. It has been suggested that

---

[45] Ibid. at 483.

[46] An example would be the interpretation of "like product" and "treatment less favourable" in Article III:4 GATT, which are argued by some to be in the process of evolving so as to accommodate distinctions based on production and processing methods (PPMs). See Section 5.4.5.

[47] AB in *US-Gasoline*, at pp. 18-19.

what must have been meant is the degree of inconsistency with the *objective* of the GATT. In this view, the meaning of "least GATT-inconsistent" is for all practical purposes equivalent to "least trade-restrictive".[48] To what extent should alternatives be considered when assessing whether a measure is "necessary"? As Article XX GATT provides exceptions for violations of all GATT obligations, including both Articles III and XI, it is clear that the alternative measures to be considered may be quite different in nature from the measure that is being assessed.[49] For instance, in the panel report in the *Thai Cigarettes* case, the panel considered that a cigarette import ban infringing Article XI did not meet the "necessary" test because an advertising ban was reasonably available. Such a ban, even if inconsistent with Article III:4, would be justified under Article XX(b) as "unavoidable and therefore necessary".[50] Likewise, it is conceivable that an import ban is found to be unnecessary because its objective could be attained by a certain tax measure.

It is sometimes difficult not to involve the level of protection sought by a measure in the assessment of alternatives to that measure. For instance, in the *Thai Cigarettes* case, the quantitative aspect of the Thai health policy objective would probably have been attained to a higher degree by an import ban than by an advertising ban.[51] Suppose that a country decided to ban smoking altogether, equally applying to domestic and imported cigarettes. Such a ban should not falter on the "necessary" test just because an advertising ban would be a less trade-restrictive alternative, since that alternative would not enable the same level of protection to be attained.[52]

After the "weighing and balancing process" laid down by the Appellate Body reports in *Korea-Beef* and *EC-Asbestos*, the interpretation of "necessary" as "least GATT-inconsistent" or "least trade-restrictive" has not explicitly been abolished. As the Appellate Body said in *Korea-Beef*, the weighing and balancing process is comprehended in the determination of whether a WTO-consistent or less WTO-inconsistent measure is "reasonably available".[53] Nevertheless, the elaboration by

---

[48] Fauchald (1998) at 311.

[49] This question may be referred to as "diagonal necessity", as an analogy to the term "diagonal proportionality" as used in Chapter 3.

[50] *Thailand-Cigarettes*, para. 78.

[51] The problem with the Thai measure was that the import ban was not accompanied by restrictions on the production or sale of domestic cigarettes. However, looking at the dispute in retrospect, that aspect of the measure would have been more appropriately addressed under the chapeau to Article XX than under the "necessary" test.

[52] Howse argues that in *Thailand-Cigarettes*, the panel ignored evidence adduced by the World Health Organisation to the effect that imported cigarettes had specifically caused an increase in smoking in several developing countries. Howse (2000) at 63, referring to *Thailand-Cigarettes*, para. 55.

[53] AB in *Korea-Beef*, para. 166.

the Appellate Body puts the least trade-restrictiveness standard into a different perspective. It is recalled that in *Korea Beef*, the Appellate Body said that it should take into account 'the relative importance of the common interests or values that the law or regulation to be enforced is intended to protect', 'the extent to which the measure contributes to the realization of the end pursued', and 'the extent to which the compliance measure produces restrictive effects on international commerce'. [54] If the relative importance of a non-trade objective, the effectiveness of a measure in attaining that objective, and the trade-restrictiveness of the measure are weighed in one basket, so to speak, this would appear to be a strict proportionality test. It could lead to the conclusion that a measure is not "necessary" because there is an alternative that is much less trade-restrictive and almost as effective in contributing to its goal.[55]

The suggestion by the Appellate Body in *Korea-Beef* that "necessary" may have a variety of meanings depending on the context in which the word appears, is difficult to reconcile with the GATT panel's finding in *Thai-Cigarettes* that "necessary" has the same meaning in paragraphs (b) and (d) of Article XX. Indeed, comparing the Appellate Body's application of the "necessary" test in paragraph (b) in *EC-Asbestos* and in paragraph (d) in *Korea-Beef*, it appears that a much more deferential position was taken in the former than in the latter. In *EC-Asbestos*, the Appellate Body applied a relatively loose test for "reasonably available alternative", probably in view of the serious health risk involved.[56] In contrast, in *Korea-Beef*, the Appellate Body replaced the defendant's view of its chosen level of protection by its own assumption of what that chosen level was. As a consequence, it did not accept the necessity of the measures chosen to guarantee the protection level alleged by the defendant, thereby also interfering with the defendant's budgetary policy. Arguably, this application of the "weighing and balancing" process tends to lean towards a strict proportionality test. If the Appellate Body has indeed provided itself with the possibility to weigh the importance of non-trade values with trade impacts and the effectiveness of measures, its more deferential exercise of that weighing exercise in *EC-Asbestos* suggests that the intensity of its weighing exercise will depend upon the importance attached to the values pursued by a measure. Which begs the question of what will be decisive: the importance attached to the non-trade value or interest by the Member applying the measure, or by the Appellate Body?

---

[54] Ibid., paras. 162-3.

[55] See the discussion on proportionality in Chapter 3.

[56] AB in *EC-Asbestos*, in particular paras. 168 and 172.

(c) "Relating to" and "Made Effective in Conjunction with…"

After the Appellate Body reports in *US-Gasoline* and *US-Shrimp-Turtle*, "relating to" appears to require that the means be "reasonably related" to the ends. There must be a "close and real" and "substantial" means-end relationship, and the measure must 'not be disproportionally wide' in its scope and reach in relation to its policy objective. These interpretations leave a great deal of flexibility as regards the extent of the relationship between means and ends that satisfies the requirement. Arguably, a "close" or "substantial" relationship is more than being "reasonably related". Moreover, the reference to being not disproportionally wide could be taken to suggest that "relating to" allows for a full proportionality test. However, it is submitted that a fully-fledged reasonableness and proportionality test would overstretch the ordinary meaning of the term "relating to".

The second element of the means-end requirement in paragraph (g) requires that the measure be 'made effective in conjunction with domestic restrictions'. The Appellate Body in *US-Shrimp-Turtle* arguably softened this obligation vis-à-vis its earlier interpretation in *US-Gasoline* as requiring "even-handedness". Since the domestic restrictions in *US-Shrimp-Turtle* were enacted as a separate law two years before the import prohibition, they were not jointly established. More importantly, it is questionable whether an import prohibition is a restriction "corresponding" to domestic requirements as regards fishing methods, enforced by monetary sanctions and civil penalties. The effect of these domestic requirements was not as absolute as the import prohibition. As long as domestic fishermen were not caught infringing the production requirements, they could sell turtle-unfriendly shrimp on the US market. Their catches were only seized in cases of "egregious" violations. In contrast, an exporter from a country hit by the import embargo could no longer sell its shrimp on the US market. Even if one has great confidence in the domestic enforcement of production requirements, to accept import bans as "corresponding" to domestic production requirements could open the door to abuse.[57] Admittedly, however, there is always the chapeau in order to address abuse.

(d) Chapeau

The "chapeau" to Article XX is likely to become the central issue in many future trade-environment disputes. The term "unjustifiable" appears somewhat tautological in an Article providing justifications for other-

---

[57] This issue relates closely to the questions discussed *infra* in Section 5.4, particularly the role of the Note Ad Article III in assessing measures based on production and processing methods (PPMs).

wise GATT-incompatible measures.[58] For instance, if a measure violates Article III because it is discriminatory or protective, it is in principle justifiable under Article XX. However, if the application of a measure constitutes "unjustifiable discrimination", it fails to meet the requirements of the chapeau, which then renders the measure "unjustifiable" under Article XX. As early as in 1969, it was questioned whether Article XX is at all necessary in relation to Article III, on the basis of the following reasoning: If the chapeau to Article XX is meant to ensure that measures falling into one of the exceptions may not be applied to protect domestic producers, recourse to Article XX is not necessary to justify internal measures protecting health, morals, etc., as Article III itself already ensures that internal measures do not discriminate or protect. Thus, the exceptions would only be necessary to justify any infringements of Article XI.[59] However, since then, internal regulations and taxes have increasingly been challenged under Article III, and a need to resort to Article XX to justify such measures has correspondingly developed. Indeed, the Appellate Body made it clear in *US-Gasoline* that Article XX applies to all GATT provisions, including Article III, and that the chapeau cannot logically refer to the same disciplines as those contained in the substantive GATT provisions whose violations are sought to be justified by resorting to Article XX.

In both *US-Gasoline* and *US-Shrimp-Turtle*, the Appellate Body said that the chapeau functions to prevent Members from abusing their right to invoke exceptions under Article XX. In *US-Shrimp-Turtle*, the Appellate Body further stated that the chapeau expresses the general principle of good faith, and that it requires the balancing and the drawing of an equilibrium line between the rights and obligations of WTO Members. Applying these general guidelines to the actual measures at issue in *US-Gasoline* and *US-Shrimp-Turtle*, the Appellate Body based quite a large number of requirements on the chapeau. Thus, according to *US-Gasoline*, the application of a measure should be "reasonable", there should be "no alternatives reasonably available", and if a measure is discriminatory in its application, the discrimination must not be "foreseen", but "inadvertent or unavoidable". The reference to "reasonably available alternatives" in an analysis of the chapeau is reminiscent of the "necessary" test applied to paragraphs (b) and (d). This is striking because it was applied to a justification under paragraph (g), which does not contain a "necessary" requirement. The Appellate Body in *US-Shrimp-Turtle* again appears to have read a "no alternatives reasonably available" requirement into the chapeau, this time specifically into "unjustifiable discrimination".[60]

---

[58] The term "unjustifiable" does not appear in Article 30 EC, the EC equivalent of Article XX GATT.

[59] Jackson (1969) at 743.

[60] AB in *US-Shrimp-Turtle*, paras. 171-172

In *US-Gasoline*, the Appellate Body largely took the three elements of the chapeau together, stating that they impart meaning to each other. However, in *US-Shrimp-Turtle*, the Appellate Body started to differentiate between the various elements of the chapeau, while in *US-Gasoline* it had taken them together. The "unjustifiability" of a discriminatory application was mostly based on whether multilateral attempts at solving the environmental problem had been made, and on whether there was sufficient flexibility in the application of the rule, e.g. whether different circumstances for different exporters had been taken into account. The "arbitrariness" of a discriminatory application focused on procedural aspects of the measure, i.e. due process requirements, such as whether exporters are duly notified of a decision affecting them, whether they can appeal against a particular decision, etc. The panel in *EC-Asbestos* took this differentiating approach further, and interpreted a "disguised trade restriction" with reference to a measure's protectionist design, architecture and structure.

A tentative synthesis of the requirements identified in the interpretation of the chapeau in *US-Gasoline*, *US-Shrimp-Turtle*, and *EC-Asbestos* is that the Member imposing a measure for which it seeks justification under Article XX must show that it has struck a balance between its own rights and obligations and those belonging to other Members. That means that it must have considered domestic as well as foreign interests and weighed the alternatives for its measure in the light of those interests. This synthesis arguably embodies the "reasonable-ness" requirement as well as the requirements of "foreseen", "not inadvertent", and "unavoidable" which were promulgated in *US-Gasoline*.

A question that remains unsolved after these reports is whether the standard in the chapeau might differ according to the substantive GATT provision which has been infringed. Judging from the first cases in which the chapeau was extensively discussed and applied, it is difficult to draw any firm conclusions on this point. *US-Gasoline* suggests that the chapeau requires that in order to justify a discriminatory internal measure, foreign interests must be taken into account to some degree. The panel in *EC-Asbestos* deemed an internal measure to be justified under Article XX(b) after finding it discriminatory under Article III. The panel found no discrimination in the context of the chapeau, however, and then concentrated on a "disguised restriction", not looking so closely at foreign interests. In *US-Shrimp-Turtle*, the conditions in exporting countries had to be taken into account to an important extent. This case involved an import prohibition, which by definition only addresses imported goods. Perhaps the degree to which foreign interests should be taken into account, as required by the chapeau is higher for Article XI infringements than for Article III infringements. Indeed, the Appellate Body and the implementation panel in *US-Shrimp-Turtle* referred to the import prohibition as the 'heaviest weapon in a Member's armoury of trade measures', its possible justification therefore deserving thorough scrutiny.[61]

---

[61] Ibid., para. 171; panel in *US-Shrimp-Turtle Implementation*, para. 5.51.

However, it is as yet unclear whether such a general conclusion can be drawn from only three cases. The measures in *US-Shrimp-Turtle* targeted production methods elsewhere, so it would seem to be logical that a fair amount of foreign interests had to be taken into account. The panel in *EC-Asbestos*, which found a violation of Article III:4, was rather deferential in applying the chapeau to Article XX. At the same time, the assessment of the unjustifiability of the discrimination in *US-Gasoline*, after a violation of Article III, was not a mild one and required a high degree of taking foreign interests into account. Perhaps the difference between *EC-Asbestos* and *US-Gasoline* in this respect is explained by the fact that the latter involved a *de jure* discrimination while the former did not. That would confirm the suggestion that the nature of the violation of the basic obligations may indeed affect the scrutiny applied under the chapeau to Article XX.

5.2.2 The TBT and SPS Agreements

Strictly speaking, one cannot speak of exceptions in either the TBT or the SPS Agreement. Neither Agreement contains a separate provision resembling Article XX GATT. The TBT and SPS Agreements integrate obligations, justifications and conditions; the basic obligations and the justifications are not differentiated as they are in the GATT. The "classic" GATT pattern of a violation of a basic obligation which can be justified under an exception if the conditions are fulfilled does not fully apply to the TBT and SPS Agreements. This makes it more difficult to assess these elements individually. However, grounds and conditions for justification, such as "means-ends tests", can still be distilled from both Agreements.

As said, the TBT Agreement contains no general exceptions article like Article XX GATT.[62] The fact that Article 2.2 refers to unnecessary trade obstacles, and elaborates on "unnecessary" by referring to "legitimate objectives", raises the question whether those objectives may also be invoked to justify infringements of the Most-Favoured Nation and National Treatment requirements in Article 2.1.

The word "unnecessary" is elaborated upon by the phrase 'shall not be more trade-restrictive than *necessary* to fulfil a legitimate objective, taking account of the risks non-fulfilment would create'. Article 2.2 thus contains an element of tautology. The phrase 'not be more trade-restrictive' in Article 2.2 TBT is reminiscent of the interpretation of "necessary" in Article XX(b) GATT.

---

[62] The same was true for the 1979 TBT Agreement. Thus, the statement in GATT (1979a) at 42 that measures deemed necessary by governments for [*inter alia*] health and environmental protection were 'excepted from the Standards Code' was subsequently removed by an erratum.

However, the different balance of obligations in Article 2.2 TBT and in Article XX GATT suggest that "necessary" need not have exactly the same meaning in Article 2.2 as in Article XX GATT.[63] The test in the TBT Agreement in addition contains a reference to the risks created by the non-fulfilment of the legitimate objective. This appears to qualify the requirement that technical regulations shall not be more trade-restrictive than necessary. It is an interesting addition, as it establishes an explicit link between the measure taken (a technical regulation) and the *fulfilment* of the legitimate objective sought by that measure. Such an explicit link between the measure and the fulfilment of the objective sought cannot be found in Article XX GATT, although it recently appears to have been read into the "necessary" test under Article XX(b) and (d) by the Appellate Body. However, according to Article 2.2 TBT, only the risk of *non-fulfilment* of the objective is to be taken into account, and not the risk created by a *lesser degree of fulfilment* of the objective.

The TBT Agreement contains no further elaboration of the risk assessment to be made by the Member applying the technical regulation, as is the case in the SPS Agreement. For assessing the risk of non-fulfilment, a non exhaustive list of 'relevant elements of consideration' is provided in the last sentence of Article 2.2. Although that list includes 'available scientific and technical information', there is no hard and fast requirement to have a scientific basis for a technical regulation as there is for sanitary or phytosanitary measures in the SPS Agreement. Accordingly, the TBT Agreement appears to provide more possibilities to base a measure on the precautionary principle than the SPS Agreement. The lack of elaboration as regards the requirement to take account of the risks of non-fulfilment raises some questions. Does a Member preparing or adopting a technical regulation have to take the risks of non-fulfilment of its objective into account when looking at each available alternative separately? Does it have to demonstrate that it has done so? Or could it be that the requirement to consider the alternatives may itself be limited because of the perceived risk of non-fulfilment caused by waiting longer to adopt a technical regulation?

An earlier version of the draft Uruguay Round Final Act contained a footnote stating that Article 2.2 was intended to incorporate a "proportionality" test to determine whether technical regulations constituted unnecessary obstacles to trade, and various authors have interpreted Article 2.2 along those lines.[64] This would imply that Article 2.2 contains a test which balances the trade effects against the non-trade objective. However, as has been signalled in the EC context, there is considerable uncertainty as to what "proportionality" exactly

---

[63] However, McGovern (1995) at 7.24-4 argues that the experience gained under Article XX GATT may be of use in determining what restrictions are necessary under Article 2.2.

[64] Ziegler (1998) at 216; Appleton (1997a) at 113; Rege (1994) at 105 note 6; Petersmann (1993a), at 66 note 45; Völker (1995) at 288.

means. Proportionality may be taken to mean the actual balancing of the trade effects and the non-trade objectives of a measure. A more limited proportionality test only balances the various means to achieve a non-trade policy goal, attempting to avoid involving the actual policy goal in its analysis. That would coincide with the usual interpretation of the "necessary" test. The question arising from the requirements in Article 2.2 itself is whether it is possible to look only at the least trade-restrictive alternative to reach a *given* policy goal, and at the same time to take account of the risks created by the non-fulfilment of that policy goal, without implicitly assessing the levels of fulfilment of the policy goal.

Finally, the SPS Agreement contains the most elaborate set of conditions, that build upon the "necessity" requirement in sub-paragraph (b) and the requirements in the chapeau to Article XX GATT, but are more detailed and more burdensome for Members to comply with. SPS measures should be applied only to the extent necessary; they should be based on scientific principles and not maintained without sufficient scientific evidence (Article 2.2); they should not arbitrarily or unjustifiably discriminate or be applied in a manner which would constitute a disguised trade restriction (Article 2.3); they should be based on international standards wherever possible and appropriate (Article 3); they should be based on a risk assessment (Article 5.1); they should be applied in order to achieve the appropriate protection level, and those levels should be applied without discrimination (Article 5.5 and Guidelines for its implementation[65]); and SPS measures should not be more trade-restrictive than required to achieve their appropriate level of protection, taking into account technical and economic feasibility, which is the case when there is no reasonably available alternative measure that achieves the appropriate protection level but is significantly less trade-restrictive (Article 5.6).

5.2.3 Justifications and "Reason"

The Appellate Body in *Japan-Alcohol* stated that:

> *WTO rules are not so rigid or so inflexible as not to leave room for reasoned judgements in confronting the endless and ever-changing ebb and flow of real facts in real cases in the real world. They will serve the multilateral trading system best if they are interpreted with that in mind. In that way, we will achieve the "security and predictability" sought for the multilateral trading system by the Members of the WTO through the establishment of the dispute settlement system*[66]

---

[65] G/SPS/W/104, 'Proposed Guidelines to Further the Practical Implementation of Article 5.5'.

[66] AB in *Japan-Alcohol*, at p. 31. In the same case, the AB used the metaphor of an accordion for the meaning of "likeness".

In *US-Gasoline,* the Appellate Body interpreted the chapeau to Article XX as a "reasonableness" requirement against the background of its purpose to prevent the abuse of Article XX. When applying the chapeau, it looked, among other things, at reasonably available alternatives. In *US-Shrimp-Turtle,* when applying the "relating to" requirement in XX(g), the Appellate Body observed that the means were "reasonably" related to the ends. When applying the requirements of the chapeau to the measure at issue, the Appellate Body remarked that an alternative course of action was *reasonably* open to the United States for securing the legitimate policy goal of its measure.[67] Also in *US-Shrimp-Turtle,* the Appellate Body said that the chapeau is an expression of the principle of good faith, prohibiting "abus de droit", which implies that the assertion of the right in Article XX 'must be exercised bona fide, that is to say, reasonably'.[68] The Appellate Body cited an author on public international law who referred to a *bona fide* and reasonable exercise of the right as one that is 'appropriate and necessary for the purpose of the right (i.e., in furtherance of the interests which the right is intended to protect)'.[69] That description of what is reasonably refers to two elements of what is called in this work proportionality *senso lutu.* The Appellate Body further clarified that the chapeau requires striking a balance between the rights of the defendant and those of the complainant, which will need to be done on a case-by-case basis. The panel in *EC-Asbestos* endorsed this interpretation and examined, within the context of the chapeau, whether the measures at issue had been "reasonably" applied.[70]

In the SPS Agreement, the words "reasonably available" feature in the Note to Article 5.6 SPS, where it functions much in the same way as in the interpretation of "necessary" in Article XX(b) and (d) GATT. In *EC-Hormones,* the Appellate Body interpreted "based on" in Article 5.1 as requiring that the results of the risk assessment must 'sufficiently warrant - that is to say, reasonably support - the SPS measure at stake', thus, that there is 'a rational relationship between the measure and the risk assessment.'[71] Furthermore, the Appellate Body in the same case found that a single divergent opinion expressed by one scientist was not "reasonably sufficient" to overturn the contrary conclusions reached in more specific scientific studies.

Thus, the Appellate Body in various instances refers to "reasonably" and "reasonableness", and has thus provided itself with a great deal of flexibility in the interpretation of open-ended norms. Other instances of such flexibility

---

[67] AB in *US-Shrimp-Turtle,* para. 171.

[68] Ibid., para. 158.

[69] Ibid., para. 158, citing Cheng (1953) at 125.

[70] Panel in *EC-Asbestos,* para. 8.226.

[71] AB in *EC-Hormones,* paras. 193 and 208.

are the "likeness" accordion in *Japan-Alcohol*, repeated in *EC-Asbestos*; and the 'continuum of meanings of "necessary"' in *Korea-Beef*. Does this mean that the Appellate Body is moving towards a general "reasonableness" or "reason" criterion in the interpretation of Article XX GATT? It is submitted that despite its increasing use of the concept of reason to interpret key provisions, the Appellate Body will not readily overlook textual and contextual differences between provisions if it wishes to interpret them in accordance with the Vienna Convention. By using such open concepts, and by referring to the line of equilibrium which accordingly moves as the kind and shape of measures vary and the factual situations of the cases differ, the Appellate Body has granted itself considerable leeway to approach the chapeau on a case-by-case basis. However, governments will want to know what sort of measures pursuing societal and environmental needs may be expected to pass the Article XX test. Although it is a difficult task, the Appellate Body will have to clarify some of the most difficult issues if governments are unwilling or unable to agree on guidelines for the interpretation of Article XX.

5.3 The Role of Protection and Discrimination

5.3.1 Introduction: Protection and Discrimination in WTO Provisions

As discussed in Section 4.2.2, according to the Appellate Body, the broad and fundamental purpose of Article III is to avoid protectionism in the application of internal tax and regulatory measures. It may be recalled that Article III:1 provides in an adhortative manner that internal taxes, and regulations affecting the sale, distribution etc. of products, should not be applied to imported or domestic products so as to afford protection to domestic production. The first paragraph is evidently not structured as a "chapeau" to Article III, and it has been argued that Article III contains ten paragraphs of equal weight.[72] Nevertheless, the Appellate Body has made it clear that the first paragraph contains a general principle that underlies the whole of Article III and "informs" the other paragraphs of Article III.[73] However, exactly how this "informing" takes place remains to be clarified, particularly in the context of Article III:4, which does not explicitly refer to Article III:1. The notion of "protection" is taken in this work as being broader than discrimination. It encompasses all instances of discrimination and in addition those situations where there is no production

---

[72] Von Moldtke (1997) at 11.

[73] AB in *Japan-Alcohol* and *EC-Asbestos*. See Section 4.2.2.

of domestic products that are "like" the imported products whose treatment is at issue, but domestic producers of products competing with the imported products are nonetheless favoured. The non-protectionism principle is not only found in Article III:1 GATT, but also in Article 2.2 TBT. Arguably, it is also embodied in the 'disguised restriction on international trade' element of the chapeau to Article XX GATT, and in Article 5.5 SPS.

Although the notion of discrimination as such does not occur in Article III:4 GATT, it is submitted that the prohibition of less favourable treatment of like imported products in that provision constitutes or at least closely resembles a non-discrimination test. Non-discrimination requirements figure in all the WTO Agreements that are central to this work. Even if the word "discrimina-tion" does not literally figure in Article III, panels have sometimes used that term when addressing this Article.[74] The panel in *Japan-Film* even spoke of *de jure* and *de facto* discrimination in the context of Article III.[75] The "less favourable treatment" standard is also found in Article 2.1 TBT, but not as such in the SPS Agreement. The word "discrimination" itself does feature in the chapeau to Article XX GATT, where it refers to the manner in which measures are applied. Article 2.3 of the SPS Agreement contains almost identical wording, albeit that it simply refers to the measures themselves, and not to their means of application. Article 5.5 SPS prohibits arbitrary or unjustifiable distinctions in protection levels deemed to be appropriate in different situations, if these result in discrimination.

A central question in relation to the national treatment provisions is whether they prohibit measures that are not linked to product origin, but may neverthe-less have as their effect the less favourable treatment of imports. The answer to this question determines to what extent WTO Members can make regulatory distinctions without infringing Article III:4. If their distinctions do not infringe Article III:4, they do not have to resort to Article XX. If their distinctions do infringe Article III:4, however, resorting to Article XX is required. Article XX lacks justification grounds such as "environmental protection" or "consumer protection" and may therefore be too limited to accommodate all the legitimate objectives for which governments make regulatory distinctions. The latter prob-lem may largely be accommodated by a wide interpretation of the grounds in Article XX. But nevertheless, there are regulatory objectives not covered by Article XX, and moreover, Article XX lays the burden of proof on the defendant to justify its measures. Thus, the scope of the prohibition in Article III:4

---

[74] For example, the GATT panel in *EC-Oilseeds*, paras. 140-141, noted that the EC Regulations at issue were capable of giving rise to discrimination, although they may not necessarily do so in the case of each individual purchase. The panel noted that the exposure of a particular imported product to a risk of discrimination in itself constitutes a form of discrimination.

[75] Panel in *Japan-Film*, para. 10.86.

has important ramifications. For example, under Article III:4, should a WTO Member be allowed to regulate cars with catalytic converters more favourably than cars without catalytic converters, e.g. by allowing cars with converters to be used during rush hours, while cars without converters are not? If cars with and without converters are found to be "like products" and "less favourable treatment" of imported cars without converters is found, the Member will need to justify its regulatory distinction under Article XX. If, on the other hand, the terms "like products" and/or "less favourable treatment" are interpreted differently, the outcome may be that the measure is not an infringement of Article III:4 in the first place.

For the purpose of the following analysis, a distinction is made between *de jure* differentiating measures and *de jure* neutral measures. *De jure* differential treatment is understood here to include not only direct references to product origin, but also references to criteria linked to product origin. An example is a national law laying down different requirements for importers and for domestic producers and traders. "*De jure* neutral" measures are defined as measures that do not differentiate between products on the basis of their origin or any factor linked to origin. Such measures may have unfavourable effects on imports. *De jure* neutral measures cannot be found to accord less favourable treatment by looking solely at the regulations themselves. For example, certain product requirements are tailored to domestic producers' wishes, or regulatory distinctions are based on criteria placing all or most imports in a disadvantaged category. It should be noted that there is no textual basis for a distinction between *de jure* differentiating and *de jure* neutral measures in Article III, as noted by the panel in *Japan-Alcohol*.[76] Although the matter has been addressed by many distinguished authors, the problem of how to assess *de jure* neutral measures that are *de facto* detrimental to imports under Article III:4 has yet to be resolved.[77]

5.3.2 *De Jure* Differentiating Measures and National Treatment

The way in which the GATT/WTO deals with *de jure* differentiation to the detriment of imports, sometimes also referred to as "explicit" or "facial" discrimination, seems relatively straightforward. If imported goods are explicitly treated differently from their "like" domestic counterparts, and the differential treatment is less favourable to imports, a violation of Article III:4 will be found. The complaining party must adduce a *prima facie* claim of an Article III:4 violation, bearing the burden of proving both elements, i.e. differential treatment of "like" products, and that that treatment is less favourable

---

[76] Panel in *Japan-Alcohol*, para. VI.16. This point was not appealed.

[77] See e.g. Roessler (1996), Mattoo and Subramanian (1998), Farber and Hudec (1994).

to imports. Then, when the party enacting the measures invokes a justification under Article XX, it is up to that party to prove that all the elements of Article XX have been fulfilled.[78] Once found to contravene Article III:4, possible justifications will have to comply with Article XX. The panel in *US-Section 337* suggested that the Member enacting *de jure* differential regulations bears part of the burden of proof under Article III:4.[79] Nonetheless, the complainant will still be required to adduce a *prima facie* case of differential treatment that is unfavourable to "like" imported products. In *US-FSC*, the implementation panel viewed the principal purpose of the "likeness" determination under Article III:4 as ascertaining whether any formal differentiation in treatment between an imported and a domestic product could be based upon the fact that the products are different -i.e. not "like"- rather than on the origin of the products involved. It noted that the distinction made in the measure at issue was solely and explicitly based on origin, and that the mere fact of having a certain origin does not render a product "unlike" an imported good.[80] In most cases where *de jure* differential treatment of "like" products has been established, finding less favourable treatment will not be a problem.[81]

5.3.3   *De Jure* Neutral Measures and National Treatment

(a)   *De Jure* Neutral Measures in GATT-WTO Dispute Settlement

The language of relevant GATT and WTO panel reports and WTO Appellate Body reports on the one hand suggests that Article III:4 goes beyond a prohibition of purely *de jure* differential treatment to the detriment of imports. On the other hand, there are few instances where *de jure* neutral measures have actually been found to be in violation of Article III:4. Under GATT 1947, the panel in *Italian Discrimination against Imported Agricultural Machines* said that 'the drafters intended to cover [...] any laws or regulations which might adversely modify the conditions of competition between the domestic and imported products on the internal market.'[82] The panel in *US-Section 337* noted in an obiter dictum that 'there may be cases where application of *formally identical* legal provisions would *in practice* accord less favourable treatment to imported products and a contracting party might thus have to apply different

---

[78]   *See* e.g. panel in *Japan-Film*, para. 10.29, Farber and Hudec (1994) at 1420, and further Section 4.7.

[79]   *US-Section 337*, para. 5.11: '[I]t is incumbent on the contracting party applying differential treatment to show that, in spite of such differences, the no less favourable treatment standard of Article III is met.'

[80]   Panel in *US-FSC Implementation*, paras. 8.132-133.

[81]   See for examples, AB in *Korea-Beef* and panel in *US-FSC Implementation*.

[82]   *Italy-Agricultural Machinery*, paras. 11-13.

legal provisions to imported products to ensure that the treatment accorded them is *in fact* no less favourable.'[83] However, these two panel reports themselves addressed *de jure* differential treatment. In *Canada-Alcohol*, a *de jure* neutral minimum price for beer was found to be inconsistent with Article III:4 to the extent that it was fixed in relation to the domestic price.[84] In *US-Beer*, a *de jure* neutral beer alcohol content requirement was found not to infringe Article III:4, since high and low alcohol beer were not considered "like products".[85] In *US-Auto Taxes*, two aspects of fuel economy requirements were found to be inconsistent with Article III:4. One because it really was not *de jure* neutral, and the other because it was not based on factors relating to the product as such.[86]

Under GATT 1994, the panel in *US-Gasoline* found that the measures infringed Article III:4 because they prevented imported gasoline from benefiting from individual baselines tied to the producer.[87] Arguably, by allowing domestic producers certain advantages not granted to importers, this measure was not *de jure* neutral. The panel in *EC-Bananas III* found aspects of the EC's banana regime to be inconsistent with Article III:4 that were, on analysis, also not *de jure* neutral.[88] The one aspect of the banana regime undisputedly *de jure* neutral was found not to infringe Article III:4.[89] The Canadian postal rates that were found to accord less favourable treatment in *Canada-Periodicals* were clearly not *de jure* neutral.[90] Finally, in *Japan-Film*, Japanese measures on the distribution and sale of photographic film that were *de jure* neutral were not found to be inconsistent with Article III:4.[91] *Japan-Film* concerned a violation claim under Article III and a non-violation claim under Article XXIII:1(b) GATT. For a non-violation claim, the application of a measure has to result in the nullification or impairment of benefits reasonably expected. As regards the causality between the measure and the nullification or impairment of benefits, the panel observed that the complainant had to show a clear causal relation between the measures and the adverse effect on the relevant competitive relationships.[92] The panel discussed the relevance of the origin-neutral nature of a measure as one aspect of this causality requirement:

---

[83] *US-Section 337*, para. 5.11.

[84] *Canada-Beer II*, para. 5.29, referring to *US-Section 337*, para. 5.11.

[85] *US-Beer*, para. 5.73.

[86] *US-Auto Taxes*, unadopted, paras. 5.47-49 and 5.50-55, respectively. See also Section 4.2.4.

[87] Panel in *US-Gasoline*, paras. 6.9-12.

[88] Panel in *EC-Bananas III*, paras. 7.180-181 on "operator categories" and paras. 7.243-250 on "hurricane licenses".

[89] Ibid., paras. 7.218-219 on "activity functions".

[90] Panel in *Canada-Periodicals*, paras. 5.32-39.

[91] Panel in *Japan-Film*, paras. 10.22-24, and 10.379-380.

[92] Ibid., para. 10.82.

[E]ven in the absence of de jure *discrimination (measures which on their face discriminate as to origin), it may be possible for the [complainant] to show* de facto *discrimination (measures which have a disparate impact on imports). However, in such circumstances, the complaining party is called upon to make a detailed showing of any claimed disproportionate impact on imports resulting from the origin-neutral measure.*[93]

The panel observed that 'WTO/GATT case law on the issue of *de facto* discrimination is reasonably well-developed [...] in regard to [...] national treatment under GATT Article III', and noted that the reasoning in that case law was equally applicable in addressing the question of *de facto* discrimination with respect to non-violation claims.[94] The panel subsequently transposed much of its reasoning to the violation claims under Article III:4. It saw no significant distinction between the standard of 'upsetting the competitive relationship' under Article XXIII:1(b), and the standard of 'upsetting the effective equality of competitive opportunities' applicable under Article III:4.[95] Referring to its findings in the non-violation context, the panel found that the measures at issue 'neither (i) discriminate on their face against imported film or paper (they are formally neutral as to the origin of products), nor (ii) in their application have a *disparate impact* on imported film or paper'. The panel's jumping from violation to non-violation and back is striking, especially considering the differences between these types of claims and the remedies which may result.[96] This was the first WTO panel report that was not appealed against, and it is not often referred to in other dispute settlement reports. Nonetheless, the report is interesting for the panel's willingness to consider *de jure* neutral measures under Article III:4 by looking at a "disparate" or "disproportionate" impact on imports. However, as said, there really are few examples in GATT/WTO case-law of *de jure* neutral measures having been assessed under Article III:4 GATT, so the panel's contention in *Japan-Film* that WTO/GATT case-law on *de facto* discrimination

---

[93] Ibid., para. 10.85.

[94] Ibid., paras. 10.85-86. The panel based its contention on one *obiter dictum* in a case involving *de jure* differentiation (*US-Section 337*), one finding on a minimum price measure to the extent that it was linked to domestic prices (*Canada-Alcohol*), one finding on a tax measure (*Japan-Alcohol*), and three findings on measures whose *de jure* neutrality is at least disputable (a requirement for imported beer and wine to use a wholesaler in *US-Beer*, differential baseline establishment rules in *US-Gasoline*, and operator categories in import licensing rules in *EC-Bananas III*).

[95] Ibid., para. 10.380.

[96] In case of non-violation complaints, there is no obligation for the WTO Member to withdraw the measure which has been found to nullify or impair benefits of another Member. See Article 26.1(b) DSU. On non-violation proceedings generally, see e.g. Petersmann (1997a) Ch. 4; Petersmann (1997) (ed.), Chapters 2 and 3; and Cho (1998).

is reasonably well-developed appears to be ill-founded. Nevertheless, as more "traditional" trade barriers are removed, regulatory differences between WTO members will come increasingly to the forefront, and *de jure* neutral measures may increasingly be challenged in trade disputes. Even if the SPS and TBT Agreements appear to be the most appropriate instruments to do so, challenges of *de jure* neutral measures under Article III:4 GATT, as in *EC-Asbestos*, will quite probably also increase.

(b) *De Jure* Neutral Measures and "Likeness"; Regulatory Distinctions, "Aim and Effect"

GATT and WTO panels have on several occasions rejected the notion of balancing less with more favourable treatment when applying Article III:4 and the first sentence of Article III:2:

> *The panel further found that the "no less favourable" treatment requirement of Article III:4 has to be understood as applicable to each individual case of imported products. The panel rejected any notion of balancing more favourable treatment of some imported products against less favourable treatment of other imported products.*[97]

It is recalled that these panel reports both concerned *de jure* differentiating measures. Yet they did not explicitly limit their refusal to balance less with more favourable treatment to such measures. However, when assessing *de jure* neutral measures, if "balancing" is not allowed, once products from different categories created by the national measure are found to be "like" in the sense of Article III:2 or III:4, it takes only one imported product from the category disadvantaged under the national rule and one "like" domestic product from the category advantaged under that national rule in order to conclude that imports are taxed in excess of (Article III:2), or treated less favourably (Article III:4) than like domestic products. This is even so when the regulatory or fiscal distinctions are made for perfectly acceptable policy reasons. Thus, a test in Article III that merely asks whether *any* imported product is treated less favourably than *any* like domestic product may lead to undesirable results in the case of *de jure* neutral measures pursuing legitimate objectives, some of which may not be covered by Article XX.[98]

---

[97] *US-Section 337*, para. 5.14, as repeated and supported by the panel in *US-Gasoline*, para. 6.14. The "balancing" of higher and lower taxation was explicitly rejected by the panel in *US-Tobacco*, para. 98, referring to *US-Section 337* as 'another Article III panel' that had ruled against balancing.

[98] Ehring (2001) at 3 (manuscript) calls this a "diagonal test".

Since the early 1990s, attempts have been made to address this problem. Initially, the focus was largely on the interpretation of "likeness". If "likeness" is interpreted strictly, Article III:4 will not easily be infringed and national regulatory autonomy will be preserved.[99] A "market-based" view of the "likeness" of products assesses "likeness" essentially from the consumer perspective.[100] If, on the other hand, the perspective of the regulating government is taken, the objectives for which regulatory distinctions between products are made may be taken into account when determining "likeness". As one author put it:

[T]he starting point of the analysis cannot be the concrete objects to which an internal tax or regulation is applied but only the abstract categories of products distinguished by the contracting party. [...] Article III:1 prescribes the perspective from which products are to be compared. [...] In determining whether two products are alike, the central issue thus is whether the product categories under which they fall have been distinguished with the intent and effect of affording protection.[101]

Taking this perspective to its extreme, "like" means 'not differing in any respect relevant to an actual non-protectionist policy'.[102] However, if "likeness" follows national regulatory distinctions, Article III:4 would in effect not discipline any de jure neutral measures. A milder version of this perspective influenced the interpretation of the two GATT panel reports in US-Beer and US-Auto Taxes, that became known for their "aims and effects" test.[103] In US-Beer, the panel considered, among other things, de jure neutral sales restrictions of beer according to its alcohol content. In the view of the panel, it was imperative that the like product determination in the context of Article III be made 'in such a way that it not unnecessarily infringe upon the regulatory authority and domestic policy options of contracting parties.'[104] In applying this approach, the panel examined whether the differentiation in the treatment of low-alcohol beer and high-alcohol beer -which were physically similar- was such as to afford protection to domestic production. The panel noted that both Canadian and US beer manufacturers produced both low and high alcohol beer and that the US laws did not differentiate between imported and domestic beer as such. The panel observed that '[t]he burdens resulting from these regulations thus do not fall more heavily

---

[99] Cf. Mattoo and Subramanian (1998) at 304.

[100] See e.g. Bronckers and McNelis (2000).

[101] Roessler (1996) at 29.

[102] See the 'aim and effect test' discussed in Section 5.3.3, and Howse and Regan (2000) at 260.

[103] While US-Beer was adopted and dealt with Article III:4 as well as Article III:2, the relevant part on 'aim and effect' of US-Auto Taxes concerned only Article III:2, first sentence, and the report remained unadopted.

[104] US-Beer, para. 5.72.

on Canadian than on United States producers'.[105] Next, the panel noted that 'the alcohol content of beer has not been singled out as a means of favouring domestic producers over foreign producers.' It concluded that high alcohol and low alcohol beer were not "like" products in terms of Article III:4. Finally, the panel added that no evidence had been submitted to it that the choice of the *particular level* of alcohol at which the measures distinguished between high and low alcohol had the *purpose or effect* of affording protection to domestic production.[106]

The panel in *US-Auto Taxes* noted that the practical interpretative issue under paragraphs 2 and 4 of Article III was:

> *which differences between products may form the basis of regulatory distinctions by governments that accord less favourable treatment to imported products? Or conversely, which similarities between products prevent regulatory distinctions by governments that accord less favourable treatment to imported products?*[107]

The panel noted that "so as to" afford protection suggested *both* aim and effect.[108] A measure had the aim of affording protection if the circumstances in which it was adopted, in particular the instruments available to achieve the declared domestic policy goal, demonstrated that a change in competitive opportunities in favour of domestic products was a *desired outcome and not merely an incidental consequence* of the pursuit of a legitimate policy goal. It had the effect of affording protection if it accorded greater competitive opportunities to domestic than to imported products.[109] After these general remarks, the panel went on to apply its "aim and effect" approach to the tax measures under Article III:2, but not to the regulatory measures under Article III:4.

The WTO panel in *US-Gasoline* did not refer to the "aim and effect" test, probably because it found *de jure* differential treatment. In *Japan-Alcohol*, which dealt with taxes under Article III:2, both the US as the claimant and Japan as the defendant claimed that an "aim and effect" test should be applied, however reaching opposite results in applying the test.[110] The panel explicitly rejected the application of an aim-and-effect test to Article III:2, first sentence. It even rejected the test with respect to the second sentence of Article III:2, which, in contrast with the first sentence (and with Article III:4) explicitly refers to Article III:1. The Appellate Body corrected the panel on this point, stating that

---

[105] Ibid., para. 5.73. Emphasis by the author.

[106] Ibid., para. 5.74. Emphasis by the author.

[107] *US-Auto Taxes*, unadopted, para. 5.6.

[108] The *US-Beer* panel had only referred to 'purpose or effect'.

[109] *US-Auto Taxes*, unadopted, para. 5.10. Emphasis added.

[110] Panel in *Japan-Alcohol*, paras. VI.14-18.

whether the tax measure in question was applied 'so as to afford protection' was a separate issue which had to be addressed individually. However, the Appellate Body made it clear that "aims" are not about subjective intentions. It is irrelevant that protectionism was not an intended objective if the particular tax measure in question is nevertheless, to echo Article III:1, 'applied to imported or domestic products so as to afford protection to domestic production'.[111] The Appellate Body then referred to the design, the architecture, and the revealing structure of a measure from which its protective application can most often be discerned. Protective application in the context of the second sentence of Article III:2 has since been accordingly interpreted in a number of disputes.[112]

In the light of the foregoing, the "aim and effect test" appears to have led a short life, at least to the extent that it was conceived in *US-Beer* and *US Auto Taxes* to inform the "likeness" determination. Nonetheless, both "aims" and "effects" may be expected to resurface in some way when determining which measures should pass the Article III:4 test and which should not. Arguments on the regulatory purpose of measures have been made by the parties in *Canada-Periodicals* and *EC-Bananas III* (in the context of GATS National Treatment).[113] The *problématique* leading to the "aim and effect" test has inspired various authors in proposing alternative tests for Article III GATT.[114]

(c)   *De Jure* Neutral Measures and "Less Favourable Treatment"

The Appellate Body in *EC-Asbestos* said that the principle of avoiding "protective application" in Article III:1 informs both "likeness" and "less favourable treatment" in Article III:4. It is recalled that the Appellate Body deduced from the principle in Article III:1 that "like" in Article III:4 is to be

---

[111] AB in *Japan-Alcohol*, at p. 28-29.

[112] See AB in *Canada-Periodicals*, *Korea-Alcohol*, and *Chile-Alcohol*, discussed in Section 4.2.3.

[113] As noted by Hudec (1998) at 636.

[114] See, in addition to those mentioned in footnotes 77 and 100-102, e.g. Cheyne (1995) at 444, arguing that national measures must employ an objective test for differentiation, and must have neither a protective intention nor a protective effect; Zedalis (1997b) at 112, arguing that the first sentence of Article III does not affect Article III:4, and protective application cannot be a criterion for determining "likeness"; Kometani (1996) at 444, proposing to interpret Article III for environmental measures by shifting the burden to the country taking the measure to prove that its measure is not aimed at protection but pursues an objective need for environmental protection. Panels should only reject such arguments in cases of manifest error or inconsistency.

interpreted to apply to products that are in a competitive relationship in the marketplace. The Appellate Body thus appears to have suggested that likeness is determined 'in the market', and thus predominantly from the perspective of the consumer rather than of the regulating government. The Appellate Body then emphasised that there is another element in Article III:4: "less favourable treatment". Thus, perhaps "less favourable treatment" may develop as the main tool by which to introduce into Article III:4 the flexibility desired to allow governments to regulate *de jure* neutrally for legitimate purposes without having to defend their measures under Article XX. However, Article III:4 does not expressly refer to Article III:1, and a *separate* consideration of protective application is not needed in order to find a violation of Article III:4.[115] This leaves open the question of how "less favourable treatment" in Article III:4 is informed by Article III:1.

In its *obiter dictum* in *EC-Asbestos*, the Appellate Body suggested that in order to find "less favourable treatment", more is needed than merely establishing that an imported product falls within the category created by the regulatory distinction that is disadvantaged, while a "like" domestic product falls within the advantaged category.[116] The Appellate Body said that if there is "less favourable treatment" of the group of "like" imported products, there is, conversely, "protection" of the group of "like" domestic products. The Appellate Body might have meant that the distinction drawn by the national measure must have protectionist effects in order to violate Article III:4. Perhaps the Appellate Body's indications as to a measure's protectionist design in *Japan-Alcohol*, as further elaborated in subsequent cases, could be of assistance here. However, it should be recalled that unlike the second sentence of Article III:2, Article III:4 does not explicitly refer to Article III:1. Moreover, the Appellate Body did not say that protection means less favourable treatment, but rather the reverse. The Appellate Body also suggested that it has to be established that a *group* of "like" *imported* products is treated less favourably than a group of "like" *domestic* products. This approach has been referred to as the "asymmetrical impact" test.[117] However, it will often be a difficult exercise to examine alleged disproportionate or asymmetrical effects on imports. For example, if low-alcohol beer and high-alcohol beer are considered to be "like" products, does a national regulation prohibiting the sale of high-alcohol beer in sports canteens afford imported beer less favourable treatment only if *all* imported beer is high-alcohol beer, and *all* domestic beer is low-alcohol beer? What if 80% of imported beer is high-alcohol beer, and 80% of domestic beer is low-alcohol beer?

---

[115] AB in *EC-Bananas III*, para. 216. Emphasis added.

[116] AB in *EC-Asbestos*, para. 100. See Section 4.2.4.

[117] Ehring (2001) at 4 (manuscript).

Another problem is that the Appellate Body's reference to "groups" of products at first sight appears to be difficult to reconcile with a consistent line of GATT and WTO dispute settlement reports in which the "balancing" of more favourable with less favourable treatment was not accepted under Article III.[118] It has been suggested that the 'no balancing' requirement should be seen in its proper context, which was a *de jure* differentiating measure, and does not necessarily apply to *de jure* neutral measures.[119] However, it should be recalled that there is no textual basis in Article III to distinguish between origin-neutral and non-origin-neutral measures. Apart from -perhaps- the *obiter dictum* in *EC-Asbestos*, there are no further panel or Appellate Body reports to support such a distinction. In *EC-Hormones*, the EC argued that there should be a comparison of the whole group of imported products with the whole group of like domestic products when assessing *de jure* neutral measures under Article III:4. According to the EC, only when assessing *de jure* differentiating measures could it be assumed that domestic production was "protected" if *any* imported product received less favourable treatment.[120] This argument was not addressed by the panel or the Appellate Body, however. In *US-FSC*, the implementation panel rejected a US argument that the treatment of classes of products had to be compared under Article III:4.[121]

(d)   *De Jure* Neutral Measures and "Inherent Competitive Disadvantages"

The suggestion to focus on "less favourable treatment" rather than "likeness" in solving the problems of assessing *de jure* neutral measures under Article III:4 was made as early as 1994.[122] Inspiration was sought in the National Treatment provision of the General Agreement on Trade in Services (GATS). Article XVII:1 GATS provides that in the sectors inscribed in the schedule to GATS, and subject to conditions and qualifications set out therein, each Member shall accord to foreign services and suppliers treatment which is no less favourable than that accorded to like domestic services and suppliers. According to Article XVII:2, Members may meet this requirement by according formally identical or formally different treatment. Article XVII:3 provides that formally identical treatment shall be considered to be less favourable if it 'modifies conditions of competition' in favour of domestic suppliers. However, the note to Article XVII:1 GATS provides that specific service commitments do not

---

[118] See e.g. *US-Section 337*, para. 5.14; panel in *US-Gasoline*, para. 6.14.

[119] Howse and Tuerk (2001); Ehring (2001) at 25 (manuscript).

[120] Panel in *EC-Hormones*, paras. 4.255-256.

[121] Panel in *US-FSC Implementation*, paras. 8.130-34.

[122] Farber and Hudec (1994) at 1427. Cf. Farber and Hudec (1996) at 72.

require any Member to compensate for any *inherent competitive disadvantages* which *result from the foreign character* of the relevant services or service suppliers.[123] The GATS National Treatment provision is not one which applies across the board like the one in the GATT, as it only applies to specific commitments made by WTO members. Moreover, the differences between services and goods should not be overlooked.[124] Nonetheless, Article XVII GATS may be useful in interpreting Article III:4 GATT. It has been suggested that the exclusion of 'inherent competitive advantages' from the category of actionable violations could be incorporated into Article III:4 GATT through the necessary interpretation of the term "less favourable treatment". However, it has not become clear what "inherent competitive disadvantages" actually are.[125]

A different kind of "inherence" criterion, this time with regard to Article III:2 GATT, can be found in the two "aim and effect" panel reports, *US-Beer* and *US-Auto Taxes*. In *US-Beer*, the claim under Article III:2 involved beneficial tax treatment for wine produced from a particular type of grape growing mostly in the south-eastern US and the Mediterranean. Although not specifically using the term "inherent", the panel did suggest that a tax categorisation based on grape varieties that could not be grown in some other countries was protectionist, in the absence of professed policy objectives other than protection. The panel found that the tax treatment *implied a geographical distinction affording protection* to local wine to the detriment of wine produced *where this particular grape could not be grown*.[126] In *US-Auto Taxes*, when the panel analysed the protective effect of the Luxury Tax, it noted that the 'regulatory distinction of $30,000 [above which the luxury tax was paid] did not create conditions of competition that divided the products *inherently* into two classes, one of [...] foreign origin and the other of domestic origin'. The panel's view of "inherence" is illustrated by its observation that there was no evidence that foreign producers did not have the 'design, production, and marketing capabilities' to sell cars below the regulatory

---

[123] An example of such an inherent competitive disadvantage is a language requirement to provide a service, which will be more difficult to meet for service providers from other countries with a different mother tongue.

[124] See Mattoo (1997).

[125] Farber and Hudec (1994) contend that a competitive disadvantage is "inherent" when the regulation producing the disadvantage is not assigned any "causal" weight in the outcome. That seems a contradiction in terms in that the word "producing" assumes a causal relationship. Moreover, the authors appear to equate the absence of causal weight with the existence of a valid regulatory purpose, which appears to the current author to be a different issue altogether.

[126] *US-Beer*, para. 5.26. The panel concluded that the distinction in favour of local wine must, on the evidence placed before it, be presumed to afford protection to local vintners and was inconsistent with Article III:2, first sentence. Even if wine produced from the special grape variety were considered "unlike" other wine, this would be inconsistent with the second sentence of Article III:2.

threshold, or that they did not produce such cars.[127] Likewise, the panel found that the distinctions drawn by the so-called Gas Guzzler Tax did not create 'inherently foreign or domestic categories', referring to technology as a pointer to such inherence.[128] It has been observed that such a view of "inherent" categorisations makes it very difficult for a complainant to find a violation of Article III:4.[129]

Thus, whereas GATS refers to inherent competitive disadvantages resulting from the foreign character of the service or its supplier, which do not have to be compensated under the national treatment requirement, the references in *US-Auto Taxes* to "inherence" in the interpretation of Article III:2 GATT suggest that any differentiation is acceptable as long as it does not create categories that are inherently domestic or foreign. In this view, only those differentiations creating favoured categories in which the foreign product *cannot possibly be placed*, for geographical, climatological, design, production, marketing or technological reasons, will be deemed to accord less favourable treatment to imports. All in all, the "inherence" criterion is fraught with a lack of clarity and consistency which means that it is unlikely to provide any decisive guidance in interpreting Article III:4.

(e)   Concluding Remarks on *De Jure* Neutral Measures

Challenging *de jure* neutral measures under Article III:4 is possible, and may be increasingly expected to occur. This is not in itself surprising, considering the potentially broad scope of Article III:4 in covering national measures 'affecting the sale, offering for sale', etc. of products. However, there is still a great deal of uncertainty as to how such measures are to be assessed. A criterion of "inherent" disadvantages for imports does not seem very helpful, as "inherence" may be interpreted in very different ways. It seems clear that to assess origin-neutral measures, panels will need information on market conditions in order to discover whether imports are being disfavoured. This raises the question whether a panel's assessment of market conditions can be appealed, in view of the limitation of appeals to issues of law and legal interpretations.[130] It appears that the Appellate Body will be able to take such assessments into account, as they are made within the framework of "less favourable treatment", which is an issue of law.

After *EC-Asbestos*, it seems that when a broad range of products are found to be in a competitive relationship and therefore "like", the analysis will concentrate

---

[127] *US-Auto Taxes*, unadopted, para. 5.14.

[128] Ibid., paras. 5.25, 5.30-31 and 5.34.

[129] Mattoo and Subrimanian (1998) at 6-7.

[130] Article 17.6 DSU.

on "less favourable treatment". The Appellate Body has suggested that the treatment of the group of imported products and of the group of domestic "like" products must be compared. This would imply that the complainant will have to adduce a *prima facie* case of "disparate" or "disproportionately unfavourable" treatment of the group of imported products as a result of the measure. The burden of proof upon the complainant may thus be significantly higher than when challenging a *de jure* differentiating measure. When assessing how products are divided into regulatory categories by the measure, it is not inconceivable that panels and the Appellate Body will take the policy objectives of the regulatory categorisations into account. In that way, "aim and effect" may still play a role in the assessment of *de jure* neutral measures, albeit in the determination of less favourable treatment rather than of likeness. "Aims" should be understood as objectives that may be ascertained from a measure's design, structure and application, rather than as subjective goals.

5.3.4 Protection and Discrimination in Justifications and Conditions

Protection and discrimination do not only play a role in the basic National Treatment obligations in Article III:4 GATT and Article 2.1 of the TBT Agreement. They also figure prominently in the chapeau to Article XX, and in several provisions of the SPS Agreement. As discussed *supra*, the panels and the Appellate Body have started to differentiate between the different elements in the chapeau. It seems that the element of "disguised restriction" is being interpreted as an anti-protectionism test, reference being made to the same yardstick of a measure's 'design, structure and architecture' which is used to assess protectionist application in Article III:2, second sentence, and possibly in Article III:4. The elements of 'arbitrary or unjustifiable discrimination between countries where the same conditions prevail' leave no doubt that there is a discrimination test in the chapeau to Article XX. Considering the interpretation of these terms in *US-Gasoline*, *US-Shrimp-Turtle*, and *EC-Asbestos* (including the implementation panel and Appellate Body report), the "unjustifiability" of the discrimination will depend on the factual background of the case. An important question in this respect is whether the nature of the violation (Article III, Article XI, Article I, etc.) sought to be justified under Article XX affects the determination of whether a discrimination is "unjustifiable".[131]

Article 2.3 of the SPS Agreement essentially repeats the elements of the chapeau to Article XX GATT.[132] As is apparent from the Section on the SPS Agreement above, that Agreement goes beyond the GATT in disciplining non-

---

[131] See Section 5.1.1.

[132] Note, however, the small difference discussed in Section 4.5.2.

discriminatory measures. A measure could be challenged under the SPS Agreement although it does not violate Article III:4 GATT, even if the latter provision disciplines *de facto* discrimination. However, SPS measures may certainly also be discriminatory; of that, there is no doubt. Often, the only way of stopping a disease or pest that has broken out in a neighbouring country from spreading into one's territory is through import-specific or discriminatory measures. Accordingly, the reference in Article 2.3 SPS to the elements of the chapeau to Article XX makes it clear that discrimination as such is not prohibited, as long as it meets the conditions in Article 2.3 and the remainder of the SPS Agreement. The other reference to discrimination in the SPS Agreement, found in Article 5.5, aims at consistency in the application of the concept of the appropriate level of sanitary or phytosanitary protection. As discussed in Section 4.5.2, Article 5.5 must be read closely together with Article 2.3. Article 5.5 applies across the board, even with regard to protection levels which are deemed to be appropriate between products that do not have a competitive relationship. However, distinctions in appropriate protection levels only violate Article 5.5 if they are arbitrary or unjustifiable, and if they result in 'discrimination or a disguised restriction on international trade'. The Appellate Body in *EC-Hormones* referred to the 'architecture and structure' of the measures as providing no indication that the distinctions at issue resulted in discrimination or a disguised restriction on international trade.

5.4   Extraterritoriality, Production Methods and Unilateral Action

5.4.1   Introduction

Trade-restrictive measures can be aimed at protecting *resources* located anywhere; partially or wholly in the importing country, partially or wholly in the country of production, partially or wholly outside any jurisdiction (e.g. the atmosphere or the high seas). A WTO Member can for instance prohibit the export of chemical waste so as to protect the populations of other Members, or the high seas. Trade-restrictive measures that try to protect environmental resources by influencing the *behaviour* of producers or governments in other countries have raised major controversies, however. Such measures are usually based on the production or processing methods (PPMs) of the products whose trade is restricted. Such measures are perceived by exporting countries to be a major threat to the trading rights they enjoy under the WTO Agreements. Illustrative of the anxiety caused by PPM-based measures is the reaction of some of the complainants to the Appellate Body report in *US-Shrimp-Turtle*. At the meeting of the Dispute Settlement Body where the Appellate Body report was discussed, Thailand pointed out that this decision permitted Members to discriminate against products based on non-product related processes and production methods (PPMs). In Thailand's view, this was a fundamental and impermissible alteration of the present balance of the rights and obligations of Members under the WTO Agreement. Thailand considered that this would result in an 'explosive growth in the number of environmental, and perhaps labour measures applied to PPMs' and justified under Article XX. The Appellate Body, of its own volition, had 'altered the balance of rights and obligations under the WTO Agreement'. Pakistan and India commented to the same effect.[133]

The relationship between the WTO rules and trade restrictive measures based on production and processing methods (PPMs) has led to a great deal of debate in academic and policy circles. Often, the discussion on PPMs is linked to the issues of "extraterritorial" or "extrajurisdictional" environmental protection, and of unilateral v. multilateral approaches to trade-related environmental problems. Even though the issues of PPMs, unilateralism and extraterritoriality are often interrelated, in this Section they are initially addressed separately, in order to avoid a confusion of arguments that may easily blur the discussion on these important issues. The OECD stipulated in 1997 that 'present trading rules do not allow one country to use trade measures for the purpose of unilaterally enforcing its own environmental preferences or requirements on other countries'.[134] This presumption of the WTO-incompatibility of unilaterally taken PPM-based measures has not remained unchallenged.[135] It will be argued in this Section that a blanket presumption of the WTO-incompatility of such measures is indeed untenable, even if they are not easily accommodated under WTO rules. Nevertheless, many officials, policy makers, non-governmental organisations and academics still assume that the WTO simply prohibits unilateral PPM-based measures.[136] At the time of writing, three years after the Appellate Body report in US-Shrimp-Turtle, the WTO website contains a similar statement.[137]

---

[133] Document WT/DSB/M/50.

[134] OECD (1997) at 6.

[135] See Howse and Regan (2000); Charnovitz (2001).

[136] Charnovitz (2001) at 25-27 provides an overview of citations from various sources to this effect.

[137] See the WTO website in its introduction 'Trading into the Future', under the heading 'The Environment-A New High Profile': 'The WTO agreements are interpreted to say two important things. First, trade restrictions cannot be imposed on a product purely because of the way it has been produced. Second, one country cannot reach out beyond its own territory to impose its standards on another country.'

5.4.2   Processes and Production Methods

The term PPMs refers to *processes and production methods*. The precise meaning of these terms is not generally agreed, and this is a point that is often overlooked in discussions of trade restrictions based on PPMs. One of the few attempts to define PPMs which may claim at least some amount of international acceptance is an OECD paper from 1997. This paper describes PPMs as 'the way in which products are manufactured or processed and natural resources extracted or harvested'.[138] The OECD paper makes the following distinction:

A process or production method can affect the characteristics of a product so that the product itself may pollute or degrade the environment when it is consumed or used (product-related PPMs). Alternatively, a process or method itself can have a negative impact on the environment through, for example, the release of pollutants into the air or water during the production stage (non-product-related PPMs).[139]

Thus, the distinction focuses on whether the environmental damage takes place during the production or during the consumption stage. However, a "product-related PPM" in OECD terminology may have negative health or environmental impacts not only during the consumption stage, but also during the production stage. Therefore, the distinction between "product-related" and "non-product-related" PPMs is not always easy to draw. An example of a measure that would seem to fall within the OECD definition of a "product-related PPM" is the treatment of cattle with growth hormones, which was at issue in *EC-Hormones*.[140] There was disagreement in that dispute as to whether the PPM actually affected the characteristics of the product. It was clear, however, that the EC's concern related to the potential effects of the PPM at the consumption stage. Arguments as to whether measures assessed under WTO rules were based on production methods were also made by the parties in the *Canada-Periodicals* dispute.[141] The main disputes involving PPM-based measures in GATT/WTO law, however, involved the incidental killing of dolphins during tuna fishing and of turtles during shrimp fishing, i.e. environmental damage during the production stage.

According to the same OECD paper, the aim of non-product-related PPM requirements is to reduce or control negative, or promote positive, environmental effects during the production stage, i.e. before a product is placed on the market

---

[138] OECD (1997) at 1.

[139] Ibid.

[140] Panel in *EC-Hormones*, (US) para. 4.252; (CND), para. 4.336.

[141] Panel in *Canada-Periodicals*, paras. 3.74, 3.80 and 3.87, on whether the Canadian difference between original-content and split-run magazines was a PPM-based measure.

for sale. PPM requirements can be designed in different ways, e.g. prescribing a PPM, prohibiting one or several PPMs, or prescribing emission or performance effects rather than the methods themselves. Moreover, there are different instru ments for implementing PPM requirements, such as regulations, labels and environmental taxes. The emphasis in this study is on regulations.[142] Countries may, for instance, apply regulatory restrictions on imported products that do not conform to specified PPM requirements in order to influence the adoption of a PPM by producers in another country. In such cases, the PPM requirements are applied to imported *products*. The OECD paper rightly noted that applying non-product-related PPM requirements to imported products is in itself not a simple exercise: 'Simple inspection of a product will not show whether a specific PPM has been used in its manufacturing. [...] The product would in most cases need to be accompanied by a certificate indicating what process was used.'[143] Applying product-related PPM requiremens to imported products will not always be a straightforward exercise either, as the manner in which a PPM affects a product's characteristics may be very difficult or costly to trace. An example of this problem is provided by genetically modified organisms (GMOs).

Subject to its obligations under international law, a country may in principle apply any production or processing requirements it wishes upon the producers under its jurisdiction. However, a country cannot regulate foreign producers. Therefore, if it wishes to extend its production requirements to foreign producers, a country may be tempted to resort to applying PPM requirements to imported products. Foreign producers must meet these requirements in order for their products to be marketed in the country applying the measure. That, however, is not a feature which is exclusive to measures based on PPMs; the same is true for regulations which determine product characteristics. PPM requirements applied to imported products in order to induce foreign producers to meet certain production standards are here referred to as 'PPM-based measures targeting producers'. Such measures define how products should be produced, or what environmental damage is acceptable in their production process. They may also be designed in terms of producer characteristics.[144] While measures defining how products should be produced have not so far been the subject of GATT and WTO disputes[145], measures involving producer characteristics have. There are also PPM-based measures restricting imports from *countries* whose authorities do not impose upon their producers PPM requirements which are equivalent to those in the importing country. Such measures are referred to here as 'PPM-based measures targeting governments'.

---

[142] On WTO rules and environmental labelling, see Appleton (1997a); on WTO rules and environmental taxes, see Fauchald (1998).

[143] OECD (1997) at 6.

[144] Charnovitz (2001) at 22.

[145] The measures at issue in *US-Shrimp-Turtle* also included certain aspects targeting producers. See *infra*.

They are applied to imports according to government policies in their country of origin. Such measures were the subject of the two *US-Tuna-Dolphin* disputes and also formed a considerable part of the measure at issue in *US-Shrimp-Turtle*.

5.4.3   Unilateral and Multilateral Approaches

Considering the cross-border and sometimes global nature of many environmental problems, multilateral action to tackle such problems is generally to be preferred over unilateral measures. A preference for multilateral solutions has been laid down in Principle 12 of the 1992 Rio Declaration on Environment and Development:

[...] Trade policy measures for environmental purposes should not constitute a means of arbitrary or unjustifiable discrimination or a disguised restriction on inter-national trade. Unilateral actions to deal with environmental challenges outside the jurisdiction of the importing country should be avoided. Environmental measures addressing transboundary or global environmental problems should, as far as possible, be based on an international consensus.[146]

Article 2.22 of Agenda 21 asks governments to encourage 'GATT, UNCTAD and other relevant international and regional economic institutions' to examine, in accordance with their respective mandates and competencies, a number of 'propositions and principles', among which is to:

(i) Avoid unilateral actions to deal with environmental challenges outside the jurisdiction of the importing country. Environmental measures addressing transborder or global environmental problems should, as far as possible, be based on an interna-tional consensus. Domestic measures targeted to achieve certain environmental objec-tives may need trade measures to render them effective. Should trade policy measures be found necessary for the enforcement of environmental policies, certain principles and rules should apply.[...]

---

[146] Principle 12 of the Rio Declaration, available at http://www.unep. org/unep/rio.htm. See also Agenda 21, paras. 39.3(d), with similar language, and paragraph 2.20: 'International cooperation in the envi-ronmental field is growing, and in a number of cases trade provisions in multilateral environment agreements have played a role in tackling global environmental challenges. Trade measures have thus been used in certain specific instances, where considered necessary, to enhance the effectiveness of environmental regulations for the protection of the environment. Such regulations should address the root causes of environmental degradation so as not to result in unjustified restrictions on trade. [...]'

The provision then refers to principles such as non-discrimination, least trade-restrictiveness, transparency and the position of developing countries. Arguably, Agenda 21 thus leaves the position on unilateral action and extrajurisdictional protection goals somewhat unclear. Whereas it states that such action should be avoided, it also appears to recognise that it may sometimes be necessary. The Marrakesh Decision on Trade and Environment refers to the Rio Declaration and Agenda 21, and considers that 'there should not be, nor need be, any policy contradiction between upholding and safeguarding an open, non-discriminatory and equitable multilateral trading system on the one hand, and acting for the protection of the environment, and the promotion of sustainable development on the other'.[147] This Decision thus leaves open the possibility that unilateral action is taken to protect the environment.

There is no agreed definition of "unilateral measure" in the WTO context, or of "unilateralism" in general public international law.[148] In public international law, the term "unilateral" is neutral. Any measure applied by a state and not mandatorily prescribed by international agreement may be dubbed "unilateral". Whether a "unilateral" measure is consistent or inconsistent with public international law will obviously depend on the type of measure and the type of international rules that apply to it. Therefore, general statements to the effect that "unilateral action" is "illegal" are meaningless. In the specific context of PPM-based trade-restrictive measures pursuing extraterritorial protection goals and/or attempting to influence behaviour abroad, "unilateral" is usually attributed a negative connotation, or even the suggestion of illegality under international law. Unilateral action having trade implications is perceived as threatening, especially by developing countries. As India put it in a communication: 'Unilateral trade measures are normally measures taken by stronger trading nations against weaker ones with a view to influencing the latter. [...] Unilateral trade measure do not find any sanction or justification either in international law or indeed in GATT/WTO law.'[149] However, also in the specific context of trade-restrictive measures, general statements to the effect that unilateral measures are illegal appear devoid of meaning. Although there is a growing body of public international law stipulating that multilateral approaches to environmental problems are to be preferred to unilateral approaches, this does not mean that unilateral measures are illegal *per se*. Thus, it has rightly been

---

[147] Marrakesh Decision on Trade and Environment, available at http://www.wto.org/english/tratop_e/envir_e.

[148] On the concept of "unilateralism" in public international law, with particular reference to trade and environment issues, see the special issue of EJIL (2000), no.2, with contributions by inter alia Sands (2000), Boisson de Chazournes (2000) and Bodansky (2000).

[149] Document WT/GC/W/123.

argued that '[e]xamining a given trade measure's legality pursuant to applicable international trade agreements, or in the absence thereof pursuant to public international law, as opposed to focusing on unilateralism *per se*, could provide greater insight into its legal implications.'[150]

How should "unilateral" be defined in the context of trade-restrictive environmental measures in the first place? The implementation panel in *US-Shrimp-Turtle* described a "unilateral measure" as a measure 'which has been designed and is applied without being expressly mandated or permitted by a multilateral agreement', without prejudice to its justification under Article XX GATT or any other provision of the WTO Agreement.[151] It should be emphasised, however, that a WTO Member that is not a member of the relevant multilateral agreement will still consider a trade-restrictive measure unilateral, even if expressly mandated or permitted by the multilateral agreement of which it is not a member.[152] Another aspect of the above desciption that needs clarification are the terms "expressly mandated or permitted" by a MEA. Does that include trade-restrictive measures taken in order to meet an objective laid down in a MEA, without the measures to be taken to achieve the objective being specified in the MEA? There seems to be a considerable grey area between measures explicitly prescribed by a MEA (such as a ban on trade in certain endangered species) and measures taken in order to pursue a goal of a MEA.[153]

The Appellate Body and the implementation panel in *US-Shrimp-Turtle* suggested that in order to address certain environmental problems, unilateral trade-restrictive measures may only be taken pending negotiations on a multilateral approach to address the environmental problem:

[I]n a context such as this one where a multilateral agreement is clearly to be preferred and where measures [...] may only be accepted under Article XX if they

---

[150] According to Appleton (1997a) at 82, the fact that both the mandatory embargo and the voluntary labelling scheme analysed in *US-Tuna-Dolphin I* were intended to further unilaterally imposed US environmental policies with extraterritorial implications, and that one scheme was accepted and the other was not, makes the legal utility of Principle 12's reliance on unilateralism as a differentiating factor questionable.

[151] Implementation panel in *US-Shrimp-Turtle*, in footnote 155.

[152] The issue of trade-restrictive measures taken pursuant to an MEA *vis-à-vis* WTO members that are non-parties to MEAs has expressly been excluded from the negotiation mandate on MEAs and WTO rules agreed in Doha in December of 2001.

[153] The EC discussion paper on the relationship between MEAs and WTO rules tabled in March of 2002 takes a broad ambit, so as to encompass all measures taken to achieve an "obligation de résultat" laid down in an MEA. It however does not clearly elaborate what is understood by such an obligation, how specific it should be expressed, and whether measures to be taken to achieve the objective should also be somehow specified in the MEA.

were allowed under an international agreement, or if they were taken further to
the completion of serious good faith efforts to reach a multilateral agreement, the
possibility to impose a unilateral measure [...] is more to be seen, for the purposes of
Article XX, as the possibility to adopt a provisional measure allowed for emergency
reasons than as a definitive "right" to take a permanent measure.[154]

The limitation to the use of unilateral trade-restrictive measures suggested by
the Appellate Body is made in the context of the justification under Article XX
GATT of a measure that would otherwise infringe the GATT rules, in this case
Article XI GATT. That Article prohibits the unilateral imposition of quantitative
restrictions. In other words, neither a general approval nor a general condemna-
tion of unilateral trade-restrictive measures should be read in this panel report.
The panel is not saying that *any* unilateral measure can only be regarded as
provisional in a context where a multilateral agreement is clearly to be preferred.
It is rather saying that in such circumstances, the possibility to justify a certain
type of unilateral measure (an import ban) under the exceptions in the GATT is
limited and needs to meet strict conditions, because such measures should really
only be taken pursuant to an international agreement.

Multilateral action regarding environmental problems may take the shape
of multilateral environmental agreements and/or standards. Some of those
agreements provide for trade-restrictive measures, as discussed in Section 4.6.
Although the relationship between the WTO rules and such agreements is
not the focus of this study, it should be noted that multilateral approaches are
also relevant in determining the WTO compatibility of unilateral measures. For
example, in *US-Tuna-Dolphin II*, the US referred to a number of international
treaties when discussing the location of the "exhaustible natural resources" in
Article XX(g).[155] The panel observed, however, that under the Vienna Convention, these treaties were not relevant as a primary means of interpreting the
text of the GATT, and were of little assistance as supplementary means of
interpretation.[156] The Appellate Body in *US-Shrimp-Turtle* referred to a number
of MEAs when interpreting "exhaustible natural resources" in Article XX(g).[157]
When interpretating in general terms the chapeau to Article XX with reference
to the objective of sustainable development as reflected in the WTO preamble,
it sought inspiration from the Marrakesh Decision on Trade and Environment,

---

[154] Panel in *US-Shrimp-Turtle Implementation*, para. 5.88.

[155] *US-Tuna-Dolphin II*, unadopted, paras. 3.21 and 3.29-31.

[156] Ibid., paras. 5.19-20.

[157] AB in *US-Shrimp-Turtle*, para. 130, referring to UNCLOS, the Biodiversity Convention, and the Resolution on Assistance to Developing Countries adopted in conjunction with the Convention on the Conservation of Migratory Species of Wild Animals, and para. 133, referring to CITES.

which in turn refers to the Rio Declaration on Environment and Development and Agenda 21.[158]

When assessing more specifically whether the US measure met the chapeau requirement of not being applied in a manner constituting "unjustifiable discrimination", the Appellate Body again referred to the Rio Declaration and Agenda 21, as well as the Inter-American Convention for the Protection and Conservation of Sea Turtles.[159] The Appellate Body clarified how a MEA may determine the interpretation of a GATT provision by noting that the parties in the Inter-American Convention had marked out the "line of equilibrium" expressed in the chapeau to Article XX.[160]

5.4.4   Extraterritorial and Extrajurisdictional Environmental Protection

Objections against PPM-based measures are often phrased in terms of their being "extraterritorial" or "extrajurisdictional". The terms "extraterritoriality" or "extraterritorial protection" may refer to measures aimed at influencing *behaviour* outside the territory of the state taking the measures, and/or to measures aimed at protecting environmental *resources* outside the territory of the state taking the measures. In some cases, such objections appear to be based on the assumption that a state taking a trade-restrictive measure based on PPMs is overstepping its jurisdiction and intruding in the jurisdiction of other states. However, it is submitted that this view is erroneous. Trade-restrictive measures may have extraterritorial and extrajurisdictional *effects*. But such measures, it will be argued below, do not amount to the exercise of extraterritorial jurisdiction, even if they are based on PPMs.

In public international law, jurisdiction refers to the regulation of activities. "Extraterritorial" jurisdiction means the assertion of jurisdiction over activities abroad. It may play a role in all three aspects of jurisdiction, i.e. executive or administrative jurisdiction (the power of a state to act in another state), judicial jurisdiction (the power of a state's courts to try cases with a foreign element), and legislative or prescriptive jurisdiction (the power to apply a state's laws to cases with a foreign element).[161] 'Extraterritorial jurisdiction' is most commonly discussed in the context of criminal law and competition law. Criminal jurisdiction is based on a number of principles, i.e. territoriality, nationality, protection, and universality. According to the nationality or personality principle, a state

---

[158] Ibid., para. 154, referring to the Marrakesh Decision on Trade and Environment, available at http://www.wto.org/english/tratop_e/envir_e.htm.

[159] Ibid., paras. 168-169.

[160] Ibid., paras. 159 and 170; see Section 4.6.

[161] See Brownlie (1998) Ch. XV; Shaw (1997) Ch.12; Malanczuk/Akehurst (1997) Ch.7.

may regulate the behaviour of its own citizens outside its territory. Within the territoriality principle, a distinction can be made between subjective and objective territoriality. If a criminal act begins in one state and ends in another (the typical example being a shooting incident across the border), the state where the act begins may assert jurisdiction on the basis of the subjective territorial principle, and the state where the act is completed on the basis of the objective territorial principle. The latter is also sometimes referred to as the "effects doctrine".[162] With regard to competition law, the discussion of "extraterritoriality" in terms of both legislative and judicial jurisdiction has led to a broader meaning of the "effects doctrine", especially in the US and the EC. According to this broader concept, a state may assume jurisdiction on the grounds that behaviour produces effects in its territory, even if that behaviour takes places wholly in another state.[163] Usually, this doctrine is qualified by the requirement that the behaviour has a direct, substantial and reasonably foreseeable effect in the territory of the state assuming jurisdiction.[164]

There is no general principle on "extraterritorial jurisdiction" in public international law. The Permanent Court of International Justice stated the following in the *Lotus* case:

> [...] *Restrictions upon the independence of States cannot [...] be presumed. Now the first and foremost restriction imposed by international law upon a State is that-failing the existence of a permissive rule to the contrary-it may not exercise its power in any form in the territory of another State. [...] It does not, however, follow that international law prohibits a State from exercising jurisdiction in its own territory, in respect of any case which relates to acts which have taken place abroad, and in which it cannot rely on some permissive rule of international law.*[165]

This judgment may be read as saying that no restrictions can be assumed to states' right to assert extraterritorial jurisdiction, as there is no general prohibition to do so and therefore no express permissive rule is needed in order to do so. However, the judgment is from 1927, it came from a deeply divided Permanent Court, and it concerned the specific field of the law of the sea. It is therefore questionable to what extent it yields answers to the issue of extraterritorial jurisdiction in general.

A state may assert personal jurisdiction over its nationals to prevent them from damaging the environment, inside or outside its territory. Thus, a state

---

[162] Malanczuk/Akehurst (1997) at 110.

[163] Shaw (1997) at 484

[164] Van Calster (2000) at 199-212.

[165] Permanent Court of International Justice Series A, No.10, at p. 18-20, available at http://www.gwu.edu/~jaysmith/Lotus.html.

may for example regulate the way its fishermen catch fish, whether they catch them within its territorial waters or on the high seas. Moreover, there is no rule in public international law that prevents states from protecting the environment located outside their territorial jurisdiction. According to Principle 21 of the 1972 Stockholm Declaration, states have the sovereign right to exploit their own resources pursuant to their own environmental policies, but at the same time have the responsibility to ensure that activities within their jurisdiction or control do not cause damage to the environment of other states or of areas beyond the limits of national jurisdiction. This formula was essentially repeated in Principle 2 of the 1992 Rio Declaration.[166] The legal status of both Principle 21 of the Stockholm Declaration as well as of Principle 2 of the Rio Declaration is somewhat problematic.[167] The inherent tension between the right and the responsibility laid down in these principles is clear. Exploiting one's own resources may lead to extraterritorial environmental damage. The pivotal question then becomes what constitutes environmental damage, and what standard of care applies to the state's responsibility to avoid such damage?[168] Importantly for the purpose of this work, these principles address the exploitation of resources, and not trade. They do not lay down a right to trade in the yields of resource exploitation. The 1992 Rio Declaration and Agenda 21 do address the issue of trade measures and environmental protection goals, but without laying down a right to trade.[169]

In view of the above observations about the status of extraterritorial jurisdiction and extraterritorial environmental protection under public international law, the following remarks are made with specific regard to trade-restrictive measures targeting foreign behaviour to protect the environment. First of all, public international law does not prevent states from protecting the environment outside their territorial jurisdiction; quite to the contrary, they have a duty to ensure that the exploitation of resources within their jurisdiction does not lead to environmental damage outside their jurisdiction. Secondly, trade-restrictive measures, even import prohibitions, may be aimed at influencing the conduct of legal subjects abroad, but they do not legally regulate their conduct by enacting legislation pertaining to foreign nationals (prescriptive jurisdiction), or trying foreign nationals (judicial jurisdiction). A trade restriction merely regulates traders, buyers, sellers etc. under the jurisdiction of the state enacting the measure, and therefore by definition does not amount to the assertion of extraterritorial

---

[166] The Rio Declaration reads the same, with two words added: 'pursuant to their own environmental *and developmental* policies' (emphasis added).

[167] See Nollkaemper (1998) at 186; however, Sands (1998) at 194 asserts that Principle 2 of the Rio Declaration reflects a general rule of customary international law.

[168] Sands (1995) at 191.

[169] See Section 5.4.3.

jurisdiction. Thirdly, under public international law, enacting trade measures and internal regulations is a prerogative of a sovereign state, and such measures are in principle lawful. There is no right under customary international law to export products to foreign markets, and no duty to grant market access.[170] If the rights of exporting producers or states are affected by such measures with "extraterritorial" or "extrajurisdictional" effects, these are treaty-based rights. Such rights or duties only exist to the extent they are laid down in treaties, such as the WTO Agreements. Thus, it is the terms of these agreements that must be interpreted when judging measures with extraterritorial effects. In the next Section, the question to what extent PPM-based measures are covered by the basic prohibitions in Articles III and XI GATT is discussed, and thereafter the possible justifications under Article XX GATT. Finally, the SPS and TBT Agreements are addressed. In sum, the use of the terms "extraterritoriality" and "extrajurisdictionality" is confusing in this context. Trade-restrictive measures may have extraterritorial effects, because they target foreign behaviour and/or aim to protect resources outside the jurisdiction of the state enacting them. But they do not amount to the assertion of extraterritorial jurisdiction.

5.4.5   PPM-Based Measures and GATT 1994

(a)   Article III or Article XI?

(i)   The "Product-Process Distinction"

Is a measure restricting imports because of their production process to be covered by Article XI GATT, or should it be considered as the application at the border of an internal regulation on domestic producers? This question remains unanswered. The *US-Tuna-Dolphin* disputes created a great deal of confusion in this respect. Both panels said that Article III does not cover, or does not permit, such measures, as they do not apply to the product as such.[171] However, not covering a measure and not permitting it are not the same things. In *US-Tuna-Dolphin I* the panel concluded on the basis of the text of Article III and the Note Ad Article III:1 that 'Article III covers only measures affecting products as such', and that '[t]he Note ad Article III covers only those measures that are applied to the product as such'.[172] The panel went on to find that the US measures at issue did not constitute internal regulations covered by the Note Ad Article III.[173] It further concluded that, even if the US provisions were

---

[170] Nollkaemper (1998); Appleton (1997a) at 77.

[171] *US-Tuna-Dolphin I*, unadopted, para. 5.14; *US-Tuna-Dolphin II*, unadopted, paras. 5.8-5.9.

[172] *US-Tuna-Dolphin I*, unadopted, paras. 5.11 and 5.13.

[173] Ibid., para. 5.14.

regarded as regulating the sale of tuna as a product, the import prohibition would not meet the requirements of Article III.[174] The panel in *US-Tuna-Dolphin II* noted that 'Article III calls for a comparison between the treatment accorded to domestic and imported like products, not for a comparison of the policies or practices of the country of origin with those of the country of importation.' The panel found that the Note Ad Article III 'could only permit' the enforcement, at the time or point of importation, of those laws, regulations and requirements that affected or were applied to the imported and domestic products considered as products. The Note therefore 'could not apply' to the enforcement, at the time or point of importation, of those laws, regulations and requirements that related to policies or practices that could not affect the product as such, and that accorded less favourable treatment to like products not produced in conformity with the domestic policies of the importing country.[175]

Both panels subsequently assessed the measures under Article XI, and their reports have both remained unadopted. Nevertheless, after these panel reports the idea has taken root that PPM-based measures in general are outside the scope of Article III, that they violate Article XI, and accordingly need justification under Article XX. This idea was articulated most clearly by the panel in *US-Tuna-Dolphin I*, when it addressed the secondary embargo on tuna imports from "intermediary countries": '[s]ince the US domestic regulations on tuna harvesting were not *applied* to tuna *as a product*, the "intermediary nations" embargo did not fall within the scope of the Note Ad Article III, and was *therefore* a quantitative restriction subject to Article XI.'[176] In the WTO *US-Shrimp-Turtles* dispute, the applicability of Article III:4 was not argued by the defendant. A violation of Article XI was found immediately and the dispute further concentrated on Article XX.

The general idea of PPM measures being outside the scope of Article III has been described as the "product-process distinction".[177] It is intimately related to the "focus on products" that some panels have read into Article III.[178] However, to limit the coverage of Article III:4 to measures directly regulating product characteristics appears irreconcilable with the very text of this provision. The yardstick for the coverage of Article III:4 is whether the 'sale, offering for sale', etc. of products is "affected" by a law, regulation or requirement. It is eminently

---

[174] Ibid, para. 5.15. 'Regulations governing the taking of dolphins incidental to the taking of tuna could not possibly *affect* tuna as a product. Article III:4 *therefore obliges* the United States *to accord* treatment to Mexican tuna no less favourable than that accorded to United States tuna, whether or not the incidental taking of dolphins by Mexican vessels corresponds to that of United States vessels.' Emphasis added.

[175] *US-Tuna-Dolphin II*, unadopted, para. 5.8.

[176] Ibid., para. 5.35. Emphasis added.

[177] Hudec (2000); Howse and Regan (2000).

[178] See Section 4.2.4.

clear from these words and from numerous GATT and WTO panel reports that the scope of Article III:4 is not limited to measures 'applied to products as such'[179] Thus, measures applied to producers, wholesalers, distributors and importers can also 'affect the sale, offering for sale' etc. of products.[180] Moreover, the sale, offering for sale, etc. of a product can be affected by a measure distinguishing (or even prohibiting) products on the basis of their PPM. For instance, with regard to intellectual property rights, a right holder in the importing country can challenge any infringements of his right that have occurred in the exporting country, including by a production process.[181] The parallel between intellectual property rights protection and environmental protection may be problematic, as the rights and interests involved are very different in nature. Arguably, in many cases of environmental protection, no individual rights are at issue. However, that does not invalidate the point that a measure based on a PPM can affect the sale, offering for sale, etc. of a product within the meaning of Article III GATT, and can therefore be covered by that provision.

Thus, a restrictive view is not warranted by the text of Article III and the Note to Article III.[182] The measures that were found to contravene Article XI in *US-Tuna-Dolphin*, and to a large extent those in *US-Shrimp-Turtle*, were designed as across the board and country-based import prohibitions targeting PPMs. They prohibited the importation of *all tuna* and *all shrimp* from *particular countries* not deemed by the US to enforce PPM requirements equivalent to those enforced upon US fishermen. It is submitted that these cases should not be taken to exclude altogether the possibility of assessing a PPM-based measure under Article III, such as a prohibition or restriction on the marketing or sale of products on the basis of PPMs. An example is a measure prohibiting the marketing or sale of tuna (or shrimp) caught in a way that leads to the death of more than x dolphins (turtles) per tonne.

(ii) The Parallel with Border Tax Adjustments

In order to substantiate its observation that 'Article III covers only measures affecting products as such', the panel in *US-Tuna-Dolphin I*

---

[179] See *Italian Agricultural Machines, Canada-FIRA, US-Section 337, US-Auto Taxes*, as well as the WTO panels in *US-Gasoline, Canada-Auto*, and *US-FSC Implementation*.

[180] See Section 4.2.4 on 'focus on products', and Howse and Regan (2000) at 255.

[181] Cf. Article 27 of the TRIPS Agreement: [...] patents shall be available for any inventions, *whether products or processes*, [...] In *US-Section 337*, the national legislation at issue concerned procedures for claims of patent infringement by products manufactured abroad, *inter alia* by means of a *process* patented in the US.

[182] See Hudec (2000); Howse and Regan (2000), and Charnovitz (2001), all making essentially the same claim.

referred to GATT practice regarding "border tax adjustment".[183] Through "border tax adjustment", countries may impose domestic taxes and charges on imports and exempt or reimburse them on exports, in order to ensure the trade neutrality of domestic taxation. The 1970 Working Party on Border Tax Adjustment concluded in its Report that

> *there was convergence of views to the effect that taxes directly levied on products were eligible for tax adjustment. [...] Furthermore, the Working Party concluded that there was convergence of views to the effect that certain taxes that were not directly levied on products were not eligible for tax adjustment. [...]*[184]

The Working Party's references to 'taxes directly levied on products' and to 'taxes that were not directly levied on products' should be read as references to indirect and direct taxes, respectively. Only "indirect" domestic taxes (levied on products) may be compensated upon import and export, while "direct taxes" (levied on persons) may not.[185] When the tax is not directly levied on the product, it is difficult or impossible to ascertain what equalisation [i.e. adjustment] requires.[186] Thus, taxing imported *products* in order to adjust a domestic *producer* tax contravenes Article III:2, because the like domestic *products* would not be subject to such a tax, even if the domestic *producers* would be. Alternatively, Article II:1(b) GATT is violated when the tax is collected at the border and is considered a charge that violates a tariff binding.[187] If only taxes levied on products as such can be adjusted, that does not mean that taxes based on production methods can never be applied to imported products. It is recalled that Article III:2 contains the words 'subject, directly or indirectly'. The major focus of the term "indirectly" seems to lie in enabling the adjustment of taxation of *inputs* in products.[188] In discussions in the Preparatory Committee, it was stated that the word "indirectly" would even cover a tax not levied on a product as such but on the *processing* of the product.[189] It is unclear, however, whether this means that

---

[183] *US-Tuna-Dolphin I*, paras. 5.13 and 5.14.

[184] Report of the Working Party on Border Tax Adjustments, BISD 185/97, para. 14.

[185] On border tax adjustment in the GATT/WTO context, see Dam (1970) at 124; Demaret and Stewardson (1994); Thaggart (1994); GATT Working party report BISD 18S/97; and a useful overview in document WT/CTE/W/47.

[186] Howse and Regan (2000) in footnote 19.

[187] As suggested by Hudec (2000), in the text accompanying footnote 10 (manuscript).

[188] Article II:2(a) GATT provides as follows: 'Nothing in this Article shall prevent any contracting party from imposing at any time on the importation of any product: (a) a charge equivalent to an internal tax imposed consistently with the provisions of paragraph 2 of Article III in respect of the like domestic product or in respect of an article from which the imported product has been manufactured or produced in whole or in part; [...]'

[189] GATT (1995), at 141, referring to original documents EPCT/A/PV/9, at p. 19 and EPCT/W/181, at p. 3.

taxes on *inputs* that are consumed domestically in *producing* a final product may be adjusted upon the import or export of the *final product*.[190]

The panel in *US Auto Taxes* considered that the border tax adjustment principles constituted a 'limitation on the range of domestic policy measures that may be applied also to imported products', which equally applied to regulations under Article III:4.[191] Can a similar argument to the one that only *taxes* 'directly levied on products' can be "adjusted" upon imported products indeed be applied to application to imports of internal *regulations*? The wording used in the first sentence of Article III:2 is 'the products [...] imported [...] shall not be *subject*, directly or indirectly, to internal taxes [...] in excess of those *applied*, directly or indirectly, to like domestic products'. The second sentence of Article III:2 refers to *applying* internal taxes or other internal charges *to* imported or domestic *products*.[192] With regard to regulations, Article III:4 refers to 'laws etc. *affecting* the internal sale, etc. *of products*.' At first sight, one could argue that "affecting" covers a broader range of measures than "subject to" and "applied to". This would suggest that Article III:4 permits a broader spectrum of regulatory "border adjustment" than Article III:2 allows border tax adjustment. In the tax situation, the argument for not allowing compensation of direct taxes by taxing imported products is that direct taxes are not necessarily passed on to the consumer, while indirect taxes are. That argument has been criticised, however.[193] Perhaps more pressing is the argument that the congruence between the tax burden on the domestic and imported products is difficult to ascertain when the tax is not levied on domestic products but producers. It is submitted that in the regulatory sphere, too, the regulatory burden upon domestic and imported products is more difficult to compare when a regulation is applied to domestic *producers* and to imported *products*. Be that as it may, the border tax adjustment parallel does not shed any conclusive light upon the question of the coverage of PPM-based *regulatory* measures by Article III:4 GATT.

(iii) The Note Ad Article III

It is recalled that the Note Ad Article III provides that any law or regulation that '*applies to* an imported product *and* to the like domestic product' is subject to Article III even if enforced upon imports at the point or time of importation.[194] PPM requirements cannot be applied to foreign *producers* directly, for reasons of jurisdictional limitations. This leads to situations in

---

[190] Demaret and Stewardson (1994) at 18.

[191] *US-Auto Taxes*, unadopted, para. 5.53.

[192] Emphasis added.

[193] Dam (1970) at 214.

[194] Note Ad Article III, reproduced in the Annex to this work. Emphasis added.

which a state regulates its domestic *producers,* and attempts to balance such regulation by regulating imported *products.* As observed above, there are practical difficulties involved in applying PPM requirements to imported *products.* It is difficult to control the observance of PPM requirements by foreign producers, especially when the PPM is not product-related. However, does that mean that no such requirements could be covered by the Note Ad Article III? This question is important, because if a PPM-based measure is covered by Article III through its Note, the discussion will focus on the issues of likeness and less favourable treatment, with the initial burden of proof being on the complainant. Only if these conditions are fulfilled will a violation of Article III be found, and the defendant will then bear the burden of proving that its measure is justified under Article XX. If a PPM-based import restriction is not covered by the Note Ad Article III, on the other hand, it will violate Article XI and the discussion will immediately shift to Article XX.

The panel in *US-Tuna-Dolphin I* was not willing to accept that an import *prohibition* coupled with domestic fishing *restrictions* were covered by the Note Ad Article III, and observed that the Note only covers measures applied to imports and domestic products that are *of the same nature.*[195] However, the WTO panel in *EC-Asbestos* has taken a somewhat wider view of the coverage of the Note Ad Article III. The panel observed that the fact that France no longer produced asbestos or asbestos-containing products (as a result of the production prohibition) did not suffice to make the Decree a measure falling under Article XI:1.[196] According to the panel, the regulations applicable to domestic products and foreign products led to the same *result.* It was not necessary that an *identical* measure be applied to the domestic product and the like imported product if the measure applicable to the imported product is to fall under Article III. The word "and" in the Note does not have the same meaning as 'in the same way as'.[197] The panel added the rhetorical question: 'Is it not equally preferable from the administrative point of view and in the interests of the importers themselves to prevent the entry of the like product into the country applying the measure rather than waiting until it is placed in a warehouse before banning its sale?'[198] The panel's observations on the Note Ad Article III were not appealed.

It may thus be assumed that in order to be covered by the Note Ad Article III, the measures applied to imports and domestic products do not need to be identical, as long as the result is the same. There must be a match between what is applied to imports and domestic products, but that match does not have to be perfect. Admittedly, the national law at issue in *EC-Asbestos* did not involve an

---

[195] *US-Tuna-Dolphin I,* para. 5.11. Emphasis added.

[196] Panel in *EC-Asbestos,* para. 8.91.

[197] Ibid., paras. 8.92-94.

[198] Ibid., para. 8.95.

import restriction based on a PPM requirement, but rather a general prohibition on manufacturing, importing, selling, or marketing a product, i.e. asbestos fibres. Nonetheless, if what the panel said is applied to PPM-based measures, it would not seem impossible *a priori* for the Note Ad Article III to cover a measure prohibiting the internal production and importation of products on the basis of their PPM, such as a prohibition on producing, marketing, selling or importing dolphin-unfriendly tuna. However, the Note would not seem to cover production *regulations* (e.g. requiring the use of certain fishing methods for catching tuna) coupled with a full import *prohibition* on the product at issue (an import prohibition on all tuna), as such measures do not lead to the same result. The same is true for an import prohibition on all tuna from certain countries that do not impose on their producers the same or equivalent PPMs as are imposed by the importing country on its producers. Such a measure *a priori* does not lead to the same result for imported and domestic tuna. It is covered by Article XI and requires justification.

Interestingly, the panel in *EC-Asbestos* did not pay explicit attention to the term "like" in the Note Ad Article III. The Note requires that the measure should apply to an imported product and the like domestic product, but the asbestos prohibition did not apply to substitute fibres. Thus, the panel must have implicitly assumed that asbestos is not "like" substitute fibres for the purposes of the Note, because otherwise it could not have found that the Note applied. Subsequently, however, the panel found that asbestos and substitute fibres are "like" for the purposes of Article III:4. That finding was reversed by the Appellate Body, but the question remains whether "likeness" in the Note ad Article III could be different from "likeness" in Article III:4. The same problem may surface in the PPM discussion. One wonders to what extent an (implicit) finding of "unlikeness" for the purposes of the Note Ad Article III may prejudge the likeness determination in Article III:4 in future cases. This is especially so after the Appellate Body has widely interpreted "likeness" in Article III:4, as discussed below.

(b)   PPM-Based Measures and Article III:4 GATT

If a PPM-based measure is assessed under Article III:4, the "likeness" of imported and domestic products will be a central issue. However, as the PPM-based measures in *US-Tuna-Dolphin* and *US-Shrimp-Turtle* were found to violate Article XI, there are to date no GATT or WTO panel or Appellate Body reports that have assessed a PPM-based measure under Article III:4. The GATT panel in *US-Beer* found that a tax differentiation based on producer size violated Article III:2 because beer from large breweries was "like" beer from small breweries. The panel said that even if the tax credits were granted on a non-discriminatory basis to small breweries inside and outside the importing country, there would still be an inconsistency with Article III:2, first sentence.[199] This report should be seen against the background of the "product-process distinction", i.e. the view that Article III only addresses measures that 'affect the product as such'.[200] As discussed above, that view is erroneous. Moreover, the case has been distinguished from measures based on environmental PPMs because the only objective of the tax credit was the protection of small breweries.[201] Still in the context of Article III:2, the GATT panel in *Japan-Alcohol (1987)* said that "likeness" must be assessed taking into account 'objective criteria such as manufacturing processes of products, and subjective criteria such as the use of the product by consumers'.[202] In *EC-Hormones*, the US argued *inter alia* that the EC had violated Article III:4 by treating hormone-treated beef less favourably than non-hormone-treated beef, while they were like products.[203] In the view of the EC, hormone-treated meat was not "like" non-hormone-treated meat, as it had substantially different properties, composition and appearance and was perceived by European consumers as a distinct product.[204] The panel and the Appellate Body in that dispute focused on the SPS Agreement; the PPM nature of the measures and the "likeness" issue were not addressed.

It is recalled that the Appellate Body in *EC-Asbestos* stated that a determination of "likeness" under Article III:4 is fundamentally a determination on the nature and extent of a competitive relationship between and among products.[205] This appears to reflect a view of "likeness" in the "market", based essentially on the consumer perspective rather than the perspective of the regulating government.[206] The Appellate Body made clear that all relevant evidence on the "likeness" issue must be taken into account and weighed by panels, before a conclusion of "likeness" or "unlikeness" can be drawn. It also suggested that products that are physically "unlike" may be found to be "like" after all, when other criteria such as end-uses and consumer tastes provide overwhelming evidence of "likeness".

This raises the question whether the reverse may also be true. May two products that are physically identical nonetheless be "unlike" in view of different

---

[199] *US-Beer*, para. 5.19.

[200] See Section 4.2.4. Hudec (2000), text accompanying footnote 29 (manuscript), mentions this case as the only adopted GATT panel report supporting the "product-process distinction".

[201] Howse and Regan (2000) at 263.

[202] *Japan-Alcohol* (1987), para. 5.7.

[203] Panel in *EC-Hormones* (US), paras. 4.223 (on SPS), 4.241 (on TBT), 4.245-251 (on GATT).

[204] Ibid., para. 4.254.

[205] Ibid., para. 99.

[206] However, Howse and Tuerk (2001) at 16 (manuscript) assert that the AB actually did take regulatory objectives into account by taking a perfectly informed consumer market as reference point, referring to para. 122 of the AB report.

consumer tastes and habits? The question is of particular importance for regulatory distinctions based on PPMs not causing any physical difference in products. It is submitted that the possibility that physically identical products are "unlike" in the marketplace does not seem to be *a priori* excluded. However, in the case of physically completely identical products, consumers will only be able to make a choice on grounds of different PPMs if they are provided with sufficient information. If the regulating government imposes a requirement to provide such information in order to enable consumers to make an informed choice, e.g. through mandatory labelling or certification, it may at the same time be steering consumers' choices.[207] The consumer and regulatory perspectives cannot always be strictly separated.[208] The regulatory perspective is itself steered by pressure groups and domestic producers.

The second aspect of an assessment under Article III:4 is 'no less favourable treatment'. In *EC-Asbestos*, the Appellate Body left open the possibility that no violation of Article III:4 is found when a regulatory distinction does not treat the "group" of imported products less favourably than the "group" of like domestic products. Although the case itself did not concern a PPM-based measure, and although the Appellate Body's remarks on less favourable treatment were *obiter dictum*, they have been interpreted as implying the possibility of making regulatory distinctions based on PPMs without violating Article III:4.[209] The Appellate Body may also have suggested that the regulatory objectives of a measure that distinguishes between products may be taken into account when assessing whether there is "less favourable treatment".[210]

(c) PPM-Based Measures and Article XX GATT: Panel and Appellate Body Reports

Arguments on "extraterritoriality" in the context of Article XX may relate to all three elements of Article XX; the exception grounds, the means-ends tests, and the conditions in the chapeau. In this Section, what has been said about "extraterritoriality" and PPM-based measures in the relevant panel and Appellate Body reports is described and discussed. A distinction is made between the location of protection goals, and the location of behaviour targeted by PPM-based measures. The next Section provides an evaluation of the arguments.

---

[207] Of course, the government will in turn be steered by consumer and/or producer pressure and lobby groups.

[208] Bronckers and McNelis (2000) appear to take the view that governments should not be allowed to steer consumer preferences in this way.

[209] Howse and Tuerk (2001).

[210] AB in *EC-Asbestos*, para. 100. See Section 4.2.4.

(i)   Location of the Resources Protected

The text of paragraphs (b) and (g) of Article XX contains no limitation regarding the location of the resources protected, and GATT and WTO dispute settlement reports are inconclusive on whether extraterritorial protection goals may be allowed. The panel in *US-Tuna-Dolphin I* noted that the text of Article XX(b) does not clarify whether it covers measures necessary to protect human, animal or plant life or health outside the jurisdiction of the contracting party taking the measure. The panel added that the concerns of the drafters of Article XX(b) focused on the use of sanitary measures to safeguard the life or health of humans, animals or plants within the jurisdiction of the importing country.[211] However, the panel did leave open the possibility of extra-jurisdictional protection. It found that 'even if Article XX(b) were interpreted to permit extra-jurisdictional protection of life and health', the measure could not be "necessary" for another reason, i.e. endangering the multilateral trade system by targeting foreign life and health policies (see below). The panel repeated its reasoning with regard to Article XX(g).

In *US-Tuna-Dolphin II*, the panel noted that previous panels had considered Article XX(g) to be applicable to policies related to migratory species of fish without making a distinction between fish caught within or outside the territorial jurisdiction of the contracting party that had invoked this provision.[212] The panel observed that measures providing different treatment to products of different origin could in principle be taken under other paragraphs of Article XX and other Articles of the General Agreement with respect to things located, or actions occurring, outside the territorial jurisdiction of the party taking the measure. It mentioned by way of example Article XX(e) concerning the products of prison labour. The negotiations of the Havana Charter and the General Agreement did not provide clear support for any particular view on the question of the location of the exhaustible natural resource in Article XX(g). Thus, the panel could see no valid reason why the provisions of Article XX(g) should only apply to policies related to the conservation of exhaustible natural resources located within the territory of the contracting party invoking the provision.[213] However, this panel, too, denied justification under the exception grounds for reasons of targeting foreign policies, as discussed *infra*.

In *US-Shrimp-Turtle*, the Appellate Body noted that sea turtles are highly migratory animals, passing in and out of waters subject to the rights of jurisdiction of various coastal states and the high seas. The sea turtle species covered by the US measure were all known to occur in waters over which the United States

---

[211] *US-Tuna-Dolphin I*, unadopted, paras. 5.25-26.

[212] Referring to *Canada-Herring and Salmon*; *US-Tuna 1982*.

[213] *US-Tuna-Dolphin II*, unadopted, paras. 5.15-20.

exercises jurisdiction. The Appellate Body decided not to rule on the question of whether there is an 'implied jurisdictional limitation' in Article XX(g), and if so, what is the nature or extent of that limitation. It merely noted that in the specific circumstances of the case before it, there was a 'sufficient nexus between the migratory and endangered marine populations involved and the United States for purposes of Article XX(g)'.[214] The Appellate Body found that the measure was provisionally justified under paragraph (g).

(ii)   Location of the Behaviour Targeted

Trade-restrictive measures regulate and thereby *immediately* target domestic behaviour, such as imports, marketing, sales, etc. They may aim to influence and thereby *eventually* target behaviour abroad, such as production, processing or catching methods.[215] As argued above, trade-restrictive measures raise no jurisdiction issues, as the behaviour they immediately target is within the jurisdiction of the state taking the measures. With regard to the location of the behaviour eventually targeted by a trade-restrictive measure, the text of Article XX is silent. Nonetheless, a number of panels and the Appellate Body have discussed precisely that issue in their interpretation of Article XX. In *US-Tuna-Dolphin*, both panels did so within the context of the means-ends tests in paragraphs (b) and (g). The panel in *US-Tuna-Dolphin I* said that to accept a broad interpretation of Article XX(b) would endanger the multilateral trading system, as 'each contracting party could unilaterally determine the life or health protection policies from which other contracting parties could not deviate without jeopardizing their rights under the General Agreement.'[216] The panel in *US-Tuna-Dolphin II* said that if Article XX were interpreted as permitting contracting parties to take trade measures so as to force other contracting parties to change their conservation policies within their jurisdiction, the balance of rights and obligations among contracting parties, in particular the right of access to markets, would be seriously impaired. The General Agreement could then no longer serve as a multilateral framework for trade among contracting parties. Thus, 'measures taken so as to force other countries to change their policies, and that were effective only if such changes occurred, could not be primarily aimed either at the conservation of an exhaustible natural resource, or at rendering effective restrictions on domestic production of consumption, in the meaning of Article XX(g)'.[217] The panel repeated this reasoning with regard to "necessary" in Article XX(b).

---

[214] AB in *US-Shrimp-Turtle*, para. 133.

[215] Cf. Howse and Regan 2000, at 278.

[216] *US-Tuna-Dolphin I*, unadopted, para. 5.27.

[217] *US-Tuna-Dolphin II*, unadopted, paras. 5.26-27.

The panel in *US-Shrimp-Turtle* relied on essentially the same argument, but this time read it into the chapeau to Article XX. In the panel's opinion, the chapeau to Article XX only allows Members to derogate from GATT provisions so long as, in doing so, they do not undermine the WTO multilateral trading system, thus also abusing the exceptions contained in Article XX. Such undermining and abuse would occur when a Member jeopardises the operation of the WTO Agreement in such a way that guaranteed market access and non-discriminatory treatment within a multilateral framework would no longer be possible. The panel was of the view that allowing Members to condition market access upon the adoption of certain policies by exporting Members would endanger the multilateral trading system. Market access for goods could become subject to an increasing number of conflicting policy requirements for the same product and this would rapidly lead to the end of the WTO multilateral trading system.[218] In support of its contention, the panel referred to *US-Tuna-Dolphin II*, and to the *Belgian Family Allowances* panel report.[219] The panel noted that the US measure conditioned access to the US market for a given product upon the adoption by exporting Members of conservation policies that the United States considered comparable to its own. Accordingly, the panel found that the US measure constituted "unjustifiable discrimination" within the meaning of the chapeau to Article XX.[220]

The panel had started its analysis with the chapeau, and had concluded that as the measure did not meet the requirements in the chapeau, it could not be justified by Article XX. The Appellate Body reversed this sequence. It first accepted the "provisional justification" of the measure under Article XX(g). Only then did it find that there was "unjustifiable discrimination" within the meaning of the chapeau, observing that 'it is not acceptable, in international trade relations, for one WTO Member to use an economic embargo to *require* other Members to adopt essentially the same comprehensive regulatory program, to achieve a certain policy goal, as that in force within that Member's territory, *without* taking into consideration different conditions which may occur in the territories of those other Members.'[221] According to the Appellate Body, the

---

[218] Panel in *US-Shrimp-Turtle*, paras. 7.44-45.

[219] Panel in *US-Shrimp-Turtle*, para. 7.46, referring to *Belgian Family Allowances*. That dispute involved a charge imposed by Belgium on the purchase by public bodies of imported products originating from countries where the law did not require companies to pay family allowance benefits for their employees, or required them to pay less than 80% of what was paid in Belgium. The panel in that dispute had considered that 'the Belgian legislation on family allowance was not only inconsistent with the provisions of Article I (and possibly with those of Article III, paragraph 2), but was based on a concept which was difficult to reconcile with the spirit of the General Agreement.'

[220] Ibid., paras. 7.48-49.

[221] AB in *US-Shrimp-Turtle*, para. 164. Emphasis in the original.

unjustifiable discrimination was also caused by other factors. First, the United States had prohibited the importation of shrimp caught using methods which were identical to those employed in the US, solely because they had been caught in the waters of countries that have not been certified by the United States.[222] Second, the United States had failed to engage all Members exporting shrimp to the United States in serious, across the board negotiations with the objective of concluding bilateral or multilateral agreements for the protection and conservation of sea turtles, before enforcing the import prohibition against the shrimp exports of those other Members.[223] Third, the US had treated exporting countries differently by allowing only some of them to make use of "phase-in periods" to adjust to its requirements, and by making different efforts to transfer relevant technology.[224]

(iii) Targeting Foreign Producers and Targeting Foreign Governments

The panel in *US-Shrimp-Turtle* emphasised that it was not addressing the potential jurisdictional scope of Article XX, but rather 'the inclusion of certain unilateral measures within the scope *ratione materiae* of Article XX'.[225] The panel noted that many domestic governmental measures can have an effect outside the jurisdiction of the government which takes them. However, it observed a difference between an import ban on a particular product (mentioning by way of example a dangerous product) and a country-based measure such as the one at issue:

> *banning the importation of a particular product does not* per se *imply that a change in policy is required from the* country *whose exports are subject to the import prohibition. [...] This is clearly different from adopting a policy pursuant to which only countries that adopt measures restricting all of their production to products considered safe by a particular Member may export to the market of that Member.*[226]

The panel considered that a measure requiring that other *Members* adopt *policies* comparable to the US policy for their domestic markets and all other markets represented a threat to the WTO multilateral trading system and was not within

---

[222] Ibid., para. 165.

[223] Ibid., paras. 166-172.

[224] Ibid., paras. 173-175.

[225] Panel in *US-Shrimp-Turtle*, para. 7.50.

[226] Ibid., para. 7.50. Emphasis in the original.

the scope of Article XX.[227] The Appellate Body rejected the panel's suggestion that unilateral measures requiring other Members to adopt certain policies are outside the scope of Article XX altogether. The Appellate Body stated that

> conditioning access to a Member's domestic market on whether exporting Members comply with, or adopt, a policy or policies unilaterally prescribed by the importing Member may, to some degree, be a common aspect of measures falling within the scope of one or another of the exceptions (a) to (j) of Article XX. [...] It is not necessary to assume that requiring from exporting countries compliance with, or adoption of, certain policies [...] prescribed by the importing country, renders a measure a priori incapable of justification under Article XX.[228]

The Appellate Body subsequently took the country-based nature of the measure into account as an important factor in the assessment of whether there was unjustifiable discrimination within the meaning of the chapeau to Article XX. Indeed, it expressly noted the fact that foreign producers meeting the PPM requirements could still not export their shrimp to the US.[229] Nevertheless, although condemning the measure at issue, the Appellate Body suggested that a PPM-based measure targeting the policies of other Members is in principle acceptable, as long as it meets certain conditions. Subsequently, the US revised the application of its measures. Under the revised implementing guidelines, shipments of shrimp from non-certified countries are accepted when accompanied by a shrimp exporters' declaration form attesting that the shrimp was harvested with fishing technology not adversely affecting sea turtles.[230] Nevertheless, to a large extent the measures still rely on country certification, and thus on targeting foreign government policies.[231] The implementation panel in *US-Shrimp-Turtle* accepted the revised measures, and the Appellate Body confirmed its findings. The Appellate Body *expressis verbis* repeated the above statement that conditioning market access on the policies of exporting countries' governments is a common aspect of measures falling within the scope of the

---

[227] Ibid., para. 7.51. Emphasis added. Earlier on in its report, in footnote 649, the panel responded to a reference by the United States to Article XX(e) as evidence that GATT refutes any argument that trade measures generally should not have any effect on the internal affairs of exporting countries. The panel noted that 'Article XX(e) does not permit a Member to make entry of imported goods into its territory conditional upon the exporting Member's *policy* on prison labour. This paragraph only refers to the *products* of prison labour.'

[228] AB in *US-Shrimp-Turtle*, para. 121.

[229] Ibid., para. 164.

[230] The possibility of accepting shrimp from non-certified countries is the subject of domestic court proceedings in the US. See the panel in *US-Shrimp-Turtle Implementation*, paras. 2.15-18 and 2.24-26.

[231] Ibid., paras. 2.23, 2.25, 2.27-32.

exceptions in Article XX. It added that its statement expresses a principle that was central to its ruling in its original report in *US-Shrimp-Turtle*. Then, it observed that a separate question arises when examining under the chapeau of Article XX a measure that provides market access conditionally.[232]

(d) PPM-Based Measures and Article XX GATT: Evaluation

(i) Relevance of Context, Object, Purpose, and Public International Law Principles

According to Article 31 of the Vienna Convention, the terms of a treaty must be given meaning in their context and in the light of their object and purpose. Together with the context, any relevant rules of international law shall be taken into account. What are the context, object and purpose of Articles III, XI, and XX GATT when addressing PPM-based measures? It may seem that measures conditioning the importation or marketing of products on their production methods are contrary to the basic rationale underlying the international trade system. That rationale is a general obligation to provide market access at bound tariffs, embodied in Articles XI and II GATT, coupled with a general obligation not to discriminate between exporting countries (Article I GATT) and against imported products once they have entered the market (Article III GATT). Any deviation from this obligation to grant market access will in that view need justification under Article XX, which is the only place where arguments on "extraterritorial effects" should play a role.

On the other hand, it has been argued that as a 'general right of access view' derogates much more from national sovereignty than a "non-discrimination" view of the trading system, the latter is the correct view. Market access cannot always be presumed; to do so would derogate from sovereignty without clear textual support.[233] That would not be in accordance with the doctrine of *in dubio mitius*, according to which in cases of doubt, treaties are to be interpreted in the way that least intrudes upon state sovereignty. Arguably, neither the "market access view" nor the "non-discrimination view" of the WTO rules is correct. There are various commitments extending beyond non-discrimination, not only in Articles II and XI GATT, but also in the TBT and SPS Agreements. On the other hand, market access can indeed not always be presumed. In this respect, it should be emphasised that the goal of the WTO as laid down in the preambles of the WTO and GATT Agreements is not "free trade" but just "expanding trade" through 'mutually advantageous arrangements directed to the substantial reduc-

---

[232] AB in *US-Shrimp-Turtle Implementation*, paras. 137-139.

[233] Howse and Regan (2000) at 276.

tion [...] of barriers to trade and to the elimination of discriminatory treatment in international trade relations'.[234]

The object and purpose of the chapeau to Article XX is to prevent unjustifiable or arbitrary discrimination or disguised trade restrictions in the application of measures that could otherwise be justified as pursuing a valid non-trade objective and meeting the means-ends tests. As the Appellate Body has stated at several occasions, the chapeau to Article XX thus aims to prevent the abuse of Article XX, and thereby to safeguard the balance of rights and obligations between WTO Members. The context of the chapeau to Article XX GATT includes the references to sustainable development and environmental protection in the preamble to the WTO Agreement. According to the Appellate Body in *US-Shrimp-Turtle*, the language of the chapeau makes it clear that the exceptions in paragraphs (a) to (j) of Article XX are *limited and conditional* exceptions from the *substantive* obligations contained in the other provisions of the GATT 1994.[235] The Appellate Body has been criticised for suggesting, by the use of these words, that the right to invoke an exception is in an inferior position *vis-à-vis* the "substantive rights" such as those in Articles III and XI.[236] Indeed, the mere fact that a provision is characterised as an exception does not *ipso facto* require a narrow interpretation.[237] The text of Article XX provides that subject to the conditions laid down in that provision, 'nothing in this Agreement shall be construed to prevent the adoption or enforcement' of protective measures. Thus, there is no textual reason for assuming that the right to invoke an exception is inferior to the "substantive rights" in Articles XI and III.

In the view of some, trade-restrictive measures are considered as intrusions on the sovereign right of states not to have their conditions and policies influenced through trade measures by other states.[238] Article XX would accordingly have to be interpreted strictly. That is only one way of looking at the issue,

---

[234] Cf. the remarks on "embedded liberalism" in the Introductory Chapter.

[235] Ibid., paras. 156-7. Emphasis added.

[236] See Charnovitz (2001) at 30-31.

[237] Cf. the AB in *EC-Hormones*, para. 104, on Article 3.3 SPS: 'Merely characterizing a treaty provision as an "exception" does not by itself justify a "stricter" or "narrower" interpretation of that provision than would be warranted by examination of the ordinary meaning of the actual treaty words, viewed in context and in the light of the treaty's object and purpose, or, in other words, by applying the normal rules of treaty interpretation.'

[238] Cf. the Swedish representative in the GATT Council in 1991 stating that 'In the GATT, parties had voluntarily accepted some limits on their sovereignty. However, the GATT did not explicitly allow action to influence conditions within another contracting party's territory, or its policies outside the trade field. [...] Contracting parties, therefore, retained a basic right to remain free from such pressures, which in many cases could effectively be brought to bear through trade measures.' As cited by Kingsbury (1994) at 21.

however. One may equally assert that the right to apply trade-restrictive measures as reflected in Article XX is itself an expression of state sovereignty, which is only limited by positive commitments to provide market access and to avoid discrimination as laid down in Articles I, II, III, and XI GATT. Thus, Article XX reflects the sovereign right to protect life and health, natural resources and other things, a right which is not conferred by the trade treaty but which already existed. Such goals sometimes override trade liberalisation objectives, as has been recognised by panels.[239] Tariff bindings and provisions such as Articles XI and III GATT may be said to confer rights of access and treatment of traded goods to WTO Members, and to that extent limit the sovereignty of other Members. But these are treaty rights. In cases of doubt, the *in dubio mitius* principle would point towards a limited interpretation of those rights in favour of the remaining state sovereignty reflected in Article XX.[240] If the chapeau is to reflect a balance of rights and obligations, "substantive rights" such as tariff bindings or expectations of market access should not be given preference *a priori* over the right to invoke an exception. A presumption against PPM-based measures would therefore seem inappropriate.

(ii) Exception grounds and Means-Ends Tests

As observed above, the text of Article XX does not exclude the possibility of extrajurisdictional resource protection or the targeting of behaviour abroad through trade restrictions. The Appellate Body in *US-Shrimp-Turtle* left open the question of whether there is an 'implied jurisdictional limitation' in Article XX(g), and noted that in the case before it, there was a "sufficient nexus" between the migratory and endangered species involved and the United States for the purposes of Article XX(g). One may actually wonder why one should be looking for *inherent* jurisdictional limitations in Article XX. In accordance with the *Lotus* principle, one could suffice by observing that there are no express jurisdictional limits in Article XX(g), and there is no general rule of international law governing the question of the location of resources protected by trade restrictive measures. One would tend to assume that the same is true for Article XX(b), although that would result in an incongruence with the SPS Agreement, which is limited to the protection of life and health within the territory of the Member taking measures. The *US-Shrimp-Turtle* reports have clarified that PPM-based measures targeting foreign government policies by making imports dependent upon them are not *a priori* excluded from being

---

[239] See e.g. *Thailand-Cigarettes*, para. 74: '[the objective of paragraphs (b) and (d) of Article XX is] to allow contracting parties to impose trade restrictive measures inconsistent with the General Agreement to pursue overriding public policy goals to the extent that such inconsistencies were unavoidable.'

[240] Cf. Howse and Regan (2000) at 276.

covered by the exceptions in Article XX. On the contrary, the Appellate Body has asserted that conditioning market access on the policies of exporting countries' governments is a 'common aspect of measures falling within the scope of the exceptions in Article XX'.

It is difficult to make general statements as to whether unilateral trade-restrictive measures based on PPMs will meet the means-ends tests in Articles (b) and (g). It is clear from cases such as *US-Tuna-Dolphin* and *US-Shrimp-Turtle*, that the *product targeted* by a measure is not necessarily the same as the resource or animal or human sought to be protected.[241] This also applies to product measures, such as an asbestos ban to protect human health. An interesting question is whether the means-ends tests also require that there be a relationship between the product targeted and the protection or conservation goal. In the sphere of PPM-based measures, such a relationship is absent when WTO Member A bans the imports of cars from Member B, because the latter does not take measures to ensure that its fishermen do not kill dolphins or turtles. Such a measure would operate as a sanction. It would not seem impossible that such a measure could be found to be "necessary" or "relating to". However, if unilaterally imposed, such a measure would appear to upset the balance of rights and obligations of WTO Members and would accordingly not meet the standards of the chapeau.

The means-ends requirements in paragraphs (b) and (g) of Article XX require a link between the measure and its goal. The relationship between a measure and its goal is also part of the assessment of "relating to" in Article XX(g), as the Appellate Body reports in *US-Gasoline* and *US-Shrimp-Turtle* show. The means must be reasonably related to the ends; the means must not be disproportionately wide in relation to the objective. The *US-Shrimp-Turtle* saga has made it clear that measures targeting foreign government policies by making imports dependent upon them can meet the means-ends tests. The contribution made by the measure to the attainment of the policy goal is also one of the factors to be taken into account in interpreting "necessary" in Article XX(d) and XX(b), along with the importance of the objective and the impact on trade.[242] Up to now, no PPM-based measures have been assessed under Article XX(b). However, it would not seem impossible that such a measure could be found to be "necessary". A thorny question is who is ultimately to decide upon the importance of the objective. The Appellate Body has been deferential in this respect in a dispute like *EC-Asbestos*. But it will face a more difficult situation when PPM-based measures are at issue. The Appellate Body will probably look for multilateral instruments as indicators for an agreement on the importance of the objective. Most thorny will be disputes involving local environmental problems upon which little or no consensus exists, such as animal welfare.

---

[241] See Charnovitz (1991).

[242] See AB in *Korea-Beef* and in *EC-Asbestos*, respectively.

Although the location of the resources protected in the first place seems relevant to the interpretation of the exception grounds, it could also play a role in interpreting the means-ends tests. It appears overly simplistic to state that the more tenuous the nexus between the territory of the country taking the measure and the location of the protection goal, the less likely it is that a measure will meet the means-ends tests. Sometimes, the absence of such a link will indeed be reflected in the measure's lack of effectiveness in contributing to its desired objective. This will especially be the case when the Member taking the measure imports only a small share of the product involved. But in other cases, there may be a strong means-end relationship between the measure and its goal, even if the protection goal is fully located within the exporting country. If a Member imports 95% of another Member's fur exports and prohibits the importation of furs from animals caught with leghold traps, the contribution to the attainment of the environmental goal of the measure may be considerable.[243] The means-ends tests may accordingly be met. In a reverse situation, a PPM-based measure may aim to protect the importing country's territory against production spills, but this will be ineffective because the product restricted by the measure is not (or is hardly) exported to the country taking the measure.

(iii) The Chapeau

Despite the disputable value of the reference to *Belgian Family Allowances*, it is submitted that the panel's point in *US-Shrimp-Turtle* was valid.[244] There is a difference between measures targeting government behaviour by making imports dependent upon it, and measures targeting producer behaviour. Measures justified under Article XX do not necessarily or commonly prescribe policies to be adopted by the authorities of exporting Members, as the Appellate Body suggests. It is normally not states that trade, but private importers and exporters. It is quite obvious that a producer or exporter must ensure that the importing country's requirements are met by its product if it wishes to sell its product on the importing country's market. In principle, this is also true for the requirements set by the importing country regarding the way the product has been produced. The importing country is not telling the

---

[243] Although the actual effect will depend on the extent to which exports are diverted to other countries.

[244] *Belgian Family Allowances* concerned a levy, not a regulatory measure, that was primarily assessed under the Most-Favoured Nation requirement, not National Treatment. Article XX was not even mentioned. Moreover, there was no relationship whatsoever between the policy in the exporting country and the imported products charged. This panel report would therefore appear to be only marginally, if at all, relevant to the assessment of environmental PPM measures under Article III. According to Hudec (2000) at 1 (manuscript), the report in *Belgian Family Allowances* is often mistakenly cited as the foundation of the "product-process doctrine".

producer in the exporting country how to produce; only how to produce if it wishes to compete on its market. It is quite another thing for the importing country to make access to its market dependent upon whether the *authorities* in the exporting country determine how their producers produce.

Measures targeting foreign policies by making imports dependent on policies of the exporting country's government treat goods on the basis of their origin. Producers in the exporting country may see the market access of their products denied by the importing country because of their origin, even if they fully comply with the importing country's PPM requirements. Such measures will accordingly more easily lead to unjustifiable or arbitrary discrimination than measures that target producers by making imports dependent on production methods, irrespective of product origin. It is submitted that unilateral PPM-based measures making imports dependent upon the adoption of certain policies by governments may endanger the multilateral trading system, because a proliferation of such measures could lead to mutually incompatible policy demands. Such a development could thus endanger the balance of rights and obligations which the chapeau is intended to preserve. This is not to say, as the panel did, that measures targeting governments are *per se* outside the scope of possibly justifiable measures under Article XX. The Appellate Body was correct in noting that there is no basis in the text of Article XX to exclude certain types of measures *a priori* from justification under Article XX. A country-based approach may sometimes be unavoidable. However, the discrimination that such an approach implies arguably needs to be justified by particular circumstances. The present author submits that the Appellate Body was right in suggesting that whether it is acceptable to make imports conditional on foreign governments' policies is a matter to be assessed under the chapeau. However, it is submitted that the Appellate Body could have made it clearer that PPM-based measures targeting governments should only be the last resort; PPM-based measures targeting producers are preferable in terms of the chapeau, as they endanger the trading system much less than measures targeting governments.

Could the balance of rights and obligations as reflected in the chapeau to Article XX be tilted by the absence of a "nexus" between the location of the resources protected and/or the behaviour targeted on the one hand, and the Member taking the measure on the other? The danger identified by the Appellate Body of eroding or rendering naught the market access rights negotiated in the WTO Agreement seems most apparent when unilateral measures are taken in order to address an environmental problem located completely within the jurisdiction of the exporting country, without any transfrontier effects. For example, a trade restriction in order to address a local animal welfare problem in the exporting country. A number of approaches have been proposed to argue that PPM-measures may even be acceptable in such cases, such as a 'new effects doctrine',[245] "universal jurisdiction",[246] and "affirmative duties" of states to contribute to the protection of the environment outside their territory.[247] This may in principle include trade policies. The idea is that by importing products produced with an environmentally harmful PPM, the importing country is contributing to the harm caused. The US in *Tuna-Dolphin II* seems to have made a claim along the lines of affirmative duties, arguing that its measures were taken in order to ensure that activities within its jurisdictional control (i.e. the importation and consumption of tuna in the US market) do not cause damage to the environment of other states or areas beyond the limits of national jurisdiction.[248]

Such approaches would only be relevant, it seems, when PPM-based measures addressing environmental problems located within the jurisdiction of the exporting Member were presumed to upset the balance of rights and obligations between Members and not to meet the standards in the chapeau. However, the current author submits that such a presumption is not warranted by the text of the chapeau in its context and in the light of its object and purpose. The argument usually invoked for a presumption that Article XX simply prohibits PPM-based measures is that of the "slippery slope" of "green protectionism", which may moreover be extended to PPMs relating not to environmental problems, but rather to labour and human rights standards. However, the current author does not regard this policy argument as a convincing basis for a legal presumption against this kind of measure. A case-by-case and rigorous application of the requirements in Article XX GATT will arguably suffice to avoid this "slippery slope". Such application may in many cases lead to findings against PPM-based measures, but that is not the same as a blanket presumption against them. Even PPM-based measures targeting environmental problems in the exporting country could in theory meet the standards of the chapeau.

Finally, the extent to which international agreement (in some form) exists on the environmental issue at stake will play an important role in the interpretation of the disciplines in Article XX, especially the chapeau. This role is not confined

---

[245] Encompassing not only international physical externalities but also 'non-physical externalities' or 'psychological or preservation spillovers', i.e., moral outrage in the importing country caused by local production and catching methods in the exporting country. Nollkaemper (1998) at 194. The link with morality raises the issue of the possible applicability of Article XX(a), which has not yet been invoked and is not further discussed here. In fact, a Member taking PPM-based measures to protect animal welfare outside its jurisdiction may have to invoke paragraph (a), as its protection goal may not qualify under paragraph (b) or (g).

[246] Jansen and Lugard (1999) at 534.

[247] Arguably, Principle 2 of the Rio Declaration requires states to prevent all activities under their jurisdiction that cause harm to other states or the commons. Nollkaemper (1998) at 199.

[248] *US-Tuna-Dolphin II*, unadopted, para. 3.18.

to the few multilateral environmental agreements that explicitly provide for trade measures. The extent to which international agreement exists or is being sought on any environmental issue may be a decisive criterion for the room for unilateral measures under Article XX GATT. The Appellate Body and the implementation panel in *US-Shrimp-Turtle* suggested that in order to address some environmental problems, unilateral measures may only be taken pending negotiations on a multilateral approach:

> *[I]n a context such as this one where a multilateral agreement is clearly to be preferred and where measures [...] may only be accepted under Article XX if they were allowed under an international agreement, or if they were taken further to the completion of serious good faith efforts to reach a multilateral agreement, the possibility to impose a unilateral measure [...] is more to be seen, for the purposes of Article XX, as the possibility to adopt a provisional measure allowed for emergency reasons than as a definitive "right" to take a permanent measure.*[249]

Although the difference between a right to take a permanent measure and a possibility to take a provisional measure can be disputed, this shows the importance that multilateral approaches may have in interpreting Article XX GATT when assessing unilateral measures.

5.4.1   PPM-Based Measures and the SPS and TBT Agreements

The definitions in the SPS Agreement make it clear that SPS measures are applied to protect human, animal or plant life or health *within the territory* of the Member taking the measure. Thus, there is no question of the protection of extraterritorially located resources under the SPS Agreement. That does not in itself mean that SPS measures cannot be based on PPMs, or cannot target health or life risks caused by production processes abroad. Indeed, the definition of an SPS measure explicitly states that SPS measures include '*inter alia* [...] processes and production methods; [...]'. However, these risks must threaten the domestic human, animal or plant population of the Member taking the measure, so PPM-based SPS measures will in the majority of cases be product-related. The only scenario in which the SPS Agreement could possibly cover a non-product-related PPM-based measure would seem to be when the measure targets a foreign PPM that threatens the life and health of humans, animals or plants in the state taking the measure not through the product but directly, e.g. through transboundary poisonous gases caused by the PPM.

The definitions of the SPS Agreement cover measures to protect human life and health from risks *arising from* foods, beverages and foodstuffs,[250] measures

---

[249] Panel in *US-Shrimp-Turtle Implementation*, para. 5.88.

[250] Annex A SPS Agreement, Article 1(b). Emphasis added.

to protect animals and plants against risks arising from the entry, establishment or spread of pests, diseases, and organisms carrying or causing diseases,[251] measures to protect humans against risks arising from diseases *carried* by animals, plants or products thereof or from the entry, establishment or spread of pests, and, finally, measures preventing and limiting other damage from the entry, establishment or spread of pests.[252] The only possibility for accommodating non-product-related PPM measures under these definitions would be by reference to measures addressing risks and damage caused by the entry, establishment or spread of pests or diseases. But the scenario of a foreign PPM threatening life or health or causing damage in the territory of the Member taking the measure by contamination through e.g. poisonous gases would not be covered by the words "pests" or "diseases". Thus, the only possibility of covering a non-product-related PPM-based measure would seem to be a measure addressing a PPM that causes a pest or disease to spread into the territory of the Member taking the measure, but which does not travel with the product.

The SPS definitions further include 'packaging and labelling requirements directly related to food safety'. This would seem to include the possibility of an SPS measure requiring a label indicating a non-product-related PPM. However, what exactly is meant by the limitation 'directly related to food safety' is as yet unclear. For instance, is a requirement to indicate on the label whether a product has been produced with genetically modified ingredients 'directly related to food safety'?

The TBT Agreement is silent on the location of the resources whose protection is sought. However, it does contain a limitation in its definitions. The definition of a mandatory "technical regulation" uses the words 'document which lays down product characteristics and *their related* processes and production methods [...] It may also include or deal exclusively with [...] marking or labelling requirements as they apply to a product, process or production method.' A voluntary standard, on the other hand, is a 'document [...] that provides [...] rules, guidelines or characteristics for products or *related* processes and production methods'.[253] Thus, "technical regulations" are only covered by the TBT Agreement if they lay down PPM requirements that are "related" to product characteristics. However, looking at the text of the definitions, there would seem to be no doubt that *labelling requirements* which refer to "non-product-related" PPMs are covered by the TBT Agreement. It has nevertheless been argued that the first sentence of these definitions overrides the second sentence, to the effect that the limitation of the coverage of the TBT Agreement to product-related PPMs also applies to the modes listed in the second sentence, such as

---

[251] Annex A SPS Agreement, Article 1(a).

[252] Annex A SPS Agreement, Article 1(c) and (d), respectively. Emphasis added.

[253] Definitions in Annex 1 TBT.

labelling requirements.[254] Most authors seem to favour a restricted scope of the TBT Agreement as covering only measures based on product-related PPMs.[255] However, it is submitted that the differences in wording between "or their related" in the definition for mandatory measures, "or related" in the definition for voluntary standards, and the absence of the word "related" in the second sentence of both definitions dealing with labelling requirements should have a conclusive meaning. It is not warranted by the text to argue that the whole of the TBT Agreement, including the parts of the definitions that address labelling, only covers national measures based on product-related PPM requirements.

The history of the TBT Agreement does not provide conclusive evidence of the precise meaning of the word "related" in the definitions, and also shows that the question to what extent PPMs should be covered by the TBT Agreement has now been contentious for some 25 years.[256] The fact that 'or their related' was inserted in the technical regulations definition indicates that the TBT Agreement was intended to discipline only a narrow group of mandatory PPM-based measures, not including non-product-related PPMs. However, the fact that the second sentence of the definitions of "technical regulations" and "standards" contained a broader reference to PPMs which was not discussed throughout the negotiations, suggests that labelling requirements referring to non-product-related PPMs, both mandatory and voluntary, may well have been intended to be within the purview of the TBT Agreement. A clarification by the WTO Members of the scope of the TBT Agreement in terms of production and processing methods is called for.[257] However, this is a politically highly contentious issue, and no progress in this respect has so far been made. The first and second Triennial Reviews of the TBT Agreement did not address the PPM issue.[258] However, in June 2001, it was decided to start a discussion on labelling in the TBT Committee which would include the PPM issue.

---

[254] Appleton (1997a) at 93 in footnote 36 cites a WTO official who stated that during the Uruguay Round negotiations, the second sentence was never treated as a stand-alone provision.

[255] Appleton (1997a) at 93 asserts that this is the generally accepted view, referring to Schultz (1994), Rege (1994), and Völker (1995) at 286-7. Petersmann (1993a) at 68-69 appears to leave open the question of "related".

[256] WTO document WT/CTE/W/10 (G/TBT/W/11), 'Negotiating History of the Agreement on Technical Barriers to Trade with Regard to Labelling Requirements, Voluntary Standards, and Processes and Production Methods Unrelated to Product Characteristics'.

[257] See on PPMs and labelling specifically, Abdel Motaal (1999), and Swiss paper, G/TBT/W/162.

[258] See WTO documents G/TBT/5 and G/TBT/9 (triennal reviews).

5.5 Concluding Remarks

The main WTO disciplines relevant to trade-related non-fiscal environmental measures have been examined in this Part. These are Articles III:4, XI, and XX of the GATT, and the TBT and SPS Agreements. The major developments in the interpretation of these disciplines are briefly summarised here.

After *EC-Asbestos*, "likeness" in Article III:4 is a potentially and traditionally wide concept. This may lead to increasing challenges under this provision. However, the same case has suggested that the concept of "less favourable treatment" may provide enough flexibility to avoid all sorts of regulatory measures being found to be in violation of Article III:4 and imposing on the regulating Member the burden of justifying them in terms of Article XX. At least with regard to *"de jure* neutral" measures, it appears to be no longer sufficient for a complainant to show that one imported product is being treated less favourably than one "like" domestic product. In any event, in most cases, *de jure* neutral measures may be expected to be covered by the SPS or TBT Agreement, and assessed accordingly. However, the relationship between the GATT and the TBT Agreement is not yet clear, and any assessment under either or both will also depend on the claims made by the complainant. More generally, the scope and burden of proof of the disciplines in the TBT Agreement still need clarification. Such clarification has been provided for the SPS Agreement in a number of dispute settlement reports, which clarify that the SPS Agreement imposes disciplines extending beyond the GATT.

In principle, Article XI covers non-fiscal "border measures" and Article III:4 covers internal regulatory measures. Nonetheless, a border measure may be covered by Article III through the Note Ad Article III. According to the panel in *EC-Asbestos*, in order to be covered by the Note Ad Article III, the internally applied measure does not have to be the same as the border measure; an import prohibition may be covered as enforcing an internal production prohibition. However, that does not necessarily mean that domestic production requirements can be enforced at the border by import restrictions and be covered by Article III. In order to be covered by the Note Ad Article III, the result for the competitive conditions of foreign products must be the same as for that of domestic products. This is obviously not the case when the importation of a product (tuna) is prohibited due to the enforcement of a domestic production requirement for tuna fishermen. Such measures are not covered by the Note Ad Article III and will be assessed under Article XI. An origin-neutral measure based on a production method, e.g. a sales prohibition on products produced in a certain way, may be enforced by a border measure and be covered by the Note Ad Article III. However, in order to check whether the PPM requirement is being met by the product, the importing Member will arguably need to resort to labelling or certification requirements. If those are not imposed upon domestic products this may cause National Treatment problems under Article III.

Violations of Article III or XI may be justified under Article XX GATT, which has been interpreted in a number of important trade-environment disputes. This provision in its subparagraphs imposes requirements as to the legitimate objective sought and the relationship between means and ends, as well as a general "reasonableness" requirement in its chapeau. Although the "necessary" requirement in paragraph (b) has traditionally been a major obstacle in justifying health protection measures, *EC-Asbestos* suggests a more deferential approach to that requirement. "Relating to" in paragraph (g) has been interpreted in *US-Gasoline* and *US-Shrimp-Turtle* as requiring a substantial and reasonable relationship between means and ends. Paragraph (g) moreover imposes the requirement 'made effective in conjunction with restrictions on domestic production or consumption', which has been interpreted as a test of "even-handedness" between domestic and import restrictions. Under the chapeau, the reasonableness of the application of the measure is assessed, which involves looking at whether the right to invoke exceptions is being abused and balancing the right to do so with the substantive rights of the complainant. In *US-Gasoline* and *US-Shrimp-Turtle*, similar arguments playing a role in the means-end requirements also seem to have influenced the interpretation of the chapeau. This raises the question to what extent there is a double test in Article XX, and whether the means-ends requirements and the chapeau may become increasingly conflated. Such conflation would imply that the difference between the measures as such and their application are not vital.

It is indisputable that both the SPS and the TBT Agreements allow WTO Members to challenge other Members' measures even if these are non-discriminatory. While the SPS Agreement lays down disciplines for sanitary and phytosanitary measures that may be border or internal measures, the TBT Agreement specifically concerns Members' internal technical regulations. Both Agreements signify a step in the WTO from rules based on non-discrimination to a trade obstacle test. However, the obstacle test is qualified in both Agreements; to put it simply, only "unnecessary" trade obstacles are prohibited. While the "unnecessary obstacles" test is the central obligation of the TBT Agreement, with other provisions essentially coming down to notification requirements, the set of disciplines to be met by a measure in the SPS Agreement is more elaborate. That Agreement contains, *inter alia*, a further elaboration of the "necessity" requirement as 'not more trade-restrictive than required to achieve the appropriate level of protection, taking into account technical and economic feasibility' (Article 5.6), detailed provisions regarding the risk assessment upon which an SPS measure is to be based (Article 5.1 to 5.4), and an obligation to avoid arbitrary or unjustifiable distinctions in the levels of protection considered appropriate in different situations, i.e., a requirement of consistency of a Member's SPS measures. Both the TBT and SPS Agreements refer to international standard-setting. Simplifying these references, they essentially come down to preferential treatment under the TBT and SPS disciplines of measures based on relevant international standards.

PART FOUR

Comparative Analysis

CHAPTER 6

Prohibitions, Justifications and Conditions

6.1 Typologies, Scope and Nature of the Prohibitions

Article 28 EC prohibits quantitative restrictions on imports and all measures having equivalent effect. Article XI GATT proscribes prohibitions or restrictions on imports (or exports) made effective through quotas, import or export licences or other measures. Article III:4 GATT prohibits the less favourable treatment of imported products in comparison to like domestic products in respect of internal regulatory measures affecting their sale, offering, distribution, transport and use. The TBT Agreement essentially prohibits unnecessary trade obstacles created by technical regulations, and the SPS Agreement -through an elaborate set of disciplines- seeks to ensure that (phyto-)sanitary measures are applied only to the extent necessary and are based on scientific principles. Moreover, both Agreements stimulate the recognition of equivalent standards and the use of international standards in their respective fields of application.

The preceding Chapters have addressed the essential questions of what measures are covered by the disciplines in the relevant EC and WTO provisions, and what these disciplines actually prohibit. The answers to these questions determine the extent to which the relevant rules of the EC and the WTO potentially limit domestic authority to regulate environmental and health problems. First of all, the coverage of the disciplines determines whether a national measure falls within or outside the disciplines. The coverage depends on the typologies used in the relevant provisions to designate the measures disciplined. Secondly, the nature of the disciplines themselves is equally important in determining which measures are disciplined and which measures are not. A rule of non-discrimination or one against protectionism is relative: it disciplines the treatment of imported goods relative to that of domestic goods, but it does not extend to non-discriminatory and non-protectionist measures. A prohibition of trade obstacles, on the other hand, is absolute in that it applies regardless of whether there is domestic production of the products at issue. It therefore also covers non-discriminatory and non-protectionist measures, inviting their justification according to the relevant provisions and the conditions attached which will be discussed hereafter. It is not surprising that the coverage of the prohibition and the typology of the measure are more important when the prohibition is absolute (trade obstacles) than when it is relative (discrimination).

6.1.1 Typologies and Nature of the Prohibitions

The EC Treaty contains only one basic provision regarding import-restrictive measures of a non-fiscal nature, i.e. Article 28 EC. However, the interpretation of this unitary provision by the Court of Justice has resulted in at least one important typological qualification. The Court focused its attention on the typology of national measures by introducing in *Keck* a separate test for "selling arrangements" which fall outside the scope of Article 28 if they are non-discriminatory. In *Keck*, the Court also represented its earlier interpretations of Article 28 as a prohibition of unjustified trade obstacles, applying essentially to product requirements. Thus, after *Keck*, one might be tempted to conclude that an obstacles test applies to product requirements and a discrimination test applies to selling arrangements.[1] However, the range of measures covered by the wide *Dassonville* formula for interpreting Article 28 is not exhausted by these two notions. According to the Court's case-law, a "third category" of national measures that are neither product requirements nor selling arrangements in principle falls within the obstacles test of *Dassonville*.[2] It has been argued above that the *Keck* limitation should also apply to "third category" measures.[3]

The typologies for non-fiscal trade barriers in the WTO Agreements are much more complicated. GATT Article XI prohibits the institution or mainte-nance of 'prohibitions or restrictions other than duties, taxes or other charges, whether made effective through quotas, import or export licences or other meas-ures, [...] on the importation (or exportation) of any product [...]'. Article III:4 prohibits the treatment of imported products less favourable than that accorded to like domestic products in respect of 'all laws, regulations and requirements affecting their internal sale, offering for sale, purchase, transportation, distribu-tion or use'. Thus, the coverage of Article III:4 plainly covers measures that would be denominated "selling arrangements" as identified by the European Court of Justice in the EC context. The TBT Agreement defines a technical regulation as a 'document which lays down product characteristics or their related processes and production methods, including the applicable administra-tive provisions, with which compliance is mandatory'. Finally, the SPS Agree-ment defines a sanitary or phytosanitary measure as a measure applied to protect animal or plant life or health from risks of pests and diseases, to protect human or animal life or health from food-borne risks, to protect human life or health from animal and plant diseases and pests, or to prevent or limit other damage from pests.

The history of the interpretation of both the EC and the GATT/WTO provi-sions regarding the liberalisation of trade in goods reflects the profound ques-tion whether such provisions should only prohibit the discriminatory or protec-tionist measures of their members, or whether they should rather go further and discipline measures that pose obstacles to trade, regardless of whether they discriminate against imports or protect domestic production. When a prohibi-

---

[1] As possibly qualified by a market access requirement, see Section 6.1.2.

[2] An example is a restriction on the use of certain goods, e.g. the use of cars during rush hours or on Sundays.

[3] See Section 3.1.2.

tion of discrimination is taken to include "material", "indirect" or *"de facto"* discrimination, trade liberalisation rules discipline national regulatory powers to a greater extent than when only facial, direct or *de jure* discrimination is prohibited. The introduction of a prohibition of trade obstacles stretches the reach of trade liberalisation commitments into national regulatory powers even further. Logically, the more intrusive an approach is taken in the interpretation of the provisions at issue, the more acutely the need arises to accommodate the legitimate regulatory objectives of the members. This can be done by limiting the scope of the basic prohibitions, e.g. by typological qualifications. It can also be done through accepting justification grounds for measures that would otherwise violate the prohibitions. The justifications and conditions attached to their acceptance are discussed *infra* in Sections 6.2 and 6.3.

As is apparent from this work, Article 28, the key provision of the EC Treaty, was interpreted by the European Court of Justice in *Dassonville* as a prohibition of trade obstacles covering a wide range of measures, enabling in principle the challenging of all kinds of measures not discriminating against imports or protecting domestic producers, and not specifically directed at limiting imports either. By contrast, GATT Article III:4 centres on a prohibition of discrimination, and Article XI only prohibits measures specifically prohibiting or restricting imports (or exports). Although such measures are not necessarily discriminatory or protective, as they may also apply in the absence of domestic production of similar or competitive products, they are only prohibited by Article XI if specifically directed at limiting imports.

However, the description of the EC regime as essentially based upon an "obstacles test" and the GATT regime as essentially based upon a "discrimination test" and a prohibition of specific import restrictions must be qualified. In the EC, the Court of Justice has never applied the obstacles test with full rigour to pricing measures, but rather a discrimination or protection test. Moreover, it has made an important qualification to the "obstacles test" in *Keck*, according to which non-discriminatory "selling arrangements" are outside the scope of Article 28. This discrimination test appears in turn to be qualified by a prohibition; if selling arrangements completely bar the market access of imported products, they may be covered by the prohibition of Article 28 after all, even if they are non-discriminatory (i.e. equally barring the market access of domestic products).[4] Finally, the Court has limited the scope of Article 28 by ruling that it does not cover measures whose trade effects are too remote or uncertain.[5] Strictly speaking, measures hindering trade but justified by a "mandatory requirement" also fall outside the ambit of Article 28. However, following the Court's approach, this study treats "mandatory requirements" as justifications

---

[4]   See Section 6.1.2.

[5]   In cases such as C-379/92 *Peralta*.

for infringements of Article 28 rather than as limitations to the coverage of the Article 28 prohibition.[6]

Under the WTO rules, internal regulatory measures not specifically directed at imports are not in violation of GATT rules as long as they do not discriminate or protect, even if they result in barring market access. However, within the GATT framework, additional disciplines to address non-discriminatory technical regulations were proposed as early as in 1973. This resulted in the 1979 Tokyo Round Agreement on Technical Barriers to Trade (TBT). Article 2.1 of the 1979 TBT Agreement prompted parties to ensure that technical regulations and standards or their application would not have the effect of creating *unnecessary obstacles to international trade.*[7] The provision appears to date back to the 1973 draft, which was even before the European Court of Justice passed its judgment in *Dassonville.*[8] It should be noted that the 1979 TBT Agreement was only binding upon the signatories, which were far fewer than the GATT contracting parties. Moreover, the 1979 TBT Agreement had its own dispute settlement provisions. However, after the Uruguay Round, the TBT Agreement was transformed into the current multilateral agreement that forms part of the "single undertaking" of the WTO Agreements, and now it is compulsory for all of its Members. The 1994 TBT Agreement also contains a prohibition of unnecessary trade obstacles (Article 2.2). The SPS Agreement does not explicitly lay down an obstacles prohibition. Yet it applies to all sanitary and phytosanitary measures 'which may, directly or indirectly, affect international trade' (Article 1.1 SPS), and contains disciplines that go beyond a non-discrimination requirement that may be read as a qualified obstacles test much in the same way as that found in the TBT Agreement.

Thus, while the prohibition of trade obstacles remains a centrepiece of the EC regime on trade and environment, there are limits to its application, and for certain types of measures, the prohibition is limited to discrimination (albeit in turn probably qualified by a prohibition to prevent market access). At the same time, while the GATT non-discrimination requirement of Article III is still one of the major WTO disciplines, the TBT and SPS Agreements have introduced disciplines going beyond that test, including a prohibition of unnecessary trade obstacles.

---

[6] They are accordingly discussed as justifications in Section 6.2 *infra*.

[7] Emphasis added.

[8] This assertion is based on the account of the negotiations by Bernier (1982) at 199, and on GATT Activities publications from 1968 to 1979.

6.1.2   Recognition and Market Access

The consequence of the obstacles test in the EC as laid down by the Court of Justice in its *Cassis de Dijon* case-law is that products lawfully marketed or produced in one Member State must be permitted market access in another Member State unless there is a justification for refusing to do so. Thus, the Court imposed the recognition of regulatory standards in other Member States, with the burden on the importing Member State of proving why it does not accept products conforming to those standards. In the EC, a complaint may be limited to merely pointing at a potential trade obstacle. The basic disciplines in the TBT Agreement also oblige Members to ensure that technical regulations are not 'prepared, adopted or applied with a view to or with the effect of creating unnecessary obstacles to international trade'. "Unnecessary" is elaborated by referring to a least trade-restrictiveness test and legitimate objectives (Article 2.2 TBT). This arguably amounts to a discipline similar to that in *Cassis de Dijon*: the application of technical regulations to imported products is only acceptable when necessary for fulfilling legitimate objectives. Hence, applying technical regulations that are not necessary to fulfil such objectives to imports would contravene the TBT Agreement. A strict application of this discipline could eventually lead to a *de facto* obligation of recognition.

However, there is a difference in the division of the burden of proof. While the interpretation of Article 28 by the ECJ presumes that a product lawfully produced and marketed in one Member State conforms to requirements pursuing legitimate objectives, with the importing Member State needing to explain why the product does not conform to its particular requirements, the TBT Agreement does not make such a presumption. Article 2.7 TBT, read in combination with Article 2.2 TBT, makes it clear that the TBT Agreement does not *oblige* Members to accept products lawfully produced and marketed in other Members. Even if the importing Member is satisfied that the exporting Member's regulations fulfil the objectives that the importing Member's regulations seek, Article 2.7 only obliges it to give positive consideration to accepting the equivalence of foreign regulations, not to accept them. Thus, the TBT Agreement does not impose the recognition of foreign technical regulations; it merely provides the exporting Member with the possibility to complain that products lawfully produced and marketed in its territory are subjected to requirements that result in unnecessary trade obstacles. An exporting WTO Member will have to adduce a *prima facie* case that this results in an unnecessary trade obstacle. Only if such a *prima facie* case is made will the importing Member need to demonstrate that the application of its technical regulation is necessary.

In the SPS Agreement, Members are obliged to accept the SPS measures of other Members as being equivalent, if the exporting Member objectively demonstrates that its measures achieve the importing Member's appropriate level of protection. Here again, the initial burden is on the exporting Member rather than on the importing Member. Thus, while imposing disciplines going beyond non discrimination requirements, and making a cautious start towards "mutual recognition", the TBT and SPS Agreements do not impose the marketability in one WTO Member of products lawfully produced and marketed in another Member subject to justification for deviations, in the same way in which the ECJ has imposed it in its interpretation of Article 28 EC.

Different understandings of the concept of "market access" may cause confusion when applied in the EC and WTO contexts. Arguably, "market access" in the WTO context means 'not being prevented by import restrictions from entering an export market'. This simply means access to the territory of another Member. Within the GATT disciplines, market access is guaranteed principally by Article I (most-favoured nation treatment with regard to *inter alia* 'rules and formalities in connection with importation and exportation'), Article II (no tariffs above the tariff bindings) and Article XI (no prohibitions or restrictions upon importation). Once on the market, i.e. having paid the tariff applicable if any and having complied with customs formalities, the competitive conditions of imported products *vis-à-vis* domestic products are protected by Article III. However, Article III does not guarantee market access as such. It only guarantees treatment which is no less favourable for imported products as compared to domestic products with regard to both fiscal and non-fiscal regulations that condition the sale, offering for sale, distribution, etc. of the product. Thus, neither Article XI nor Article III guarantees that imported products can actually be marketed in the importing country. All that market access amounts to in the WTO context is getting a product across the border and not being discriminated thereafter. That is not the same as ensuring that the product can actually be offered for sale or be sold.

In the EC, on the other hand, "market access" appears to be associated not only with entering the territory of another Member State, but also with the product not being prevented from actually being put on the market. That involves a great deal more than merely passing customs formalities; it includes meeting all sorts of product requirements and other internal regulatory requirements. As the EC Commission puts it, 'placing on the market is the initial action of making a product available for the first time on the Community market, with a view to distribution or use in the Community'.[9] Moreover, in order to be marketed, a product must in most cases also be transported and distributed. The ECJ's reference to measures preventing market access in *Keck* suggests that "market access" comprises even more than this. If a "selling arrangement" having the result that an imported product cannot be sold at all is caught by the prohibition in Article 28 and needs justification, "market access" could be taken to mean that a product should be able to pass all customs formalities, to be

---

[9]   EC Commission (2000a), at 18.

marketed, *and* to be sold. The concept could arguably be stretched even further, so as to include all other internal prohibitions that are capable of making it *de facto* impossible for imported products to compete on the market. Examples are prohibitions on registering, using, possessing or disposing of certain products. In other words, an extensive reading of the concept of "market access" would seem to equal the absence of obstacles to trade in the sense of the *Dassonville* formula.

Articles XI and III GATT do not warrant a similar obstacles-based understanding of "market access". All sorts of internal requirements that affect the marketing, sale, use, transport or distribution of goods once they have entered a Member's territory are covered by Article III GATT and not by Article XI, even if they result in preventing the product at issue from being marketed, sold, used etc. They are consequently subject to a non-discrimination requirement, and not to an obstacles requirement. This is even so when such requirements are applied at the border in the case of the imported product, as the Note Ad Article III makes clear.[10] Thus, a prohibition to distribute or use a product does not need justification under GATT rules, while it does under EC rules. A prohibition on selling a product does not need justification under GATT rules, while it might under EC rules (if the reference by the Court of Justice to market access in *Keck* has a separate meaning, see *infra*). These differences are attenuated by the TBT and SPS Agreements, to the extent that measures barring the market access of imported products may be typified as technical regulations or SPS measures. The TBT and SPS Agreements go beyond the GATT rules by enabling WTO Members to seek market access, e.g. by disciplining non-discriminatory internal measures.

In the EC context, the typological reference to "selling arrangements" by the Court of Justice in *Keck* has been criticised. Why should a ban on selling cigarettes from machines be excluded from the scope of Article 28, while a ban on smoking in public places does fall within the scope of Article 28 and need justification?[11] The same question can be posed when there is a restriction on the sale of cars without a catalytic converter and a restriction on the use of such cars, respectively. There appears to be no logical explanation for applying a preliminary non-discrimination test to selling arrangements, while treating "third category measures", i.e. measures that regulate neither product requirements nor selling arrangements, as covered by the obstacles test and requiring justification, whether they are discriminatory or not. In addition to creating uncertainty by introducing the term "selling arrangements", the Court was

---

[10] In *EC-Asbestos*, for instance, an internal prohibition on the manufacture, sale, offering for sale, and use of asbestos was applied at the border by means of an import prohibition. It was covered by Article III and not XI, even if completely barring market access for the imported product.

[11] Weiler (1999) at 372.

somewhat unclear in *Keck* as to the role to be played by "market access". The Court left it open whether its statement on selling arrangements preventing market access in paragraph 17 should be seen as a stand-alone requirement or rather as flowing from the non-discrimination test in paragraph 16. It has been argued that as selling arrangements that are non-discriminatory in law and in fact may prevent market access altogether, there is indeed a separate market access requirement, failing which the measure at issue will need to be justified.[12] The current author supports this view.

The discontent with the Court's typology of "selling arrangements" and the lack of clarity as regards the role played by market access have led to proposals to apply a more general "market access test" to Article 28 EC. Under such a test, *de jure* discriminatory measures always need justification. Arguably, the same goes for product characteristics, even if they are *de jure* equally applicable to domestic and imported products, because they *per se* prevent products lawfully produced and marketed elsewhere but not conforming to the product requirement, from being marketed.[13] Other non-discriminatory measures that substantially impede access to the market (including the extreme case of preventing market access altogether) breach Article 28 and need justification.[14] Some have coupled a proposed general market access test to a proposal to drop the reference to "selling arrangements".[15] The test would hence also apply to "third category measures" such as restrictions on the distribution, transportation, registration, use, and disposal of goods. It has also been proposed to limit the market access test to a requirement that justification is only needed for those measures that prevent market access altogether, rather than for all those measures substantially restricting market access.[16]

Thus, according to these proposals, when discrimination is found, justification is always needed. However, the content of the discrimination test in some proposals is confined to *de jure* discrimination, while in others it includes *de facto* discrimination.[17] The main question that remains is what to do with those measures impeding trade that are difficult or impossible to tackle on the basis

---

[12] Barnard (2001) at 48; Eeckhout (2000); Weatherill (1996).

[13] AG Jacobs in Case C-412/93 *Leclerc-Siplec*, para. 44.

[14] Barnard (2001) at 52; cf. Weatherill (1996), Chalmers (1994) at 401, and AG Jacobs in Case C-412/93 *Leclerc-Siplec*, paras. 41-47 of his opinion.

[15] Weiler (1999) at 372; Weatherill (1996).

[16] Weiler (1999) at 372-73, regards this market access rule as a 'special rule of free movement', which complements a 'general rule of free movement' that stipulates that national provisions that are discriminatory in law or in fact need justification.

[17] Weatherill (1996) and AG Jacobs in Case C-412/93 *Leclerc-Siplec* propose a *de jure* test, while the Court itself in *Keck* applies a *de jure* and *de facto* test, which Weiler (1999) appears to endorse as a general rule.

of a discrimination test? Of course, the group of remaining measures is larger when only *de jure* discrimination is prohibited than when *de facto* discrimination is included. In any event, when no discrimination is found, "market access" plays a predominant role in the proposed tests, determining whether non-discriminatory measures need justification or not. Again, "market access" in such tests is understood in the wide sense of being able to access a Member State's territory, to be transported, distributed, marketed, offered for sale, sold, and possibly even used and disposed of. The rationale behind market access tests is the objective of an internal market:

> *If an obstacle to inter-State trade exists, it cannot cease to exist simply because an identical obstacle affects domestic trade. [...] from the point of view of the Treaty's concern to establish a single market, discrimination is not a helpful criterion: from that point of view, the fact that a Member State imposes similar restrictions on the marketing of domestic goods is simply irrelevant. The adverse effect on the Community market is in no way alleviated; nor is the adverse effect on the economies of the other Member States, and so on the Community economy.*[18]

It is recalled that achieving an internal market is not an objective or instrument of the WTO. Nevertheless, the question what to do with measures that impede trade, but are difficult to tackle on the basis of a non-discrimination test, has also presented itself in the WTO context. It has been suggested that a combination of a prohibition of non-discrimination and of preventing market access as seen in the EC reflects the GATT situation.[19] However, this argument is based on a wide reading of Article XI GATT that is not reflected in its wording or interpretation, and is arguably not warranted by the structure of the GATT obligations in Articles XI and III.[20] Moreover, surprisingly, the wide interpretation of Article XI GATT is deduced from the panel report in the *EC-Hormones* case, which did not address the European hormone beef ban under Article XI, but under the SPS Agreement.[21] The SPS and TBT Agreement indeed go beyond the GATT in disciplining non-discriminatory measures. However, from that fact alone one

---

[18] AG Jacobs in Case C-412/93 *Leclerc-Siplec*, paras. 39-40.

[19] Weiler (1999) at 356.

[20] According to Weiler, Article XI in principle prohibits not only quotas but also 'measures the effect of which is to prevent, like a quota, access to the market', unless such measures are justified. In his view, '[a]ny measure effectively preventing an imported product from being put into the stream of commerce [...] would be caught by the prohibition' in Article XI. Ibid. at 356.

[21] Ibid. at 374: 'The GATT until recently never took seriously its own Article XI and the prohibition contained therein. [...] it was rare to challenge non-discriminatory quantitative restrictions even where those totally barred access of imported products to a domestic market. [...] *Hormones* represents the bending of the GATT towards the obstacles rationale of the EC.'

cannot infer a wider reach of GATT Article XI. On the contrary, further-reaching obligations were negotiated precisely within the confines of the SPS and TBT Agreements, not the GATT. It would seem that the wider obligations on non-discriminatory trade obstacles in these Agreements were not intended to widen the prohibitions in the basic GATT provisions.

6.2 Justifications for Measures Otherwise Infringing Prohibitions

6.2.1 Justification Grounds

The exceptions provision in the EC Treaty, Article 30 EC, refers to 'prohibitions or restrictions [...] justified on grounds of [...] the protection of health and life of humans, animals or plants', and Article XX GATT refers in paragraph (b) to 'measures [...] necessary to protect human, animal or plant life or health' and in paragraph (g) to 'measures [...] relating to the conservation of exhaustible natural resources [...]'. When comparing Articles 30 EC and XX GATT, the first thing that strikes one is that the exception of protecting exhaustible natural resources in Article XX(g) is not included in Article 30 EC. As the drafters of the EC Treaty, and in particular of Article 30 thereof, clearly had the text of Article XX GATT before them, one wonders why that ground for an exception was omitted. Perhaps one of the answers is that exhaustible natural resources were partially covered by the ECSC and Euratom treaties. Probably more importantly, to allow trade restrictive measures to be justified under Article 30 would have opened the door to economic considerations in that provision. Article 30 was not intended to cater for purely economic considerations, as the Court subsequently consistently held.[22] In an internal market, the free movement of production factors should in principle include that of raw materials. One of the objectives of the Community environmental policy is the prudent and rational utilisation of natural resources (see Article 174(1) EC).

Originally, Article XX(g) was drafted in order to allow countries to restrict exports of natural resources such as minerals.[23] Article XX(g) has since been interpreted to include living resources, which results in a considerable overlap with Article XX(b).[24] Thus, it appears that the exception in paragraph (g) was originally intended for purposes of economic policy, and was subsequently reinterpreted as an environmental exception. Arguably, measures for the protec-

---

[22] See e.g. Cases 72/83 *Campus Oil*, C-203/96 *Dusseldorp*, C-379/98 *Preussen Elektra*. In *Campus Oil*, the Court did accept economic considerations that were intricately linked to security motives.

[23] See Charnovitz (1991) at 45, and Fauchald (1998) at 330.

[24] See *Canada-Herring and Salmon*, *US-Tuna* (1982), and the AB in *US-Shrimp-Turtle*.

tion of fish and other animals justified under Article XX(g) could be justified under the life and health exception too. However, as long as Article XX(g) contains conditions that are more easily met than those in paragraph (b) (see *infra*), Members will continue to invoke it for such objectives. In addition, the reference to exhaustible natural resources, already interpreted to cover "clean air" in *US-Gasoline*, arguably enables the justification of measures aimed at addressing important environmental problems such as ozone depletion or climate change.

Once non-discriminatory measures began to be challenged under the wide interpretation of the basic discipline in Article 28 EC, the need was felt to expand upon the limited exceptions Article, which had been conceived at a time when such a wide interpretation of the basic prohibition had arguably not been foreseen. Thus, in *Cassis de Dijon* the Court of Justice invented the concept of "mandatory requirements" that could justify "indistinctly applicable" measures that were potentially within the scope of the widely interpreted basic prohibition and not covered *ratione materiae* by the exceptions in Article 30. The Court's case-law is not always clear and consistent on the interpretation of the concept of "indistinctly applicable", i.e. whether it refers only to "directly", "facially" or *"de jure"* discriminatory measures or also to "indirect", "material" or *de facto* discrimination. This author submits that "indistinctly applicable" should be understood as a formal criterion, i.e. excluding only those measures that differentiate on the basis of product origin or are otherwise linked to product origin. This approach implies that formally neutral measures that are *de facto* detrimental to imports and would be prohibited by Article 28 may nevertheless be justified by a mandatory requirement.

In the WTO context, under the disciplines of Articles XI and III GATT, only measures specifically targeting imports and discriminatory internal measures can be challenged. It has been argued in this work that most cases in which internal regulatory measures have been assessed under Article III GATT have involved differentiations somehow linked to product origin, i.e. formal or *de jure* discrimination. However, the text of Article III:4 also enables Members to challenge *de facto* discriminatory measures, and in a small number of cases this has been done.[25] The possibility of assessing *de jure* neutral measures under National Treatment provisions was expressly laid down in the equivalent GATS provision, Article XVII.[26] Nevertheless, as the GATT disciplines were never interpreted as widely as the general trade obstacles test for Article 28 EC, the need for the expansion of the justification grounds in addition to those found in the

---

[25] See e.g. the GATT panels in *Canada-Alcohol, US-Beer,* and *US-Auto Taxes* (unadopted) and the WTO panels in *EC-Bananas III* and *EC-Asbestos.*

[26] Even if the meaning of 'inherent competitive disadvantages' in that provision is unclear. See Section 5.3.3.

GATT's main exceptions provision, Article XX, was not felt to the same extent as in the EC. During the Uruguay Round negotiations, Article XX was not changed so as to include "environmental protection". Apparently, parties deemed environmental protection to be sufficiently covered by the Article XX exceptions, and no need was felt to make this explicit in Article XX.[27] However, in a development to some extent parallel to the EC situation, when basic disciplines were agreed on in the TBT Agreement reaching beyond the GATT disciplines, the list of legitimate objectives in the TBT Agreement was also added to in comparison with Article XX GATT, by referring to *inter alia* "environmental protection".

6.2.2 Justifying Formally Discriminatory Environmental Measures in the EC

The ECJ, after having stated for over 40 years that the exception grounds in Article 30 need to be narrowly interpreted, has arguably started to extend the scope of the 'protection of animal life and health' in the *Bluhme* case.[28] Moreover, in a number of judgments it has used the words "environmental protection" in the context of Article 30 justifications, suggesting that (some) environmental protection goals can be read into the grounds of the exception provision.[29] Still, environmental objectives are conceivable that are not even covered by a wide interpretation of the exception ground in Article 30. Examples are the prevention of litter not posing any health risk, at issue in *Danish Bottles*, and other environmental measures taken for aesthetic rather than life or health reasons, such as measures protecting certain countryside landscapes. Considering the traditional requirement that measures need to be "indistinctly applicable" in order to qualify for justification under a mandatory requirement, such objectives cannot be pursued by formally discriminatory measures. Proposals by Austria, Germany and a reflection group to add the ground of "environmental protection" to Article 30 during the 1996 Intergovernmental Conference that led to the Amsterdam Treaty did not succeed.[30] The 2000 Treaty of Nice again did not result in such a change.

---

[27] When Article XIV GATS, the exceptions provision that parallels Article XX GATT, was discussed during the Uruguay Round, a draft discussion paper by the GATT Secretariat stated that 'the common understanding of Parties, based on the opinion of the GATT legal service division, is confirmed that measures necessary to protect human, animal and plant life and health are understood to include measures necessary to protect the environment'. C2-ART, Revised Secretariat draft based on discussions, 29 November 1991, as cited by Wilkinson (1994) at 401.

[28] See Section 2.2.1.

[29] See Case 125/88 *Improsol* and Case C-473/98 *Toolex Alpha*.

[30] IGC Briefing No.32: European Environmental Policy and the 1996 IGC, at the time available on the website of the European Parliament.

Nonetheless, Member States have occasionally felt the need to take formally discriminatory measures in order to pursue legitimate objectives such as environmental protection not mentioned in the treaty exceptions of Article 30. Advocate-General Jacobs has even gone as far as asserting that

> *[n]ational measures for the protection of the environment are* inherently *liable to differentiate on the basis of the nature and origin of the cause of harm, and are therefore liable to be found discriminatory, precisely because they are based on such accepted principles as that 'environmental damage should as a priority be rectified at source' [...]. Where such measures* necessarily *have a discriminatory impact of that kind, the possibility that they may be justified should not be excluded.*[31]

Although the words "inherently" and "necessarily" appear somewhat exaggerated, as many environmental protection objectives not covered by the life and health exception can arguably be attained by means of non-discriminatory measures, Jacobs convincingly makes the point that, sometimes, environmental measures simply need to discriminate. And indeed, this need has prompted the ECJ to accept environmental objectives as justifying discriminatory measures, in spite of its usual statement that "mandatory requirements" can only justify "indistinctly applicable measures".[32] The fact that the Court has so far shied away from making its change of mind explicit is probably due to a fear of possible spillovers to other mandatory requirements, and perhaps also to other free movement clauses than those concerning goods.

6.2.3   Justifying Formally Discriminatory Environmental Measures in the WTO

It is not inconceivable that a need will arise in the WTO context similar to that in the EC, when a WTO Member applies a formally discriminatory measure with an environmental objective not covered by Article XX GATT. It should be noted, however, that infringements of Article III or XI GATT may to a large extent be justified by an extensive interpretation of the justification grounds in Article XX GATT, even if that provision - just as Article 30 EC - does not explicitly mention "environmental protection". For instance, the Appellate Body has adopted a wide interpretation of the term "exhaustible natural resources" in Article XX(g) in *US-Shrimp-Turtle*. Even more importantly, in the same case it endorsed a dynamic interpretation of that term in the light of the reference to sustainable development in the preamble to the WTO Agree-

---

[31] AG Jacobs in his opinion in Case C-379/98 *Preussen Elektra*, para. 233. Emphasis added.

[32] See Cases C-2/90 *Walloon Waste*, C-389/96 *Aher Waggon*, C-314/98 *Snellers*, and C-379/98 *Preussen Elektra*.

ment. This indicates that a large part of the need to discriminate in order to protect the environment can be accommodated with reference to Article XX GATT. Nonetheless, discriminatory measures that are aimed at protecting the environment and not covered by any of the existing paragraphs of Article XX are conceivable. The same examples mentioned in the EC context may come to mind, such as measures against littering and for landscape protection. Measures pursuing such environmental objectives not covered by Article XX GATT may be challenged as violations of Article III:4 GATT. Perhaps they may in part be saved by a flexible interpretation of "less favourable treatment", as suggested by the Appellate Body in *EC-Asbestos*. This may save some environmental measures that do not differentiate on the basis of product origin but are nevertheless challenged as having discriminatory effects. It would however be difficult to save *de jure* discriminatory environmental measures in this way.

Unlike Article XX GATT, the TBT Agreement does explicitly refer to "environmental protection". This is a welcome reference, since, as discussed above, the TBT Agreement disciplines non-discriminatory measures that are not prohibited by GATT Articles XI and III. It seems only reasonable to have more justification grounds at Members' disposal as a complement to such further-reaching disciplines. However, the TBT Agreement contains no general exceptions article like Article XX GATT. This raises the question how discriminatory technical regulations could be justified, if at all. The structure of the TBT Agreement suggests that the "legitimate objectives" in Article 2.2 are not available to justify breaches of the National Treatment (and Most-Favoured Nation Treatment) obligations in Article 2.1. That would imply that the TBT flatly prohibits any discriminatory technical regulations and that Members accused of breaching Article 2.1 TBT would have to refer in defence of such regulations to Article XX GATT.[33] The problem of how to justify formally discriminatory environmental measures does not present itself in the SPS Agreement, the disciplines of which apply to both discriminatory and non-discriminatory SPS measures. An SPS measure may discriminate, as long as the discrimination is not unjustifiable or arbitrary, and as long as the other requirements of the SPS Agreement are met.

6.2.4 Comparison: How Big is the Problem?

How large or small is the group of strictly environmental aims that may not be covered by an extensive interpretation of Article 30 EC and/or the acceptance of the mandatory requirement of environmental protection as a justification for discriminatory measures in the EC? Likewise, in the WTO, how many measures will not be covered by the reference to "environmental

---

[33] This view is expressed by Hudec (1998) at 644.

protection" in the TBT Agreement and an extensive interpretation of Article XX GATT? Considering the wide interpretation of Article XX GATT, the group of environmental measures that are not accommodated by the WTO rules appears to be rather small. Examples given above are measures against non-dangerous litter and landscape protection. Considering the lack of reference to exhaustible natural resources, the group of environmental measures not accommodated by Article 30 EC appears to be somewhat larger. Whether measures addressing e.g. climate change or ozone depletion are covered by the life and health exception in Article 30 EC depends on the causal connection required between the measure and its objective. If such measures do qualify under the exception of Article 30 EC, it will in any event be more difficult for them to fulfil the conditions attached to justification discussed *infra*, as they protect life and health only indirectly.

Much of the problem in the EC would be resolved by a clear stance by the ECJ on its acceptability of the justification of discriminatory measures under the mandatory requirement of environmental protection. As signalled in Part 2, the Court tends to accept such justifications, but only tacitly. Measures addressing resources such as clean air, an intact ozone layer or a climate not unduly changed by fossil fuel burning can arguably be covered by the concept of "environmental protection". In *Preussen Elektra*, the Court did not explicitly choose either "environmental protection" or Article 30, but anyhow it found discriminatory measures aiming at stimulating green energy to be acceptable with reference to the Community's policy to combat climate change. However, the Court's reasoning in that case was unsatisfactory. The Court not only failed to clarify whether a discriminatory measure may be justified by the mandatory requirement of environmental protection, but also omitted any reference to proportionality. As a result, the failure of the measure at issue to accept green electricity from other Member States that was equally capable of contributing to combating greenhouse gases was not properly addressed.[34]

6.2.5 Justifications and their Relationship to Prohibitions

Prohibitions are difficult to separate from justifications. Even in the EC, which aims to achieve an internal market, prohibiting trade obstacles *per se* would lead to absurd and undesirable results as long as there are differences between Member States. Such differences may relate to e.g. natural endowments, and cultural habits and preferences of local populations. Such differences will not be completely 'harmonised away' by Community legislation. Accordingly, they must be accommodated by accepting trade obstacles that are justified by national regulatory objectives. Hence 'obstacles to movement within

---

[34] See Goossens and Emmerechts (2001).

the Community resulting from disparities between the national laws relating to the marketing of the products in question must be accepted in so far as those provisions must be recognised as being necessary in order to satisfy mandatory requirements' (*Cassis de Dijon*). In other words, the obstacles test in Article 28 EC is not absolute. Likewise, in the application of a prohibition of discrimination, regulatory objectives may be taken into account as the reasons for which differentiations are made. Therefore, although the basic prohibitions discussed in this work may be isolated from the justifications for the sake of structuring the study, just as they are separated by adjudicators and dispute parties for the sake of dividing the burden of proof, these separations should not obscure the fact that basic disciplines and justifications are intimately related. The less far-reaching the basic discipline, the less resort to justifications is required, and *vice versa*.

Looking at the basic prohibitions and exceptions in the EC Treaty and the GATT, at first sight the following pattern emerges. First, a violation of one of the basic prohibitions (Article 28 EC, Article XI or III GATT) is alleged. If such a violation is indeed found, the EC Member State or WTO Member defending its measure will invoke one of the exceptions in Article 30 EC or Article XX GATT, and will argue that the conditions attached to these exceptions have been fulfilled. However, this pattern becomes much less straightforward once the basic prohibition is extensively interpreted (as in the EC) or added to by other provisions (as in the WTO), and the possibilities for justification are accordingly widened. In the EC, *Cassis de Dijon* made an explicit link between the prohibition ("obstacles"), the justification ("mandatory requirements") and the condition ("necessary"). However, the ECJ treats justifications under mandatory requirements in the same way as under Article 30 EC: a trade obstacle is challenged and the Member State needs to rebut the claimed breach of Article 28 EC by reference to a mandatory requirement and by showing that the relevant conditions have been fulfilled.

Under the WTO rules, an infringement of the obstacle discipline in the TBT Agreement is only found when the obstacle is unnecessary, i.e. more trade-restrictive than necessary to fulfil a legitimate objective. A GATT publication discussing the 1979 TBT Agreement stated that the problem had been to 'strike a balance between [...] essential needs [...] and the demand of exporters that their goods should not unreasonably or unfairly be excluded from the market.'[35] The similarity with the language employed by the European Court of Justice in the *Dassonville* and *Cassis de Dijon* judgments is striking. The 1994 TBT Agreement explicitly includes "environmental protection" among the "legitimate objectives" whose fulfilment may render a technical regulation 'not more trade-restrictive than necessary' and hence not an "unnecessary trade obstacle". Here, too, the

---

[35]   GATT (1979b) at 62.

prohibition, the justification and the conditions attached to that justification cannot be neatly separated as in the "classic" pattern. Thus, the 1994 TBT Agreement reflects a development that parallels that in *Dassonville* and *Cassis de Dijon*: extending the basic prohibition, at the same time providing for more justification possibilities, and blurring the dividing line between the two. The claimant bears a heavier burden of proof than under Article 28 EC, however; it will not be sufficient to limit the claim to the existence of a trade obstacle, because arguments as to the lack of necessity of that obstacle will need to be adduced.

Also in the SPS Agreement, the disciplines, justifications and conditions cannot meaningfully be separated. Even under Articles III and XX GATT, the distinction between prohibition and justification may not be so clear-cut after all. It has been argued that national treatment is inherently unstable, and 'with time and pressure seems to metamorphose into more rigorous tests'. National treatment testing of *de jure* equally applicable measures easily shades into necessity testing.[36] Indeed, if the reason for regulatory distinctions is evaluated in order to assess whether there is *de facto* discrimination under Article III, one may wonder what is the remaining role for the exceptions in Article XX in justifying *de facto* discriminatory measures. Suppose a measure is found to *de facto* discriminate under Article III because the regulatory distinction made is not justified by the regulatory objective. Could the measure then still be justified under Article XX, especially its chapeau which refers to 'unjustifiable or arbitrary discrimination'? Up to now, this problem has been largely avoided by GATT and WTO panels and the Appellate Body. After *Japan-Alcohol* and *EC-Asbestos*, it seems clear that the consideration of regulatory objectives does not play a role in determining "likeness" under Article III GATT. It is still open to debate to what extent such objectives may play a part in determining whether *de jure* neutral regulatory measures assessed under Article III:4 treat imports less favourably than like domestic products and thereby protect domestic production. It may be expected that the consideration of regulatory objectives will be kept outside Article III:4 assessments as far as possible. The question under Article III:4 is whether a measure, e.g. a regulatory distinction, treats imports less favourably than like domestic products. The questions under Article XX are whether the measure - and not the distinction it makes - has a regulatory objective covered by one of the exception grounds, whether the measure - not the distinction it makes - meets the means-ends tests, and whether the application of the measure constitutes unjustifiable or arbitrary discrimination or a disguised trade restriction. Thus, arguments that have been made in the context of Article III are most likely to resurface in the context of the chapeau, where the question

---

[36] Trachtman (1998) at 60-61.

is addressed whether the regulatory distinction made is unjustifiable or arbitrary in its application.[37]

The two-tiered approach in which the prohibition and the justification are neatly divided is sometimes even problematic in cases of *de jure* discrimination where a justification is argued for the very distinction made, as illustrated by the ECJ's conceptual struggle in *Walloon Waste*. A parallel may be drawn with the ECJ's case-law on internal taxation under Article 90, which also centres upon a non-discrimination assessment. There are no treaty exceptions for that provision, but the ECJ has taken regulatory objectives into account when assessing whether there is discrimination in the first place. A similar issue may arise in the WTO, if a defendant argues that a regulatory distinction challenged under Article III:4 is justified by an objective not covered by Article XX GATT, and that as a result, there is no less favourable treatment of like products and no violation of Article III:4. If regulatory objectives are taken into account in determining whether Article III:4 is being violated, what will be the remaining role for the subsequent analysis under Article XX if there is a violation? WTO panels and the Appellate Body may be expected to choose an extensive and flexible interpretation of Article XX rather than allowing regulatory objectives to play a role in the assessment of Article III:4. However, considering the *obiter dictum* in *EC-Asbestos*, it is not inconceivable that such objectives are invoked as a defence, to the effect that a regulatory distinction does not result in less favourable treatment.

The ECJ has in the application of Article 28 largely avoided the problem of how discrimination tests, regulatory objectives and justifications should relate to each other by relying on an obstacles test instead of a *de facto* discrimination test, thus enabling it to maintain a two-tiered approach. However, its *Keck* case-law has introduced a preliminary discrimination test for certain types of measures, which includes *de facto* discrimination. Therefore, depending on how *de facto* discrimination is assessed, the assessment of discrimination and of regulatory objectives as justifications could take place in the EC context when addressing "selling arrangements". However, up to now, it appears that the test of *de facto* discrimination as aid down in *Keck* is objective, in that it does not take regulatory objectives into consideration.[38] This in turn raises the question of how *de facto* discriminatory "selling arrangements" may be justified; under Article 30 only, or also by mandatory requirements? The Court in *De Agostini* chose

---

[37] Cf. in the sphere of tax measures under Article III:2, the panel in *Argentina-Hides*, para. 11.303 and footnotes 560 and 564.

[38] See Joined Cases C-34-36/95 *De Agostini*, where the Court suggested that there was indeed *de facto* discrimination, but left the decision to the national court; C-405/98 *Gourmet* and C-254/98 *TK Heim-dienst*, where the Court itself decided that the measure at issue did not meet the *de facto* discrimination test, without however at that stage of the analysis considering the measure's regulatory objectives.

the latter option. This reinforces the view adhered to by the present author that the condition laid down by the Court of being "indistinctly applicable" in order to qualify for justification by a "mandatory requirement" is a formal criterion of *de jure* equal applicability. If a selling arrangement is *de facto* but not *de jure* discriminatory, it can be justified under both Article 30 and mandatory requirements.

6.3   Conditions Applicable to Justifications

6.3.1   Terminology and Factors Taken into Account

Article 30 EC states that Article 28 shall not preclude import prohibitions or restrictions "justified" on the grounds of, *inter alia*, the protection of health and life. The ECJ in *Cassis de Dijon* spoke of national provisions "necessary" in order to satisfy mandatory requirements. Paragraph (b) of Article XX GATT requires that measures be "necessary", and paragraph (g) that they are "relating to" the conservation of exhaustible natural resources and "made effective in conjunction with" domestic restrictions. In addition, the second sentence of Article 30 EC and the chapeau to Article XX GATT require that measures seeking justification do not constitute a means of arbitrary (or unjustifiable) discrimination or a disguised restriction on trade.[39]

When discussing the conditions which a measure seeking justification must meet, be it on the basis of Article 30 EC or of a mandatory requirement, the European Court of Justice usually refers to the requirement of "proportionality". In this work, "proportionality" in the wide sense of the term is defined as encompassing, (1) a measure's suitability to achieve an environmental goal, (2) its necessity, in the sense that there are no alternatives available that are less trade-restrictive while guaranteeing the same level of environmental protection; and (3) whether the measure is proportionate in the narrow sense, in other words, whether it strikes a reasonable balance between trade and environment.[40] There is no uniform interpretation of the terms "necessity" and "proportionality". The ECJ itself sometimes applies both, sometimes one of them, and sometimes simply refers to "least trade-restrictiveness". The first element of "proportionality" in the wide sense as described above is the appropriateness or suitability of a measure to contribute to its objective, i.e. the existence of a causal link between the measure and its goal. Some include this element as part of a wider concept of "necessity", which also encompasses "least trade-restric-

---

[39] The adjective "unjustifiable" is found in Article XX GATT but not in Article 30 EC.

[40] See De Búrca (1993); Emiliou (1996a); Jans (2000b) and AG Fennelly in Case C-217/99 *Commission v. Belgium.*

tiveness".[41] A minority includes "proportionality" *stricto sensu* in the concept of "necessity".[42] In its Communication on the Single Market and the Environment, the European Commission applies still different definitions: it describes the causal link requirement as "necessity", and the "least trade-restrictiveness" requirement as "proportionality".[43]

What is important is not so much the name given to the conditions applied to justifications, but rather what factors are taken into account when applying them, and how these factors are taken into account. Factors potentially playing a role in assessing the relationship between means and ends are the importance of the objective, the level of protection chosen, the contribution made to the objective by the chosen measure, the impact of the measure on trade, and the domestic costs of the measure. A "necessary" test applied in the sense of "least trade-restrictiveness" compares the trade impact of alternative measures, assuming that the alternatives will prove equally effective in attaining the chosen level of protection. This assumption could be made explicit by adding the requirement that the alternatives that are compared must be equally effective, and must guarantee the same level of protection. Though such a test would not take domestic costs into account, those costs could be taken into consideration by requiring not only that there should be no measure which is less trade-restrictive, but also that the alternative should be "reasonably available".

A strict proportionality test assesses whether the obstacle to trade is proportionate to the regulatory objective in the abstract, or to the contribution it is capable of making to the achievement of the objective pursued.[44] Strict proportionality may assess the relationship between an obstacle to trade and its objective (or the achievement thereof) directly, or in comparison with alternative measures. Comparative proportionality takes into account the relationship between the impact on trade and the objective of alternative measures in order to assess whether the trade impact of a measure is disproportionate. Non-comparative proportionality only considers whether this relationship is not disproportionate for the particular measure at issue, irrespective of alternatives. Comparative proportionality testing is closely connected to "necessity" or "least trade-restrictiveness testing". However, unlike "necessity" testing, comparative proportionality testing openly compares measures that differ in their contribution to the regulatory objective.[45]

---

[41] See e.g. AG Jacobs in Case C-169/89 *Van den Burg*; Montini (1997).

[42] See e.g. T. Weiler (1998).

[43] COM(99)263f at 8.

[44] See AG Van Gerven in Case C-169/89 *Van den Burg*.

[45] See Trachtman (1998) on the various tests.

6.3.2   The ECJ and Proportionality

Notwithstanding the fact that the second sentence of Article 30 expressly mentions the conditions that measures shall not constitute a means of arbitrary discrimination or a disguised restriction on trade between Member States, the Court often does not explicitly apply these conditions. Rather, they seem to be the underlying rationale of the Court's "proportionality test" in the wide sense, which it applies to justifications under both Article 30 and the "mandatory requirements". Apparently, the Court thinks that when a measure does not satisfy the proportionality requirement, it *ipso facto* breaches that sentence. The condition of being "indistinctly applicable" in order to qualify for justification under the "mandatory requirements" has become somewhat uncertain, now that the Court appears to have accepted environmental protection as a justification for "distinctly applicable" measures.[46] For all practical purposes, the other conditions applicable to justifications under Article 30 and the "mandatory requirements" appear to be identical.

It is argued in this work that strict proportionality testing is controversial because it may lead to substituting the court's view for that of the Community or the national legislator. It is difficult to attune to the Court's professed view that it is up to Member States to determine the appropriate level of protection of interests such as environmental protection, in the absence of Community action on the matter at issue. Not surprisingly, therefore, the Court has shown restraint in assessing strict proportionality in its vertical relationship, i.e. when checking the compatibility of Member States' measures with the EC Treaty. It has only very rarely actually applied strict proportionality in its full rigour. The only instances this author has found were *Danish Bottles* and, somewhat less clearly, *Monsees*.[47] In *Stoke-on-Trent*, one of the cases on Sunday trading rules preceding *Keck*, the Court instructed national courts to weigh the national interest in attaining a legitimate aim against the Community interest in ensuring the free movement of goods.[48] The reaction of a British court illustrates the controversial nature of such testing:

Weights would be attributed to the interests respectively of free movement and the socio-cultural object of the particular measure, and the court would then decide whether the latter outweighed the former. Something of the kind is often involved in the legislative process [...] But to perform this task in a judicial context would in all but the most obvious cases be a difficult matter.[49]

---

[46] In cases such as C-2/90 *Commission v. Belgium (Walloon Waste)*, C-389/96 *Aher Waggon*, and possibly C-379/98 *Preussen Elektra*.

[47] Langer and Wiers (2000).

[48] Case C-169/91 *Stoke-on-Trent* at para. 15.

[49] High Court of Justice, Queen's Bench Division in *WH Smith Do-It-All Ltd.* v. *Peterborough City Council* [1990] 2 CMLR 577, as cited in Trachtman (1998) at 77.

In its horizontal institutional relationship with the Community legislator, the ECJ checks the proportionality of Community legislation. However, even if the Court applies all three elements of proportionality *sensu lato* separately in a more consistent way than when assessing national measures, it does so in a deferential manner. It verifies whether the measure is not manifestly inappropriate to its objective (suitability), whether the legislator has not made a manifest error of assessment in deciding that there were no alternatives that were equally effective without entailing significant additional costs to the public purse (necessity), and finally, whether the damage to individual rights does not outweigh the benefit to the general interest (strict proportionality).[50] In *Omega Air*, Advocate General Alber has proposed to apply a more intrusive "necessary" test for Community law.[51] As regards strict proportionality, although separately address-ing this element, the Court often points to the fact that the Community legis-lature makes social policy choices or complex technical assessments, and the Court accordingly demonstrates a great deal of restraint in assessing the balance struck by the Community legislature.[52] When assessing Community legislation, the Court mostly defines proportionality *stricto sensu* as a matter of balancing damage to individual rights versus the common good. This approach should be seen in the context of the types of cases in which the Court is asked to look at the proportionality of Community legislation. These are mostly claims for the annulment of Community acts under Article 230 EC. In order for such a claim to be admissible, an individual must establish that the Community legislative act is of individual and direct concern to him. Thus, when the Court assesses proportionality in this context, individuals have been identified whose rights have been damaged by the Community act, and the damage to their interests is weighed against the general benefit of the act in question.

The above situation does not necessarily present itself when a national court or the European Court of Justice is asked to assess the proportionality of national measures in the context of the free movement of goods. The Court may make such assessments either in direct actions in which the Commission or another Member State challenges the measure (Articles 226 and 227 EC, respectively), or by way of a preliminary ruling under Article 234 EC. In the former case, the Court examines whether the national legislator has taken Community in-terests sufficiently into account when enacting its measure. In the latter case, the Court assists the national court in its function of controlling the national legislator, part of which involves ensuring that the national legislature has taken Community interests into account. It is not clear whether the Court should only give general directions or whether it should itself decide on the

---

[50] See Case T-125/96 *Boehringer*.

[51] Opinion in Joined Cases C-27/00 and C-122/00 *Omega Air*. The Court however did not follow his suggestion.

[52] See Cases C-84/94 *UK v. Council* and C-127/95 *Norbrook Laboratories*.

328

proportionality question in preliminary rulings; its decisions provide examples of both approaches.[53] In both cases, the individual interests affected are not necessarily as easily identifiable as in the situation where the Court assesses the proportionality of Community legislation. In direct actions under Articles 226 and 227, a national measure may be challenged on behalf of all producers and traders in another Member State or in all other Member States. And in preliminary rulings, the individual rights affected will depend on who is bringing the case in the national court and on the standing requirements there.

Thus, it is far from clear that the weighing of interests required by a strict proportionality test neatly pitches damage to *individual* rights against benefits to the *common* good. In fact, the rights of individual traders and producers in other Member States coincide with the more general Community interest in ensuring the free movement of goods. The benefit to the common good, for example an environmental or health objective, may be local, regional, national, transnational, or global. But in all cases, it can be said to coincide with the general Community interest in a high level of environmental and health protection. Thus, when a national court or the ECJ assesses the proportionality of national measures *stricto sensu*, it is really weighing general interests against general interests. This is the domain of legislators. It may be the Community legislature if it has competence and if there is a political will to harmonise the balance between free movement and the environmental or health interest at the Community level. It will be national legislatures if such competence or will is lacking.

In *Danish Bottles* and *Monsees*, the Court of Justice applied a comparative proportionality test, examining whether there were alternatives that struck a different balance between trade impacts and regulatory goals by impacting less on trade, while safeguarding the regulatory goal to an extent deemed sufficient by the Court. A comparative proportionality test thus combines least trade-restrictiveness with the level of attainment of the regulatory objective. It is highly questionable whether the Court of Justice is in a proper position to balance these elements and thereby to interfere with the chosen level of protection by a Member State in a field that has not been harmonised by Community secondary legislation. This is why the strict proportionality test has been criticised here and elsewhere.[54] A non-comparative proportionality test may be of assistance when the "necessary" test does not yield clear results. This may occur e.g. because there is no agreement on the extent to which less trade-restrictive alternatives are equally capable of attaining the level of protection chosen, or whether such alternatives are reasonably available. However, even if applied only in this moderate manner and only in those cases where a qualified neces-

---

[53] See Jans (2000b); Jarvis (1998).

[54] See Section 3.2.2; Langer and Wiers (2000); Jans (2000a); Krämer (1993a).

sary test does not yield satisfactory results, proportionality testing still involves adjudicative bodies in attaching relative weight to incommensurable values, and therefore raises important issues of legitimacy.

Thus, it is submitted that when addressing national measures under Articles 28-30 EC, a strict proportionality test should at the very most only apply in the most egregious cases. It would have to be a test which would only censure cases where the legislature could not reasonably have arrived at the balance struck by its measure. Such strict proportionality testing should moreover be applied in negative terms ('not manifestly disproportionate') and be non-comparative. In most, if not all, such cases, however, there will be something amiss with the measure that can be addressed either under the preliminary question of the existence of an environmental or health goal covered by Article 30 or the mandatory requirements, or under the first or second element of proportionality in the wide sense - the suitability and necessity requirements.

The "necessary" or "least trade-restrictive" test also entails a risk of substituting the legislator by accepting less trade-restrictive alternatives that might prove less effective as a means of attaining the environmental goal. To some extent, this is true for all "means-ends tests", as they are all conditions attached to invoking exceptions in order to control governments in their regulatory choices and to ensure that they do not neglect the Community interest in the free movement of goods. However, the substitution of the national legislator by the Court leads to possible interference with the chosen level of protection only when strict proportionality is applied, or when "necessary" is applied without due regard to the effectiveness in attaining the level of protection sought of the various alternatives considered. The "necessary" requirement should therefore be applied with due regard to the effectiveness of the alternatives. Recent applications by the Court of Justice suggest that it is taking this into account.[55] In sum, although far from consistent in the terminology used, the European Court of Justice appears to apply the means-ends tests with due restraint. However, it is regrettable that in some of the cases where the Court appears to have accepted the justification of discriminatory measures by the mandatory requirement of environmental protection, it has omitted the means-ends tests altogether.[56]

6.3.3 Means-Ends Tests in Article XX GATT

GATT and WTO panels and the Appellate Body have interpreted Article XX GATT in a manner which is more closely related to the actual text of the provision than the case-law of the ECJ has been related to the text of

---

[55] See e.g. Case C-473/98 *Toolex Alpha*, Case C-217/99 *Commission v. Belgium*.

[56] See Cases C-2/90 *Commission v. Belgium (Walloon Waste)*, and C-379/98 *Preussen Elektra*.

Articles 28-30 EC.[57] Having identified whether a measure has an environmental goal covered by a relevant paragraph, for our purposes mainly (b) or (g), the conditions in those paragraphs are first addressed. Is the measure "necessary" (paragraph b), or is it a measure "relating to" and 'made effective in conjunction with...' (paragraph g)? Only if these requirements are satisfied will the conditions in the chapeau to Article XX be addressed: does the measure in its application constitute a means of arbitrary or unjustifiable discrimination between countries where the same conditions prevail, or a disguised restriction on international trade?

The requirement of "relating to the conservation of exhaustible natural resources" was interpreted under GATT 1947 as meaning "primarily aimed at". After the Appellate Body's interpretation of "relating to" in *US-Gasoline* and *US-Shrimp-Turtle*, it has been further refined as requiring a "substantial relationship" between a measure and its purpose. According to the Appellate Body report in *US-Gasoline*, the measure under appraisal must be 'not merely incidentally or inadvertently aimed at' the conservation goal. And, according to the Appellate Body in *US-Shrimp-Turtle*, the measure must not be disproportionately wide in its scope and reach in relation to the policy objective; the means must be reasonably related to the ends. The use of the words "not disproportionately" and "reasonably related" might suggest that the Appellate Body applied a strict proportionality test. However, this would seem to overstretch the ordinary meaning of the words "relating to". The words used by the Appellate Body could also be read as referring to the appropriateness or suitability of a measure to contribute to its objective, i.e. the first element of proportionality *senso latu*.

The second element of the means-end test in Article XX(g), "made effective in conjunction with", requires a certain even-handedness between restrictions imposed domestically and on imports. However, it does not require the identical treatment of domestic and imported products.[58]

"Necessary" in paragraph (b) of Article XX was interpreted by the GATT panel in *Thailand-Cigarettes* as requiring that the "least GATT-inconsistent" measure reasonably available was chosen. "Least GATT-inconsistent" may be equated with "least trade-restrictive". The "least trade-restrictive reasonably available" test was reiterated in interpretations of "necessary" in the WTO era, for example in *US-Gasoline*. It was further elaborated in *EC-Asbestos*, after a similar elaboration had first taken place in *Korea-Beef* in the context of Article XX(d). According to the Appellate Body in *EC-Asbestos*, assessing "necessary" involves

---

[57] Article 31.1 of the the Vienna Convention mandates a treaty to be interpreted in accordance with the *ordinary meaning of the terms* of the treaty in their context and in the light of its object and purpose. Emphasis added. See the Annex to this work for the full text of the provision. The Appellate Body often has recourse to a dictionary when interpreting WTO provisions.

[58] See the AB in *US-Gasoline*, at p. 21-22.

a process of weighing and balancing factors, such as the contribution of the measure to the goal, the importance of the interest protected, and the measure's trade impacts. The 'contribution of the measure to the goal' can be read as referring to the suitability of the measure to pursue its goal, which would coincide with the first element of wide proportionality. However, if the importance of the goal and the contribution of the measure to the goal are to be weighed against trade impacts, then panels and the Appellate Body will be balancing the importance of the interest protected with the accompanying trade impacts. That means that when they apply the "necessary" requirement, they are assessing proportionality in the strict sense.

In its actual application of the "necessary" test, the Appellate Body in *EC-Asbestos* merely noted that the interest protected, in that case human health, was vital and important to the highest degree. It added that any alternative measure might compromise the chosen level of health protection. Thus, the Appellate Body in that case did not really balance the measure and its goal: only reasonably alternative measures that guarantee the same level of attainment of the protection goal should be considered. However, in *Korea-Beef*, the Appellate Body suggested that "necessary" may have different meanings in the different paragraphs in which it occurs in Article XX. This report dealt with Article XX(d), under which measures may be justified as "necessary" to secure compliance with laws or regulations which are not themselves GATT-inconsistent. In applying the balancing process involved in assessing "necessity" in *Korea-Beef*, the Appellate Body was arguably quite severe. Although paying lip service to the right of Members to establish their desired level of protection, the Appellate Body thought it unlikely that Korea intended to establish a very high level of protection. Arguably, this second-guessing of Korea's intentions effectively limits the right of Members to establish their own protection levels. Read together with the more deferential application of "necessary" in *EC-Asbestos*, *Korea-Beef* could be taken to mean that "necessary" involves a more severe test in paragraph (d) than in paragraph (b). The explanation of this difference probably lies in the relative importance of the interests pursued under both paragraphs.

According to the Appellate Body in *Korea-Beef*, when interpreting a treaty, account may be taken of the relative importance of the common interests or values that the law or regulation to be enforced is intended to protect. The importance of the interest protected will not easily be doubted in cases involving Article XX(b), such as *EC-Asbestos*. Under paragraph (d), the defending Member will be expected to invoke some other interest or value pursued by the law or regulation that the measure at issue enforces.[59] Most of the interests protected by

---

[59] Paragraph (d) speaks of 'laws or regulations [...] including those relating to customs enforcement, the enforcement of monopolies [...], the protection of patents, trade marks and copyrights, and the prevention of deceptive practices'.

laws whose enforcement measures are sought to be justified under paragraph (d) are of an economic nature. In *Korea Beef*, the interest invoked was the prevention of fraud, or of "deceptive practices", as paragraph (d) refers to it. Economic interests are perhaps more easily weighed against trade impacts than such non-economic interests as environmental protection. However, as the reference to the protection of patents, trade marks and copyrights in paragraph (d) itself indicates, such economic interests are sometimes related to individual rights. This make it a difficult exercise to weigh them against trade impacts. Moreover, it is submitted that a correct interpretation of "necessary" in paragraph (d) should concentrate on the relationship between the actual measure at issue and its objective, which is the enforcement of another GATT consistent law or regulation. It should not impose a "necessary" requirement on the relationship between the enforcement measure at issue and the objective of the underlying regulation. As a matter of fact, paragraph (d) explicitly employs "relating to" as the test for the relationship between the means and ends of the underlying laws or regulations, which in its ordinary meaning is less strict than "necessary".

The current author questions whether the approach taken in *Korea-Beef* is desirable. A very flexible interpretation of "necessary" may lead to much legal uncertainty. Moreover, it is recalled that the Appellate Body questioned the high level of protection professed by Korea and in fact substituted its own assessment of the level of protection chosen by Korea.[60] The Appellate Body then observed that Korea could have achieved that level through WTO-consistent measures.[61] If the Appellate Body really intended to balance the importance of the interest with the trade impacts and the measure's effectiveness, and in the process to second-guess Korea's chosen level of enforcement, it arguably went a step too far. Even in the realm of enforcement measures under Article XX(d), strict proportionality testing is not warranted. Arguments as to the professed level of protection of the objective of a measure would seem to relate to the existence of a legitimate objective and the suitability of a measure to attain such objective. If the Appellate Body really meant that Korea used its measure to discriminate or protect its domestic production, it should have addressed this in the context of the chapeau rather than under the "necessary" test.

It has been argued that testing "necessity" easily shades into recognition. After all, is it "necessary" to impose one's own regulation on an imported product when that product meets the exporting country's equivalent regulation?[62] Likewise, it has been argued that what is often referred to as "mutual recognition" in the EC context is really no more than "functional parallelism", and that this is 'a very conservative and fully justified application of the principle

---

[60] AB in *Korea-Beef*, para. 178.

[61] Ibid., paras. 180-82.

[62] Trachtman (1998) at 65-67 and at 73, respectively.

of proportionality'.[63] In this view, 'insisting on a specific technical standard, even if a different standard is functionally parallel in achieving the desired result, is to have adopted a measure which is not the least restrictive possible'.[64] And, still according to the same author, if the logic of functional parallelism is rooted in the necessity requirement, a similar doctrine will inevitably emerge in the GATT, as a state could not justify excluding an imported product which meets functionally parallel regulation as "necessary", as has already been acknowledged in the SPS and TBT regimes.[65]

However, that view does not seem fully correct in that it fails to look at the scope of the basic provisions that precede the consideration of means-ends tests. If a basic provision such as a prohibition of trade obstacles or a non-discrimination rule is not violated in the first place, no justification or proportionality assessment is needed. If mutual recognition or "functional parallelism" are rooted in "proportionality" and "necessity", it must be assumed that *any* measure must be "proportionate" or "necessary". This is not true in the GATT situation, where Article III only prohibits regulatory measures that discriminate. Thus, in principle, any product requirement equally applicable to imported and domestic products could be applied consistently with Article III GATT. Only if the basic discipline were to be extended beyond non-discrimination to include non-discriminatory trade obstacles could Members be forced to accept imported products that do not meet their requirements but do meet the desired result of those requirements. Admittedly, the TBT and SPS Agreements have changed the lack of disciplines for non-discriminatory requirements in the GATT, although as argued above they do not go as far as imposing recognition. The interpretation of the "necessary" tests in these Agreements may go some way towards *de facto* imposing recognition. But to imply "mutual recognition" or "functional parallelism" from the "necessary" requirement in Article XX GATT appears to be mistaken, because Articles III or XI GATT cannot be regarded as implying a general "obstacles test".[66] Moreover, there is no *general* "necessity" requirement in the GATT; while measures protecting life and health must be "necessary", measures protecting exhaustible natural resources only need to be "relating to" their objective. Finally, if "necessary" in Article XX GATT led to "mutual recognition", the need to conclude separate SPS and TBT Agreements would be less clear. That need can only be explained by the need to extend the disciplines beyond those contained in the basic GATT provisions.

---

[63] Weiler (1999) at 367.

[64] Ibid.

[65] Ibid.

[66] Article XI only prohibits those trade obstacles posed by import-specific measures and Article III prohibits less favourable treatment of like imported products.

6.3.4 The Conditions in the Chapeau to Article XX GATT

In *US-Gasoline*, the Appellate Body said that the three elements of the chapeau to Article XX may be read side-by-side, and that 'they impart meaning to one another.' Nevertheless, in *US-Shrimp-Turtle*, the Appellate Body began to differentiate between the different elements found in the chapeau, and this approach was taken a step further by the panel in *EC-Asbestos*. That panel observed that under the chapeau, it has first to be established whether there is discrimination, which is an objective fact. Only if this is the case, must the question whether the discrimination is unjustifiable or arbitrary be addressed, which involves determining whether the measure has been reasonably applied, with due regard to the duties of the defendant and the rights of the claimant. The same panel interpreted "disguised restriction" to mean restrictions concealing trade-restrictive [protectionist] objectives. In order to discern the protective application of a measure, its design, architecture and revealing structure should be assessed. The panel further said that a protectionist *effect* does not normally mean that the measure has a protectionist *aim*, as long as that effect remains within certain limits. This suggests that extensive and disproportionate protectionist effects may lead to the conclusion that a measure has been applied so as to constitute a disguised restriction on international trade.

With regard to violations of Article III GATT that are sought to be justified under Article XX, the questions to be asked are the following. Does the measure result in less favourable treatment of imported products than of like domestic products? Does the measure pursue a legitimate objective mentioned in Article XX, and does it (as a whole, in its general design) meet the applicable means-end(s) test(s)? Finally, does the measure in its application constitute discrimination that is unjustifiable or arbitrary, or a disguised restriction on international trade? Certain problems and overlaps in the different parts of the analysis are likely to occur. According to the Appellate Body in *Gasoline*, '[t]he chapeau by its express terms addresses, not so much the questioned measure or its specific contents as such, but rather *the manner* in which that measure is *applied*.'[67] However, it is questionable whether the measure and its application can always usefully be distinguished. The design of a measure itself may of necessity lead to certain applications of it that may not meet the standards of the chapeau. Does it make any difference in such cases whether the measure or its application is assessed? In fact, the Appellate Body itself appears to have looked at the measure itself rather than its application when it assessed the chapeau in *US-Gasoline*.[68]

---

[67] The Appellate Body referred to the GATT panel in *US-Spring Assemblies* that had made the same observation.

[68] As noted by the panel in *Argentina-Hides*, in note 566.

A second problem is that of the overlap of requirements. The Appellate Body in *US-Gasoline* and in *US-Shrimp-Turtle* looked at available alternatives in the context of the chapeau. Whether one wishes to call this a "necessary" test or not,[69] there is a risk of an overlap between the tests in the chapeau and paragraphs (b), (d) and (a). There is also a risk that as a result of the interpretation of the chapeau, a measure justified under paragraph (g) will after all be subjected to a "necessary" test. Overlaps may occur between the non-discrimination requirements in e.g. Articles I and III GATT and the chapeau to Article XX. The question whether there is discrimination under the chapeau is likely to refer back to findings under these substantive provisions. Likewise, findings of protective application under the second sentence of Article III:2, and possibly also under Article III:4, may be expected to influence the analysis of "disguised restriction" in the chapeau.[70]

6.3.5 The Conditions in the TBT and SPS Agreements

Although the conditions that measures must meet in order to be justified under the SPS and TBT Agreements resemble those found in Article XX GATT, there are a number of differences. First of all, there are no separate exceptions provisions in the SPS and TBT Agreements. The "substantive obligations" and "exceptions" cannot be separated in these Agreements; they are integrated. Accordingly, the means-ends tests and other conditions found in these Agreements do not only come into play once a violation has been found, as is the case under the GATT provisions. As a result, it is possible to complain under the SPS and TBT Agreements that a measure is not "necessary", which would not be possible under the GATT rules.[71] Secondly, as there are no separate exceptions provisions, there is no structure that resembles that of Article XX GATT, with a chapeau and paragraphs. Reflections of the chapeau are found in the preamble and Article 2.3 of the SPS Agreement, and in the preamble to the TBT Agreement, but not in its actual provisions. Both Agreements contain elaborations of the "necessary" requirement.

The TBT Agreement elaborates the "necessity" condition as 'not more trade-restrictive than necessary to fulfil a legitimate objective, taking account of the risks non-fulfilment would create'. The test in the TBT has been identified by some authors as a proportionality test, albeit perhaps an embryonic one.[72] In the run-up to the 1999 Seattle Ministerial Conference, the European Community called for the clarification of the TBT Agreement, including the proportion-

---

[69] See Waincymer (1996); McGovern (1995). Appleton (1997b) argues *contra*.

[70] On protective application and less favourable treatment, see the AB in *EC-Asbestos*, para. 100.

[71] As noted by Desmedt (2001) at 461.

[72] Trachtman (1998) at 70; Montini (1997); T.Weiler (1998).

ality of measures.[73] A footnote to Article 2.2 in an earlier version of the TBT Agreement actually confirmed that this provision was to ensure proportionality 'between regulations and the risks non-fulfilment of legitimate objectives would create'. However, that footnote was subsequently dropped, so there is no explicit reference to proportionality in the TBT Agreement.[74] It has nevertheless been argued that Article 2.2 TBT authorises tribunals to go further than the "necessary" analysis of GATT Article XX in order to resolve the most difficult cases in this area, including measures that are necessary but disproportionate, and that WTO tribunals are quite likely to engage in such [advanced] balancing, regardless of the governing legal standard.[75] It has also been argued that a panel could find under Article 2.2 TBT that the trade obstacle outweighs the risk of non-fulfilment, and that a technical regulation could be considered to be disproportionate even in the absence of an alternative less trade-restrictive alternative.[76]

The current author concurs with the view that 'taking into account the risks non-fulfilment would create' is indeed reminiscent of proportionality *stricto sensu*. However, by only taking into account the risks of *non-fulfilment* of the legitimate objective, this is only a very limited proportionality. The risks of *less fulfilment* of the legitimate objective cannot be taken into account in this test. Another argument against reading a strict proportionality test in Article 2.2 TBT is that the preamble of the TBT Agreement recognises that 'no country should be prevented from taking measures necessary to ensure [...] the protection of human, animal or plant life or health, or the environment [...] at the levels it considers appropriate [...].' It has been suggested that panels' willingness to interfere with Members' technical regulations may ultimately depend on the legitimate objective at stake.[77]

The SPS Agreement contains the most elaborate set of means-ends conditions. SPS measures should be applied only to the extent necessary, be based on scientific principles and not be maintained without sufficient scientific evidence (Article 2.2). They should not arbitrarily or unjustifiably discriminate or be applied in a manner which would constitute a disguised trade restriction (Article 2.3). They should be based on a risk assessment (Article 5.1), and be applied in order to achieve their appropriate protection level. Appropriate protection levels should be applied consistently (Article 5.5 and Guidelines for its implementation). SPS measures should not be more trade-restrictive than required to achieve their appropriate level of protection, taking into account technical and

---

73 Document WT/GC/W/274.

74 Petersmann (1993a).

75 Hudec (1998) at 643.

76 Desmedt (2001) at 459-460.

77 Ibid. at 460.

economic feasibility, which is the case when there is no reasonably available alternative measure that achieves the appropriate protection level but is significantly less trade-restrictive (Article 5.6).

The SPS Agreement thus requires that SPS measures be "necessary", but also that they be based on a risk assessment. It has been argued that the "necessary" requirement in Article 2.1 SPS includes an obligation to demonstrate a causal link between the measure and its aim.[78] The requirement in Article 5.1 SPS, on the other hand, requires a causal link, or "rational connection" between the measure and a risk assessment.[79] Thus, it has been argued that the SPS Agreement imposes a double obligation in terms of appropriateness or suitability, the first element of proportionality in the wide sense of the term. This double obligation has been contrasted with the EC situation, where no distinction is explicitly made between the causal link between the measure and its objective, and between the measure and the risk.[80] However, the current author doubts whether it is useful to distinguish the aim of a measure from the risks it seeks to avert. According to the definitions in the SPS Agreement, the aim of an SPS measure is to protect humans, animals or plants from certain risks. Thus, it would seem that the obligation of a risk assessment and the existence of a risk are part of the preliminary question whether a measure is an SPS measure in the first place and the question of the causal link or suitability. The necessity of the measure rather relates to the reasonable availability of less trade-restrictive alternatives to achieve the aim, as further elaborated in Article 5.6 SPS. The test in Article 5.6 may be seen as the most elaborate refinement of the sometimes rough instrument of necessity as least trade-restrictiveness. By stipulating that alternatives must be reasonably available taking into account technical and economic feasibility, the domestic regulatory costs of a measure can be accounted for. Moreover, by adding "significantly" to "less trade-restrictive", it is ensured that a slightly more trade-restrictive measure will not fail the test.

6.3.6   Comparison: Proportionality in Article XX GATT?

In *Gasoline* and *Shrimp-Turtle*, the Appellate Body referred to the role of the chapeau in ensuring that the exceptions in Article XX are not abused, and that thus, the appropriate balance between rights and obligations of the WTO Members is maintained. The Appellate Body observed that the chapeau to Article XX is but one expression of the principle of good faith that controls the exercise of rights by states. It further observed that one application

---

[78] Desmedt (2001) at 454.

[79] AB in *EC-Hormones*, para. 193.

[80] Desmedt (2001) at 454.

of this principle, the doctrine of *abus de droit*, enjoins that whenever the assertion of a right 'impinges on the field covered by [a] treaty obligation, it must be exercised *bona fide*, that is to say, reasonably.' Moreover, the Appellate Body cited an author on public international law who referred to a *bona fide* and reasonable exercise of the right as one that is 'appropriate and necessary for the purpose of the right (i.e., in furtherance of the interests which the right is intended to protect)'.[81] This terminology strongly calls to mind the terminology used by the ECJ when assessing justifications under Articles 28-30 EC. As signalled in Chapter 5, the Appellate Body appears to be increasingly resorting to the concepts of "reason" and "reasonability".[82]

It is recalled that the European Court of Justice has repeatedly stated that the requirement of proportionality underlies the second sentence of Article 30 EC. Could it likewise be said that, proportionality derives from the requirements in the chapeau to Article XX GATT? Various authors have suggested that the chapeau to Article XX may be used to test proportionality.[83] It should be stressed, however, that the notion of "proportionality" is itself interpreted in different ways. Sometimes, the term is used to refer to strict proportionality only, sometimes it is equated with "necessity", and sometimes it is taken in the widest sense to include both, as well as "appropriateness". Therefore, simply saying that the chapeau calls for proportionality testing does not answer the question of what is to be understood by a proportionality test. Moreover, it is recalled that Article 30 EC refers to prohibitions or restrictions which are "justified" on the grounds of a number of stated objectives. It does not further differentiate the means-ends tests for different exception grounds, like Article XX GATT does. Accordingly, the ECJ usually treats Article 30 as one integrated whole. In most cases, it does not explicitly refer to the second sentence of Article 30, but merely lays down the "proportionality" requirement, in one of the many forms it has presented that requirement.

The question arises whether an "overall" requirement of "proportionality" and/or "reasonableness" could similarly be applied to Article XX GATT, and whether that would also lead to an approach that integrates all the elements of Article XX GATT into one general test. If the EC parallel were followed, such a test would probably lead to an "appropriateness" and "necessity" test, in which the chapeau requirements would be subsumed. One advantage of an integrated approach to the means-ends tests and the chapeau would be that the

---

[81] AB in *US-Shrimp-Turtle*, para. 158, citing Cheng (1953) at 125.

[82] On the concept of "reason" in public international law, see Corten (1999).

[83] Mathis (1991) at 49; Cameron and Campbell (1998) at 223; Manzini (1999) at 840; Hilf and Puth (2001).

overlaps now occurring between the assessment of the means-ends tests under the paragraphs and the chapeau could be avoided. These overlaps risk resulting in double necessity tests for justifications under paragraph (b) and necessity tests for justifications under paragraph (g) even if that paragraph does not contain a necessary requirement. Avoiding such overlaps would alleviate the burden on the defendant under Article XX.

However, an "integrated approach" to Article XX GATT is not without its problems. Even if a measure and its application are not always easy to separate, an integrated approach would be difficult to reconcile with the text of Article XX GATT. Up to now, Article XX has been applied in a two-tiered manner, treating the tests in the paragraphs as addressing the measure and the tests in the chapeau as addressing its application. A textual approach to Article XX acknowledges that "relating to" in paragraph (g) is essentially an appropriateness test, in other words the first element of proportionality *sensu lato*. "Necessary" may have different meanings in paragraphs (a), (b) and (d), as the Appellate Body suggested in *Korea Beef*. "Necessary" seems to always include appropriateness, and also compares whether there are equally effective less trade-restrictive alternatives available. Looking for alternatives in the context of Article XX GATT may include a whole range of different types of measures, as Article XX applies to the whole GATT Agreement. Thus, when the necessity of a quantitative restriction found to infringe Article XI is assessed under Article XX, alternatives looked at may include taxation or internal regulatory measures. This wide range of possible alternatives may be contrasted with the EC situation. There, measures having equivalent effect to a quantitative restriction may be compared, but including taxation measures in assessing "diagonal proportionality" is less obvious, considering the fact that the exceptions in Article 30 do not apply to the provision on tax measures in Article 90 EC. Going back to "necessary" in Article XX GATT, arguably, in spite of the Appellate Body's suggestions in *Korea-Beef* and *EC-Asbestos*, "necessity" does not include strict proportionality.

The chapeau to Article XX GATT does not warrant strict proportionality testing either. The chapeau rather invites the adjudicator to look at whether the measure has been applied reasonably, with due regard to the interests concerned, by checking for qualified forms of discrimination and disguised restrictions. It should be emphasised that the measures in *US-Gasoline* and *US-Shrimp-Turtle* were found not to meet the standards in the chapeau mainly because they unjustifiably discriminated, not because they were disproportionate. It has been argued that there is no 'single overarching (unwritten) proportionality principle' in WTO law, and that it would not be appropriate for WTO dispute settlement organs to assert such a principle at this stage of the WTO's development.[84] The current author agrees with this view. It is submitted that the arguments raised

---

[84] Desmedt (2001) at 479-80.

above against the application of a strict proportionality test to national measures in the EC apply with even greater force to WTO panels and the Appellate Body.

6.4 Concluding Remarks on Prohibitions, Justifications and Conditions

Summarising the above considerations, the following pattern can be discerned when comparing the EC and WTO rules regarding trade-restrictive environmental and health measures.

- National measures taken for health or environmental reasons that specifically target imported products as such violate Article 28 and Article XI GATT, and need justification under Article 30 EC and Article XX GATT, respectively. When such measures are taken for sanitary or phytosanitary protection, they are disciplined by the SPS Agreement, which prohibits them if they are more trade-restrictive than required, not based on scientific principles and a risk assessment, or if they amount to arbitrary or unjustifiable discrimination or a disguised trade restriction.
- National internal regulatory measures taken for health or environmental reasons that lay down product characteristics with reference to product origin violate Article 28 EC and Article III:4 GATT as well as Article 2.1 TBT. They require justification under Article 30 EC and Article XX GATT. When taken for sanitary or phytosanitary protection, they are covered by the SPS Agreement (see above).
- National internal regulatory measures taken for health or environmental reasons that lay down product characteristics without reference to product origin violate Article 28 EC but can be justified under Article 30 EC or by mandatory requirements. They do not violate the GATT, but do violate Article 2.2 TBT if more trade-restrictive than necessary. When taken for sanitary or phytosanitary protection, they are disciplined by the SPS Agreement (see above).
- National internal regulatory measures taken for health or environmental reasons that restrict or prohibit certain selling arrangements violate Article 28 EC only if they discriminate *de facto* or *de jure* or completely prevent the market access of imported goods. If they do, they can be justified under Article 30 EC or by mandatory requirements, except if *de jure* discriminatory, in which case only Article 30 EC is available. Such measures violate Article III:4 GATT only if they are discriminatory; if so, they may be justified by Article XX GATT.
- National internal regulatory measures taken for health or environmental reasons that do not lay down product characteristics, and do not prohibit or restrict certain selling arrangements, i.e. those dubbed as "third category

measures" in the EC context, violate Article 28 EC unless their trade effects are too remote or uncertain. If they violate Article 28 EC, they can be justified under Article 30 EC or by mandatory requirements, except if they are *de jure* discriminatory, in which case only Article 30 EC is available. Such measures violate Article III:4 GATT only if discriminatory; if so, they can be justified by Article XX GATT.

- When measures require justification under Article 30 EC or the mandatory requirements, they need to pursue an acceptable (environmental or health) objective, be appropriate to pursue that objective, and be necessary in the sense that no alternative less trade-restrictive measures are available that are equally capable of attaining the same level of protection. Under Article 30 EC, they must not arbitrarily discriminate or constitute a disguised trade restriction. When measures require justification under Article XX GATT, the TBT or SPS Agreement, they need to pursue an acceptable (environmental or health) objective, be appropriate to pursue that objective (explicit in paragraph (g) and implicit in other paragraphs and in the TBT and SPS Agreements), be necessary in the sense that no alternative less trade-restrictive measures are reasonably available that are equally capable of attaining the same level of protection, and must not arbitrarily or unjustifiably discriminate or constitute a disguised trade restriction (chapeau to Article XX and SPS).

Thus, the main differences between the two legal regimes are, first, the ECJ's separate treatment of "selling arrangements"; secondly, the WTO's separate treatment of SPS measures; and thirdly, the different treatment of "third category" measures. The first difference is really not that great in that it amounts to a national treatment test for selling arrangements similar to that in Article III:4 GATT. However, it is qualified by the ECJ by a market access test, which has been argued in this work to constitute an additional requirement and is not found in GATT Article III:4. The second difference is a typological one rather than one resulting in essentially different tests. The ECJ has made it clear that Member States may set their own level of life and health protection, but that they must take into account the interests of traders and producers in other Member States and scientific evidence, and must avoid double testing. These requirements closely resemble the conditions which SPS measures must fulfil in the WTO. Finally, it has been argued in this work that there is no reason not to extend the EC regime applicable to "selling arrangements" to "third category measures". This would unify the EC test for measures not specifically targeting imports and not laying down product requirements as a non-discrimination test, qualified by a market access test. It would signify further alignment with the WTO regime under Article III:4 GATT, with the exception of that same market access requirement, which is appropriate in an internal market but not in the

WTO. Considering the different contexts in which they operate, the similarities between the relevant provisions and their interpretations are striking. However, two fields in which the similarities between the EC and the WTO are less obvious remain to be discussed: that of harmonisation and that of extraterritoriality and PPMs.

CHAPTER 7

Harmonisation, Extraterritoriality and Production and Processing Methods

7.1 Treaty Provisions and Harmonised Environmental Standards

What effects does harmonisation have upon the assessment of trade restrictive environmental measures as investigated above? Once environmental standards are harmonised, to what extent are measures still assessed under the rules discussed in this work? This question is addressed here for both the EC and WTO contexts, with focus being placed on product standards, as they provide the most grounds for a comparative approach.

7.1.1 Harmonisation, Legislative Powers and International Standards

"Harmonisation" denotes a range of policy instruments, from the adoption of completely unified international standards to the recognition by one state of the equivalence of another state's standards.[1] "Standards" is used here in a wide sense, as encompassing what the TBT Agreement calls mandatory "technical regulations", voluntary "standards", as well as conformity assessment rules. When the word "harmonisation" is used in the EC context, it usually refers to the enactment of so-called secondary Community legislation. Such legislation may also encompass the whole range of harmonisation instruments, from legislation setting unified standards to legislation imposing recognition.[2] EC harmonising legislation reflects a political compromise in striking a balance between the imperatives of the free movement of goods and those of other interests, such as environmental ones.

The WTO, on the other hand, lacks the powers to enact comparable instruments. The WTO Agreements do not empower the institutions of that organisation to enact legislation as the EC Treaty empowers the Council of Ministers and the European Parliament to issue directives, regulations, and decisions. In principle, it is not impossible that substantive environmental standards become part of the WTO set of commitments. The Members of the WTO could commit themselves to anything, including substantive environmental standards. Substantive harmonisation has taken place in the TRIPS Agreement, which includes substantive norms of intellectual property protection (e.g. the minimum protection to be given to intellectual property rights). Likewise, Members could add an Agreement on Trade and Environment to the WTO "single package". However, it is difficult to imagine what kind of substantive environmental standards could be incorporated into such an agreement. WTO Members differ

---

[1]   See Sykes (1999a and b); Trebilcock and Howse (1998).

[2]   Legislation imposing recognition even had its own basis in the EC Treaty in the old Article 100b, introduced by the Single European Act but abolished by the Amsterdam Treaty.

greatly in terms of their natural and climatological endowments and their levels of technological and economic development. Moreover, as has rightly been observed, the TRIPS Agreement recognises individual intellectual property rights and provides that right-holders can have these rights enforced in their domestic judicial systems.[3] These features appear quite difficult to transpose into environmental standards. Thus, although the TRIPS can be taken as a precedent for incorporating substantive standards within the WTO, it appears highly unlikely that standards in the environmental sphere will be incorporated or set in a WTO Agreement. It has been argued that in many cases, substantive environmental harmonisation is even unsound from an economic viewpoint.[4] Another problematic question is why, if at all, such standard-setting should take place within the WTO, as that organisation mostly consists of trade experts and lacks expertise in environmental and health issues, which is present in other international fora. Less ambitious and more feasible is for WTO Agreements to refer to substantive standards which have been agreed upon elsewhere. That is precisely what the TBT and SPS Agreements do.

As most of the TBT Agreement and some of the SPS Agreement deal with product standards, the provisions in these agreements that refer to international standards and their consequences for the WTO compatibility of national measures are best compared to Article 95 of the EC Treaty. Article 95 EC, it is recalled, provides legislative authority to enact 'measures for the approximation of the provisions laid down by law, regulation or administrative action in Member States which have as their object the establishment and functioning of the internal market'. Most of the Community legislation based upon Article 95 harmonises product standards. Article 95(3) EC provides that the Commission must take as a basis for its legislative proposals a high level of health, safety, environmental and consumer protection, and that the Council and the European Parliament will also seek to achieve this objective when enacting the legislation. Article 95(4-6) EC at the same time lays down conditions under which Member States are allowed to maintain or introduce stricter standards than those laid down in the harmonising legislation, including the application of such standards to imported products.

According to the EC's "New Approach", the harmonisation instrument itself, usually a directive, only lays down "essential requirements" that products must meet in order to be allowed free movement in the internal market. The harmonisation of the more detailed technical standards is left to standardisation bodies.[5] These bodies in turn refer to international standards wherever possible.[6] Prod-

---

[3] Enders in Van Dijck and Faber (1996) at 71.

[4] See e.g. Esty and Geradin (1998).

[5] The three European standardisation bodies are CEN (general standardisation), CENELEC (electrical standardisation) and ETSI (telecom standardisation).

[6] Mainly ISO (general standardisation) and IEC (electrical standardisation) standards.

ucts manufactured in conformity with harmonised standards are presumed to
conform to the essential requirements and thus enjoy free movement.[7] Once a
product conforms to harmonised standards and is thus presumed to meet the
essential requirements laid down in the relevant Community directive, Member
States may still apply additional national provisions to protect in particular workers, consumers, or the environment. However, these provisions must comply
with the Treaty, in particular Articles 28-30 thereof. This means that they
may neither require modifications to the product nor influence the conditions
for its placement on the market.[8] The New Approach has not been applied
to all product requirements in the EC. Important sectors such as foodstuffs,
chemical products and pharmaceuticals have been excluded.[9] Nonetheless, the
harmonisation of product standards not following the New Approach is likewise
usually coupled with a free movement clause, which ensures that Member
States in principle cannot refuse market access to products conforming to the
harmonised standards. Thus, as a general rule for the harmonisation of product
standards in the EC, Member States can in principle enact stricter standards, but
can only apply them to their own producers. The main exception to this general
rule is provided in paragraphs 4-6 of Article 95 EC, which provide a possibility
for Member States to apply stricter standards, including to imports, but only
under strict conditions and under Commission scrutiny.

The SPS Agreement (Article 3.4) provides that Members shall play a full
part 'in the relevant international organisations and their subsidiary bodies,
in particular the Codex Alimentarius Commission, the International Office of
Epizootics, and the international and regional organisations operating within
the framework of the International Plant Protection Convention, to promote
within these organisations the development and periodic review of standards,
guidelines and recommendations'. In its Annex A, the SPS Agreement defines
'international standards, guidelines and recommendations' by reference to these
three organisations, adding that the SPS Committee may identify appropriate
standards promulgated by other international organisations which are open
for membership to all WTO Members for matters not covered by the above
organisations.

The TBT Agreement is less clear as to what should be understood by "inter-
national standards". It does not define them or list organisations as the SPS
Agreement does. It does provide in Annex 1 that the terms in the ISO/IEC
Guide on General Terms and Their Definitions Concerning Standardisation
and Related Activities shall have the same meaning when used in the TBT
Agreement, but subsequently adds its own definitions of a technical regulation,

---

7   See Council Resolution on the New Approach to Technical Harmonisation, OJ 1985 C136/1, and further
explanations at http://europa.eu.int/comm/enterprise/newapproach.

8   EC Commission (2000a), at 9.

9   See EC Commission (2000a).

a standard and a conformity assessment procedure.[10] An explanatory note to the definition of "standard" adds to the lack of clarity. It provides that whereas standards prepared by "the international standardisation community" -a term that remains undefined- are based on consensus, the TBT Agreement also covers documents that are not based on consensus.[11] It is unclear whether "documents" refers to documents laying down standards that have been internationally agreed upon, but not by 'the international standardisation community', or rather to national standards or technical regulations, or to both. Probably, international standards not based on consensus are meant. Understandably, the lack of clarity as to what is an international standard under the TBT Agreement is one of the items under discussion in the TBT Committee.[12]

In the WTO, as said, there is no harmonising legislative authority, so there are no instruments equivalent to Community directives. However, both the SPS and TBT Agreements oblige Members to base their measures on international standards, except if they wish to apply stricter standards (Article 3.1 and 3.3 SPS) or deem the international standard to be ineffective or inappropriate (Article 2.4 TBT). There is a presumption of conformity with the SPS Agreement and the GATT on the part of SPS measures conforming to international standards (Article 3.2 SPS), and a presumption of conformity with the main discipline in the TBT Agreement for technical regulations in accordance with international standards (Article 2.5 TBT). Thus, although in the WTO there is no presumption of free movement for products conforming to international standards, national product requirements conforming to international standards will generally not hamper the importation of a product that conforms to the same international standards. However, in the absence of a notion like "essential requirements" and of a free movement presumption, a Member can always oppose an additional product requirement being applied to the importation of a product, even if it conforms to an international standard. Conformity with an international standard, in other words, does not exhaust the range of objectives that national product requirements may pursue. For example, a product may conform to an international safety standard and nevertheless be refused because it does not meet an environmental standard. Moreover, the SPS and TBT Agreements leave ample room for Members to impose stricter standards than relevant international standards.

The only way for EC Member States to oppose the importation of a product meeting harmonised standards based on Article 95 is to invoke paragraphs 4-6

---

[10] Annex 1 TBT further defines an 'international body or system' as a boy or system whose membership is open to the relevant bodies of at least all WTO Members. However, that reference is relevant to voluntary standards rather than mandatory technical regulations on which this work concentrates.

[11] Explanatory Note to the definition of "standard" in Annex 1 TBT.

[12] See e.g. documents G/TBT/W/121 (Japanese proposal, with correction); G/TBT/W/87 and 133 (EC proposals); G/TBT/W/143 (Canadian proposal), and G/TBT/W/131 (Communications from the IEC and ISO).

of that provision. As these paragraphs are invoked by Member States to apply
national measures that deviate from harmonised protection levels, the Commission applies the conditions in these paragraphs strictly. WTO Members, on
the other hand, can determine that an international standard is inappropriate,
ineffective or insufficient to achieve their chosen protection level. Although a
challenge under the SPS or TBT Agreement may oblige them to demonstrate
that this is indeed the case, their stricter standards are not subjected to approval
by a WTO body, as is the case under Article 95 EC. A further important
difference between the EC and the WTO in this respect is that Article 95(3)
lays down the Community's ambition to achieve a high level of health and
environmental protection when enacting harmonising legislation. Both the TBT
and SPS Agreements lack any such reference to the high protection levels of
international standards.

Harmonisation of environmental and health standards is not only based on
Article 95 EC, but also on Article 175 EC and Article 152(4) EC. As the Court
has said, the Community rules do not seek to effect complete harmonisation in
the area of the environment.[13] Article 176 EC allows Member States to maintain
or introduce more stringent protective measures than the protective measures
adopted pursuant to Article 175 EC. This provision affirms that stricter national
standards must be compatible with the Treaty, but does not subject such standards to Commission approval. Arguably, the looser wording of Article 176 EC as
compared to Article 95(4-6) is precisely the result of the type of standards that
are normally harmonised under Articles 175 and 95 respectively. Under Article
175, standards for air quality, surface water, nature protection reserves etc.
are harmonised. Such standards are not applied to products and have less
bearing on the free movement of goods, and the same holds true for stricter
national standards. It is not entirely clear to what extent Article 175 may be
used for harmonising product standards. If this were done, there might be an
evasion of paragraphs 4-6 of Article 95, which guarantee that once standards
are harmonised and thereby a Community level of protection has been agreed,
the application of stricter standards to imports remains exceptional. Thus, the
harmonisation of product standards should preferably take place on the basis
of Article 95, not 175 EC. Production methods may also be harmonised under
Article 175. Such standards cannot as such be applied to products, as they
address manufacturers. However, it is argued in this work that the proper
legal basis is Article 95 if the production methods have a significant impact
on production costs. Finally, Article 152(4) explicitly allows stricter national
measures in the case of the harmonisation of quality and safety standards for
organs and human substances, and explicitly excludes harmonisation of health-
incentive measures. It also provides for the harmonisation of veterinary and

---

[13]　Case C-318/98 *Fornasar*, para. 46.

phytosanitary measures with the direct objective of protecting human health, without clarifying whether stricter measures are allowed.

International standard-setting not only takes place within the organisations the TBT and SPS Agreements explicitly refer to. Standards developed within international bodies not expressly mentioned may also play a role in interpreting WTO provisions. Moreover, an important part of international environmental law is laid down in multilateral environmental agreements (MEAs). Such agreements contain principles and rules, but sometimes also substantive environmental standards. The WTO Agreements do not currently expressly refer to such agreements. However, MEAs already play a role in interpreting GATT provisions, and are increasingly likely to do so in the future.[14]

If environmental standards are unlikely to be agreed upon within the WTO, they will continue to be set outside the WTO. Their relationship with WTO commitments, as well as who is to decide upon that relationship, will therefore continue to be a potential problem.[15] Clarification of the relationship between WTO commitments and MEAs is part of the post-Doha negotiating agenda, at least with regard to WTO members that are also parties to MEAs. However, agreement will be difficult to find, and clarification may be sought through dispute settlement procedures. Many MEAs are based on a non-contentious model, and have no or less efficient dispute settlement procedures than the WTO. As a result of this, and of the relatively efficient and successful WTO dispute settlement procedures, governments may be expected to resort to WTO dispute settlement rather than dispute settlement under MEAs or the International Court of Justice.

This expected tendency creates two problems. First, why should those aspects which governments cannot agree upon at even the highest political level be left to international dispute settlement bodies? Although there is no easy answer to this question, it should be noted that where treaties contain widely formulated norms and provide for dispute settlement procedures, these norms can be seen as a mandate for the adjudicatory body to interpret them.[16] In principle, states can always interfere if they are unhappy about the results of such interpretation. However, it is difficult to agree politically, as was demonstrated by the difficult decision-making process at recent Ministerial Conferences. Thus, the responsibility laid upon the adjudicatory body is heavy, and that body may accordingly be expected to search for ways to show deference to states' choices in its interpretations. Secondly, if any dispute settlement body is going to decide on

---

[14] See also Sections 4.6.1 and 5.4.3.

[15] The Committee on Trade and Environment has carried out important work in co-operation with secretariats of a large number of MEAs in taking stock of potential conflicts. See in particular documents WT/CTE/W/160, Matrix on Trade Measures Pursuant to Selected MEAs, and WT/CTE/W/191, Compliance and Dispute Settlement Provisions in the WTO and in Multilateral Environmental Agreements.

[16] Trachtman (1999) at 362. Cf. Bronckers (1999a and 1999b).

the relationship between trade and environment commitments, why that of the
WTO? The preference of the complainant is likely to be the WTO in most cases,
as it will typically be the complainant who wants trade interests to prevail and
who wishes to see a swift resolution of the dispute.[17]

The problem of which disputes concerning the intersection between international commitments on trade and on environment are brought before the
Appellate Body could be accommodated by agreeing in MEAs on dispute settlement procedures with a clear mandate, and by deference to such procedures on
the part of WTO panels and the Appellate Body. However, as said, MEAs do
not necessarily rely on dispute settlement, which is not always an appropriate
manner to tackle global environmental challenges. Moreover, problems may
arise when parties to a dispute disagree on what is the appropriate forum for
their dispute.[18] Perhaps the International Court of Justice is best suited to decide
upon such problems of competence. However, the WTO Dispute Settlement
Understanding rather coercively stipulates that Members are to have recourse to
the DSU rules if they seek redress of a violation of WTO obligations or other
nullification or impairment of benefits under the WTO Agreements.[19] Thus, if
a party challenges an environmental measure pursuant to an MEA under the
WTO rules, the Appellate Body will play a decisive role as the forum in which
the intersection of international trade law and international environmental law
is addressed.[20] Although the Appellate Body does not consist of experts on international environmental law, experience up to now provides reason to assume
that the Appellate Body will show due diligence in properly taking developments
in international environmental law into account. Nevertheless, a modification of
the DSU provision mentioned above and involvement of the ICJ in disputes over
competence to decide over disputes at the intersection of international trade law
and international environmental law are worth consideration.

7.1.2 Interplay between the Legislature and the Adjudicator

In the EC, a "horizontal interplay" between the adjudicator and
the legislator takes place in all subject areas where the EC and its Member States
share competencies, and where both Community harmonisation and national
measures are controlled by primary Community law. The trade-environment
nexus is a good example of this interplay. In the absence of harmonisation, if

---

[17] See Ohloff and Schloeman (1998).

[18] The swordfish dispute between the EC and Chile is a case in point. Complaints were brought both in the
WTO and before the Law of the Sea Tribunal. However, the dispute was settled amicably. See OJ (2000)
L 96/67, and www.europa.eu.int/comm/trade/miti/dispute/swordfish.html.

[19] Article 23.1 DSU.

[20] Trachtman (1999) at 364.

a national trade-related environmental measure is challenged before a national court (e.g. by a trader) or before the ECJ (e.g. by the Commission), there are two possible outcomes: either the measure is found to violate the EC Treaty and must be modified by the national legislator, or the measure is upheld. In the latter case, the distortions to the functioning of the internal market caused by the measure may nevertheless be removed through legislative action at the Community level. As the Commission stated in its communication after the *Cassis de Dijon* judgment, its harmonisation work is mainly directed at national laws posing barriers to trade that are admissible under the Court's criteria for Articles 28-30.[21] The European Commission, in its role as a "guardian of the Treaties", plays a strategic part in this interplay. It has the sole right of initiative to enact proposals for legislation concerning the internal market. It also has the discretion whether or not to commence infringement actions against Member States. Thus, to some extent the Commission is able to influence the direction of solutions to trade-environment conflicts. It may commence an infringement action against a Member State's environmental legislation if it deems that legislation to be too restrictive of intra-Community trade. If the Court agrees, the Member State will have to repeal or amend its legislation. If the Court upholds the national legislation, the Commission can still propose legislation in order to 'harmonise away' the trade-restrictive effects of the national legislation, or at least part of it.

The Court has determined that a measure adopted on the basis of Article 95 of the Treaty must genuinely have as its object the improvement of the conditions for the establishment and functioning of the internal market, i.e. the elimination of obstacles to free movement or the elimination of distortions of competition.[22] It has been argued that the Community may, on the basis of Article 95, only legislate as regards those matters falling within the ambit of Article 28 EC.[23] This would imply that the Community could not harmonise "selling arrangements" meeting the *Keck* test on the basis of Article 95. More generally, it implies that the Court's interpretation of Article 28 is instrumental in determining the scope of the Community's legislative mandate in Article 95. However, there have also been instances of harmonisation under Article 95 concerning subject-matters that had little to do with trade.[24] Moreover, there are no instances in which the Court itself has made explicit the linkage between Articles 28 and 95.[25] In any event, this point illustrates that the inter-

---

[21] OJ 1980 C 256/2.

[22] Case C-376/98 *Germany v. Parliament and Council* at paras. 83-84.

[23] See Weiler (1999) at 372: '[T]he broader the catch of Article 30 [now 28], the broader the legislative competences of the Community.'

[24] Such as the harmonisation of daylight saving time: See Directive 94/21, mentioned by Schrauwen (1997) at 194. Further on this subject, Mortelmans (1994), and Mortelmans and Van Ooik (2001).

[25] As noted by Mortelmans and Van Ooik (2001) at 126, who argue that it would be logical that only those measures falling within the prohibition of Article 28 could be harmonised under Article 95.

play between the Commission and the Court works both ways. If the Commission can somewhat steer the direction of trade-environment issues by deciding against which trade obstacles to address in infringement procedures, its legislative proposals for harmonisation will in turn be influenced by the Court's findings as to the scope of Article 28, which may vary over time. Moreover, the horizontal interplay in the EC is not confined to the relationship between the Commission and the Court; the Council and European Parliament also play a role in disputes concerning the proper legal basis of harmonising legislation. On that point there is also vertical interplay, as illustrated by cases in which Member States that have been overruled in the Council when harmonisation was enacted then challenge its legal basis.[26]

Horizontal interplay between the adjudicator and the legislator present in the EC is largely absent in the WTO. The WTO legislator is the Ministerial Conference that convenes once every two years. Recent Ministerial Conferences and the continuing deadlock in the Committee on Trade and Environment demonstrate how difficult it is for over 140 Members to "legislate", i.e. to change or add to the existing agreements. The General Council, which is composed of representatives of all the Members, convenes once a month and conducts the functions of the Ministerial Conference in the intervals between its meetings.[27] The Ministerial Conference and the General Council have the exclusive authority to adopt interpretations of the WTO Agreements.[28] Amendments to the Agreements must be decided by the Ministerial Conference.[29] Both authoritative interpretations and amendments are very difficult to agree on. Thus, in the WTO, there is a bias for "negative integration" without accompanying "positive integration".[30] This may result in a "regulatory gap", when national environmental measures are struck down for violating WTO commitments, and international measures cannot be politically agreed upon.[31] In some respects, this situation may be compared to the situation prevailing in the EC before the 1987 Single European Act made it possible to enact harmonising legislation by qualified majority. During the 1970s and early 1980s, a great deal of environmental harmonisation was precluded by the fact that Member States had a veto. During that same period, the ECJ gave an important impetus to the internal market by interpreting the relevant provisions quite liberally. This impetus in turn paved the way for renewed legislative activity under the Commission's plan to achieve the internal market by 1992.

---

[26] As in Case C-376/98 *Germany* v. *Parliament and Council* mentioned above.

[27] Article IV:1 and IV:2 of the WTO Agreement.

[28] Article IX:2 of the WTO Agreement.

[29] Article X of the WTO Agreement.

[30] Cf. Trachtman (1998) at 51.

[31] Cf. the "regulatory gap" referred to in the EC context in Micklitz and Weatherill (1994).

In the absence of legislative capacity in the WTO comparable to that in the EC, a similar judicial-legislative dynamic appears impossible in the WTO. It should be noted, moreover, that the "judicial activism" of the ECJ did not only result in a "pro-trade" attitude. If Article 28 was given its wide interpretation of prohibiting trade obstacles and imposing recognition during this period, the Court at the same time accepted the mandatory requirements as justifications for national measures. Moreover, it accepted that environmental protection is one of the Community's essential objectives, and that it constitutes a mandatory requirement.[32] The remaining question is whether similar "judicial activism" is called for in the WTO, as long as governments do not agree on positive integration inside or outside the WTO. It is submitted that in view of the different objectives of the WTO and the EC, similar activism is not called for. The WTO is not striving to attain an internal market. Panels and the Appellate Body should respect the textual limitations of the agreements they interpret, and not read into them more trade liberalisation commitments than their text warrants. At the same time, WTO dispute settlement will need to take on board all external "positive integration", i.e. all environmental standards and principles that have been internationally agreed upon and that are potentially relevant to it when interpreting WTO provisions in trade-environment disputes. Moreover, it should be recalled that harmonisation is not confined to standards and principles; it includes the recognition of equivalence. The more environmental standards are recognised as being equivalent, the less trade barriers will be caused by their application to imports. The WTO can play an important role in this respect, as the TBT and SPS Agreements contain the beginnings of recognition requirements.[33]

7.2 Extraterritoriality, Production Methods and Unilateralism

The above considerations regarding harmonisation demonstrate that it is not always easy to compare the EC and the WTO. The same is true for the issues of extraterritoriality, production and processing methods (PPMs) and unilateralism. Although disputes concerning these issues have been presented to both the ECJ and the GATT and WTO dispute settlement bodies, the manner in which they have been presented and addressed differs to an important extent. In the WTO, the three disputes in which unilateral measures based on PPMs were taken to pursue extraterritorial environmental objectives, *US-Tuna-Dolphin I* and *II* and *US-Shrimp-Turtle*, all concerned import prohibi-

---

[32] See Cases 240/83 *ADBHU* and 302/86 *Danish Bottles*, respectively.

[33] Cf. Van Calster (2000) at 544-549.

tions of products from exporting Members whose authorities did not impose
PPMs that were equivalent to the PPMs imposed domestically by the importing
Member.[34] In the EC, most of the relevant cases concerned export rather than
import restrictions. Only in *Gourmetterie van den Burg* and *Preussen Elektra* were
imports at issue. The ECJ has as yet not taken a clear position on extraterritorial
protection, PPM-based measures, and unilateralism. However, it has in fact
given contradictory hints as to its position. In most of the ECJ cases on these
issues, there was relevant secondary Community legislation, which enabled the
Court not to take a definite stance on whether unilateral PPM-based measures
protecting the environment outside the Member State taking the measure are
principally prohibited, or rather allowed in principle but subject to strict conditions.

7.2.1   Extraterritoriality, Unilateralism, and PPMs in the EC

The Court is unclear concerning the acceptability of extraterritorial resource protection under Articles 28-30 EC. Extraterritorial environmental objectives may be allowed and even mandated by Community harmonisation
instruments.[35] However, at least in a situation where there was relevant harmonisation, the Court has shown itself to be sceptical about unilateral extraterritorial protection measures extending beyond the protection offered in the
Community instrument. In *Van den Burg*, the Court found that Article 30 'read
in conjunction with' the Wild Birds directive cannot justify extraterritorial protection measures. Although the Court's position might have been different had
unilateral measures been taken in the absence of any relevant harmonisation,
its mention of Article 30 suggests that it did not favourably regard import restrictions for extraterritorial protection reasons under that provision.[36] However, not
only was there relevant harmonisation, but the species sought to be protected
in *Van den Burg* were confined to one Member State and were not migratory or
endangered. Therefore, *Van den Burg* does not appear altogether to exclude the
possibility that unilateral extraterritorial measures pursuing transnational and
global environmental protection objectives can be justified under Article 30 (and
arguably the mandatory requirements).

The Court's sceptical position with regard to extraterritorial protection goals
that are confined to other Member States can also be seen in the context
of export restrictions in the *Nertsvoederfabriek*, *Hedley Lomas*, and *Compassion
in World Farming* cases. In the latter case, as in *Van den Burg*, there was

---

[34] The second *US-Tuna-Dolphin* dispute in addition concerned an 'intermediary nation embargo', i.e. an
import prohibition from GATT contracting parties that did not certify and prove that they had not
imported tuna subjected to the primary embargo.

[35] See Cases C-202/94 *Van der Feesten* and C-149/94 *Vergy*.

[36] Cf. Scott (2000) at 128.

relevant Community legislation. And again, the Court found that the provision in that legislation allowing Member States to take stricter measures was to be interpreted as being confined to its own territory. In both cases, the Court observed that the secondary Community legislation exhaustively regulated the Member States' powers with regard to the protection goal at issue.[37] There was an important difference, though. The provision on stricter national measures in the directive at issue in *Compassion* explicitly provided for such territorial limitation, while the provision in the Wild Birds directive at issue in *Van den Burg* did not. Nevertheless, as said, the Court thought it inappropriate for one Member State to take trade restricting measures to protect a bird that received no special protection under the directive and was lawfully hunted in another Member State in accordance with the directive.

On the other hand, in *Inter-Huiles* and *Dusseldorp*, again in the context of export restrictions, the Court appears to admit the possibility of extraterritorial protection, when the importing Member State does not offer the same extent of protection as the exporting Member State. Although not explicitly, the Court also appears to accept trade-restrictive measures aimed at protecting global commons, at least when there are relevant instruments of international law regarding the protection of these commons. Thus, in *Bluhme*, the Court accepted a trade-restrictive measure with reference to the Biodiversity Convention, and in *Preussen Elektra*, it accepted an obligation to purchase locally produced green electricity as part of a strategy to combat climate change, with reference to the Kyoto Protocol. The latter case suggests that even discriminatory measures can be taken to protect the global commons. The Court in all four cases mentioned above did not pay explicit attention to the location of the resources protected. Nonetheless, considering the Court's case-law, it may be argued that in the absence of relevant harmonisation, the possibility that extraterritorial protection measures are acceptable under Articles 28-30 EC exists. Obviously, the proportionality test may be expected to apply with particular vigour in such cases. The appropriateness of the measure in terms of its contribution to the environmental objective will not always be easy to show, and the necessity requirement will imply that the Member State taking the measure will need to explain why it had to resort to a unilateral measure. This will probably include a requirement of having first attempted to fulfil the conservation goal in the other Member State by entering into negotiations with that Member State, and by raising the matter in the appropriate Community institutions. *Preussen Elektra* and *Bluhme* suggest that the Court may be more lenient in its appraisal of unilateral extraterritorial protection measures when the protection of global commons is at stake than when the protection objective is confined to the limits of another Member State and has no transnational aspect to it. Both cases also suggest that such measures

---

[37] Cases C-169/89 *Van den Burg*, para. 9; C-1/96 *Compassion*, paras. 56-62.

will be more acceptable when there is relevant international environmental
law regarding the problem the measure aims to address.

The issue of unilateralism in the EC is closely connected to the existence or
absence of harmonising legislation. In *Hedley Lomas*, the UK was not allowed
to restrict exports of live sheep because it thought Spain did not duly apply the
obligations in the Community directive on slaughtering methods. The Court
based this observation on Article 10 of the EC Treaty, the obligation of loyalty
towards the Community, which precludes Member States from taking the law
into their own hands. Indeed, Member States have various possibilities at
their disposal as alternatives to unilateral action when they are of the opinion
that another Member State is infringing Community law. They may start an
infringement procedure against that Member State under Article 227 EC. They
may also ask the Commission to check the behaviour of the other Member State,
which may - upon the discretion of the Commission - lead to infringement
procedures under Article 226 EC. Whether unilateralism is acceptable is less
clear in the absence of Community legislation on the subject-matter at hand.
In such cases, the subject-matter has not been "occupied" by the Community;
therefore, Member States are in principle free to take unilateral measures, as
long as they respect primary Community law. Thus, the question whether or
not unilateral measures are allowed will have to be answered by interpreting
Articles 28 and 30. However, if a Member State feels that its industry, consumers or animals suffer from PPMs applied in another Member State, Article 10
EC commits it to ask the Commission to present proposals for legislation to
harmonise that PPM in the Community rather than to take unilateral measures.
Again, the Commission has discretion; but especially if the Member State
succeeds in mobilising other Member States, the Commission is unlikely to
ignore its call.

As discussed in Chapter 3, the ECJ has accepted tax differentiation on
the basis of PPMs in a number of cases.[38] Internal taxes may differentiate on
the basis of objective criteria without regard to product origin, including the
raw materials used or production processes employed, as long as there is no
discrimination or protection, i.e. as long as any tax advantages are extended to
imports. Moreover, tax differentiation is compatible with Community law only
if it pursues objectives which are themselves compatible with the Treaty and
its secondary legislation. In *Outukumpu Oy*, the Court explicitly stated that a
tax differentiation according to PPMs based on environmental considerations is
acceptable, as long as importers are given an opportunity to demonstrate the
PPM applied in producing the imported electricity so as to qualify for a favourable rate.[39] Considering this consistent case-law regarding tax differentiations,

---

[38] See Cases 127/75 *Bobie*, 148/77 *Hansen*, 21/79 *Commission* v. *Italy* (Regenerated Oils), 140/79 *Chemial*
Farmaceutici.

[39] Case C-213/96 *Outukumpy Oy*.

the question arises whether a national *regulatory* measure that differentiates products according to their production methods might be acceptable under Articles 28-30 EC, if it allows imported products to be marketed if they are accompanied by a certificate or label stating their production method.

The European Court of Justice has as yet not been confronted with measures making imports dependent on the policies of the governments of exporting Member States, as has been the case in the WTO. The situation in *Hedley Lomas* can to some extent be compared to the WTO disputes, in that the export restrictions were motivated by the perceived failure by the authorities in the importing country to duly implement a Community directive. In view of the institutional framework in the EC, and of the obligation of solidarity laid down in Article 10 EC, it appears that unilateral measures to target government policies in other Member States, e.g. by making imports dependent on policies regarding production methods, is not acceptable under Articles 28-30 EC. On the other hand, as argued above, it does not seem to be impossible from the outset that measures making the marketing or sale of products, including imports, dependent on how products are produced can be justified by Article 30 or the mandatory requirement of environmental protection. The ECJ has also not been faced with such measures up to now. Perhaps this is because production methods are partially harmonised in the EC. It is recalled that according to the *Cassis de Dijon* case-law, there is a presumption that products lawfully produced in a Member State should have access to the entire Community market, unless obstacles to such access can be justified. The obligation to purchase locally produced green electricity at issue in *Preussen Elektra* referred to the production method of electricity. At the same time, it excluded all imported electricity, including green electricity from other Member States. It may be argued that if such a discriminatory measure can be justified, a measure based on a PPM that equally applies to imported and domestic goods should also be able to find justification for the trade obstacles is causes. If so, the case-law on regulatory measures would be brought into line with that on tax measures.

The question as to whether a PPM-based labelling requirement is acceptable under Articles 28-30 EC may need to be addressed by the European Court of Justice in the near future. A Dutch legislative proposal currently pending essentially requires all wooden products placed on the Dutch market to bear a mark indicating whether or not the product originates from an area subject to a management plan for sustainable forestry. This management plan must be approved by a body recognised either by the Dutch Council for Accreditation or by any organisation with which the Council for Accreditation has a mutual recognition agreement.[40] A declaration made on the basis of a document issued

---

[40] Dutch Parliament, proposal to amend the Wet milieubeheer (Dutch Environmental Management Act), Kamerstukken 23982 and 26998, especially the proposed Articles 9.2, 9.4-9.8, and 9.16; the addition on foreign accreditation organisations was added later.

by a foreign organisation and recognised by the Dutch Environment Minister is
equated with this approval. Likewise, permission to issue a certificate conferring
the right to apply a "positive mark" on sustainably produced wood is granted
by a body recognised either by the Dutch Council for Accreditation or by any
organisation with which the Council for Accreditation has a mutual recognition
agreement. Such permission may be equated with a declaration by a recognised
body that the applicant meets the requirements in the Dutch law or equivalent
requirements. In turn, such a declaration may be issued on the basis of a document issued by a foreign organisation recognised by the Dutch minister that is
capable of assessing the sustainability of wooden products in an independent,
reliable and expert manner.[41]

The proposal was notified to the European Commission in accordance with
the directive on the notification of technical regulations.[42] The Commission and
ten Member States as well as Norway delivered detailed opinions criticising the
proposal.[43] In its detailed opinion, the Commission acknowledged that sustainable forest management is an acceptable objective, and thus did not question
the acceptability of the extraterritorial nature of the Netherlands' protection
objective. However, the Commission raised serious doubts as to the appropriateness, necessity and proportionality of the proposed measure, with regard to
wood products both from within the Community and from third countries.[44]
Subsequently, in its reaction to the Dutch response to the detailed opinions, the
Commission did question the extraterritorial nature of the measure's protection
goal. In addition, it pointed at the Community's initiatives towards a common
policy regarding the protection of tropical forests, and stated that in its view,
voluntary labelling would be more appropriate and a less trade-restrictive measure to fulfil the objective pursued.[45] At the time of writing, the Dutch government still has to sign the legislative bill. If it does so, the Commission intends to
commence infringement procedures.

7.2.2 Extraterritoriality, Unilateralism, and PPMs in the WTO

In the WTO, the nature of the measures at issue in *US-Tuna-
Dolphin* and *US-Shrimp-Turtle* has arguably shaped much of the debate, including a misunderstanding that PPM-based measures are WTO-incompatible *per se*,
as violations of Article XI GATT not justified by Article XX GATT. The current

---

[41] Proposed Articles 9.4 and 9.8 of the Wet Milieubeheer.

[42] Directive 98/34, OJ 1998 L 204/34.

[43] Detailed opinions within the meaning of Article 9(2) of Directive 98/34. The only Member States not
having reacted are Denmark, Greece, Luxembourg and Ireland.

[44] Documents on file with the author.

[45] Ibid.

author does not argue that PPM-based measures that make imports dependent upon government policies in exporting countries are covered by the Note Ad Article III, and should therefore be assessed under Article III rather than Article XI. However, PPM-based measures that do not target products according to whether the authorities in the exporting country impose the same PPMs as the country taking the measure could well be assessed under Article III including the Note thereto. It has been argued in this work that measures restricting the sale, offering for sale, etc. of products on the basis of PPMs can be assessed under Article III:4 rather than Article XI GATT. The discussion of such measures will concentrate on the issues of "likeness" and "less favourable treatment", before any justification under Article XX becomes relevant. Admittedly, there are no examples of panel or Appellate Body reports that have actually found products "unlike" on the basis of their PPMs. The issue of the compatibility with Articles III and XX GATT of a PPM-based internal regulatory measure has as yet not been presented in any dispute. However, within the realm of tax discrimination, a GATT panel has suggested that differentiation on the basis of PPMs may affect "likeness".[46] Moreover, as the Appellate Body in *EC-Asbestos* has called for an evaluation of all relevant factors in determining "likeness", it does not seem to be ruled out that products are not "like" despite their physical similarity. Finally, the Appellate Body in the same case has suggested that "less favourable treatment" may in the future receive a more flexible interpretation than previously. This may also be relevant to regulatory measures that do not differentiate on the basis of product origin but on the basis of PPMs.

As regards Article XX, an evolution can be discerned in the GATT/WTO interpretations of both the issue of extraterritorial protection goals and that of unilateral PPM-based measures. As to the location of the resources protected, the first panel in *US-Tuna-Dolphin* left it open whether Article XX could allow the protection of animals or resources outside the jurisdiction of the country taking the measure, and the second thought that in principle Article XX allowed to do so.[47] The Appellate Body in *US-Shrimp-Turtle* specifically declined to rule on this point, but it did accept a sufficient link to US jurisdiction of the migratory species whose protection was sought, thus suggesting that Article XX could indeed accommodate measures seeking to protect animals that spend most of their time outside the jurisdiction of the protecting Member. As regards the principal question whether Article XX could at all be invoked to justify unilateral PPM-based measures, both panels in *US-Tuna-Dolphin* as well as the panel in *US-Shrimp-Turtle* condemned the measures at issue essentially because they

---

[46] *Japan-Alcohol 1987*, para. 5.7: '[...] the "likeness" of products must be examined taking into account not only objective criteria (such as the composition and *manufacturing processes* of products) but also the more subjective consumers' viewpoint (such as consumption and use by consumers) [...]'. Emphasis added.

[47] On the second panel report, see Weiss (1995a).

feared that the multilateral trading system would be endangered if it allowed
measures making imports dependent on the exporting states adopting certain
policies. The Appellate Body in *US-Shrimp-Turtle*, however, rejected this view
and even stated that most measures seeking justification under Article XX
condition imports on the adoption of policies by other countries. While this
statement is not entirely correct in the author's view, it marks an important shift
in dispute settlement on unilateral PPM-based trade restrictive measures. Now,
the door appears to have been opened for such measures. As the implementation dispute in *US-Shrimp-Turtle* shows, even measures targeting countries and
violating Article XI may be justified by Article XX. However, if such measures
are to be accepted, the Member taking them will have to show that it has made
serious efforts to reach international agreement on the protection objective with
all the countries it is targeting, and is not arbitrarily or unjustifiably discriminating by not taking into account differing circumstances in exporting countries,
or by not allowing sufficient guarantees of due process in the administration
of its measures.

Phrasing PPM-based measures in a non-import-specific and non-discriminatory manner in order to have them assessed under Article III rather than Article
XI GATT looks promising, but is not without its own problems. First of all,
some Members perceive import restrictions as the only way to address a number
of pressing environmental problems, because they fear that market-based non-
discriminatory measures such as a prohibition of selling dolphin-unfriendly
tuna, cannot be effectively enforced and thus lose most of their anticipated effect
on foreign producers. If this problem is real, it seems to be accommodated by the
Appellate Body's acceptance, in principle, of unilateral origin-based measures
when strict conditions are fulfilled. Secondly, and related thereto, how can a non-
origin-based and non-discriminatory PPM-based measure effectively be applied
to imports? An obligation to label or certify imported products appears to be the
only viable way in which to do this. This raises questions such as the following:
Should the labelling obligation be extended to domestic producers even if their
production is already regulated? To what extent should foreign certification be
accepted? Is mandatory labelling or certification based on PPMs covered by the
TBT, by GATT or by both? Such questions are at issue in discussions on the
WTO compatibility of the Dutch wood labelling legislative proposal mentioned
above. After the notification of this proposal under the TBT Agreement, several
WTO Members commented upon it, most of them criticising it as an unnecessary obstacle to international trade within the meaning of Article 2.2 TBT and
asking for further explanations as to its justification under Article 2.5 TBT.[48]

The US argued in *US-Tuna-Dolphin II* that the position taken by the EC to
the effect that Article XX GATT did not allow extraterritorial protection was

---

[48] Notification: G/TBT/Notif.98.448. Reactions from Canada, Malaysia, Thailand, Indonesia, Norway and
Poland on file with the author. The Malaysian reaction is documented as G/TBT/W/96. Discussions on
the proposal are found in documents G/TBT/M13 and G/TBT/W/102.

inconsistent with the position it had taken with respect to Article 30 EC in *Van den Burg*.[49] The Commission had in this case unequivocally argued that Article 30 could cover the protection of animals outside the jurisdiction of the Member State taking the measure. The EC responded that the US had misread the Court's judgment in *Van den Burg*, and that in any event, Article XX GATT should not be interpreted by reference to Article 30 EC, which had gone through a wholly different evolution of interpretation in the common market.[50] This example illustrates that the EC does not necessarily take the same view of the acceptability of unilateral PPM-based measures with extraterritorial protection objectives within the EC and in the external sphere. Indeed, the line with regard to such measures may be drawn differently in the EC and in the WTO, in view of the respective objectives and institutional frameworks of both organisations. However, the EC has also taken a rather ambiguous position on the issue of the compatibility with WTO rules of unilateral measures based on PPMs as such. This ambiguity can be explained to some extent by the fact that the Community is an amalgam of institutions with differing objectives and preferences. Even within the Commission, several directorates have different agendas on issues such as trade and environment.

For example, the European Parliament in 1998 passed a resolution reflecting the view that PPMs should play a role in "likeness" determinations under Article III GATT in accordance with the aim and effect test.[51] In preparations for the WTO's 1999 Seattle Ministerial Conference, the Community suggested as one of the priority issues 'a clarification of the relationship between WTO rules and Non-Product Related Processes and Production Methods requirements and, in particular, of the WTO-compatibility of eco-labelling schemes.' Subject to transparency and non-discrimination in the creation and administration of such schemes being safeguarded in a multilateral framework, 'there should be scope for a clear understanding that there is room within the WTO to use such market based, non-protectionist instruments as a means of achieving environmental objectives and of allowing consumers to make informed choices.' The Commu-

---

[49] The US accused the Netherlands, which acted as co-complainant in *US-Tuna-Dolphin II* representing the Netherlands Antilles, of similar inconsistency.

[50] *US-Tuna-Dolphin II*, unadopted, paras. 3.25 and 3.48, respectively.

[51] European Parliament Resolution A4-0125/98, adopted on 30 April 1998: 'Urges the Commission to advocate [...] that the WTO should draw up a Statement of Understanding concerning the application of the principle of "like products" which enables otherwise identical products to be differentiated where the production or processing of such products have different impacts on the environment. This Statement of Understanding should elaborate on the findings of the Panel on the US tax treatment of automobiles (the so-called "Gas Guzzlers" ruling).'

nity also suggested establishing rules on eco-labelling schemes based on a life-cycle approach in the context of the TBT Agreement.[52]

In contrast, as said above, the Community in the second *Tuna-Dolphin* dispute argued against extraterritorial protection. In its submissions to the panel in the *Japan-Alcohol* dispute, the Commission warned that 'the aim-and-effect test could open the door to claims that the extraterritorial application of environmental regulations concerning non-product related processes and production methods is not contrary to Article III.'[53] Interestingly, the EC itself has taken various legislative initiatives that resemble the measures at issue in the GATT/WTO disputes on PPMs and extraterritoriality. Many of these initiatives do not so much aim to protect animals threatened with extinction, but rather animal welfare. For instance, a recent Council regulation provides for the compulsory labelling of eggs on the basis of farming methods. The compulsory labelling applies to all eggs sold in the European Community, whether they are produced in the EC or emanate from third countries. However, in the case of third-country eggs, indication of the farming method may be replaced by the indication 'farming method not specified', and by an indication of origin if third country procedures do not offer sufficient guarantees as to equivalence with the technical rules and standards applicable to Community procedures.[54] Arguably, the latter indications may function as a negative label much in the same way as the not 'certified to be sustainably produced' label proposed by the Netherlands. The Community has notified the egg labelling regulation under the TBT Agreement.[55] Its WTO compatibility has so far not been challenged. Other examples of EC unilateral action also aiming at PPMs in third countries are the proposed leghold trap regulation that eventually was not applied,[56] and

---

[52]   See documents WT/GC/W/194 and WT/GC/W/274, as well as 'The EU Approach to the Millennium Round', Communication from the Commission to the Council and the European Parliament, July 1999, and Council Conclusions of 25 October 1999 on the Millennium Round preparation, on file with the author.

[53]   [original footnote 46] 'According to the Community, the generally accepted view is that an imported product and a domestic product manufactured in accordance with different non-product related PPMs [...] are still "like" and cannot therefore be treated differently under internal regulations. This interpretation is supported by the two unadopted panel reports on [*US-Tuna-Dolphin I and II*]. Under the aim-and-effect test one could argue that tuna harvested with a high rate of incidental dolphin killing is not like to other tuna because the distinction does not have a protectionist purpose.'

[54]   Council Regulation 5/2001 amending Council Regulation 1907/90, OJ 2001 L 2/1. Interestingly, neither of these two regulations refers to any specific Treaty Article as their legal basis. They are based upon Council Regulation 2771/75, which refers to Articles 36 and 37 (common agricultural policy).

[55]   WTO document G/TBT/Notif.00/428.

[56]   Regulation 3254/91, OJ 1991 L 308/1. See Nollkaemper (1996).

proposals to prohibit animal testing of cosmetics that initially included an import prohibition.[57]

At some stage, a WTO challenge to EC legislation unilaterally prescribing PPMs for third country goods is likely to occur. What will then happen will be interesting not only from the point of view of WTO law, but also for the EC itself. As said, a legislative proposal for the mandatory labelling of wood products in one Member State has been vehemently criticised by the Commission, and may lead to both internal EC proceedings and WTO proceedings. It will be interesting to see whether the Community is of the opinion that while one Member State is not allowed to impose PPM-based measures on third-country imports, the Community as a whole is allowed to do so. Other EC measures may be expected to pose less problems of WTO compatibility, as they are based on MEAs. Examples are regulations restricting trade in products damaging the ozone layer pursuant to the Montreal Protocol,[58] restricting trade in hazardous waste pursuant to the Basel Convention,[59] and restricting trade in endangered species pursuant to the Convention on International Trade in Endangered Species of Flora and Fauna.[60] Sometimes, the Community measures go further than their obligations under the MEA require them to do, which may raise questions of international law regarding the relationship between these MEAs and the WTO commitments.

---

[57] Council Directive 76/768, modified by Council Directive 93/35 (sixth modification), provided in Article 4 that Member States had to prohibit the marketing of animal-tested cosmetics, irrespective of whether they were produced in the EC or in third countries. For fear of WTO incompatibility, in the proposal for the seventh modification, COM(2000)189, the cosmetics directive no longer prohibits the marketing of animal-tested cosmetics, but only the carrying out of animal tests within the EC.

[58] Regulation 3093/94, OJ L 1994 333/1. A proposed revision is found in COM(98)398.

[59] Regulation 259/93 OJ L 1993 30/1.

[60] Regulation 338/97, OJ L 1997 61/1

CHAPTER 8

National Environmental Measures and Third-Country Products in the EC

EC and WTO Requirements

8.1 Introduction

This Section addresses a particular question arising from the
fact that EC Member States need to comply with both EC and WTO disciplines:
What is the legal status of the application by EC Member States of trade-
restrictive environmental measures to products from third countries? That legal
status will in the first place be examined from the point of view of EC law,
but the relevance of WTO law will also be discussed. A customs union like
the European Community requires a certain degree of uniformity in external
trade policies, in order to avoid trade diversions in its internal market. For
example, a Member State that wishes to individually ban the imports of a
third-country product will need authorisation by the Community to do so. In
order to effectively implement its ban, it will moreover need to ensure that
the third-country product is not indirectly imported into its territory, through
another Member State that does allow the importation and marketing of the
third-country product. The ensuing internal trade barrier will also require Community authorisation.

A certain degree of external uniformity of the trade policies of a customs
union is also required by Article XXIV GATT. The question is, how far does
this requirement go, both from the point of view of a well-functioning internal
market, and from the point of view of WTO obligations? Does it only concern
measures specifically regulating trade flows with third countries, such as import
and export restrictions? Or does it extend to all sorts of internal legislative
measures that may have a trade-hindering effect on third-country goods? In
other words, does the Community's common commercial policy cover the application to third-country products of those national measures that fall within the
notion of 'measures having equivalent effect' to quantitative restrictions in intra-
Community trade? Does a Member State need authorisation for each and every
instance in which it applies its internal legislation to a third-country product, or
can such authorisation be implied in the Treaty or secondary Community legislation? Or should no distinction be made between the treatment of third-country
products and products of Community origin once they are on the Community
market? These questions are addressed below, with particular attention to the
interpretation of the Community's common import and export regulations and
the concept of free circulation.

8.2 The European Community as a Customs Union and Third-Country Products

8.2.1 The European Community as a Customs Union

Article 23 EC stipulates that the Community shall be based on a customs union which shall cover all trade in goods and which shall involve the prohibition between Member States of customs duties and charges having equivalent effect and the adoption of a common customs tariff in their relations with third countries. This formulation suggests that the EC customs union is a narrow concept, confined to the internal elimination and external uniformisation of customs duties and charges having equivalent effect.[1] However, this narrow concept is largely rectified with regard to the internal side of the customs union. Articles 3(1)(a) and 28-31 EC make it clear that internally, not only customs duties and charges having equivalent effect, but also quantitative restrictions and measures having equivalent effect are prohibited. Furthermore, products from third countries benefit from these prohibitions once they are in free circulation in the Community. Article 23(2) EC provides that Article 25 (the prohibition of customs duties and charges having equivalent effect within the Community) and Articles 28-31 (the prohibition of quantitative restrictions on imports and exports within the Community, the exceptions thereto, and the provision on state trading monopolies) shall apply to both products originating in the Community and products coming from third countries that are in free circulation in Member States. Article 24 defines third-country products to be in "free circulation" when import formalities have been complied with and customs duties or charges having equivalent effect have been levied.

8.2.2 The Customs Union Externally; the Common Commercial Policy

Article 3(1)(b) of the EC Treaty mentions among the European Community's activities a "common commercial policy". According to Article 131 EC, by establishing a customs union between themselves the Member States aim to contribute, in the common interest, to 'the harmonious development of world trade, the progressive abolition of restrictions on international trade and the lowering of customs barriers'. Article 133 of the EC Treaty provides that the common commercial policy 'shall be based on uniform principles, particularly in regard to changes in tariff rates, the conclusion of tariff and trade agreements, the achievement of uniformity in measures of liberalisation, export policy and

---

[1]   This is narrower than what a customs union should substantially eliminate internally and uniformise externally according to Article XXIV:8(a) GATT, as discussed *infra*.

measures to protect trade such as those to be taken in the event of dumping or
subsidies'.[2] Article 133 EC makes it clear that the EC Treaty is aimed at establishing a customs union within the meaning of Article XXIV:8 GATT, despite the
narrow description of the customs union in Article 23(1).[3] However, the non-
exhaustive nature of the measures listed leaves the scope of the Community's
competence to conduct a common commercial policy somewhat unclear.

In disputes over whether the Community has been competent to act on the
basis of Article 133, the Court has tended to take a broad view of the common
commercial policy. As early as in 1973, it stated that the proper functioning of
the customs union justifies a wide interpretation of Article 133 and of the powers
it confers on the institutions to allow them thoroughly to control external trade
by measures taken both independently and by agreement.[4] In its Opinion 1/78
on the International Rubber Agreement, the Court observed that the common
commercial policy could not be restricted to the use of instruments 'intended to
have an effect only on the traditional aspects of external trade to the exclusion of
more highly developed mechanisms'. The Court went on to state that:

> [T]he question of external trade must be governed from a wide point of view and
> not only having regard to the administration of precise systems such as customs and
> quantitative restrictions. [...] the enumeration in article 113 [now 133] of the subjects
> covered by commercial policy [...] must not, as such, close the door to the application
> in a Community context of any other process intended to regulate external trade.
> A restrictive interpretation of the concept of common commercial policy would risk
> causing disturbances in intra-Community trade [...].[5]

In the *Chernobyl 1* case, in which the legal basis of a Community regulation
governing the imports of third-country agricultural products after the accident
at the Chernobyl nuclear power station was at issue, the ECJ again took a broad
view of the scope of Article 133.[6] The Court referred to Opinion 1/78 cited above

---

[2] The changes to Article 133 brought about by the 2000 Treaty of Nice mainly concern the conclusion
of agreements concerning trade in services and trade-related intellectual property rights, which are not
further discussed here.

[3] Demaret (1987) at 154.

[4] Case 8/73 *Massey-Ferguson*, para. 4. However, this case should not too easily be taken as an authority.
The Court made this statement while in the very same sentence admitting that Article 235 [now 308]
and not Article 133 had rightly been chosen as the legal basis for a Community regulation on customs
valuation. That appears typically the kind of measure one would assume that Article 133 should cover.

[5] Opinion 1/78 *Re International Agreement on Natural Rubber*, paras. 44-45. Emphasis added.

[6] Case 62/88 *Chernobyl 1*, paras. 16-20. 'Articles 130r and 130s [now 174 and 175] [...] leave intact the
powers held by the Community under other provisions of the Treaty, even if the measures to be taken
under the latter provisions pursue at the same time any of the objectives of environmental protection.'

in the *Werner* and *Leifer* cases, which concerned national licensing requirements for the export of so-called dual-use goods to Libya and Iraq, respectively, and are further discussed below. It held that 'a measure [...] whose *effect* is to prevent or restrict the export of certain products, cannot be treated as falling outside the scope of the common commercial policy on the ground that it has foreign policy and security objectives.'[7] The Court added that a Member State should not be able to restrict the scope of the common commercial policy by freely deciding, in the light of its own foreign policy or security requirements, whether a measure is covered by Article 133.[8] In other words, even if trade-restrictive measures pursue a health or security objective, they may still be covered by the concept of a common commercial policy.

In Opinion 1/94, the Commission asked the Court to decide upon the Community's competence to conclude the WTO Agreement.[9] The Commission phrased its questions in a somewhat unclear way, and the Court appears to have deliberately rephrased them in terms not of competence as such, but of exclusive competence.[10] The Court decided that pursuant to Article 133 EC, the Community had exclusive competence to conclude the Multilateral Agreements on Trade in Goods, which include *inter alia* the GATT and the TBT and SPS Agreements.[11] The Community and the Member States were jointly competent to conclude the GATS and TRIPS Agreements.[12] As regards the TRIPS Agreement, the Court held that with the exception of the provisions concerning counterfeit goods, the TRIPS Agreement was not within the scope of Article 133.[13] According-ing to the Court, even if there is a connection between intellectual property and trade in goods, this does not bring them within the scope of Article 133; intellectual property rights 'do not *relate specifically* to international trade'.[14] The Court's restrictive interpretation of Article 133 as regards the TRIPS Agreement does not extend to measures affecting trade in goods covered by the Multilateral Agreements on Trade in Goods. These Agreements do not only discipline specific trade policy instruments such as tariffs and quantitative restrictions, but also the internal legislation of WTO Members regarding, for example, taxation and regulation (Article III GATT) and technical regulations (TBT Agreement). Clearly, such internal legislation does not 'relate specifically

---

[7]   Case C-70/94 *Werner,* para. 10. Emphasis added.

[8]   Ibid., para. 11.

[9]   Opinion 1/94 *Re the Uruguay Round Agreements* has been extensively discussed elsewhere. See e.g. Bourgeois (1995), Hilf (1995), Jans (1996).

[10]   On this point, see Jans (1996).

[11]   Opinion 1/94 *Re the Uruguay Round Agreements*, paras. 31-34.

[12]   Ibid., paras. 98 and 105.

[13]   Ibid., para. 55.

[14]   Ibid., paras. 55 and 56. Emphasis added.

to international trade'. The present author therefore does not think that Opinion 1/94 implies a *general* retreat *vis-à-vis* the Court's earlier case-law on the scope of Article 133 EC.

Admittedly, the Court's recent opinion regarding the legal basis of the Cartagena Biosafety Protocol seems to indicate a cautious approach towards the scope of Article 133. The central objective of the Protocol is that its parties shall ensure that the development, handling, transport, use, transfer and release of any living modified organisms are undertaken in a manner that prevents or reduces the risks to biological diversity.[15] Thus, the activities within the scope of the Protocol no doubt include trade. Accordingly the Commission had argued for a double legal basis (Articles 175 and 133) for the Biosafety Protocol. However, the Court refused to accept a double legal basis, and advised a single environmental basis (Article 175). The question remains open of whether this opinion should be interpreted as a general limitation to the scope of Article 133, or should rather be seen as an expression of the Court's reluctance to accept a double legal basis.[16] The present author tends to take the latter view. Thus, even if the Court has become more cautious in interpreting Article 133 in recent opinions, its earlier case-law is arguably still valid: the common commercial policy is an evolutive concept that loses its effectiveness when interpreted restrictively.

8.2.3 Exclusivity of Community Competence and "Specific Authorisation"

The common commercial policy consists of both conventional measures, i.e. international agreements, and autonomous measures, i.e. Community legislation regulating trade with third countries. With respect to conventional measures, the above cases and opinions indicate a general tendency to widely interpret the scope of the common commercial policy. Does this mean that a prohibition of 'measures having equivalent effect' to quantitative restrictions imposed on third-country goods can be considered to be part of the common commercial policy? In a number of free trade and association agreements with third countries concluded by the Community on the basis of Article 133 EC, 'measures having equivalent effect' have been expressly included as part of a prohibition. Moreover, even if these words do not figure in the WTO Agreements, these Agreements do discipline many measures that have been dubbed 'measures having equivalent effect' within the Community. Thus, the Community is clearly allowed to conclude, on the basis of Article 133 EC, agreements disciplining 'measures having equivalent effect'. However, the scope of Article 133 is somewhat less clear with respect to autonomous Community

---

[15] Article 2 Biosafety Protocol, available at http://www.biodiv.org/biosafety

[16] See Case C-42/97 *Parliament v. Council.*

measures, and with respect to the leeway for Member States to act individually in the absence of such measures.

In principle, Community legislation regulating imports and/or exports from and/or to third countries may be expected to be based on Article 133 EC. Examples are the common import and export regulations that are discussed *infra*, and the antidumping and anti-subsidy regulations.[17] However, many pieces of secondary legislation do not exclusively regulate trade with third countries but also the internal market, or they pursue other objectives in addition to the regulation of trade flows. Accordingly, the Community legislature often chooses a different legal basis, or a combination of Article 133 and another legal basis. For example, most Community legislation laying down product requirements applies to both Community and third-country goods. Such Community legislation is usually based on Article 95, not Article 133.[18] Community legislation may also contain a combination of general measures that apply to internal and third-country products alike, and measures specifically addressing third-country goods. A combined legal basis of Articles 95 and 133 would appear appropriate in such cases.[19] Community legislation may also have other objectives in addition to regulating international trade. For example, the Court has held with regard to agricultural goods that the mere fact that Community legislation also concerns imports into the Community does not suffice to make Article 133 applicable.[20] In the environmental sphere, a joint legal basis of Articles 133 and 175 is indeed possible.[21] However, a considerable number of Community measures that also specifically regulate imports and exports from and to third countries are based on Article 175 alone, instead of Article 133 or a combination of both.[22]

With regard to the situation where the Community has not enacted autonomous measures on the basis of Article 133 EC, are the Member States in principle free to act individually with regard to third-country goods? The answer

---

[17] Regulation 384/96 on protection against dumped imports, OJ 1996 L 56/1, Regulation 3284/94 on protection against subsidised imports, OJ 1994 L 349/22.

[18] E.g. Directive 91/157/EEC on Batteries and Accumulators containing Certain Dangerous Substances, OJ 1991 L 78/38.

[19] E.g. Regulation 259/93 on the supervision and control of shipments of waste within, into and out of the European Community, OJ 1993 L 30/1, which is based on Article 175 but in the present author's view should rather have been based on Articles 133 and 95, as the Commission had proposed.

[20] See Case C-131/87 *Commission v. Council*, para. 28. However, it may be recalled that the Court stated in Case 62/88 *Chernobyl I* that the fact that a regulation pursues a health objective is not enought to remove it from the ambit of Article 133 EC.

[21] See e.g. Regulation 3254/91 on animals caught with leghold traps, OJ 1991 L 308/1.

[22] See e.g. Regulation 2455/92 on the import and export of certain dangerous chemicals, OJ 1992 L 251/13; and Regulation 259/93 on waste shipments within, into and out of the Community (Basel Regulation), OJ 1993 L 30/1. See Jans (2000a) at 77.

to that question appears to be negative, because the Court has consistently held
that the Community's powers under Article 133 EC are exclusive. This means
that Member States are in principle precluded from acting. The Court as early as
in 1975 observed that the common commercial policy is conceived in the context
of the operation of the common market, for the defence of the common interests
of the Community. This conception, according to the Court, 'is incompatible
with the freedom to which the Member States could lay claim by invoking
a concurrent power, so as to ensure that their own interests were separately
satisfied in external relations, at the risk of compromising the effective defence
of the common interests of the Community.' 'It cannot therefore be accepted
that, in a field [...] covered by [...] the common commercial policy, the Member
States should exercise a power concurrent to that of the Community's.[23] In its
judgment in the *Donckerwolcke* case, the ECJ clarified the following consequence
of the exclusive character of the Community's competence under Article 133:

> As full responsibility in the matter of commercial policy was transferred to the
> Community by means of article 113(1) [now 133(1)] measures of commercial policy of
> a national character are only permissible after the end of the transitional period by
> virtue of specific authorization by the Community.[24]

Thus, Member States are only allowed to take commercial policy measures with
specific Community authorisation, because such measures are part and parcel
of the Community's exclusive competence to adopt a common commercial policy
under Article 133. The scope of this common commercial policy is therefore
of obvious importance. The wider its scope, the more specific authorisation is
needed by Member States to act individually.

8.2.4 Common Rules for Imports and Exports

Among the measures taken on the basis of Article 133, the Community's regulation laying down common rules for imports based on Article
133 deserves specific mention.[25] The preamble to the common import regulation
states *inter alia* that 'the starting point for the common rules for imports is
liberalization of imports, namely the absence of any quantitative restrictions;
[...]'. Article 1 of the regulation stipulates that imports of products originating
from third countries 'shall be freely imported into the Community and accordingly [...] shall not be subject to any quantitative restrictions.' The language of

---

[23] Opinion 1/75 *Re Local Cost Standard.*

[24] Case 41/76 *Donckerwolcke*, para. 32.

[25] Regulation 3285/94, OJ 1994 L 349/53.

'measures having equivalent effect' found in Article 28 EC does not appear here. The common import regulation also contains exceptions. According to Article 24(2)(a), '[w]ithout prejudice to other Community provisions, this Regulation shall not preclude the adoption or application by Member States (i) of prohibitions, quantitative restrictions or surveillance measures on grounds of [...] the protection of health and life of humans, animals or plants [...]'. The reference to life and health protection forms part of an enumeration of exception grounds that parallels the one in Article 30 EC. However, there are some differences between the two exceptions provisions. While Article 24(2)(a) of the common import regulation uses the words 'prohibitions, quantitative restrictions or surveillance measures', Article 30 EC uses the wider terms 'prohibitions or restrictions'. Moreover, the second sentence of Article 30, which adds that such prohibitions or restrictions should not constitute a means of arbitrary discrimination or a disguised restriction on trade [between the Member States], is absent in Article 24(2) of the common import regulation.

The prohibition in the common import regulation currently in force has, to this author's knowledge, not been the subject of any decisions by the European Court of Justice. However, the identically worded prohibition in one of its predecessors was interpreted in the *EMI* case, where the Court found that the prohibition related only to quantitative restrictions and not to measures having equivalent effect.[26] The prohibition in the common *export* regulation has similar wording as that in the import regulation.[27] The Court has interpreted the common export regulation on a number of occasions.[28] In *Bulk Oil*, the ECJ stated that the common export regulation does not prohibit a Member State from imposing new 'quantitative restrictions or measures having equivalent effect' on its exports of oil to non-member countries.[29] The Court's reference to 'measures having equivalent effect' in this case has been interpreted in a contrasting fashion. Some have read it as confirming that measures having equivalent effect were not covered by the prohibition in the common export regulation in the first place.[30] Others have suggested that the judgment implies that the prohibition also covers such measures.[31] In any event, the relevance of this case to the interpretation of the common import regulation is doubtful. The case concerned

---

[26] Case 51/75 *EMI*, para. 20, on Regulation 1439/74, OJ 1974 L 159/1.

[27] The exceptions provision in the common export regulation is confined to "quantitative restrictions" and thus differs somewhat from the exceptions in the common import regulation, which in addition refers to "prohibitions". However, quantitative restrictions arguably include prohibitions, so the difference is not that great.

[28] Regulation 2603/69, OJ 1969 L 324/25, as amended by regulation 3918/91, OJ 1991 L 372/91.

[29] Case 174/84 *Bulk Oil*, para. 37.

[30] Völker (1993) at 106.

[31] Lauwaars (1988) at 78.

a particular provision containing temporary exceptions to the prohibition of
quantitative restrictions for oil and a number of other products, which is not
found in the common import regulation.

In *Aimé Richardt*, certain export restrictions on materials considered strategic by Luxembourg were at issue. Advocate-General Jacobs argued in his opinion
that the common export regulation was applicable to the export restriction. He
furthermore contended that in the light of the objectives of the regulation and its
structure and wording it was clear that the regulation 'embodies a fundamental
rule that, subject to the exceptions specified, exports from the Community
to non-member States are unrestricted.'[32] Jacobs thought it unreasonable to
conclude from the absence of the words 'measures having equivalent effect' in
the export regulation that all such measures were excluded from its scope. That
was not to say, however, that the scope of the prohibition in the regulation is the
same as that of the relevant Treaty provision regarding intra-Community trade.[33]
However, an export licensing system would be within the scope of the export
regulation if its effect is to preclude all exports of a particular product. Jacobs
rejected a parallel with *EMI*, positing that the scope of the various provisions
in Community legislation depends not on the formulation used, but on their
context and purposes. He then referred to Article XI GATT, which explicitly
refers to licenses or other measures, and concluded that the measures at issue
were prohibited by the common export regulation, unless justified under its
exceptions. The Court, however, did not address the common export regulation
in its judgment.

Subsequently, Jacobs essentially repeated his position in his joined opinion
in the *Werner* and *Leifer* cases, which again involved national export restrictions
on goods that can be used for military purposes. Jacobs referred to the first
part of Article 1(2) of the common export regulation, which provides that the
exportation of products from the Community shall be free, as a "principle" and
as a 'basic rule of the common commercial policy'.[34] This time, the Court did
address the common export regulation in its judgment. It observed that it does
not follow from the absence of any reference to 'measures having equivalent
effect' as found in Article 29 that the concept of quantitative restrictions used
in a regulation concerning trade between the Community and non-member
countries must be interpreted as excluding any measure having equivalent effect
within the meaning of Article 34 [now 29] of the Treaty.[35] The Court stated that
provisions of Community law must be interpreted by considering not only their

---

[32] AG Jacobs in Case C-367/89 *Aimé Richardt*, para. 18 of his opinion.

[33] Ibid., para. 20 of his opinion, erroneously referring to Article 30 [now 28] EC instead of Article 34
     [now 29] EC.

[34] AG Jacobs in Cases C-70/94 *Werner* and C-83/94 *Leifer*, paras. 31 and 38 of his opinion.

[35] Case C-70/94 *Werner*, para. 20.

wording, but also their context and the objectives of the rules of which they are part. The Court added that:

> A regulation based on Article 113 [now 133] of the Treaty, whose objective is to implement the principle of free exportation at the Community level, as stated in Article 1 of the Export Regulation, cannot exclude from its scope measures adopted by the Member States whose effect is equivalent to a quantitative restriction where their application may lead, as in the present case, to an export prohibition.[36]

The Court then referred to Article XI GATT, 'which can be considered to be relevant for the purposes of interpreting a Community instrument governing international trade.' It observed that Article XI GATT uses the wording 'prohibitions or restrictions other than duties, taxes or other charges, whether made effective through quotas, import or export licences or other measures'. The Court concluded that the measures at issue were covered by the prohibition in the common export regulation and accordingly proceeded to examine whether they could be justified under its exceptions. In both cases, the Court found that this was indeed the case for the security exception invoked.

8.2.5 Prohibitions, Justifications and Conditions

After the *Werner* and *Leifer* judgments, it is clear that at least some measures having equivalent effect to quantitative restrictions are covered by the prohibition in the common export regulation. It may be assumed that by analogy, the same is true for the common import regulation. However, does that mean that all measures having equivalent effect covered by the prohibition in Article 28 EC in intra-Community trade are also covered by the import regulation, or merely some of them? On the one hand, one could argue that the sentence 'where their application may lead, as in the present case, to an export prohibition' functions by way of example, and was added because the preliminary question concerned such a situation. In that view, the sentence does not necessarily limit the range of measures having equivalent effect prohibited by Article 1 of the export regulation. On the other hand, a more restrictive view can be taken, according to which Article 1 of the export regulation only prohibits those measures having equivalent effect that may lead to an export prohibition. The Court suggested in *Werner* and *Leifer* that in interpreting the common export regulation, Article XI GATT should be followed. Article XI GATT only covers prohibitions and restrictions specifically addressing imports and exports, and not internal regulatory measures, even if they formally discriminate against imports or exports. Internal measures are covered by Article III. Therefore,

---

[36] Ibid., para. 22.

despite the use of the words "other measures" in Article XI GATT, the reference
to Article XI suggests that the more restrictive view of Article 1 of the common
export regulation should be taken.[37] Then again, the Court did not say that Article XI is the only GATT provision relevant to interpreting the common export
regulation. Could the common export and import regulations also cover those
'measures having equivalent effect' that are covered by Article III GATT, i.e.
discriminatory internal regulatory measures? It is difficult to answer this question, because *Werner* and *Leifer* were preliminary rulings that only concerned
export certificates.

Whether one takes a broad or restrictive view of what the Court said in
Werner and *Leifer*, the words "quantitative restrictions" in any event have a wider
meaning in the common export regulation than in Article 29 EC. Obviously, a
wider interpretation of "quantitative restrictions" in Article 29 EC is not necessary, because that provision itself already explicitly refers to 'measures having
equivalent effect'. It has been suggested above that what was said in *Werner* and
Leifer should also apply to the prohibition in the common import regulation.
Admittedly, the import and export regulations do not necessarily have the same
scope. Therefore, the words 'measures having equivalent effect' do not necessarily have the same meaning in the common export regulation as in the
common import regulation. After all, these words have not received the same
interpretation in Articles 28 and 29 EC, despite the identical wording of these
provisions. However, a counter-argument to a diverging interpretation of "quantitative restrictions" in the import and export regulations is that they are both to
be interpreted taking into account Article XI GATT, which addresses import and
export restrictions in the same manner. In any event, it would seem illogical to
assume that the prohibition in the common export regulation is wider than the
prohibition in the common import regulation.

If one adopts a broad interpretation of the prohibition in the common import
regulation, then all measures having equivalent effect that are covered by Article
28 EC are also covered by the prohibition in the common import regulation.
A consequence would be that a Member State would infringe the prohibition
if it applied an indistinctly applicable product requirement to a third-country
product, unless the Member State could justify the resulting trade obstacle. If
that position is accepted, it makes sense to accept justifications for reasons of
mandatory requirements too.[38] It is recalled that the exceptions provision in
the common import regulation lists similar grounds as Article 30 EC. If the
prohibition in the common import regulation is to reflect Article XI GATT, the
exceptions provision may be expected to reflect Article XX GATT. However,
the exceptions provision does not list a number of grounds that are listed in

---

[37]   Support is found in the conclusion of AG Geelhoed in Case C-296/00 *Carbone*.

[38]   As argued by Demaret (1994) at 296, and Jans (2000a) at 84.

Article XX, such as the conservation of exhaustible natural resources. Finally, as regards the conditions which are applicable to exceptions, it may be recalled that the exceptions in the common import regulation are not accompanied by a clause requiring that any restrictions shall not constitute a means of arbitrary discrimination or a disguised trade restriction. Nevertheless, the Court has stated that the exceptions provision in the common export regulation must be interpreted in a way which does not extend its effects beyond what is necessary for the protection of the interests which it is intended to guarantee. Accordingly, it must be assessed whether the measure is necessary and appropriate to achieve the objective pursued and whether or not the objective could have been attained by less restrictive measures.[39]

Does the exceptions provision in the common import regulation constitute a "specific authorisation" within the meaning of the *Donckerwolcke* judgment? In *Bulk Oil*, the ECJ accepted that an exception to the prohibition of quantitative restrictions in the common export regulation for certain products mentioned in an annex to it such as oil, constituted a specific authorisation.[40] However, the Court at the same time stressed that this exception applied on a "transitional" basis.[41] The exception provided that 'until such time as the Council [...] shall have introduced common rules in respect of the products listed in the annex to this regulation, the principle of freedom of export from the Community as laid down in Article 1 shall not apply to those products'. Arguably, the nature of this exception is indeed more temporary than the general public policy exceptions in Article 11 of the common export regulation or Article 24 of the common import regulation. Nonetheless, in *Werner* and *Leifer,* the Court referred to its judgments on specific authorisation in *Donckerwolcke* and *Bulk Oil*, and stated that 'the export of goods from the Community to non-member countries is *therefore* governed by [...] the Export Regulation'.[42] The Court concluded that Article 133, and in particular Article 11 of the export regulation, did not preclude the national provisions at issue. Thus, in these cases, the Court appears to have implicitly accepted that the exceptions in the export regulation constitute a specific authorisation for Member States to take individual measures.

8.2.6 Does Article 133 EC Prohibit 'Measures having Equivalent Effect'?

If a restrictive reading of the *Werner* and *Leifer* judgments is taken, the common import and export regulations only prohibit measures

---

[39] Case C-83/94 *Leifer,* paras. 33-34.

[40] Case 174/84 *Bulk Oil*, para. 33.

[41] Ibid., paras. 32 and 35.

[42] Case C-70/94 *Werner,* para. 13. Emphasis added.

having equivalent effect that may lead to import or export prohibitions. Could a
wider prohibition be read in Article 133 itself? Could Article 133 be interpreted
as a parallel to the internal market provisions regarding the free movement of
goods? If stretched to its extreme, a parallel interpretation would mean that
Article 133 contains a prohibition with the same scope as that in Article 28 EC.
As Article 133 gives the Community exclusive competence, this would imply that
Member States are precluded from applying to third-country imports any of their
internal laws that, in intra-Community trade, would be covered by the prohibition in Article 28 EC. Any such application would constitute a *per se* violation
of Article 133. In line with the Court's judgment in *Donckerwolcke*, a Member
State would require "specific Community authorisation" for any derogation from
this prohibition.

An objection against reading Article 133 in parallel with the internal market
provisions is that there is no textual basis for this in the EC Treaty. The
text of Article 133 does not prohibit measures having equivalent effect, and
such a prohibition with regard to third-country trade cannot arguably be found
elsewhere in the EC Treaty, or be deduced or implied from the Community's
objectives or tasks as laid down in Articles 2 and 3 of that Treaty. Internally,
Articles 28-30 (as well as 25 and 90) EC provide for negative integration and
Article 95 EC for positive integration. It has been argued that Article 133 is
merely a Community policy provision, i.e. it provides for positive but not negative integration.[43] However, does not the very exclusiveness of the Community's
competence in matters falling within the scope of Article 133 imply a prohibition
on Member States taking any unilateral measures (or concluding any agreements), and therewith a negative integration effect?[44] Thus, it would seem that
Article 133 comprises aspects of both negative and positive integration. What is
the nature of Article 133 as the external dimension of such provisions? There is
a clear difference between the Community's competence in the internal market
and its competence with regard to the common commercial policy. Internally,
Member States are competent to adopt measures to protect human, animal or
plant life and health and the environment, as long as the Community has not
acted to harmonise on the basis of Article 95 and as long as they respect the
requirements of Articles 28-30 EC. If this state of affairs applied equally to
external trade, Member States would be allowed to act as long as the Community
had not acted on the basis of Article 133.[45] Thus, the exclusive character of the
Community's competence under Article 133 would thereby be compromised.[46]

---

[43] Lauwaars (1998) at 79.

[44] Leefmans (1998) at 127.

[45] As argued by Eeckhout (1994) at 348.

[46] As noted by Schrauwen (1997) at 219.

Various approaches have been taken to deal with the dual nature of Article 133 EC as comprising both a positive and a negative integration aspect and the exclusive character of the Community's competence under this provision. They all attempt to limit the scope of the prohibition to be read into Article 133. For example, it has been proposed that Article 133 EC only prohibits measures 'directly affecting trade with third countries', or only discriminatory measures.[47] It has also been proposed to distinguish between measures specifically regulating international trade and measures that do not specifically regulate international trade, but may have an impact on it.[48] Only the former are part of the common commercial policy and Member States cannot enact them individually without specific Community authorisation. Measures not specifically regulating international trade are not part of the Community's common commercial policy, or only part of it if their "predominant purpose" is to affect international trade patterns or flows. It is obviously problematic to determine what the predominant purpose of a measure is.[49] If a measure falls outside the scope of the common commercial policy, Member States are not *ipso facto* precluded from individually applying such measures to products from third countries. They are precluded from doing so only when the Community has enacted specific legislation in the area covered by such measures.

Another aspect of a parallel approach to Articles 28-30 and 133 concerns of course the justification possibilities. The possibilities provided under Article 30 EC and the "mandatory requirements" could also be extended to Article 133 EC.[50] However, the parallelism is unbalanced if on the one hand, the prohibition is confined to measures directly affecting trade in third-country goods or discriminatory measures, and on the other hand, mandatory requirements are available as justifications. If that were the case, justifications would be available externally to the same extent as internally, while the prohibition is not as wide externally as it is internally.

In order to accommodate the possibility for Member States to act with the exclusive character of the Community's competence, a broad reading of the concept of "specific Community authorisation" is needed. Accordingly, any measure having equivalent effect applied to third-country goods that is justified by an exception or a mandatory requirement would need to be considered to have "specific authorisation". As will be argued below, the present author is of the opinion that the concept of "free circulation" renders attempts at interpreting Article 133 or the import and export regulations parallel to Articles 28-30 EC unnecessary.

---

[47] Timmermans (1986), Eeckhout (1994).

[48] Bourgeois (1981 and 1983); Ehlermann (1984).

[49] As noted by Ehlermann (1984) at 152-56.

[50] As proposed by Demaret (1994) and Jans (2000a) for the common import regulation; see *supra*.

8.3   Imports from Third Countries in Free Circulation

According to Article 23(2) of the EC Treaty, the prohibitions in Articles 28 and 29 EC and the exceptions in Article 30 apply both to products originating in Member States and to products coming from third countries which are in free circulation in Member States. Article 24 EC further stipulates that products coming from third countries are considered to be in free circulation in a Member State if the import formalities have been complied with and any customs duties or charges having equivalent effect which are payable have been levied in that Member State. Thus, a third-country product in free circulation has equal status to a product originating in the Community. As the Court said in *Donckerwolcke*,

The result of this assimilation is that the provisions of article 30 [now 28] concerning the elimination of quantitative restrictions and all measures having equivalent effect are applicable without distinction to products originating in the Community and to those which were put into free circulation in any one of the Member States, irrespective of the actual origin of these products.[51]

An exception to the above rule is found in Article 134 EC. If a Member State is specifically authorised to apply or maintain commercial policy measures, such as quantitative restrictions on certain third-country goods, such measures are easily circumvented if those third-country goods can be imported elsewhere in the Community, be put into free circulation, and then be reimported into the Member State applying the measures. Accordingly, under Article 134, the Commission may allow Member States to take protective measures in order to ensure that commercial policy measures taken in accordance with the Treaty by any Member State are not obstructed by a deflection of trade, or where differences between such measures lead to economic difficulties for one or more Member States. However, recourse to this provision is exceptional and becoming increasingly rare, which is understandable as such protective measures go against the concept of an internal market in which intra-Community border checks have been abolished.

Apart from restrictions based on Article 134, does the requirement of free circulation mean that any restrictions to intra-Community trade in third-country products are permitted only to the extent that they are justified under the exceptions in Article 30 or the mandatory requirements accepted by the Court of Justice? One would assume that this is the most logical conclusion, and one may indeed find confirmation of this in the Court's observations in *Donckerwolcke*

---

[51]   See Case 41/76 *Donckerwolcke*, para. 18.

cited above.[52] Any other approach would seem to contradict the logic of the internal market.

Having been lawfully imported and brought into free circulation does not necessarily correspond to having been lawfully marketed in a Member State.[53] As regards product safety requirements, the two have been assimilated by a Community regulation (based on Article 133), which ensures that national customs authorities competent to release goods for free circulation also exercise control on product safety and on conformity with both Community and national rules.[54] Generally speaking, however, the test of whether a product can be lawfully marketed in a Member State is not necessarily fulfilled at the same time the customs formalities have been fulfilled.[55] What constitutes being lawfully marketed depends on the product at issue and the applicable rules. For some products, prior authorisation will be needed in order to be marketed, while for others, there will be general rules for marketing in combination with *ex post facto* controls to check whether these rules are being adhered to.[56] In the latter situation, a good that has been put into free circulation may not be allowed to be marketed according to national requirements, and if it is marketed anyway it may be removed from the shops when it turns out that it does not meet these requirements.

If, according to Articles 23(2) and 24 EC as interpreted by the Court in *Donckerwolcke*, the prohibition of quantitative restrictions and measures having equivalent effect in Article 28 EC fully applies to goods in free circulation, to what extent can Member States impose their national requirements to prevent the marketing of those goods on their territory? Is there any difference in this respect between goods originating in the Community and goods originating in third countries? Does a product in free circulation enjoy full freedom of movement according to Articles 28-30 EC, or does it first need to be lawfully

---

[52] See also Case 119/78 *Peureux*, para. 26: 'The prohibition of measures having an effect equivalent to quantitative restrictions in intra-Community trade has the same scope as regards products imported from another Member State after being in free circulation there as for those originating in the same Member State.'

[53] Völker (1993) at 93-94; Eeckhout (1994) at 274 in his footnote 54.

[54] Article 2 of Regulation 339/93, OJ 1993 L 40/1, provides as follows: 'When, in the context of checks which they carry out in respect of goods declared for release for free circulation, the customs authorities find [...] that a product or batch of products is not accompanied by a document or not marketed in accordance with the Community or national rules on product safety applicable in the Member State in which release for free circulation is sought, they shall suspend release of the product or batch of products concerned and immediately notify the national authority responsible for monitoring the market.'

[55] Cf. AG Geelhoed in Case C-296/00 *Carbone*.

[56] Eeckhout (1994) at 274.

marketed in a Member State in order to do so? It is recalled that in *Cassis de Dijon*, the Court said that under Article 28, absent mandatory requirements, there is no valid reason why products should not be introduced into any other Member State, provided they have been lawfully *produced and marketed* in one of the Member States.[57] In subsequent judgments, the Court dropped the reference to "produced" and confined its statement to "lawfully marketed".[58] This suggests that once lawfully *imported and marketed* anywhere in the Community, third-country goods should be treated in the same manner as goods lawfully *produced and marketed* in the Community. In other words, third-country goods that are in free circulation and lawfully marketed in any Member State can be marketed in any other Member State, except if mandatory requirements or an exception in Article 30 can be invoked and the corresponding conditions are fulfilled.[59]

A number of situations can be envisaged. First, a third country good put into free circulation can be lawfully marketed in the Member State of importation. Articles 28-30 prescribe that the good can also be marketed in other Member States, unless Article 30 or a mandatory requirements prevents this. Second, a third country product cannot be lawfully marketed in the Member State where it has been put into free circulation, but it can be lawfully marketed in another Member State. Once such marketing elsewhere has taken place, Article 28 can be invoked to seek marketing in the Member State of first importation. Whether the national measure impeding its marketing is justified will be assessed under Article 30 or the mandatory requirements. It has been argued that in such a situation, the requirement of having been lawfully marketed in another Member State does not apply to each individual product; it would be sufficient that one item of the product at issue has been lawfully marketed.[60] It has further been suggested that the Court's "circumvention" or "U-turn" case-law regarding goods which have been exported solely in order to be reimported so as to enjoy free movement could be applicable here *mutatis mutandis*.[61] However, the actual marketing of the product in another Member State as well as discussions on whether this is done to create a "U-turn" construction can be avoided if Article

---

[57] See Case 120/78 *Cassis de Dijon*, and the Commission Communication following that judgment, both discussed in Chapter 2. Emphasis added.

[58] See e.g. Cases 27/80 *Fietje*.

[59] E.g. Völker (1993), Eeckhout (1994), and Tegeder (1994). *Contra*, White (1989) at 263, basing his argument on Case 41/76 *Donckerwolcke*, paras. 24-25, where the Court said that the assimilation of goods in free circulation to products originating within the Member States may only take full effect if these goods are subject to the same conditions of importation both with regard to customs and commercial considerations, irrespective of the State in which they were put into free circulation.

[60] Eeckhout (1994) at 275, in his footnote 57.

[61] See Tegeder (1994) at 93; Eeckhout (1994) at 275.

28 can be invoked directly, without the good actually having been marketed in another Member State.

The present author submits that considering the fact that Article 28 EC, as interpreted in *Dassonville*, also covers *potential* trade barriers, it would seem sufficient that the product *can* be lawfully marketed in any Member State to invoke this provision. One could argue that if Article 28 is invoked to challenge a national measure impeding marketing in the Member State of importation of a third country good, there is no sufficient connection to intra-Community trade to invoke Article 28. However, it would appear possible to invoke Article 28 if the national measure also applies to imports from other Member States.[62] Of course, being able to invoke Article 28 does not mean that the measure is found to violate that provision. Whether that is the case depends on the justification and proportionality assessment.

The third situation that can be envisaged occurs when a third country product cannot be lawfully marketed in the Member State where it has been put into free circulation, and cannot be lawfully marketed in any other Member State. Such a product is in the same situation as a product produced in the Community which cannot be lawfully marketed in any Member State. Article 28 can be invoked to challenge national measures preventing its marketing, but these may be justified under Article 30 or mandatory requirements.

In sum, a third-country product in free circulation that has been or can be lawfully marketed in any Member State is really in the same position as a product of Community origin that has been or can be lawfully marketed in any Member State. Both enjoy free movement with the presumption of "mutual recognition". If a Member State disallows the marketing of a directly imported third-country product, while the product can be lawfully marketed in another Member State, the importer can arguably rely on Articles 28-30 EC to have the product marketed after all. There is no danger of trade deflections, except if actual marketing in another Member State is required. However, it is submitted that the possibility of being lawfully marketed in another Member State suffices, which would make deflections unnecessary.

The above considerations were based on the assumption that there is no relevant secondary Community law regarding rules for the marketing of products. In reality, both Community and third-country products must increasingly meet harmonised Community standards in order to be lawfully marketed. It has been argued that extending "mutual recognition" to third-country products is undesirable, as third-country producers would have access to the entire Community market once their products could be marketed in one Member State, while similar advantage is not granted to Community producers on third-country markets.[63] However, the extension of "mutual recognition" to products in free

---

[62] By analogy with Case C-448/98 *Guimont*.

[63] White (1989); cf. Tegeder (1994).

circulation appears to be the only way in which to ensure a functioning internal market. Any other approach would make it necessary to distinguish between Community and third-country products after they have been put into free circulation. Apart from the practical problems this would create, it would be very difficult to apply such a distinction in legal terms. Should the prohibition in Article 28 be less broad for third-country products, and/or should Member States bear a less onerous burden of proof in justifying their measures when applied to third-country goods? The present author disagrees with the argument against extending "mutual recognition" to third country goods in free circulation. In fact, to treat third-country products different from products from other Member States with regard to technical regulations may be difficult to reconcile with the Most-Favoured Nation requirement found in the TBT Agreement, as discussed in Section 8.4.

8.4 WTO Requirements

8.4.1 The Requirements for Customs Unions in Article XXIV:8 GATT

Article XXIV GATT addresses customs unions and free trade areas. The idea behind this provision is that smaller groups of countries, that are often geographically, economically and/or politically close to each other, may reach a degree of economic integration going further than the multilateral system is able to attain. GATT Article XXIV:4 recognises that such integration can increase freedom of trade within such groups, and accepts them as long as their purpose is not to raise external trade barriers.[64] Accordingly, Article XXIV acts as an exception that allows customs unions and free trade areas to derogate from substantive GATT obligations, such as most-favoured nation treatment.[65] In other words, members of a customs union or free trade area can allow a degree of free movement of goods in their internal trade which is not necessarily accompanied by similar external openness. However, Article XXIV:5 provides that 'the provisions of this Agreement shall not prevent [...] the *formation* of a customs union or of a free trade area [...].'[66] As the Appellate Body has stated with regard to the customs union between the EC and Turkey, paragraph 5

---

[64] On Article XXIV GATT, see e.g. Jackson (1969), Dam (1970), Marceau and Reiman (2001), and Mathis (2001).

[65] See the AB in *Turkey-Textiles*, para. 45: 'Article XXIV may, under certain conditions, justify the adoption of a measure which is inconsistent with certain other GATT provisions, and may be invoked as a possible "defence" to a finding of inconsistency.'

[66] Emphasis added.

indicates that Article XXIV can justify the adoption of a measure which is inconsistent with certain other GATT provisions only if the measure is introduced upon the formation of a customs union, and only to the extent that the formation of the customs union would be prevented if the introduction of the measure were not allowed.[67] Moreover, Article XXIV:5 imposes the condition that the level of protection applied by the customs union or free trade area to trade with third countries shall not be higher than the level of protection previously applied by its constituent members.

Article XXIV:8 is of central importance. It defines a customs union and a free trade area, and its definitions contain requirements as to both the internal and external trade of a customs union. Article XXIV:8(a)(i) addresses internal trade, providing that in a customs union, duties and 'other restrictive regulations of commerce' (except, where necessary, those permitted under Articles XI, XII, XIII, XIV, XV and XX) are eliminated with respect to substantially all the trade between the constituent territories of the union, or at least with respect to substantially all the trade in products originating in such territories.[68] Article XXIV:8(a)(ii) GATT concerns external trade. It provides that substantially the same duties and 'other regulations of commerce' are to be applied by each of the members of a customs union to third-country trade. As the panel in *Turkey-Textiles* observed, the implied ultimate (and ideal) situation is that a complete single common foreign trade regime is adopted by the constituent members of the customs union.[69] It is to be noted that both the word "restrictive" and the reference to GATT exceptions found in paragraph 8(a)(i) are absent in paragraph 8(a)(ii). Thus, according to Article XXIV:8(a) as a whole, regulations of commerce need to be substantially eliminated internally only to the extent that they are restrictive and not covered by any of the exceptions mentioned, while they need to be substantially unified externally, regardless of whether they are restrictive or could be covered by Articles XI-XV or XX GATT.

The meaning of the word "substantially" and the phrase 'other (restrictive) regulations of commerce' is not addressed in the WTO Understanding on the Interpretation of Article XXIV GATT. In the *Turkey-Textiles* dispute, the panel said that the ordinary meaning of the term "substantially" in the context of sub-paragraph 8(a) appears to provide for both qualitative and quantitative components. In the panel's view, the standard laid down by "substantially" would be

---

[67] AB in *Turkey-Textiles*, para. 46.

[68] Incidentally, the last part of this sentence appears very odd in a definition of a customs union. According to Demaret, this phrase relates to a situation where the constituents of a customs union have not previously agreed on the distribution of the revenues of customs duties, in which case internal checks are needed. This will not be further dealt with, as it is irrelevant to the Communit where customs revenues flow into the Community resources. See Demaret (1987) at 141-42.

[69] Panel in *Turkey-Textiles*, para. 9.144.

met by 'comparable trade regulations having similar effects'.[70] The Appellate
Body agreed that "substantially" comprises both quantitative and qualitative
aspects. However, it did not agree with the panel that comparable trade regulations would be sufficient, and said that 'a higher degree of "sameness"' is
required by the terms of sub-paragraph 8(a)(ii).[71] That, of course, still leaves
much to be clarified. Importantly for the purposes of this Section, the panel
and the Appellate Body in *Turkey-Textiles* did not address the coverage of 'other
regulations of commerce' in Article XXIV:8. However, the term 'other regulations of commerce' also features in paragraph 5 of Article XXIV, which, it is
recalled, lays down the requirement that a customs union or free trade area
should not on the whole be more trade-restrictive to third-country trade than its
constituent members were before the formation of the customs union or free
trade area. In *Turkey-Textiles*, the panel observed that while there is no agreed
definition between Members as to the scope of this concept of 'other regulations
of commerce', it is clear that this concept includes quantitative restrictions. It
added the following interesting remark:

> *More broadly, the ordinary meaning of the terms 'other regulations of commerce'*
> *could be understood to include any regulation having an impact on trade (such as*
> *measures in the fields covered by WTO rules, e.g. sanitary and phytosanitary, customs*
> *valuation, anti-dumping, technical barriers to trade; as well as any other trade-related*
> *domestic regulation, e.g. environmental standards, export credit schemes). Given the*
> *dynamic nature of regional trade agreements, we consider that this is an evolving*
> *concept.[72]*

This interpretation was not appealed against. At first sight, one might be
tempted to think that the term 'other regulations of commerce' should be
given the same meaning in another paragraph of the same Article. However,
to transpose this interpretation of 'other regulations of commerce' to Article
XXIV:8(a)(ii) appears to be problematic.[73] It would mean that any policies that
may have an impact on trade would need to be substantially harmonised by the
customs union. Considering the fact that this is very much not the case even in
the most advanced of all customs unions, the EC, it would seem virtually impossible for any customs union to meet the requirement in Article XXIV:8(a)(ii). It
should be noted that paragraphs 5 and 8 pursue different objectives. Whereas
paragraph 5 seeks to ensure that a customs union is not on the whole more
protectionist than its constituent members were before its formation, paragraph

---

[70] Panel in *Turkey-Textiles*, para. 9.148.

[71] AB in *Turkey-Textiles*, para. 50.

[72] Panel in *Turkey-Textiles*, para. 9.120. Emphasis added.

[73] Cf. Kuijper (1991) at 53, note 4.

8(a)(ii) merely seeks to ensure a certain degree of uniformity in the external trade policy of the customs union.

There are divergent views in academic literature on the correct interpretation of the term 'other regulations of commerce' for the purpose of Article XXIV:8(a)(ii). A strict interpretation covers only measures specifically relating to imports, and not internal measures.[74] On the other hand, it has been argued that Article XXIV:8(a)(ii) implies that all trade obstacles that have to be eliminated within the customs union need to be made uniform externally.[75] The same author has contended that the notion of 'other restrictive regulations of commerce' in paragraph (8)(a)(i) covers measures having equivalent effect to quantitative restrictions.[76] This would *a fortiori* mean that 'other regulations of commerce' in paragraph (8)(a)(ii), which are not necessarily restrictive, must also include measures having equivalent effect to quantitative restrictions.

Arguably, a requirement to recognise other states' standards within a customs union, such as laid down in the *Cassis de Dijon* case-law, violates the MFN requirement if not extended to third-country products. Such a violation cannot be excused under Article XXIV GATT, as it will not pass the test of Article XXIV:5 laid down by the Appellate Body: the formation of the customs union would not be prevented if the introduction of the measure were not allowed. This issue has to the author's knowledge not been raised in dispute settlement. If third-country products in free circulation are fully assimilated to products of Community origin, as argued in Section 8.3, it will not arise as there is no MFN violation.

The beginning of recognition of standards between WTO Members is laid down in the SPS and TBT Agreements. Article XXIV GATT only applies to GATT obligations, and not to other WTO Agreements, such as the TBT and SPS Agreements. Thus, in the case of customs unions, Article XXIV:8(a) in itself imposes no obligation to substantially unify or harmonise its members' SPS measures or technical regulations, internally or externally. However, that does not necessarily mean that Article XXIV is irrelevant to other WTO agreements. Its possible relevance to other WTO Agreements is as yet untested, except in the particular case of a WTO Agreement that explicitly refers to GATT 1994.[77]

---

[74] White (1989) at 262-63.

[75] Demaret (1988) at 73-74.

[76] Demaret (1987) at 142.

[77] As in the Agreement on Textiles and Clothing (ATC). See the AB in *Turkey-Textiles*, in its footnote 13: 'The chapeau of [Article XXIV] paragraph 5 refers only to the provisions of the GATT 1994. It does not refer to the provisions of the *ATC*. However, Article 2.4 of the *ATC* provides that "[n]o new restrictions ... shall be introduced *except under* the provisions of this Agreement or *relevant GATT 1994 provisions.*" (emphasis added) In this way, Article XXIV of the GATT 1994 is incorporated in the *ATC* and may be invoked as a defence to a claim of inconsistency with Article 2.4 of the *ATC*, provided that the conditions set forth in Article XXIV for the availability of this defence are met'.

It could be argued that the absence of a clause concerning customs unions and free trade areas in the TBT Agreement may lead EC Member States to violate the Most-Favoured Nation clause in Article 2.1 of the TBT Agreement. This would be the case when they do not extend to directly imported third-country products the recognition of equivalence that is imposed upon them by the *Cassis de Dijon* line of decisions by the ECJ with regard to intra-Community trade.[78] The same could be said about the prohibition of discrimination in Article 2.3 of the SPS Agreement, to the extent that this provision demands most-favoured nation treatment. However, the problem there is more minor than with regard to the TBT Agreement, as many SPS measures are import-specific. Only some SPS measures will be the kind of equally applicable internal regulations to which the recognition of equivalence in *Cassis* applies. Moreover, the SPS Agreement goes further than the TBT Agreement in demanding the recognition of equivalence, so the discrepancies with the EC internal regime may be smaller. Article 4 of the SPS Agreement obliges WTO Members to recognise the equivalence of other Members' SPS measures, albeit upon proof that they meet the importing Member's appropriate level of protection. Article 2.7 TBT only provides that Members 'shall give positive consideration' to accepting the equivalence of other Members' technical regulations.

As formally, Article XXIV GATT is not applicable to the TBT and SPS Agreements, the possible tension between Most-Favoured Nation requirements and preferential recognition schemes within free trade areas or customs unions will have to be addressed with reference to the terms of these Agreements. However, as argued in Section 8.3, the present author opines that the problem described above does not arise in reality as a result of Articles 23(2) and 24 EC. A third-country good is assimilated to goods of Community origin after customs formalities have been complied with. From that moment on, the good is in free circulation and there will be no difference in treatment as between goods originating in third countries and goods originating in other Member States.

8.4.2 The EC and its Member States as WTO Members

In Opinion 1/94, the Court addressed the Commission's objections to shared competence in the GATS and TRIPS Agreements. The Commission was afraid that Member States would seek to express their views individually on matters within their competence, and that there would be interminable discussions to determine under whose competence a given matter falls. The Community's unity of action and its negotiating power would thus be undermined and weakened. The Court responded that such fears could not affect the competence question, which is a prior issue. However, the Court did

---

[78] Cf. Eeckhout (1994) at 276-77 with regard to the Tokyo Round TBT Agreement.

point out that it was essential to ensure close co-operation between the Member States and the Community institutions, not only in the negotiations but also in the fulfilment of the commitments entered into. The obligation to co-operate flows from the requirement of unity in the international representation of the Community, and is all the more imperative in the case of the WTO Agreements, which are inextricably linked and provide for the possibility of cross-retaliation measures.[79] Shortly after the Court had delivered its opinion, delegations from the Council of Ministers and from the Commission held negotiations in order to draft a code of conduct between the Member States and the Community in WTO matters. The code was never agreed on, however, and was accordingly not made public.[80] However, the Community and its Member States have generally succeeded in keeping their internal differences outside the WTO meeting rooms. The Commission represents the Member States in WTO dispute settlement procedures, apparently without the question of competence being raised.

Both the EC and its Member States are WTO Members, and accordingly, both have to act in conformity with WTO provisions.[81] The Multilateral Agreements on Trade in Goods discipline a great number of measures that would be qualified as 'measures having equivalent effect to quantitative restrictions' in intra-Community trade. As a matter of public international law, Member States are obliged *vis-à-vis* other WTO Members to respect the Multilateral Agreements on Trade in Goods.[82] Therefore, their internal environmental and health legislation has to be in conformity with the obligations found in the GATT, SPS and TBT Agreements. Moreover, as these Agreements have been concluded on the basis of Article 133 EC, Member States have the same obligation *vis-à-vis* the Community as a matter of Community law.[83] This obligation is confirmed by the solidarity requirement in Article 10 EC. This is not to say that the scope of the Multilateral Agreements on Trade in Goods determines the scope of the exclusive powers of the Community under Article 133, which is ultimately a Community matter. However, other WTO Members can hold both Member States and the Community itself liable for not adhering to WTO obligations. It is up to the Community how responsibilities are divided internally and who responds to violation claims.[84]

---

[79] Opinion 1/94 *Re the Uruguay Round Agreements*, paras. 106-109.

[80] Interview with a Community official who whill remain anonymous.

[81] On the WTO compatibility of some of the Community's trade policy measures, see Section 7.2.2.

[82] Article XVI:4 WTO Agreement: 'Each Member shall ensure the conformity of its laws, regulations and administrative procedures with its obligations as provided in the annexed Agreements.'

[83] See Articles 133(3) and 300(7) EC.

[84] On the representation of the Member States by the Community in WTO dispute settlement proceedings, see the panel in *EC-LAN*, paras 4.9-15 and 8.15-17.

Increasing Community harmonisation and the assimilation of third-country goods in free circulation to Community goods make it unlikely that a Member State's internal regulations are challenged in the Community for breaching WTO rules. Suppose an importer of Chinese beer is precluded from marketing its beer in Germany because of the German beer purity rules. The importer will invoke Articles 28-30 EC and if possible rely on the fact that Chinese beer can be lawfully marketed in another Member State, rather than trying to rely directly on WTO rules in a national court in a Member State, or asking China to challenge the beer purity laws in the WTO. Nevertheless, it is not inconceivable that the Court of Justice is called upon to determine whether a measure by a Member State as applied to third-country goods, violates the WTO rules. The question of the direct effect of WTO law in national courts is not addressed in this work.[85] Rather, the situation envisaged is a challenge to the WTO-compatibility of a national measure *as a matter of EC law,* in a direct action before the ECJ, e.g. an infringement action on the basis of Articles 226 or 227 EC. It is recalled that compliance with WTO obligations is not only an obligation for Member States because they are WTO Members; it is also part of their obligations under the EC Treaty. As the Court has said, the provisions of 'agreements such as those concerning free trade where the obligations entered into extend to many areas of a very diverse nature' form an integral part of the Community legal system.[86] Even if this was said in the context of free trade agreements with future Member States, it would seem to apply to the WTO Agreement too. The fact that the "direct effect" of WTO obligations has been denied by the ECJ in no way affects the obligation of the Community and its Member States to ensure that it is observed.[87]

WTO challenges to national measures may occur when a national measure meets the WTO requirements (i.e. prohibitions, justifications and conditions) but not the EC requirements, or vice versa. An example would be a technical regulation that lays the burden of proving the equivalence of a foreign technical regulation upon the importer.[88] It is also conceivable that a mandatory label based on production methods in exporting countries is acceptable under Article XX GATT, but not under EC rules. On the other hand, if an individual Member State were to take a measure like the one at issue in *US-Shrimp-Turtle,* it would

---

[85] The direct effect of WTO rules has been consistently denied by the ECJ; see e.g. Case C-149/96 *Portugal v. Council.* However, WTO rules do have "indirect effect" in the EC legal order, which may have profound implications over time. See e.g. Cases C-89/99 *Schieving-Nijstadt,* and the opinion of AG Alber in Joined Cases C-122/00 and 27/00 *Omega Air.*

[86] Case 104/81 *Kupferberg,* paras. 12-13. See also Case 181/73 *Haegeman.*

[87] Cf. Ehlermann (1986) at 138 with regard to the GATT.

[88] This would not be acceptable under the *Cassis de Dijon* line of decisions on Article 28 EC, but would be acceptable under Article 2.7 TBT.

most likely not be allowed to apply its measure to direct imports from third countries, as an import prohibition is obviously covered by the common import regulation. The question would accordingly be whether such application could be justified under the exceptions in the common import regulation. The requirement of interpreting the regulation in conformity with WTO rules would not oppose such justification, although the logic of the internal market would. Opposite scenarios are also conceivable, where a national measure is WTO incompatible, but EC compatible. Suppose that the EC had not had a Community-wide prohibition in place to administer growth hormones, and hormones were administered in some Member States but not in others. If individual Member States had instituted an import ban on hormone-treated beef, the ECJ might have accepted such a ban in those circumstances as a proportionate means to address a potential health risk.[89] The same ban might have been unacceptable under the SPS Agreement. If such scenarios were to materialise, third-country goods could not be precluded from being marketed, sold or used in a Member State while the same Member State was allowed to prevent their marketing, sale or use under Articles 28-30 when the goods originated in another Member State. Deflections through third countries might be the result.

The Dutch legislative proposal for the mandatory labelling of wood products that has been referred to in the Introduction to this study illustrates that the above considerations are not merely hypothetical. Wood products are to be labelled according to whether they emanate from sustainably managed forests.[90] After the proposed Act had been notified within the framework of the Community's notification procedure, the Commission in its detailed opinion did not mention Article 133, but concentrated on its compatibility with Articles 28-30 EC and with the TBT Agreement.[91] This suggests that the Commission does not regard the application to third-country goods of indistinctly applicable measures having equivalent effect to quantitative restrictions as an infringement of Article 133 EC.[92] Nonetheless, as argued above, a violation of the TBT Agreement by an individual Member State would also constitute a violation of Community law, so the Commission could challenge the Dutch Act before the ECJ, alleging a

---

[89] Cf. De Búrca and Scott (2001) at 10.

[90] Dutch Parliament, proposal to amend the Wet milieubeheer (Environmental Management Act), Kamerstukken nos. 23 982 and 26 998, available in Dutch at http://www.overheid.nl/op. A brief account of the Dutch law in English can be found in WTO document G/TBT/Notif.98.448, available at http://docsonline.wto.org.

[91] Originally, the Dutch proposal prohibited the imports of wood products not sustainably produced. The Commission had argued that the original proposal not only violated Articles 28-30, but also Article 133.

[92] If the Commission commences an infringement procedure on the basis of Article 226 EC and fails to mention Article 133 in its reasoned opinion, the Court will not decide on this point unless another Member State raises the issue.

violation of the TBT Agreement. If the Act is formally adopted by the Dutch parliament and other WTO Members start dispute settlement proceedings challenging its compatibility with WTO rules, the Commission will indeed be externally defending the Dutch Act that it is attacking internally.

If the Court were to find that the Dutch Act is an unjustified violation of Articles 28-30 EC, would the Act then have to be abolished altogether, or could it still be applied to third-country goods as long as its incompatibility with the WTO rules has not been established? A violation found in an infringement procedure obliges the Member State concerned to 'take the necessary measures to comply with the judgement' (Article 228 EC). This would seem to imply a requirement to amend the Act so as to remove the violation, not to repeal it altogether. Thus, as a matter of EC law, a Member State could continue to apply an indistinctly applicable marketing requirement to both national products and directly imported third-country products. However, such continued application may violate national rules regarding equality of treatment and reverse discrimination.[93] Moreover, if the legislation is amended so as to remove products in free circulation from its ambit, its continued application to directly imported third-country goods may be challenged under Article 28 EC, as argued in Section 8.3.

8.5   Conclusions on Third-Country Goods in the EC

Article 133 EC functions both to provide the Community with powers to enact legislation and conclude international agreements, and to preclude autonomous Member State action. This double function and the exclusivity of the Community's competence render the scope of Article 133 EC a difficult issue. The Court has generally held that the Community enjoys broad powers to conclude international agreements and to take autonomous measures under Article 133. Indeed, the Community has concluded international agreements with third countries in which not only quantitative restrictions, but also 'measures having equivalent effect to quantitative restrictions' are prohibited. It has also concluded the WTO Multilateral Agreements on Trade in Goods on the basis of Article 133, which discipline not just "classic" trade-specific measures, but also all sorts of internal regulatory measures, as is clear from the WTO part of this study. At the same time, most autonomous Community commercial policy measures that are based only on Article 133 EC specifically regulate trade with third countries.

The scope of Article 133 EC as providing competence to act conventionally and autonomously necessarily has repercussions on the Member States' auton-

---

[93] See Case C-448/98 *Guimont* and Section 2.1.6.

omy with regard to trade in third-country goods. If a 'measure having equivalent effect to a quantitative restriction' falls within the scope of the common commercial policy, the exclusivity of Community competence implies that a Member State is precluded from taking such a measure autonomously, save with "specific Community authorisation". Article 133 EC unites the external aspects of both Articles 28-30 EC and Article 95 EC. However, the parallel is not perfect. Internally, there are concurrent powers. As long as the Community has not enacted legislation, e.g. on the basis of Article 95 EC, Member States may take appropriate measures, as long as they respect Articles 28-30 EC. Externally, the Community has exclusive competence, and Member States are precluded from acting save with authorisation. Should the prohibition on acting externally be equally broad as internally? Should the exception grounds in Article 30 EC and the mandatory requirements also be considered to apply externally, functioning as Community authorisation? Textually, the Community's common import and export regulations do not go that far.

In the *Werner* and *Leifer* judgments, the Court has suggested that at least some 'measures having equivalent effect to quantitative restrictions' are prohibited under the common export regulation. It may be assumed that the same must be true for the common import regulation. However, the Court referred to Article XI GATT and the cases themselves concerned export certificates. It is therefore as yet unclear to what extent, if at all, these regulations prohibit the application to imports from third countries the kind of internal regulatory 'measures having equivalent effect to quantitative restrictions' as are prohibited by Article 28 EC in intra-Community trade. From the same judgments, it appears that the exceptions in the common export and import regulations constitute "specific authorisation" for Member States to apply individual trade-restrictive measures to third-country products. Whether such measures could also be justified by "mandatory requirements" has not been decided, and this logically depends on the scope attributed to the prohibition. If all 'measures having equivalent effect to quantitative restrictions' prohibited by Article 28 EC were also prohibited by the common import regulation or Article 133 EC, a parallel application of the "mandatory requirements" would be called for.

The present author argues that the scope of the prohibition of the common import and export regulations is restricted to measures covered by Article XI GATT, and does not extend to internal measures covered by Article III GATT. Neither the common import and export regulations nor Article 133 EC *per se* preclude Member States from applying internal regulatory measures to third-country imports. That does not mean, however, that Member States are free to apply to third-country imports trade-restrictive measures having equivalent effect to quantitative restrictions. Rather, the rules on the free movement of goods within the internal market are applicable to the application of internal measures to third-country goods. Once duly imported into the Community and hence brought into free circulation, third-country goods are assimilated to goods of Community origin. The Court has made it clear that such goods enjoy full free movement as guaranteed by Articles 25, 28-30 and 90 EC, thus including the broad prohibition in Article 28 EC. Therefore, a Member State will need to justify any obstacle to the importation or marketing of any product in free circulation, wherever it was produced or imported into the Community. The present author is of the opinion that this approach also applies when marketing is sought in the same Member State where the product was imported from a third country, even if the product has not moved to another Member State. In order to invoke Article 28 with regard to the marketing of a third-country product in free circulation, it is sufficient that the product can *potentially* be marketed in another Member State.

Whatever view is taken of the scope of Article 133 EC and of the common import and export regulations, both the EC and its Member States must act in conformity with WTO requirements when dealing with third-country goods. In addition to the disciplines imposed by the WTO Agreement, Member States may be precluded from applying to third-country goods measures having equivalent effect to quantitative restrictions because there is internal Community legislation that already regulates the aspects they seek to regulate, e.g. product characteristics laid down in Community harmonising legislation on the basis of Article 95. Such Community legislation may apply to goods of both Community and third-country origin.

Finally, Article XXIV GATT imposes certain requirements on customs unions, which the EC should meet. The scope of these requirements is unclear, in particular the obligation to substantially apply externally 'substantially the same duties and other regulations of commerce'. This work does not address the question of the "direct effect" of WTO rules in the EC legal order. However, it has speculated as to the possibility that a trade-restrictive measure of a Member State can be challenged within the EC, e.g. by the Commission, for a breach of WTO obligations. Such challenges are most likely to occur with regard to issues where EC and WTO obligations diverge. The Commission may find itself in an awkward position of defending a Member State in the WTO while attacking it internally. However, generally speaking, challenges to Member States' measures will be based on EC law rather than WTO law.

CHAPTER 9

Similarities and Differences

Europe as a Model for the WTO?

9.1 Introduction

As is clear from the foregoing, trade and environment conflicts and the relevant rules in the EC and WTO show remarkable similarities. Nevertheless, as discussed in the Introductory Chapter, the backgrounds of these organisations in terms of their objectives, institutional structure, and membership are quite different. Despite these differences, it has been argued by some that the rules of then EC and the WTO are not only similar, but also converging, and that the European rules and their development could provide a "model" for the WTO. Others have criticised such views and emphasised the differences between both sets of rules and their institutional framework. Both such assertions are discussed in this Chapter, with particular attention being paid to the idea of "constitutionalising" the WTO, which is largely based on the process EC law has gone through over the past decades.

9.2 Europe as a "Model" for the 'International Economic Law Revolution'

Some have used the term 'international economic law revolution' when describing *inter alia* WTO law, and sometimes also developments in the EU.[1] This "revolution" has been described as 'a new era of international legislation and constitutionalisation, driven by international economic law and challenging the Westphalian system of international law and its basic concepts of sovereignty, domaine reservé, sovereign equality, and territorial jurisdiction'. The "revolution" is said to have germinated in the EC, and to be 'spreading as the European Union spreads and as its principles of free trade and multilateralism are adopted in other regions and in the multilateral system'.[2] The same author contends that '[w]hile global economic integration is far more difficult an enterprise than European economic integration, it is also ineluctable', and that 'its end result would be *similar* to the goal of the EC: to achieve a single market without diseconomies due to the existence of national borders *and national regulation*'.[3] This statement is useful to demonstrate the concept of the EC as a "model" or "forerunner" of global economic integration, even if it may be criticised as being overly broad. Although the EC indeed has as one of its goals

---

[1]   This term, to the current author's knowledge coined by Joel Trachtman, has since occurred in writings by other authors, among whom is Petersmann. See Trachtman (1996b) at 36 and 47, and e.g. Petersmann (1998).

[2]   Trachtman (1996b) at 37.

[3]   Trachtman (1992). Emphasis added.

the creation of an internal market, this does not imply that it aims to erase *any* diseconomies arising from different national regulations. Legitimate differences between Member States and their regions may and will persist. This is shown both by the justifications for obstacles to free movement accepted in the EC Treaty and the ECJ's case-law, and by the possibilities for Member States to adopt stricter measures offered in the EC Treaty and in harmonisation measures.[4] The WTO does not aim to achieve an internal market. Therefore, even more "diseconomies" between Members may be expected to remain in the WTO, which itself has no legislative power to even out regulatory differences.[5]

Building upon the liberal notion in international relations theory that states are not the only actors, the "liberal paradigm" in international law has been said to contain 'an expanding world of liberal states, spreading out from the Western heartland [...], characterised by tendencies toward [...] representative liberal democracies with independent judiciaries and flourishing domestic and trans-border civil societies; free, if regulated, market economies [...] increasingly dense patterns of transnational interactions [...], and the erosion of significant distinctions between the international and the domestic.'[6] According to this view, the international legal system should reflect these developments by comprising 'norms of interaction for individuals and groups in transnational civil society [...]; rules and decisions promulgated by state institutions in transnational dialogue with other relevant institutions; and the law controlling state action, which will be a mixture of international agreements and national law, and will generally be subject to enforcement in national courts and in supranational courts of which the EU's European Court of Justice is the prototype.'[7]

"Model" or "forerunner" concepts may lead to even more ambitious visions about how the European experience could or should lead the way for global developments. Consider the following statement by the President of the European Commission:

> *Our European model of integration is the most developed in the world. Imperfect though it still is, it nevertheless works on a continental scale. Given the necessary institutional reforms it should continue to work well after enlargement, and I believe we can make a convincing case that it would also work globally.*[8]

---

4   See especially Article 95 (4-9) EC.

5   Trachtman does however acknowledge in the same article that according to the principle of subsidiarity, certain social functions are more effectively addressed at lower levels of organisation, and that economic integration does not thus erase the state and sub-national entities.

6   Kingsbury (1994) at 32-33.

7   As accounted by Kingsbury (1994) at 37-38, who himself expresses doubts about the tendency to centre on the Western model, and as to the value of the EU, the 'beloved archetype of liberal theorists', as a model for the future of global organisation..

8   Prodi (2000) at 6.

The Commission's President further states that a future system of world governance must be based on shared values such as justice and fair play, sustainability
and subsidiarity, transparency and democratic accountability, and that the EU
already enshrines and promotes precisely those values.[9] Although this statement
is not a shining example of self-criticism, it reflects a vision of economic integration closely associated with values such as justice and democracy. Others, too,
have linked the phenomenon of globalisation with the spreading of values
perceived as European, or Western, such as democracy and individualism.[10]

9.3   European Difficulties and Idiosyncrasies

Various voices have emphasised differences rather than similarities between the EC and the WTO, thus illustrating the possible difficulties
of regarding the European experience as a "model" for the WTO. For example,
it has been asserted that 'as the expansive vision of EU is being called into
question even in Europe, its value as a model for the future of global organisation must remain very doubtful'.[11] In this view, although the existing WTO
framework for trade and environment conflicts will evolve somewhat, the WTO
cannot be expected to model itself on an economic integration organisation like
the EU. Likewise, it has been stressed that the European Union has evolved
into a body for "social co-ordination", and that it should not be assumed that
such an evolution can be replicated on a global scale.[12] The EU has even been
depicted as a model for how the international trade law order should *not* develop.
In this view, the EU has been structured by 'the interaction of an economic and
a political idea which track, in some sense, the cosmopolitan and metropolitan
sensibilities animating the broader international legal and political regime.'[13]
The EU's economic idea combines deregulation and technocratic expertise,
while its political idea combines centralisation with sectoral functionalism. The
result is 'a political culture with a technocrat and legal face, in which politics is
treated as having somehow already happened elsewhere.'[14] In this view, the EU
appears to track one's worst fears about the internationalisation of public life.

---

[9]   Prodi (2000) at 7.

[10]   See e.g. Cohen (1998) at 118: '[...] Adam Smith's book The Wealth of Nations was written before
the beginning of the industrial revolution; a revolution that Smith himself apparently was unable to
imagine. We may likewise soon discover that the current wave of globalization is spreading production
techniques as much as the (individualist? democratic?) values in which they are grounded.'

[11]   Kingsbury (1994) at 37 and 40.

[12]   Nichols (1996a) at 694.

[13]   Kennedy (1994) at 20.

[14]   Ibid. at 21.

The political has become technocratic, the government exists only to serve the market.[15] This would appear to provide a warning sign rather than a model for international trade law. This position is qualified, however, by adding that the process of technocratisation and market domination obscuring the locus for political engagement is not unique to the EU. It essentially takes place at national and even sub-national levels too. Moreover, at those levels, it has been shown that this problem is not solved merely by reinvigorating the institutions of public sovereignty.

Criticism of the European experience in the specific realm of market integration is expressed in work discussing 'federalism and responsibility'. It is argued that the allocation of competence between the EC and its Member States is often unclear. If it is unclear who has competence to regulate, then it is unclear who bears responsibility when things go wrong. Where the fixing of responsibility is obscured by the imprecision of competence allocation, responsibility may vanish into a "black hole", the 'chasm between state and market'. The "state" at the national level is restricted in its capacity for action by obligations arising under primary Community law. For its part, the Community either does not have the competence to act, or is politically unable to do so. This policy problem, it has been argued, occurs *inter alia* in environmental policy.[16] Even though the WTO could not be compared to a "federal" structure, this criticism seems to apply to the WTO too, and possibly even more seriously. After all, while states are limited in their actions by the WTO rules they have agreed on as they are interpreted through dispute settlement, no competencies whatsoever to legislate in the relevant fields (such as consumer or environmental protection) are conferred upon the WTO. Thus, assuming that both EC and WTO trade liberalisation commitments limit national government action, the gap between "market" and "state" is even greater in the WTO than in the EC. Perhaps on a global scale, at least part of the regulatory functions can be fulfilled by international co-operation, in the shape of multilateral environmental agreements and standards agreed upon in international bodies. However, the WTO as such has no authority to bring about such co-operation.

9.4 European "Constitutionalism"

The experiences in European integration are often captured by the concepts of "constitutionalisation" and "constitutionalism".[17] Since the

---

[15] Ibid. at 22.

[16] Micklitz and Weatherill (1994) at 33-34. On the relationship between the "market" and the "state" in Europe, see Joerges (1996) and Poiares Maduro (1997) and (1998a).

[17] Weiler and Trachtman (1997).

early 1980s, an impressive body of literature has addressed the "constitutional" aspects of the European construct, from a legal perspective, but also from political science backgrounds.[18] The concepts of "constitutionalisation" and "constitutionalism" are now increasingly employed in the discourse of other international organisations, among which is the WTO.[19] It has been argued that 'it is time to view European constitutionalism as a model that may be copied, if and to the extent that its structure seems useful in other contexts.'[20] In academic literature, there is increasing mention of a "constitutional" approach to the WTO.[21] At the same time, however, such an approach is criticised. Interestingly, one of the authors who proposed to use European constitutionalism as a model for other contexts like the WTO some years ago has since depicted the 'constitutionalisation of the GATT in structural terms' as a "simplistic dream", and deemed the school of thought arguing for grafting the constitutionalisation of the EU onto the GATT 'wholly misguided'.[22] Others have argued that the WTO lacks, and will lack in the foreseeable future, the sources of legitimacy that would need to underpin a "constitutional" status.[23]

Far-reaching ambitions for drawing inspiration from the European "constitutional" experience at the world stage can be found in various writings by Petersmann.[24] The emphasis in this "constitutional" approach is on judicially enforceable individual rights. Petersmann stresses the importance of citizens' rights as checks on the trade policy powers of their own nations. Such rights, he argues, are laid down in both the EC and WTO treaties.[25] European experi-

---

[18] It is not the intention of this work to provide an exhaustive bibliography of European constitutionalism. A survey is provided in Weiler and Trachtman (1997)

[19] Weiler and Trachtman (1997) argue that despite the alleged uniqueness of the European experience and its "constitutionalism", it is time to recognise that EC law is not a different species of law, but rather a mutation of the same species [of international law].

[20] Weiler and Trachtman (1997) at 392.

[21] See e.g. various works by Petersmann; Cottier (2000); and various papers presented at the June 2000 Harvard Kennedy School conference entitled 'Efficiency, Equity and Legitimacy: the Multilateral Trading System at the Millennium', available at http://www.ksg.harvard.edu/cbg/trade/papers.htm. In one of these papers, Roessler (2000) examines the role of the "judicial organs" of the WTO *vis-à-vis* the "legislative branch" (WTO Membership) and the "executive authorities" (the various Committees in the WTO), asserting that decision-making in the WTO is divided 'in a manner akin to the trias politica of modern states'.

[22] Weiler (1999) at 374, and Weiler in Weiler (ed.) (2000), respectively.

[23] Howse and Nicolaidis (2000).

[24] See Petersmann (2000), (1999), (1998), (1997b), and (1993b). The basis for Petersmann's "constitutional approach" to international trade law is found in Petersmann (1991a).

[25] In the EC, in this view, 'freedom of trade as a fundamental right' protects the freedom to trade of Community citizens with partners both inside and outside the EC. Petersmann (1993b) at 24. This work has inspired a study on the treatment of GATT/WTO law by the European Court of Justice, with particular focus on the EC banana regime: Kuilwijk (1996).

ence shows that trade policy powers are most effectively "constitutionalised" by incorporating 'international prohibitions of trade barriers' into domestic laws and by enabling private traders, producers and consumers to enforce these in domestic courts.[26] Thus, Petersmann strongly advocates a 'human rights approach' to WTO law, inspired by the European experience,[27] and based on 'the dignity and worth inherent in the human person': 'As in EC Law, "we the citizens" must become the main subjects and beneficiaries of WTO rules. The protection of our freedom, legal equality, and peaceful cooperation across frontiers should be recognised as WTO goals that are morally and legally more important than economic utilitarianism.'[28] This line of reasoning assumes important similarities in the EC and the WTO. More importantly, the author appears to read individual freedoms and rights into the WTO Agreements that have not as such been acknowledged by its Members.[29] Furthermore, on the basis of this view of the WTO, he asserts that "WTO integration law" sets precedents for the adjustment of other international organisations such as the United Nations to 'the modern globalisation, deregulation and democratisation of national economies and polities'.[30] This approach appears to be characteristic of a prescriptive attitude towards WTO law, strongly influenced by developments in EC law as well as European human rights law. Rather than discussing *whether* WTO law serves 'constitutional functions' and contains 'constitutional principles', it concentrates on what can be learned from the WTO to reform the UN, thereby implicitly assuming the "constitutional" character of WTO law.

9.5 "Constitutionalising" the WTO?

Considering the voices for and against a "constitutional" approach to WTO law inspired by the European experience, the question of to what extent, if at all, the European "constitutional model" could be applied to the WTO deserves some further exploration. In order to address this question, it is important first to agree on what "constitutionalisation" and "constitutionalism" mean in the EC context. The emphasis in one definition of these concepts is

---

[26] Petersmann (1993b) at 49.

[27] Including not only the EU and EC but also the European Convention on Human Rights and its institutions.

[28] Petersmann (2000) at 24. On the asserted universal validity of this moral basis, see Petersmann (1998) at 201.

[29] Petersmann provides intellectual property rights as protected by the WTO's TRIPS Agreement as the only concrete example provided for a much wider claim to the existence of such rights as freedom, non-discrimination, and due process. See Petersmann (1998) at 194 and 203.

[30] Petersmann (1998) at 203.

on the evolution into a 'vertically integrated legal regime, conferring judicially enforceable rights and obligations on all legal persons and entities', and on the 'alleged shift from a legal order founded by international treaties negotiated by the governments of states under international law and giving birth to an international organisation, to a Community which has evolved and behaves as if its founding instrument were not a treaty governed by international law but, to use the language of the European Court of Justice, the "constitutional charter of a Community based on the rule of law."'[31] How does the WTO experience so far fit the description of the key elements of "European constitutionalism", i.e., a vertically integrated legal regime conferring judicially enforceable rights and obligations on all legal persons and entities, and the interpretation of the founding treaty as a "constitution"?

9.5.1 The WTO: A 'Vertically Integrated Legal System'?

Does the WTO constitute a 'vertically integrated legal system'? Power is shared vertically between different levels of government in the EC and in the United States, whether or not one wishes to use the term "federal" or "semi-federal" for the EC. Hence the question *at what level* should decisions be taken becomes of central importance in such systems. In addressing that question, the concepts of "pre-emption" and "subsidiarity" play a role. The doctrine of "pre-emption" originates in US constitutional law, but it is increasingly applied in the EC context too.[32] Subsidiarity, which originates in canonical law, has in modern times mostly been applied in the EC context.[33] It is sometimes also proposed in the global context of the WTO.[34] From the point of view of EC law, the use of the word "subsidiarity" in the WTO context could appear somewhat bewildering, as it applies in the EC context to those areas in which the Community and its Member States share competencies, such as in the environmental

---

[31] See the ECJ's opinion 1/91 *re the European Economic Area*, para. 21.

[32] Simplifying the intricacies of the doctrine, it comes down to the idea that laws issued by federal bodies preclude the corresponding regulatory powers of the states in the federation. See Goucha Soares (1998), with references to pre-emption in both the US and the EC.

[33] Simplifying again, subsidiarity may be described as the idea that regulation should take place by the level of government closest to the task at hand. Some of the literature on subsidiarity in the EC deals specifically with environmental policy. See e.g. the special issue of (2000) 10 *European Environment* on Subsidiarity and Environmental Policy in the EU.

[34] 'We believe that the spirit of embedded liberalism needs to be recovered and reinterpreted under the new conditions of globalization. This can be done again in part through inspiration from the EU, not in its constitutional guise but by incorporating some of the institutional and political features associated with the thinking on subsidiarity.' Howse and Nicolaides (2000) (at 11 of the Internet version of the paper).

sphere.[35] Arguably, the equivalent situation does not exist in the WTO, which has no legislative competencies. Surely, WTO bodies take decisions, but they cannot harmonise Members' legislation.[36]

The only competencies that resemble legislative powers are the provisions in the WTO Agreement allowing the Ministerial Conference and the General Council to adopt authoritative interpretations, and allowing the Ministerial Conference to make amendments to the WTO Agreement or the Multilateral Trade Agreements.[37] Formally, WTO Members can be bound to such interpretations or amendments against their will, as these provisions provide for decisions to be taken by three-fourths and two-thirds majorities. In practice, however, decisions in the WTO are usually made by consensus, and voting is only resorted to if consensus cannot be arrived at.[38] Moreover, WTO Members may withdraw from the WTO Agreement at any time. In the case of important amendments, the Ministerial Conference may explicitly decide that a Member that has not accepted an amendment may decide either to withdraw, or to remain a Member with the consent of the Ministerial Conference.[39] Hence, it is difficult to draw a parallel with the legislative powers conferred to the EC institutions. There, even if the Council of Ministers represents the Member States and decides whether or not to adopt legislation, the Commission and European Parliament as supranational institutions play an important part in the legislative process. Member States that have been outvoted in a qualified majority decision in the Council are not free to withdraw from the EC. Even if the references in the TBT and SPS Agreements to international standards may to some extent be considered to be parallel to harmonised Community standards, the former are agreed upon outside the WTO framework and the latter within the EC framework, including procedures that safeguard a precarious institutional balance.

9.5.2 Judicial Law-making in the WTO?

There are no legislative vertical power shifts in the WTO context similar to the conferral of legislative authority to the European Community. However, agreeing on open-ended trade liberalisation commitments and exceptions, and subsequently leaving it up to a dispute settlement body to decide upon

---

[35] See Article 5 EC and the Protocol on the Application of the Subsidiarity and Proportionality Principles, attached to the EC Treaty (as amended by the 1997 Amsterdam Treaty), and the 1993 Interinstitutional Agreement on the application of the subsidiarity principle.

[36] On the decision-making powers of WTO bodies, see Kuijper (2001)

[37] See Articles IX:2 and X of the WTO Agreement.

[38] See Article IX:1 WTO Agreement. To this author's knowledge, voting had not occurred during the first five years of the WTO's existence (information from the WTO Secretariat).

[39] Article X:3 WTO Agreement.

their interpretation can be seen as a shift of the level at which decisions should be taken. Thus, 'adjudicative vertical power shifts' may be said to take place in the WTO to the extent that panels and the Appellate Body actively scrutinise domestic policy acts that balance interests. Obviously, the scope of such *judicial* powers depends on the type of rules agreed upon; are they abstract and open, or concrete and detailed?[40] When interpreting the WTO Agreements, panels and the Appellate Body have an opportunity to replace domestic policy-makers' decisions on how to balance, for example, trade and environmental interests with their own decisions on such trade-offs. Admittedly, the WTO does not share formal powers over, for example, environmental or health protection with its Members in a way which is similar to federal structures like the US or the EC. However, the interpretation of WTO provisions in effect does reflect choices over the level at which decisions should be taken. Thus, vertical power shifts do occur in the WTO constellation.[41] Considerable deference to national policy-makers' choices by a panel or the Appellate Body in the interpretation of trade and environment provisions will result in more decision-making power at lower levels, while activism in the interpretation of such provisions will effectively shift more decision-making power to the level of the WTO.[42]

Judicial power is also circumscribed by the agreed status of the outcome of the exercise of such powers, as well as by the possibilities to overrule such outcomes. In the context of the WTO, panels and the Appellate Body issue a report interpreting WTO provisions.[43] Whereas the Appellate Body is a standing body increasingly regarded as a "tribunal" or "court", the panel procedure still reflects elements of the practice under the pre-WTO GATT to seek diplomatic rather than strictly judicial solutions to trade disputes. Panellists are still appointed on an *ad hoc* basis, albeit from an indicative list of suitable individuals held by the WTO Secretariat. Parties to a dispute may oppose nominations of panellists in their dispute for compelling reasons. However, the parties cannot block the formation of a panel; failing agreement between the parties, the WTO Director-General determines the composition of the panel.[44] A panel or Appellate Body report formally contains no more than recommendations.[45] However,

---

[40] See on this issue Trachtman (1999), distinguishing between "rules" that specify in advance the conduct to which it is applied, and "standards" that do not.

[41] According to Trachtman, most, if not all, international economic law may involve transactions in jurisdiction, either horizontal or vertical. Trachtman (1996a), at 454.

[42] For an extensive analysis along these lines, see Trachtman (1998).

[43] Although according to Article 3.2 DSU, the dispute settlement system serves to "clarify" rather than "interpret" WTO provisions, the Appellate Body does refer to "interpretations", e.g. in *US-Shrimp-Turtle*, para. 107.

[44] Article 8 DSU.

[45] See Article 19 DSU.

the reports are subsequently adopted by the Dispute Settlement Body (DSB) which consists of representatives of the WTO Membership, unless there is a consensus not to adopt them. This procedure means that, in practice, reports have up to now always been adopted, and consequently, recommendations made by panels or the Appellate Body acquire significant importance as legal interpretations. On the other hand, according to the Dispute Settlement Understanding, 'recommendations and rulings of the DSB cannot add to or diminish the rights and obligations provided in the covered agreements'.[46] Although WTO Members are obliged to ensure the conformity of their laws and regulations with WTO obligations, nowhere in the WTO Agreements is it explicitly stated that Members must comply with recommendations in panel or Appellate Body reports adopted by the DSB by bringing their legislation into conformity with the WTO Agreements.[47] Hence there is some uncertainty as to the legal status of panel and Appellate Body reports adopted by the Dispute Settlement Body, in terms of the precise obligations that ensue for WTO Members.[48]

With the caveat of the above particularities of WTO dispute settlement, it seems safe to say that a significant amount of "judicial" (or, if one wishes, quasi-judicial) law-making is taking place in the WTO. This is an important conclusion in the light of the absence of *legislative* powers in the WTO noted above. It is in this judicial (or quasi-judicial) realm that the WTO's Dispute Settlement Body, through panels and the Appellate Body, is asked to interpret rules in conflicts that bear resemblance to the way in which the European Court of Justice (ECJ) interprets the EC rules in disputes within the Community.

9.5.3   Conferring Enforceable Rights on Individuals?

"Direct effect" in the sense of WTO law mandatorily being able to be invoked by individuals in domestic courts is highly unlikely to be agreed upon by the Members. It is even more unlikely to be 'imposed from above' by a panel or the Appellate Body in the same way as the European Court of Justice has done for European law. As noted by a WTO panel, even though the WTO legal order has implications for individuals, it does not comprise them as its subjects.[49] As to the possibility of "direct effect" being unilaterally provided by WTO Members themselves, there seems little chance of a breakthrough, since the major players, the US and the EC, have explicitly refused to do so. If the possibilities for individuals to invoke WTO law before their domestic courts are limited or absent, there will also be little incentive for co-operation between

---

[46] See Article 3.2 and Article 19.2 DSU.

[47] See Article XVI WTO Agreement and Article 21 DSU.

[48] See e.g. Hippler Bello (1996) and Jackson (1997).

[49] Panel in *US-Section 301*, paras. 7.72-78, speaking of "indirect effect".

national courts and the WTO in the interpretation of WTO law. A "preliminary ruling" type of procedure is therefore highly unlikely to come about in the WTO.[50] However, the declarations denying direct effect are just statements made when ratifying the WTO Agreements, and they do not necessarily preclude national courts from applying WTO law in national disputes. In fact, although ruling out the direct effect of WTO provisions covered by Community competence, the ECJ has left it to the national courts in the EC's Member States to decide whether to allow the direct effect of WTO provisions covered by national competence.[51] The possibility of WTO law being directly applied in national courts is certainly not altogether excluded.[52] Moreover, even in the absence of "direct effect", WTO law can affect domestic legal orders in a variety of ways.[53]

9.5.4   Constitutionalisation of the Founding Treaties

As to the second key element of the "constitutional approach", the "constitutionalisation" of the founding treaties, some developments in the WTO context may be noted. A steadily growing body of panel and Appellate Body reports leads academics and policy-makers to search for consistency, principles, and structure.[54] Thus, through these reports, and their doctrinal interpretations, a system of law is being built.[55] The influence of EC discourse is seen

---

[50] Weiler and Trachtman note proposals which have been made for a preliminary ruling-like procedure in the GATT, however without providing exact references. Weiler and Trachtman (1997) at 354.

[51] Case C-300/98 Dior, para. 49: 'In a field in respect of which the Community has not yet legislated and which consequently falls within the competence of the Member States, [...] Community law neither requires nor forbids that the legal order of a Member State should accord to individuals the right to rely directly on [a WTO provision] or that it should oblige the courts to apply that rule of their own motion.'

[52] For example, the Dutch constitution provides in Article 93 that '[p]rovisions of treaties and of resolutions by international institutions, which may be binding on all persons by virtue of their contents shall become binding after they have been published', and in Article 94 that '[s]tatutory regulations in force within the Kingdom shall not be applicable if such application is in conflict with provisions of treaties that are binding on all persons or of resolutions by international institutions'. A variety of international legal rules have been invoked before Dutch courts.

[53] See e.g. the duty to interpret national law in conformity with WTO requirements in Cases C-300/98 Dior and C-89/99 Schieving; the so-called Nakajima case-law from the GATT era as repeated in the WTO era in Case C-149/96 Portugal v. Council, providing limited opportunities to directly invoke GATT/WTO law after all; and the suggestion by AG Alber in Joined Cases C-122/00 and 27/00 Omega Air that WTO law may influence the assessment of the necessity and proportionality of Community secondary legislation. The Court did not follow the AG's approach in its judgment in March of 2002.

[54] See e.g. Palmeter and Mavroidis (1998); Senti (2000).

[55] Work on the sources of this system is being done inter alia by Thomas Skouteris and Mary Footer (Ph.D. theses in progress).

in this system-building. A number of recent comparisons between the EC and WTO have focused on the role of principles and the structural implications thereof in both legal systems.[56] Interestingly, a first attempt by one author to embark on a "principled approach" to WTO law argues that similarities with EC law can be observed when considering the 'typical conflict between economic rules and non-economic interests', such as trade and environment.[57] The author states that nearly every trade conflict affects a number of rules and principles, and a balancing process is needed in which no rule or principle involved should be left to redundancy or inutility. Having pointed at a number of differences between the EC and the WTO, he concludes that the consideration of legal principles in the decision-making process of both dispute settlement bodies is nevertheless rather similar. According to him, the necessary balancing process can only be guided by the sensitive process of applying the principle of proportionality. Even though this principle is not as such expressed in WTO law, its criteria for finding an appropriate, necessary and reasonable balance between conflicting interests and principles seem to have been applied by WTO panels and the Appellate Body.[58] Other comparisons between the EC and the WTO have taken principles like "necessity" and "proportionality" as a basis.[59] It should be recalled, however, that the current author argues that WTO law does not contain a "strict proportionality" requirement.[60]

Another author discussing the (future) interpretation of WTO law appears to be heavily inspired by the EC experience, and the role of its court therein. He asks, rhetorically so it seems, whether the fact that the WTO is not an integrated system like the EC will prevent WTO 'to construe in a hierarchical way a system of WTO law' through its dispute settlement. He points at the institutional basis and the wider goals pursued by the WTO in contrast with its predecessor, the GATT. Moreover, he asserts, while the only "superseding principle" of the GATT was that of good faith, the WTO in pursuing wider goals adds other "superseding principles". In the light of these changes, he thinks that 'in the future the WTO will construe WTO Agreements taking into account not only the wording of their provisions, but also the objectives and the values that the WTO has in common with the EC. He adds that it is his conviction that the WTO 'will be capable of a dynamic development similar to that of the EC, thanks to its case law'.[61] Already now, in accordance with the Vienna Convention, the WTO rules

---

[56] Hilf (1999) and (2001); Mengozzi (1998) and (1999).

[57] Hilf (1999) at 20.

[58] Hilf (1999) at 21. Hilf and Puth (2001) have further elaborated on proportionality in WTO law.

[59] Montini (1997), concluding that there is a common core concept of the principles of necessity and proportionality in the EC and WTO.

[60] See Section 6.3.6 and, concurring, Desmedt (2001).

[61] Mengozzi (1999) at 13.

are being interpreted in the light of their context and objectives. However, as discussed in the Introductory Chapter, the reference to common values is more problematic in the WTO context than in the EC context. It was also argued there that the objectives of the EC and the WTO are not really the same. It is therefore far from self-evident to speak of the two organisations as having certain objectives in common.

In sum, the definition of "constitutionalism" provided above includes the constitutionalisation of the founding treaties, as well as a vertically integrated legal regime conferring domestically enforceable individual rights. In the absence of a vertical power shift in the sense of a conferral of legislative authority to the WTO level and of directly enforceable individual rights, the applicability of constitutional language inspired by European (and federal) experiences in the context of the WTO appears doubtful. However, leaving the interpretation of open-ended rules such as non-discrimination requirements and environmental exceptions open to dispute settlement results in *de facto* adjudicative vertical power shifts in the WTO. Moreover, even in the absence of "direct effect", WTO law is binding on its Members, and has several important indirect effects in their legal orders. Finally, the search for principles and the building of a system of WTO law may be expected to continue. Whether one wishes to apply a more narrow meaning to terms like "constitutionalism" or "constitutionalisation" to describe these phenomena obviously depends on one's definition of these words.[62]

One could speak of "partial" or "low-key" constitutionalism in the WTO context. However, when doing so, one should be well aware that the notion of "constitutionalisation" of WTO law along the lines of a European "model" easily leads to misconceptions. Because of the similarity of many EC and WTO rules, it may be tempting to ascribe certain characteristics of EC law to WTO law. However, it is recalled that the WTO lacks an institutional framework similar to the EC, including far-reaching legislative powers. Therefore, a top-down imposition of such characteristics as supremacy over national law and direct effect as has taken place through the judicial activism of the European Court of Justice appears inconceivable in the WTO. Even if such characteristics were to be ascribed to WTO law, the question would arise why they should not apply to all other public international law. The WTO lacks the considerable degree of autonomy from general international law that appears to go hand in hand with the evolution of a "constitutional order." EC law has reached considerable autonomy, not in the sense of not being bound by public international law (quite to the contrary), but in the sense of its effects in national legal orders and on their citizens.

---

[62] Jackson (1998a) at 129, note 1, mentions the WTO "constitution", albeit somewhat hesitantly, constantly placing the term between quotation marks.

CHAPTER 10

Concluding Remarks

10 Concluding Remarks

As seen above, various approaches have been taken to compare developments in the EC and the WTO, among which are "constitutional", "liberal", "principle-based", "systemic", "value-based" and "process-based" approaches. The similarities in the trade liberalisation rules and their interpretation have invited some to speculate as to whether one organisation or set of rules could be a "model" for the other, and whether the interpretations of the relevant rules may be converging. One author speaks of a 'strong convergence manifest in many areas', and asserts that the convergence in the material law of disparate international trade regimes lies at the heart of the emergent 'common law of international trade'.[1] Perhaps this 'material convergence thesis' may seem the most modest way of looking at similarities in the EC and WTO.[2] Nevertheless, the current author would like to emphasise the different contexts and backgrounds of the trade liberalisation commitments in the EC and WTO. There is no equivalent to secondary Community law in the WTO. If the WTO rules on interpretations and amendments to the Agreements can be compared to the European construct at all, it would be to the European Union's procedures for Treaty revisions in intergovernmental conferences. For the above reasons, it appears inconceivable that the WTO could achieve, through its (quasi-)judicial Dispute Settlement Body, similar effects for WTO rules in its Members' legal orders as the ECJ has done for European law in the Member States' legal orders. Institutionally, there is no equivalent to supranational bodies like the European Commission or the European Parliament in the WTO. The WTO Secretariat does not function as the guardian of the Agreements in the way the Commission does in the EC. Thus, the kind of intensive institutional interplay witnessed in the EC does not occur in the WTO. The term "horizontal federalism" applied in the context of the EC is not appropriate in the WTO.

Do the rules of the EC or the WTO regarding trade and environment need to be changed? This question is particularly topical in the WTO context, where public concern about the balance struck between trade liberalisation and non-trade interests appears to be much greater than in the WTO. For example, it has been argued that the problems engendered by "trade and..." conflicts may not be solved by asking WTO panels to 'struggle openly' with regard to these conflicts.[3] For the interpretation of WTO rules in "trade and..." conflicts, clear authority or shared understandings are generally lacking. Such conflicts are rendered effectively non-justiciable and politicised. "Political" choices by WTO

---

[1]   See Weiler (1999).

[2]   Cf. Pescatore, Davey, and Lowenfeld (1991), Chapter II.B, where it is asserted that the WTO will have to evolve along the line of the *Cassis de Dijon* case-law of the ECJ.

[3]   Dunoff (1998a) at 388.

panels and the Appellate Body may lead to a crisis of legitimacy putting the entire trading system at risk. For these reasons, it has been suggested, "trade and..." conflicts urge us to rethink the foundations of the international trade regime.[4] Several attempts have been made to limit the potential role of the WTO dispute settlement system in interpreting open-ended rules, as it is felt that domestic policy choices are effectively substituted by such interpretations. Especially with regard to "trade and..." conflicts, various authors have argued for deference by panels and the Appellate Body to domestic policy decisions in WTO Members. The problem of course is how such deference should be devised. Proposed tests include the creation by panels of a "doctrine" that allows national laws 'to survive' which reflect a societal interest and whose impact on trade is incidental. The burden of proof in the application of such a test should be laid on the country defending its law or regulation.[5] This proposal appears to stipulate a general "rule of reason" for WTO law, based on the purpose of national legislation. It may be criticised to the extent that it does not take into account the different nature of the various WTO provisions that can be infringed, and is heavily based on ascertaining the purpose of a measure, which is not a desirable exercise.[6] Another test proposes to define the conditions in which the international trade system should yield to 'national democratic impulses' by applying "filters" identifying national measures which are "authentic" and "self-sacrificing".[7] The WTO rules on antidumping measures provide a special deference standard, which is not however applicable to other WTO Agreements.[8] Some authors suggest that WTO panels should seek inspiration in "passive virtues" strategies developed by domestic and international courts to avoid certain types of contested issues.[9]

In one author's view, considering the contested issues underlying "trade and..." conflicts, even 'more artful treaty language' will not solve them.[10] This

---

[4] Dunoff (1998a).

[5] Nichols (1996a) at 713 and 716.

[6] Nichols arguably reads too much of a "purpose" test into the case-law of the ECJ, and bases his reading of GATT/WTO dispute settlement on the much disputed 'aim and effect' panel reports in *US-Alcohol* and *US-Auto-Taxes*, unadopted, which have subsequently been rejected by the Appellate Body in *Japan-Alcohol* and *EC-Bananas III*. Nichols (1996a) at 715-16.

[7] Atik (1998) at 252.

[8] Article 17.6 Antidumping Agreement. On this deference standard, see Croley and Jackson (1997). However, there appear to be potential spillovers to the Subsidies Agreement. Croley and Jackson (1997) refer to a Declaration on Dispute Settlement pursuant to the AD Agreement and SCM Agreement, in which Ministers recognise the need for the consistent resolution of disputes arising from AD and countervailing measures.

[9] Dunoff (1999a) at 757-760, building in large part upon Dunoff (1996); Davey (2001).

[10] Dunoff (1999a) at 756.

view may be contrasted with pleas for more precise treaty rules in the WTO Agreements, so as not to leave important decisions to dispute settlement.[11] It has also been argued that the main task of dispute settlement bodies set up by trade agreements is to ensure that the various interests at stake have been duly taken into account in the domestic policy process. The interests to be taken into account are not confined to domestic ones, and trade liberalisation provisions as well as exception clauses ensure that those interests are duly taken into consideration. Such process-based approaches have been applied to the case-law of the European Court of Justice, and have been said to also be of relevance to WTO dispute settlement.[12] Some of the Appellate Body's decisions indeed show signs of a process-based approach to trade-environment conflicts.[13] However, although they provide a promising way of looking at *inter alia* trade and environment problems, process-based approaches are not a panacea. They raise important questions, which arguably cannot be solved by relying purely on the domestic decision-making process, such as: which non-domestic interests have to be taken into account, how should this be done, and what weight should they be accorded? How does the taking into account of non-domestic interests, e.g. those of particular foreign producers, fit into the democratic model, if it is clear that those producers cannot vote in the state whose policy-makers are supposed to take their interests into account? Although more study is needed on this issue, it appears that generally speaking, taking non-domestic interests into account in the domestic policy-making process is a concept easier to achieve in the context of the EC than in the WTO, with its 140-plus Members.

The present author concludes that in principle, the relevant rules in both the EC and the WTO provide sufficient room for a balanced outcome of disputes on trade and environmental protection in the broad sense. Treaty changes are not needed, provided that the adjudicatory bodies in both organisations ensure that certain conditions are met. Some of these merely reflect their actual practice, while others require that they provide additional clarification. To start with the WTO, it is submitted that panels and the Appellate Body should ensure that:
- The "less favourable treatment" test in Article III:4 GATT is clarified, taking due account of the fact that the TBT and SPS Agreements are the primary instruments to address origin-neutral national regulatory measures, which suggests that such measures will only fall foul of Article

---

[11] Bronckers (1999a and 1999b).

[12] See Scott (2000), envisaging a process-based approach for balancing trade-environment conflicts in both the EC and the WTO and referring to Poiares Maduro (1998).

[13] In *US-Gasoline*, the AB found that the US authorities had not taken into account foreign producers' costs, and in *US-Shrimp-Turtle* found that the US had provided insufficient guarantees for foreign producers in a domestic process of assessing whether they met the US requirements. See on interest representation in these cases, Hansen (1999).

III:4 GATT if they result in overall less favourable treatment for imported products *vis-à-vis* like domestic products (See Sections 5.1.2 and 5.3.3).

- The grounds in Article XX GATT are interpreted sufficiently broadly so as to accommodate environmental concerns (See Sections 5.2.1 and 6.2.1).
- No strict proportionality test is applied in the sense of weighing the trade impacts of a measure with the importance of its non-trade objectives, such as environmental protection, and
- When looking at less trade-restrictive alternatives in testing necessity, only reasonably available alternatives that are equally effective in achieving the non-trade objective are assessed (See Sections 5.2.1 and 6.3.3).
- All relevant international environmental law is fully taken into account when interpreting WTO provisions, in accordance with Article 31.3(c) of the Vienna Convention (See Sections 4.1 and 4.6).
- The conditions of Article XX GATT are applied strictly when assessing unilateral PPM-based measures that make imports dependent upon the policies of the government in the exporting country, because they endanger the multilateral system. It should be made clear that such measures are only acceptable as a last resort, in situations in which PPM-based measures targeting producers, wherever they come from, are not feasible (See Sections 5.4.5 and 7.2.2).

As regards the European Community, the European Court of Justice will continue to ensure a balanced outcome of trade and environment disputes if it ensures that:

- Measures that neither lay down product requirements nor restrict or prohibit selling arrangements but nevertheless are capable of hindering intra-Community trade, which have been dubbed "third category measures", are treated in the same way as measures regulating selling arrangements, i.e., they only need justification if they directly or indirectly discriminate or prevent the market access of imported goods altogether (See Sections 3.1.2 and 6.1.1).
- It is clearly recognised that the mandatory requirement of environmental protection may justify "distinctly applicable" or discriminatory measures, but at the same time, that the proportionality requirement applies to such measures. That requirement will ensure that distinctly applicable measures are not justified if the same result could have been achieved by an indistinctly applicable measure, or by a less trade-restrictive distinctly applicable measure (See Sections 3.3.3 and 6.2.2).
- Strict proportionality testing is not applied, because in those areas where there is no harmonising legislation, i.e., where no balance between trade and environmental protection has been struck at the Community level, it is not up to the ECJ but to the EC legislature, if need be, to modify the balance struck by national authorities (See Sections 3.2.4-6 and 6.3.2).

- It is recognised that extraterritorial protection goals are acceptable, but that measures targeting the policies of governments of other Member States cannot be justified, and that PPM-based measures targeting producers in other Member States can only be justified if serious efforts have been made to address the perceived distortion caused by a production process in another Member State through the appropriate institutional procedures of the Community (See Sections 3.4.6 and 7.2.1).

If the above conditions are met, the interpretation of the relevant EC and WTO provisions results in considerable similarity. As regards the basic disciplines, both sets of rules include a prohibition of import restrictions and of unnecessary obstacles caused by product requirements, and a discrimination test for other measures that may hinder trade. The remaining difference would be the prohibition of measures preventing market access altogether in the EC (selling arrangements and third category measures if the suggestions above were to be followed). As regards the justification possibilities, environmental justifications would be possible for all measures, be they discriminatory or not. It should be noted, though, that "environmental protection" as such is not mentioned either in Article XX GATT or in Article 30 EC. Accordingly, if the possibility suggested here were to be made explicit, treaty changes would be necessary. However, this is not really necessary, as the ECJ appears to tacitly accept environmental justifications for discriminatory measures, and the Appellate Body has interpreted Article XX sufficiently broadly to encompass virtually all conceivable environmental objectives. Scientific justification for life and health measures would be needed under both sets of rules, although the role of the precautionary principle is interpreted somewhat more broadly within the EC. Finally, as regards the conditions applying to justifications, under both sets of rules, a measure must have an identifiable environmental objective, be appropriate and necessary to achieve its objective, and must not arbitrarily discriminate or operate as a disguised trade restriction. The differences here are, first, that Article XX(g) GATT only requires a measure to be "relating" to its objective, not "necessary". Secondly, while the proportionality test (in the broad sense) and the requirement concerning arbitrary discrimination or disguised trade restrictions are usually integrated in the ECJ's test, they are separate steps in the WTO. Moreover, the chapeau to Article XX GATT adds "unjustifiable discrimination" to "arbitrary discrimination", while Article 30 EC does not.

The present author does not agree with those asserting that EC law provides a "model" for WTO law, or that EC and WTO law in the field of trade in goods are "converging" into one general "common international trade law". It is submitted that the backgrounds to both sets of rules are too different to support such statements. The main difference lies not so much in the effects of the rules in domestic legal orders, because even in the absence of "direct effect", WTO law certainly has profound effects on Members' legal orders. It is rather the "in house" legislative authority in the EC that is missing in the WTO, as well as the accompanying interplay between the ECJ, the EC legislature, national authorities and the national courts. According to the EC Treaty, environmental concerns are supposed to be integrated in all Community policies, including all secondary legislation.[14] Although not impossible, substantive environmental standard-setting is not likely to occur within the WTO as it happens in the EC. International environmental standards are more likely to be set in other international fora than in the WTO. If the process of environmental standard-setting as it now stands is regarded as too dispersed, establishing an overarching World Environmental Organisation would in the current author's view be a better approach than trying to bring substantive environmental agreements into the WTO.[15] It is submitted that environmental standard-setting within the WTO is not desirable.[16] The WTO lacks expertise in environmental matters, and there is no need to transfer issues to the WTO provided that they are adequately dealt with in other international organisations. Such transfers would arguably put too much strain on an already overburdened WTO, which could result in an overall collapse or deadlock. That would imply that the baby had been thrown out with the bath water; all the advantages of a rules-based trading system would be lost, which would arguably be detrimental to developing countries.

As long as WTO Members do not wish to add substantive environmental standards to their obligations under the WTO Agreements, the interplay between the national and supranational courts and legislatures found in the EC cannot be replicated in the WTO, even if WTO rules are interpreted in a manner that is perfectly open to developments in international environmental law. This makes the danger of a "regulatory gap", i.e. the situation in which a national environmental measure is struck out in dispute settlement on the basis of trade liberalisation rules while no international agreement is attained in order to address the environmental problem, greater in the WTO than in the EC, where environmental and internal market legislation is agreed upon by qualified majority voting. Accordingly, panels and the Appellate Body cannot be expected to demonstrate "judicial activism" in the sense of providing a strong impetus to trade liberalisation as the ECJ has demonstrated, especially during the 1970s and 1980s. The ECJ provided this impetus by emphasising the importance of the free movement of goods and the internal market. Both of these concepts are alien to the WTO, which only aims at continuing liberalisation, not at free trade as such. There is no overriding trade liberalisation principle in the WTO,

---

[14] Article 6 EC.

[15] As proposed by *inter alia* former WTO Director General Ruggiero (Speech at the High-Level Symposium on Trade and the Environment, Geneva, March 1999).

[16] *Contra*, Bronckers (2001), proposing that the WTO could be turned into a World Economic Organisation, provided that certain changes are made to the organisation; Strauss (1998a) and (1998b).

and it should also not be read into its rules.[17] It should be stressed that the "judicial activism" of the ECJ did not only result in a wide interpretation of the prohibition in the EC Treaty, but also to a widening of justification possibilities. In that regard, the Appellate Body has arguably already demonstrated a degree of "activism", in interpreting Article XX GATT in accordance with the exigencies of modern times.

Around the time when the manuscript of this thesis was completed, the fourth WTO Ministerial Conference was held at Doha. In the build up to Doha, the focus was on the inclusion of the developing world in the international trading system. In view of this focus on the needs of developing countries, and their general disapproval of discussing trade and environment issues, the environment has been given relatively little consideration. The European Union has been the most persistent to try to keep the debate alive. Indeed, if it were not for the efforts of the EU, the environment would probably not have been discussed at Doha at all. The EU initially demanded that a new trade round should include negotiations on the relationship between multilateral environmental agreements (MEAs) and the WTO, on a clarification of the use of labelling schemes under the TBT Agreement, and on the inclusion in WTO law of the precautionary principle as defined in the Rio Declaration on Environment and Development. The latter theme has been considered to be an absolute non-issue by other Members. Moreover, many developing countries are afraid that any clarification of the provisions of the TBT Agreement will increase the possibilities for trade-restrictive labelling schemes.

At Doha, Members agreed to put the relationship between WTO rules and MEAs on the agenda for a new round, albeit only with respect to the relationship between WTO Members that are parties to MEAs. Members also agreed to negotiate procedures for co-operation between the WTO Secretariat and MEA secretariats, and market access for environmental goods and services. Furthermore, the Committee on Trade and Environment has been instructed to focus its debate on certain issues, among which are labelling, market access issues and the relevant provisions of the TRIPS agreement. The Committee is to make recommendations to the fifth Ministerial Conference where appropriate, including the desirability of negotiations.[18] Negotiations on the three topics mentioned above are expected to start in the first half of 2002.[19]

The language of the Doha mandate on trade and environment issues does not appear particularly forceful, and it may be considered an empty gesture. Moreover, as said, the main objective of the new round is the inclusion of devel-

---

[17] Cf. Bronckers (2001) and Howse and Regan (2000), and the discussion on "embedded liberalism" by Dunoff (1999a). *Contra*, see Hilf (2001).

[18] See document WT/MIN(01)/DEC/1.

[19] Postscript: the EC has posted a first paper regarding the relationship between WTO rules and MEAs in March of 2002.

oping countries in the multilateral trading system. The new round has been dubbed the Doha Development Agenda. Considering the contentious nature of most trade-environment issues between developed and developing countries and the limited mandate agreed upon at Doha, little clarification or other progress may be expected from the new round with regard to trade and environment. However, the question is whether this is regrettable. As argued, the present author opines that the rules as they are provide sufficient room for a balanced solution to trade and environment issues, provided that certain conditions are met. In fact, especially in its interpretation of Article XX GATT, the Appellate Body has arguably done more to "green" the WTO than could conceivably have been achieved trough intergovernmental negotiations.[20] One would expect that public support of the WTO in developed countries had benefited from the "green" outcome of decisions such as *US-Shrimp-Turtle* and *EC-Asbestos*. This does not really seem to be the case in reality, however. Perhaps environmental critics of the WTO in these countries do not sufficiently realise how "green" the outcome in these cases is.

The current author submits that in *US-Shrimp-Turtle*, the Appellate Body has possibly been even a little too "green", by allowing a unilateral PPM-based measure that targeted government rather than producer behaviour in the exporting country, without making it very clear that such measures must remain highly exceptional so as not to endanger the multilateral nature of the trade system. Indeed, governments of a large number of developing countries are highly critical of the outcome of this dispute, as it appears to open the door to power politics by developed members to the detriment of the export opportunities of developing countries. Accordingly, one of the major challenges for the WTO as an organisation, including its Dispute Settlement Body, will be to find sufficient support on both sides of the "North-South divide", in conflicts that at least at first sight pitch trade and development interests of developing countries against environmental and health interests in developed countries. Major examples of such conflicts that are likely to surface over the next few years concern eco-labelling requirements, and various sanitary, phytosanitary and technical requirements seeking to apply the high protection level chosen by developed countries to imports from developing countries. If the EC wants to be a "model", it should address the concerns of developing countries over such matters, and enhance the external coherence of its trade, environment, development and other policies. It should moreover reflect upon the question of whether the Community can enact certain measures, such as unilateral PPM-based trade-restrictive measures, while disallowing individual Member States to do the same.

---

[20] Cf. Weinstein and Charnovitz (2001).

Bibliography

ABBOTT, K. (1989)

"Modern International Relations Theory: A Prospectus for
International Lawyers", (1989) 14 *Yale Journal of International Law* 335

ABBOTT, K. (1996)

"International Economic Law: Implications for Scholarship", (1996) 17
U. Pa. J. Int'l. Econ. L. 505-511

ABBOUD, W. (2000)

"The WTO's Committee on Trade and Environment: Reconciling
GATT 1994 with Unilateral Trade-Related Environmental Measures",
(2000) *EELR* 147

ABDEL MOTAAL, D. (1999)

"The Agreement on Technical Barriers to Trade, the Committee on
Trade and Environment, and Eco-labelling", in Sampson, G. (ed.),
Trade, Environment, and the Millennium, New York, United Nations
University Press, 1999

AKANDE, D. (1996)

"The Legal Imperatives Towards Supranationalism Inherent in the
Process of Economic Integration", in *Proceedings of the Annual
Conference of the Afr. Soc. Int. Comp. Law*, 1996

ALA'I, P. (1999)

"Free Trade or Sustainable Development? An Analysis of the WTO
Appellate Body's Shift to a More Balanced Approach to Trade
Liberalization", (1999) 14 *Am. U. Int'l. L. Rev.* 1129-1171

ANDERSON, K. AND BLACKHURST, R. (EDS.) (1992)

The Greening of World Trade Issues, Hemel Hempstead, Harvester
Wheatsheaf, 1992

APPLETON, A. (1997A)

*Environmental Labelling Programmes - International Trade Law
Implications*, London, Kluwer Law International, 1997

APPLETON, A. (1997B)

"GATT Article XX's Chapeau: A Disguised 'Necessary' Test?: The
WTO Appellate Body's Ruling in *United States - Standards for
Reformulated and Conventional Gasoline*", (1997) 6 *RECIEL* 131-138

APPLETON, A. (1999)

"Shrimp/Turtle: Untangling the Nets", (1999) 2 *JIEL* 477-496

ATIK, J. (1998)

"Identifying Antidemocratic Outcomes: Authenticity, Self-Sacrifice,
and International Trade", (1998) 19 *U. Pa. J. Int'l. Econ. L.* 229-262

BALASSA, R. (1961)

The Theory of Economic Integration, Homewood, Irwin, 1961

BARNARD, C. (2001)

"Fitting the Remaining Pieces into the Goods and Persons Jigsaw?",
(2001) 26 *ELRev* 35

BARNARD, C. AND HARE, I. (1997)

"The Right to Protest and the Right to Export: Police Discretion and the Free Movement of Goods", (1997) 60 *The Modern Law Review* 394-411

BECKER, U. (1991)

Der Gestaltungsspielraum der EG-Mitgliedstaaten im Spannungsfeld zwischen Umweltschutz und Freiem Wahrenverkehr, Baden-Baden, Nomos, 1991

BEGHIN, J. AND POTIER, M. (1997)

"Effects of Trade Liberalisation on the Environment in the Manufacturing Sector", (1997) 20 *The World Economy* 435-456

BÉRAUD, R (1968)

"Les mesures d'effet équivalent au sens des articles 30 et suivants du Traité de Rome", (1968) 4 *RTDE* 265-292

BERNARD, N. (1996)

"Discrimination and Free Movement in EC Law", (1996) 45 *ICQL* 82-108

BERG, G. (1996)

"An Economic Interpretation of 'Like-Product'", (1996) 30 *JWT* 195-209

BERNIER, I. (1982)

"Product Standards and Non-Tariff Obstacles: The GATT Code on Technical Barriers to Trade", in Quinn, J. and Slayton, P. (eds.), *Non-Tariff Barriers After the Tokyo Round*, Montreal, Institute of Research on Public Policy, 1982

BHAGWATI, J. (1992)

"The Threats to the World Trading System", (1992) 15 *The World Economy* 443-456

BHAGWATI, J. (1998)

"Trade Linkage and Human Rights", in Bhagwati, J. and Hirsch, M. (eds.), *The Uruguay Round and Beyond - Essays in Honour of Arthur Dunkel*, Berlin, Springer, 1998

BHAGWATI, J. AND HUDEC, R. (EDS.) (1997)

Fair Trade and Harmonization - Prerequisites for Free Trade?, Cambridge, MIT Press, 1996

BHANDARI, J. AND SYKES, A. (EDS.) (1997)

Economic Dimensions in International Law - Comparative and Empirical Perspectives , Cambridge, Cambridge University Press, 1997

BLACKHURST, R., MARIAN, N., AND TUMLIR, J. (1977)

Trade Liberalization, Protectionism and Interdependence, Geneva, GATT, 1977

BODANSKY, D. (2000)

"What's So Bad about Unilateral Action to Protect the Environment?", (2000) 11 *EJIL* 339-347

BOISSON DE CHAZOURNES, L. (2000)

"Unilateralism and Environmental Protection: Issues of Perception and Reality of Issues", (2000) 11 *EJIL* 315-338

BOUCKAERT, B. AND DE GEEST, G. (2000)

"Encyclopedia of Law and Economics", Cheltenham, Elgar, 2000

BOURGEOIS, J. (1981)

"Some Comments on the Practice", in Timmermans, C. and Völker E. (eds.), *Division of Powers between the European Communities and their Member States in the Field of External Relations*, Deventer, Kluwer, 1981

BOURGEOIS, J. (1983)

"The Common Commercial Policy-Scope and Nature of the Powers", in Völker, E. (ed.), *Protectionism and the European Community*, Deventer, Kluwer, 1983

BOURGEOIS, J. (1993)

"Trade Policy-Making Institutions and Procedures in the European Community", Hilf, M. and Petersmann, E.-U. (eds.), *National Constitutions and International Economic Law*, Deventer, Kluwer, 1993

BOURGEOIS, J. (1995)

"The EC in the WTO and Advisory Opinion 1/94: an Echternach Procession", (1995) 32 *CMLRev* 763

BOURGEOIS, J. (1999)

"External Relations Powers of the European Community", (1999) 22 *Fordham Int'l. L.J.* 149-173

BRAND, R. (1996)

"Semantic Distinctions in an Age of Legal Convergence", (1996) 17 *U. Pa. J. Int'l. Econ. L.* 3-7

BREIER, S. (1993)

"Die völkerrechtlichen Vertragsschlußkompetenzen der Europäischen Gemeinschaft und ihrer Mitgliedstaaten im Bereich des Umweltschutzes", (1993) 28 *Europarecht* 340

BRIETZKE, P. (1994)

"Insurgents in the 'New' International Law", (1994) 13 *Wisconsin International Law Journal* 1-56

BRONCKERS, M. (1999A)

"Better Rules for a New Millennium", (1999) 2 *JIEL* 547

BRONCKERS, M. (1999B)

"Une mise en garde contre des tendances antidémocratiques à l'OMC : de meilleures règles pour un nouveau millénaire", (1999) *RMC* 683

BRONCKERS, M. (2001)

"More Power to the WTO?", (2001) *JIEL* 41

BRONCKERS, M. AND MCNELIS, N. (2000)

"Rethinking the 'Like Product' Definition in GATT 1994", in Cottier, T. and Mavroidis, P. (eds.), *Regulatory Barriers and the Principle of Non-Discrimination in World Trade Law*, Ann Arbor, University of Michigan Press, 2000

BROWNLIE, I. (1998)

Principles of Public International Law (5th ed.), Oxford, Clarendon, 1998

BRUSASCO-MACKENZIE, M. AND KISS, A. (1989)

"Les relations extérieures des Communautés européennes en matière de protection de l'environnement", (1989) 35 *Annuaire français du droit international* 702

CAMERON, J. AND CAMPBELL, K. (1998)

"Challenging the Boundaries of the DSU trough Trade and Environment Disputes", in Cameron, J. and Campbell, K. (eds.), *Dispute Resolution in the World Trade Organisation*, London, Cameron May, 1998

CAMERON, J. AND ORAVA, S. (1999)

"Where Do We Go Now And How Do We Get There: Moving the Trade and Environment Debate Forward in the New Millennium", on file with author, 1999

CAMERON, J. AND GRAY, K. (2001)

"Principles of International Law in the Dispute Settlement Body", (2001) 50 *ICLQ* 248-298

CAPPELLETTI, M., SECCOMBE, M., AND WEILER, J. (1985)

"Integration Through Law: Europe and the American Federal Experience-A General Introduction", in Cappelletti, M., Seccombe, M., and Weiler, J. (eds.), *Integration Through Law-Europe and the American Federal Experience*, Florence, EUI, 1985

CARNEY, T. (1998)

"The EU's *Locus Standi* in GATT Article III Disputes: A Reappraisal", (1998) 3 *European Foreign Affairs Review* 95-114

CASS, R. (1997)

"Introduction: Economics and International Law", in Bhandari, J. S. and Sykes A. O. (eds.), *Economic Dimensions in International Law - Comparative and Empirical Perspectives*, Cambridge, Cambridge University Press, 1997

CHALMERS, D. (1995)

"Environmental Protection and the Single Market: An Unsustainable Development. Does the EC Treaty need a Title on the Environment?", (1995) *LIEI* 65-98

CHALMERS, D. (1998)

"External Relations and the Periphery of EU Environmental Law", in Weiss, F , Denters, E., and de Waart, P. (eds.), *International Economic Law with a Human Face*, The Hague, Kluwer Law International, 1998

CHANG, H. (1998)

"An Economic Analysis of Trade Measures to Protect the Environment", in Howse, R. (ed.), *The World Trading System-Critical Perspectives on the World Economy*, London, Routledge, 1998

CHARNOVITZ, S. (1991)

"Exploring the Environmental Exceptions in GATT Article XX", (1991) 25 *JWT* 37-55

CHARNOVITZ, S (1993A)

"Environmentalism Confronts GATT Rules: Recent Developments and New Opportunities", (1993) 27 *JWT* 37

CHARNOVITZ, S. (1993B)

"A Taxonomy of Environmental Trade Measures", (1993) 6 *Georgetown Int'l. Env. L.Rev.* 1-46

CHARNOVITZ, S. (1994)

"Green Roots, Bad Pruning: GATT Rules and their Application to Environmental Trade Measures", (1994) 7 *Tulane Environmental Law Journal* 299

CHARNOVITZ, S. (1997A)

"The World Trade Organization and the Environment", (1997) 8 *Yearbook of International Environmental Law* 98-116

CHARNOVITZ, S. (1997B)

"Case note on the WTO's *Alcoholic Beverages* Report", (1997) 6 *RECIEL* 198-203

CHARNOVITZ, S. (1998A)

"Free Trade, Fair Trade, Green Trade: Defogging the Debate", in Howse, R. (ed.), *The World Trading System - Critical Perspectives on the World Economy*, London, Routledge, 1998

CHARNOVITZ, S. (1998B)

"Linking Topics in Trade Treaties", (1998) 19 *U. Pa. J. Int'l. Econ. L.* 329-346

CHARNOVITZ, S. (2000)

"World Trade and the Environment: A Review of the New WTO Report", (2000) 12 *Georgetown International Environmental Law Review* 523

CHARNOVITZ, S. (2001)

"Solving the Production and Processing Methods (PPMs) Puzzle", Graduate Institute of International Studies, 2001

CHENG, B. (1953)

General Principles of Law as Applied by International Courts and Tribunals, London, Stevens and Sons, 1953

CHEYNE, I. (1995)

"Environmental Unilateralism and the GATT/WTO System", (1995) 24 *Georgia Journal of International and Comparative Law* 433-465

CHO, S.-J. (1998)

"GATT Non-Violation Issues in the WTO Framework: Are They the Achilles' Heel of the Dispute Settlement Process?", (1998) 39 *Harvard International Law Journal* 311-355

CHURCHILL, R. AND KÜTTING, G. (1994)

"International Environmental Agreements and the Free Movement of Goods in the EC: the Case of the Montreal Protocol", (1994) 3 *EELR* 329-335

COASE, R. (1988)

The Firm, the Market and the Law, Chicago, University of Chicago Press, 1988

COHEN, D. (1998)

The Wealth of the World and the Poverty of Nations, Cambridge, The MIT Press, 1998

COLAS, B. (1991)

"Acteurs, sources formelles et hierarchie des normes en droit international economique", (1991) 22 *Revue Générale de Droit* 385-391

COLEMAN, M. (1993)

"Environmental Barriers to Trade and European Community Law", (1993) 2 *EELR* 295-314

COOPER, J. (1999)

"Spirits in the Material World: A Post-Modern Approach to United States Trade Policy", (1999) 14 *Am. U. Int'l. L. Rev.* 957-1023

CORCELLE, G. AND JOHNSON, S. (1995)

The Environmental Policy of the European Community, (2nd), London, Kluwer, 1995

CORTEN, O. (1999)

"The Notion of "Reasonable" in International Law: Legal Discourse, Reason and Contradictions", (1999) 48 *ICLQ* 613

COTTIER, T. (1998)

"Dispute Settlement in the World Trade Organization: Characteristics and Structural Implications for the European Union", (1998) 35 *CMLRev.* 325-378

COTTIER, T. (2000)

"Limits to International Trade: The Constitutional Challenge", paper presented at the 2000 meeting of the American Society of International Law

CRAIG, P. AND DE BÚRCA, G. (1999)

EU Law, (2nd ed.), Oxford, Oxford University Press, 1999

CROLEY, S. AND JACKSON, J. (1997)

"WTO Dispute Procedures, Standard of Review, and Deference to National Governments", (1997) 90 AJIL 193-213

CROSBY, S. (1991)

"The Single Market and the Rule of Law", (1991) 16 ELRev 451-465

DAM, K. (1970)

The GATT - Law and International Economic Organization, Chicago, University of Chicago Press, 1970

DASHWOOD, A. (1996)

"The Limits of European Community Powers", (1996) 21 *ELRev.* 113-128

DASHWOOD, A. (1998)

"External Relations Provisions of the Amsterdam Treaty", (1998) 35 *CMLRev* 1019-1045

DASHWOOD, A. (1999)

"Treatment of Public International Law by European Community Law", 1999

DAVEY, W. (2001)

"Has the WTO Dispute Settlement System Exceeded its Authority?", (2001) 4 *JIEL* 79

DE BÚRCA, G. (1993)

"The Principle of Proportionality and its Application in EC Law", (1993) 13 *Yearbook of European Law* 105-150

DE BÚRCA, G. AND SCOTT, J. (2001)

"The Impact of the WTO on EU Decision-Making", De Búrca, G. and Scott, J. (eds.), *The EU and the WTO: Legal and Constitutional Issues*, Hart, 2001

DEMARET, P. (1987)

"Le régime des échanges internes et externes de la Communauté à la lumière des notions d'union douanière et de zone de libre-échange", in Capotorti et al. (eds.), *Liber Amicorum Pierre Pescatore*, Baden Baden, Nomos, 1987

DEMARET, P. (1994)

"Trade-Related Environmental Measures (TREMs) in the External Relations of the European Community", Cameron, J., Demaret, P., and Geradin, D. (eds.), *Trade and the Environment: The Search for Balance*, London, Cameron May, 1994

DEMARET, P. (2000)

"The Non-Discrimination Principle and the Removal of Fiscal Barriers to Intra-Community Trade", in Cottier, T. and Mavroidis, P. (eds.), *Regulatory Barriers and the Principle of Non-Discrimination in World Trade Law*, Ann Arbor, University of Michigan Press, 2000

DEMARET, P. (ED.) (1988)

Rélations extérieures da la Communauté européenne et marché intérieur: aspects juridiques et fonctionnels, Gent, Story-Scientia, 1988

DEMARET, P. AND STEWARDSON, R. (1994)

"Border Tax Adjustments under GATT and EC Law and General Implications for Environmental Taxes", (1994) 28 *JWT* 5-65

DEMARET, P., BELLIS, J.-F., AND GARCIA JIMENEZ, G. (EDS.) (1997)

Regionalism and Multilateralism after the Uruguay Round, Brussels, European Interuniversity Press, 1997

DEMIRAY, D. (1994)

"The Movement of Goods in a Green Market", (1994) *LIEI* 73-110

DENZA, E. (1999)

"Two Legal Orders: Divergent or Convergent?", (1999) 48 *ICLQ* 257-284

DESMEDT, A. (2001)

"Proportionality in WTO Law", (2001) *JIEL* 441-480

DIEM, A. (1996)

Freihandel und Umweltschutz in GATT und WTO, Baden-Baden, Nomos, 1996

DIXON, M. AND MCCORQUODALE, R. (1991)

Cases and Materials on International Law, (2nd), London, Blackstone, 1991

DONA-VISCARDINI, W. (1973)

"Les mesures d'effet équivalent à des restrictions quantitatives", (1973) 16 *RMC* 224-233

DOUMA, W. AND JACOBS, M. (1999)

"The Beef Hormones Dispute and the Use of National Standards under WTO Law", (1999) 8 *EELR* 137

DRIESSEN, B. (1999)

"New Opportunities or Trade Barrier in Disguise? The EC Eco-Labelling Scheme", (1999) *EELR* 5-15

DRIJBER, B. AND PRECHAL, S. (1997)

"Gelijke behandeling van mannen en vrouwen in horizontaal perspectief", (1997) *SEW* 122-167

DUNOFF, J. (1994)

"Resolving Trade-Environment Conflicts: The Case for Trading Institutions", (1994) 27 *Cornell Int'l. L.J.* 607-629

DUNOFF, J. (1996)

"'Trade and': Recent Developments in Trade Policy and Scholarship - And Their Surprising Political Implications", (1996) 17 *Northw. J. Int.'l L. & B'ness.* 759

DUNOFF, J. (1998A)

"Rethinking International Trade", (1998) 19 *U.Pa.J.Int'l Econ.L.* 347-389

DUNOFF, J. (1998B)

"The Misguised Debate about NGO Participation in the WTO", (1998)
1 *JIEL* 433

DUNOFF, J. (1999A)

"The Death of the Trade Regime", (1999) 10 *EJIL* 733-762

DUNOFF, J. (1999B)

"Border Patrol at the World Trade Organization", (1999) *Yearbook of
International Environmental Law* 20

EC COMMISSION (1996A)

"Communication to the Council and to the Parliament on Trade and
Environment", February 1996

EC COMMISSION (1996B)

"Proposal for the EC Submission to the WTO Committee on Trade and
Environment on Item 1 of the Work Program", 1996

EC COMMISSION (1999A)

"The Internal Market and the Environment", 1999

EC COMMISSION (1999B)

"EU Activities With the World Trade Organisation - Report to the
European Parliament", 1999

EC COMMISSION (2000A)

"Guide to the Implementation of Directives Based on New Approach
and Global Approach", EC, 2000

EC COMMISSION (2000B)

"Communication on the Application of the Precautionary Principle",
COM (2000) 1

EECKHOUT, P. (1994)

The European Market and International Trade: A Legal Analysis, Oxford,
Clarendon, 1994

EECKHOUT, P. (1997)

"The Domestic Legal Status of the WTO Agreement: Interconnecting
Legal Systems", (1997) 34 *CMLRev* 11-57

EECKHOUT, P. (2000)

"After Keck and Mithouard: Free Movement of Goods in the EC,
Market Access, and Non-Discrimination", in Cottier, T. and Mavroidis,
P. (eds.), *Regulatory Barriers and the Principle of Non-Discrimination in
World Trade Law*, Ann Arbor, University of Michigan Press, 2000

EGLIN, R. (1998)

"Trade and Environment", in Bhagwati, J. and Hirsch, M. (eds.), *The
Uruguay Round and Beyond - Essays in Honour of Arthur Dunkel*, Berlin,
Springer, 1998

EHLERMANN, C.-D. (1984)

"The Scope of Article 113 of the EEC Treaty", in Manin, P. et alii (eds.),
Mélanges offerts à Pierre-Henri Teitgen, Paris, Pedone, 1984

EHLERMANN, C.-D. (1986)
"Application of GATT Rules in the European Community", in Hilf, M., Jacobs, F., and Petersmann, E.-U. (eds.), *The European Community and GATT*, Deventer, Kluwer, 1986

EHLERMANN, C.-D. (1987)
"The Internal Market Following the Single European Act", (1987) 24 *CMLRev* 361

EHLERMANN, C.-D. (1995)
Increased Differentiation or Stronger Uniformity, Florence, European University Institute, 1995

EHRING, L. (2001)
"Non-Discrimination in WTO Law: National and Most-Favoured Nation Treatment or Equal Treatment?", manuscript on file with author, 2001

EMILIOU, N. (1996A)
The Principle of Proportionality in European Law - A Comparative Study, London, Kluwer Law International, 1996

EMILIOU, N. (1996B)
"The Death of Exclusive Competence?", (1996) 21 *ELRev.* 294-311

EMILIOU, N. AND O'KEEFFE, D. (EDS.) (1996)
The European Union and World Trade Law After the Uruguay Round, Chichester, Wiley, 1996

EPINAY, A. (2000)
"Welthandel und Umwelt -Ein Beitrag zur Dogmatik der Art. III, IX [sic], XX GATT", (2000) 115 *Deutsches Verwaltungsblatt* 77-148

ESPÓSITO, C. (2001)
"International Trade and National Legal Orders : the Problem of Direct Applicability of WTO Law", (2001) 24 *Polish yearbook of international law* 169

ESTY, D. (1994)
Greening the GATT: Trade, Environment, and the Future, 1994

ESTY, D. AND GERADIN, D. (1998)
"Environmental Protection and International Competitiveness: A Conceptual Framework", (1998) 32 *JWT* 5-46

EVANS, A. (1998)
A Textbook on EU Law, Oxford, Hart, 1998

FALK, R. (1995)
"Environmental Protection in an Era of Globalization", (1995) 6 *YIEL* 3-25

FARBER, D. (1996)
"Stretching the Margins: The Geographic Nexus in Environmental Law", (1996) 48 *Stanford Law Review* 1235-1278

FARBER, D. AND HUDEC, R. (1994)

"Free Trade and the Regulatory State: A GATT's-Eye view of the Dormant Commerce Clause", (1994) 47 *Vanderbilt Law Review* 1401-1440

FARBER, D. AND HUDEC, R. (1996)

"GATT Legal Restraints on Domestic Environmental Regulations", Bhagwati, J. and Hudec, R. (eds.), *Fair Trade and Harmonization - Prerequisites for Free Trade?*, Cambridge, MIT Press, 1996

FAUCHALD, O. (1998)

Environmental Taxes and Trade Discrimination, London, Kluwer Law International, 1998

FAURE, M. (1998)

"Harmonisation of Environmental Law and Market Integration: Harmonising for the Wrong Reasons?", (1998) 7 *EELR* 169

FEDDERSEN, C. (1998)

"Focusing on Substantive Law in International Economic Relations: The Public Morals of GATT's Article XX(a) and "Conventional" Rules of Interpretation", (1998) 7 *Minnesota Journal of Global Trade* 75-122

FEKETEKUTY, G. (1993)

"The Link Between Trade and Environmental Policy", (1993) 2 *Minnesota Journal of Global Trade* 171-205

FINLAYSON, J. AND ZACHER, M. (1981)

"The GATT and the Regulation of Trade Barriers: Regime Dynamics and Functions", (1981) 35 *International Organization* 561-602

FLETCHER, G. (1999)

Basic Concepts of Legal Thought, Oxford, Oxford University Press, 1999

FLORY, TH. (1999)

"Les facteurs non-économiques dans la jurisprudence de la Cour de Justice des Communautés européennes et dans les Instances de l'OMC -Rapport introductif", Colloque Jean Monnet, 1999

FORD RUNGE, C., ORTALO-MAGNE, F., AND VANDEKAMP, PH. (1994)

Freer Trade, Protected Environment, New York, Council on Foreign Relations, 1994

FOY, G. (1992)

"Toward Extension of the GATT Standards Code to Production Processes", (1992) 26 *JWT* 121-131

FRENCH, D. (2000)

"The Changing Nature of 'Environmental Protection': Recent Developments Regarding Trade and the Environment in the European Union and the World Trade Organisation", (2000) 47 *NILR* 1

FUKUYAMA, F. (1992)

The End of History and the Last Man, New York, The Free Press, 1992

GAFFNEY, J. (1999)

"Due Process in the World Trade Organization: The Need for
Procedural Justice in the Dispute Settlement System", (1999) 14
American University International Law Review 1173-1221

GAINES, S. (1997)

"Rethinking Environmental Protection, Competitiveness, and
International Trade", (1997) *University of Chicago Legal Forum* 231-290

GARCIA, F. (1998A)

"Trade and Justice: Linking the Trade Linkage Debates", (1998) 19
Un.P.J.Int.Econ.L. 391-434

GARCIA, F. (1998B)

"The Trade Linkage Phenomenon: Pointing the Way to the Trade Law
and Global Social Policy of the 21st Century", (1998) 19 *U. Pa. J. Int'l.
Econ. L.* 201-208

GARRETT, G. (1995)

"The Politics of Legal Integration in the European Union", (1995) 49
International Organization 171-81

GATT (1971)

"Industrial Pollution Control and International Trade", Geneva, GATT,
1971

GATT (1979A)

"GATT Activities in 1978", Geneva, GATT, 1979

GATT (1979B)

"The Tokyo Round of Multilateral Trade Negotiations", Geneva, GATT,
1979

GATT (1991)

"Trade and Environment - Factual Note by the Secretariat", Geneva,
GATT, 1991

GATT (1992)

"Trade Provisions in MEAs - Note by the Secretariat", Geneva, GATT,
1992

GATT/WTO (1994)

"Marrakesh Decision on Trade and Environment", Geneva, GATT,
1994

GERADIN, D. (1993)

"Trade and Environmental Protection: Community Harmonization
and National Environmental Standards", (1993) *YEL* 151-199

GERADIN, D. (1997)

Trade and the Environment - A Comparative Study of EC and US Law,
Cambridge, Cambridge University Press, 1997

GINTHER, K., DENTERS, E., AND DE WAART, P. (EDS.) (1995)

Sustainable Development and Good Governance, Dordrecht, Martinus
Nijhoff, 1995

GOH, G. AND ZIEGLER, A. (1998)

"A Real World Where People Live and Work and Die - Australian SPS Measures After the WTO Appellate Body's Decision in the Hormones Case", (1998) 32 JWT 271

GONZÁLEZ VAQUÉ, L. (2000)

"La jurisprudence relative a l'article 28 CE apres l'arret "Keck et Mithouard"", (2000) Revue du Droit de l'Union Europeenne 395-419

GOOSSENS, A. AND S. EMMERECHTS (2001)

"Note on Case C-379/98 Preussen Elektra", (2001) 38 CMLRev 991-1010

GORMLEY, L. (1985)

Prohibiting Restrictions on Trade Within the EC, Amsterdam, North Holland, 1985

GOUCHA SOARES, A. (1998)

"Pre-emption, Conflicts of Powers and Subsidiarity", (1998) 23 ELRev 132

GOVAERE, I. (1997)

Note on Cases C-70/94 Werner and C-83/94 Leifer, (1997) 34 CMLRev 1019-1037

GRAF, M. (1972)

Der Begriff 'Massnahmen gleicher Wirkung wie mengenmässige Einfuhrbeschränkungen in dem EWG-Vertrag, Köln, Carl Heymans Verlag, 1972

GREENAWAY, D. (1983)

International Trade Policy, London, Macmillan, 1983

HANSEN, P. (1999)

"Transparency, Standards of Review, and the Use of Trade Measures to Protect the Global Environment", (1999) 39 Virginia Journal of International Law 1017-68

HANSON, B. (1998)

"What Happened to Fortress Europe? External Trade Policy Liberalization in the European Union", (1998) 52 International Organization 55-85

HARRYVAN, A. VAN DER HARST J. (EDS.) (1997)

Documents on European Union, London, MacMillan, 1997

HARTLEY, T. (1994)

The Foundations of European Community Law, (Third), Oxford, Clarendon, 1994

HELLER, T. AND PELKMANS, J. (1985)

"The Federal Economy: Law and Economic Integration and the Positive State-The USA and Europe Compared in an Economic Perspective", Cappelletti, M., Seccombe, M., and Weiler, J. (eds.), Integration Trough Law-Europe and the American Federal Experience, Florence, EUI, 1985

HERTZ, N. (2000)
> *The Silent Takeover*, London, Heinemann, 2000

HEWISON, H. (1994)
> "Multilateral Efforts to Protect the Environment and International Trade: the case of Driftnet Fishing", Paper Presented at the GATT Symposium on Trade, Environment and Sustainable Development, GATT, 1994

HEY, E. (2000)
> "Considerations Regarding the Hormones Case, the Precautionary Principle and International Dispute Settlement Procedures", (2000) 13 *LJIL* 239

HEYVAERT, V. (2001)
> "Balancing Trade and Environment in the European Union: Proportionality Substituted?", (2001) 13 *JEL* 391-407

HIERONYMI, O. (1973)
> *Economic Discrimination Against the United States in Western Europe (1945-1958)*, Geneva, Droz, 1973

HILF, M. (1995)
> "The ECJ's Opinion 1-94 on the WTO - No Surprise, but Wise?", (1995) 6 *EJIL* 245

HILF, M. (1999)
> "A Principle-Oriented Approach to WTO Law", Colloque Jean Monnet, 1999

HILF, M. (2001)
> "Power, Rules and Principles - Which Orientation for WTO/GATT Law?", (2001) *JIEL* 111

HILF, M., JACOBS, F., AND PETERSMANN, E.-U. (EDS.) (1986)
> *The European Community and GATT*, Deventer, Kluwer, 1986

HILF, M. AND PETERSMANN, E.-U. (EDS.) (1993)
> *National Constitutions and International Economic Law*, Deventer, Kluwer, 1993

HILF, M. AND PUTH, S. (2001)
> "The Principle of Proportionality on its Way into WTO/GATT Law", manuscript on file with the author, 2001 *(to be published in Festschrift Ehlermann)*

HILPOLD, P. (1999)
> *Die EU im GATT/WTO System*, Frankfurt, Peter Lang, 1999

HILSON, C. (1999)
> "Discrimination in Community Free Movement Law", (1999) 24 *ELRev* 445-462

HIPPLER BELLO, J. (1996)
> "The WTO Dispute Settlement Understanding: Less is More (Editorial Comment)", (1996) 90 *AJIL* 416-418

HORNG, D.-C. (1999)
"The Principle of Mutual Recognition - The European Union's Practice and Development", (1999) 22 *Journal of World Competition* 135-55

HOUSMAN, R., GOLDBERG, D., VAN DYKE, B., AND ZAELKE, D. (1995)
"The Use of Trade Measures in Select Multilateral Environmental Agreements", Geneva, UNEP, 1995

HOWSE, R. (1998)
"The Turtles Panel - Another Environmental Disaster in Geneva", (1998) 32 *JWT* 73-100

HOWSE, R. (2000)
"Adjucative Legitimacy and Treaty Interpretation in International Trade Law: The Early Years of WTO Jurisprudence", in Weiler, J. (ed.) (2000), *The EU, the WTO and the NAFTA - Towars a Common Law of International Trade*, Oxford, Oxford University Press, 2000

HOWSE, R AND TREBILCOCK, M. (1997)
"The Free Trade-Fair Trade Debate: Trade, Labor, and the Environment", in Bhandari, J. and Sykes A. (eds.), *Economic Dimensions in International Law - Comparative and Empirical Perspectives*, Cambridge, Cambridge University Press, 1997

HOWSE, R. AND REGAN, D. (2000)
"The Product/Process Distinction - An Illusory Basis for Disciplining Unilateralism in Trade Policy", (2000) 11 *EJIL* 249

HOWSE, R. AND NICOLAIDIS, K. (2000)
"Legitimacy and Global Governance: Why Constitutionalizing the WTO is a Step Too Far", paper presented at the Harvard conference on "Efficiency, Equity and Legitimacy", 2000

HOWSE, R. AND TUERK, E. (2001)
"The WTO Impact on Internal Regulations - A Case Study of the Canada-EC Asbestos Dispute", manuscript on file with author, 2001 *(published in De Búrca and Scott (eds.), The EU and the WTO, Oxford, Hart, 2001)*

HUDEC, R. (1990)
The GATT Legal System and World Trade Diplomacy, (2nd ed.), Salem, New Hampshire, Butterworth Legal Publishers, 1990

HUDEC, R. (1996A)
"Introduction to the Legal Studies", Bhagwati, J. and Hudec, R. (eds.), *Fair Trade and Harmonization - Prerequisites for Free Trade?*, Cambridge, MIT Press, 1996

HUDEC, R. (1996B)
"GATT Legal Restraints on the Use of Trade Measures against Foreign Environmental Practices", in Bhagwati, J. and Hudec, R. (eds.), *Fair Trade and Harmonization - Prerequisites for Free Trade?*, Cambridge, MIT Press, 1996

HUDEC, R. (1996c)

"Differences in National Environmental Standards: The Level-Playing-Field Dimension", (1996) 5 *Minnesota Journal of Global Trade* 1-28

HUDEC, R. (1998)

"GATT/WTO Constraints on National Regulation: Requiem for an "Aims and Effects" Test", (1998) 32 *The International Lawyer* 619-649

HUDEC, R. (1999)

"Tiger Tiger, in the House: A Critical Appraisal of the Case Against Discriminatory Trade Measures", in Hudec, R. E., *Essays on the Nature of International Trade Law*, London, Cameron May, 1999

HUDEC, R. (2000)

"The Product-Process Doctrine in GATT/WTO Jurisprudence", manuscript on file with author, 2000 *(published in Bronckers, M. and Quick, R. (eds.), New Directions in International Economic Law, Essays in Honour of John Jackson, London, Kluwer Law International, 2000)*

HUNTINGTON, S. (1996)

The Clash of Civilisations and the Remaking of World Order, New York, Simon and Schuster, 1996

IISD (1994)

"Trade and Sustainable Development: Principles", IISD, 1994

INAMA, S. AND VERMULST, E. (1999)

Customs and Trade Laws of the European Community, London, Kluwer Law International, 1999

IRWIN, D. (1996)

Against the Tide: An Intellectual History of Free Trade, Princeton, Princeton University Press, 1996

JACKSON, J. (1969)

World Trade and the Law of GATT, (1st ed.), Charlottesville (VA), Michie, 1969

JACKSON, J. (1988)

"Strengthening the International Legal Framework of the GATT-MTN System: Reform Proposals for the New GATT Round", in Petersmann, E.-U. and Hilf, M. (ed.), *The New GATT Round of Multilateral Trade Negotiations*, Deventer, Kluwer, 1988

JACKSON, J. (1989 AND 1997)

The World Trading System: Law and Policy of International Economic Relations, (1st and 2nd ed.) Cambridge, MIT Press, 1989 and 1997

JACKSON, J. (1994)

"The Legal Meaning of a GATT Dispute Settlement Report: Some Reflections", in Blokker, N. and Muller, S. (eds.), *Towards More Effective Supervision by International Organizations*, Dordrecht, Martinus Nijhoff Publishers, 1994

JACKSON, J. (1995A)

"The World Trade Organization: Watershed Innovation or Cautious Small Step Forward?", (1995) *The World Economy* 11-27

JACKSON, J. (1995B)

"International Economic Law: Reflections on the 'Boilerroom' of International Relations", (1995) 10 *Am.U.J. Int. L.& Pol'y* 595-606

JACKSON, J. (1996A)

"Reflections on International Economic Law", (1996) 17 *U. Pa. J. Int'l. Econ. L.* 17-28

JACKSON, J. (1996B)

"The World Trade Organization and the 'Sovereignty' Question", (1996) *LIEI* 179-187

JACKSON, J. (1997)

"The WTO Dispute Settlement Understanding - Misunderstandings on the Nature of Legal Obligations", (1997) 91 *AJIL* 60-64

JACKSON, J. (1998A)

The World Trade Organization - Constitution and Jurisprudence, London, Royal Institute of International Affairs, 1998

JACKSON, J. (1998B)

"The Uruguay Round and National Sovereignty", in Bhagwati, J. and Hirsch, M. (eds.), *The Uruguay Round and Beyond - Essays in Honour of Arthur Dunkel*, Berlin, Springer, 1998

JACKSON, J., MATSUSHITA, M., AND LOUIS, J.-V. (1984)

Implementing the Tokyo Round, University of Michigan Press, 1984

JACKSON, J., DAVEY, W., AND SYKES, A. (1995)

Legal Problems of International Economic Relations, (3rd), St.Paul, Minn., West, 1995

JACOBS, F. (1999)

"Recent Developments in the Principle of Proportionality in European Community Law", in Ellis, E. (ed.), *The Principle of Proportionality in the Laws of Europe*, Oxford, Hart, 1999

JANS, J. (1992)

"Evenredigheid: ja, maar waartussen?", (1992) 40 *SEW* 751-770

JANS, J. (1995)

European Environmental Law, (1st ed.), London, Kluwer Law International, 1995

JANS, J. (1996)

Noot bij advies 1/94, (1996) 44 *SEW* 110

JANS, J. (1999)

The Status of the Self-sufficiency and Proximity Principles with regard to the Disposal and Recovery of Waste in the European Community", 11 (1999) *JEL* 121-156

JANS, J. (2000A)

European Environmental Law, (2nd ed.), Groningen, Europa Law
Publishing, 2000

JANS, J. (2000B)

"Proportionality Revisited", (2000) 27 LIEI 239-265

JANSEN, B. AND LUGARD, M. (1999)

"Some Considerations on Trade Barriers Erected for Non-Economic
Reasons and WTO Obligations", (1999) 2 JIEL 530-536

JARVIS, M. (1998)

The Application of EC Law by National Courts - The Free Movement of
Goods, Oxford, Clarendon, 1998

JENNINGS, R. WATTS A. (EDS.) (1992)

Oppenheim's International Law, (9th), Harlow, Longman, 1992

JEUCKEN, M. (1998)

"Milieu als comparatieve factor in internationale handel", (1998) 62
Maandschrift Economie 52-75

JOERGES, C. (1996)

"The Market without the State? States without a Market? Two Essays
on the European Economy", European University Institute, 1996

JOERGES, C. (2000)

"Law, Science and the Management of Risks to Health at National,
European and International Level", Revised Contribution to the
Seminar on 'Regulatory Interventions in a Market Economy', Moscow,
December 1999, 2000

JOERGES, C., LADEUR, K.-H., AND VOS, E. (EDS.) (1997)

Integrating Scientific Expertise into Regulatory Decision-Making:
National Traditions and European Innovations, Baden-Baden, Nomos,
1997

JOLIET, R. (1994)

"La libre circulation des marchandises: l'arrêt Keck et Mithouard et
les nouvelles orientations de la jurisprudence", (1994) Journal des
tribunaux du droit européen 1

KANT, I. (1991)

Political Writings, (Edited by Hans Reiss), Cambridge, Cambridge
University Press, 1991

KAPTEIJN, P. VERLOREN VAN THEMAAT, P., AND GORMLEY, L. (1998)

Introduction ot the Law of the European Communities (3rd ed.), London,
Kluwer Law International, 1998

KENNEDY, D. (1994)

"Receiving the International", (1994) 10 Connecticut Journal of
International Law 1-26

KENNEDY, D. (1995)

"The International Style in Postwar Law and Policy: John Jackson and the Field of International Economic Law", (1995) 10 *Am. U. J. Int'l. L. & Pol'y* 671-716

KENNEDY, D. (1997)

"New Approaches to Comparative Law: Comparativism and International Governance", (1997) *Utah Law Review* 545-634

KENNEDY, D. (1999)

"The Disciplines of International Law and Policy", (1999) 12 *LJIL* 9-133

KENNEDY, D. AND TENNANT, C. (1994)

"New Approaches to International Law: A Bibliography", (1994) 35 *Harvard Int'l L J'l* 417-460

KINGSBURY, B (1994)

"The Tuna-Dolphin Controversy, the World Trade Organization, and the Liberal Project to Reconceptualize International Law", (1994) 5 *Yearbook of International Environmental Law* 1-40

KINGSBURY, B. (1998)

"Sovereignty and Inequality", (1998) 9 *EJIL* 599

KIRIYAMA, N. (1998)

"Institutional Evolution in Economic Integration: A Contribution to Comparative Institutional Analysis for International Economic Organization", (1998) 19 *U. Pa. J. of Int'l. Econ. L.* 53

KLABBERS, J. (1992)

"Jurisprudence in International Trade Law - Article XX of GATT", (1992) 26 *JWT* 63-94

KLEIN, N. (1999)

No Logo, New York, Picador, 1999

KOHONA, P. (1997)

"The WTO and Trade and Environment Issues - Future Directions", (1997) 20 *World Competition* 87-111

KOMESAR, K. (1994)

Imperfect Alternatives - Choosing Institutions in Law, Economics and Public Policy, Chicago, University of Chicago Press, 1994

KOMETANI, K. (1996)

"Trade and Environment: How Should WTO Panels Review Environmental Regulations Under GATT Articles III and XX?", (1996) 16 *Northwestern Journal of International Law & Business* 441-477

KOMMERS, D. AND WAELBROECK, M. (1985)

"Legal Integration and the Free Movement of Goods: The American and European Experience", in Cappelletti, M., Seccombe, M., and Weiler, J. (eds.), *Integration Trough Law-Europe and the American Federal Experience*, Florence, EUI, 1985

KOOPMANS, T. (1986)

Vergelijkend publiekrecht, (2nd), Deventer, Kluwer, 1986

KRÄMER, L. (1990)

EEC Treaty and Environmental Protection, London, Sweet & Maxwell, 1990

KRÄMER, L. (1992; 1997)

Focus on European Environmental Law, (1st and 2nd ed.), London, Sweet & Maxwell, 1992; 1997

KRÄMER, L. (1993A)

"Environmental Protection and Article 30 EEC Treaty", (1993) 30 *CMLRev* 111

KRÄMER, L. (1993B)

European Environmental Law Casebook, London, Sweet & Maxwell, 1993

KRÄMER, L. (1995)

EC Treaty and Environmental Law, London, Sweet & Maxwell, 1995

KRÄMER, L. (1996)

"Environmental Protection and Trade - the Contribution of the European Union", in Wolfrum, R. (ed.), *Enforcing Environmental Standards: Economic Mechanisms as a Viable Means?,* Berlin, Springer, 1996

KRÄMER, L. (2000)

EC Environmental Law, (4th ed.), London, Sweet & Maxwell, 2000

KRESS, A. (1949)

The Documents of Economic Diplomacy-A Selection of Commercial Treaties and Documents, Washington, DC, Georgetown University, 1949

KROMAREK, L. (1990)

"Environmental Protection and Free Movement of Goods: The Danish Bottles Case", (1990) 2 *JEL* 89

KRUEGER, A. (ED.) (1998)

The WTO as an International Organization, Chicago, University of Chicago Press, 1998

KUIJPER, P.-J. (1991)

"The Influence of the Elimination of Physical Frontiers in the Community on Trade in Goods with Third States", in Hilf, M. and Tomuschat, C. (ed.), *EG und Drittstaatsbeziehungen nach 1992,* Baden-Baden, Nomos, 1991

KUIJPER, P.-J. (1996)

"Booze and Fast Cars: Tax Discrimination under GATT and the EC", (1996) *LIEI* 129-144

KUIJPER, P.-J. (1997)

Review of Kuilwijk, K.-J. (1996), (1997) 45 *SEW* 250-252

KUIJPER, P.-J. (2001)

"Decision-Making in the WTO", manuscript on file with author, 2001 (to be published in Liber Amicorum Robert Hudec, 2002)

KUIK, O., VERBRUGGEN, H., AND HOEFNAGEL, S. (1996)

"The Consequences of the Uruguay Round Agreements for Dutch National and International Environmental Policies", Institute for Environmental Studies, 1996

KUILWIJK, K.-J. (1996)

The European Court of Justice and the GATT Dilemma: Public Interest versus Individual Rights, Beuningen, Nexed Editions, 1996

LAMY, P. (2001)

"Global Policy without Democracy?", 2001

LANE, R. (1993)

"New Community Competences under the Maastricht Treaty", (1993) 30 CMLRev 939

LANG, W. (ED.) (1995)

Sustainable Development and International Law, London, Graham&Trotman/Martinus Nijhoff, 1995

LANGER, J. AND WIERS, J. (2000)

"Danish Bottles and Austrian Animal Transport: the Continuing Story of Free Movement, Environmental Protection and Proportionality", (2000) RECIEL 188

LARENZ, K. AND CANARIS, C.-W. (1995)

Methodenlehre der Rechtwissenschaft, (3rd), Berlin, Springer, 1995

LASOK, K. (2000)

"Role and Efficacy of the Commission's Reasoned Opinion in Article 169/170 Proceedings", in Weiss, F. (ed.), Improving WTO Dispute Settlement, London, Cameron May, 2000

LAUWAARS, R. (1988)

"Scope and Exclusiveness of the Common Commercial Policy-Limits of the Powers of the Member States", in Schwarze (ed.), Discretionary Powers of the Member States in the Field of Economic Policies and their Limits under the EEC Treaty, Baden-Baden, Nomos, 1988

LEEFMANS, P. (1998)

Externe Milieubevoegdheden, Deventer, Kluwer, 1998

LEENEN, A. (1984)

"Participation of the EEC in International Environmental Agreements", (1984) LIEI 93

LENAERTS, K. AND VERHOEVEN, A. (2000)

"Towards a Legal Framework for Executive Rule-Making in the EU? The Contribution of the New Comitology Decision", (2000) 37 CMLRev 645

LONDON, C. AND LLAMAS, M. (1995)

EC Law on Protection of the Environment and the Free Movement of Goods, London, Butterworths, 1995

LONG, A. AND BAILEY, T (1997)

"The Single market and the Environment: the European Union's Dilemma: The Example of the Packaging Directive", (1997) 6 *EELR* 214-219

LOWENFELD, A. (1996)

"The USA, the EEC, and the GATT: The Road Not Taken", (1996) 17 *U. Pa. J. Int'l. Econ. L.* 533-538

MAGGI, G. (1999)

"The Role of Multilateral Institutions in International Trade Cooperation", (1999) 89 *The American Economic Review* 191

MALANCZUK, P. AND AKEHURST, M. (1997)

Modern Introduction of International Law, (7th ed.), London, Routledge, 1997

MANZINI, P. (1999)

"Environmental Exceptions of Article XX GATT 1994 Revisited in the Light of the Rules of Interpretation of General International Law", in Mengozzi, P. (ed.), *International Trade Law on the 50th Anniversary of the Multilateral Trade System*, 1999

MARCEAU, G. (1991)

"Some Evidence of a New International Economic Order in Place", (1991) 22 *Revue Générale de Droit* 385-395

MARCEAU, G. (1997)

"Dispute Settlement Mechanisms - Regional or Multilateral: Which One is Better?", (1997) 31 *JWT* 169-179

MARCEAU, G. AND REIMAN, C. (2001)

"When and How Is a Regional Trade Agreement Compatible with the WTO?" (2001) 28 *LIEI* 297-336

MARENGO, G. (1984)

"Pour une interprétation traditionelle de la notion de mesure d'effet équivalent à une restriction quantitative", (1994) 20 *Cahiers du Droit Européen* 291-364

MARESCEAU, M. (ED.) (1993)

The European Community's Commercial Policy after 1992: The Legal Dimension, Dordrecht, Kluwer, 1993

MARKS, S. (1997)

"The End of History? Reflections on Some International Legal Theses", (1997) 8 *EJIL* 449

MARTHA, R. (1997)

"Precedent in World Trade Law", (1997) 44 *NILR* 347-377

MASKUS, K. (2000)
"Regulatory Standards in the WTO-Comparing Intellectual Property
Rights with Competition Policy, Environmental Protection, and Core
Labor Standards", Institute for International Economics, 2000

MATHIS, J. (1991)
"Trade Related Environmental Measures in the GATT", (1991) 2 LIEI
37

MATHIS, J. (2001)
Regional Trade Agreements in the GATT/WTO: Article XXIV and the
Internal Trade Requirement, The Hague, TMC Asser Press, 2002

MATTOO, A. (1997)
"National Treatment in the GATS - Corner-Stone or Pandora's Box?",
(1997) 31 JWT 107-136

MATTOO, A. AND SUBRAMANIAN, A. (1998)
"Regulatory Autonomy and Multilateral Disciplines: The Dilemma and
a Possible Resolution", WTO Staff Working Paper, 1998

MCDONALD, F. AND DEARDEN, S. (ED.) (1999)
European Economic Integration, (3rd), Harlow, Addison Wesley
Longman, 1999

MCDOUGALL, M. LASSWELL H. MILLER J. (1994)
The Interpretation of International Agreements and World Public Order,
New Haven, New Haven Press, 1994

MCGEE, R. (1995)
"The Moral Case for Free Trade", (1995) 29 JWT 69-76

MCGOVERN, E. (1986)
International Trade Regulation. GATT, the United States and the
European Community, (Second), Globefield University Press, 1986

MCGOVERN, E (1995)
International Trade Regulation (looseleaf version), Exeter, Globefield
Press, 1995 and subsequent supplements

MCNELIS, N. (2001)
"The Role of the Judge in the EU and WTO - Lessons from the BSE and
Hormones Cases", (2001) JIEL 189-208

MENGOZZI, P. (1997)
"The Present State of Research Carried Out by the English-speaking
Section of the Centre for Studies and Research", in Centre for Studies
and Research in International Law and International Relations, The
World Trade Organization, The Hague, Kluwer Law International, 1997

MENGOZZI, P. (1998)
"Les valeurs de l'intégration européenne face à la globalisation des
marchés", (1998) RMUE 5-12

MENGOZZI, P. (1999)

"WTO Structures and Principles in the Light of the Implementation of DSB Recommendations in the Bananas case", Colloque Jean Monnet, 1999

MICKLITZ, H. AND WEATHERILL, S. (1994)

"Federalism and Responsibility", in Micklitz, H., Roethe, T., and Weatherill, S. (eds.), *Federalism and Responsibility*, London, Graham & Trotman, 1994

MIDDLETON, R. (1980)

"The GATT Standards Code", (1980) 14 *JWT* 201

MINISTERIE VAN BUITENLANDSE ZAKEN (DUTCH MINISTRY OF FOREIGN AFFAIRS)

Jaarboek Buitenlandse Zaken 1952-53, The Hague, Ministry of Foreign Affairs, 1953

MONTAGUTI, E. AND LUGARD, M. (2000)

"The GATT 1994 and other Annex 1A Agreements: Four Different Relationships?", (2000) 3 *JIEL* 473-484

MONTAÑA Y MORA, M. (1996)

"Equilibrium: A Rediscovered Basis for the Court of Justice of the European Communities to Refuse Direct Effect to the Uruguay Round Agreements?", (1996) 30 *JWT* 43-59

MONTINI, M. (1997)

"The Nature and Function of the Necessity and Proportionality Principles in the Trade and Environment Context", (1997) 6 *RECIEL* 121-130

MORTELMANS, K. (1994)

"De interne markt en het facettenbeleid na het Keck-arrest: nationaal beleid, vrij verkeer of harmonisatie", (1994) *SEW* 236

MORTELMANS, K. (1997)

"Excepties bij non-tarifaire intracommunautaire belemmeringen: assimilatie in het nieuwe EG-Verdrag?", (1997) 45 *SEW* 182-190

MORTELMANS, K. AND VAN OOIK, R. (2001)

"Het Europese verbod op tabaksreclame: verbetering van de interne markt of bescherming van de volksgezondheid?", (2001) 50 *Ars Aequi* 114

NEERGAARD, U. (1999)

"Free Movement of Goods from a Contextual Perspective, A Review Essay", (1999) 6 *Maastricht Journal of European and Comparative Law* 151-167

NERI, S. AND SPERL, H. (EDS.) (1960)

Traité instituant la Communauté Economique Européenne, Luxembourg, European Economic Community, 1960

NEUWAHL, N. (1991)
"Joint Participation in International Treaties and the Exercise of Power by the EEC and its Member States: Mixed Agreements", (1991) 28 CMLRev 717

NEUWAHL, N. (1996)
"Shared Powers or Combined Incompetence? More on Mixity", (1996) 33 CMLRev 667-687

NEVILLE BROWN, L. (1985)
"General Principles of Law and the English Legal System", in Cappelletti, M., Seccombe, M., and Weiler, J. (eds.), Integration Through Law: Europe and the American Federal Experience-A General Introduction, Florence, EUI, 1985

NICHOLS, P. (1996A)
"Trade Without Values", (1996) 90 Northwestern Un. L. Rev. 658-719

NICHOLS, P. (1996B)
"Realism, Liberalism, Values, And the World Trade Organization", (1996) 17 U. Pa. J. Int'l. Econ. L. 851-882

NICHOLS, P. (1998)
"Forgotten Linkages - Historical Institutionalism and Sociological Institutionalism and Analysis of the World Trade Organization", (1998) 19 U. Pa. J. Int'l. Econ. L. 461-512

NOGUEIRA, G. (1996)
"The First WTO Appellate Body Review: United States - Standards for Reformulated and Conventional Gasoline", (1996) 30 JWT 5-29

NOLLKAEMPER, A. (1996)
"The Legality of Moral Crusades Disguised in Trade Laws: An Analysis of the EC 'Ban' on Furs from Animals Taken by Leghold Traps", (1996) 8 JEL 237

NOLLKAEMPER, A. (1998)
"Rethinking States' Rights to promote Extra-territorial Environmental Values", in Weiss, F., Denters, E., and de Waart, P. (eds.), International Economic Law with a Human Face, The Hague, Kluwer Law International, 1998

NOTARO, N. (2000)
"The New Generation Case Law on Trade and Environment", (2000) 25 ELRev 467

NUSSBAUMER, J. (1984)
"The GATT Standards Code in Operation", (1984) 18 JWT 542

O'KEEFFE, D. AND SCHERMERS, H. (EDS.) (1983)
Mixed Agreements, Deventer, Kluwer, 1983

O'KEEFFE, D AND TWOMEY, P. (EDS.) (1994)
Legal Issues of the Maastricht Treaty, London, Chancery Law Publishing, 1994

OECD (1994)
"An Historical and Current Perspective of the Provisions of the GATT and PPMs", OECD, 1994

OECD (1997)
"PPMs: Conceptual Framework and Considerations on Use of PPM-based Trade Measures", 1997

OHLOFF, S. AND SCHLOEMANN, H. (1998)
"Rational Allocation of Disputes and 'Constitutionalisation': Forum Choice as an Issue of Competence", in Cameron, J. and Campbell, K. (eds.), *Dispute Resolution in the World Trade Organisation*, London, Cameron May, 1998

OLIVER, P. (1982, 1988, 1996)
Free Movement of Goods in the European Community, (1st, 2nd and 3rd ed.), London, Sweet & Maxwell

OLIVER, P. (1999)
"Some Further Reflections on the Scope of Articles 28-30 (Ex 30-36) EC", (1999) 36 *CML Rev* 783-806

PALMETER, D. (1993)
"Environment and Trade: Much Ado About Little? - Review Issue of *The Greening of World Trade Issues* by Anderson, K. and Blackhurst, R. (eds.)", (1993) 27 *JWT* 55-70

PALMETER, D. (1996)
"The WTO Appellate Body's First Decision", (1996) 9 *LJIL* 337-360

PALMETER, D. AND MAVROIDIS, P. (1998)
"The WTO Legal System: Sources of Law", (1998) 92 *AJIL* 398-413

PALMETER, D. AND MAVROIDIS, P. (1999)
Dispute Settlement in the World Trade Organization, The Hague, Kluwer Law International, 1999

PARDO QUINTILLAN, S. (1999)
"Free Trade, Public Health Protection and Consumer Information in the European and WTO Context - Hormone-treated Beef and Genetically Modified Organisms", (1999) 33 *JWT* 147-197

PAUL, J. (1995)
"The New Movements in International Economic Law", (1995) 10 *Am. U. J. Int'l. L. & Pol'y* 607-617

PAUWELYN, J. (1999)
"The WTO Agreement on Sanitary and Phytosanitary Measures as Applied in the First Three SPS Disputes", (1999) 2 *JIEL* 241

PELKMANS, J. (1997)
European Integration - Methods and Economic Analysis, Heerlen, Addison Wesley Longman, 1997

PESCATORE, P. (1998)
"Notes for the Conference on Free World Trade and the European Union", on file with author, 1998

PESCATORE, P. (1999)

"Opinion 1/94 on "Conclusion" of the WTO Agreement: Is There an Escape from a Programmed Disaster?", (1999) 36 CMLRev. 387 403

PESCATORE, P., DAVEY, W., AND LOWENFELD, A. (1991-1999 ETC.)

Handbook of GATT/WTO Dispute Settlement, The Hague, Kluwer Law International, 1991-1999 etc.

PETERSMANN, E.-U. (1988)

"Grey Area Policy and the Rule of Law", (1988) 22 JWT 23-44

PETERSMANN, E.-U. (1991A)

Constitutional Functions and Constitutional Problems of International Economic Law, Fribourg, Fribourg University Press, 1991

PETERSMANN, E.-U. (1991B)

"Trade Policy, Environmental Policy and the GATT - Why Trade Rules and Environmental Rules Should Be Mutually Consistent", (1991) 46 Aussenwirtschaft 197-221

PETERSMANN, E.-U. (1993A)

"International Trade Law and International Environmental Law - Prevention and Settlement of International Disputes under GATT", (1993) 27 JWT 43-81

PETERSMANN, E.-U. (1993B)

"National Constitutions and International Economic Law; Limited Government and Unlimited Trade Policy Powers? Why Effective Judicial Review and a Liberal Constitution Depend on Individual Rights", in Hilf, M. and Petersmann, E.-U. (eds.), National Constitutions and International Economic Law, Deventer, Kluwer, 1993

PETERSMANN, E.-U. (1994)

"Settlement of International Environmental Disputes in GATT and the EC - Comparative Legal Aspects", Blokker, N. and Muller, S. (eds.), Towards More Effective Supervision by International Organizations, Dordrecht, Martinus Nijhoff Publishers, 1994

PETERSMANN, E.-U. (1995)

International and European Trade and Environmental Law after the Uruguay Round, London, Kluwer Law International, 1995

PETERSMANN, E.-U. (1996)

"Trade and the Protection of the Environment after the Uruguay Round", in Wolfrum, R. (ed.), Enforcing Environmental Standards: Economic Mechanisms as Viable Means?, Berlin, Springer, 1996

PETERSMANN, E.-U. (1996-7)

"Constitutionalism and International Organizations", (1996-7) 17 Northwestern Journal of International Law & Business 398-469

PETERSMANN, E.-U. (1997A)

The GATT/WTO Dispute Settlement System - International Law, International Organizations and Dispute Settlement, London, Kluwer Law International, 1997

PETERSMANN, E.-U. (1997B)

"How to Reform the UN System? Constitutionalism, International
Law, and International Organizations", (1997) 10 *Leiden Journal of
International Law* 421-474

PETERSMANN, E.-U. (1998)

"How to Reform the United Nations? Lessons from the 'International
Economic Law Revolution'", (1998) 53 *Aussenwirtschaft* 193-231

PETERSMANN, E.-U. (1999)

"How to Promote the International Rule of Law? Contributions
by the WTO Appellate Review System", http://www.law.harvard.edu/
Programs/JeanMonnet/seminar/dpapers, 1999

PETERSMANN, E.-U. (2000)

"The WTO Constitution and Human Rights", (2000) *JIEL* 19-25

PETERSMANN, E.-U. (ED.) (1997)

International Trade Law and the GATT/WTO Dispute Settlement System,
London, Kluwer Law International, 1997

POIARES MADURO, M. (1997)

"Reforming the Market or the State? Article 30 and the European
Constitution: Economic Freedom and Political Rights", (1997) 3
European Law Journal 55-82

POIARES MADURO, M. (1998A)

*We The Court - The European Court of Justice and the European Economic
Constitution; a Critical Reading of Article 30 of the EC Treaty*, Oxford,
Hart, 1998

POIARES MADURO, M. (1998B)

"The Saga of Article 30 EC Treaty: To Be Continued", (1998) 5
Maastricht Journal of European and Comparative Law 298-316

PREEG, E.(1995)

Traders in a Brave New World, Chicago, University of Chicago Press,
1995

PRODI, R. (2000)

"Europe and Global Governance", Speech, 2000

QUICK, R. (1995)

"The Agreement on Technical Barriers to Trade in the Context of the
Trade and Environment Discussion", in Bourgeois, J. Berrod F. Gippini
Fournier E. (eds.), *The Uruguay Round Results - A European Lawyer's
Perspective*, Brussels, European Interuniversity Press, 1995

REGE, V. (1994)

"GATT-Law and Environment-related Issues Affecting the Trade of
Developing Countries", (1994) 28 *JWT* 95

REITERER, M. (1994)

"GATT/WTO: Internationaler Handel und Umwelt", (1994) 49
Aussenwirtschaft 477-494

REITZ, C. (1996)

"International Economic Law", (1996) 17 *U. Pa. J. Int'l. Econ. L.* 29-32

REPETTO, R. (1994)

"Trade and Sustainable Development", Geneva, UNEP, 1994

REUTER, P. (1995)

Introduction to the Law of Treaties, London, Kegan Paul International, 1995

RICHARDSON, M. (2000)

Globalisation and International Trade Liberalisation: Continuity and Change, Cheltenham, Elgar, 2000

RIDEAU, J. (1990)

"Les Accords internationaux dans la jurisprudence de la Cour de Justice des Communautés européennes", (1990) 94 *Revue Générale de Droit International Public* 289

RIESENFELD, S. (1997)

"Legal Systems of Regional Economic Integration", (1997) 20 *Hastings Int'l. & Comp. L. Rev.* 539-569

ROESSLER, F. (1996)

"Diverging Domestic Policies and Multilateral Trade Integration", Bhagwati, J. and Hudec, R. (eds.), *Fair Trade and Harmonization - Prerequisites for Free Trade?*, Cambridge, MIT Press, 1996

ROESSLER, F. (1998)

"Domestic Policy Objectives and the Multilateral Trade Order: Lessons from the Past", (1998) 19 *U.Pa.J.Int'l Econ.Law* 513

ROESSLER, F. (2000)

"The Institutional Balance Between the Judicial and the Political Organs of the WTO", 2000

RUGGIE, J. (1982)

"International Regimes, Transactions, and Changes: Embedded Liberalism in the Postwar Economic Order", (1982) 36 *International Organization* 379

RUNGE, C., ORTALO-MAGNE, F., AND VANDE KAMP, P. (1994)

Freer Trade, Protected Environment: Balancing Trade Liberalization and Environmental Interests, New York, Council on Foreign Relations, 1994

SACK, J. (1995)

"The European Community's Membership of International Organizations", (1995) 32 *CMLRev* 1227

SANDS, P. (1994)

"GATT 1994 and Sustainable Development - Paper Presented at the GATT Symposium on Trade, Environment and Sustainable Development", GATT, 1994

SANDS, P. (2000)

"'Unilateralism', Values, and International Law", (2000) 11 *EJIL*
291-302

SCHLAGENHOFF, M. (1995)

"Trade Measures Based on Environmental Processes and Production
Methods", (1995) 29 *JWT* 123-155

SCHLOEMANN, H. AND OHLHOFF, S. (1999)

"'Constitutionalization' and Dispute Settlement in the WTO: National
Security as an Issue of Competence", (1999) 93 *AJIL* 424-451

SCHOENBAUM, T. (1997)

"International Trade and Protection of the Environment: The
Continuing Search for Reconciliation", (1997) 91 *AJIL* 268-313

SCHRAUWEN, A. (1997)

Marché intérieur - recherches sur une notion, Amsterdam, 1997

SCHREUER, C. (1979)

"New Haven Approach und Völkerrecht", in Schreuer, C. (ed.),
Autorität und internationale Ordnung , Berlin, Duncker & Humblot,
1979

SCHRIJVER, N. (1995)

"The Dynamics of Sovereignty in a Changing World", in Ginther, K.,
Denters, E., and de Waart, P. (eds.), *Sustainable Development and Good
Governance*, Dordrecht, Martinus Nijhoff, 1995

SCHULTZ, J. (1994)

"Environmental Reform of the GATT/WTO International Trading
System", (1994) 18 *World Competition* 77-113

SCHULTZ, J. (1995)

"The GATT/WTO Committee on Trade and the Environment - Toward
Environmental Reform", (1995) 89 *AJIL* 423-439

SCHWARZE, J. (1992)

European Administrative Law, London, Sweet & Maxwell, 1992

SCOTT, J. (1998)

EC Environmental Law, London, Longman, 1998

SCOTT, J. (2000)

"On Kith and Kine (And Crustaceans): Trade and Environment in
the EU and WTO", in Weiler, J. (ed.), *The EU, the WTO and the
NAFTA - Towards a Common Law of International Trade*, Oxford, Oxford
University Press, 2000

SEDEMUND, J. (1988)

"Statement on the Concept of the Free Movement of Goods and the
Reservation for National Action under Article 36 EEC Treaty", in
Schwarze, J. (ed.), *Discretionary Powers of the Member States in the Field
of Economic Policies and their Limits under the EEC Treaty*, Baden-Baden,
Nomos, 1988

SEIDL-HOHENVELDERN, I. (1967)

"Der EWG-rechtliche Begriff der Massnahme gleicher Wirkung wie eine mengenmässige Einfuhrbeschränkung", (1967) NJW 2081

SEIDL-HOHENVELDERN, I (1992 AND 1999)

International Economic Law, (2nd and 3rd ed.), The Hague, Kluwer Law International, 1992 and 1999

SENTI, R. (2000)

WTO-System und Funktionsweise der Welthandelsordnung, Zurich, Schulthess, 2000

SEUNG WHA CHANG (1997)

"GATTing a Green Trade Barrier - Eco-Labelling and the WTO Agreement on Technical Barriers to Trade", (1997) 31 JWT 137-159

SEVENSTER, H. (1992)

Milieubeleid en Gemeenschapsrecht: het interne juridische kader en de praktijk, Deventer, Kluwer, 1992

SEVENSTER, H. (1998)

Eco-imperialisme binnen de Europese Unie; een juridisch probleem? (inaugural speech), Deventer, Tjeenk Willink, 1998

SHAW, M. (1997)

International Law, (4th), Cambridge, Cambridge University Press, 1997

SHAW, N. (1995)

"Linking Trade and Environment to Promote Sustainable Development", in Sander, H. and Inotai, A. (eds.), World Trade After the Uruguay Round: Prospects and Policy Options for the 21st Century, London, Routledge, 1995

SHAW, S. (1997)

"Trade and Environment: The Post-Singapore Agenda", (1997) 6 RECIEL 105-111

SHENK, M. (1996)

"United States - Standards for Reformulated and Conventional Gasoline (Casenote)", (1996) 90 AJIL 669-674

SIEBERT, H. (1996)

"Trade Policy and Environmental Protection", (1996) The World Economy - Global Trade Policy 1996 183-194

SITTMANN, J. (1997)

"Das Streitbeilegungsverfahren der World Trade Organisation (WTO)", (1997) 43 Recht der Internationalen Wirtschaft 749-753

SLAUGHTER, A.-M. (1995)

"Liberal International Relations Theory and International Economic Law", (1995) 10 Am. U. J. Int'l. L. & Pol'y 717-743

SLOAN, R. AND CARDONNEL, P. (1995)

"Exemptions from Harmonization Measures under Article 100a(4): The Second Authorization of the German Ban on PCP", (1995) 4 *EELR* 45

SLOTBOOM, M. (1999)

"The Hormones Case: an Increased Risk of Illegality of Sanitary and Phytosanitary Measures", (1999) *CMLRev* 471

SLYNN, G. (1988)

"The Concept of the Free Movement of Goods and the Reservations for National Action Under Article 36 EEC Treaty", in Schwarze, J. (ed.), *Discretionary Powers of the Member States in the Field of Economic Policies and their Limits under the EEC Treaty*, Baden-Baden, Nomos, 1988

SNELSON, J. (1996)

"Can GATT Article III Recover From Its Head-On Collision With *United States-Taxes on Automobiles?*", (1996) 5 *Minnesota Journal of Global Trade* 467-502

SNYDER, F. (1998)

International Trade and Customs Law of the European Union, London, Butterworths, 1998

SPIERMANN, O.

"The Other Side of the Story: An Unpopular Essay on the Making of the Community Legal Order", (1999) 10 EJIL 763-789

SPRANCE, W. (1998)

"The World Trade Organization and United States Sovereignty: The Political and Procedural Realities of the System", (1998) 13 *Am. U. Int'l. L. Rev.* 1225-1265

STAFFIN, E. (1996)

"Trade Barrier or Trade Boon? A Critical Evaluation of Environmental Labelling and Its Role in the 'Greening' of World Trade", (1996) 21 *Columbia Journal of Environmental Law* 205-286

STEENBERGEN, J. (1993)

"Is there a Need for Constitutional Reforms of the Foreign Trade Law of the EEC?", in Hilf, M. and Petersmann, E.-U. (ed.), *National Constitutions and International Economic Law*, Deventer, Kluwer, 1993

STEGER, D. (1997)

"WTO Dispute Settlement: Revitalization of Multilateralism After the Uruguay Round", (1997) 9 *LJIL* 319-335

STEINBERG, R. (1997)

"Trade-Environment Negotiations in the EU, NAFTA, and WTO: Regional Trajectories of Rule Development", (1997) 91 *AJIL* 231-267

STEPHAN, P. (1995)

   "Barbarians Inside the Gate: Public Choice Theory and International
   Economic Law", (1995) 10 *Am. U. J. Int'l. L. & Pol'y* 745-767

STEPHENSON, S. (1997)

   "Standards, the Environment and Trade Facilitation in the Western
   Hemisphere: Negotiating the FTAA", (1997) 31 *JWT* 137-170

STERN, B. (1997)

   "Can the United States set Rules for the World?", (1997) 31 *JWT* 5-26

STERN, R. (1996)

   "Conflict and Cooperation in International Economic Policy and Law",
   (1996) 17 *U. Pa. J. Int'l. Econ. L.* 539-554

STEWART, T. (1992)

   "International Trade and Environment, Lessons from the Federal
   Experience", (1992) 49 *Washington & Lee Law Review* 1329

STEWART, T. (ED.) (1993)

   The GATT Uruguay Round - A Negotiating History (1986-1992),
   Deventer, Kluwer, 1993

STRAUSS, A. (1998A)

   "The Case for Utilizing the World Trade Organization as a Forum for
   Global Environmental Regulation", (1998a) 3 *Widener Law Symposium
   Journal* 309

STRAUSS, A. (1998B)

   "From GATTzilla to the Green Giant: Wining the Environmental
   Battle for the Soul of the World Trade Organization", (1998b) 19 *U. Pa.
   J. Int'l. Econ. L.* 769-821

SUCHARIPA-BEHRMANN, L. (1994)

   "Austrian Legislative Efforts to Regulate Trade in Tropical Timber and
   Tropical Timber Products", (1994) 46 *Austrian Journal of Public and
   International Law* 283-292

SUMMERS, R. (1993)

   "A Formal Theory of the Rule of Law", (1993) 6 *Ratio Juris* 127-42

SYKES, A. (1995)

   Product Standards for Internationally Integrated Goods Markets,
   Washington D.C., The Brookings Institution, 1995

SYKES, A. (1999A)

   "Regulatory Protectionism and the Law of International Trade", (1999)
   66 *University of Chicago Law Review* 1-46

SYKES, A. (1999B)

   "The (Limited) Role of Regulatory Harmonization in International
   Goods and Services Markets", (1999) 2 *JIEL* 49-70

TEGEDER, J. (1994)

   "Applying the Cassis de Dijon Doctrine to Goods originating in Third
   Countries", (1994) 19 *ELRev* 86-94

TEMMINK, H (2000)

"From Danish Bottles to Danish Bees: The Dynamics of Free Movement of Goods and Environmental Protection-a Case Law Analysis", (2000) *Yearbook of European Environmental Law* 61-102

THAGGART, H. (1994)

"A Closer Look at the Tuna-Dolphin Case: 'Like Products' and 'Extrajurisdictionality' in the Trade and Environment Context", in Cameron, J., Demaret, P., and Geradin, D. (eds.), *Trade and the Environment: The Search for Balance*, London, Cameron May, 1994

THORN, G. AND CARLSON, M. (2000)

"The Agreement on the Application of Sanitary and Phytosanitary Measures and the Agreement on Technical Barriers to Trade", (2000) 31 *Law and Policy in International Business* 841

TIETJE, C. (1995)

"Voluntary Eco-Labelling Programmes and Questions of State Responsibility in the WTO/GATT Legal System", (1995) 29 *JWT* 123-158

TIETJE, C. (1998)

Normative Grundstrukturen der Behandlung nichttarifärer Handelshemmnisse in der WTO/GATT Rechtsordnung , Berlin, Duncker & Humblot, 1998

TIMMERMANS, C. (1982)

"Verboden discriminatie of geboden differentiatie", (1982) 30 *SEW* 426-460

TIMMERMANS, C. (1986)

"La libre circulation des marchandises et la politique commerciale commune", in Demaret, P. (ed.), *Relations extérieures de la Communauté européenne et marché intérieur: aspects juridiques et fonctionnels*, Bruges, Story-Scientia, 1986

TIMMERMANS, C. (1999)

"The EU and Public International Law", (1999) 4 *European Foreign Affairs Review* 181-194

TINBERGEN, J. (1954)

International Economic Integration, London, MacMillan, 1954

TRACHTMAN, J. (1992)

"l'Etat, c'est nous: Sovereignty, Economic Integration and Subsidiarity", (1992) 33 *Harvard Int'l Law Journal* 459-473

TRACHTMAN, J. (1997)

"Externalities and Extraterritoriality: The Law and Economics of Prescriptive Jurisdiction", in Bhandari, J. S. and Sykes A. O. (eds.), *Economic Dimensions in International Law - Comparative and Empirical Perspectives*, Cambridge, Cambridge University Press, 1997

TRACHTMAN, J. (1996A)

"The Theory of the Firm and the Theory of the International Economic Organization: Toward Comparative Institutional Analysis", (1996) 17 *Northwestern School of Law Journal of International Law & Business* 470

TRACHTMAN, J. (1996B)

"The International Economic Law Revolution", (1996) 17 *U. Pa. J. Int'l. Econ. L.* 33-61

TRACHTMAN, J. (1998)

"Trade and...Problems, Cost-Benefit Analysis and Subsidiarity", (1998) 9 *European Journal of International Law* 32-85

TRACHTMAN, J. (1999)

"The Domain of WTO Dispute Resolution", (1999) 40 *Harvard International Law Journal* 333-377

TREBILCOCK, M. AND HOWSE, R. (1998)

"Trade Liberalization and Regulatory Diversity: Reconciling Competitive Markets with Competitive Politics", (1998) 6 *European Journal of Law and Economics* 5-37

TREBILCOCK, M. AND HOWSE, R. (1999)

The Regulation of International Trade, (2nd ed), London, Routledge, 1999

TRIDIMAS, T. (1999)

"Proportionality in European Community Law: Searching for the Appropriate Standard of Scrutiny", in Ellis, E. (ed.), *The Principle of Proportionality in the Laws of Europe*, Oxford, Hart, 1999

TWINING, W. (1999)

"Globalization and Comparative Law", (1999) 6 *Maastricht Journal of European and Comparative Law* 217-234

UIMONEN, P. (1995)

"Trade Rules and Environmental Controversies During the Uruguay Round and Beyond", (1995) 18 *The World Economy* 71-86

UIMONEN, P. AND WHALLEY, J. (1997)

Environmental Issues in the New World Trading System, New York, St. Martin's Press, 1997

VAN BEERS, C. AND VAN DEN BERGH, J. (1996)

"An Overview of Methodological Approaches in the Analysis of Trade and Environment", (1996) 30 *JWT* 143-167

VAN CALSTER, G. (1996)

"The World Trade Organisation Committee on Trade and Environment: Exploring the Challenges of the Greening of Free Trade", (1996) 5 *EELR* 44-51

VAN CALSTER, G. (1999)

"The WTO Appellate Body in Shrimp/Turtle: Picking up the Pieces", (1999) *EELR* 111-115

VAN CALSTER, G. (2000)

International and EU Trade Law - The Environmental Dimension,
London, Cameron May, 2000

VAN DIJCK, P. AND FABER, G. (EDS.) (1996)

Challenges to the New World Trade Organisation, The Hague, Kluwer,
1996

VAN GERVEN, W. (1999)

"The Effect of Proportionality on the Actions of Member States of
the European Community: National Viewpoints from Continental
Europe", in Ellis, E. (ed.), The Principle of Proportionality in the Laws of
Europe, Oxford, Hart, 1999

VEDDER, H. (2001)

"Environmental Protection and Free Competition: A New Balance?",
28 (2001) LIEI 105-116

VEIL, E. (1965)

Die Wohlstandswirkungen der Handelspolitischen Integration
Westeuropas, PhD thesis, München, 1965

VERLOREN VAN THEMAAT, P. (1967)

"Bevat Artikel 30 van het EEG Verdrag slechts een non-discriminatie-
beginsel ten aanzien van invoerbeperkingen?", (1967) SEW 632-643

VERLOREN VAN THEMAAT, P. (1970)

"EEG richtlijnen betreffende discriminerende aankoopppolitiek
overheidsinstellingen, discriminerende prijsvoorschriften en andere
maatregelen van gelijke werking als kwantitatieve invoerbeperkingen",
(1970) SEW 258-266

VERLOREN VAN THEMAAT, P. (1981)

The Changing Structure of International Economic Law, Den Haag,
Martinus Nijhoff, 1981

VERLOREN VAN THEMAAT, P. (1998)

"In hoeverre wordt het economisch recht nu ook nog
gemondialiseerd?", (1998) SEW 82-85

VÖLKER, E. (1993)

Barriers to External and Internal Community Trade, Deventer, Kluwer,
1993

VÖLKER, E. (1995)

"The Agreement on Technical Barriers to Trade", in Bourgeois, J.,
Berrod F., Gippini Fournier E. (eds.), The Uruguay Round Results -
A European Lawyer's Perspective, Brussels, European Interuniversity
Press, 1995

VÖLKER, E. AND TIMMERMANS, C. (EDS.) (1981)

Division of Powers between the European Communities and their Member
States in the Field of External Relations, Deventer, Kluwer, 1981

VON MOLDTKE, K. (1997)

"When the Appellate Body Errs", Bridges - ICTSD, 1997

WAELBROECK, M, (1969)

In Ganshof van der Meersch, W., *Droit des Communautés européennes,* Bruxelles, Ferdinand Larcier, 1969

WAELDE, T. (1998)

"A Requiem for the 'New International Economic Order'", in Hafner, G., Loibl, A., Sucharipa-Behrmann, L., and Zemanek, K. (ed.), *Liber Amicorum Professor Seidl-Hohenfeldern-in honour of his 80th birthday,* The Hague, Kluwer Law International, 1998

WAINCYMER, J. (1996)

"*Reformulated Gasoline* under Reformulated WTO Dispute Settlement Procedures: Pulling Pandora out of a Chapeau?", (1996) 18 *Michigan Journal of International Law* 141-181

WALKER, S. (1993)

Environmental Protection versus Trade Liberalization: finding the Balance, Bruxelles, Facultés universitaires Saint-Louis, 1993

WALKER, V. (1998)

"Keeping the WTO from Becoming the 'World Trans-Science Organisation': Scientific Uncertainty, Science Policy, and Factfinding in the Growth Hormones Dispute", (1998) 31 *Cornell Int'l Law Journal* 251

WALLACH, L. (1998)

Whose Trade Organisation? Corporate Globalization and the Erosion of Democracy, Washington, Public Citizen, 1998

WARD, H. (1997)

"Trade and Environment Issues in Voluntary Eco-labelling and Life Cycle Analysis", (1997) 6 *RECIEL* 139-147

WASMEIER, M. (2001)

"The Integration of Environmental Protection as a General Rule for Interpreting Community Law", (2001) 38 *CMLRev* 159

WEATHERILL, S. (1996)

"After *Keck* : Some Thoughts on How to Clarify the Clarification", (1996) 33 *CMLRev* 885

WEATHERILL, S. (1999)

"Recent Case Law Concerning the Free Movement of Goods: Mapping the Frontiers of Market Regulation", (1999) 36 *CMLRev* 51-85

WEATHERILL, S. AND BEAUMONT, P. (1995)

EC Law, (Second), London, Penguin, 1995

WEILER, J. (1981)

"The Community System: the Dual Character of Supranationalism", (1981) *Yearbook of European Law* 268

WEILER, J. (1991)

"The Transformation of Europe", (1991) 100 *Yale Law Journal* 2403

WEILER, J. (1999)

"The Constitution of the Common Market Place: Text and Context in the Evolution of the Free Movement of Goods", in Craig, P. and De Búrca, G. (eds.), *The Evolution of EU Law*, Oxford, Oxford University Press, 1999

WEILER, J. (ED.) (2000)

The EU, the WTO and the NAFTA - Towards a Common Law of International Trade, Oxford, Oxford University Press, 2000

WEILER, J. AND TRACHTMAN, J. (1997)

"European Constitutionalism and Its Discontents", (1997) 17 *Northwestern School of Law J. of Int. L. & B'ness* 354-397

WEILER, T. (1998)

"Interpreting the Necessity Principle in Selected WTO Agreements", 1998

WEINSTEIN, M. AND CHARNOVITZ, S. (2001)

"The Greening of the WTO", *Foreign Affairs*, 15 November 2001

WEISS, F. (1995A)

"The Second Tuna GATT Panel Report", (1995) 8 *IJIL* 135-150

WEISS, F. (1995B)

"The GATT 1994: Environmental Sustainability of trade or environmental protection sustained by trade?", in Ginther, K., Denters, E., and de Waart, P. (eds.), *Sustainable Development and Good Governance*, Dordrecht, Martinus Nijhoff, 1995

WEISS, F. (1998)

"The WTO and the Progressive Development of International Trade Law", (1998) 29 *Netherlands Yearbook of International Law* 71-117

WEISS, F. (1999)

"Non-Economic Factors in the Case-Law of the ECJ and in the WTO ", colloque Jean Monnet, 1999

WEISS, F., DENTERS, H., AND DE WAART, P. (EDS.) (1996)

International Economic Law with a Human Face, The Hague, Kluwer Law International, 1996

WERKSMAN, J. (1999)

"Greenhouse Gas Emissions Trading and the WTO", (1999) 8 *RECIEL* 1

WHITE, E. (1989)

"In Search of the Limits to Article 30 of the EEC Treaty", (1989) 26 *CMLRev* 235-280

WIERS, J. (1998A)

"Regional and Global Approaches to Trade and Environment: The EC and the WTO", (1998) 25 *LIEI* 93-115

WIERS, J. (1998B)

"The WTO's Rules of Conduct for Dispute Settlement", (1998) 11 *LJIL*
265-274

WIERS, J. (1999)

"Garnalen, schildpadden en de Wereldhandelsorganisatie", (1999) 26
Milieu en Recht 103-107

WIERS, J. (2001)

"Responsible Decision-makers, Do It Yourself: The Panel Report in the
Asbestos Case", (2001) 28 *LIEI* 117-126

WIERS, J. AND MATHIS, J. (2001)

"The Report of the Appellate Body in the Asbestos Dispute", (2001)
28 *LIEI* 211-225

WILKINSON, D. (1994)

"NAFTA and the Environment: Some Lessons for the Next Round of
GATT Negotiations", (1994) 17 *World Economy* 395

WINHAM, G. (1992)

The Evolution of International Trade Agreements, Toronto, University of
Toronto Press, 1992

WINTER, G. (ED.) (1996)

European Environmental Law - A Comparative Perspective, Aldershot,
Dartmouth, 1996

WIRTH, D. (1994)

"The Role of Science in the Uruguay Round and NAFTA Trade
Disciplines", Geneva, UNEP, 1994

WORLD BANK (2001)

"Globalization, Growth and Poverty: Building an Inclusive World
Economy", Washington, World Bank, 2001

WTO (1995)

"Analytical Index-Guide to GATT Law and Practice", Geneva, WTO,
1995

WTO (1998)

"Globalization and Trade", Geneva, WTO, 1998

WTO (1999)

"Trade and Environment", Geneva, WTO, 1999

WYATT, D. AND DASHWOOD, A. (1993)

European Community Law, (3rd), London, Sweet & Maxwell, 1993

ZAELKE, D., ORBUCH, P., AND HOUSMAN, R. F. (EDS.) (1993)

Trade and the Environment: Law, Economics, and Policy, Washington
D.C., Island Press, 1993

ZAMORA, S. (1996)

"International Economic Law", (1996) 17 *U. Pa. J. Int'l. Econ. L.* 63-67

ZARRILLI, S. (1997)

"Trade and Environment - The Rules, Panels and Debate on the World Trade Organization", (1997) 20 *World Competition* 93-130

ZEDALIS, R. (1997A)

"The Environment and the Technical Barriers to Trade Agreement: Did the *Reformulated Gasoline* Panel miss a Golden Opportunity?", (1997) 44 *NILR* 186-208

ZEDALIS, R. (1997B)

"Product v. Non-Product Based Distinctions in GATT Article III Trade and Environment Jurisprudence: Recent Developments", (1997) 6 *EELR* 108-112

ZIEGLER, A. (1996)

Trade and Environmental Law in the European Community, Oxford, Clarendon, 1996

ZIEGLER, A. (1998)

"WTO Rules Supporting Environmental Protection", in Weiss, F., Denters, E., and de Waart, P. (eds.), *International Economic Law with a Human Face*, The Hague, Kluwer Law International, 1998

GATT Panel Reports

WTO Panel Reports

WTO Appellate Body Reports

Annex: Treaty Provisions

Vienna Convention on the Law of Treaties

Article 31. General Rule of Interpretation

1. A treaty shall be interpreted in good faith in accordance with the ordinary meaning to be given to the terms of the treaty in their context and in the light of its object and purpose.
2. The context for the purpose of the interpretation of a treaty shall comprise, in addition to the text, including its preamble and annexes:
(a) any agreement relating to the treaty which was made between all the parties in connexion with the conclusion of the treaty;
(b) any instrument which was made by one or more parties in connexion with the conclusion of the treaty and accepted by the other parties as an instrument related to the treaty.
3. There shall be taken into account, together with the context:
(a) any subsequent agreement between the parties regarding the interpretation of the treaty or the application of its provisions;
(b) any subsequent practice in the application of the treaty which establishes the agreement of the parties regarding its interpretation;
(c) any relevant rules of international law applicable in the relations between the parties.
4. A special meaning shall be given to a term if it is established that the parties so intended.

Article 32. Supplementary Means of Interpretation

Recourse may be had to supplementary means of interpretation, including the preparatory work of the treaty and the circumstances of its conclusion, in order to confirm the meaning resulting from the application of article 31, or to determine the meaning when the interpretation according to article 31:
(a) leaves the meaning ambiguous or obscure; or
(b) leads to a result which is manifestly absurd or unreasonable.

General Agreement on Tariffs and Trade 1994

Article III. National Treatment on Internal Taxation and Regulation

1.The contracting parties recognize that internal taxes and other internal charges, and laws, regulations and requirements affecting the internal sale, offering for sale, purchase, transportation, distribution or use of products, and internal quantitative regulations requiring the mixture, processing or use of products in specified amounts or proportions, should not be applied to imported or domestic products so as to afford protection to domestic production.
2.The products of the territory of any contracting party imported into the territory of any other contracting party shall not be subject, directly or indirectly, to internal taxes or other internal charges of any kind in excess of those applied, directly or indirectly, to like domestic products. Moreover, no contracting party shall otherwise apply internal taxes or other internal charges to imported or domestic products in a manner contrary to the principles set forth in paragraph 1.
[...]
4.The products of the territory of any contracting party imported into the territory of any other contracting party shall be accorded treatment no less favourable than that accorded to like products of national origin in respect of all laws, regulations and requirements affecting their internal sale, offering for sale, purchase, transportation, distribution or use. The provisions of this paragraph shall not prevent the application of differential internal transportation charges which are based exclusively on the economic operation of the means of transport and not on the nationality of the product.
[...]

Interpretative Notes Ad Article III and Ad Article III:2[1]

Ad Article III

Any internal tax or other internal charge, or any law, regulation or requirement of the kind

---

[1] The Note Ad Article III:1 is not reproduced here as it is of no relevance to the purpose of this work.

referred to in paragraph 1 which applies to an imported product and to the like domestic product and is collected or enforced in the case of the imported product at the time or point of importation, is nevertheless to be regarded as an internal tax or other internal charge, or a law, regulation or requirement of the kind referred to in paragraph 1, and is accordingly subject to the provisions of Article III.

Ad Paragraph 2
A tax conforming to the requirements of the first sentence of paragraph 2 would be considered to be inconsistent with the provisions of the second sentence only in cases where competition was involved between, on the one hand, the taxed product and, on the other hand, a directly competitive or substitutable product which was not similarly taxed.

Article XI. General Elimination of Quantitative Restrictions
1. No prohibitions or restrictions other than duties, taxes or other charges, whether made effective through quotas, import or export licences or other measures, shall be instituted or maintained by any contracting party on the importation of any product of the territory of any other contracting party or on the exportation or sale for export of any product destined for the territory of any other contracting party.
2. The provisions of paragraph 1 of this Article shall not extend to the following:
(a) Export prohibitions or restrictions temporarily applied to prevent or relieve critical shortages of foodstuffs or other products essential to the exporting contracting party;
(b) Import and export prohibitions or restrictions necessary to the application of standards or regulations for the classification, grading or marketing of commodities in international trade;
(c) Import restrictions on any agricultural or fisheries product, imported in any form,[2] necessary to the enforcement of governmental measures which operate:
    (i) to restrict the quantities of the like domestic product permitted to be marketed or produced, or, if there is no substantial domestic production of the like product, of a domestic product for which the imported product can be directly substituted; or
    (ii) to remove a temporary surplus of the like domestic product, or, if there is no substantial domestic production of the like product, of a domestic product for which the imported product can be directly substituted, by making the surplus available to certain groups of domestic consumers free of charge or at prices below the current market level; or
    (iii) to restrict the quantities permitted to be produced of any animal product the production of which is directly dependent, wholly or mainly, on the imported commodity, if the domestic production of that commodity is relatively negligible. [...]

Article XX. General Exceptions
Subject to the requirement that such measures are not applied in a manner which would constitute a means of arbitrary or unjustifiable discrimination between countries where the same conditions prevail, or a disguised restriction on international trade, nothing in this Agreement shall be construed to prevent the adoption or enforcement by any contracting party of measures:
(a) necessary to protect public morals;
(b) necessary to protect human, animal or plant life or health;
[...]
(d) necessary to secure compliance with laws or regulations which are not inconsistent with the provisions of this Agreement, including those relating to customs enforcement, the enforcement of monopolies operated under paragraph 4 of Article II and Article XVII, the

---

2   Note Ad Article XI:2 (c): 'The term "in any form" in this paragraph covers the same products when in an early stage of processing and still perishable, which compete directly with the fresh product and if freely imported would tend to make the restriction on the fresh product ineffective.'

protection of patents, trade marks and copyrights, and the prevention of deceptive practices;

(e) relating to the products of prison labour;

[...]

(g) relating to the conservation of exhaustible natural resources if such measures are made effective in conjunction with restrictions on domestic production or consumption;

(h) undertaken in pursuance of obligations under any intergovernmental commodity agreement which conforms to criteria submitted to the CONTRACTING PARTIES and not disapproved by them or which is itself so submitted and not so disapproved;[3]

[...]

Agreement on Technical Barriers to Trade

Annex 1

1. *Technical regulation*

Document which lays down product characteristics or their related processes and production methods, including the applicable administrative provisions, with which compliance is mandatory. It may also include or deal exclusively with terminology, symbols, packaging, marking or labelling requirements as they apply to a product, process or production method.

2. *Standard*

Document approved by a recognized body, that provides, for common and repeated use, rules, guidelines or characteristics for products or related processes and production methods, with which compliance is not mandatory. It may also include or deal exclusively with terminology, symbols, packaging, marking or labelling requirements as they apply to a product, process or production method.

3. *Conformity assessment procedures*

Any procedure used, directly or indirectly, to determine that relevant requirements in technical regulations or standards are fulfilled.

Article 2. Preparation, Adoption and Application of Technical Regulations by Central Government Bodies

With respect to their central government bodies:

2.1 Members shall ensure that in respect of technical regulations, products imported from the territory of any Member shall be accorded treatment no less favourable than that accorded to like products of national origin and to like products originating in any other country.

2.2 Members shall ensure that technical regulations are not prepared, adopted or applied with a view to or with the effect of creating unnecessary obstacles to international trade. For this purpose, technical regulations shall not be more trade-restrictive than necessary to fulfil a legitimate objective, taking account of the risks non-fulfilment would create. Such legitimate objectives are, *inter alia:* national security requirements; the prevention of deceptive practices; protection of human health orsafety, animal or plant life or health, or the environment. In assessing such risks, relevant elements of consideration are, *inter alia:* available scientific and technical information, related processing technology or intended end-uses of products.

2.3 Technical regulations shall not be maintained if the circumstances or objectives giving rise to their adoption no longer exist or if the changed circumstances or objectives can be addressed in a less trade-restrictive manner.

2.4 Where technical regulations are required and relevant international standards exist or their completion is imminent, Members shall use them, or the relevant parts of them, as a basis for their technical regulations except when such international standards or relevant parts would

---

[3] Note Ad Article XX(h): 'The exception provide for in this sub-aragraph extends to any commodity agreement which conforms to the principles approved by the Economic and Social Council in its resolution 30 (IV) of 28 March 1947.'

be an ineffective or inappropriate means for the fulfilment of the legitimate objectives pursued, for instance because of fundamental climatic or geographical factors or fundamental technological problems.

[...]

2.6 With a view to harmonizing technical regulations on as wide a basis as possible, Members shall play a full part, within the limits of their resources, in the preparation by appropriate international standardizing bodies of international standards for products for which they either have adopted, or expect to adopt, technical regulations.

2.7 Members shall give positive consideration to accepting as equivalent technical regulations of other Members, even if these regulations differ from their own, provided they are satisfied that these regulations adequately fulfil the objectives of their own regulations.

2.8 Wherever appropriate, Members shall specify technical regulations based on product requirements in terms of performance rather than design or descriptive characteristics.

[...]

Agreement on the Application of Sanitary and Phytosanitary measures

Annex A

1. *Sanitary or phytosanitary measure* - Any measure applied:

(a) to protect animal or plant life or health within the territory of the Member from risks arising from the entry, establishment or spread of pests, diseases, disease-carrying organisms or disease-causing organisms;

(b) to protect human or animal life or health within the territory of the Member from risks arising from additives, contaminants, toxins or disease-causing organisms in foods, beverages or feedstuffs;

(c) to protect human life or health within the territory of the Member from risks arising from diseases carried by animals, plants or products thereof, or from the entry, establishment or spread of pests; or (d) to prevent or limit other damage within the territory of the Member from the entry, establishment or spread of pests.

Sanitary or phytosanitary measures include all relevant laws, decrees, regulations, requirements and procedures including, inter alia, end product criteria; processes and production methods; testing, inspection, certification and approval procedures; quarantine treatments including relevant requirements associated with the transport of animals or plants, or with the materials necessary for their survival during transport; provisions on relevant statistical methods, sampling procedures and methods of risk assessment; and packaging and labelling requirements directly related to food safety.

Article 1. General Provisions

1. This Agreement applies to all sanitary and phytosanitary measures which may, directly or indirectly, affect international trade. Such measures shall be developed and applied in accordance with the provisions of this Agreement

[...]

Article 2. Basic Rights and Obligations

1. Members have the right to take sanitary and phytosanitary measures necessary for the protection of human, animal or plant life or health, provided that such measures are not inconsistent with the provisions of this Agreement.

2. Members shall ensure that any sanitary or phytosanitary measure is applied only to the

extent necessary to protect human, animal or plant life or health, is based on scientific principles and is not maintained without sufficient scientific evidence, except as provided for in paragraph 7 of Article 5.

3. Members shall ensure that their sanitary and phytosanitary measures do not arbitrarily or unjustifiably discriminate between Members where identical or similar conditions prevail, including between their own territory and that of other Members. Sanitary and phytosanitary measures shall not be applied in a manner which would constitute a disguised restriction on international trade.

4. Sanitary or phytosanitary measures which conform to the relevant provisions of this Agreement shall be presumed to be in accordance with the obligations of the Members under the provisions of GATT 1994 which relate to the use of sanitary or phytosanitary measures, in particular the provisions of Article XX(b).

Article 3. Harmonization

1. To harmonize sanitary and phytosanitary measures on as wide a basis as possible, Members shall base their sanitary or phytosanitary measures on international standards, guidelines or recommendations, where they exist, except as otherwise provided for in this Agreement, and in particular in paragraph 3.

2. Sanitary or phytosanitary measures which conform to international standards, guidelines or recommendations shall be deemed to be necessary to protect human, animal or plant life or health, and presumed to be consistent with the relevant provisions of this Agreement and of GATT 1994.

3. Members may introduce or maintain sanitary or phytosanitary measures which result in a higher level of sanitary or phytosanitary protection than would be achieved by measures based on the relevant international standards, guidelines or recommendations, if there is a scientific justification, or as a consequence of the level of sanitary or phytosanitary protection a Member determines to be appropriate in accordance with the relevant provisions of paragraphs 1 through 8 of Article 5.[4] Notwithstanding the above, all measures which result in a level of sanitary or phytosanitary protection different from that which would be achieved by measures based on international standards, guidelines or recommendations shall not be inconsistent with any other provision of this Agreement. [...]

Article 5. Assessment of Risk and Determination of the Appropriate Level of Sanitary or Phytosanitary Protection

1. Members shall ensure that their sanitary or phytosanitary measures are based on an assessment, as appropriate to the circumstances, of the risks to human, animal or plant life or health, taking into account risk assessment techniques developed by the relevant international organizations.

2. In the assessment of risks, Members shall take into account available scientific evidence; relevant processes and production methods; relevant inspection, sampling and testing methods; prevalence of specific diseases or pests; existence of pest- or disease-free areas; relevant ecological and environmental conditions; and quarantine or other treatment.

3. In assessing the risk to animal or plant life or health and determining the measure to be applied for achieving the appropriate level of sanitary or phytosanitary protection from such risk, Members shall take into account as relevant economic factors: the potential damage in terms of loss of production or sales in the event of the entry, establishment or spread of a pest

---

[4] 'For the purposes of paragraph 3 of Article 3, there is a scientific justification if, on the basis of an examination and evaluation of available scientific information in conformity with the relevant provisions of this Agreement, a Member determines that the relevant international standards, guidelines or recommendations are not sufficient to achieve its appropriate level of sanitary or phytosanitary protection.'

or disease; the costs of control or eradication in the territory of the importing Member; and the relative cost-effectiveness of alternative approaches to limiting risks.

4. Members should, when determining the appropriate level of sanitary or phytosanitary protection, take into account the objective of minimizing negative trade effects.

5. With the objective of achieving consistency in the application of the concept of appropriate level of sanitary or phytosanitary protection against risks to human life or health, or to animal and plant life or health, each Member shall avoid arbitrary or unjustifiable distinctions in the levels it considers to be appropriate in different situations, if such distinctions result in discrimination or a disguised restriction on international trade. Members shall cooperate in the Committee, in accordance with paragraphs 1, 2 and 3 of Article 12, to develop guidelines to further the practical implementation of this provision. In developing the guidelines, the Committee shall take into account all relevant factors, including the exceptional character of human health risks to which people voluntarily expose themselves.

6. Without prejudice to paragraph 2 of Article 3, when establishing or maintaining sanitary or phytosanitary measures to achieve the appropriate level of sanitary or phytosanitary protection, Members shall ensure that such measures are not more trade-restrictive than required to achieve their appropriate level of sanitary or phytosanitary protection, taking into account technical and economic feasibility.[5]

7. In cases where relevant scientific evidence is insufficient, a Member may provisionally adopt sanitary or phytosanitary measures on the basis of available pertinent information, including that from the relevant international organizations as well as from sanitary or phytosanitary measures applied by other Members. In such circumstances, Members shall seek to obtain the additional information necessary for a more objective assessment of risk and review the sanitary or phytosanitary measure accordingly within a reasonable period of time.

8. When a Member has reason to believe that a specific sanitary or phytosanitary measure introduced or maintained by another Member is constraining, or has the potential to constrain, its exports and the measure is not based on the relevant international standards, guidelines or recommendations, or such standards, guidelines or recommendations do not exist, an explanation of the reasons for such sanitary or phytosanitary measure may be requested and shall be provided by the Member maintaining the measure.

---

[5] 'For purposes of paragraph 6 of Article 5, a measure is not more trade-restrictive than required unless there is another measure, reasonably available taking into account technical and economic feasibility, that achieves the appropriate level of sanitary or phytosanitary protection and is significantly less restrictive to trade.'

Treaty Establishing the European Community

Article 28
Quantitative restrictions on imports and all measures having equivalent effect shall be prohibited between Member States.

Article 29
Quantitative restrictions on exports, and all measures having equivalent effect, shall be prohibited between Member States.

Article 30
The provisions of Articles 28 and 29 shall not preclude prohibitions or restrictions on imports, exports or goods in transit justified on grounds of public morality, public policy or public security; the protection of health and life of humans, animals or plants; the protection of national treasures possessing artistic, historic or archaeological value; or the protection of industrial and commercial property. Such prohibitions or restrictions shall not, however, constitute a means of arbitrary discrimination or a disguised restriction on trade between Member States.

Article 95
1. By way of derogation from Article 94 and save where otherwise provided in this Treaty, the following provisions shall apply for the achievement of the objectives set out in Article 14. The Council shall, acting in accordance with the procedure referred to in Article 251 and after consulting the Economic and Social Committee, adopt the measures for the approximation of the provisions laid down by law, regulation or administrative action in Member States which have as their object the establishment and functioning of the internal market.
2. Paragraph 1 shall not apply to fiscal provisions, to those relating to the free movement of persons nor to those relating to the rights and interests of employed persons.
3. The Commission, in its proposals envisaged in paragraph 1 concerning health, safety, environmental protection and consumer protection, will take as a base a high level of protection, taking account in particular of any new development based on scientific facts. Within their respective powers, the European Parliament and the Council will also seek to achieve this objective.
4. If, after the adoption by the Council or by the Commission of a harmonisation measure, a Member State deems it necessary to maintain national provisions on grounds of major needs referred to in Article 30, or relating to the protection of the environment or the working environment, it shall notify the Commission of these provisions as well as the grounds for maintaining them.
5. Moreover, without prejudice to paragraph 4, if, after the adoption by the Council or by the Commission of a harmonisation measure, a Member State deems it necessary to introduce national provisions based on new scientific evidence relating to the protection of the environment or the working environment on grounds of a problem specific to that Member State arising after the adoption of the harmonisation measure, it shall notify the Commission of the envisaged provisions as well as the grounds for introducing them.
6. The Commission shall, within six months of the notifications as referred to in paragraphs 4 and 5, approve or reject the national provisions involved after having verified whether or not they are a means of arbitrary discrimination or a disguised restriction on trade between Member States and whether or not they shall constitute an obstacle to the functioning of the internal market.
In the absence of a decision by the Commission within this period the national provisions referred to in paragraphs 4 and 5 shall be deemed to have been approved.

Article 133

1. The common commercial policy shall be based on uniform principles, particularly in regard to changes in tariff rates, the conclusion of tariff and trade agreements, the achievement of uniformity in measures of liberalisation, export policy and measures to protect trade such as those to be taken in the event of dumping or subsidies.

2. The Commission shall submit proposals to the Council for implementing the common commercial policy.

3. Where agreements with one or more States or international organisations need to be negotiated, the Commission shall make recommendations to the Council, which shall authorise the Commission to open the necessary negotiations. The Commission shall conduct these negotiations in consultation with a special committee appointed by the Council to assist the Commission in this task and within the framework of such directives as the Council may issue to it. The relevant provisions of Article 300 shall apply.

4. In exercising the powers conferred upon it by this Article, the Council shall act by a qualified majority.

5. The Council, acting unanimously on a proposal from the Commission and after consulting the European Parliament, may extend the application of paragraphs 1 to 4 to international negotiations and agreements on services and intellectual property insofar as they are not covered by these paragraphs.

Article 152

1. A high level of human health protection shall be ensured in the definition and implementation of all Community policies and activities.

Community action, which shall complement national policies, shall be directed towards improving public health, preventing human illness and diseases, and obviating sources of danger to human health. Such action shall cover the fight against the major health scourges, by promoting research into their causes, their transmission and their prevention, as well as health information and education.

The Community shall complement the Member States' action in reducing drugs-related health damage, including information and prevention.

2. The Community shall encourage cooperation between the Member States in the areas referred to in this Article and, if necessary, lend support to their action.

Member States shall, in liaison with the Commission, coordinate among themselves their policies and programmes in the areas referred to in paragraph 1. The Commission may, in close contact with the Member States, take any useful initiative to promote such coordination.

3. The Community and the Member States shall foster cooperation with third countries and the competent international organisations in the sphere of public health.

4. The Council, acting in accordance with the procedure referred to in Article 251 and after consulting the Economic and Social Committee and the Committee of the Regions, shall contribute to the achievement of the objectives referred to in this Article through adopting:

a) measures setting high standards of quality and safety of organs and substances of human origin, blood and blood derivatives; these measures shall not prevent any Member State from maintaining or introducing more stringent protective measures;

b) by way of derogation from Article 37, measures in the veterinary and phytosanitary fields which have as their direct objective the protection of public health;

c) incentive measures designed to protect and improve human health, excluding any harmonisation of the laws and regulations of the Member States.

The Council, acting by a qualified majority on a proposal from the Commission, may also adopt recommendations for the purposes set out in this Article.

5. Community action in the field of public health shall fully respect the responsibilities of the Member States for the organisation and delivery of health services and medical care. In particular, measures referred to in paragraph 4(a) shall not affect national provisions on the donation or medical use of organs and blood.

Article 174

1. Community policy on the environment shall contribute to pursuit of the following objectives:
- preserving, protecting and improving the quality of the environment;
- protecting human health;
- prudent and rational utilisation of natural resources;
- promoting measures at international level to deal with regional or worldwide environmental problems.

2. Community policy on the environment shall aim at a high level of protection taking into account the diversity of situations in the various regions of the Community. It shall be based on the precautionary principle and on the principles that preventive action should be taken, that environmental damage should as a priority be rectified at source and that the polluter should pay.

In this context, harmonisation measures answering environmental protection requirements shall include, where appropriate, a safeguard clause allowing Member States to take provisional measures, for non-economic environmental reasons, subject to a Community inspection procedure.

3. In preparing its policy on the environment, the Community shall take account of:
- available scientific and technical data;
- environmental conditions in the various regions of the Community;
- the potential benefits and costs of action or lack of action;
- the economic and social development of the Community as a whole and the balanced development of its regions.

4. Within their respective spheres of competence, the Community and the Member States shall cooperate with third countries and with the competent international organisations. The arrangements for Community cooperation may be the subject of agreements between the Community and the third parties concerned, which shall be negotiated and concluded in accordance with Article 300.

The previous subparagraph shall be without prejudice to Member States' competence to negotiate in international bodies and to conclude international agreements.

Article 175

1. The Council, acting in accordance with the procedure referred to in Article 251 and after consulting the Economic and Social Committee and the Committee of the Regions, shall decide what action is to be taken by the Community in order to achieve the objectives referred to in Article 174.

2. By way of derogation from the decision-making procedure provided for in paragraph 1 and without prejudice to Article 95, the Council, acting unanimously on a proposal from the Commission and after consulting the European Parliament, the Economic and Social Committee and the Committee of the Regions, shall adopt:
- provisions primarily of a fiscal nature;
- measures concerning town and country planning, land use with the exception of waste management and measures of a general nature, and management of water resources;
- measures significantly affecting a Member State's choice between different energy sources and the general structure of its energy supply.

The Council may, under the conditions laid down in the preceding subparagraph, define those matters referred to in this paragraph on which decisions are to be taken by a qualified majority.

3. In other areas, general action programmes setting out priority objectives to be attained shall be adopted by the Council, acting in accordance with the procedure referred to in Article 251 and after consulting the Economic and Social Committee and the Committee of the Regions.

The Council, acting under the terms of paragraph 1 or paragraph 2 according to the case, shall adopt the measures necessary for the implementation of these programmes.

4. Without prejudice to certain measures of a Community nature, the Member States shall finance and implement the environment policy.

5. Without prejudice to the principle that the polluter should pay, if a measure based on the provisions of paragraph 1 involves costs deemed disproportionate for the public authorities of a Member State, the Council shall, in the act adopting that measure, lay down appropriate provisions in the form of:

- temporary derogations, and/or
- financial support from the Cohesion Fund set up pursuant to Article 161.

Article 176

The protective measures adopted pursuant to Article 175 shall not prevent any Member State from maintaining or introducing more stringent protective measures. Such measures must be compatible with this Treaty. They shall be notified to the Commission.

Literature

AJIL	American Journal of International Law
CMLRev	Common Market Law Review
EELR	European Environmental Law Review
EJIL	European Journal of International Law
ELRev	European Law Review
ICLQ	International Comparative Law Quarterly
JEL	Journal of Environmental Law
JIEL	Journal of International Economic Law
JWT	Journal of World Trade
LIEI	Legal Issues of Economic Integration (from vol. 27)
LIEI	Legal Issues of European Integration (vol. 1-26)
LJIL	Leiden Journal of International Law
NILR	Netherlands International Law Review
NJB	Nederlands Juristen Blad
NTER	Nederlands Tijdschrift voor Europees Recht
RECIEL	Review of European Community and International Environmental Law
RMC	Revue du Marché Commun
RMUE	Revue du Marché commun et de l'Union Européenne
RTDE	Revue Trimestrielle du Droit Européen
SEW	Sociaal-Economische Wetgeving

Other

AB	Appellate Body
AG	Advocate General
DSU	Understanding on Rules and Procedures Governing the Settlement of Disputes
EC	European Community
ECJ	European Court of Justice
ECSC	European Coal and Steel Community
EEC	European Economic Community
EU	European Union
EAEC (Euratom)	European Atomic Energy Community
GATS	General Agreement on Trade in Services
GATT	General Agreement on Tariffs and Trade
ICJ	International Court of Justice
NAFTA	North American Free Trade Agreement
SPS	Agreement on the Application of Sanitary and Phytosanitary measures
TBT	Agreement on Technical Barriers to Trade
TPR	Trade Policy Review
TRIPS	Agreement on Trade-Related Aspects of Intellectual Property Rights
WTO	World Trade Organisation

Index